THE CHILD'S RIGHT TO PARTICIPATE IN FAMILY LAW PROCEEDINGS

THE CHILD'S RIGHT TO PARTICIPATE IN FAMILY LAW PROCEEDINGS

Represented, Heard or Silenced?

Charlotte Mol

INTERSENTIA

Cambridge – Antwerp – Chicago

Intersentia Ltd
8 Wellington Mews
Wellington Street | Cambridge
CB1 1HW | United Kingdom
Tel: +44 1223 736 170
Email: mail@intersentia.co.uk
www.intersentia.com | www.intersentia.co.uk

Distribution for the UK and
Rest of the World (incl. Eastern Europe)
NBN International
1 Deltic Avenue, Rooksley
Milton Keynes MK13 8LD
United Kingdom
Tel: +44 1752 202 301 | Fax: +44 1752 202 331
Email: orders@nbninternational.com

Distribution for Europe
Lefebvre Sarrut Belgium NV
Hoogstraat 139/6
1000 Brussels
Belgium
Tel: +32 (0)800 39 067
Email: mail@intersentia.be

Distribution for the USA and Canada
Independent Publishers Group
Order Department
814 North Franklin Street
Chicago, IL 60610
USA
Tel: +1 800 888 4741 (toll free) | Fax: +1 312 337 5985
Email: orders@ipgbook.com

The Child's Right to Participate in Family Law Proceedings. Represented, Heard or Silenced?

ISBN 978-1-83970-255-6
D/2022/7849/57
NUR 822

British Library Cataloguing in Publication Data. A catalogue record for this book is available from the British Library.

ACKNOWLEDGEMENTS

This volume is a revised version of my doctoral dissertation completed in September 2021 and publicly defended at Utrecht University. There are many people who have made the completion of my PhD research and this volume possible and I would like to thank them all.

In particular I would like to thank my supervisors, prof. Wendy Schrama and dr. Merel Jonker, for their exceptional guidance, encouragement, support and feedback throughout the process. I am indebted to the members of the doctoral examination committee – prof. dr. dr. h.c. mult. Katharina Boele-Woelki, prof. dr. Ursulla Kilkelly, prof. dr. Charlotte Declerck, prof. dr. Mariëlle Bruning and prof. dr. Janneke Gerards – for their valuable comments on my dissertation and critical questions at my defence. A note of thanks also to the Netherlands Organisation for Scientific Research for funding my PhD research through a Research Talent Grant.

I am very grateful to Intersentia Ltd and Ahmed Hegazi, publisher, and Ella Brice-Jeffreys, editor, in particular. I would also like to thank the Organising Committee of the Commission on European Family Law (CEFL) for accepting my manuscript as a volume in the European Family Law Series.

A final and special thank you to my friends, parents, sister and partner for their endless support and encouragement over these past years.

CONTENTS

LIST OF TABLES AND FIGURES

TABLES

FIGURES

LIST OF ABBREVIATIONS

ACWRC	African Charter on the Rights and Welfare of the Child
ADR	Alternative Dispute Resolution
CA	Content Analysis
CAQDAS	Computer Assisted Qualitative Data Analysis Software
CoE	Council of Europe
CFREU	Charter of Fundamental Rights of the European Union
CRC Committee	United Nations Committee on the Rights of the Child
ECECR	European Convention on the Exercise of Children's Rights
ECHR	European Convention on Human Rights
ECtHR	European Court of Human Rights
EU	European Union
GCFJ	Guidelines on Child-Friendly Justice
ICCPR	International Covenant on Civil and Political Rights
ICESCR	International Covenant on Economic, Social and Cultural Rights
NGO	Non-governmental organization
QCA	Qualitative Content Analysis
TEU	Treaty on European Union
TFEU	Treaty on the Functioning of the European Union
UDHR	Universal Declaration of Human Rights
UN	United Nations
UNCRC	United Nations Convention on the Rights of the Child
UNHCHR	United Nations High Commissioner for Human Rights
UNICEF	United Nations Children's Fund

LIST OF INTERNATIONAL AND EUROPEAN INSTRUMENTS AND SOURCES

COUNCIL OF EUROPE

Action Plan Third Summit of Heads of State and Government of the Council of Europe (Warsaw, 16–17 May 2005).

Brussels Declaration, adopted at the High-Level Conference on the future of the European Court of Human Rights, 27 March 2015.

CoE Parliamentary Assembly, *Recommendation 874 (1979) European Charter on the Rights of the Child.*

—— *Recommendation 1121 (1990) Rights of Children.*

—— *Recommendation 1864 (2009) Promoting the participation by children in decisions affecting them.*

CoE Resolution (72)29 on the lowering of the age of full capacity, adopted by the Committee of Ministers on 19 September 1972.

Convention for the Protection of Human Rights and Fundamental Freedoms, Rome, 4 November 1950, ETS No. 005.

Council of Europe, *Building a Europe for and with children 2009–2011: the Stockholm strategy*, 27 November 2008.

Council of Europe, *Strategy for the Rights of the Child (2012–2015)*, 15 February 2012.

—— *Strategy for the Rights of the Child (2012–2015): Implementation report*, 2016.

—— *Strategy for the Rights of the Child (2016–2021)*, March 2016.

Directorate of the Jurisconsult, *Guide on Article 8 of the European Convention on Human Right*, Strasbourg: Council of Europe/European Court of Human Rights 2018.

—— *Practical Guide on Admissibility Criteria*, Strasbourg: Council of Europe/European Court of Human Rights, 2019.

European Convention on the Exercise of Children's Rights, Strasbourg, 25 January 1996, ETS No. 160.

European Council, *Conclusions of the Presidency*, 7–10 December 2000, Nice, available at: www.europarl.europa.eu/summits/nice1_en.htm.

European Court of Human Rights, *Guide on Article 8 of the Convention – Right to respect for private and family life*, Council of Europe/European Court of Human Rights 2020 (available at: www.echr.coe.int/documents/guide_art_8_eng.pdf).

European Ministers of Justice, *Resolution No. 2 on child-friendly justice*, 28th Conference of the European Ministers of Justice, 2007, MJU-28 (2007) Resol. 2E.

Explanatory Memorandum to the Guidelines on child-friendly justice, Council of Europe 2011.

Explanatory Report to the European Convention on the Exercise of Children's Rights, 25 January 1996, ETS No. 160.

Group of Specialists on Child-Friendly Justice, *Report of the 1st Meeting of the Group of Specialists on Child-Friendly Justice*, CJ-S-CH (2009) 3.
—— *Draft Report of the 2nd Meeting of the Group of Specialists on Child-Friendly Justice*, CJ-S-CH (2009) 15.
—— *Report of the 3rd Meeting of the Group of Specialists on Child-Friendly Justice*, CJ-S-CH (2009) 18 rev. 1.
—— *Report of the 4th Meeting of the Group of Specialists on Child-Friendly Justice*, CJ-S-CH (2010) 8 E.
Guidelines of the Committee of Ministers of the Council of Europe on Child-Friendly Justice, 17 November 2010.
Public Relations Unit, *The European Court of Human Rights in Facts & Figures 2019*, European Court of Human Rights 2020, available at: https://echr.coe.int/Documents/Facts_Figures_2019_ENG.pdf.
Recommendation CM/Rec(2012)2 of the Committee of Ministers to member States on the participation of children and young people under the age of 18 (Adopted by the Committee of Ministers on 28 March 2012 at the 1138th meeting of the Ministers' Deputies), no. 1.
Registry of the European Court of Human Rights, 'Access of children to justice – Specific focus on the access of children to the European Court of Human Rights as well as its case law related to children's access to national jurisdictions', in: Council of Europe, *Compilation of Texts Related to Child-Friendly Justice*, Directorate General of Human Rights and Legal Affairs, 2009.
Report by the Secretary General on the Review of Council of Europe Conventions, SG/Inf(2012)12.

EUROPEAN UNION

Charter of Fundamental Rights of the European Union, 2000/C 364/01.
Council Regulation (EC) No 2201/2003 of 27 November 2003 concerning jurisdiction and the recognition and enforcement of judgments in matrimonial matters and the matters of parental responsibility, repealing Regulation (EC) No 1347/2000.
Council Regulation (EU) 2019/1111 of 25 June 2019 on jurisdiction, the recognition and enforcement of decisions in matrimonial matters and the matters of parental responsibility, and on international child abduction (recast).
European Commission, 'An EU Agenda for the Rights of the Child', Brussels, 15 February 2011, COM(2011) 60 final.
Explanations relating to the Charter of Fundamental Rights, 2007/C 303/02.
Treaty of Lisbon amending the Treaty on European Union and the Treaty establishing the European Community (OJ C 306), 13 December 2007.

UNITED NATIONS

Declaration on the Rights of the Child, Records of the Fifth Assembly, Supplement No. 23, League of Nations Official Journal 1924.

Optional Protocol to the Convention on the Rights of the Child on a communications procedure, adopted and opened for signature, ratification and accession by General Assembly resolution A/RES/66/138 of 19 December 2011.

UN Commission on Human Rights, *Report of the 34th Session 6 February – 10 March 1978*, E/1978/34 or E/CN.4/1292.

UN Committee on the Rights of the Child, *General Comment No 5 (2003): General measures of implementation of the Convention on the Rights of the Child*, 27 November 2003, CRC/GC/2003/5.

—— *General Comment No. 7 (2005): Implementing child rights in early childhood*, 20 September 2006, CRC/C/GC/7/Rev.1.

—— *General Comment No. 12 (2009): The right of the child to be heard*, 1 July 2009, CRC/C/GC/12.

—— *General Comment No. 14 (2013) on the right of the child to have his or her best interests taken as a primary consideration (art. 3, para. 1)*, 29 May 2013, CRC/C/GC/14.

—— *General Comment No. 19 (2016) on public budgeting for the realization of children's rights (art. 4)*, 20 July 2016, CRC/C/GC/19.

—— *General Comment No. 20 (2016) on the implementation of the rights of the child during adolescence*, 6 December 2016, CRC/C/GC/20.

—— *General Comment No. 25 (2021) on children's rights in relation to the digital environment*, 2 March 2021, CRC/C/GC/25.

—— *Recommendations: Day of General Discussion on Children without Parental Care*, 17 March 2006, CRC/C/153.

—— *Recommendations: Day of General Discussion on the Right of the Child to Be Heard*, 29 September 2006.

UN Convention on the Rights of the Child, 20 November 1989, United Nations, Treaty Series, vol. 1577, p. 3.

UN Economic and Social Council Commission on Human Rights, *Question of a Convention on the Rights of the Child: Note Verbale Dated 5 October 1979 Addressed to the Division of Human Rights by the Permanent Representation of the Polish People's Republic to the United Nations in Geneva*, 17 January 1980, E/CN.4/1349*.

—— *Report of the Working Group on a Draft Convention on the Rights of the Child*, 17 February 1981, E/CN.4/L.1575.

UN General Assembly, *Declaration on the Rights of the Child*, 20 November 1959, A/RES/1386(XIV).

UN General Assembly 31/169 on an International Year of the Child adopted on 21 December 1976.

UN High Commissioner for Human Rights, *Access to justice for children*, A/HRC/25/35, 16 December 2013.

UN Human Rights Council, *Report of the open-ended working group to explore the possibility of elaborating an optional protocol to the Convention on the Rights of the Child to provide a communications procedure*, A/HRC/13/43, 21 January 2010.

UN Office of the High Commissioner for Human Rights, *Legislative History of the Convention on the Rights of the Child* (vol. I), 2007.

LIST OF CASES

COURT OF JUSTICE OF THE EUROPEAN UNION

EUROPEAN COURT OF HUMAN RIGHTS

Paulsen-Medalen and Svensson v. Sweden (dec.) (Appl. No. 47411/99), 30 September 2003 .... 150, 153, 179, 219, 223, 233, 265–266, 276

UN COMMITTEE ON THE RIGHTS OF THE CHILD

CHAPTER 1
INTRODUCTION

'I said it must be interesting to be able to see people without them seeing you. It seemed to me that children were often treated in the same way, as witnesses whose presence was somehow not taken into account ... "That's true", he said. "At least until the divorce proceedings start. Then everyone's after them for their vote."'

– Rachel Cusk, *Transit*[1]

1. INTRODUCTION

Family law disputes, such as those concerning divorce, custody or parentage, have a great impact on all those involved as they touch upon our personal lives and affect the relationships we share with those closest to us. Many of these family law disputes concern and impact children. Not only does the existence of conflict affect children, but the disputed topic often concerns children's lives. For example, when parents separate, there may be conflict over the custody of the child, their living situation or how much time the child will spend with each parent. Family law disputes, especially those concerning parental separation, are often submitted to courts. Children and their lives are at the centre of these disputes, but they are generally not party to the proceedings. In that sense, children are silent witnesses. However, the position of children in family law proceedings has in the past few decades been the subject of increased attention. Through international and European human rights instruments, the child's right to participate in family law proceedings has evolved considerably. Most notably, children have been afforded the right to participate in these proceedings through Article 12 of the United Nations Convention on the Rights of the Child 1989 (UNCRC). Whereas historically children were seen as objects as illustrated by the 19th-century proverb that 'children should be seen and not heard',[2] the

1 R. Cusk, *Transit*, London: Faber & Faber Ltd 2018, p. 52.

2 See e.g. J. Fortin, *Children's Rights and the Developing Law*, Cambridge: Cambridge University Press 2009, p. 7.

children's rights movement in the 1970s and 1980s led to the recognition of children as rights-holders with 'personhood, integrity and autonomy'.[3] Since the entry into force of the UNCRC in 1990 and through its almost universal ratification,[4] the child's right to participate is a fundamental human right of the child.

In the quote above, the protagonist in *Transit* reflects upon the fact that children are often shrouded in a cloak of invisibility, as their presence is not taken into account. Another character in the novel disagrees, remarking that this is not the case in divorce proceedings, where the child's 'vote' is sought by both parents, for example, in favour of living with them. This response reflects a common misconception that children can decide with which parent they want to live after divorce or separation. In reality, the child's right to participate in family law proceedings is more nuanced: according to Article 12 UNCRC, children have the right to express their views on the matter and these views must be given due weight by the court. In short, children have a voice, but not an unrestricted choice.

By listening to children's voices we, as a society, include them as citizens and recognize their autonomy.[5] Children are taken seriously as persons in their own right, with their own perspectives and wishes if they are granted the opportunity to express their views on matters affecting them, and these views are taken into account. More generally, regular participation in various areas of life has been shown to help children develop their 'self-esteem, cognitive abilities, social skills and respect for others'.[6] In family law proceedings

3 See P. Alston & J. Tobin, *Laying the Foundations for Children's Rights: An Independent Study of Some Key Legal and Institutional Aspects of the Impact of the Convention on the Rights of the Child*, Florence: United Nations Children's Fund 2005, pp. 3–8; J.E. Doek, 'What Does the Children's Convention Require?', *Emory International Law Review*, Vol. 20, No. 1, 2006, pp. 199–208; M. Freeman, 'Towards a Sociology of Children's Rights', in: M. Freeman (ed.), *Law and Childhood Studies*, Oxford: Oxford University Press 2012, pp. 29–38, p. 30; A. Parkes, *Children and International Human Rights Law: The Right of the Child to Be Heard*, Abingdon: Routledge 2013, pp. 1–2.

4 At present, only one state (the USA) has signed the UNCRC but has not yet ratified it. See the Interactive Dashboard for the Status of Ratification, United Nations Office of the High Commissioner of Human Rights, available at: https://indicators.ohchr.org/.

5 See UN Committee on the Rights of the Child, *General Comment No. 12 (2009): The Right of the Child to Be Heard*, 1 July 2009, CRC/C/GC/12, para. 1, in which the recognition of the 'legal and social status of children' is noted. See also U. Kilkelly, *Listening to Children about Justice: Report of the Council of Europe Consultation with Children on Child-Friendly Justice*, CJ-S-CH (2010) 14 rev., Strasbourg, 5 October 2010, p. 13; G. Lansdown, *Every Child's Right to Be Heard: A Resource Guide on the UN Committee on the Rights of the Child General Comment No. 12*, London: Save the Children Fund 2011, pp. 4–9.

6 See Lansdown 2011, p. 4.

specifically, allowing children to participate provides parents, judges and others with insights into their unique perspectives on the matter.[7] Child participation leads to more inclusive, more informed and therefore better decision-making and outcomes.[8] Additionally, the process of participation is presumed to be beneficial for children.[9] By participating in family law proceedings, children can feel recognized, acknowledged and respected, and may feel that they have some control over the situation.[10] With regard to child protection (or care) proceedings specifically, research shows that children appreciate being listened to as it makes them feel valued; in contrast, when they are not heard, it may lead to 'feelings of desperation'.[11] Children themselves also generally think that they should have a say in family law proceedings, although children with experience of family law proceedings express a more nuanced view.[12] While some children

7 This is also known as the 'enlightenment rationale', see R.A. Warshak, 'Payoffs and Pitfalls of Listening to Children', *Family Relations*, Vol. 52, No. 4, 2003, pp. 373–384, p. 374.

8 See P. Parkinson & J. Cashmore, *The Voice of a Child in Family Law Disputes*, Oxford: Oxford University Press 2008, pp. 12–13; Kilkelly 2010, p. 13; Lansdown 2011, p. 4; J. Cashmore, 'Children's Participation in Family Law Decision-Making: Theoretical Approaches to Understanding Children's Views', *Children and Youth Services Review*, Vol. 33, No. 4, 2011, pp. 515–520, p. 517; R.H. Ballard et al., 'Hearing the Voice of the Child in Divorce', in: M.K. Miller, J. Chamberlain & T. Wingrove (eds.), *Psychology, Law, and the Wellbeing of Children*, Oxford: Oxford University Press 2014, pp. 122–135, pp. 123–124; and M.R. Bruning et al., *Kind in proces: van communicatie naar effectieve participatie*, Nijmegen: Wolf Legal Publishers 2020, p. 126.

9 This is also known as the 'empowerment rationale'; see Warshak 2003, p. 374.

10 P. Parkinson, J. Cashmore & J. Single, 'Parents' and Children's Views on Talking to Judges in Parenting Disputes in Australia', *International Journal of Law, Policy and the Family*, Vol. 21, No. 1, 2007, pp. 84–107, p. 90; Cashmore 2011, p. 517; Bruning et al. 2020, p. 205.

11 See e.g. S. Bessel, 'Participation in Decision-Making in Out-of-Home Care in Australia: What Do Young People Say?', *Children and Youth Services Review*, Vol. 33, No. 4, 2011, pp. 497–501, p. 498; and G.G. van Bijleveld, C.W.M. Dedding & J.F.G. Bunders-Aelen, 'Children's and Young People's Participation within Child Welfare and Child Protection Services: A State-of-the-Art Review', *Child & Family Social Work*, Vol. 20, No. 2, 2015, pp. 129–138, p. 133.

12 Parkinson, Cashmore & Single 2007, p. 89; J. Cashmore & P. Parkinson, 'Children's and Parents' Perceptions on Children's Participation in Decision Making after Parental Separation and Divorce', *Family Court Review*, Vol. 46, No. 1, 2008, pp. 91–104, pp. 94–95; Parkinson & Cashmore 2008, p. 20; Kilkelly 2010, p. 29 (also in relation to other types of legal proceedings); Cashmore 2011, p. 517; R. Fitzgerald & A. Graham, '"Something Amazing I Guess": Children's Views on Having a Say about Supervised Contact', *Australian Social Work*, Vol. 64, No. 4, 2011, pp. 487–501, p. 496; Ballard et al. 2014, pp. 124–125; European Union Fundamental Rights Agency, *Child-Friendly Justice. Perspectives and Experiences of Children Involved in Judicial Proceedings as Victims, Witnesses or Parties in Nine EU Member States*, Luxembourg: Publications Office of the European Union 2017, pp. 52–54; and Bruning et al. 2020, p. 196.

are ambivalent or do not personally wish to participate – for example, due to the potential response of their parents or a fear of hurting a parent[13] – this does not detract from the core view that children should have the opportunity to participate if they wish to. With regard to voice and choice – or the 'voting' referred to in the quote given above – it is important to emphasize that most children think they should have a say, but do not want to make the decision themselves.[14]

Considering the value of child participation and children's rights more generally, it is no surprise that the child's right to participate has gained increasing attention. The UNCRC and Article 12 specifically have served as a catalyst for the (further) development of the child's right to participate domestically, regionally and internationally.[15] It has provided the inspiration for the inclusion of the child's right to participate in other human rights instruments, including Article 4(2) of the African Charter on the Rights and Welfare of the Child (ACRWC) and various instruments in Europe, such as the European Convention on the Exercise of Children's Rights of 1996 (ECECR) and the 2010 Guidelines on Child-Friendly Justice (GCFJ).[16]

Additionally, although the European Convention on Human Rights 1950 (ECHR) does not include an article on children's rights or their right to participate, in the case law of the European Court of Human Rights (ECtHR), child participation in family law proceedings has increasingly been considered. The ECHR is known as a 'living instrument' and the ECtHR, as a unique international authority, has through its evolutive interpretation gradually expanded the rights provided in the ECHR.[17] The case law of the ECtHR has

---

13 Cashmore & Parkinson 2008, p. 95; Cashmore 2011, p. 518 and Fitzgerald & Graham 2011, p. 496.

14 However, some research shows this is different when it comes to children who have faced abuse. See e.g. Parkinson & Cashmore 2008, p. 20; Cashmore 2011, p. 517 and R. Birnbaum & M. Saini, 'A Scoping Review of Qualitative Studies about Children Experiencing Parental Separation', *Childhood*, Vol. 20, No. 2, 2012, pp. 260–282, p. 278.

15 See e.g. M.R. Bruning et al., 'Conclusion', in: W. Schrama et al. (eds.), *International Handbook on Child Participation in Family Law*, Cambridge: Intersentia 2021, pp. 359–367, p. 363.

16 This will be further discussed in Chapter 3. See also M.R. Bruning & C.R. Mol, 'Child Participation in International and Regional Human Rights Instruments', in: Schrama et al. 2021, pp. 13–40, pp. 14–15.

17 See e.g. U. Kilkelly, *The Child and the European Convention on Human Rights*, Aldershot: Ashgate 1999, pp. 13–14; A. Mowbray, 'The Creativity of the European Court of Human Rights', *Human Rights Law Review*, Vol. 5, No. 1, 2005, pp. 57–79, pp. 60–64 and M. Burbergs, 'How the Right to Respect for Private and Family Life, Home and Correspondence Became the Nursery in Which New Rights are Born', in: E. Brems & J. Gerards (eds.), *Shaping Rights in the ECHR: The Role of the European Court of Human Rights in Determining the Scope of Human Rights*, Cambridge: Cambridge University Press 2014, pp. 315–329, p. 319.

subsequently brought children's rights within the scope of protection of the ECHR. There are two articles in the ECHR of (potential) relevance for the child's right to participate in family law proceedings: Article 6 (the right to a fair trial) and Article 8 (the right to respect for family and private life). With regard to Article 6, it has been argued that not hearing children in family law proceedings should be a breach of their right to a fair trial under the civil limb of Article 6.[18] However, whether the child's right to participate in family law proceedings has been recognized under the civil limb by the ECtHR has not been further investigated in previous research. In contrast to Article 6, the ECtHR's case law on Article 8 has considered the topic of child participation in family law proceedings and, more recently, has even introduced the child's right to participation. Previous authors have analysed the child's right to participate in family law proceedings on the basis of a number of landmark cases. Authors have done so when assessing the child's right to participation specifically,[19] or children's rights in general under the ECtHR,[20] or in the context of specific areas of family law, such as contact cases following parental separation.[21]

---

18 A. Daly, 'The Right of Children to Be Heard in Civil Proceedings and the Emerging Law of the European Court of Human Rights', *International Journal of Human Rights*, Vol. 15, No. 3, 2011, pp. 441–461, p. 445.

19 Kilkelly 1999, pp. 116–122; Daly 2011; Parkes 2013, pp. 111–113; U. Kilkelly, 'The CRC in Litigation under the ECHR', in: T. Liefaard & J.E. Doek (eds.), *Litigating the Rights of the Child: The UN Convention on the Rights of the Child in Domestic and International Jurisprudence*, Dordrecht: Springer 2015, pp. 193–209; Bruning et al. 2020, pp. 102–108; C. Fenton-Glynn, *Children and the European Court of Human Rights*, Oxford: Oxford University Press 2021, pp. 283–289.

20 M. Woolf, 'Coming of Age? The Principle of "the Best Interests of the Child"', *European Human Rights Law Review*, 2003, pp. 205–221; S. Choudhry & J. Herring, *European Human Rights and Family Law*, Oxford: Hart Publishing 2010, pp. 221–224; F. Ippolito, '(De)Constructing Children's Vulnerability under European Law', in: F. Ippolito & S. Iglesias Sanchez (eds.), *Protecting Vulnerable Groups: The European Human Rights Framework*, Oxford: Hart Publishing 2015, pp. 23–47; European Union Agency for Fundamental Rights and Council of Europe, *Handbook on European Law Relating to the Rights of the Child*, Luxembourg: Publications Office of the European Union 2017.

21 Regarding case law on custody and access or contact, see: E. Merckx, 'Het EHRM over ouderlijk gezag en verblijf in het belang van het kind na relatiebreuk', *Tijdschrift voor Familierecht*, No. 9, 2017, pp. 241–264; E. Vertommen, 'Balancing the Rights of Parent and Child in Case of Non-compliance with Contact Arrangements: A Case Law Analysis', in: K. Boele-Woelki & D. Martiny (eds.), *Plurality and Diversity of Family Relations in Europe*, Cambridge: Intersentia 2019, pp. 175–201; E. Merckx, 'The ECtHR on Parental Authority and Contact after Separation: Towards a More Child-Centered Perspective', in: P. Czech et al. (eds.), *European Yearbook on Human Rights 2020*, Cambridge: Intersentia 2020, pp. 97–133; and European Court of Human Rights, *Guide on Article 8 of the Convention – Right to respect for private and family life*, Council of Europe/European Court of Human Rights 2020, para. 312.

While previous studies have addressed the landmark cases on child participation or have discussed it as one factor in the ECtHR's case law on substantive matters of family law (for example, contact cases), there has been no broad and systematic review of the ECtHR's case law on child participation in family law proceedings. Therefore, uncertainty remains as to the scope, requirements and conditions of the child's right to participation under Articles 6 and 8 ECHR. For example, if the right to be heard is dependent on the circumstances of the case, which circumstances are these? As the topic of child participation is considered in cases concerning a variety of family law proceedings, it is fragmented throughout the ECtHR's case law. Relying solely on so-called landmark cases gives a distorted view for two reasons. First, it is unclear whether these landmark cases reflect the standards set by the ECtHR in *all* cases where participation is raised in family law proceedings. When only considering the landmark cases, themes and developments occurring in the broader case law may remain unexposed. Second, the discussions on landmark cases focus on those cases where the ECtHR has responded at length to complaints on participation, while it does not consider why the ECtHR does consider complaints in some cases and not in others. At present, there is insufficient knowledge of the existing standards on child participation and their relationship to each other, the types of proceedings and circumstances. This book addresses this gap in knowledge by extensively examining the ECtHR's case law through an innovative and systematic approach: a qualitative content analysis. In doing so, the standards set by the ECtHR regarding child participation in family law proceedings are examined.

The analysis of the ECtHR's case law on child participation provides many new and important insights regarding the child's right to participate. Relying and building on these insights, this book goes a step further. European states are not only bound to the standards set by the ECHR and the ECtHR, but must also meet the human rights standards in other international and European instruments. In the field of child participation, as mentioned earlier, the UNCRC is the core international source which is supplemented at the European level by the ECECR, the GCFJ, the 2012 Recommendation on the participation of children, and Article 24 of the Charter of Fundamental Rights of the European Union (CFREU). The accumulation of international and European human rights instruments dealing with the right to participate has strengthened the rights of children, but has also led to diverging concepts

Regarding case law on adoption, see: C. Fenton-Glynn, 'The Child's Voice in Adoption Proceedings: A European Perspective', *International Journal of Children's Rights*, Vol. 21, No. 4, 2013, pp. 590–615.

and interpretations. This development has been accentuated by the fact human rights standards contain open-ended requirements and discretion is often afforded to states as to how the rights can be implemented in national legislation and practice. Take, for example, the issue of whether or not age may form the sole condition for participation.[22] Article 12 UNCRC speaks of the child 'capable of forming his or her own views', a norm that is open to interpretation, whereas the ECECR and the GCFJ speak of 'sufficient understanding', and the ECtHR has seemingly relied on the age and maturity of the child in question. What is meant by these conditions? Are they similar or not in light of all of these instruments? Can European states use age as a condition for a child's participation in family law proceedings and, if so, should it?

For the European states parties to the international and European human rights instruments, it is crucial that the obligations to which they are bound are known. There are 47 European states bound to at least the UNCRC and the ECHR, but most of these 47 states are also bound to the other instruments (see Figure 1.1 below). Having clarity as to the binding standards is important not only so that states can work towards and ensure compliance with the human rights instruments themselves, but also to provide a framework by which researchers can evaluate whether states meet their human rights obligations. Even more important is the fact that children in particular, but also parents, professionals and others, should know the rights children have regarding their participation in family law proceedings. Overall, the broader societal importance of a clear international and European framework for the right of children to participate is that it may lead to the improved realization of children's rights.

While much has been written about child participation, to date there has yet to be a systematic comparison and analysis of the international and European human rights instruments addressing the child's right to participate in family law proceedings. The analysis and comparison of the standards in all these instruments is not only relevant for Europe, but also raises questions and provides new input for the understanding and realization of the right of the child to participate in family law proceedings internationally, as per the UNCRC amongst others. Therefore, while this book primarily addresses the rights of European children to participate in the 47 European states shown in Figure 1.1 below, the conclusions drawn – especially regarding the UNCRC – are also relevant for the more than 140 other states worldwide and the children residing there.

22 See e.g., Parkes 2013, pp. 113–117.

Figure 1.1. Map of Europe with instruments to which states are party[23]

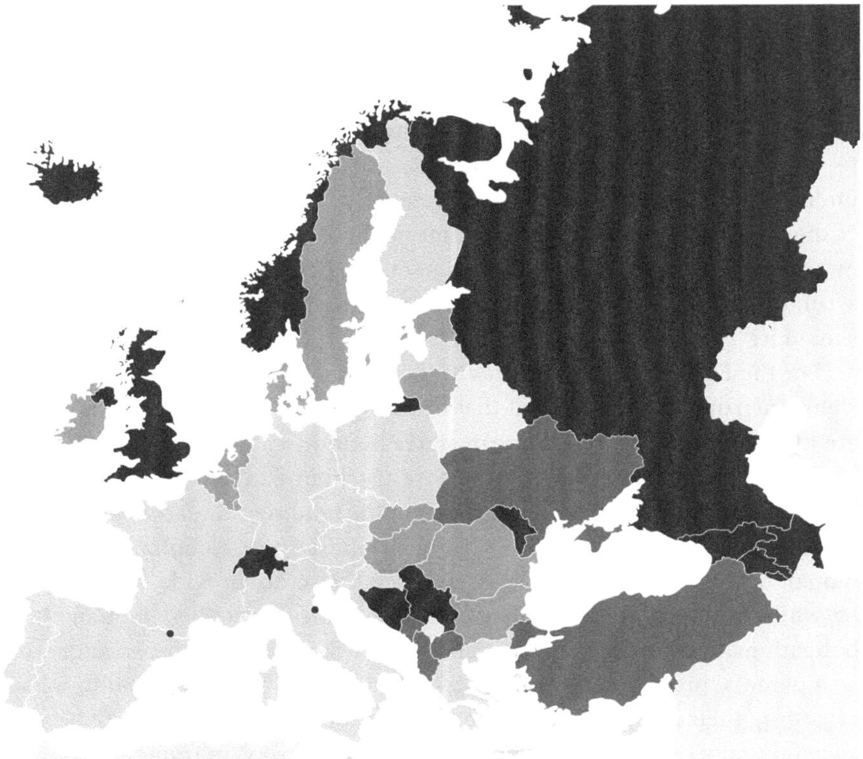

- UNCRC, ECHR, GCFJ and Recommendation
- UNCRC, ECHR, CFREU, GCFJ and Recommendation
- UNCRC, ECHR, ECECR, GCFJ and Recommendation
- UNCRC, ECHR, ECECR, CFREU, GCFJ and Recommendation

Source: Compiled by the author.

In light of the above, this book provides an in-depth analysis of the different international and European human rights instruments on child participation in family law proceedings. By means of comparison, the standards that European states have to meet are provided and, subsequently, the international and

[23] UN Convention on the Rights of the Child (UNCRC); European Convention on Human Rights (ECHR); European Convention on the Exercise of Children's Rights (ECECR); Charter of Fundamental Rights of the European Union (CFREU); Guidelines on Child-Friendly Justice (GCFJ); Recommendation on the participation of children (Recommendation).

European framework of the child's right to participate in family law proceedings is evaluated.

The analysis in this book consists of two steps. In the first step, the standards under the international and European human rights instruments are determined and analysed.[24] Instrument by instrument, the standards are described and their internal coherence is considered. For example, Article 12 UNCRC is analysed as such, but also in relation to other relevant articles in the UNCRC. Additionally, as a central part of this research, the ECHR and the case law of the ECtHR on child participation in family law proceedings are systematically analysed to determine the development and existence of coherent standards under Articles 6 and 8 ECHR.

In the second step, the standards are compared, and the international and European framework is evaluated in relation to the standards that can be aligned and strengthened. Considering the different origins, aims, scopes and degrees of specificity of these instruments, and the varying aspects and interpretations of the right to participate, there is much to compare. Recognizing that there are different approaches to child participation and the discretion afforded to states to most effectively (and efficiently) implement the child's right, this book aims to provide clarity as to the applicable standards where it is currently unclear. Throughout this book, the international and European framework is evaluated to determine how they can be aligned and strengthened.

The aim of children's participation in family law proceedings is central to this evaluation. As noted above, in the past few decades, children have increasingly been recognized as rights-holders instead of being solely viewed as 'object[s] of care and protection'.[25] The fundamental principle of the protection of children has been enriched with the empowerment of children and the recognition of their autonomy. In the balance between protection and empowerment, the child's right to participate has played a pivotal role in providing children more autonomy. This right provides children with the opportunity to express their views and have due weight accorded to these views. This is a circumscribed autonomy; children are not given *full* autonomy or a right to choose because a balance continues to be sought between empowerment and protection. In this book, the aim of child participation is understood to be to empower children by having their views on the matter considered in the decision-making process. The aim is not to determine the objective truth, but to give children the space to express their views, opinions and truths. In addition to empowering children, child participation is presumed to improve decision-making on matters

24 Standards are understood in this research as the legal obligations as well as the surrounding norms, guidelines and soft law which together form the legal framework.

25 Doek 2006, p. 199.

concerning the child. This aim is not articulated explicitly in the international and European instruments, but it lies beneath the development and provision of the child's right to participate.[26]

In order to advance the child's right to participate in family law proceedings, this book aims to align and strengthen the framework where the current standards or interpretations differ, conflict or provide room for improvement. The *alignment* of the framework is sought through comparing and evaluating the standards for their coherence and consistency, both in relation to each other and in relation to the aim of child participation, as expressed above. Aligning the framework is a first step towards strengthening the framework. Beyond evaluating the coherence and consistency, where difference or conflicts are found, suggestions to *strengthen* the framework are made by considering the aim of child participation (both the empowerment of children by providing circumscribed autonomy and the improvement of the decision-making process) and in light of this, the potential (practical) benefits between different options to help realize the aim of child participation. Where relevant, the human rights of others, specifically those of parents, are also considered in the strengthening of the framework.

In the following section, four central concepts in this book are defined (section 2). Subsequently, the structure of the research is set out (section 3).

2. CENTRAL CONCEPTS

Four central concepts must be defined before diving into the substance: child(ren); child participation; family law proceedings and international and European human rights instruments.

2.1. CHILD(REN)

The term 'child' or 'children' is used to refer to any person under the age of 18. This definition mirrors Article 1 UNCRC, the age of legal capacity as recommended by the Committee of Ministers of the Council of Europe, and the generally accepted European age of majority.[27]

---

26 See also ECtHR, *M. and M. v. Croatia* (App. No. 10161/13), 3 September 2015, para. 171, as discussed in Chapter 5, section 1.

27 Council of Europe (CoE), *Resolution (72)29 on the Lowering of the Age of Full Capacity*, adopted by the Committee of Ministers on 19 September 1972. See Explanatory Report to the European Convention on the Exercise of Children's Rights, 25 January 1996, para. 11.

2.2. CHILD PARTICIPATION

Participation is a word which can take on a myriad of meanings depending on the context in which it is used. In the normal meaning of the word, participation is the act of taking part in something. Whereas the term does not appear in the text of Article 12, it is commonly used in the debate surrounding the implementation of Article 12.[28] The Committee on the Rights of the Child (hereinafter 'the CRC Committee') has also drawn attention to the fact that the term 'participation' is 'now widely used' as Article 12 'has been broadly conceptualized as participation'.[29] In the context of children's rights, participation is an umbrella term. It has been subject to debate; Milne criticizes it as a 'buzzword' which captures 'both everything and nothing',[30] while other authors have noted that it is a 'multi-faceted concept' or 'container concept'.[31] In that sense, Herbots and Put suggest that 'participation' is 'not easily encapsulated by a single definition'.[32] Various academics have developed models to conceptualize child participation.[33]

---

28 See e.g. F. Ang et al., 'Participation Rights in the UN Convention on the Rights of the Child', in: F. Ang et al. (eds.), *Participation Rights of Children*, Antwerp: Intersentia 2006, pp. 9–26; E.E. Sutherland, 'Listening to the Voice of the Child: The Evolution of Participation Rights', *New Zealand Law Review*, Vol. 26, No. 3, 2013, pp. 335–355 and R. Thorburn Stern, *Implementing Article 12 of the UN Convention on the Rights of the Child: Participation, Power and Attitudes*, Leiden: Brill Nijhoff 2017.

29 UN Committee on the Rights of the Child, *General Comment No. 12 (2009): The Right of the Child to Be Heard*, 1 July 2009, CRC/C/GC/12, para. 3.

30 B. Milne, *Rights of the Child: 25 Years after the Adoption of the UN Convention*, Cham: Springer 2015, p. 88.

31 See Sutherland 2013, p. 354; and K. Herbots & J. Put, 'The Participation Disc: A Conceptual Analysis of (a) Child ('s Right to) Participation', *International Journal of Children's Rights*, Vol. 23, No. 1, 2015, pp. 154–188, p. 166.

32 Herbots & Put 2015, p. 156.

33 Based on Arnstein's ladder of citizen participation, Hart's ladder of child participation is perhaps the most well-known model of participation (R.A. Hart, *Children's Participation: From Tokenism to Citizenship*, Florence: UNICEF International Child Development Centre 1992 – see p. 8 for a figure of the ladder). This ladder has been further amended by, amongst others, P. Treseder, *Empowering Children and Young People: Training Manual; Promoting Involvement in Decision-Making*, London: Save the Children 1997. Other models include Shier's model (H. Shier, 'Pathways to Participation: Openings, Opportunities and Obligations: A New Model for Enhancing Children's Participation in Decision-Making, in Line with Article 12.1 of the United Nations Convention on the Rights of the Child', *Children & Society*, Vol. 15, No. 2, 2001, pp. 107–117 – see p. 111 for a figure), Thomas' theory (N. Thomas, 'Towards a Theory of Children's Participation', *International Journal of Children's Rights*, Vol. 15, No. 2, 2007, pp. 199–218), Lundy's model of child participation (L. Lundy, '"Voice" is Not Enough: Conceptualizing Article 12 of the United Nations Convention on the Rights of the Child', *British Educational Research Journal*, Vol. 33, No. 6, 2007, pp. 927–942 – see p. 932 for a figure of the model), and the participation disc of Herbots and Put (Herbots & Put 2015 – see p. 167 for a figure). See also Parkes 2013, pp. 15–23; and D.J.H. Smeets & S. Rap, 'Child Participation in Family Law Proceedings: Pedagogical Insights on Why and How to Involve Children', in: W.M. Schrama et al. (eds.), *International Handbook on Child Participation in Family Law*, Cambridge: Intersentia 2021, pp. 41–66, pp. 47–50.

These models concern participation in all contexts and recognize different levels of participation (for example, tokenistic participation to shared decisions) or emphasize important elements for child participation (such as Lundy's model, which defines space, voice, audience and influence).[34]

In this book, child participation refers to the act of expressing views, being heard and having these views considered in the decision-making process, specifically by courts in family law proceedings. Child participation embraces various modes of participation. There are no standard participation modes and there is no common terminology for the different modes of participation. However, one can broadly distinguish between direct participation (i.e. being heard by the decision-maker, such as a judge or state body) and indirect participation: either through representation (for example, by a guardian ad litem or separate legal representative) or through reports (for example, by experts or social workers).[35] Throughout this book, the different modes of participation and how to distinguish between them will be further examined and specified. Not included under child participation are children providing witness statements or testimony in legal proceedings, as these are modes of ascertaining evidence instead of the child's views on the matter.

2.3. FAMILY LAW PROCEEDINGS

Family law proceedings in this book are understood as including parentage, adoption, parental responsibilities, custody, access, international child abduction and child protection or care proceedings.[36] Most of the focus is on proceedings concerning parental authority, custody and access following the separation of parents.[37] However, proceedings on parentage, adoption and child protection or care are also considered. The latter may not always be understood as forming part of family law, because of the involvement of states or the public law nature of the proceedings, as opposed to parental conflicts, which are typically understood to fall under private law. However, as care proceedings do concern the relations

---

34 See Lundy 2007.

35 See e.g. Parkinson & Cashmore 2008, pp. 47–53; Parkes 2013, pp. 93–105 and Ballard et al. 2014, p. 127.

36 Proceedings regarding a child's first name, surname or gender are not included here.

37 Although the broader concept of parental responsibilities is more modern and better recognizes that the relationship between parents and children consists of both rights and duties of the parent, the terms 'parental authority', 'custody' and 'access' are used throughout this research to run in parallel with the terms used in many of the instruments studied. See specifically Chapter 4, section 7 below with regard to the case law of the ECtHR on this issue. On the topic of parental responsibilities, see further K. Boele-Woelki et al., *Principles of European Family Law Regarding Parental Responsibilities*, Antwerp: Intersentia 2007.

between parents and children and certainly affect children's rights and lives, this has been included, as child participation can play an important role.

This book focuses on contested and uncontested matters which enter the court system; therefore, the phrase 'family law *proceedings*' is used instead of 'family law *disputes*'. Family law disputes can also be resolved through alternative dispute resolution, most commonly through mediation, and child participation is equally important in alternative dispute resolution (ADR) processes.[38] Although the human rights framework will also apply (to a certain extent) to these processes, the specifics of child participation in ADR are beyond the scope of this book.

2.4. INTERNATIONAL AND EUROPEAN HUMAN RIGHTS INSTRUMENTS

A definition of international and European human rights instruments is not required here, but some words are needed to clarify their scope. Human rights instruments are treaties and other texts which serve as legal sources for human rights law. These instruments include well-respected soft law and case law. In this book, a distinction is made between international human rights instruments (in this case the UNCRC) and European human rights instruments. The European human rights instruments studied have been introduced above: on the one hand, the Council of Europe instruments (the ECHR and the case law of the ECtHR, the ECECR, the GCFJ and the 2012 Recommendation); and, on the other hand, the EU instrument (CFREU).

3. STRUCTURE OF THE BOOK

This book is divided into three parts: Part I, 'The Child's Right to Participate in International and European Human Rights Instruments'; Part II, 'The Child's Right to Participate in the Case Law of the ECtHR' and Part III, 'Comparative Remarks and Conclusions'.

In Part I, the international and European human rights instruments are subject to legal doctrinal research to determine the standards set. To determine and analyse the standards provided in the international and European human rights instruments, three aspects are addressed per instrument: (1) brief

38 See e.g. Parkinson & Cashmore 2008, pp. 43–47; A.L. James et al., 'The Voice of the Child in Family Mediation: Norway and England', *International Journal of Children's Rights*, Vol. 18, 2010, pp. 313–333; M. Vonk, 'Het Kind als (Vol)waardige Partij bij Mediation', in: J.H. de Graaf et al. (eds.), *Rechten van het Kind en Waardigheid*, Nijmegen: Ars Aequi Libri 2013, pp. 219–228 and Ballard et al. 2014, p. 123.

historical remarks regarding the introduction of the instrument; (2) the scope (material and personal) and nature (including enforceability) of the instrument and (3) the specific standards provided in the instrument concerning the right of children to participation in family law proceedings. Chapter 2 examines the child's right to participate according to the UN Convention on the Rights of the Child, whereas Chapter 3 examines the standards set by the European human rights instruments, with the exclusion of the ECHR.

Part II of this volume dives into the case law of the ECtHR. It presents the first qualitative content analysis (QCA) of the case law of the ECtHR on child participation in family law proceedings. The analysis aims to clarify how the Court has interpreted the children's right to participate in family law disputes in light of Articles 6 (the right to a fair trial) and 8 (the right to respect for private and family life) ECHR. Originating from the social sciences, QCA is a method used to meticulously examine text on the basis of a set coding frame.[39] This method was borrowed and adapted for this research, where a selection of 182 judgments and decisions of the ECtHR were subjected to the rigorous method of QCA. In doing so, the analysis systematically dissected each of the individual cases for the issues of child participation raised by the applicants and governments, and how child participation is dealt with by the ECtHR. New insights on the development, scope and content of the ECtHR's standards on child participation have been brought to light. The conclusions are of great relevance for understanding the European human rights framework on child participation in family law proceedings. In Chapter 4, the ECHR and the ECtHR are further introduced as well as the QCA method used, the structure of the analysis and the applicants, the types of proceedings, and the modes of participation present in the case law. The introduction of the case law analysis is followed by the analysis itself. In Chapters 5–8, the analysis is divided into four core themes of child participation as determined inductively and deductively in the case law analysis.[40] These themes are: (in)sufficient participation (Chapter 5); the weight accorded to the child's views (Chapter 6); the maturity of the child (Chapter 7) and 'influence' on the views of the child (Chapter 8). Subsequently, the conclusions of the case law analysis are brought together in Chapter 9, simultaneously signalling the end of Part II.

This leads us to Part III, where the standards from both Parts I and II are brought together, and opportunities to align and strengthen the international and European human rights framework on child participation are sought.

---

39 On the method of qualitative content analysis, see P. Mayring, 'Qualitative Content Analysis', *Forum: Qualitative Social Research Sozialforschung*, Vol. 1, No. 2, 2000; M. Schreier, *Qualitative Content Analysis in Practice*, London: SAGE 2012; M. Schreier, 'Qualitative Content Analysis', in: U. Flick (ed.), *The SAGE Handbook of Qualitative Data Analysis*, Los Angeles: SAGE 2014.

40 For further explanation, see Chapter 4, section 5.

The synthesis begins with the comparison of the standards in Chapter 10, examining the similarities and differences and providing some explanations for these. In the concluding Chapter 11, final recommendations and remarks are made for a strengthened and aligned framework for the child's right to participate in family law proceedings, addressing (European) states, courts, the CRC Committee, the ECtHR, future applicants, parents, children and academics.

PART I

THE CHILD'S RIGHT TO PARTICIPATE IN INTERNATIONAL AND EUROPEAN HUMAN RIGHTS INSTRUMENTS

CHAPTER 2

THE CHILD'S RIGHT TO PARTICIPATE IN THE UN CONVENTION ON THE RIGHTS OF THE CHILD

'There is a need for a better understanding of what Article 12 entails and how to fully implement it for every child.'

– UN Committee on the Rights of the Child[41]

1. INTRODUCTION

The United Nations Convention on the Rights of the Child (UNCRC) is for most children an invisible presence – a piece of paper with text that will likely not be understood. In fact, for many adults, the Convention will also be a blur of legalese. However, unbeknownst to most, the UNCRC has been the catalyst for the expansion and implementation of children's rights. More specifically, it has set in motion the existence and acceptance of the child as a legal subject, and Article 12 UNCRC is the cornerstone for the child's right to participate. As a children's rights instrument, the UNCRC is unparalleled, because of its international reach, being almost universally binding, and the broad scope of children's rights it provides.

In the quest to determine, align and strengthen the international and European human rights framework for the child's right to participate in family law proceedings, Article 12 and the UNCRC as a whole form the starting point. It is not possible to fully grasp the framework without first conducting a deep dive into the UNCRC. And this chapter will provide an in-depth study of this because, as the UN Committee on the Rights of the Child (CRC Committee) rightfully expressed in the quote above, there is much to be said about Article 12 and how to implement it.

In this chapter, the first step is to set out the international and European human rights framework for the child's right to participate and to determine how

41 UN Committee on the Rights of the Child, *General Comment No. 12 (2009): The Right of the Child to Be Heard*, 1 July 2009, CRC/C/GC/12, para. 4.

this framework can be aligned and strengthened: the UNCRC and Article 12 in particular are put through the x-ray machine. In doing so, the different aspects making up the right to participation will be lit up, as bones in the body. In addition, other UNCRC rights of relevance to the understanding and implementation of Article 12 will also be discussed, as the joints which allow our bones to connect and move. While doing so, the internal alignment (i.e. consistency and coherence) of the standards are considered and areas of uncertainty are reflected upon. When combined, an image of the child's rights under Article 12 UNCRC will be produced to determine the standards of the child's right to participate in family law proceedings under the UNCRC.

This chapter will proceed as follows. First, the UNCRC and the CRC Committee will be introduced with some historical remarks and by explaining the UNCRC's nature and scope (section 2). Subsequently, the bones of Article 12 are discussed (section 3). This consists of a detailed analysis of the text of Article 12 and is supplemented by the implementation steps required by the CRC Committee. With the bones in place, the relationship between Article 12 and other articles of the UNCRC will be analysed (section 4). In doing so, the contours of Article 12 will be further clarified. In section 5, the individual communications to the CRC Committee (i.e. its jurisprudence) regarding Article 12 will be examined for final clues. In the conclusion, all the above will be brought together to determine which standards the UNCRC dictates in terms of the child's right to participate in family law proceedings (section 5).

2. THE NATURE AND SCOPE OF THE UNCRC

Let us first consider the history of the Convention. With the introduction of the UNCRC in 1989, full human rights were granted to children for the first time as independent human beings.[42] The Convention was preceded by two Declarations on the Rights of the Child, but both were welfare-oriented and did not include civil and political rights or participation rights.[43] The League of Nations adopted the Geneva Declaration in 1924,[44] which inspired the subsequent Declaration on

42 United Nations Convention on the Rights of the Child, 20 November 1989, United Nations, Treaty Series, vol. 1577, p. 3. See also R.M. Stahl, '"Don't Forget about Me": Implementing Article 12 of the United Nations Convention on the Rights of the Child', *Arizona Journal of International & Comparative Law*, Vol. 24, No. 3, 2007, p. 805.

43 See D. Fottrell, 'One Step Forward or Two Steps Sideways? Assessing the First Decade of the Children's Convention on the Rights of the Child', in: D. Fottrell (ed.), *Revisiting Children's Rights: 10 Years of the UN Convention on the Rights of the Child*, The Hague: Kluwer Law International 2000, pp. 1–14, p. 2 and J. Tobin, 'Introduction: The Foundation for Children's Rights', in: J. Tobin (ed.), *The UN Convention on the Rights of the Child: A Commentary*, Oxford: Oxford University Press 2019, pp. 1–20, pp. 4–5.

44 *Declaration on the Rights of the Child*, Records of the Fifth Assembly, Supplement No. 23, League of Nations Official Journal 1924.

the Rights of the Child adopted by the UN General Assembly in 1959.[45] In light of the twentieth anniversary of the latter Declaration, 1979 was proclaimed as the 'International Year of the Child' by the UN General Assembly in 1976.[46] The International Year of the Child prompted the Polish government to propose a draft for a binding international convention on the rights of the child in 1978.[47] It subsequently took the established Working Group ten years to draft the Convention, whereby it is notable that non-governmental organizations were involved and that the final text was adopted on the basis of consensus.[48] The Convention was adopted by the UN General Assembly on 20 November 1989 and came into force on 2 September 1990.

Since the adoption of the UNCRC, it has achieved almost universal ratification, the sole exception being the USA.[49] This is unique for a human rights treaty and signifies the value given to children's rights from a political and moral point of view.[50] From a legal point of view, the UNCRC is a binding international convention for all states that have ratified it. Upon ratification, states parties have the obligation to implement the UNCRC according to Article 4. As will be further discussed in section 4.3 below, this includes 'ensuring that … the Convention's principles and provision can be directly applied and appropriately enforced'.[51] However, the practical reality is that the UNCRC cannot always be successfully invoked directly before national judicial or administrative authorities.[52] Legal challenges barring the invocation of UNCRC rights include 'the absence of a domestic constitution in which children's rights have been embedded or on the basis of which international law is regarded as

---

45 UN General Assembly, *Declaration on the Rights of the Child*, 20 November 1959, A/RES/1386(XIV).

46 UN General Assembly 31/169 on an International Year of the Child adopted on 21 December 1976. See also Tobin 2019, p. 5.

47 The complete draft can be found as an annex to UN Commission on Human Rights, *Report of the 34th Session 6 February–10 March 1978*, E/1978/34 or E/CN.4/1292.

48 For a brief discussion of the drafting process, see Tobin 2019, pp. 5–7. See also N. Cantwell, 'Are Children's Rights Still Human?', in: A. Invernizzi & J. Williams (eds.), *The Human Rights of Children: From Visions to Implementation*, Abingdon: Routledge 2011, pp. 51–70, pp. 53–54.

49 The USA has signed the UNCRC but has not ratified it. Both Somalia and South Sudan did ratify the Convention in 2015, making the UNCRC an almost universal treaty. See the Interactive Dashboard for the Status of Ratification, United Nations Office of the High Commissioner, available at: https://indicators.ohchr.org.

50 See M-F. Lücker-Babel, 'The Right of the Child to Express Views and to Be Heard: An Attempt to Interpret Article 12 of the UN Convention on the Rights of the Child', *International Journal of Children's Rights*, Vol. 3, No. 3/4, 1995, pp. 391–404, p. 391 and Fottrell 2000, p. 1.

51 UN Committee on the Rights of the Child, *General Comment No. 5 (2003): General Measures of Implementation of the Convention on the Rights of the Child*, 27 November 2003, CRC/GC/2003/5, para. 1. See also J. Zermatten, 'Foreword', in: T. Liefaard & J.E. Doek (eds.), *Litigating the Rights of the Child*, Dordrecht: Springer 2015, p. vii.

52 See T. Liefaard & J.E. Doek, 'Litigating the Rights of the Child: Taking Stock after 25 Years of the CRC', in: T. Liefaard & J.E. Doek (eds.), *Litigating the Rights of the Child*, Dordrecht: Springer 2015, pp. 1–12, p. 2.

higher law'.[53] Another key legal challenge is the fact that children often have no standing to bring claims on their own behalf and must instead rely on their legal representatives.[54] There can also be practical and cultural reasons which can limit the potential of litigating UNCRC rights in legal systems[55] – for example, issues of corruption or a weak rule of law,[56] limited access to international documents, and cultural attitudes.[57]

The implementation of the UNCRC by states is monitored by the CRC Committee, which was introduced by means of Articles 43 and 45 UNCRC. The CRC Committee is a treaty-based UN organ consisting of 18 experts, with the responsibility to monitor the implementation of the Convention through state reporting procedures.[58] The CRC Committee also drafts General Comments, which may give interpretations for specific articles, deal with general issues or address themes covered by multiple articles.[59] General Comments have been described best by Alston as 'a means by which a UN human rights expert committee distils its considered views on an issue which arises out of the provision of the treaty whose implementation it supervises and presents those views in the context of a formal statement of its understanding to which it attaches major importance'.[60] General Comments are not legally binding on states parties; instead, they are 'secondary soft law instruments' and are understood to include norms which 'interpret and add detail' to UNCRC rights.[61]

53 Liefaard & Doek 2015, p. 3.

54 See e.g. W. Vandenhole, 'Belgium: The Convention on the Rights of the Child in Belgian Case Law', in: T. Liefaard & J.E. Doek (eds.), 2015, pp. 105–122, p. 108. This is similarly the situation in Australia, China, the Netherlands, New Zealand, Norway and Romania; see C.R. Mol, 'Child Participation in Family Law Proceedings Compared', in: W. Schrama et al. (eds.), *International Handbook on Child Participation in Family Law*, Cambridge: Intersentia 2021a, pp. 335–358, p. 346.

55 Liefaard & Doek 2015, p. 2.

56 See e.g. N. Vučković Šahović & I. Savić, 'Serbia: Strategic Litigation on the Rights of the Child in Serbia', in: T. Liefaard & J.E. Doek (eds.), *Litigating the Rights of the Child*, Dordrecht: Springer 2015, pp. 139–156, pp. 154–155.

57 See e.g. K. Filali, 'Algeria: Experiences in Algeria with the Use of the CRC in Legal Proceedings', in: T. Liefaard & J.E. Doek (eds.), *Litigating the Rights of the Child: The UN Convention on the Rights of the Child in Domestic and International Jurisprudence*, Dordrecht: Springer 2015, pp. 157–175, pp. 162 and 174–175.

58 See M. Verheyde & G. Goedertier, 'Articles 43–45: The UN Committee on the Rights of the Child', in: A. Alen et al. (eds.), *A Commentary on the United Nations Convention on the Rights of the Child*, Leiden: Martinus Nijhoff 2006, pp. 3–4.

59 See Verheyde & Goedertier 2006, p. 39–40.

60 P. Alston, 'The Historical Origins of the Concept of "General Comments" in Human Rights Law', in: L. Boisson de Chazournes & V. Gowlland-Debas, *The International Legal System in Quest of Equity and Universality: Liber Amoricum Georges Abi-Saab*, The Hague: Martinus Nijhoff 2001, pp. 763–776, p. 764. See also H. Keller & L. Grover, 'General Comments of the Human Rights Committee and Their Legitimacy', in: H. Keller & G. Ulfstein (eds.), *UN Human Rights Treaty Bodies: Law and Legitimacy*, Cambridge: Cambridge University Press 2012, pp. 116–198, p. 117.

61 Keller & Grover 2012, p. 129.

In 2011, the Optional Protocol to the UNCRC on a communications procedure was adopted.[62] This Third Optional Protocol entered into force on 14 April 2014 and provides for individual communications to the CRC Committee. This means that children can, either individually or as a group, submit complaints of non-compliance or a violation of the Convention to the CRC Committee.[63] The CRC Committee will consider the admissibility of the communication and will invite the state to respond to the complaint.[64] Subsequently, a friendly settlement is sought and when this is not achieved, the CRC Committee will consider the communication and 'adopt views' (i.e. issue an opinion with recommendations) on the communication.[65] The adopted views and recommendations are binding for the state party involved and the Third Optional Protocol provides for a follow-up procedure by which the CRC Committee invites the state party to inform the Committee on the actions taken in response to the views and recommendations.[66] It is worth noting that the individual communications procedure is limited to violations by those states that have ratified the Third Optional Protocol (at present 46 states).[67]

The substantive scope of the UNCRC is broad. The Convention consists of 40 substantive children's rights, including civil, political, economic, social and cultural rights, protective rights and participatory rights. In this volume Article 12, with its right to express views, is the central focus. It is also considered to be one of the four 'general principles' by the CRC Committee.[68] The four general principles are considered to be the Convention rights which are vital for the interpretation and effective implementation of all the guaranteed Convention rights.[69] The right to be heard in Article 12 is one of these four general principles, together with the principle of non-discrimination (Article 2), the principle that the best interests of the child should be a primary consideration (Article 3), and the right to life, survival and development (Article 6). As one of the general principles, the right to be heard provides a vehicle for children to exercise all

---

62 Optional Protocol to the Convention on the Rights of the Child on a communications procedure, adopted and opened for signature, ratification and accession by General Assembly Resolution A/RES/66/138 of 19 December 2011.

63 Article 5 of the Third Optional Protocol. See also R. Smith, 'The Third Optional Protocol to the UN Convention on the Rights of the Child? Challenges Arising Transforming the Rhetoric into Reality', in: M. Freeman (ed.), *The Future of Children's Rights*, Leiden: Koninklijke Brill NV 2014, pp. 178–195, p. 181.

64 Articles 7 and 8 of the Third Optional Protocol.

65 Articles 9 and 10 of the Third Optional Protocol. See Smith 2014, pp. 181–182.

66 Article 11 of the Third Optional Protocol. See Smith 2014, p. 182.

67 Currently 46 states have ratified the Third Optional Protocol, with an additional 18 signatories (8 December 2020). See the Interactive Dashboard for the Status of Ratification, United Nations Office of the High Commissioner, available at: https://indicators.ohchr.org/.

68 UNCRC General Comment No. 5 (2003), para. 12.

69 UNCRC General Comment No. 12 (2009), para. 2.

the other rights contained in the UNCRC.[70] This means that Article 12 not only provides a substantive right as a means in itself, but also that it is a procedural right in relation to the other articles of the UNCRC.[71] Before we turn to the relationship between Article 12 and the other UNCRC rights, the content and scope of Article 12 UNCRC itself will be discussed.

3. THE RIGHT TO PARTICIPATE: ARTICLE 12 UNCRC

Article 12 UNCRC determines that children should be provided with the opportunity to express their views in all matters concerning them and that these views should be given due weight. More specifically, in paragraph 2, the child's right to be heard is safeguarded, whether directly or through a representative, in any judicial and administrative proceedings affecting the child. In the following section, Article 12 will be further analysed to determine the scope and content of this right to participation. The analysis will begin with the text of the article, before moving on to look at some themes more generally.

3.1. ANALYSIS OF THE TEXT OF ARTICLE 12 UNCRC

In this analysis, the text of Article 12 UNCRC will be dissected. The phrasing of the article reveals a great deal. Before diving into specifics, let us introduce the text of Article 12, which reads as follows:

> 1. States Parties shall assure to the child who is capable of forming his or her own views the right to express those views freely in all matters affecting the child, the views of the child being given due weight in accordance with the age and maturity of the child.
> 2. For this purpose, the child shall in particular be provided the opportunity to be heard in any judicial and administrative proceedings affecting the child, either directly, or through a representative or an appropriate body, in a manner consistent with the procedural rules of national law.

The article consists of two paragraphs. The first paragraph provides the more general right to express views in all matters and situations affecting the child, while the second paragraph more specifically concerns judicial and administrative proceedings. Thus, one can say that the second paragraph is a

---

70 A. Parkes, *Children and International Human Rights Law: The Right of the Child to Be Heard*, Abingdon: Routledge 2013, p. 5.

71 R. Hodgkin & P. Newell, *Implementation Handbook for the Convention on the Rights of the Child*, New York: UNICEF 2007, p. 150.

lex specialis, as it provides additional specifics for the right to express views in judicial and administrative proceedings.[72] Both paragraphs will be discussed separately, but it is important to remember the distinction between the more general nature of the first paragraph compared to the second paragraph.

3.1.1. Article 12(1) UNCRC

The core of Article 12 is found in the first paragraph of the article. This paragraph provides for the right of the child to express his or her views freely in all matters affecting the child and for these views to be given due weight in accordance with the age and maturity of the child. In analysing this first paragraph, the text can be divided into six phrases of importance: States Parties (1) *shall assure* to the child who is (2) *capable of forming his or her own views* the right to (3) *express those views freely* in (4) *all matters affecting the child*, the (5) *views of the child being given due weight* (6) *in accordance with the age and maturity of the child.*

3.1.1.1. 'Shall Assure'

The paragraph starts with the phrase that states 'shall assure' this right. As with all Convention rights, Article 12 is in essence an obligation for states parties. As signatories to the Convention text, they have bound themselves to fulfilling the duties contained in the text. According to the CRC Committee, the use of the term 'assure' strengthens the legal obligation of states to implement the right provided in Article 12: it is a 'strict obligation' with 'no leeway' for discretion.[73] This interpretation has been reiterated by various authors.[74] Within the UNCRC, the term 'assure' is only used in Article 12. More common are the phrases 'shall ensure', 'shall undertake' or 'shall respect'.

The drafting history of Article 12 does not clarify why the term 'assure' was used. It was discussed whether the article should have started with 'shall enable the child' or 'shall assure to the child'.[75] The sole comment in the drafting history with regard to this discussion is: 'One speaker pointed out that the state is under no obligation, as a matter of law, towards children: the child should have a degree of freedom comparable to that enjoyed by an individual under the

---

72 L. Lundy, J. Tobin & A. Parkes, 'Art. 12: The Right to Respect for the Views of the Child', in: Tobin 2019, pp. 397–434, p. 420.

73 UNCRC General Comment No. 12 (2009), para. 19.

74 L. Lundy, '"Voice" is Not Enough: Conceptualizing Article 12 of the United Nations Convention on the Rights of the Child', *British Educational Research Journal*, Vol. 33, No. 6, 2007, pp. 927–942, pp. 933–934; E.E. Sutherland, 'Listening to the Voice of the Child: The Evolution of Participation Rights', *New Zealand Law Review*, Vol. 26, No. 3, 2013, pp. 335–355, p. 341 and Lundy, Tobin & Parkes 2019, p. 416.

75 UN Economic and Social Council Commission on Human Rights, *Report of the Working Group on a Draft Convention on the Rights of the Child*, 17 February 1981, E/CN.4/L.1575, para. 77.

Covenants and comparable instruments'.[76] This comment does not provide any explanation as to why 'assure' is more suitable than 'enable'. The remark that the state has no legal obligation towards children is problematic. In drafting, signing and ratifying an international treaty on children's rights, states have agreed to respect and ensure children's rights, and thus have created legal obligations for themselves towards the children under their jurisdiction. Regarding the second half of the statement, does the speaker mean to say that an obligation to provide rights to children hinders the freedom of children? In principle, the answer should be no. States' human rights obligations generally do not limit the freedom of persons, but instead may offer more freedom. The legal obligation to assure or enable the right of children to express views is a good example of this. Perhaps the second half of the statement is the speaker suggesting that children should have the 'degree of freedom' to express views comparable to the freedom granted to adults to express their views. All in all, while the drafting history does not offer any guidance as to the use of the term 'assure' and the strength of the legal obligation, this strength has been widely accepted by the CRC Committee and in the legal literature.[77]

The strict obligation to provide children with the right to express views has also not been curbed through any reservations by states parties.[78] There are three states parties that have, in their declaration, stated (amongst other things) that the rights provided by Article 12 UNCRC 'shall be exercised with respect for parental authority' in accordance with their national customs and traditions.[79] The lack of reservations means that Article 12 must be implemented regardless of the cultural or traditional differences between states parties. However, the CRC Committee has remarked that cultural and traditional attitudes towards children are a serious obstacle towards implementing Article 12 effectively in all states, including those who have not made any declarations regarding national customs and traditions.[80]

3.1.1.2. 'Capable of Forming His or Her Own Views'

The right to express views is not granted unconditionally. Article 12 provides the child 'capable of forming his or her own views' with the right to express views.

---

76 UNCHR Report of the Working Group 1981, para. 77.

77 As discussed above, see UNCRC General Comment No. 12 (2009), para. 19; Lundy 2007, pp. 933–934; Sutherland 2013, p. 341 and Lundy, Tobin & Parkes 2019, p. 416.

78 See the United Nations Treaty Collection website for all the reservations and declarations made regarding the UNCRC: https://treaties.un.org/Pages/ViewDetails.aspx?src=IND&mtdsg_no=IV-11&chapter=4&clang=_en.

79 Kiribati, Poland and Singapore. See the United Nations Treaty Collection website for all the reservations and declarations made regarding the UNCRC: https://treaties.un.org/Pages/ViewDetails.aspx?src=IND&mtdsg_no=IV-11&chapter=4&clang=_en.

80 UN Committee on the Rights of the Child, *Recommendations: Day of General Discussion on the Right of the Child to Be Heard*, 29 September 2006, para. 9.

This phrase originated in the revised Polish draft of 1979, where it was included in the proposed Article 7.[81] During the discussion of the Working Group in 1981, the proposal from the USA for Article 3 (which included what later evolved into Article 12(2)) used the phrasing 'the age of reason'.[82] An unspecified delegate opposed the use of this phrase, finding 'the characterization of "the age of reason" ... very difficult'.[83] The Working Group agreed to replace the phrase with being 'capable of forming his or her own views', following the suggestion of an observer of the International Association of Penal Law.[84] The choice not to adopt the 'age of reason' proposal can be understood as a choice not to include a qualitative requirement or, in light of the drafting history, a choice for a requirement that is less difficult to 'characterize'.[85] However, the question is whether it was not in fact swapping one qualitative requirement, 'age of reason', with another one, 'capable of forming his or her own views', and whether the latter is easier to characterize.

Thus, 'capability' to form views constitutes the requirement for the right to participate in the first paragraph of Article 12. The CRC Committee notes that this phrase should not be seen as a limitation of the right to express views, but that it is an 'obligation for states parties to assess the capacity of the child to form an autonomous opinion'.[86] What does this mean? The CRC Committee tries to positively spin the capability requirement. However, it remains the case that the right is not provided to all children unconditionally. 'Capability' must be assessed, whether as 'the capacity of the child to form an autonomous opinion' or otherwise (as we will see below). What is meant by forming an 'autonomous opinion' is not clarified and nor is it made clear how states should assess this in practice. The CRC Committee subsequently notes that as it is not a limitation, states 'cannot begin with the assumption that the child is incapable'.[87] Instead, there is a presumption of capacity to which states parties should adhere: 'it is not up to the child to first prove her or his capacity'.[88] Alderson remarks that the Committee somewhat contradicts itself with these statements: if there is a

---

81 UN Economic and Social Council Commission on Human Rights, *Question of a Convention on the Rights of the Child: Note Verbale Dated 5 October 1979 Addressed to the Division of Human Rights by the Permanent Representation of the Polish People's Republic to the United Nations in Geneva*, 17 January 1980, E/CN.4/1349*.

82 UNCHR Report of the Working Group 1981, para. 20.

83 UNCHR Report of the Working Group 1981, para. 29.

84 UNCHR Report of the Working Group 1981, para. 29.

85 See A. Daly, *Children, Autonomy and the Courts: Beyond the Right to Be Heard*, Leiden: Brill 2018a, p. 46; and Lundy, Tobin & Parkes 2019, p. 404.

86 UNCRC General Comment No. 12 (2009), para. 20.

87 UNCRC General Comment No. 12 (2009), para. 20.

88 UNCRC General Comment No. 12 (2009), para. 20, see also L. Krappmann, 'The Weight of the Child's View (Article 12 of the Convention on the Rights of the Child)', *International Journal of Children's Rights*, Vol. 18, No. 4, 2010, pp. 501–513, p. 507 and G. Lansdown, *Every Child's Right to Be Heard: A Resource Guide on the UN Committee on the Rights of the Child General Comment No. 12*, London: Save the Children Fund 2011, p. 20.

presumption of capacity for all children, then why is the assessment of capacity as an obligatory starting point?[89] The phrasing of the first statement should perhaps be inverted: it is an obligation for states parties to assess the incapacity, as capacity is presumed.[90]

A subsequent question is how to understand this 'capability' requirement. Clear guidance from the CRC Committee is that the article does not impose an age limit and that there should not be an age limit 'either in law or in practice which would restrict the child's right to be heard'.[91] It has also stated previously that 'age should not be a barrier to the child's right to participate fully in the justice process'.[92] If 'capability' is not to be defined by age, how can it be understood within Article 12? The CRC Committee provides a few additional interpretive comments.

The first is that young children can be capable of forming views, even if they are not yet able to express them verbally.[93] 'Views' may also be understood as including 'feelings, insights, interpretations, concerns and ideas'.[94] Thus, young or disabled children must also be provided with the opportunity to participate, even if non-verbally. This has also been reaffirmed in the General Comment on implementing child rights in early childhood, where the CRC Committee emphasized that 'even the youngest children are entitled to express their views'.[95] According to Krappmann, the Committee's recommendation to hear young children is to 'find out whether their views can contribute to good solutions'.[96]

Second, according to the CRC Committee, it is 'not necessary that the child has comprehensive knowledge of all aspects of the matter affecting him or her'.[97] A child does not need to be able to understand all aspects of the matter or be able to foresee the consequences of their views; instead, he or she needs to have 'sufficient understanding to be capable of appropriately forming her or his own views'.[98] But what is 'sufficient understanding' and when has a child 'appropriately' formed views? 'Sufficient understanding' may be understood as

---

89 P. Alderson, 'Giving Children's Views "Due Weight" in Medical Law', *International Journal of Children's Rights*, Vol. 26, No. 1, 2018, p. 21.

90 C.R. Mol, 'Maturity and the Child's Right to Be Heard in Family Law Proceedings: Article 12 UNCRC and Case Law of the ECtHR Compared', in: K. Boele-Woelki & D. Martiny (eds.), *Plurality and Diversity of Family Relations in Europe*, Cambridge: Intersentia 2019a, pp. 237–254, p. 239.

91 UNCRC General Comment No. 12 (2009), para. 21.

92 UNCRC Recommendations: Day of General Discussion 2006, para. 51.

93 UNCRC General Comment No. 12 (2009), para. 21.

94 Lansdown 2011, p. 21.

95 UN Committee on the Rights of the Child, *General Comment No. 7 (2005): Implementing Child Rights in Early Childhood*, 20 September 2006, CRC/C/GC/7/Rev.1, para. 14.

96 Krappmann 2010, p. 507.

97 UNCRC General Comment No. 12 (2009), para. 21.

98 UNCRC General Comment No. 12 (2009), para. 21.

having some 'idea on the issue' and 'what is at stake', as suggested by Lücker-Babel,[99] or may be understood as forming a higher threshold. In any case, it may be assumed that it cannot form a very high threshold as that would contradict the remarks made that very young children may also be capable When views are 'appropriately' formed is also vague and may lead to 'subjective assessments' by decision-makers, just as 'sufficient understanding' may.[100] The phrasing calls for more substance.

A third interpretative comment can be extracted from the previously mentioned remark by the CRC Committee that it is an 'obligation for states parties to assess the capacity of the child to form an autonomous opinion'.[101] The criterion of forming an 'autonomous opinion' as a means of determining capability does not provide a clear-cut interpretative guidance. Neither the CRC Committee nor legal scholars have further identified what is meant by forming an 'autonomous opinion'. Based on the ordinary meaning of the phrase, it can be understood to mean that a child ought to be able to form an independent opinion free from the influence of others, such as his or her parents in family law proceedings. With the topic of influence often raised within debates on child participation in family law proceedings, the use of the term 'autonomous opinion' may further raise the threshold for the child to express his or her views.

The interpretative comments proffered in the General Comment do not offer enough to apply the 'capability' criterion in practice. The language of the commentary is 'vague, problematic and exclusionary', as noted by Daly.[102] The CRC Committee relies on interpretation by negation, employing a mainly negative explanation as to when a child is capable of forming his or her own views, dismissing age criteria or the requirement of comprehensive knowledge. Additionally, using 'capability' and phrases such as 'sufficient understanding', 'appropriately' forming views and 'autonomous opinion' does not offer any further tools for interpretation. Of course, it is inherent to the nature of open norms that they are vague to a certain extent, and the lack of clarity provided by the CRC Committee may be further explained by the fact that the first paragraph of Article 12 concerns participation 'all matters' and not specifically in judicial proceedings.

A reason why the vague phrasing may be 'problematic and exclusionary' is because the open-norm allows for adults to assess and decide when a child is 'capable'.[103] They can be 'interpreted to impose a qualitative test on children's ability to form views which could be used to deny some children the benefit of

---

99 Lücker-Babel 1995, p. 397.
100 Lundy, Tobin & Parkes 2019, p. 405.
101 UNCRC General Comment No. 12 (2009), para. 20.
102 Daly 2018a, p. 47.
103 Daly 2018a, p. 47; Lundy, Tobin & Parkes 2019, p. 406.

having a right to express their views'.[104] This brings with it the risk that adults may place a high threshold which could exclude certain children. As strongly stated by Archard and Skivenes, 'a child should not be judged against a standard of competence by which even most adults would fail'.[105] It is therefore important that the 'capability' criterion is not applied too strictly to avoid the unjust exclusion of certain children.[106]

3.1.1.3. Right to Express Views Freely

The third phrase to be analysed is that the child has the right to 'express those views freely'. This phrase strengthens the position of the child in three ways. First, the word 'views' indicates a broader right than being able to express 'wishes' or 'opinions', which were suggested at earlier stages of the drafting process.[107] In the technical review of the draft Convention, the United Nations Children's Fund (UNICEF) commented on the replacement of the word 'wishes' with 'views', as this would suit the intention 'to take into account of all views and not only those which constitute wishes'.[108] The other two aspects strengthening the position of the child in the phrase are linked to the term 'freely'. 'Freely' expresses that a child has the choice whether or not to exercise his or her right to express views.[109] Article 12 provides a right for the child to participate, but not an obligation to do so. 'Freely' also conveys that there should be no undue pressure or influence placed on the child when expressing his or her views.[110] In that regard, the CRC Committee also refers to the use of the term 'own views' in Article 12 UNCRC: the child has the right to express their views, not the views of others.[111] The child should be able to express his or her views safely. He or she should be supported in expressing his or her views and should not fear criticism or punishment.[112]

While providing children with a stronger position, the phrase that the child has the right to 'express those views freely' is worth little without the connected right to have those views given 'due weight'. As we will see below, this is a valuable

---

104 Lundy, Tobin & Parkes 2019, p. 406.

105 D. Archard & M. Skivenes, 'Balancing a Child's Best Interests and a Child's Views', *International Journal of Children's Rights*, Vol. 17, No. 1, 2009, pp. 1–21, p. 10.

106 Lücker-Babel 1995, p. 397.

107 See the wording of Article 7 in the Polish Revised Draft Convention in UNCHR Note verbale 1980; and the wording of the Australian proposal in the UNCHR Report of the Working Group 1981, para. 74. See also Lundy, Tobin & Parkes 2019, p. 407.

108 See the text taken from E/CN.4/1989/WG.1/CRP.1 in United Nations Office of the High Commissioner of Human Rights, *Legislative History of the Convention on the Rights of the Child* (vol. I), 2007, p. 441.

109 UNCRC General Comment No. 12 (2009), para. 16 and 22; and Sutherland 2013, p. 344.

110 UNCRC General Comment No. 12 (2009), para. 22.

111 UNCRC General Comment No. 12 (2009), para. 22.

112 Lansdown 2011, p. 22.

addition and a core difference between the right to freedom of expression in Article 13 and the right provided in Article 12.

3.1.1.4. 'In All Matters Affecting the Child'

In the first paragraph of Article 12 UNCRC, it is specified that the right to express views is granted in 'all matters affecting the child'. This phrase provides for a very broad application of the right.[113] This is even more the case given the drafting process of this phrase. In the first draft of the Convention (the revised Polish draft of 1979), the right was limited to expressing views 'in matters concerning his own person, and in particular, marriage, choice of occupation, medical treatment, education and recreation'.[114] During the 1981 Working Group discussions, the USA suggested a revised version of Article 7, expanding the list of matters by adding 'religion, political and social beliefs, matters of conscience, cultural and artistic matters'.[115] However, most delegations[116] called for the removal of the list as they were of the opinion that the right should not 'be subject to the limits of a list'.[117] The Working Group thus opted to delete the list and instead adopted the text with the phrase 'in all matters'.[118] During the second reading at the Working Group discussion of 1989, the Finnish delegation suggested adding to the phrase 'affecting the child'.[119] The Working Group discussed two options – 'affecting the child' and 'affecting the rights of the child' – finally adopting the phrase 'in all matters affecting the child'.[120] This phrase is inclusive, also covering matters affecting the rights of the child, as noted by the Finnish observer.[121] This development in drafting ensured a less restrictive formulation in the first paragraph of Article 12.[122]

The phrase 'in all matters affecting the child' is therefore not restrictive with regard to legal or non-legal matters, although the term 'affecting' does signal that there must be a connection between the child and the matter.[123] Lücker-Babel has argued that this requires a 'restrictive interpretation' to those matters 'affecting them directly'.[124] Similarly, Cantwell has noted that these matters should be those 'directly pertinent to the life of the child concerned';

---

113 Sutherland 2013, pp. 343–344.
114 UNCHR Note verbale 1980.
115 UNCHR Report of the Working Group 1981, para. 76.
116 It is not stated which delegations these were, but representatives of 21 states attended the Working Group meetings in 1981; see UNCHR Report of the Working Group 1981, para. 5.
117 UNCHR Report of the Working Group 1981, para. 76.
118 UNCHR Report of the Working Group 1981, paras. 79 and 80.
119 UNCHR Report of the Working Group 1989, para. 235.
120 UNCHR Report of the Working Group 1989, para. 253.
121 UNCHR Report of the Working Group 1989, paras. 242 and 243.
122 Lundy, Tobin & Parkes 2019, p. 408; and Krappmann 2010, p. 504.
123 Lundy, Tobin & Parkes 2019, p. 408.
124 Lücker-Babel 1995, p. 396.

children would then have the freedom of expression in more general matters.[125] However, as there is nothing in the drafting history to hint at a restrictive interpretation and the General Comment makes no reference to any need for direct effect, it can be agreed that the matter does not need to directly affect the child; it solely needs to affect the child.[126] In this regard, it is important to note that the matters affecting the child are not limited to those affecting individual children (such as family law proceedings that form the focus of this volume), but also encompass matters affecting groups of children.[127] The latter matters include, for example, policy-making in fields affecting all children or in specific fields with children who have experience in that field (e.g. juvenile justice), or a class of children with regard to policy at school.[128]

3.1.1.5. Views of the Child Given Due Weight

The first paragraph of Article 12 concludes with the phrase that the states parties shall assure 'the views of the child being given due weight in accordance with the age and maturity of the child'. This phrase is of great relevance for the right to participation provided by Article 12 UNCRC. It formulates the obligation for states to give serious consideration to the child's views when making a decision.[129] As the CRC Committee notes, 'simply listening to the child is insufficient'.[130] The subsequent step of due weight is necessary.

Let us start with a brief historical note. Originally, in the Article 3 proposal of the USA, the phrase was that 'views shall be taken into account'.[131] Once the paragraph was moved to Article 7, the Australian representative proposed the phrasing of 'due weight'.[132] There is no explanation in the Working Group reports as to why this phrase was chosen over the other. Krappmann interprets the amendment as expanding and strengthening the original proposals.[133]

Turning to the interpretation, in order to correctly understand the obligation placed on states, the phrase 'due weight' indicates that Article 12 UNCRC is a

125 Cantwell 2011, p. 65.

126 F. Ang et al., 'Participation Rights in the UN Convention on the Rights of the Child', in: F. Ang et al. (eds.), *Participation Rights of Children*, Antwerp: Intersentia 2006, pp. 9–26, p. 17; and Lundy, Tobin & Parkes 2019, p. 409.

127 UNCRC General Comment No. 12 (2009), para. 9. See also Ang et al. 2006, p. 17; and Lundy, Tobin & Parkes 2019, p. 409.

128 UNCRC General Comment No. 12 (2009), paras. 9, 105 and 127. See also Ang et al. 2006, p. 17; and Lundy, Tobin & Parkes 2019, p. 409.

129 Lansdown 2011, p. 23.

130 UNCRC General Comment No. 12 (2009), para. 28.

131 UNCHR Report of the Working Group 1981, para. 20.

132 UNCHR Report of the Working Group 1981, para. 75.

133 Krappmann 2010, p. 503.

right to participation, not a right to self-determination.[134] Due weight signals that the views of the child can be given more or less weight. In the General Comment, the CRC Committee provides no interpretation of 'due weight' beyond stating that 'the views of the child have to be seriously considered'.[135] As observed by Parkes, 'due weight' has 'not been given any definitive meaning'.[136] Most likely, the lack of a definitive or 'specific'[137] meaning is due to the open nature of the concept 'due weight'. If we break down the concept, a definition is in fact possible. In legal dictionaries, the term 'due' is defined as 'proper under law'[138] or as 'just; proper; regular; lawful; sufficient'.[139] More generally, the *Oxford English Dictionary* defines it as 'that ought (by right, in fairness, etc., or in the opinion of the writer or speaker) to be given, granted, or carried out; requisite; merited, deserved'.[140] The definition of 'weight' in this context is provided as 'the relative importance or authority accorded something' in the *Merriam-Webster Legal Dictionary*.[141] Combining the above, this research suggests the following definition: 'proper or just relative importance accorded'. In this definition, the term 'relative' is of key importance as it emphasizes how due weight cannot be determined *in abstracto*; instead, what is 'due' will depend on the circumstances of each individual case.

The relative nature of due weight also explains why neither 'due weight' nor the definition above provide what would be 'due', 'proper or just' importance for the views of children. The decision-maker will need to come to that determination himself or herself, taking different factors into account. According to Article 12 UNCRC, a relevant factor that must be considered when doing so is the 'age and maturity' of the child. This key factor will be discussed further below (see section 3.1.1.6). The Convention does not explain whether any further factors are relevant for due weight. However, the CRC Committee appears to refer to one other factor.[142] Somewhat inconspicuously, when attempting to define maturity, the Committee notes that 'the impact of the matter on the child must also be taken into consideration'.[143] This is followed by the comment that the 'greater the impact of the outcome on the life of the child, the more relevant the appropriate assessment of the maturity of the child'.[144] The last part of that

134 R. Thorburn Stern, *Implementing Article 12 of the UN Convention on the Rights of the Child: Participation, Power and Attitudes*, Leiden: Brill Nijhoff 2017, p. 53.
135 UNCRC General Comment No. 12 (2009), para. 28.
136 Parkes 2013, p. 35.
137 Thorburn Stern 2017, p. 62.
138 *Merriam-Webster*, https://www.merriam-webster.com/dictionary/due.
139 *Black's Law Dictionary*, https://thelawdictionary.org/due/.
140 *Oxford English Dictionary Online*, Oxford University Press, September 2019, www.oed.com/.
141 *Merriam-Webster*, https://www.merriam-webster.com/dictionary/weight, no. 7a.
142 Lundy, Tobin & Parkes 2019, p. 414.
143 UNCRC General Comment No. 12 (2009), para. 30.
144 UNCRC General Comment No. 12 (2009), para. 30.

comment is strange; one would expect that the greater the impact, the more weight should be granted to the views of the child. This is also how most authors would understand this additional factor.[145]

In the literature, more additional factors have been suggested. Multiple authors refer to a list of factors presented by Willow in her research regarding children's right to be heard in child protection cases following violence.[146] The factors formulated by Willow are: the extent to which the decision will impact the child, the extent to which other children and adults will be affected by the decision, the strength of the child's views, how the rights of the child and the rights of others will be affected by the decision, and what the consequences are if the child's views are not followed.[147] Daly, referring to common-law case law, also identifies a number of factors used by courts to determine the weight due to the views of the child.[148] These include: the strength and duration of the child's views[149] and the validity of the views (i.e. whether they are 'rational' and their 'own').[150] It is suggested here that there can also be other factors relevant for the question of due weight. Considering that Article 12(1) applies to all matters – ranging from decisions within the family, to school matters, to judicial proceedings – it is to be expected that the factors can also differ depending on the subject matter. Even within the scope of judicial proceedings, one could argue that the subject matter of the proceedings may bring with it different considerations for due weight.

Turning away from the (potential) factors in determining due weight, the argument has been made that 'due weight' as such should be amended.

Notably, Daly advocates that the views of the child should be determinative, unless significant harm to the child would arise from doing so.[151] In proposing this, Daly does not rely on 'due weight', but proposes a 'children's autonomy principle'.[152] She thereby reframes the question of participation and due weight. The suggested principle is limited to 'best interests proceedings'. Daly defines these as proceedings in which 'the principle of the best interests of the child is *the* primary consideration – it determines the case'.[153] These proceedings render

---

145 See Lansdown 2011, p. 23; Ang et al. 2006, pp. 18–19; Lundy, Tobin & Parkes 2019, p. 414; and W. Vandenhole, G.E. Türkelli & S. Lambrechts, *Children's Rights: A Commentary on the Convention on the Rights of the Child and its Protocols*, Cheltenham: Edward Elgar 2019, p. 150.

146 See e.g. Parkes 2013, p. 35; Thorburn Stern 2017, p. 62; and Vandenhole, Türkelli & Lambrechts 2019, p. 150.

147 C. Willow, *Children's Right to Be Heard and Effective Child Protection: A Guide for Governments and Children Rights Advocates on Involving Children and Young People in Ending All Forms of Violence*, Bangkok: Save the Children Sweden 2010, p. 40.

148 Daly 2018a, p. 293.

149 Daly 2018a, pp. 303–304.

150 Daly 2018a, pp. 304–311.

151 Daly 2018a, p. 10.

152 Daly 2018a, p. 10.

153 Daly 2018a, p. 72.

'substitute decisions' on matters which adults would decide for themselves, she argues.[154] They are decisions taken 'because the individual is a child', i.e. they are proceedings which do not exist for adults.[155] Daly refers to contact, residence and adoption cases as well as medical decisions.[156] In these proceedings, Daly argues that the child should be able to choose the outcome, unless significant harm would arise from doing so.[157] In effect, that would mean that the child's views are determinative and no other factors or interests should be considered in the decision-making process, except if they prove 'significant harm'. Daly's proposal is radical. It goes further than Article 12 UNCRC as it sets aside the principle of due weight. In doing so, it disqualifies the consideration of other factors or interests. It also assumes that a child's views will include a clear position against or in favour of a certain decision. Although there will be situations in which this is the case, many children (especially in family law proceedings) may not have a clear choice or want to be responsible for the decision. Daly's definition of 'best interests proceedings' as 'substitute decisions' makes sense, but her assertion that in these proceedings the best interests of the child are *the* primary consideration can be questioned. Of course, in disputes concerning contact, residence or the care of children, their best interests will be a primary consideration, as Article 3 UNCRC also posits; however, that does not mean they must be *the* primary consideration. All in all, the proposition of Daly for an autonomy principle in these proceedings can be debated.

At the other end of the spectrum is Brighouse, who takes the 'paternalistic position' (as he calls it) that children's voices should be 'consultative, but not authoritative, where their interests are at stake'.[158] His argument is in direct opposition to that of Daly, as he claims that 'we should regard children's voices as consultative even in situations in which we would normally be obliged to regard an adult's view as authoritative'.[159] Instead, the adult 'morally charged with protecting the interests' of the child is authoritative, although the adult should be guided by their 'good faith understanding of what is in the child's interests'.[160] Regarding custody and divorce proceedings, Brighouse sticks to his argument, noting that the 'responsible adult (the divorcing parents, or when they are in serious dispute, the judge)' must determine the child's views and consider whether they are in the child's interests.[161] He does not further expand

154 Daly 2018a, p. 6.
155 Daly 2018a, p. 7.
156 She excludes international child abduction cases under The Hague Convention, because the best interests of children are generally to be considered in those proceedings as a quick return is aimed for. See Daly 2018a, pp. 103–104 and 109–112.
157 Daly 2018a, p. 10.
158 H. Brighouse, 'How Should Children Be Heard?', *Arizona Law Review*, Vol. 45, No. 3, 2003, pp. 691–711, p. 692.
159 Brighouse 2003, p. 693.
160 Brighouse 2003, pp. 693–694.
161 Brighouse 2003, p. 707.

on the fact that adults are not always 'responsible' or neutral when faced with divorce. Contrary to the proposition of Daly, the position of Brighouse does not contradict the text of Article 12 UNCRC,[162] although it can be seen as a very conservative interpretation.

More suitable is the interpretation of due weight given by Lundy, Tobin and Parkes, who note that it is possible for the views of a child to be determinative 'when a child has reached a level of maturity or competency with respect to a matter affecting him which is equivalent to that required of an adult, then the child's views must be determinative of their best interests'.[163] The authors argue that there would be no legal or moral justification not to do so. In these situations, the child's views can be determinative with respect to their best interests; these will still have to be balanced against the impact of the decision on other children and adults or any other legitimate considerations.[164]

To conclude, while the CRC Committee has not provided for a definition of 'due weight' the meaning of the phrase is simple. Defined in this research as 'proper or just relative importance accorded', the standard of due weight is clear, but the application cannot be determined *in abstracto*. The context of each individual matter will determine what 'due' means as the discretion lies with the decision-maker. In order to determine 'due weight' for the views of the child, the key factor will be the child's age and maturity. Other factors may also be considered, such as the impact of the decision on the child and, by extension, the matter or type of proceeding concerned.

3.1.1.6. Due Weight in Accordance with Age and Maturity of the Child

As previously mentioned, the text of Article 12 refers to the 'age and maturity' factor, according to which due weight must be granted to the views of the child. According to the CRC Committee, this phrase refers to the 'capacity of the child'.[165] The use of the term 'capacity' raises questions as to the relationship with the term 'capable' required for the right to express views, as discussed above. We will come back to this point in section 3.2.2.2 below. Let us instead consider the phrase 'age and maturity', which consists of two factors. The reason for the duality is that age, by itself, is insufficient to determine a child's capacity or the significance that should be attributed to his or her views according to the CRC Committee.[166] The Committee notes that age does not uniformly relate to a child's understanding. Thus, it refers to factors drawn from research that also contribute to a child's development: information, experience, environment,

162 Brighouse 2003, p. 695.
163 Lundy, Tobin & Parkes 2019, p. 413.
164 Lundy, Tobin & Parkes 2019, p. 413.
165 UNCRC General Comment No. 12 (2009), para. 28.
166 UNCRC General Comment No. 12 (2009), para. 29.

social and cultural expectations, and levels of support.[167] These factors have not been further elaborated upon by the CRC Committee, nor has a reference been provided for the research mentioned. In reference to these factors, the Committee instructs the views of the child to be 'assessed on a case-by-case examination'.[168]

Moving on to the second factor, 'maturity', the CRC Committee explains the term as 'the ability to understand and assess the implications of a particular matter'.[169] According to the CRC Committee, 'maturity is difficult to define', but should be understood in the context of Article 12 as 'the capacity of a child to express her or his views on issues in a reasonable and independent manner'.[170] In General Comment No. 20 on the rights of the child during adolescence, the Committee reaffirms the importance of 'maturity' adding to it the necessity for 'understanding', when stating that 'States Parties need to ensure that appropriate weight is afforded to the views of adolescents as they acquire understanding and maturity'.[171] Finally, in the literal analysis of the phrase in General Comment No. 12, the CRC Committee notes that the 'greater the impact' of the decision on the life of the child, 'the more relevant the assessment of the maturity'.[172] As discussed above, the CRC Committee thereby introduces an additional factor for 'due weight' and authors recognize this as a separate factor for due weight.[173] However, the CRC Committee raises it as a factor in assessing the maturity of the child. This could be understood as meaning that the more impact a decision has, the more attention should be placed in assessing the maturity. This is sensible insofar as the first paragraph of Article 12 is broad and concerns 'all matters' rather than only legal proceedings. One could argue that assessing maturity in family law proceedings – for example, regarding custody decisions – must be done more carefully as the decision will have more impact on the child compared to, say, the assessment of maturity for participation in school policy. The CRC Committee's comment could also mean that the less maturity the child has, the more impact the decision must have for the child's views to be given more weight. However, this makes less sense.

The existence of the dual criteria 'age and maturity' has been criticized by children's rights scholars, especially the term 'maturity'. The critique is that the term 'maturity' and the reference to 'capacity' are open to interpretation, and thus

---

167 UNCRC General Comment No. 12 (2009), para. 29.

168 UNCRC General Comment No. 12 (2009), para. 29.

169 UNCRC General Comment No. 12 (2009), para. 30.

170 UNCRC General Comment No. 12 (2009), para. 30.

171 UN Committee on the Rights of the Child, *General Comment No. 20 (2016) on the Implementation of the Rights of the Child during Adolescence*, 6 December 2016, CRC/C/GC/20, para. 22.

172 UNCRC General Comment No. 12 (2009), para. 30.

173 Lundy, Tobin & Parkes 2019, p. 414; and Lansdown 2011, p. 23.

are open to 'paternalistic restriction'.[174] It is argued by Lundy that determining the child's capacity is generally dependent on adults' perceptions, and adults may underestimate the capacity of a child.[175] Thorburn notes that maturity may lead to young children's views not being given anything other than 'marginal weight'.[176] Archard and Skivenes therefore recommend that the assessment of the child's maturity 'be made independently of an evaluation of the child's opinion', because otherwise immaturity may be concluded simply because the adult disagrees with the child's view.[177]

To conclude, the duality of the 'age and maturity' criteria is key. When considering the weight to be granted to the child's views, the decision-maker must consider the child's development and understanding more broadly than simply relying on his or her age.

3.1.2. Article 12(2) UNCRC

The second paragraph of Article 12 UNCRC contains the child's right to be heard in judicial and administrative proceedings. It continues on the right of the first paragraph, providing 'special guidance' for judicial and administrative proceedings.[178] In analysing this second paragraph, its text can be divided into four relevant phrases: For this purpose, the child shall in particular be provided the (1) *opportunity to be heard* in (2) *any judicial and administrative proceedings affecting the child*, (3) *either directly, or through a representative or an appropriate body*, in a (4) *manner consistent with the procedural rules of national law.*

Before diving into this analysis, it is important to consider the drafting history of the UNCRC. The content of this paragraph was introduced by the USA as a paragraph to Article 3 on the best interests of the child.[179] Although some representatives were of the opinion that the paragraph added nothing new, with the child's right to express views already incorporated in another article, most were in agreement that the specific reference to legal proceedings had added value and that it was logical to include it in Article 3, as the views of the child would be a way to ascertain their best interests.[180] However, in 1979 the paragraph was moved to Article 7 (what is now Article 12 UNCRC) by the Working Group because the scope of the paragraph overlapped with that of Article 7.

174 Parkes 2013, p. 35.
175 Lundy 2007, p. 937–938.
176 Thorburn Stern 2017, p. 63.
177 Archard & Skivenes 2009, p. 10.
178 Lundy, Tobin & Parkes 2019, p. 404. See also Thorburn Stern 2017, p. 64.
179 UNCHR Report of the Working Group 1981, para. 20.
180 UNCHR Report of the Working Group 1981, paras. 27 and 28.

Additionally, it was more logical to include it in the general participation principle.[181] The latter is also emphasized by the start of the paragraph, which shows that the second paragraph contains the specific right for children to express their views and have them taken into account in legal proceedings. An important effect of this is that the child must meet the capability and maturity requirements of paragraph 1 to rely on the rights provided in paragraph 2.[182]

3.1.2.1. The Opportunity to be Heard

The second paragraph of Article 12 provides children with the 'opportunity to be heard'. The term 'opportunity' signals that a child may make use of the right to be heard if he or she so wishes. In order to effectively provide the opportunity, the CRC Committee suggests that states should make legal proceedings accessible and child-appropriate, and barriers, such as costs and lack of legal counsel, must be eliminated.[183] According to Krappmann, the term 'heard' is more juridical than the phrase of expressing views as used in the first paragraph.[184] However, there is no sign that the term has a different meaning, either from the General Comment or the legislative history, so one can conclude that it encompasses the same. Finally, although the term 'heard' can have the connotation of referring only to children directly expressing their views to the decision-maker, this is not how it is to be understood in Article 12 UNCRC. This is crystal-clear from the continuation of paragraph 2, with the phrase 'either directly, or through a representative or an appropriate body' (see section 3.1.2.3 below).

3.1.2.2. Any Judicial and Administrative Proceedings Affecting the Child

The phrase that the right to be heard is to be provided for 'in any judicial and administrative proceedings affecting the child' makes the second paragraph of Article 12 specific to the legal arena. In understanding this phrase, the use of 'any' signals that the scope of proceedings is broad. As emphasized by the CRC Committee, the phrase refers to 'all relevant judicial proceedings affecting the child, without limitation'.[185] The CRC Committee provides a non-exhaustive list of judicial and administrative proceedings, including family law proceedings such as the separation of parents, custody, care and adoption.[186] The term 'proceedings' also includes alternative dispute mechanisms.[187] Additionally, the

181 UNCHR Report of the Working Group 1989, paras. 128 and 236. See also Hodgkin & Newell 2007, p. 155.
182 Lundy, Tobin and Parkes 2019, p. 420.
183 UNCRC General Comment No. 12 (2009), para. 34; and Lansdown 2011, p. 52.
184 Krappmann 2010, p. 506.
185 UNCRC General Comment No. 12 (2009), para. 32.
186 UNCRC General Comment No. 12 (2009), para. 32. See also Parkes 2013, p. 37.
187 UNCRC General Comment No. 12 (2009), para. 32. See also Thorburn Stern 2017, p. 65.

CRC Committee has clarified that no distinction should be made between proceedings initiated by the child himself or herself and those initiated by others – Article 12(2) applies to all.[188] This means that the scope of judicial and administrative proceedings is broad. However, these proceedings must still be 'affecting the child'. This phrasing mirrors the language in paragraph 1 and as paragraph 2 is a specified version of the rights under paragraph 1, we must assume that the conditions of paragraph 1 must be met. Therefore, the proceedings must 'affect the child' as clarified in section 3.1.1.4.

3.1.2.3. Directly, or through a Representative or an Appropriate Body

Where Article 12(1) provides for the general right to express views, Article 12(2) formulates ways in which the child can express these views in judicial or administrative proceedings. The text of Article 12(2) states that the child's opportunity to be heard should be provided 'either directly, or through a representative or an appropriate body'.

What is meant by this phrase will be discussed below, starting by briefly looking at the development of the phrase in the drafting of the UNCRC. In the initial version of the paragraph, which the USA proposed should fall under (what has remained) Article 3, the opportunity was to be granted to the child 'as an independent party to the proceedings'.[189] In discussion of the Working Group, the representative of the Netherlands suggested that the phrase 'directly or indirectly through a representative' be added to the draft and other representatives also suggested that the word 'independent' to be removed.[190] The paragraph after the first reading thus stated that children should be provided the opportunity to be heard, 'either directly or indirectly through a representative, as a party to the proceedings'.[191] Subsequently, when the Finnish representative (on behalf of a drafting group) proposed moving the paragraph from Article 3 to what is now Article 12 UNCRC, the phrase was again amended. The part 'as a party to the proceedings' was removed and 'or an appropriate body' was added.[192] The *travaux préparatoires* do not provide any explanation as to why these changes were made. The amendments are relevant as the removal of 'as a party to the proceedings' clarifies that children are not provided with the same procedural rights as adults. Additionally, it signals that Article 12 UNCRC does not provide children with the right to initiate proceedings, the right to access

188 UNCRC General Comment No. 12 (2009), para. 33. See also Lundy, Tobin & Parkes 2019, p. 421.

189 UNCHR Report of the Working Group 1981, para. 20.

190 UNCHR Report of the Working Group 1981, para. 30.

191 UNCHR Draft Convention on the Rights of the Child 1987, p. 6.

192 UNCHR Report of the Working Group 1989, para. 235.

to court or the right to a remedy.[193] While the CRC Committee does recognize that it may be possible for proceedings to be initiated by children, referring to 'complaints against ill-treatment and appeals against school exclusion',[194] neither Article 12 nor the Committee suggests that children should be afforded a right to initiate family law proceedings.

Knowing that Article 12(2) does not enable children to become a party to the proceedings, it is time to ask what is provided and meant by the right to be heard directly, through a representative or an appropriate body.

In the General Comment, the first aspect that was singled out by the CRC Committee is that this phrase provides the child with a second choice. Once he or she has opted to be heard in a proceeding, he or she 'will have to decide how to be heard'.[195] The child should be able to opt between the different modes of participation – being heard directly, indirectly through a representative or indirectly through an appropriate body – if they are provided for. Whether this choice means that all three modes have to be provided to all children in all proceedings is not immediately clear from Article 12(2) or the General Comment. The most far-reaching interpretation of this phrase would be that, yes, all three modes do have to be provided to all children in all types of proceedings so that children would at all times have the option to decide how they wish to be heard. However, children's rights scholars do not back this interpretation. Instead, Lundy, Tobin and Parkes argue that it would be 'unreasonable to demand' that all three modes are made available to a child in 'every' (emphasis added by the authors) proceeding.[196] They provide two examples: there may be proceedings whose nature may give rise to a preferred mode of participation in light of the child's best interests or there may be proceedings in which adults may only participate through representation and so children should too.[197] One could also argue that it would be unreasonably burdensome for states to provide all three modes of participation in all (types) of proceedings in light of the potential costs attached. Hodgkin and Newell note that states have the discretion to determine how the child's views should be heard.[198] Their interpretation would mean that the child does not have a choice in terms of how to be heard, while the CRC Committee specifically states that the child can decide how to be heard.[199] Thorburn argues that the 'method chosen should be determined with

---

193 Stahl 2007, p. 811; and D. O'Donnell, *The Right of Children to Be Heard: Children's Right to Have Their Views Taken into Account and to Participate in Legal and Administrative Proceedings* (Innocenti Working Paper), UNICEF 2009, p. 2–3.

194 UNCRC General Comment No. 12 (2009), para. 33.

195 UNCRC General Comment No. 12 (2009), para. 35.

196 Lundy, Tobin & Parkes 2019, p. 423.

197 Lundy, Tobin & Parkes 2019, p. 423.

198 Hodgkin & Newell 2007, p. 157.

199 UNCRC General Comment No. 12 (2009), para. 35.

reference to the particular situation and to the child itself', also considering the evolving capacities of the child and the best interests principle.[200] This is more burdensome for states as it requires a personalized method per child; in order to be able to choose, more than one mode of participation would have to be available in proceedings. Sutherland provides a more balanced interpretation, noting that states have 'a degree of latitude' as to how they implement Article 12, but alternative mechanisms of participation 'should be accessible and effective' to comply with the Convention.[201] The CRC Committee recommends that 'wherever possible, the child must be given the opportunity to be directly heard in any proceedings'.[202] Additionally, Parkes has interpreted Article 12(2) as implying that having a representative must be available as an option to children in proceedings.[203] However, neither the Article itself nor the CRC Committee places an obligation on states to provide for a mode of child representation in legal proceedings. To conclude, it can be argued that states cannot simply decide to provide children in all types of proceedings with only one manner in which to be heard;[204] instead, they should ensure that there are accessible and effective modes of participation available to children. This would mean that various modes of participation should be available; however, it does not mean that in all proceedings, for all children, all the different modes have to be offered – valid exceptions may apply. If we consider the underlying aim of Article 12, then whether the child has the opportunity to make use of a *specific* mode of participation is less relevant than whether the child has the opportunity to effectively express his or her views – although specific modes of participation may assist in providing the child with the opportunity to do so.

After considering the need for multiple modes of participation, let us look at each of the three modes mentioned in Article 12(2). The phrase first introduces the option of being heard directly. In the literal analysis, the CRC Committee does not disclose what is meant by this. However, it does recommend hearing children directly wherever possible.[205] In the literature, it is presumed that a child is heard directly if he or she is heard in person by the decision-maker or decision-making body in the legal or administrative proceedings.[206] The person who hears the child will depend on the context. In the light of Article 12 as a whole, the CRC Committee refers to adults involved in the matter, such

[200] Thorburn Stern 2017, p. 66.

[201] Sutherland 2013, p. 345.

[202] UNCRC General Comment No. 12 (2009), para. 35.

[203] Parkes 2013, p. 98.

[204] See also C.R. Mol, 'Children's Representation in Family Law Proceedings: A Comparative Evaluation in Light of Article 12 of the United Nations Convention on the Rights of the Child', *International Journal of Children's Rights*, Vol. 27, No. 1, 2019b, pp. 66–98, p. 70.

[205] UNCRC General Comment No. 12 (2009), para. 35.

[206] Parkes 2013, p. 37; and Lundy, Tobin & Parkes 2019, p. 424.

as teachers, social workers and caregivers, but also decision-makers, such as a judge or administrator, or specialists, such as psychologists or other experts.[207] If we consider judicial and administrative proceedings specifically, the person who would hear the child directly would likely be the decision-maker – for example, the judge or administrative body. However, the direct hearing by a judge or administrator is contentious in certain jurisdictions for a variety of reasons concerning the court environment, the capacity of decision-makers and the issue of confidentiality.[208] Hearing the child through an expert or social worker is more accepted in certain jurisdictions, but it is not self-evident whether this would be a delegated direct hearing, a form of representation or the hearing by an appropriate body (see below).[209]

The second form of participation mentioned in the phrase is that of a 'representative'. The General Comment provides additional information as to who 'a representative' should be. The CRC Committee notes that various persons can be the representative of a child in proceedings: the parent(s), a lawyer or another person.[210] Representation is therefore not limited to qualified lawyers in the context of Article 12(2).[211] However, one must be cautious in relation to having the parent(s) as a representative. Although they are the most obvious representatives, there is the risk in proceedings that there may be a conflict between the child and the parent(s), or between the two parents who ought to represent the child's interests jointly.[212] In such situations, a legal or other lay representative is necessary. Whichever type of representative is chosen, the CRC Committee notes that they should have sufficient knowledge and understanding of the proceedings and have experience in working with children.[213] The representative should ensure that the views of the child are 'transmitted correctly to the decision maker' and thus should also exclusively represent the interests of the child and not those of other persons.[214] With regard to the latter, it is important that the representative does not confuse his or her role with the obligation contained in Article 3 UNCRC to have the child's best interests as a primary consideration.[215] The representative represents the child's views and not their own views as to what is in the best interests of that child. Therefore, the representative 'must actually obtain the views of a child' as emphasized by

207 UNCRC General Comment No. 12 (2009), para. 42.
208 For a brief discussion on this topic, see Lundy, Tobin & Parkes 2019, p. 426.
209 See Mol 2021a, pp. 345–346.
210 UNCRC General Comment No. 12 (2009), para. 36.
211 Lundy, Tobin & Parkes 2019, p. 427.
212 UNCRC General Comment No. 12 (2009), para. 36.
213 UNCRC General Comment No. 12 (2009), para. 36.
214 UNCRC General Comment No. 12 (2009), paras. 36 and 37.
215 Lansdown 2011, p. 25.

Lundy, Tobin and Parkes.[216] Finally, in relation to representatives, the CRC Committee notes briefly that codes of conduct should be developed.[217]

The last mode of participation mentioned in the phrase is the option of an 'appropriate body'. The inclusion of this phrase is not motivated in the drafting documents and no guidance is offered in the General Comment either. However, it has been understood in the literature as meaning that the child need not be represented by an individual, but may also be represented by an institution, whether governmental or non-governmental in nature.[218]

3.1.2.4. In a Manner Consistent with the Procedural Rules of National Law

Article 12(2) UNCRC concludes with the phrase that the right to be heard in proceedings should be provided 'in a manner consistent with the procedural rules of national law'. As stressed by the CRC Committee, this should not be read as permitting procedural rules of national law to restrict or prevent the enjoyment of the child's right to be heard.[219] Instead, the states are encouraged to ensure that the child's right to be heard complies with 'the basic rules of fair proceedings'.[220] Parkes notes that this phrase is intended to emphasize that states ought to ensure specific procedures are in place to ensure effective implementation of Article 12(2).[221] Within this scope of effective implementation, the phrase provides states with discretion as to how they wish to do this.[222]

3.2. IMPLEMENTATION OF ARTICLE 12 UNCRC

In General Comment No. 12, the CRC Committee sets out five steps for the 'effective' implementation of Article 12 UNCRC.[223] These steps consist of multiple requirements and will draw on the content of Article 12 as also described above. The five steps, as phrased by the CRC Committee, are: (1) preparation; (2) the hearing; (3) assessment of the capacity of the child; (4) information about the weight given to the views of the child (the feedback) and (5) complaints, remedies and redress.[224] These steps concern the three phases in the process of child participation: the preparation prior to participation (step 1), the participation

216 Lundy, Tobin & Parkes 2019, p. 428.
217 UNCRC General Comment No. 12 (2009), para. 37.
218 Parkes 2013, p. 38; and Lundy, Tobin & Parkes 2019, p. 431.
219 UNCRC General Comment No. 12 (2009), para. 38.
220 UNCRC General Comment No. 12 (2009), para. 38; and Lansdown 2011, p. 26.
221 Parkes 2013, p. 39.
222 Thorburn Stern 2017, p. 67.
223 UNCRC General Comment No. 12 (2009), paras. 40–47.
224 See UNCRC General Comment No. 12 (2009), paras. 40–47.

itself (steps 2–3), and the feedback and options post-participation (steps 4–5). Each of these phases will now be discussed in relation to family law proceedings.

3.2.1. Before Participation

In order for children to be able to participate in legal proceedings, it is necessary that they are aware of the proceedings and are informed of the opportunities to participate. This is addressed in the first step of 'preparation'.[225] According to the CRC Committee, the key requirement for the preparation of the child is that the child must be informed regarding the right to express views.[226] In the brief paragraph addressing this requirement, the CRC Committee comments on what information has to be given to the child and by whom.

To begin with, the information that must be provided to the child is fourfold. First, the child has to be informed of his or her right to express an opinion – both generally 'in all matters affecting the child', as well as specifically in 'any judicial and administrative decision-making processes' affecting them.[227] This is the starting point; a child must know that he or she has the possibility to share their views. Second, the child has to be informed 'about the impact that his or her expressed views will have on the outcome'.[228] Prior to expressing his or her views, the child must be aware of the potential impact of these views. This is not the same as being informed about how his or her specific views have been given due weight in the matter at hand (that is addressed by the feedback to be given post-participation).[229] Instead, it means that the child should be informed in general terms what weight the decision-maker could give to his or her views – for example, that these views will not be determinative. The CRC Committee subsequently also notes that the child should be informed of the options between the modes of participation: 'either communicating directly or through a representative'.[230] This third piece of information has to be supplemented, according to the CRC Committee, as the consequences of the decision between direct and indirect participation must also be shared with the child.[231] The fourth and final piece of information to be imparted to the child is an explanation before the hearing 'as to how, when and where the hearing will take place and who the participants will be'.[232] Knowing these details will allow the child to be prepared for the hearing. Lansdown has grouped the first three

225 UNCRC General Comment No. 12 (2009), para. 41.
226 UNCRC General Comment No. 12 (2009), para. 41.
227 UNCRC General Comment No. 12 (2009), para. 41.
228 UNCRC General Comment No. 12 (2009), para. 41.
229 See UNCRC General Comment No. 12 (2009), para. 45 and section 3.2.3 below.
230 UNCRC General Comment No. 12 (2009), para. 41.
231 UNCRC General Comment No. 12 (2009), para. 41.
232 UNCRC General Comment No. 12 (2009), para. 41.

pieces of information as information on the 'children's role in the proceedings' and the latter as information on 'the practical arrangements'.[233]

With regard to who should inform the child of all the above, the CRC Committee makes a distinction between the information on the 'children's role in the proceedings' (i.e. the right to be heard, the impact of their views and the choice of modes) and the information on 'the practical arrangements' (how, when, where and who). The CRC Committee refers, on the one hand, to 'those responsible for hearing the child' and, on the other hand, to 'the decision maker'.[234] It is possible that the person responsible for hearing the child is also the decision-maker, but that need not be the case as the decision-maker might have delegated the hearing of the child to another person, such as a representative. According to the CRC Committee, the decision-maker is responsible for 'adequately prepar[ing] the child before the hearing' by providing practical information regarding the how, when, where and who.[235] In contrast, for the information on the child's role, 'those responsible for hearing the child have to ensure that the child is informed'.[236] Not only is this broader than the decision-maker, but those responsible are not tasked with informing the child themselves; according to the General Comment, they need only to *ensure* that the child has been informed. This means that others, such as parents, social workers, etc., could be tasked with informing the child upon the request of the decision-maker.

Towards the end of the General Comment, the CRC Committee notes some 'basic requirements' for all processes of participation. The first two thereof concern the phase prior to participation, in that the process of participation must be 'transparent and informative' and 'voluntary'.[237] In making the process transparent and informative, the Committee emphasizes that children 'must be provided with full, accessible, diversity-sensitive and age-appropriate information'.[238] In addition, the breadth of the information to be provided is again noted. With regard to the voluntary nature of participation, the child also ought to 'be informed that they can cease involvement at any stage'.[239]

To conclude, the first step in ensuring the effective realization of the child's right to be heard is preparing the child through informing him or her of his or her right to express views and the conditions thereof. The CRC Committee does not go so far as to speak of a right to information, but does strongly request states parties to provide the child – especially in judicial proceedings – with the necessary information to participate effectively.

233 Lansdown 2011, pp. 51–52.
234 UNCRC General Comment No. 12 (2009), para. 41.
235 UNCRC General Comment No. 12 (2009), para. 41.
236 UNCRC General Comment No. 12 (2009), para. 41.
237 UNCRC General Comment No. 12 (2009), para. 134.
238 UNCRC General Comment No. 12 (2009), para. 134(a).
239 UNCRC General Comment No. 12 (2009), para. 134(b).

3.2.2. *During Participation*

After the child has been prepared for participation and chooses to express views, the participation process continues with the actual participation. This consists of the next two steps specified by the Committee: (2) the hearing; and (3) the assessment of capacity of the child.

3.2.2.1. The Hearing

The hearing is the moment when the child has the opportunity to express his or her opinion on the matter affecting him or her. The CRC Committee phrased three additional recommendations in its steps for implementation with regard to the hearing. The first of these is the 'context' or the environment in which the child is heard ought to be 'enabling and encouraging'.[240] This means that the person hearing the child must 'be willing to listen and seriously consider what the child has decided to communicate', but also that the child 'can be sure' that this holds true.[241] In that regard, the CRC Committee emphasizes the requirement of due weight from the text of Article 12, the serious consideration of the child's views and, additionally, that the child must feel that they are being heard and taken seriously.[242] It is unclear how the child should be made to feel 'sure' that the adult is willing to listen and will seriously consider the child's views. However, it likely addresses the demeanour and posture of the decision-maker and the environment of the hearing, which is also the topic of the second recommendation. The CRC Committee recommends that the hearing should 'have the format of a talk rather than a one-sided examination'.[243] The third and final recommendation regarding the hearing is that it is preferable to hear children 'under conditions of confidentiality' and not 'in open court'.[244] The CRC Committee does not further elaborate which level of confidentiality should be provided. Options could include full confidentiality, confidentiality insofar as the child wishes, or confidentiality as to the precise wording of the child.[245] These three additional recommendations regarding the hearing of the child should be seen in combination with the comments made regarding the text of Article 12 UNCRC, as discussed above.[246]

The recommendations are also supplemented by a number of 'basic requirements' for all processes of participation noted by the CRC Committee.

240 UNCRC General Comment No. 12 (2009), para. 42.
241 UNCRC General Comment No. 12 (2009), para. 42.
242 See also Lansdown 2011, p. 52.
243 UNCRC General Comment No. 12 (2009), para. 43.
244 UNCRC General Comment No. 12 (2009), para. 43.
245 See also Mol 2021a, p. 340.
246 See sections 3.1.1.3, 3.1.1.4, 3.1.2.2 and 3.1.2.3.

With regard to the hearing itself, these basic requirements note that the process should be 'respectful', 'child-friendly', 'inclusive', 'supported by training' and 'safe and sensitive to risk'.[247] These requirements strengthen the recommendations made by the CRC Committee throughout the General Comment regarding the manner in which adults (i.e. the decision-maker, representative or other person) ought to hear the child and the environment which should be provided during the hearing. 'Child-friendly' participation requires 'environments and working methods', which are 'adapted to children's capacities'.[248] 'Inclusive' participation means that there should be no discrimination on any grounds[249] – as the relationship between Article 12 and Article 2 UNCRC also calls for.[250] In addition, while the capacity of a child can be limited due to disabilities, the CRC Committee urges states to ensure that children with disabilities are provided with the necessary means to be able to express their views.[251] To ensure respectful, child-friendly, inclusive, safe and effective participation, adults may require training – for example, in listening skills.[252] Finally, safe participation requires those involved considering whether the expression of views may bring any risks for the child, to 'violence, exploitation or other negative consequences'.[253]

Through the recommendations on implementation and basic requirements together, the CRC Committee has further expanded on the conditions needed for child participation. While the text of Article 12 UNCRC itself does not delve into these additional conditions – for example, regarding the context in which the child is heard – the CRC Committee has recognized their importance.

3.2.2.2. The Assessment of Capacity of the Child

The third step described by the CRC Committee in the process of participation is the 'assessment of capacity of the child'. The Committee starts by noting that 'the child's views must be given due weight, when a case-by-case analysis indicates that the child is capable of forming her or his own views'. This explanation causes confusion as the CRC Committee combines two seemingly separate aspects of Article 12(1) UNCRC: the giving of due weight and the requirement that the child is capable of forming his or her own views. The latter is, in the text of Article 12, a requirement related to the question of whether a child may express views.[254]

---

247 UNCRC General Comment No. 12 (2009), para. 134.

248 UNCRC General Comment No. 12 (2009), para. 134(e). See also examples in Lansdown 2011, p. 54.

249 UNCRC General Comment No. 12 (2009), para. 134(f).

250 See also section 4.1 below.

251 UNCRC General Comment No. 12 (2009), para. 78.

252 UNCRC General Comment No. 12 (2009), para. 134(g).

253 UNCRC General Comment No. 12 (2009), para. 134(h).

254 See section 3.1.1.2 above.

The former, the question of due weight has a seemingly different requirement attached to it, namely the 'age and maturity' of the child.[255] As we have seen in the analysis of the text of Article 12 UNCRC above, the article contains two criteria concerning maturity: (1) the child 'capable of forming his or her own views' has the right to express views; and (2) 'in accordance with the age and maturity of the child', these views should be given due weight by the decision-maker. This third step of implementation exposes the existing discussion as to whether there is a distinction between these two criteria. This discussion was also ignited by the recurring use of the term 'capacity' by the CRC Committee in the legal analysis of both criteria.[256] Is the 'presumed capacity' for being capable of forming views the same 'capacity' referred to by the Committee to explain 'age and maturity' with regard to due weight? In essence, is there a distinction between the two criteria: 'capable of forming his or her own view' and 'age and maturity'?[257]

Before answering this question, let us consider why this question matters in practice. If the answer to the question is that there is *no* distinction between the two criteria, i.e. that the two are in fact one and the same criterion, then that would mean that the child's maturity would be evaluated against one required level of capacity. This single evaluation would then determine whether the child can make use of his or her right to be heard and affect the weighing of the child's views. On the other hand, if the answer to the question is that there *is* a distinction between the two criteria, then these will need to be assessed separately in legal proceedings, even if at the same point in time. These separate evaluations of the child's maturity are then split between, first, the question of granting the child the opportunity to express views and, subsequently, the question of how much weight should be attached to the child's views.

We now turn to the following question: is there a distinction between the two criteria, capable of forming views and age and maturity, or are they in fact one and the same? One would at first glance assume that the answer is *yes*, they are two distinct criteria. The criteria are phrased differently in the article itself and are discussed separately in the literal analysis of Article 12 in the General Comment. The legal analysis of Article 12 UNCRC also commences by noting that the article establishes the right to express views 'and the subsequent right for those views to be given due weight, according to the child's age and maturity'.[258] The use of the word 'subsequent' hints at a separation between expressing views

255 See section 3.1.1.6 above.

256 See section 3.1.1.6 above.

257 This question and the answer thereto have been discussed by the author previously in Mol 2019a, pp. 241–243.

258 UNCRC General Comment No. 12 (2009), para. 15.

and due weight for these views, thus arguing for two distinct criteria. This interpretation is also favoured by multiple authors.[259] Stahl, for example, argues that Article 12 'recognizes that age and maturity are important to the analysis of how to implement the right of participation, but not whether a child possess the right [to participate]'.[260]

Notwithstanding these considerations, which point to there being two distinct criteria, the General Comment raises confusion. The phrasing at several points suggests that the answer to the question may in fact be *no*, the two criteria are in essence one criterion. As noted previously in this chapter, in the legal analysis on the due weight clause, the CRC Committee repeatedly uses phrases which appear to refer to the analysis of the 'capable of forming views' criterion.[261] More specifically, this occurs at three points in the legal analysis. First, the CRC Committee states that 'the views of the child have to be seriously considered when the child is *capable of forming her or his own views*'.[262] Subsequently, when discussing factors relevant for maturity other than age, it should be noted that these factors 'contribute to the development of a child's *capacities to form a view*'.[263] Instead of referring to the capacity to form views, one would have expected the CRC Committee to focus on the relevance of these factors in giving due weight to the child's views. Finally, within the scope of Article 12 UNCRC, the CRC Committee defines maturity as 'the *capacity of a child to express her or his views* on issues in a reasonable and independent manner'.[264] These repeated references to the capacity or capability of forming or expressing views appear to suggest that the two criteria are compounded. As noted at the beginning of this section, the CRC Committee similarly muddles the two criteria in the third step of implementation on 'the assessment of capacity of the child', when it states:

> The child's views must be given due weight, when a case-by-case analysis indicates that the child is *capable of forming her or his own views*. If the child is *capable of forming her or his own views* in a reasonable or independent manner, the decision maker must consider the views of the child as a significant factor in the settlement of the issue.[265]

---

259 See e.g. Lücker-Babel 1995, pp. 397 and 399; Thorburn Stern 2017, pp. 56–58 and 62–64; A. Daly, 'No Weight for "Due Weight"? A Children's Autonomy Principle in Best Interest Proceedings', *International Journal of Children's Rights*, Vol. 26, No. 1, 2018b, pp. 61–92, p. 68 and E.K.M. Tisdall, 'Challenging Competency and Capacity? Due Weight to Children's Views in Family Law Proceedings', *International Journal of Children's Rights*, Vol. 26, No. 1, 2018, pp. 159–182, p. 165.

260 Stahl 2007, p. 807.

261 See also section 3.1.1.6 above.

262 UNCRC General Comment No. 12 (2009), para. 28. Emphasis added.

263 UNCRC General Comment No. 12 (2009), para. 29. Emphasis added.

264 UNCRC General Comment No. 12 (2009), para. 30. Emphasis added.

265 UNCRC General Comment No. 12 (2009), para. 44. Emphasis added.

While addressing the giving of due weight to the views expressed by the child, no reference is made to the criterion of age and maturity. It is also notable that in the previous step regarding the hearing itself, there is no mention of assessing whether the child is capable of forming or expressing views. That would have been more fitting in light of the text of Article 12 UNCRC. Finally, when commenting on the relationship between Article 12 and Article 5 UNCRC on the evolving capacities of the child, the CRC Committee states that Article 12 'stipulates that the child's views must be given due weight, whenever the child is capable of forming his or her own views'.[266]

Does the CRC Committee mean to say that once the child's capacity to form views has been determined, due weight must be given without a separate assessment of the child's age and maturity to determine what would be 'due'? Arguably, no. In addition to the reasons advanced above as to why there are two distinct criteria, three additional reasons argue in support of this.

First, the CRC Committee's reference to capacity or capability of forming views in light of due weight – for example, in the third step of implementation or in relation to Article 5 – can be explained both ways. It may signal that being capable of forming views is a criterion for due weight, but it can also be understood as being a reference to the first step – participation – which is necessary before even getting to the second step of due weight. If children are capable of forming their own views, then they have the right to express views. Once this right has been granted, then these views should be given due weight. Due weight does not mean determinative weight; instead, it is a 'proper or just' weight that is dependent on various factors, such as the interests of the child and other parties involved and, as provided by Article 12 UNCRC, the age and maturity of the child.[267] The latter criterion is at times missing in the explanation of the CRC Committee, but that does not mean that age and maturity is the same criterion as being capable of forming views. Especially because the reasoning cannot be turned around: age and maturity should not determine the right to express views. The Committee explicitly discourages age limits in that regard.[268]

Second, it seems improbable that the CRC Committee meant to say that the views of young (even non-verbal)[269] children are to be given due weight to the extent of being a 'significant factor' in the decision. Instead, the separate criteria of 'age and maturity' will be relevant for the amount of weight given: a capable young non-verbal child may express views, but these views may be given less weight because of the child's youth.

This leads us to the third reason; the CRC Committee might be distinguishing between the two separate criteria with two forms of capacity to express views.

[266] UNCRC General Comment No. 12 (2009), para. 85.
[267] See also section 3.1.1.5 above.
[268] UNCRC General Comment No. 12 (2009), para. 21. See also section 3.1.1.2 above.
[269] See UNCRC General Comment No. 12 (2009), para. 21. See also section 3.1.1.2 above.

When read carefully, the difference between the capacity criteria appears to be that in relation to the right to express views, a child ought to be 'capable of forming her or his own views' and these views should be given due weight, but for the views to be a 'significant factor' – in line with the 'age and maturity' requirement – a child ought to be capable of forming his or her views 'in a reasonable or independent manner'.[270]

To conclude, is there a distinction between the two criteria: 'capable of forming his or her own view' and 'age and maturity'? Yes, most arguments point towards the understanding that the two criteria are different. In order to have the opportunity to express views, the child must be 'capable of forming his or her own view' or have the capacity to form and express their views (which is to be presumed).[271] Subsequently, the decision-maker has to give due weight to the expressed views. The extent to which these views are given weight should in part be determined by the 'age and maturity' of the child. The at times ambiguous phrasing of the CRC Committee might have been on purpose, but it may also simply be a human slip-up. In the drafting of the General Comment, the CRC Committee might have lost sight of their phrasing and repeated use of capability and capacity.

In any case, the capacity of the child will have to be assessed by the decision-maker during the participation process. While it may be presumed for the hearing, the age and maturity of the child will be considered when the decision-maker has to weigh their views.

3.2.3. *After Participation*

The process of participation should not end abruptly after the child has been heard and their views given due weight. The CRC Committee recognizes two final steps when implementing Article 12 UNCRC: (4) providing the child with information about the weight given to his or her views (the feedback) and (5) providing children with the procedures for complaints, remedies and redress.[272] These two steps occur after the decision has been taken.

The fourth step mirrors the first step. Information has to be provided prior to participation, but also afterwards. More specifically, according to the CRC Committee, 'the decision maker has to inform the child of the outcome of the process and explain how her or his views were considered'.[273] This is meant to 'guarantee' that the child's views are taken seriously,[274] as the decision-maker must respond to the child's views through reporting back to the child. The CRC

270 UNCRC General Comment No. 12 (2009), paras. 30 and 44.
271 See also section 3.1.1.2 above.
272 See UNCRC General Comment No. 12 (2009), paras. 40–47.
273 UNCRC General Comment No. 12 (2009), para. 45.
274 UNCRC General Comment No. 12 (2009), para. 45.

Committee notes that in judicial proceedings, this feedback may prompt the child to 'file an appeal or a complaint', referring to the next step.[275] The CRC Committee's explanation places the burden on the decision-maker to inform the child. It is unclear whether the Committee suggests that it should always be the decision-maker informing the child, or whether the decision-maker must ensure that the child is informed, but can delegate the practical duty of informing the child.

The fifth and final step described in the General Comment is the requirement to ensure that there are procedures for children's complaints, with remedies and redress if their rights under Article 12 UNCRC have been 'disregarded and violated'.[276] Law has to be enacted which provides for this. Specifically, with regard to judicial and administrative proceedings, 'the child must have access to appeals and complaints procedures which provide remedies for rights violations'.[277] These procedures have to 'provide reliable mechanisms' so that children can use them.[278]

By addressing the need for feedback and complaints and remedy procedures, the CRC Committee clarifies the importance of a participation process that goes further than hearing the child and considering his or her views. Together with the requirement of informing the child prior to the participation, the CRC Committee spells out a complete process by which the child's right under Article 12 UNCRC is given colour.

4. THE RELATIONSHIP BETWEEN ARTICLE 12 AND OTHER UNCRC ARTICLES

Articles within a convention cannot be seen in isolation. The context of the Convention and the other rights provided offer further understanding of, in this case, Article 12 UNCRC. As Article 12 is considered to be one of the four 'general principles' of the Convention, it is of relevance in the interpretation and implementation of all UNCRC rights.[279] The other three are the right to non-discrimination (Article 2), the primary consideration of the child's best interests (Article 3), and the right to life and development (Article 6). With regard to these 'general principles', Hanson and Lundy note that there is a lack of 'consistency and clarity' with regard to the meaning of the concept of 'general principles'

275 UNCRC General Comment No. 12 (2009), para. 45.
276 UNCRC General Comment No. 12 (2009), para. 46.
277 UNCRC General Comment No. 12 (2009), para. 47.
278 UNCRC General Comment No. 12 (2009), para. 47.
279 UNCRC General Comment No. 12 (2009), para. 2.

and the 'interpretation and application' thereof.[280] In that regard, they suggest renaming the set of four provisions to 'cross-cutting standards' and also switching Article 6 with Article 5 (evolving capacities of the child), as will be discussed in section 4.4.[281] According to Hanson and Lundy, as one of the 'cross-cutting standards', Article 12 'cross-cut[s] or intersect[s] with and appl[ies] to all other articles' in the UNCRC and provides a 'substantial norm' which must be met.[282]

In light of this, it would be possible to discuss the relationship between Article 12 and each of the more than 30 rights contained in the UNCRC. However, in this research, the relationship between Article 12 and other UNCRC rights will only be discussed insofar as the other rights impact the interpretation of the child's right to participation in family law proceedings. There are a number of articles within the Convention which have an especially relevant relationship to Article 12 in that regard and which will therefore be discussed in this section: Article 2 (non-discrimination), Article 3 (best interests of the child), Article 4 (implementation), Article 5 (evolving capacities of the child), Article 9 (separation from parents), Article 13 (freedom of expression), Article 17 (access to information from the media) and Article 21 (adoption).

4.1. ARTICLES 2 AND 12 UNCRC

The right to non-discrimination in Article 2 UNCRC is one of the four general principles of the Convention. In this regard, the principle of non-discrimination is relevant for the interpretation and implementation of all the rights contained in the UNCRC. Although the principle of non-discrimination is one that is common to human rights law, with regard to children, it is important to recognize that it addresses discrimination both between children and adults as well as between children and children (on grounds of race, sex, etc.).[283] As a general principle, the right to non-discrimination applies equally in the context of Article 12 UNCRC. As stressed by the CRC Committee, the right provided in Article 12 must be provided to children without discrimination on the grounds of race, colour, sex, language, religion, political or other opinion, national, ethnic or social origin, property, disability, birth or other status.[284] Article 2 requires states to both 'respect and ensure' the UNCRC rights without discrimination.

---

280 K. Hanson & L. Lundy, 'Does Exactly What it Says on the Tin? A Critical Analysis and Alternative Conceptualisation of the So-Called "General Principles" of the Convention on the Rights of the Child', *International Journal of Children's Rights*, Vol. 25, No. 2, 2017, pp. 285–306, p. 302.

281 Hanson & Lundy 2017, pp. 301–302.

282 Hanson & Lundy 2017, p. 302.

283 S. Besson & E. Kleber, 'Art. 2: The Right to Non-discrimination', in: Tobin 2019, pp. 41–72, p. 42.

284 UNCRC General Comment No. 12 (2009), para. 75.

This is a twofold duty: to refrain from discrimination, i.e. to 'respect', on the one hand and the obligation to actively 'ensure' non-discrimination on the other.[285] With regard to Article 12, the CRC Committee notes that states must ensure that vulnerable or marginalized groups of children are also afforded the opportunity to be heard.[286]

4.2. ARTICLES 3 AND 12 UNCRC

Article 3(1) UNCRC contains the key principle that the best interests of the child shall be a primary consideration in all actions concerning them. Article 3 is interdependent with Article 12 UNCRC according to the Committee, which stresses the importance of the relationship between the two articles.[287] In the General Comment from 2009, concerning Article 12, the CRC Committee qualified the relationship as 'complementary' with 'no tension' between the articles.[288] This position recurs in the General Comment on Article 3 from 2013.[289] In both General Comments, the CRC Committee subsequently explains the complementary role of the two articles. Article 3(1) 'aims to realize the child's best interests' and Article 12 'provides the methodology for reaching the goal of hearing either the child or the children'.[290] The symbiotic relationship between the two articles is stressed: Article 3(1) reinforces Article 12 by 'facilitating the essential role of children in all decisions affecting their lives' and the right to be heard of Article 12 is indispensable for the correct application of Article 3.[291] What exactly is meant by this complementary role? To answer this question, a distinction needs to be made between the two aspects of child participation: (1) the expression of views; and (2) the weighing of these views. These two aspects relate in different ways to Article 3(1) UNCRC, even more so because the child's best interests concept is also 'threefold' according to the Committee:[292] it is a 'substantive right', a 'fundamental, interpretative legal principle' and a 'rule of procedure'.[293]

---

285 See Besson & Kleber 2019, pp. 50–51.

286 Lansdown 2011, p. 32; and UNCRC General Comment No. 12 (2009), paras. 77 and 78.

287 UNCRC General Comment No. 12 (2009), para. 68; and UN Committee on the Rights of the Child, *General Comment No. 14 (2013) on the Right of the Child to Have His or Her Best Interests Taken as a Primary Consideration (Art. 3, Para. 1)*, 29 May 2013, CRC/C/GC/14, para. 43.

288 UNCRC General Comment No. 12 (2009), para. 74.

289 UNCRC General Comment No. 14 (2013), para. 43.

290 UNCRC General Comment No. 12 (2009), para. 74; and UNCRC General Comment No. 14 (2013), para. 43.

291 UNCRC General Comment No. 12 (2009), para. 74; and UNCRC General Comment No. 14 (2013), para. 43.

292 UNCRC General Comment No. 14 (2013), para. 6.

293 UNCRC General Comment No. 14 (2013), para. 6.

4.2.1. *Expression of Views: Articles 3 and 12 UNCRC*

The first aspect is the opportunity for the child to express their views in proceedings. This is a 'mandatory' procedural step according to the CRC Committee or the 'methodology' for hearing the child.[294] One of the dimensions of Article 3(1) is that the child's best interests have to be assessed and determined in all actions concerning him or her, which makes it a 'rule of procedure' as well as a 'substantive right' of the child.[295] This is why the CRC Committee considers both Article 3 and Article 12 to be obligatory procedural steps when taking decisions affecting the child.[296] In General Comment No. 14 concerning Article 3(1), the CRC Committee specifically emphasizes the right of the child to express views as one of the procedural safeguards to assess and determine the child's best interests.[297] In this manner, the two articles have a complementary relationship. However, there may be potential tension between the two, as the child's opportunity to participate could be limited by reason of his or her best interests.

Take the practical example in which a court decides not to hear the child as it considers that this would not be in the best interests of the child. The question then becomes whether this is based on a general presumption that involving children in legal proceedings may harm them[298] or whether the court has made this decision in light of the specific circumstances of the individual case. According to Lansdown, the best interests principle should not be used to 'trump' the child's right to be heard.[299] Article 12 UNCRC and the interpretation offered by the CRC Committee do not provide any basis whereby the child's best interests could be used as a reason for limiting child participation, either as a general presumption or in relation to specific circumstances.

Another example of potential tension concerns the determination of the child's capability to form views. Thomas and O'Kane note that adults (i.e. the decision-makers) can hold the tacit assumption that when 'children use different criteria for making choices, those are necessarily defective or at least inferior to adult criteria'.[300] If adults have a certain view of what is in the best interests of the child in light of certain criteria and this conflicts with the child's views on

---

294 UNCRC General Comment No. 12 (2009), paras. 70 and 74.

295 UNCRC General Comment No. 14 (2013), paras. 6 and 85.

296 UNCRC General Comment No. 12 (2009), para. 70.

297 UNCRC General Comment No. 14 (2013), paras. 89–91.

298 See F.E. Raitt, 'Judicial Discretion and Methods of Ascertaining the Views of a Child', *Child & Family Law Quarterly*, Vol. 16, No. 2, 2004, pp. 151–164, p. 153; and C. Piper, 'Assumptions about Children's Best Interests', *Journal of Social Welfare and Family Law*, Vol. 22, No. 3, 2000, pp. 261–276, p. 262.

299 Lansdown 2011, p. 33.

300 N. Thomas & C. O'Kane, 'When Children's Wishes and Feelings Clash with Their "Best Interests"', *International Journal of Children's Rights*, Vol. 6, No. 2, 1998, pp. 137–154, p. 151.

the subject, then it may be that the adult considers the child to be insufficiently capable. In that way, the child's best interests (from the point of view of the decision-maker) may hamper his or her opportunity to express views.[301] Neither the text of the Convention nor the CRC Committee refers to the child's best interests as relevant in determining whether a child should have the opportunity to express views; the only condition is that a child is capable of forming his or her own views. In determining whether a child is capable of forming views, as discussed above, the presumption of capacity applies.

The conclusion in short is that there is a potential for tension between Articles 3 and 12 UNCRC, but this tension should be limited to exceptional situations. In principle, Articles 3 and 12 UNCRC are complementary, as recognized by the CRC Committee. The right of the child to express views is in his or her best interests. Children should have the opportunity to express views without any assessment as to whether this is in their interests. The child's interests are protected by the fact that the right to be heard is a voluntary right; children can choose whether or not to make use of their opportunity to express views. There may be circumstances in which the decision-maker finds (further) participation to seriously hinder the child's interests, but these should be extremely exceptional as the CRC Committee emphasizes that the environment in which the child is heard should be 'enabling and encouraging', and the process voluntary, respectful, child-friendly, inclusive and safe.[302] Additionally, a decision-maker should not anticipate whether the child's views will be 'defective' or 'invalid' because they (potentially) conflict with their own views on the subject. To conclude, the relationship between Article 3 and Article 12 UNCRC should only strengthen the child's right to participate.

4.2.2. Due Weight: Articles 3 and 12 UNCRC

The second phase of the right contained in Article 12 UNCRC is the giving of 'due weight' to the views of the child. The child has been given the opportunity to speak and express his or her views; now the question is how much weight these views should be given by the decision-maker. As Article 3(1) provides, at its core, the right of the child to have his or her best interests assessed and taken as a primary consideration, the question of due weight intrinsically links Article 3 and Article 12 UNCRC. According to the CRC Committee, the expressed views of the child are one of the elements to be considered in the assessment of a child's best interests.[303] The CRC Committee notes that the rights of Article 12 must be included in the assessment and that the views expressed by the child

301 See also Lundy, Tobin & Parkes 2019, p. 405.
302 See section 3.2.2.1 below; UNCRC General Comment No. 12 (2009), paras. 42 and 134.
303 UNCRC General Comment No. 14 (2013), paras. 52–54.

are to be weighed in the assessment of the child's best interests increasingly as the child matures.[304] What does this mean in practice? It means that the child's views should be a fundamental component in the assessment of the child's best interests. If decision-makers seriously consider the views of the child when deciding in the child's best interests, then there will be no possibility for tension between Article 3 and Article 12 UNCRC.

In order to understand this complementary relationship between the two articles, a different way of looking at the child's views in family law disputes may be necessary. When discussing the relationship between Article 3 and Article 12 UNCRC, it is often presumed that a child's views are clear and speak in favour of or against a specific outcome. Let us take as an example a dispute regarding access rights: parent X has requested access and the court can either decide to grant access (option A) or can decide not to (option B). Most authors appear to argue from the perspective that the child will either be in favour of option A or in favour of option B. If the court decides to grant access (option A), but the child voices strong feelings against it (option B), then one would argue that that the decision goes against the child's views.[305] This perspective – that children generally have a clear stance for or against in the dispute – should not be the starting point. Instead, one could presume that in family law proceedings, a child will not want to make a decision themselves between A or B. It is more likely that a child has many different, perhaps even conflicting, thoughts about the dispute.[306] This is important to take into account not only in the relationship between Article 3 and Article 12 UNCRC, but also in relation to the questions we ask children when they are heard. Is the question phrased as a choice between one option and the other? Is the child asked what he or she 'wants' or is he or she asked what he or she would consider to be in his or her best interests? Is the child given the space to reflect on his or her short-term versus long-term wishes or not? The latter questions provide more opportunities for children to express nuanced views. Departing from the perspective that children in family law proceedings do not generally express a choice between A or B, but express nuanced views on the dispute and their lives makes the complementary relationship between Article 3 and Article 12 somewhat easier to understand as explained in the following.

Multiple authors refer to the tension between Article 3 and Article 12 UNCRC. They do so by considering the situation in which a court's assessment of the child's best interests – separate from the child's views – finds an option A

304 UNCRC General Comment No. 14 (2013), paras. 43 and 44.

305 See e.g. Archard & Skivenes 2009, p. 16; E.K.M. Tisdall, 'Children and Young People's Participation: A Critical Consideration of Article 12', in: W. Vandenhole et al. (eds.), *Routledge International Handbook of Children's Rights Studies*, Abingdon: Routledge 2015, pp. 185–200, p. 196 and Vandenhole, Türkelli & Lambrechts 2019, p. 152.

306 See Daly 2018a, pp. 39–40, who notes that it is only in protracted family law proceedings – especially those regarding access – that children may insist on a preference.

to be best, but the child's views are firmly in favour of option B. If the child's best interests and his or her views are considered separately, then there is a potential – as in this example – for tension between the two. As noted by Archard and Skivenes, this tension arises because the UNCRC requires decision-makers to, essentially paternalistically, determine the best interests of the child, while at the same time considering the child's (potentially contradictory) views.[307] The question becomes how to align the best interests of the child and the child's view, and authors question which of the two should prevail. One argument is that Article 3 UNCRC prevails because the decision between A and B ultimately lies with the court as the decision-maker, which has to make a final determination of the child's best interests.[308] Alternatively, as Lundy notes, the child's best interests are to be *a* primary consideration, not *the* primary consideration.[309] Thus, there is no unequivocal primacy of Article 3 UNCRC. Similarly, there is also no reason to suggest that Article 12 UNCRC prevails. Article 12 does not provide children with a right to self-determination. It is therefore possible that the court weighs the views of the child in favour of option B, but ends up deciding on option A for other reasons. As Lücker-Babel comments, there needs to be a 'fine balance, constantly sought' between the child's rights under Article 3 and Article 12 UNCRC.[310]

However, the question should not be which of the two prevail or how to conduct a 'balance' between the child's best interests and the child's views as posed above; instead, as the child's views are considered to be one of the elements in assessing his or her best interests and often will be more nuanced than a simple preference for B, in order for due weight to be accorded to them, the child's views should always be considered as a factor in his or her best interests.

This means that the child's views should play a role in the judgement of what is in the child's best interests.[311] According to the CRC Committee, the child's best interests are to be assessed on the basis of multiple elements. The child's views form one element, but there are also other relevant elements. For example with regard to access proceedings, the child's identity, the preservation of the family environment and maintaining relations, and the care, protection and safety of the child are also relevant elements.[312] The court may consider option A to be in the child's best interests on the basis of all the other elements (i.e. on the basis of an 'objective' assessment),[313] but the child's views – as a final

307 Archard & Skivenes 2009, p. 2.

308 See Sutherland 2013, p. 347; Tisdall 2015, p. 196 and Lundy, Tobin & Parkes 2019, p. 413.

309 Lundy 2007, p. 938.

310 Lücker-Babel 1995, p. 394.

311 Archard & Skivenes 2009, pp. 15–16.

312 UNCRC General Comment No. 14 (2013), paras. 52–74.

313 See also J. Eekelaar, 'The Interests of the Child and the Child's Wishes: The Role of Dynamic Self-Determinism', *International Journal of Law and the Family*, Vol. 8, No. 2, 1994, pp. 42–61, pp. 46–48.

element – may sway the decision towards another option. Perhaps this will be option B if the child is more mature and very steadfast in his or her preference,[314] but it is also possible that a third option is discovered in between A and B to meet the child's nuanced wishes. The former is also in keeping with Article 12 UNCRC, as due weight has to be accorded in the light of the child's age and maturity.

It is also possible that even after considering the child's steadfast views in favour of option B, the court's best interests assessment leads to a decision in favour of option A. This does not automatically mean that the court has not given due weight to the child's views. It simply means that all things considered, option A is the better option for the child in light of his or her interests. In this situation, Archard and Skivenes see an additional benefit of knowing and weighing the child's views in the best interests assessment: the court can take into account the costs that deciding against the child's views will have.[315] This of course can also play a role in the court's best interests assessment when the child's views are more nuanced. In these situations, where the court is faced with a difficult decision due to the tension between the child's views and his or her best interests, it is especially relevant that the court provides good reasoning as to the balancing of the child's views and other factors in the best interests assessment.

The child's views being given due weight as an element in the best interests assessment can also be seen in other examples. For example, the child's nuanced views may also run parallel to the court's assessment of the child's best interests on the basis of other elements. Another option is that the child's views may be determinative in the assessment of his or her best interests where the 'objective' assessment of these interests does not lead to a preferential outcome. For example, consider residence proceedings where there is shared custody and in which there are no objective reasons favouring either the mother's or the father's residence. The child's views can then tilt the scales towards one of the two, acting as a deciding factor in the assessment of his or her best interests.

To conclude, the relationship between Article 3 and Article 12 UNCRC is definitely complementary, as stated by the CRC Committee. The procedural rights contained in both articles must be guaranteed in all proceedings affecting children, as must the right for the child's best interests to be a primary consideration and the right for his or her views to be given due weight. This means, as strongly worded by the CRC Committee in the General Comment on Article 3, that 'as the child matures, his or her views shall have increasing weight in the assessment of his or her best interests'.[316] Decision-makers must consider

314 See Lundy, Tobin & Parkes 2019, p. 413; and J. Eekelaar & J. Tobin, 'Art. 3 The Best Interests of the Child', in: Tobin 2019, pp. 73–107, p. 87.

315 Archard & Skivenes 2009, p. 16.

316 UNCRC General Comment No. 14 (2013), para. 44.

the child's views and give them due weight when assessing his or her best interests. This is not to say that the relationship between Article 3 and Article 12 is always complementary; in individual cases, a very real tension may exist between a child's best interests and their views. For those situations, Articles 3 and 12 UNCRC do not provide a clear answer or simple solution.

4.3. ARTICLES 4 AND 12 UNCRC

States are imposed with the obligation to implement the UNCRC in Article 4. The text of Article 4 reads as follows:

> States Parties shall undertake all appropriate legislative, administrative, and other measures for the implementation of the rights recognized in the present Convention. With regard to economic, social and cultural rights, States Parties shall undertake such measures to the maximum extent of their available resources and, where needed, within the framework of international co-operation.

In the first sentence, the core obligation is contained that states should take 'all appropriate legislative, administrative, and other measures for the implementation of the rights' contained in the UNCRC. What is meant by 'all appropriate' measures? According to the CRC Committee, measures are appropriate 'when they are relevant to directly or indirectly advancing children's rights in a given context'.[317] Tobin, referencing the similar phrasing contained in Article 2(1) of the International Covenant on Economic, Social and Cultural Rights (ICESCR), concludes that states may themselves decide what is most appropriate; however, it must lead to effective implementation and the state must demonstrate this effectiveness.[318] Measures may be legislative, administrative or other measures. With regard to legislative measures, the CRC Committee has clarified that one obligation to ensure full compliance with the UNCRC is a 'comprehensive review of all domestic legislation'.[319] Additionally, the CRC Committee emphasizes that the general principles of the UNCRC – including Article 12 – should be reflected in domestic law.[320] In this sense, the first sentence of Article 4 can be understood to mean that states are obligated to ensure that their legislation complies with, in this case, the right provided in Article 12 UNCRC. Yet, a question that remains is to what extent states must comply with the rights provided in the UNCRC when

---

[317] UN Committee on the Rights of the Child, *General Comment No. 19 (2016) on Public Budgeting for the Realization of Children's Rights (Art. 4)*, 20 July 2016, CRC/C/GC/19, para. 22.

[318] Tobin 2019, pp. 112–113.

[319] UNCRC General Comment No. 5 (2003), para. 18.

[320] UNCRC General Comment No. 5 (2003), para. 22.

they are at times too idealistic in light of other interests, such as public budgets. For example, with regard to Article 12 UNCRC, must states provide multiple modes of participation in all legal proceedings for all children or may they opt to provide only one mode for a certain proceeding?[321] It may be expected that the CRC Committee recommends more participation modes, as will children's rights activists and scholars; however, it may not be realistic. The second sentence of Article 4 UNCRC may provide some clues in that regard.

In the second sentence of Article 4, a distinction is made with regard to economic, social and cultural rights. States are to undertake measures to implement these rights 'to the maximum extent of their available resources and, where needed, within the framework of international cooperation'. According to the CRC Committee, this second sentence reflects the 'realistic acceptance that lack of resources – financial and other resources – can hamper the full implementation of economic, social and cultural rights'.[322] As with the ICESCR, there will be a 'progressive realization' of these rights.[323] On the contrary, the International Covenant on Civil and Political Rights (ICCPR) requires immediate full implementation, with no reference to the question of resources.[324] This differentiation between types of rights and their subsequent implementation is difficult within the framework of the UNCRC. As the CRC Committee itself has concluded: 'There is no simple or authoritative division of human rights in general or of Convention rights into the two categories.'[325] In comparing the UNCRC to the ICCPR and the ICESCR, Articles 7, 8, 13–17 and 37(a) are definitely civil and political rights (as also recognized by the CRC Committee's reporting guidelines and the CRC Committee),[326] and Articles 24, 26, 27, 28, 30 and 32 can be recognized as economic, social and cultural rights. However, for the many remaining rights, including Article 12 UNCRC, it is not immediately clear into which category they fall. This is in part because a number of rights protected in the UNCRC are unique to children and therefore no equivalent exists in other human rights treaties. Article 12 UNCRC is one of these rights. The CRC Committee has underlined that 'children's rights are interdependent and indivisible' and therefore 'caution should be exercised in differentiating between economic, social and cultural rights on the one hand, and civil and political rights on the other'.[327] It has also noted that 'many other articles contain elements which constitute civil/political rights', including Article 12, together with Articles 2, 3 and 6 (i.e. the four general principles), without

---

321 See section 3.1.2.3 above.
322 UNCRC General Comment No. 5 (2003), para. 7.
323 UNCRC General Comment No. 5 (2003), para. 7.
324 See Article 2(2) ICCPR; and Tobin 2019, p. 109.
325 UNCRC General Comment No. 5 (2003), para. 6.
326 UNCRC General Comment No. 5 (2003), para. 6.
327 UNCRC General Comment No. 19 (2016), para. 9.

specifying whether this means that this excludes them from the second sentence of Article 4 UNCRC.[328] The second sentence of Article 4 may therefore mean that pragmatic choices are made at the national level in light of the available resources. Considering the example mentioned above, this would entail that states may opt to choose certain modes of participation to ensure the child's right to participate to the fullest extent possible instead of having to provide for multiple modes of participation in all proceedings for all children.

Notwithstanding the unclear position of Article 12, the implementation of the child's right to be heard has been repeatedly emphasized. States should take all necessary measures to implement and ensure the child's rights under Article 12 UNCRC.[329]

4.4. ARTICLES 5 AND 12 UNCRC

Article 5 UNCRC is a unique provision – there is nothing like it in other human rights instruments – and it has introduced the principle of 'evolving capacities' which has started to take on a life of its own.[330] Article 5 requires states parties to 'respect the responsibilities, rights and duties of parents' (or other legal guardians and sometimes the extended family)[331] to 'provide, in a manner consistent with the evolving capacities of the child, appropriate direction and guidance' to the child in exercising his or her Convention rights. The right concerns the triangular relationship between the child, the parents and the state, and contains rights or obligations for all three.[332] Central is the right of children to 'receive appropriate direction and guidance' from their parents to exercise their Convention rights,[333] but Article 5 also provides parents with the right to provide this direction and guidance, and contains an obligation for the state to respect parents' rights in doing so.[334] In relation to Article 12 UNCRC, Article 5

---

328 UNCRC General Comment No. 5 (2003), para. 6.

329 UNCRC General Comment No. 12 (2009), paras. 48–49. See Vandenhole, Türkelli & Lambrechts 2019, p. 113.

330 G. Lansdown, *The Evolving Capacities of the Child*, Florence: United Nations Children's Fund 2005, p. 3; J. Tobin & S. Varadan, 'Art. 5: The Right to Parental Direction and Guidance Consistent with a Child's Evolving Capacities', in: Tobin 2019, pp. 159–185, p. 159 and S. Varadan, 'The Principle of Evolving Capacities under the UN Convention on the Rights of the Child', *International Journal of Children's Rights*, Vol. 27, No. 2, 2019, pp. 306–338.

331 The article mentions 'parents or, where applicable, the members of the extended family or community as provided for by local custom, legal guardians or other persons legally responsible for the child'. This was meant to accommodate cultural diversity; see E.E. Sutherland, 'The Enigma of Article 5 of the United Nations Convention on the Rights of the Child: Central or Peripheral?', *International Journal of Children's Rights*, Vol. 28, No. 3, 2020, pp. 447–470, p. 454. In this research, the focus will be on the parents.

332 See Sutherland 2020, p. 448.

333 Tobin & Varadan 2019, p. 161.

334 Sutherland 2020, p. 455; and Tobin & Varadan 2019, p. 161.

is relevant in two ways. First, in light of due weight accorded to children's views, the shifting equilibrium between the direction and guidance of parents and children's independent decision-making powers in Article 5 UNCRC will be discussed in section 4.4.1 below. Second, the principle of 'evolving capacities' plays a role both with regard to participation and due weight, as will be further elaborated upon in section 4.4.2 below.

4.4.1. The Relationship between Article 5 and Article 12

The relationship between Article 5 and Article 12 UNCRC has been described by the CRC Committee. In General Comment No. 12 concerning Article 12, the CRC Committee notes the relevance of the child's views being given due weight for the shifting equilibrium between parents and children.[335] The transformation from parents giving 'direction and guidance' to giving 'reminders and advice' and finally to 'an exchange on an equal footing' is said to occur in combination with the increasing opportunity for children to express their own views.[336] According to the CRC Committee, as children 'acquire capacities', they are 'entitled to an increasing level of responsibility for the regulation of matters affecting them'.[337] The continually shifting equilibrium between children and their parents is in that sense closely linked to the child's right to be heard.[338] However, there is a distinct difference between the child's right under Article 12 and the right under Article 5 within the decision-making process. Where Article 5 provides for the child's right to be the 'joint decision maker' together with their parents and at a certain point as the main decision-maker, Article 12 only goes so far as to allow the child to have his or her views taken into account by the decision-maker.[339] In other General Comments, the CRC Committee also reflects on the relationship between Article 5 and Article 12. For example, in General Comment No. 7 on implementing rights in early childhood, the CRC Committee considers the principle of 'evolving capacities' and notes that a young child's interests and wishes have to be taken into account for the level of support and guidance that parents give.[340]

In all these comments, the relationship between Article 12 and Article 5 focuses on the giving of guidance and direction by parents to their children. This is primarily relevant for the right to be heard within the setting of the

335 UNCRC General Comment No. 12 (2009), paras. 84 and 85.
336 UNCRC General Comment No. 12 (2009), para. 84.
337 UNCRC General Comment No. 12 (2009), para. 85.
338 Lansdown 2011, pp. 36–37.
339 Lansdown 2005, p. 4. See also Sutherland 2020, p. 466, who notes that Article 5 is broader than Article 12, because it extends to children's agency more generally than solely the child's views.
340 UNCRC General Comment No. 7 (2005), para. 17.

family or in healthcare,[341] i.e. for the first paragraph of Article 12, but less so for children's participation in legal proceedings as provided by Article 12(2). Within the family, parents and children will need to find a balance between children's autonomy and parents' authority for many topics, including daily decisions and bigger decisions regarding education, health, etc. Within the scope of legal proceedings, the opportunity for parents to reach a consensus has often passed or was never available to children – for example, in family law proceedings, where mediation has been unsuccessful or where a passage to court is required. A decision-maker (i.e. a judge or court) is tasked with adjudicating, which makes the direction and guidance of a parent less relevant. The child is not a 'joint decision maker' with the court, so the right of Article 12 to participate is more relevant than the right of Article 5.[342] The intended scope of Article 5 by the drafters of the Convention[343] – focusing on parental direction and guidance – is therefore less relevant for the relationship with Article 12(2). However, as mentioned at the start of this section, the phrase 'evolving capacities' has taken on a life of its own. In doing so, the concept of 'evolving capacities' has become relevant for the child's right to be heard in family law proceedings.

4.4.2. 'Evolving Capacities' and Article 12 UNCRC

The concept of 'evolving capacities' has gained increasing importance within the framework of the UNCRC. Through the work of the CRC Committee, 'evolving capacities' has become relevant for the interpretation and implementation of many UNCRC rights.[344] There have even been calls to recognize it as a general principle.[345] Before we turn to the value of 'evolving capacities' as a principle, let us first consider what is meant by this phrase. According to the CRC Committee, 'evolving capacities' refers to 'the processes of maturation and learning whereby children progressively acquire knowledge, competencies and understanding'.[346] It is a 'positive and enabling process, not an excuse for authoritarian practices'.[347] The CRC Committee's comments also show that 'evolving capacities' is not determined solely by age, the 'individual variations in the capacities of children of the same age' must also be taken into account.[348]

'Evolving capacities' has been recognized as a concept or principle of various kinds. Most critically, Liebel claimed that as a principle 'evolving capacities' can

341 See UNCRC General Comment No. 12 (2009), paras. 91 and 100.
342 Lansdown 2005, p. 4.
343 See also Varadan 2019, pp. 315–316.
344 Tobin & Varadan 2019, p. 162.
345 Hanson & Lundy 2017, pp. 300–301; Tobin & Varadan 2019, p. 162.
346 UNCRC General Comment No. 7 (2005), para. 17.
347 UNCRC General Comment No. 7 (2005), para. 17.
348 UNCRC General Comment No. 7 (2005), para. 17. See also Sutherland 2020, p. 466.

be understood 'as a limitation of the rights exercised by children' or, in contrast, 'as a stimulant for the recognition of the special capacities of children and their promotion'.[349] He argues, rather pessimistically, that 'as long as adults possess the definition power on capacities, the principle will be used in the sense of a limitation'.[350] Taking a more positive approach, Lansdown distinguishes between three conceptual frameworks through which 'evolving capacities' can be understood in relation to other Convention rights:[351] first, as a developmental concept by which the fulfilment of Convention rights should be ensured so as to promote the development of children to reach their 'optimum capacities';[352] second, that as a participatory or emancipatory concept, 'evolving capacities' is meant to assist in 'recognising and respecting children's capacities' through the 'shifting of responsibility for the exercise of rights from adults to children';[353] and, third and finally, that as a protective concept, 'evolving capacities' acknowledges that children have the right to protection because they are still developing.[354] Of these three concepts set out by Lansdown, 'evolving capacities' as a participatory concept is most clearly linked to Article 12 UNCRC. As she notes, the concept of 'evolving capacities' stresses that children are not all the same and that the 'capacities and context of the individual child' must be taken into account, amongst other things in the determination of due weight in accordance with age and maturity.[355]

Varadan has more recently formulated 'evolving capacities' as three different principles, which represent the different roles and functions given to 'evolving capacities' by the CRC Committee.[356] 'Evolving capacities' is seen as: (1) an enabling principle; (2) an interpretative principle; and (3) a policy principle.[357] The CRC Committee itself has also personally referred to 'evolving capacities' as an enabling principle in General Comment No. 7.[358] As an enabling principle, the principle of 'evolving capacities' is 'used to empower children in the exercise of their rights under the UNCRC'.[359] As an interpretative principle, 'evolving capacities' is used to interpret UNCRC provisions 'in a manner that recognizes children's capacities in the exercise of their rights'.[360] Finally, as a policy principle,

[349] M. Liebel, 'From Evolving Capacities to Evolving Capabilities: Contextualizing Children's Rights', in: D. Stoecklin and J.-M. Bonvin (eds.), *Children's Rights and the Capability Approach*, Dordrecht: Springer Science+Business Media 2014, pp. 67–84, p. 69.
[350] Liebel 2014, p. 69.
[351] Lansdown 2005, p. 15.
[352] Lansdown 2005, pp. 15–16 and 22.
[353] Lansdown 2005, pp. 15 and 22.
[354] Lansdown 2005, pp. 15 and 31.
[355] Lansdown 2005, pp. 22–23.
[356] Varadan 2019. See also Varadan & Tobin 2020, pp. 178–182.
[357] Varadan 2019, p. 309.
[358] UNCRC General Comment No. 7 (2005), para. 17.
[359] Varadan 2019, p. 316.
[360] Varadan 2019, p. 316.

'evolving capacities' is 'used to guide states in policy-making and programming on children's rights'.[361] Of these three principles, the first two are key in relation to Article 12 UNCRC.

As an enabling and interpretative principle, 'evolving capacities' is relevant for the first phase of child participation, i.e. whether a child may express views. Where Article 12(1) itself refers to a child being 'capable of expressing views', the principle can be used to interpret the phrase in such a way as to enable children.[362] The CRC Committee does not explicitly refer to 'evolving capacities' in the interpretation. However, in emphasizing that even the youngest children should be able to express views (for example, through non-verbal forms of communication), the CRC Committee refers to the research of Lansdown on the child's evolving capacities.[363] As an interpretative principle, 'evolving capacities' is also a relevant consideration in the discussion concerning the use of minimum age limits for child participation. Age is not explicitly mentioned in Article 5 UNCRC – however, it has been accepted that age limits do not have to conflict with the principle of 'evolving capacities'.[364] Minimum age limits are sometimes needed in practice, because assessing every child's capacity is not realistic in many areas of the law.[365] To comply with the principle of 'evolving capacities', the minimum age limits should be justified – for example, to protect the child and his or her rights – and should not unreasonably interfere with his or her evolving capacities.[366]

'Evolving capacities' is even more relevant as an enabling and interpretative principle for the second phase of child participation: giving due weight to the child's views.[367] The CRC Committee itself notes that 'evolving capacities' must be taken into consideration in the comments on 'being given due weight in accordance with the age and maturity of the child'.[368] The CRC Committee does not further elaborate on how that should be done in the General Comment regarding Article 12 UNCRC, but it has in the General Comment on Article 3(1) recognized a role for 'evolving capacities' in the relationship between the child's best interests and his or her views being given due weight.[369] According to the CRC

361 Varadan 2019, p. 316.
362 See Varadan 2019, p. 323.
363 See UNCRC General Comment No. 12 (2009), para. 21 and fn. 6, referring to Lansdown 2005.
364 See Lansdown 2005, pp. 49–53; Lansdown 2011, p. 37; Varadan & Tobin 2020, p. 182 and S. Rap, E. Schmidt & T. Liefaard, 'Safeguarding the Dynamic Legal Position of Children: A Matter of Age Limits', *Erasmus Law Review*, No. 1, 2020, pp. 4–12, p. 6
365 Lansdown 2011, p. 37.
366 Varadan & Tobin 2020, p. 182.
367 See also Varadan 2019, p. 324.
368 UNCRC General Comment No. 12 (2009), para. 31.
369 UNCRC General Comment No. 14 (2013), para. 44.

Committee, as children mature, their views should be given increasing weight in the assessment of their best interests.[370] This interpretation of relationship between Articles 3(1), 5 and 12 UNCRC was reaffirmed with regard to children's rights in adolescence, where the CRC Committee 'stresses that when determining best interests, the child's views should be taken into account, consistent with their evolving capacities and taking into consideration the child's characteristics'.[371] In this sense, the CRC Committee uses the principle of 'evolving capacities' in lieu of the phrase 'in accordance with the age and maturity of the child'. According to Sutherland, the former 'both overlaps with, and is broader than' the condition of 'age and maturity' from Article 12.[372] Sutherland notes that 'evolving capacities' is broader because it is not only determined by age,[373] but this in fact mirrors the CRC Committee's comments that 'age and maturity' are dual criteria, and that age alone cannot determine the weight to be granted.[374] The actual reason why 'evolving capacities' can be considered to be broader is because it encapsulates the child's development, while 'age and maturity' is more static. The broader nature of 'evolving capacities' can also be attributed to its place within Article 5 – which provides an ongoing right – whereas Article 12 tends to focus more on fixed matters affecting the child. For example, in legal proceedings affecting the child, the child should be heard at a specific point in time, while Article 5 calls for a constant balance between a child's agency and the direction and guidance of their parents. The ongoing nature of Article 5 versus the more static right under Article 12 also explains why the phrasing of 'evolving capacities' is more suitable in the text of Article 5 than 'age and maturity', even though the two are highly similar. The child's evolving capacities should constantly (un)consciously be considered by the parents, while the child's age and maturity will need to be considered by decision-makers at a set point when deciding how much weight to attach to the child's views.

In conclusion, the concept of 'evolving capacities' has started to take on a life of its own. Through the work of Lansdown and Varadan, the different dimensions and functions of the principle have become clear. With regard to the child's right to participate in family law proceedings, this principle is of more interpretative importance than the right provided in Article 5 UNCRC as such. As we have seen above, the child's evolving capacities should be considered both in terms of his or her right to express views and in the granting of due weight to his or her views.

---

370 UNCRC General Comment No. 14 (2013), para. 44.

371 UNCRC General Comment No. 20 (2016), para. 22.

372 Sutherland 2020, p. 466.

373 Sutherland 2020, p. 466, also referring to UNCRC General Comment No. 7 (2005), para. 17.

374 UNCRC General Comment No. 12 (2009), para. 29; see also section 3.1.1.6 above.

4.5. ARTICLES 9 AND 12 UNCRC

Article 9 UNCRC provides children the right not to be separated from their parents, unless it is necessary in terms of being in their best interests. This article contains multiple rights which strengthen this presumption against family separation, including a substantive test and procedural requirements.[375] More specifically, in proceedings where the child is to be separated from his or her parents and placed in alternative care, Article 9(2) UNCRC requires that 'all interested parties shall be given an opportunity to participate in the proceedings and make their views known'. The phrase 'all interested parties' includes children, their parents and others who have a substantial interest in the case, such as siblings.[376] The child who is the subject of the proceedings must thus be given the opportunity to participate and to be heard.[377] In this regard, Article 9 UNCRC reaffirms the right to participate as provided under Article 12 UNCRC.[378] It is not understood to go any further than the scope of Article 12 UNCRC, as there is nothing to suggest that. For example, the text of Article 9, the drafting history and (to date) the CRC Committee all do not suggest or require access to legal representation for the interested parties.[379] In addition, there is nothing to be found which further specifies how interested parties ought to participate and make their views known, or on how weight is to be accorded to these views.[380] On the Day of General Discussion in 2005 on 'Children without Parental Care', the CRC Committee recommended – in light of Article 12 – that children should be heard 'throughout the protection measure process, before making the decision, while it is implemented and also after its implementation'.[381] With regard to children, the right to participation under Article 12 UNCRC can therefore be considered of key importance to understand the procedural requirement included in Article 9 UNCRC.[382]

---

375 J. Tobin & J. Cashmore, 'Art. 9: The Right Not to Be Separated from Parents', in: Tobin 2019, pp. 307–341, p. 309.

376 Tobin & Cashmore 2019, p. 312 and 327.

377 Lansdown 2011, p. 66.

378 See J.E. Doek, 'Article 8: The Right to Preservation of Identity, and Article 9: The Right Not to Be Separated from His or Her Parents', in: Alen et al. 2006a, p. 27 and Vandenhole, Türkelli & Lambrechts 2019, p. 113.

379 Tobin & Cashmore 2019, p. 328.

380 Tobin & Cashmore 2019, pp. 328–329.

381 UN Committee on the Rights of the Child, *Recommendations: Day of General Discussion on Children without Parental Care*, 17 March 2006, CRC/C/153, para. 664.

382 See e.g. Tobin & Cashmore 2019, p. 329 regarding due weight. Note also that the UN Guidelines for the Alternative Care of Children provide no further specifications regarding the participation of the child in alternative care.

4.6. ARTICLES 12, 13 AND 17 UNCRC

The child's right to be heard in Article 12 UNCRC is a broad one that is not solely limited to legal proceedings, but is also provided within the scope of the family, education and political settings. In light of the latter, two of the civil rights and freedoms articles in the UNCRC – Articles 13 and 17 – are closely related to Article 12. Article 13 provides the right to freedom of expression and Article 17 provides the right to have access to appropriate information through mass media. According to the CRC Committee, both articles are 'crucial prerequisites' for the child to effectively exercise his or her right to be heard.[383]

The child's right to freedom of expression in Article 13 distinguishes itself from the child's right to be heard in Article 12 because of its scope and nature. First, Article 13 is broader in scope as it concerns the child's right to have and express any and all opinions regarding any matter, while Article 12 is restricted to 'all matters affecting the child'.[384] Second, the right provided is of a different nature. As noted by the CRC Committee, Article 12 'imposes an obligation on States parties to introduce' legal frameworks and mechanisms to ensure that a child can express his or her views and that due weight is given to these views, while Article 13 imposes an obligation on states parties to 'refrain from interference' in the expression of views.[385] While Article 12 is a positive obligation, Article 13 is a negative obligation and a more classical human right. Both articles provide that children should be able to freely express their views and strengthen each other in that way, however different they are.[386] These differences explain why within the scope of family law disputes, Article 13 is of no further relevance in relation to Article 12 UNCRC.

In Article 17 UNCRC, the child is provided with the right to have access to appropriate information by the 'mass media'. This latter phrase narrows the scope of this article, as it focuses on encouraging the availability of and access to beneficial information for the child through the media and protecting the child against harmful information or material.[387] It is interesting that the CRC Committee refers to Article 17 in stressing that the child has the right to access information 'on all issues of concern to them', including information concerning 'their rights, any proceedings affecting them, national legislation, regulations

---

383 UNCRC General Comment No. 12 (2009), para. 80.

384 UNCRC General Comment No. 12 (2009), para. 81.

385 UNCRC General Comment No. 12 (2009), para. 81. See also Lundy, Tobin & Parkes 2019, p. 401.

386 UNCRC General Comment No. 12 (2009), para. 81. See also Lansdown 2011, p. 35.

387 See S.W. Sacino, 'Article 17: Access to a Diversity of Mass Media Sources', in: A. Alen et al. (eds.), *A Commentary on the United Nations Convention on the Rights of the Child*, Leiden: Martinus Nijhoff Publishers 2012, p. 1; and J. Tobin & E. Handsley, 'Art. 17: The Mass Media and Children: Diversity of Sources, Quality of Content, and Protection against Harm', in: Tobin 2019, pp. 600–644, p. 602.

and policies'.[388] It would have been more fitting to (also) refer to Article 13, which, as a dual right, also provides children the right to information.[389] Article 13 not only affords children the right to communicate or express ideas, but also grants children the right to seek and receive information and ideas.[390] Either way, the provision of information is no doubt important in order for children to effectively realize their right to express views. However, as the ambit of Article 17 mostly concerns children's access to the media and the provision of quality content, it is less relevant for the implementation of the child's right to participation in legal proceedings. This is notwithstanding the fact that the media can assist in creating awareness for children's rights,[391] for example, in television shows, books and online.

All in all, while Articles 13 and 17 both strengthen the emancipation of children and their right to information, both articles above all provide children with civil and political rights. They are therefore key for the child's right to participate in society. With regard to participation in family law proceedings, the articles are not as relevant. Article 12 is by itself sufficient in this respect: it provides children with the right to express views in family law proceedings, and access to information is recognized, by the Committee, as part of the implementation processes.[392]

4.7. ARTICLES 12 AND 21 UNCRC

Adoption is one type of family law proceeding for which the UNCRC contains a separate provision. Article 21 UNCRC addresses the adoption of children and provides a number of standards and safeguards which states must uphold in adoption proceedings.[393] In Article 21(a), the UNCRC provides safeguards for the authorization of adoption, including three preconditions,[394] one of which is that 'if required, the persons concerned, where appropriate, have given their informed consent'. While this precondition does not explicitly mention the child, 'the persons concerned' are understood to include the child.[395] This precondition is not absolute; the phrase 'if required' grants states parties the discretion as to

388 UNCRC General Comment No. 12 (2009), para. 82. See also Lansdown 2011, p. 36.
389 See also Tobin & Handsley 2019, p. 611.
390 See Sacino 2012, p. 6.
391 UNCRC General Comment No. 12 (2009), para. 82.
392 UNCRC General Comment No. 12 (2009), para. 134.
393 See P. Alston, N. Cantwell & J. Tobin, 'Art. 21: Adoption', in: Tobin 2019, pp. 759–816, p. 761, where the authors note the 'neutral position' that the UNCRC takes towards adoption, neither mandating adoption nor prohibiting it.
394 See Alston, Cantwell & Tobin 2019, p. 785.
395 S. Ferreira, 'It is My Adoption, But is Anyone Listening to Me?', *New Zealand Law Review*, Vol. 26, No. 3, 2013, pp. 335–355, p. 377; and Alston, Cantwell & Tobin 2019, p. 793.

whether or not to require informed consent by law and/or which exceptions may apply for informed consent.[396]

With regard to the relationship between Article 21 and Article 12 UNCRC, it is important to note the difference between informed consent and the right to express views. Consent is the legally binding agreement or permission to do something – for example, an adoption. It is 'informed' when the person giving consent has a full understanding of the consequences and gives it voluntarily without undue pressure.[397] Informed consent is a matter of yes or no. Expressing views, as is meant by Article 12 UNCRC, is much more than that. Children can express their feelings, experiences and opinions on their current and future situations. Granting children the right to express their views is broader than asking them a yes or no question. An additional important difference between informed consent and participation is that expressed views must be given due weight, while informed consent (when required) is in principle decisive. Article 12 UNCRC does not grant children a veto power or a right to self-determination, while requirements of informed consent do.[398]

In the General Comment on Article 12, the CRC Committee has underscored the vital importance of hearing children in adoption (or Islamic *kafalah*) proceedings.[399] The CRC Committee also mentions Article 21 UNCRC to emphasize the importance of considering the child's views in determining the child's best interests – which are to be of paramount consideration in adoption proceedings.[400] No reference is made to the condition of informed consent in Article 21 UNCRC.

All things considered, Article 12 UNCRC and the child's right to be heard are of importance in adoption proceedings. Article 21 UNCRC does not further solidify or increase the child's right to participate. The standard put forward by Article 21 for informed consent of those persons concerned, if appropriate and if required, is of a different nature from the right provided by Article 12 UNCRC.

Article 21 UNCRC is the last article to be discussed in relation to Article 12 UNCRC. In this section, we have seen the interplay between the child's right to participation and other rights and principles, including the principles of non-discrimination, the child's best interests and evolving capacities. This section has also clarified the implementation obligation according to Article 4, and the difference between Article 12 and the child's civil rights and freedoms protected in Articles 13 and 17 UNCRC. Finally, with regard to the specific

---

396 See S. Vité & H. Boéchat, 'Article 21: Adoption', in: A. Alen et al. (eds.), *A Commentary on the United Nations Convention on the Rights of the Child*, Leiden: Martinus Nijhoff Publishers 2008, p. 39; and Alston, Cantwell & Tobin 2019, p. 792.

397 Alston, Cantwell & Tobin 2019, p. 794.

398 See also section 3.1.1.5 above.

399 UNCRC General Comment No. 12 (2009), para. 55.

400 UNCRC General Comment No. 12 (2009), para. 56. See also Vité & Boéchat 2008, p. 39.

proceedings in which children are separated from their parents (Article 9) and adoption proceedings (Article 21), the relevance of Article 12 UNCRC has been addressed in addition to the broader procedural requirements included in these articles.

5. INDIVIDUAL COMMUNICATIONS TO THE UN COMMITTEE ON THE RIGHTS OF THE CHILD

Having discussed Article 12 UNCRC in detail, and also in relation to other UNCRC rights and principles, the final section of this chapter addresses the individual communications decided upon by the CRC Committee regarding Article 12 UNCRC. As was noted at the start of this chapter,[401] in 2014 the Third Optional Protocol to the UNCRC, which provides for individual communications to the Committee, entered into force. In effect, this means that children can individually or as a group complain to the CRC Committee about non-compliance or violation of the UNCRC by states parties that have ratified the Third Optional Protocol.[402] In this section, the individual communications to the UNCRC which have been decided upon are considered to determine whether the CRC Committee has provided further interpretation to the standards of Article 12 UNCRC.

5.1. SEARCH AND SELECTION

At present, the jurisprudence of the CRC Committee is steadily increasing, but is not yet substantive. This makes a search and analysis of the relevant individual communications manageable. For this analysis, the jurisprudence database of the United Nations Human Rights Office of the High Commissioner was searched for the selection of individual communications.[403] The search was conducted without search terms, using only filters available through the detailed search. The following two filters were used: first, as the selection only concerns the jurisprudence of the CRC Committee, the filter by bodies was used, selecting 'CRC'; and second, the filter by articles was used selecting for Article '12', '12-1' and '12-2' so as to search for all communications concerning Article 12 UNCRC. This search resulted in a total of 27 results.[404]

---

401 See section 2.2 above.

402 At present 46 states; see also section 2.2 above.

403 The database is available at: https://juris.ohchr.org/search/Documents.

404 The final search was conducted on 28 January 2021.

To determine which of these decisions on individual communications contains further interpretation of the CRC Committee with regard to the standards of Article 12 UNCRC, a quick scan was conducted of all 27 decisions. A discontinuance decision was given in six of these communications, as there are no views given by the CRC Committee, either as to the admissibility or the merits of the communication; these decisions will not be considered further here.[405] Subsequently, four communications are not further considered because they were found to be inadmissible on grounds unrelated to Article 12 UNCRC – more specifically, on the grounds of the non-exhaustion of all available domestic remedies,[406] *ratione temporis*[407] or because the alleged victims were not minors at the time of the alleged violation.[408] Following this quick scan, we are left with 18 decisions on individual communications.[409]

5.2. ARTICLE 12 IN INDIVIDUAL COMMUNICATIONS

In 18 individual communications decided upon by the CRC Committee, Article 12 UNCRC is considered. In the following sections, these 18 decisions will be discussed. First, those concerning family law proceedings will be addressed. Subsequently, those concerning migration and asylum proceedings will be briefly discussed, taking into account the question whether the Committee's interpretation of Article 12 UNCRC in these proceedings also applies to family law proceedings.

5.2.1. Individual Communications on Family Law Proceedings

Out of the 18 individual communications, four concern family law proceedings. All four were found to be inadmissible by the CRC Committee on the ground of being insufficiently substantiated. These inadmissibility decisions do not contain an adoption of views by the Committee, but in finding the claims insufficiently

---

405 UNCRC, *M.B. v. Spain* (CRC/C/78/D/39/2017), 12 June 2018; UNCRC, *J.G. v. Switzerland* (CRC/C/81/D/47/2018), 28 June 2019; UNCRC, *M.I.M. v. Spain* (CRC/C/82/D/54/2018), 13 November 2019; UNCRC, *E.H.R.S., A.I.R.S. and A.H.R.S. v. Argentina* (CRC/C/85/D/90/2019), 4 November 2020; UNCRC, *J.J., O.L., A.J. and A.S. v. Finland* (CRC/C/85/D/87/2019), 11 November 2020 and UNCRC, *L.D. v. Spain* (CRC/C/85/D/37/2017), 28 September 2020, para. 9.

406 UNCRC, *D.C. v. Germany* (CRC/C/83/D/60/2018), 4 February 2020.

407 UNCRC, *J.A. and E.A. v. Switzerland* (CRC/C/85/D/53/2018), 28 September 2020.

408 UNCRC, *Y.M. v. Spain* (CRC/C/78/D/8/2016), 31 May 2018; and UNCRC, *A.D. v. Spain* (CRC/C/80/D/14/2017), 1 February 2019.

409 One decision contained two individual communications – one of which was discontinued, the other on which the Committee did adopt views. This is why there remain 18 decisions and not 17. See UNCRC, *L.D. v. Spain* (CRC/C/85/D/37/2017), 28 September 2020; and UNCRC, *B.G. v. Spain* (CRC/C/85/D/38/2017), 28 September 2020.

substantiated, the Committee does consider the substance of the case. In doing so, it at times indirectly responds to the claims regarding Article 12 UNCRC.

All four individual communications concerning family law proceedings were brought by a parent on behalf of their child (or children). They concerned high-conflict separations, in the sense that the parents had been engaged in a large amount of litigation regarding custody, contact or visitation, allegations of verbal and/or physical abuse and a (seemingly) high degree of anger, hostility and distrust.[410] The first communication, *Y. and Z. v. Finland* (2019), was brought by a mother on behalf of her two children and concerned the granting of custody to the father and the enforcement of contact rights.[411] In *L.H.L. and A.H.L. v. Spain* (2019), a father submitted an individual communication on behalf of his two children concerning the denial of the Spanish courts to return the children to Switzerland and the failure to enforce his access rights.[412] The third communication, *A.R.G. v. Spain* (2020), submitted by a mother on behalf of her son, concerned a visitation schedule of the child's father which the mother argued should be suspended because of alleged sexual abuse by the father.[413] Finally, *L.H.A.N. v. Finland* (2020) concerned residence proceedings with a mother submitting the communication on behalf of her son.[414] Three parents complained of a violation of a whole list of UNCRC rights: 14 articles,[415] 15 articles[416] and 23 articles respectively.[417] A possible explanation may be that all three of these parents were not represented by counsel.[418] In *A.R.G. v. Spain* (2020), the mother (represented by counsel) complained of a violation of five UNCRC articles.[419]

One can question whether parents engaged in high-conflict separations should be authoring communications to the CRC Committee on behalf of their children. In *L.H.A.N. v. Finland* (2020), the state party argued that the complaint should be inadmissible because there is no proof of the child's consent to the communication, while the 'child's age is above 10 years, his opinion should be considered', and that given the circumstances 'there is a manifest conflict of interests' between mother and child.[420] The CRC Committee did not go along

410 For one definition of high-conflict divorce, see Z. Levite & O. Cohen, 'The Tango of Loving Hate: Couple Dynamics in High-Conflict Divorce', *Clinical Social Work Journal*, Vol. 40, No. 1, 2012, pp. 46–55, p. 46.

411 UNCRC, *Y. and Z. v. Finland* (CRC/C/81/D/6/2016), 15 May 2019, para. 3.1.

412 UNCRC, *L.H.L. and A.H.L. v. Spain* (CRC/C/81/D/13/2017), 15 May 2019, paras. 3.2–3.5.

413 UNCRC, *A.R.G. v. Spain* (CRC/C/85/D/92/2019), 28 September 2020, paras. 1.1 and 2.1.

414 UNCRC, *L.H.A.N. v. Finland* (CRC/C/85/D/98/2019), 28 September 2020, para. 3.1.

415 UNCRC, *Y. and Z. v. Finland* (CRC/C/81/D/6/2016), 15 May 2019, para. 3.1.

416 UNCRC, *L.H.L. and A.H.L. v. Spain* (CRC/C/81/D/13/2017), 15 May 2019, paras. 1.1 and 3.1.

417 UNCRC, *L.H.A.N. v. Finland* (CRC/C/85/D/98/2019), 28 September 2020, para. 3.1.

418 UNCRC, *Y. and Z. v. Finland* (CRC/C/81/D/6/2016), 15 May 2019, para. 1; UNCRC, *L.H.L. and A.H.L. v. Spain* (CRC/C/81/D/13/2017), 15 May 2019, para. 1.1; UNCRC, *L.H.A.N. v. Finland* (CRC/C/85/D/98/2019), 28 September 2020, para. 1.1.

419 UNCRC, *A.R.G. v. Spain* (CRC/C/85/D/92/2019), 28 September 2020, paras. 1.1 and 3.3.

420 UNCRC, *L.H.A.N. v. Finland* (CRC/C/85/D/98/2019), 28 September 2020, para. 4.5.

with this argument, noting that the mother had joint custody and the submission of the communication was not 'clearly against' the child's best interests.[421]

Amongst the different articles complained about, in all four communications a violation of Article 12 UNCRC was alleged. In two of these communications, no further explanation was provided by the parent as to why Article 12 UNCRC had been violated in the domestic proceedings.[422] In the other two communications, the complaint was substantiated. In *Y. and Z. v. Finland* (2019), the mother claimed that 'the children's opinion that they did not want to live with their father was not considered' and that the children had not been heard in any of the proceedings.[423] In *L.H.A.N. v. Finland* (2020), the mother claimed that Article 12 UNCRC was breached because the national authorities had 'failed to listen to the child when he voiced his own opinions' and instead had listened to 'what the child said after the father had manipulated him'.[424] The complaint is not that the child had not been heard, but that the child's views should not have been taken into account as 'the father controlled the child's thinking' and the child had been alienated from the mother which 'affected the child's views'.[425]

Notwithstanding the specific complaints, in all four communications, the CRC Committee did not go into the merits of the complaints regarding Article 12. Instead, the Committee consistently determines that the claims were insufficiently substantiated because the parent had 'not demonstrated' that the assessment of the facts and evidence by the courts or authorities was 'clearly arbitrary or amounted to a denial of justice'.[426] The Committee relied on the following principle: 'it is for the national authorities to examine the facts and evidence and to interpret and enforce domestic law, unless their assessment has been clearly arbitrary or amounts to a denial of justice'.[427] The Committee would not reassess the facts or evidence, but would 'ensure that their assessment was not arbitrary or tantamount to a denial of justice and that the best interests of the child were a primary consideration in that assessment'.[428] As the CRC Committee itself notes, it is not a 'court of fourth-instance', as is also the case

---

421 UNCRC, *L.H.A.N. v. Finland* (CRC/C/85/D/98/2019), 28 September 2020, para. 7.2.

422 UNCRC, *L.H.L. and A.H.L. v. Spain* (CRC/C/81/D/13/2017), 15 May 2019, para. 7.3; and UNCRC, *A.R.G. v. Spain* (CRC/C/85/D/92/2019), 28 September 2020, para. 3.3.

423 UNCRC, *Y. and Z. v. Finland* (CRC/C/81/D/6/2016), 15 May 2019, para. 3.2.

424 UNCRC, *L.H.A.N. v. Finland* (CRC/C/85/D/98/2019), 28 September 2020, para. 3.3.

425 UNCRC, *L.H.A.N. v. Finland* (CRC/C/85/D/98/2019), 28 September 2020, para. 3.3.

426 UNCRC, *Y. and Z. v. Finland* (CRC/C/81/D/6/2016), 15 May 2019, para. 9.8; UNCRC, *L.H.L. and A.H.L. v. Spain* (CRC/C/81/D/13/2017), 15 May 2019, para. 9.5; UNCRC, *A.R.G. v. Spain* (CRC/C/85/D/92/2019), 28 September 2020, para. 4.2 and UNCRC, *L.H.A.N. v. Finland* (CRC/C/85/D/98/2019), 28 September 2020, para. 7.5.

427 UNCRC, *Y. and Z. v. Finland* (CRC/C/81/D/6/2016), 15 May 2019, para. 9.8; UNCRC, *L.H.L. and A.H.L. v. Spain* (CRC/C/81/D/13/2017), 15 May 2019, para. 9.5; UNCRC, *A.R.G. v. Spain* (CRC/C/85/D/92/2019), 28 September 2020, para. 4.2 and UNCRC, *L.H.A.N. v. Finland* (CRC/C/85/D/98/2019), 28 September 2020, para. 7.5.

428 UNCRC, *Y. and Z. v. Finland* (CRC/C/81/D/6/2016), 15 May 2019, para. 9.8.

with respect to other UN treaty bodies.[429] This means that 'the committees are competent to consider possible violations of the rights guaranteed by the treaties concerned, but not to act as an appellate instance with respect to national courts and tribunals'.[430] With regard to the four communications, the CRC Committee found that claims had not been sufficiently substantiated because the cases had all been dealt with by the national courts or authorities. For example, in *L.H.L. and A.H.L. v. Spain* (2019), the CRC Committee commented that the alleged abduction and lack of contact had been 'subject to a detailed analysis by the Spanish courts'.[431]

All four communications were found to be inadmissible as a whole, but let us zoom in on the complaints regarding Article 12 UNCRC. In only one of the four communications does the CRC Committee specifically comment on the child's participation. In response to the allegation of manipulated views in *L.H.A.N. v. Finland* (2020), the Committee found that the child had been heard in the decision-making and that a social report had 'stated that the child's own thoughts were clearly his own'.[432] While finding the communication inadmissible and not considering the merits, the Committee did inadvertently clarify that with regard to allegations of influence, national courts can be helped by reports on the child's behaviour and wishes. In the other three communications, the CRC Committee does not make any remarks regarding child participation. In two of these communications, there are also no signs of a violation, because the state notes that the children had been heard by the courts[433] or because the parent's claim goes no further than noting a violation.[434] In the third communication, *Y. and Z. v. Finland* (2019), the Committee does not comment on Article 12, even though the mother claimed that the children had not been heard. Perhaps the Committee considered the state's argument to be sufficient, namely that a forensic psychiatry working group had 'reviewed the ability of the children to be interviewed' (in light of the criminal investigation) and had concluded that the children could not be interviewed 'due to their age and the prolonged nature of the custody dispute' and that interviewing the children would not have been in their best interests.[435] This would be noteworthy, as the working group assessed

---

429 UNCRC, *L.H.A.N. v. Finland* (CRC/C/85/D/98/2019), 28 September 2020, para. 4.6. See also UN Human Rights Council, *Report of the Open-Ended Working Group to Explore the Possibility of Elaborating an Optional Protocol to the Convention on the Rights of the Child to Provide a Communications Procedure*, A/HRC/13/43, 21 January 2010, para. 80.

430 J. Cardona Llorens, 'The Legal Value of the Views and Interim Measures Adopted by United Nations Treaty Bodies', *Spanish Yearbook of International Law*, Vol. 23, 2019, pp. 146–165, p. 151.

431 UNCRC, *L.H.L. and A.H.L. v. Spain* (CRC/C/81/D/13/2017), 15 May 2019, para. 9.5.

432 UNCRC, *L.H.A.N. v. Finland* (CRC/C/85/D/98/2019), 28 September 2020, para. 7.5.

433 UNCRC, *L.H.L. and A.H.L. v. Spain* (CRC/C/81/D/13/2017), 15 May 2019, para. 7.12.

434 UNCRC, *A.R.G. v. Spain* (CRC/C/85/D/92/2019), 28 September 2020.

435 UNCRC, *Y. and Z. v. Finland* (CRC/C/81/D/6/2016), 15 May 2019, para. 8.9.

the children's possibility to be interviewed for allegations of suspected violence by their father,[436] while interviews for the purpose of criminal investigations are very different from children expressing views in family law proceedings. The purpose of children expressing views under the scope of Article 12 UNCRC is not to 'obtain reliable information' on alleged violence – as suggested by the state –[437] but to allow children to express their opinions as to custody and contact. In finding this communication to be inadmissible and not commenting any further on Article 12 UNCRC, the CRC Committee has left a key question unanswered: can children's right to be heard in family law proceedings be limited because it is considered not to be in their best interests?

Perhaps this question will be answered in a future individual communications procedure. On the basis of these four inadmissibility decisions, the tentative conclusion can be made that highly litigious parents dissatisfied with the outcome of family law proceedings will generally not be successful in complaining in the name of their child of breaches under the UNCRC. The CRC Committee is not a 'court of fourth-instance' and seemingly does not want to burn its hands on these drawn-out high-conflict proceedings. If future authors of individual communications do want a response regarding a violation of Article 12 in family law proceedings, they will likely have to be very explicit and clearly substantiate the violation to pass the admissibility test of 'clearly arbitrary or a denial of justice'. A communication by a child himself or herself, or by a parent assisted by counsel, focusing on only a number of UNCRC articles – and not a full sweep – will potentially be considered substantively by the Committee.

5.2.2. *Individual Communications on Migration or Asylum Proceedings*

Aside from the four individual communications on family law proceedings, the other 14 communications concerned migration or asylum proceedings. Of these 14 decisions, a majority concerned comparable complaints regarding the process for the determination of the age of an alleged unaccompanied minor. In addition to complaints regarding a whole list of UNCRC articles, these 12 communications all share similar complaints regarding Article 12 UNCRC: the minor did not have (timely) access to legal assistance that would have enabled him to express views throughout the age determination process and to have kept him informed.[438] One of these 12 complaints was found to be

436 UNCRC, *Y. and Z. v. Finland* (CRC/C/81/D/6/2016), 15 May 2019, para. 8.2.

437 UNCRC, *Y. and Z. v. Finland* (CRC/C/81/D/6/2016), 15 May 2019, para. 8.2.

438 UNCRC, *N.B.F. v. Spain* (CRC/C/79/D/11/2017), 27 September 2018, para. 7.2; UNCRC, *D.K.N. v. Spain* (CRC/C/80/D/15/2017), 1 February 2019, paras. 3.1 and 3.3; UNCRC, *A.L. v. Spain* (CRC/C/81/D/16/2017), 31 May 2019, paras. 3.6 and 7.7; UNCRC, *J.A.B. v. Spain* (CRC/C/81/D/22/2017), 31 May 2019, para. 3.8; UNCRC, *M.T. v. Spain* (CRC/C/82/D/17/2017), 18 September 2019, para. 3.4; UNCRC, *R.K. v. Spain* (CRC/C/82/D/27/2017), 18 September 2019, paras. 3.5, 6.10 and 6.11; UNCRC, *A.D. v. Spain* (CRC/C/83/D/21/2017), 4 February 2020,

inadmissible.[439] In the other 11 communications, the Committee did adopt views, finding a violation of Article 12 (in combination with Article 3) in all these communications, in particular due to the absence of a (legal) representative or guardian.[440] These 11 communications provide a clear principle for the representation of alleged unaccompanied minors in the age determination process.[441] As this context is very different from that of children in family law proceedings who do have legal guardians (i.e. their parents) and are not facing a determination which will strip them of their rights as children, it is unlikely that the CRC Committee would require the same immediate representation of minors in family law proceedings.

The remaining two communications concern other situations of migration or asylum proceedings in which a complaint under Article 12 UNCRC was brought, because the children had not been heard in the proceedings.[442] In *C.E. v. Belgium* (2018), the foster parents under a *kafalah* arrangement of a young Moroccan girl submitted an individual communication to the CRC Committee on behalf of the girl, C.E, complaining of various violations in the denial of a humanitarian visa for C.E. to reside in Belgium.[443] In *E.A. and U.A. v. Switzerland* (2020), a mother submitted a communication on behalf of her two sons concerning

para. 3.5; UNCRC, *M.A.B. v. Spain* (CRC/C/83/D/24/2017), 7 February 2020, paras. 3.5 and 6.5; UNCRC, *M.B.S. v. Spain* (CRC/C/85/D/26/2017), 28 September 2020, para. 3.4; UNCRC, *M.B. v. Spain* (CRC/C/85/D/28/2017), 28 September 2020, paras. 3.4 and 7.3; UNCRC, *B.G. v. Spain* (CRC/C/85/D/38/2017), 28 September 2020, paras. 3.4 and 7.3 and UNCRC, *S.M.A. v. Spain* (CRC/C/85/D/40/2017), 28 September 2020, para. 5.9.

439 UNCRC, *D.K.N. v. Spain* (CRC/C/80/D/15/2017), 1 February 2019, para. 11.5.

440 UNCRC, *N.B.F. v. Spain* (CRC/C/79/D/11/2017), 27 September 2018, para. 12.9; UNCRC, *A.L. v. Spain* (CRC/C/81/D/16/2017), 31 May 2019, para. 12.9; UNCRC, *J.A.B. v. Spain* (CRC/C/81/D/22/2017), 31 May 2019, para. 13.9; UNCRC, *M.T. v. Spain* (CRC/C/82/D/17/2017), 18 September 2019, para. 13.6; UNCRC, *R.K. v. Spain* (CRC/C/82/D/27/2017), 18 September 2019, para. 9.9; UNCRC, *A.D. v. Spain* (CRC/C/83/D/21/2017), 4 February 2020, para. 10.16; UNCRC, *M.A.B. v. Spain* (CRC/C/83/D/24/2017), 7 February 2020, para. 10.9; UNCRC, *M.B.S. v. Spain* (CRC/C/85/D/26/2017), 28 September 2020, para. 9.15; UNCRC, *M.B. v. Spain* (CRC/C/85/D/28/2017), 28 September 2020, para. 9.14; UNCRC, *B.G. v. Spain* (CRC/C/85/D/38/2017), 28 September 2020, para. 10.15 and UNCRC, *S.M.A. v. Spain* (CRC/C/85/D/40/2017), 28 September 2020, para. 7.14.

441 UNCRC, *N.B.F. v. Spain* (CRC/C/79/D/11/2017), 27 September 2018, para. 12.8; UNCRC, *A.L. v. Spain* (CRC/C/81/D/16/2017), 31 May 2019, para. 12.8; UNCRC, *J.A.B. v. Spain* (CRC/C/81/D/22/2017), 31 May 2019, para. 13.7; UNCRC, *M.T. v. Spain* (CRC/C/82/D/17/2017), 18 September 2019, para. 13.5; UNCRC, *R.K. v. Spain* (CRC/C/82/D/27/2017), 18 September 2019, para. 9.8; UNCRC, *A.D. v. Spain* (CRC/C/83/D/21/2017), 4 February 2020, para. 10.14; UNCRC, *M.A.B. v. Spain* (CRC/C/83/D/24/2017), 7 February 2020, para. 10.8; UNCRC, *M.B.S. v. Spain* (CRC/C/85/D/26/2017), 28 September 2020, para. 9.13; UNCRC, *M.B. v. Spain* (CRC/C/85/D/28/2017), 28 September 2020, para. 9.12; UNCRC, *B.G. v. Spain* (CRC/C/85/D/38/2017), 28 September 2020, para. 10.13 and UNCRC, *S.M.A. v. Spain* (CRC/C/85/D/40/2017), 28 September 2020, para. 7.12.

442 UNCRC, *C.E. v. Belgium* (CRC/C/79/D/12/2017), 27 September 2018, para. 3.7; and UNCRC, *E.A. and U.A. v. Switzerland* (CRC/C/85/D/56/2018), 28 September 2020, paras. 3.2 and 3.4.

443 UNCRC, *C.E. v. Belgium* (CRC/C/79/D/12/2017), 27 September 2018, para. 1.

asylum proceedings in Switzerland in which both she and her children were to be deported to Italy.[444] In both communications, the Committee adopted views and found a violation of Article 12 UNCRC, because the children had not been heard.[445] In both communications, the respective states argue that the children had been too young to express their views,[446] but this argument is not accepted by the Committee. In *C.E. v. Belgium* (2018), the CRC Committee referred to previous General Comments emphasizing that 'Article 12 imposes no age limit' and that 'the fact that the child is very young or in a vulnerable situation … does not deprive him or her of the right to express his or her views'.[447] In light of this, the Committee found that as C.E. was five years old at the time of the second visa decision, 'she would have been perfectly capable of forming views of her own'.[448] In *E.A. and U.A. v. Switzerland* (2020), the Committee found the 'absence of a direct hearing of the children constituted a violation of Article 12', noting that Article 12 does not impose an age limit and that states are discouraged from introducing age limits.[449] The children were eight and three years old during the proceedings, and the domestic laws determined a presumption of discernment at 14 years.[450] In the latter communication, the Committee also did not agree with the state party's argument that the children did not need to be heard because their mother could represent their interests; instead, children's interests should be assessed separately.[451]

The CRC Committee's adopted views in these two communications have in common the fact that the Committee remains steadfast with regard to discouraging states from introducing or using age limits. In both communications, the Committee found that the children should have been heard directly. The possibility for the mother to bring forward the interests of the children was not accepted as a reason not to hear the children. Both of these communications concerned migration or asylum proceedings, so it is not clear whether the Committee would be of the same opinion if the communications had concerned family law proceedings. One might assume that as the General Comment makes no strong distinction between migration/asylum proceedings and family law proceedings that the same standards would apply, but as the Committee has found all four individual communications to date concerning family law

---

444 UNCRC, *E.A. and U.A. v. Switzerland* (CRC/C/85/D/56/2018), 28 September 2020, para. 1.1.

445 UNCRC, *C.E. v. Belgium* (CRC/C/79/D/12/2017), 27 September 2018, para. 8.9; and UNCRC, *E.A. and U.A. v. Switzerland* (CRC/C/85/D/56/2018), 28 September 2020, para. 7.3.

446 UNCRC, *C.E. v. Belgium* (CRC/C/79/D/12/2017), 27 September 2018, para. 4.13; UNCRC, *E.A. and U.A. v. Switzerland* (CRC/C/85/D/56/2018), 28 September 2020, para. 4.15.

447 UNCRC, *C.E. v. Belgium* (CRC/C/79/D/12/2017), 27 September 2018, para. 8.7.

448 UNCRC, *C.E. v. Belgium* (CRC/C/79/D/12/2017), 27 September 2018, para. 8.8.

449 UNCRC, *E.A. and U.A. v. Switzerland* (CRC/C/85/D/56/2018), 28 September 2020, para. 7.3.

450 UNCRC, *E.A. and U.A. v. Switzerland* (CRC/C/85/D/56/2018), 28 September 2020, para. 4.13.

451 UNCRC, *E.A. and U.A. v. Switzerland* (CRC/C/85/D/56/2018), 28 September 2020, paras. 4.13 and 7.3.

and Article 12 UNCRC to be inadmissible, that is debatable. Perhaps the CRC Committee does find migration or asylum proceedings to be of a different nature from family law proceedings and therefore requires a direct hearing regardless of the young ages of the children involved.

6. CONCLUSION

This chapter opened with a quote from the CRC Committee, which noted that there is a 'need for a better understanding of what Article 12 entails'. This quote was drawn from the starting paragraphs of the Committee's General Comment on Article 12 UNCRC from 2009. As we have seen throughout this chapter, the Committee's General Comment has to a great extent provided a better understanding of Article 12 and the requirements for implementation. However, this chapter has also shown that the CRC Committee's work has not provided all the answers with regard to child participation in family law proceedings, as certain aspects remain unclear, with different interpretations being possible. Perhaps one cannot expect the Committee to do so, given the nature of the UNCRC, the breadth of Article 12 and the limitations inherent in General Comments. The task of providing interpretative guidelines for such a unique right applicable in many different contexts in one – relatively short – document is a difficult one. The remaining uncertainty as to the interpretation of Article 12 UNCRC leaves room for discussion. This chapter has addressed these discussions and has attempted to thoroughly ascertain the standards that the UNCRC sets for child participation in family law proceedings. The nuance and detail of the standards will not be repeated here; instead, the core standards will now be presented as the first building block of the international and European framework for the child's right to participate.

To preface the following standards, it is important to emphasize that the right to participate contained in Article 12 applies in all matters affecting the child and specifically in judicial and administrative proceedings, including ADR processes.[452] The child's right to participate in family law proceedings is covered as one of the many matters affecting children. The relationship between Article 12 and Articles 9 and 21 further clarifies that in cases concerning the separation of children from their parents or those relating to adoption, the right of the child to express his or her views, as provided by Article 12, is of importance.[453] Articles 9 and 21 provide to 'all interested parties' and 'the persons concerned' respectively opportunities to participate or even provide informed consent (with regard to adoption proceedings). The child's right to express views as provided by Article 12 is not further specified in either of these articles.

---

452 See sections 3.1.1.4 and 3.1.2.2 above.

453 See sections 4.5 and 4.7 above.

A central conclusion with regard to Article 12 is that the child's right to participation consists of two parts: (1) the right to express views; and (2) the right for those views to be given due weight. Let us consider the core standards for each step.

To start with the first step, Article 12 UNCRC provides children with *the right to express views*.[454] This is a strong right and children should be informed that they have the right not to speak if they do not wish to.[455] The right to express views is not unconditional as it is granted to those children who are capable of forming their own views. What this means precisely remains to some extent up in the air. However, there are two key things to take away from this. First, states ought to rely on a presumption of capacity for the child's right to express views.[456] This brings with it the understanding of a child's 'evolving capacities' and that young children should also be afforded the opportunity to express views.[457] Second, states should not impose an age limit on the child's right to express views, either in law or in practice.[458] This has also been upheld by the CRC Committee's more recent adoption of views in individual communications.[459] The CRC Committee's explanation of how 'capability' should be understood and that it should be assessed on a case-by-case examination is to a certain extent ambitious in the context of family law proceedings. It requires judges and other legal actors, who are not schooled in the development of children, to determine which children are capable or to communicate and listen to very young children. Perhaps the breadth of matters addressed by the first paragraph of Article 12, including, for example, the right to express views within the family or at school, can explain this interpretation by the CRC Committee. Non-verbal participation of children at home regarding decisions within the family without age limits is more realistic than the similar situation in family law proceedings. The question thus becomes whether the CRC Committee would persistently maintain the current interpretation also in respect of family law proceedings and, if so, how states should implement Article 12 in such a way within their budgetary constraints. While 'capability' is an explicit condition for the right to express views, in light of the relationship between Article 3 and Article 12 UNCRC, the child's best interests should not form a ground to restrict his or her right to express views; only in exceptional circumstances may this be the case.[460]

As to how the child's right to express views is to be put into practice in legal proceedings, Article 12(2) provides for three modes of participation: directly,

454 See section 3.1.1.3 above.
455 See sections 3.1.1.3 and 3.2.2.1 above.
456 See sections 3.1.1.2 and 3.2.2.2 above.
457 See sections 3.1.1.2 and 4.4.2 above.
458 See section 3.1.1.2 above.
459 See section 5.2.2 above.
460 See section 4.2.1 above.

through a representative or through an appropriate body. Party status in legal proceedings is not provided.[461] With regard to the three modes of participation, there is no requirement that states have to provide all the modes for all children in every type of proceeding. Instead, effective and accessible modes should be available and, if possible, the child should be allowed to choose between modes.[462] This is the most feasible interpretation of the provision for states. With regard to the modes specifically, direct participation should be understood to mean an in-person meeting between the child and the decision-maker.[463] Representation can be provided by different persons and in different ways; however, the CRC Committee is steadfast that the task of the representative is to represent the child's views and is not in his or her best interests.[464] Regardless of the mode employed, the hearing of the child should occur in an enabling, encouraging, child-friendly and safe environment.[465]

Turning to the second step of participation, after the child has expressed views, these *views should be given due weight*. As a starting point, due weight clarifies that Article 12 UNCRC provides a right to participation, not a right to self-determination. Although the CRC Committee has not further defined 'due weight', the following definition is proposed: 'proper or just relative importance accorded'.[466] Due weight cannot be determined *in abstracto*; the weight accorded to the child's views will depend on the circumstances of the case and other interests involved (both of the child and other parties).[467] The principal factor in the weighing of a child's views will be his or her age and maturity – the duality of this criteria is of special importance.[468] As the child matures, his or her views shall have increasing weight in the assessment of his or her best interests.[469] The relationship between Article 12, Article 3 and the principle of evolving capacities of Article 5 is key in this respect. A number of other factors which may impact on the weighing of a child's views have been suggested in the literature, but only one additional factor is referred to by the CRC Committee: the impact of the decision on the child's life.[470] In conclusion, due weight should be given to the child's views in the decision as such, but more specifically the views of the child should be considered in the assessment of the child's best interests.[471] In that regard, the relationship between Article 12 and Article 3 is crucial, and

---

461 See section 3.1.2.3 above.
462 See section 3.1.2.3 above.
463 See section 3.1.2.3 above.
464 See section 3.1.2.3 above.
465 See section 3.2.2.1 above.
466 See section 3.1.1.5 above.
467 See section 3.1.1.5 above.
468 See section 3.1.1.6 above.
469 See sections 3.1.1.6, 4.2.2 and 4.4.2 above.
470 See section 3.1.1.5 above.
471 See section 4.2.2 above.

the perspective of the child's views as enmeshed within his or her interests should be widely adopted.[472] The latter requires decision-makers to consider the child's views when assessing his or her best interests – for example, allowing the child's views to push the scales in favour of two comparable options or towards a third option.

In this regard, the type of proceeding concerned is relevant, as it determines whether there are more than two options. For example, must the judge decide between custody or no custody, or are there multiple options available to the judge, such as no access, access or limited access in combination with safeguards? If the judge only has the option between yes or no, then a potential conflict between the child's views and his or her best interests (as assessed by the decision-maker) may be more difficult to resolve. The child's best interests, as determined by other aspects or factors, may then outweigh the views of the child. This is in keeping with Article 3 UNCRC, by which the child's best interests are to be a primary consideration in decisions affecting his or her, and with Article 12 UNCRC, by which the views of children must be given due weight, but which does not grant a right to self-determination.

In light of this, it is important to emphasize that Article 12 UNCRC provides a right to participation, not a right to initiate proceedings or a right to decide in proceedings. While the right to participate empowers children, providing an opportunity for children to express their views in proceedings from which they have previously been excluded, participation is a limited form of autonomy. Children may express their views, but these views are not directly decisive, although they are to be given due weight. In that sense, a balance is sought between autonomy and the protection of children. One can identify three moments in legal proceedings during which the law can provide children with autonomy, i.e. a choice, or not.[473] These three moments are shown in Figure 2.1, where the black line represents the course of legal proceedings and the boxes represent the moments at which children may be involved.

Figure 2.1. Autonomy of children in legal proceedings

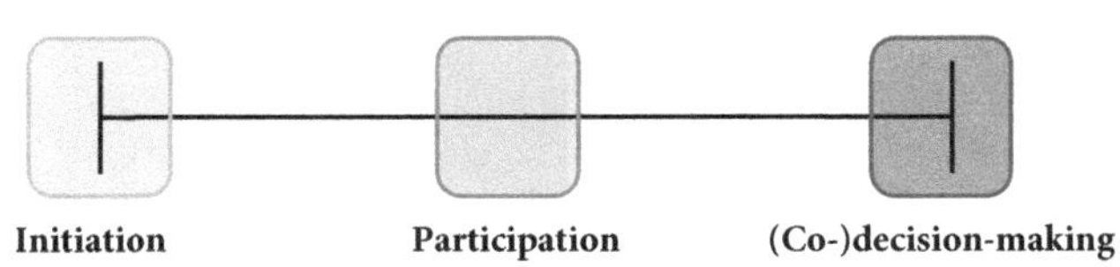

Source: Mol, Bou-Sfia & Huijer 2020, p. 95 (translated by the author).

472 See section 4.2.2 above.

473 See C.R. Mol, S. Bou-Sfia & J. Huijer, 'Mijn wil is wet! De autonomie van minderjarigen in het Nederlandse personen- en familierecht', in: W. Schrama & S. Burri (eds.), *De rol van de staat in het personen- en familierecht*, The Hague: Boom juridisch 2020, pp. 91–147.

The text of Article 12 and the General Comment clarifies that while it may be possible that children are allowed to initiate proceedings or have the power to decide the outcome, Article 12 only sees to the child's right to participation. In that regard, Daly's proposal for a 'children's autonomy principle' in which children are granted outcome autonomy – i.e. the right to decide – unless this would cause significant harm goes beyond the scope of Article 12 UNCRC. In contrast, informed consent in adoption proceedings does provide children with outcome autonomy.[474] While the UNCRC does not require that children should be afforded more autonomy in the form of the right to initiate proceedings or the right to decide in disputes (as proposed by Daly), it is a possibility to be further considered by states.

In General Comment No. 12, the CRC Committee not only provides a legal analysis of the text of Article 12 UNCRC, but also sets out five steps for 'effective' implementation. These steps address the entire participation process: before, during and after.[475] An important aspect of this, as emphasized by the CRC Committee, is the information that should be imparted to the child. Information on the participation process should be shared with the child in preparation of the opportunity to express views, regarding his or her rights, the process, the potential impact of his or her views and the practicalities of the modes of participation.[476] Following the decision, the child must be informed about the weight given to his or her views and the available mechanisms for complaints, remedies and redress.[477] In addition to informing the child, in these steps for implementation, the Committee also recognizes that children are not a homogeneous group, so the process of participation should be 'diversity-sensitive' and 'inclusive', with no discrimination on any grounds and adaptions made where necessary – for example, for children with disabilities.[478] Besides these requirements, the CRC Committee spells out quite a number of additional requirements for implementation. These additional requirements – for example, that the environment in which the child is heard must be 'enabling and encouraging' or that the child should have access to remedies – are relevant for the context in which participation occurs. These requirements are necessary for 'effective' implementation, but one can argue that they go beyond the minimum level of implementation of Article 12 UNCRC. These additional requirements are not necessary to achieve a basic level of child participation, but if implemented assist and ensure that child participation is effective and child friendly.

The above standards address child participation in family law proceedings, but it is important to note that not all family law disputes will lead to judicial proceedings.

---

474 See also section 4.7 above.

475 See section 3.2 above.

476 See section 3.2.1 above.

477 See section 3.2.3 above.

478 See sections 3.2.1 and 3.2.2.1 above.

Disputes may instead be resolved in administrative proceedings, ADR or at home. Article 12 UNCRC also provides children with the right to participate in these settings. Although the implementation may differ, the core obligation of granting children the opportunity to express views and giving due weight to these views applies equally.

In conclusion, Article 12 places a strong obligation on states to implement the child's right to participation.[479] Understanding and implementing the right to participation is not simple; states will have to carefully consider and address the multitude of standards provided by the UNCRC and the CRC Committee.

479 See sections 3.1.1.1 and 4.3 above.

CHAPTER 3
THE CHILD'S RIGHT TO PARTICIPATE IN EUROPEAN HUMAN RIGHTS INSTRUMENTS

'Convinced that the rights and best interests of children should be promoted and to that end children should have the opportunity to exercise their rights, in particular in family proceedings affecting them …'

– Preamble to the European Convention on the Exercise of Children's Rights

1. INTRODUCTION

While the United Nations Convention on the Rights of the Child (UNCRC) is the beacon of children's rights, in the past few decades the Council of Europe (CoE) and the European Union (EU) have also increasingly committed themselves to the topic. Within Europe, both have worked towards 'building a pan-European space fit for children'[480] by further strengthening children's rights. In doing so, children's rights have seeped into the European human rights framework. Nowadays, a myriad of European human rights instruments address children's participation. Most of these are new instruments, either drafted specifically to address children's rights (for example, the European Convention on the Exercise of Children's Rights, as the quote above shows) or more general human rights instruments which include children's rights (for example, the Charter of Fundamental Rights of the European Union (CFREU)). Many of the 47 Council of Europe Member States are bound to one or more of these new instruments in addition to the UNCRC, as we have seen in Chapter 1, Figure 1.1.

In this chapter, four of the five European human rights instruments which address child participation in family law proceedings are studied: the European Convention on the Exercise of Children's Rights (ECECR), the Guidelines on Child-Friendly Justice (GCFJ), the Recommendation on the participation of children and the CFREU.[481] The aim is to determine the standards set by these

480 Council of Europe, *Strategy for the Rights of the Child (2012–2015)*, 15 February 2012, p. 18.

481 The fifth instrument is the European Convention on Human Rights and the case law of the European Court of Human Rights; this instrument will be discussed in Part II below.

instruments regarding children's right to participation in family law proceedings in Europe. These four instruments add to the core instruments: the UNCRC, as discussed in the previous chapter, and the ECHR with the case law of the ECtHR, as will be discussed in depth in Part II. All six instruments combined and aligned form the international and European framework of the child's right to participate in Europe.

To fully comprehend the four different instruments and their understanding of child participation, this chapter approaches each of them similarly. First, the nature and scope of the human rights instrument is addressed. Is it a binding or non-binding instrument and what is its material and personal scope? Then the following core question is asked: what are the specific rights provided in the instrument which concern the child's right to participation in family law proceedings? The interpretation of these rights is done with reference to Explanatory Reports or memoranda, literature and, where relevant, case law. While the chapter concludes with short remarks regarding the European human rights instruments, the comparison of the different standards – between themselves, with the UNCRC and with the ECtHR case law analysed in Part II – is covered in Chapter 10. There the set of standards will be taken together and viewed as the existing framework of children's right to participate in family law proceedings in Europe, and the possibilities to align and strengthen this framework will be evaluated in Chapter 11.

Within Europe, there are two actors: the CoE and the EU. The CoE is the 'continent's leading human rights organisation',[482] a regional intergovernmental organization with 47 Member States. The leading achievement of the CoE is the European Convention on Human Rights (ECHR), adopted in 1950, and its most well-known body, the European Court of Human Rights (ECtHR). The Convention and the case law of the ECtHR are not discussed here, but are the subject of Part II, which provides a comprehensive ECtHR case law analysis.

The CoE may be best known for the ECHR, but it has also introduced many other instruments, including in the field of children's rights. In 1979, ten years before the adoption of the UNCRC, the Parliamentary Assembly recommended the creation of a European Charter on the Rights of the Child.[483] This plan never materialized as the recommendation was not passed by the Committee of Ministers.[484] Eleven years later, in light of the adoption of the UNCRC, the Parliamentary Assembly recommended considering the possibility of an additional protocol to the ECHR on the rights of the child.[485] Again, this

482 As per the Council of Europe website: http://coe.int/en/web/about-us/who-we-are.

483 CoE Parliamentary Assembly, *Recommendation 874 (1979) European Charter on the Rights of the Child*, para. 17.

484 E. Verhellen, 'Children's Rights in Europe', *International Journal of Children's Rights*, Vol. 1, Nos. 3–4, 1993, pp. 357–376, p. 369.

485 CoE Parliamentary Assembly, *Recommendation 1121 (1990) Rights of Children*.

never came into being. However, it did set the tone and it led to the European Convention on the Exercise of Children's Rights adopted in 1996. This is the first instrument relevant to child participation that will be discussed (see section 2).

In the twenty-first century, children's rights again received increasing attention from the CoE. Following a mandate by the Third Summit of Heads of State and Government in 2005,[486] the 'Building a Europe for and with Children' programme was launched in 2006. This programme subsequently led to strategy cycles,[487] the first being the Stockholm Strategy of 2009–2011,[488] followed by the Monaco Strategy of 2012–2015[489] and the current Sofia Strategy of 2016–2021.[490] These strategies all had the promotion of children's access to justice as an objective. At the same time, the CoE adopted various instruments to specifically deal with child participation. The Parliamentary Assembly Recommendation of 2009, 'Promoting the participation by children in decisions affecting them', called for further action by the Committee of Ministers and Member States' governments.[491] The Guidelines on Child-Friendly Justice were adopted in 2010 in response to conclusions by the European Ministers of Justice in 2007,[492] the Stockholm Strategy and the Recommendation.[493] These guidelines provide relevant standards for child participation, so it is the second instrument of the CoE that will be discussed here (see section 3). The third and final CoE instrument that will be discussed is the Committee of Ministers' Recommendation on the participation of children and young people under the age of 18 of 2012 (see section 4).

Finally, the last instrument analysed in this Chapter is the CFREU (see section 5). The EU differs from the CoE, as it is a unique economic and political union with broad legislative competences. As such, it has introduced its own human rights charter which must be considered in order to provide a complete overview of European norms.

---

486 Action Plan, Third Summit of Heads of State and Government of the Council of Europe (Warsaw, 16–17 May 2005).

487 R. Jensdottir, 'The Council of Europe Action in Favour of Children's Rights: Helping Professionals Working with Children Make the Best Use of the Available Standards', *Irish Journal of Applied Social Sciences*, Vol. 15, No. 2, 2015, pp. 12–24, pp. 13–14.

488 Council of Europe, *Building a Europe for and with Children 2009–2011: The Stockholm Strategy*, 27 November 2008.

489 Council of Europe, *Strategy for the Rights of the Child (2012–2015)*, 15 February 2012.

490 Council of Europe, *Strategy for the Rights of the Child (2016–2021)*, March 2016.

491 CoE Parliamentary Assembly, *Recommendation 1864 (2009) Promoting the participation by children in decisions affecting them*.

492 European Ministers of Justice, *Resolution No. 2 on Child-Friendly Justice*, 28th Conference of the European Ministers of Justice, 2007, MJU-28 (2007) Resol. 2E.

493 Guidelines of the Committee of Ministers of the Council of Europe on Child-Friendly Justice, 17 November 2010.

2. THE ECECR

The ECECR was the CoE's reaction to the UNCRC.[494] In 1990, the CoE gave the Committee of Experts on Family Law the task of preparing a convention with the aim of complementing and implementing Article 12 UNCRC.[495] Although discussions were held within the Committee concerning potential additional substantive rights which could be afforded to children (e.g. consent or veto rights for certain proceedings such as adoption) the ECECR sticks to procedural rights,[496] specifically procedural rights which are aimed at facilitating children's exercise of their substantive rights.

2.1. THE NATURE AND SCOPE OF THE ECECR

The ECECR entered into force in 2000 following ratification by three states. At present, it has been ratified by 20 states[497] and signed by a further eight states.[498] Although it is not considered a 'key' convention, it is active and has regular ratifications.[499] It is binding for the 20 states that have ratified the Convention (see also Chapter 1, Figure 1.1). For the other states – those who have signed but not ratified, as well as those who have not signed but are members of the CoE – the ECECR functions to a limited extent as an influential interpretative instrument through the case law of the ECtHR. The ECtHR has used the ECECR as a source of law in case law on child participation, even when the state against which the complaint was addressed has not ratified the ECECR.[500]

The scope of the ECECR is limited in two ways: the children to whom it grants rights and the proceedings in which it does so.

In general, the Convention applies to all children who have not reached the age of 18. This is in accordance with the age of legal capacity previously recommended by the Committee of Ministers and the generally accepted

---

494 European Convention on the Exercise of Children's Rights, Strasbourg, 25 January 1996, ETS No. 160.

495 K. Herbots, 'Het nieuwe Europees Verdrag inzake de uitoefening van de rechten van het kind en de situatie in België', *Tijdschrift voor Privaatrecht*, 1997, pp. 1763–1823, p. 1766.

496 I. Jansen 'Europees Verdrag inzake de uitoefening van rechten van kinderen', *Tijdschrift voor Familie- en Jeugdrecht*, No. 6, 1996, pp. 132–138.

497 Albania, Austria, Croatia, Cyprus, the Czech Republic, Finland, France, Germany, Greece, Italy, Latvia, Malta, Montenegro, Poland, Portugal, Slovenia, Spain, the former Yugoslav Republic of Macedonia, Turkey and Ukraine.

498 Hungary, Iceland, Ireland, Luxembourg, the Russian Federation, Serbia, the Slovak Republic and Sweden.

499 See the Report by the Secretary General on the Review of Council of Europe Conventions, SG/Inf(2012)12. In 2015, both Malta and Spain ratified the Convention.

500 See e.g. ECtHR, *N.Ts. and others v. Georgia* (Appl. No. 71776/12), 2 February 2016, para. 76. See also Chapter 9, section 5.6.

European age of majority.[501] According to the Explanatory Report, children who are under the national age of majority but are older than 18 may 'still be helped by the Convention'. This remark has been criticized for being inconsistent with the treaty text, or too vague and non-binding.[502]

Not all the rights provided by the ECECR are granted to children under the age of 18. Multiple rights, including the right to express views directly and, if states so wish, the right to apply for the appointment of a special representative, are limited to children considered to have 'sufficient understanding'.[503] The interpretation of 'sufficient understanding' is left to the states. The guidance provided by the Explanatory Report in this regard is rather unclear for a Convention that is meant to assist in the implementation of the UNCRC. First, the Explanatory Report notes that states are left to define the criteria in order to be able to evaluate 'whether or not children are capable of forming and expressing their own views'.[504] This phrasing is a clear referral to the text of Article 12 UNCRC, which provides the right to 'the child capable of forming his or her own views'. However, it does not appear that 'sufficient understanding' is a simple rephrasing of the same criteria. It seems that the Explanatory Report allows – if not suggests – states to fix a specific age as a criteria for 'sufficient understanding'.[505] The Explanatory Report states that 'it is left to states to define the criteria enabling them to evaluate whether or not children are capable of forming and expressing their own views and states are naturally free to make the age of children one of those criteria'.[506] Additionally, it suggests using 'age' as a presumption for sufficient understanding, noting that if 'internal law has not fixed a specific age in order to indicate the age at which children are considered to have sufficient understanding', the court or administrative authority will need to determine the level of understanding needed.[507]

The focus of the ECECR is on family proceedings. Although the Explanatory Report does suggest that states can opt to apply it to any other proceedings,[508] the material scope is limited to family proceedings (Article 1(3) ECECR). These include judicial proceedings before an administrative authority (Article 2(a) ECECR). The scope is especially limited because the states that ratify the

501 CoE *Resolution (72)29 on the lowering of the age of full capacity*, adopted by the Committee of Ministers on 19 September 1972. See Explanatory Report to the European Convention on the Exercise of Children's Rights, 25 January 1996, para. 11.

502 Jansen 1996, p. 133; and Herbots 1997, p. 1769.

503 See Articles 3 and 4 ECECR.

504 Explanatory Report 1996, para. 35.

505 Explanatory Report 1996, para. 36. See also Jansen 1996; and C. Sawyer, 'One Step Forward, Two Steps Back: The European Convention on the Exercise of Childrens Rights', *Child and Family Law Quarterly*, Vol. 11, No. 2, 1999, pp. 151–166.

506 Explanatory Report 1996, para. 36.

507 Explanatory Report 1996, para. 36.

508 Explanatory Report 1996, para. 15.

Convention only need to specify a minimum of three categories of family law proceedings to which the Convention is to apply.[509] The Explanatory Report provides a non-exhaustive list of examples: custody, residence, questions of parentage, administration of property, care procedures, medical treatments, etc.[510] The opting-in to certain categories makes it easier for states to ratify and implement the ECECR on the one hand,[511] but on the other hand allows – or even endorses – the fragmentation of children's rights in family law proceedings. Children could have potentially far-reaching procedural rights in three types of proceedings, but have no procedural rights in all other family law proceedings.[512] This fragmentation restricts the purpose of promoting children's rights. As Lowe notes, 'it allows states to nominate relatively narrow areas' and there is the danger that 'there may be no uniformity on which areas are covered by the Convention'.[513] In practice, some states have declared the ECECR to be applicable to three types of proceedings,[514] whereas others have listed multiple and broad types of proceedings.[515]

2.2. THE CONTENT OF THE ECECR

The ECECR provides mandatory procedural rights and optional procedural rights for children in family law proceedings. In the following sections, these mandatory and optional rights are introduced (see section 2.2.1), followed by an analysis of the different modes of participation provided by these rights (see section 2.2.2).

2.2.1. Mandatory and Optional Rights of Participation

There are two main mandatory rights provided by the ECECR. Article 3 provides the child with the right to be informed and to express his or her views

---

509 Article 1(4) ECECR. For the declarations of all ratifying states, see: www.coe.int/en/web/conventions/full-list/-/conventions/treaty/160/signatures?p_auth=Ba3WgC9J.

510 Explanatory Report 1996, para. 17.

511 Jansen 1996, p. 134.

512 Herbots 1997, p. 1774.

513 N. Lowe, 'The Impact of the Council of Europe on European Family Law', in: J.M. Scherpe (ed.), *European Family Law Volume I: The Impact of Institutions and Organisations on European Family Law*, Cheltenham: Edward Elgar 2016, pp. 95–123, p. 104.

514 See e.g. Austria (custody, access/contact and adoption), Finland (establishment of paternity adoption, and proceedings concerning the taking of a child into care) or Greece (custody, communication between parents and children, and adoption).

515 See e.g. the Czech Republic, whose declaration included 'any other family proceedings affecting the rights of the child', or Spain, whose declaration following a list of proceedings included 'any family proceedings in which the rights of minors may be affected by the decision that is taken'.

in proceedings if he or she is of sufficient understanding. This right is mirrored into the obligation of the judicial authority to ensure that the child has been informed and is able to express his or her views in Article 6. According to Article 6, the judicial authority shall also 'give due weight to views expressed by the child'. The second mandatory right is included in Articles 4 and 9: the appointment of a special representative when the holder(s) of parental responsibility cannot represent the child due to a conflict of interests. This special representative can be appointed either following a child's application (Article 4) or *ex officio* (Article 9).

The optional procedural rights which states can grant to children and which they are obliged to consider granting are provided in Article 5 ECECR. These rights are provided in ascending order, starting with the right to apply to be assisted by an appropriate person of their choice when expressing their views, followed by the right to apply for the appointment of a separate representative and the right to appoint their own representative. The article ends with the most far-reaching expansion of children's procedural rights: the right to exercise some or all of the rights of parties to such proceedings.

2.2.2. *Modes of Participation*

In these mandatory and optional rights, the ECECR includes various modes of participation. These will now be discussed in the following order: consultation, representation and party status.

The first mode is *consultation* by the judge in person or through other persons or bodies provided in Articles 3(b) and 6(b) ECECR. The term 'consultation' is not defined, but seemingly refers to the meeting between a judge and the child, i.e. what is sometimes also termed 'judicial meetings' or a direct hearing of the child.[516] According to the Explanatory Report, the judicial authority, i.e. judge, is 'under a duty to consult the child unless this is manifestly contrary to his or her best interests'.[517] The Explanatory Report also suggests that it is preferable for the judge to consult the child directly and in person, although it is also possible for the judge to request another person or body to consult the child and report back as to the child's views.[518]

The second mode provided in the ECECR is *representation*. Article 2(c) ECECR defines a representative as 'a person, such as a lawyer, or a body appointed to act before a judicial authority on behalf of a child'. There are four types of representatives mentioned in the Convention: the special representative, the separate representative, the 'own' representative and the

516 Explanatory Report 1996, para. 45.
517 Explanatory Report 1996, para. 45.
518 Explanatory Report 1996, para. 45.

holders of parental responsibilities. The special representative can be requested and appointed according to Articles 4 and 9(1) ECECR in cases where there is a conflict of interests between the child and his or her parent(s) or guardian. No examples are given as to who the special representative can or should be. The separate representative is an option which states parties can consider, according to Articles 5(b) and 9(2) ECECR. The example given of a separate representative is a lawyer, and it is explained that it is someone other than the parents or guardians. The difference between a separate representative and a special representative is not clarified. The Explanatory Report only notes that there is a difference, not what this entails.[519] Whether there is a difference between the separate representative of Article 5(b) and the own representative of Article 5(c) is also left unanswered. The final type of representative is the holder of parental responsibilities. Although extensively mentioned in the Explanatory Report, the Convention only refers to this type of representative in Article 10(2). The ECECR requires states to consider extending the duties of representatives to parents or guardians. In many jurisdictions, the law provides that parents or guardians can represent their children; however, according to the Explanatory Report, this does not automatically mean that parents or guardians must fulfil the duties provided for in Article 10.[520] Instead, they are considered representatives under the Convention only when they have specifically been appointed as representative by the judicial authority.[521] It is problematic that parents and guardians would only have to respect the child's right to express views when they have been officially appointed as representatives, as they should also do so in their capacity as a parent. On the flipside, if parents or guardians are appointed as representatives, is it appropriate for them to do so in family law proceedings? Can parents embroiled in family law proceedings provide neutral, unbiased and fair representation for their children? Even if there is no direct conflict of interests, in many family law proceedings this is often not considered to be the case.[522]

Notwithstanding the differences between the different forms of representation and whom the representative can or should be, Article 10 ECECR sets out the task of these representatives. The role of the representatives is threefold. They must: (a) 'provide all relevant information to the child'; (b) explain the 'possible consequences' of the child's views or actions to the child and (c) 'determine the views of the child and present these views to the judicial authority'. The first two tasks of the representative are conditional upon the sufficient understanding of the child. According to the Explanatory Report, states can decide whether the

519 Explanatory Report 1996, para. 53.
520 Explanatory Report 1996, para. 56.
521 Explanatory Report 1996, paras. 26 and 53.
522 Jansen 1996, p. 135; Herbots 1997, p. 1788 and Sawyer 1999, p. 153.

representative ought to have additional functions.[523] Although not mentioned in the text of Article 10 ECECR, the Explanatory Report also notes that the representative may also 'give their own views on the best interests of the child'.[524] There appears to be no distinction made as to the role of the representatives depending on the type of representative concerned.

The final mode of child participation included in the Convention is the child as a *party* in Article 5(d). This suggestion is not further discussed in the explanatory report, but is simply presented as an option for states to consider.[525]

2.3. CONCLUSION

The ECECR is an interesting Convention as it provides both mandatory and optional participation rights for children which states may introduce in their family law proceedings. It is also a very specific Convention focusing on the procedural rights of children in family law proceedings. The ECECR provides states with a great deal of discretion – both as to the proceedings to which the ECECR will apply and the rights that states wish to introduce – which may lead to fragmented implementation. In light of this discretion, it is also noteworthy that more than half of the CoE states have yet to ratify. The ECECR provides children with the right to participate through consultation and the right to a special representative, and explicitly places the duty on states to ensure these rights. The other forms of representation and party status included in the ECECR are optional, but are provided and may act as an impetus as states can consider these options. In addition to participation rights, the ECECR includes an obligation for the judicial authority and the different representatives to inform the child.

3. THE GCFJ

The CoE did not sit still in the years following the development and entry into force of the ECECR. As mentioned in the introduction, children's rights, including participation, remained on the agenda. In late 2010, this led to the adoption of the GCFJ by the Council of Ministers of the CoE.[526] The aim was to add to the existing children's rights framework through providing further guidance and examples of good practice to Member States' legislators and professionals.[527]

---

523 Explanatory Report 1996, para. 54.

524 Explanatory Report 1996, para. 55.

525 See Explanatory Report 1996, para. 42.

526 Guidelines of the Committee of Ministers of the Council of Europe on Child-Friendly Justice, 17 November 2010.

527 Explanatory Memorandum to the Guidelines on Child-Friendly Justice, Council of Europe 2011, para. 16.

The GCFJ was prepared as a response to barriers children face in participating in decisions affecting them, among other things in judicial proceedings. These barriers were identified by the European Ministers of Justice in 2007 and backed by the Parliamentary Assembly, prompting further examination of the issue by the CoE.[528] A multidisciplinary group of specialists on child-friendly justice was formed. With input from experts, non-governmental organizations and a large-scale consultation with children, the group subsequently drafted and finalized the GCFJ.[529]

3.1. THE NATURE AND SCOPE OF THE GCFJ

The GCFJ is not legally binding in nature.[530] However, it can – to a limited extent – be considered influential. As Liefaard notes, it has political and (limited) legal value.[531] It also has political value in the sense that it adopts a clear stance on children's rights. Within Europe, the GCFJ reinforces the message that the right to participation provided by the UNCRC should be effectively implemented. Inclusion of the GCFJ in children's rights strategies and agendas of the CoE and the EU reflects this political message.[532] The legal value of the GCFJ is present in relation to the ECtHR. The GCFJ forms an additional legal source for the Court, as noted by the Group of Specialists when deciding on the legal form of the GCFJ and in the literature by Liefaard.[533] This is also affirmed by the case law analysis conducted later on in this volume (see also Chapter 9, section 6).

---

528 European Ministers of Justice, *Resolution No. 2 on child-friendly justice*, 28th Conference of the European Ministers of Justice, 2007, MJU-28 (2007) Resol. 2E; Parliamentary Assembly, *Recommendation 1864 (2009) Promoting the participation by children in decisions affecting them*, Appendix, para. 14.

529 Group of Specialists on Child-Friendly Justice, *Report of the 1st Meeting of the Group of Specialists on Child-Friendly Justice*, CJ-S-CH (2009) 3; Group of Specialists on Child-Friendly Justice, *Draft Report of the 2nd Meeting of the Group of Specialists on Child-Friendly Justice*, CJ-S-CH (2009) 15; Group of Specialists on Child-Friendly Justice, *Report of the 3rd Meeting of the Group of Specialists on Child-Friendly Justice*, CJ-S-CH (2009) 18 rev. 1; Group of Specialists on Child-Friendly Justice, *Report of the 4th Meeting of the Group of Specialists on Child-Friendly Justice*, CJ-S-CH (2010) 8 E and U. Kilkelly, *Listening to Children about Justice: Report of the Council of Europe Consultation with Children on Child-Friendly Justice*, CJ-S-CH(2010) 14 rev., Strasbourg, 5 October 2010.

530 Explanatory Memorandum 2011, para. 15.

531 T. Liefaard, 'Child-Friendly Justice: Protection and Participation of Children in the Justice System', *Temple Law Review*, Vol. 88, No. 4, 2016, pp. 906–927, pp. 913–914.

532 Liefaard 2016, p. 913. See Council of Europe, *Council of Europe Strategy for the Rights of the Child (2012–2015)*, 2012; Council of Europe, *Council of Europe Strategy for the Rights of the Child (2016–2021)*, 2016 and European Commission, *An EU Agenda for the Rights of the Child*, Brussels, 15 February 2011, COM(2011) 60 final, p. 8.

533 Group of Specialists on Child-Friendly Justice, *Report of the 4th Meeting of the Group of Specialists on Child-Friendly Justice*, CJ-S-CH (2010) 8 E; and Liefaard 2016, pp. 913–914.

The non-binding nature of the GCFJ may explain its broad material scope. To begin with, the GCFJ covers all areas of law by which children may be confronted: criminal, civil and administrative law.[534] This covers the entire range from youth justice proceedings to family law proceedings and to asylum proceedings. Although some parts of the GCFJ are only of importance in certain types of cases – for example, the section on the deprivation of liberty – the guidelines are not differentiated according to the area of law. The second way in which the scope of the GCFJ is broad is that the guidelines deal with both judicial proceedings and forms of ADR.[535] The Explanatory Memorandum remarks that ADR, such as mediation, is a positive development. However, the child's right to participate should not be brushed aside and dismissed in ADR;[536] therefore, the GCFJ explicitly includes ADR. This leads us to the final aspect of the material scope – the encompassing of all phases of proceedings (before, during and after). The GCFJ thereby stress the need for child-friendly provision of information to the child both prior to and following the judicial proceedings.[537]

3.2. THE CONTENT OF THE GCFJ

Bearing in mind the broad scope but also the non-binding nature of the guidelines, the content of the GCFJ will now be discussed.

To begin with, when discussing the GCFJ, the definition of 'child-friendly justice' is important to consider. According to Guideline II(c), 'child-friendly justice' refers to 'justice systems which guarantee the respect and the effective implementation of all children's rights at the highest attainable level', taking into account the fundamental principles included in the GCFJ and 'giving due consideration to the child's level of maturity and understanding and the circumstances of the case'. It notes that, amongst other things, it includes respecting the rights 'to participate in and to understand the proceedings'. This definition is rather broad as it concerns all proceedings concerning children, including, for example, 'the right to due process', a right of more importance in youth justice or asylum proceedings and of less relevance for family law proceedings. Family law cases are not further defined in the GCFJ; the Explanatory Memorandum only refers to some examples, such as 'parentage, custody, parental abduction' cases.[538]

The rest of this section provides an overview of the guidelines which provide for or further define the child's right to participate as relevant for

534 GCFJ, I(2).
535 GCFJ, I(1).
536 Explanatory Memorandum 2011, para. 81.
537 See e.g. GCFJ, IV(B) 25 and IV(E) 75.
538 Explanatory Memorandum 2011, para. 51.

family law proceedings. In this research, the guidelines have been grouped into eight relevant aspects, which are presented in Table 3.1 below and will be discussed in that order.

Table 3.1. Relevant aspects and related guidelines

Relevant aspect	**Guidelines**
Fundamental principles	III(A)–(E)
Information and feedback	IV(A) 1–4 IV(B) 25 IV(D) 48–49 IV(E) 75 and 77
Access to court	IV(D) 34–35
Right to be heard	IV(D) 44–47
Representation	IV(D) 37–42 IV(E) 75 and 77
Organization of proceedings	IV(D) 54–62
ADR	IV(B) 24 and 26
Training of professionals	IV(A) 14–15 IV(D) 39

Source: Compiled by the author.

3.2.1. Fundamental Principles

The GCFJ refers to five fundamental principles as derived from the existing European and international instruments, and expand on these principles. The first fundamental principle is the *right to participation*. Although the principle leans on its predecessors, particularly Article 12 UNCRC,[539] its phrasing is different. Guideline III(A) 1 reads as follows:

> The right of all children to be informed about their rights, to be given appropriate ways to access justice and to be consulted and heard in proceedings involving or affecting them should be respected. This includes giving weight to the children's views bearing in mind their maturity and any communication difficulties they may have in order to make this participation meaningful.[540]

This guideline speaks of the right to be consulted and heard, and that due weight should be given, bearing in mind the child's maturity. It also speaks of 'access [to] justice'. This is a different concept from participation or child-friendly justice. Neither the UNCRC nor the ECHR speaks of access to justice.

539 See Explanatory Memorandum 2011, para. 32.

540 GCFJ, III(A) 1.

Is there a substantive difference? According to Liefaard, there is.[541] He argues that the distinguishing feature between the concepts is the focus on the ability to obtain remedies with access to justice,[542] which is not the focus of the right to participation. He bases this argument on the report of the United Nations High Commissioner for Human Rights (UNHCHR) entitled 'Access to justice for children'.[543] This report defines access to justice as the ability to obtain remedies.[544] However, in the UNHCHR report, the understanding of access to justice appears to be broader. In the continuation of the report, the focus lies largely on child participation in proceedings. The legal framework focuses on Article 12 UNCRC, and the barriers and good practices described concern participation. The UNHCHR report also contains a separate section on participation in proceedings. The concepts can be understood as related and closely intertwined, but also as different, as access to justice includes the right to participation and also the right to effective remedies, and the right to initiate proceedings in that regard.

Guideline III(A) 1 also places explicit emphasis on the importance of informing children of their right to participate. The relevance of providing information is also reflected in other guidelines, as will be discussed later on. Finally, it mentions the issues which children may face in communicating, a factor which needs to be considered in order for participation to be 'meaningful'.

This guideline on the right to participation is supplemented with a guideline noting that in exercising the right to participation, a child's capacity should be taken into account.[545] The Explanatory Memorandum refers extensively to Article 12 UNCRC and the corresponding General Comment in relation to this guideline. In doing so, the Explanatory Memorandum reiterates that states should not use standardized age limits and clarifies that the reference to capacity should not constrain children's right to participate.[546] The presumption of capacity is considered to be relevant in that regard.[547]

In the Explanatory Memorandum, family law cases are specifically mentioned with regard to this right to participation: 'all measures to ensure that children are included in the judicial proceedings should be the responsibility of the judge, who should verify that children have been effectively included in the process and are absent only when children themselves have declined to participate or are

541 See Liefaard 2016, p. 905, fn. 6.

542 T. Liefaard, 'Access to Justice for Children', in: *Preadviezen KNVIR: Protecting the Rights of Families and Children in a Changing World*, The Hague: Asser Press 2017, pp. 35–88, p. 43.

543 UN High Commissioner for Human Rights (UNHCR), *Access to Justice for Children*, A/HRC/25/35, 16 December 2013.

544 UNHCR 2013, para. 4.

545 GCFJ, III(A) 2.

546 Explanatory Memorandum 2011, paras. 33–34.

547 Explanatory Memorandum 2011, para. 33.

of such maturity and understanding that their involvement is not possible'.[548] The responsibility to ensure the child's participation in family law proceedings lies squarely with the judge, but the Explanatory Memorandum also calls upon voluntary organizations and ombudspersons to 'ensure that children are included in family law proceedings and are not faced with a fait accompli'.[549] With regard to the 'fait accompli', reference is made to custody and access cases in which parents are penalized for not complying with the judgment, while it is in fact the child who refuses to comply, but who has never been granted the opportunity to express their views on the matter.[550]

The second fundamental principle is that the *best interests of the child* ought to be a primary consideration in all matters involving or affecting them (Guideline III(B) 1). This principle is a raison d'être for the guidelines. Subsequently, Guideline III(B) 2 explicitly states that in assessing the best interests of a child, his or her views must be given due weight. In the Explanatory Memorandum, there is no further discussion as to how the views must be given due weight in assessing the child's best interests.

The third and fourth fundamental principles concern *dignity*[551] and *protection from discrimination*.[552] Treating children with dignity and not discriminating against them on any grounds are straightforward principles, although the implementation thereof may be more difficult. What does 'respecting dignity' mean for child participation in family law proceedings? The Explanatory Memorandum provides no explanation. One could argue that providing child-friendly justice and, as such, respecting the child's right to participate leads the child to be treated with dignity, i.e. treated in the way in which adults would like to be treated themselves.

Finally, the fifth fundamental principle is that the *rule of law* should apply to children as it does to adults.[553] Under the rule of law, the guidelines emphasize elements of due process and the provision of complaints mechanisms.[554]

3.2.2. *Information and Feedback*

Following the fundamental principles, the second aspect of the GCFJ that is relevant to the right to participation is the provision of child-friendly information and feedback. This aspect is a recurring theme in the GCFJ. As one of the general elements of child-friendly justice,[555] the provision of information and

548 Explanatory Memorandum 2011, para. 35.
549 Explanatory Memorandum 2011, para. 35.
550 See Explanatory Memorandum 2011, fn. 13.
551 GCFJ, III(C) 1 and 2.
552 GCFJ, III(D) 1 and 2.
553 GCFJ, III(E) 1.
554 GCFJ, III(E) 2 and 3.
555 GCFJ, IV(A) 1–4.

feedback is relevant before,[556] during[557] and after judicial proceedings.[558] At all stages, children should receive all relevant and necessary information promptly and in a manner which they can understand.[559] The GCFJ calls for the direct provision of information to children, not (only) through the parents, to ensure that they receive objective and complete information.[560] In that regard, the Explanatory Memorandum notes that 'parents may not always share all pertinent information, and what they give may be biased'.[561] Regarding the information provided to children on how they may participate during the proceedings, the GCFJ emphasizes that children should be made aware that their views may not determine the decision.[562] This is meant to dispel the common myth which children may believe about expressing their views. When judicial proceedings have been concluded, feedback by means of judgments understandable for children and, if applicable, from the child's lawyer, the guardian ad litem or other representative is necessary according to the GCFJ.[563] The latter should include information on available measures or remedies open to children, such as appeal or complaint mechanisms.[564]

3.2.3. *Access to Court*

Of course, information and feedback are not of any use unless the child can participate. This leads us to the next aspect of the GCFJ: access to court. Access to court is more far-reaching than the expression of views in proceedings. It provides children with a direct means of entry to proceedings and a recourse to remedies. In that regard, access to court falls under the broader access to justice and not child participation in the strict sense. The guidelines recommend access to court for 'children who have sufficient understanding of their rights'.[565] Thus, access to court is limited by a maturity requirement. The Explanatory Memorandum briefly delves into the discussion on age limits or open notions of maturity. The benefits and risks of both options are mentioned, as is the possibility of a flexible age limit.[566] It remains a choice between legal certainty and objectivity versus a margin of appreciation and inclusivity, and the question is: who ought to carry the burden of proof that the child is sufficiently mature? The GCFJ does not provide an answer to this. The Explanatory Memorandum

556 GCFJ, IV(B) 25.
557 GCFJ, IV(D) 48–49.
558 GCFJ, IV(E) 75.
559 See Explanatory Memorandum 2011, paras. 50 and 53.
560 GCFJ, IV(A) 3. See also Explanatory Memorandum 2011, para. 52.
561 Explanatory Memorandum 2011, para. 52.
562 GCFJ, IV(D) 48.
563 GCFJ, IV(D) 49 and IV(E) 75.
564 GCFJ, IV(E) 75 and 77.
565 GCFJ, IV(D) 34.
566 Explanatory Memorandum 2011, para. 95.

does appear to lean towards open notions instead of age limits, as these are said to tend 'to be too rigid and arbitrary'.[567]

While the Explanatory Memorandum notes that the access to court should also be applied in civil proceedings, it is questionable whether the GCFJ aims to suggest that children should be granted access to court in family law proceedings. According to the Explanatory Memorandum, 'it goes without saying that children, like adults, should have a solid legal basis to bring a case to court'.[568] This can be understood as granting children a right to access to court only insofar as domestic laws provide for a legal basis to do so. The Explanatory Memorandum generally notes two situations in which access to court may be necessary. First, children 'should' have the possibility to have a case reviewed when the 'child's rights have been violated or need defending' and their legal representative 'does not do so on behalf of the child'.[569] With regard to family law proceedings, one could interpret this to mean that the child should have the possibility to bring a case where his or her rights are violated – for example, if the child has not been granted the right to participate, and may not have a general right to apply to court for family law proceedings. Second, the Explanatory Memorandum states that 'access to court for children may also be necessary in cases where there can be a conflict of interests between the child and the legal representatives'.[570] With regard to family law proceedings, especially those concerning a conflict between parents, this potentially calls for a broader access to court for children. However, the Explanatory Memorandum uses the term 'may' and does not strongly or explicitly call for a general possibility of access to court for children in family law proceedings.

When providing access to court to children, the guidelines note that any obstacles should be removed.[571] Obstacles may include costs for proceedings, lack of legal counsel and, in family law proceedings, where there may be a conflict of interests, the requirement of parental consent.[572] The GCFJ does not specify how these obstacles should be removed – for example, whether children ought to have the right to free legal aid.

3.2.4. *The Right to be Heard*

With regard to the right to participation, the GCFJ stresses the child's right to be heard. This right is set out in six guidelines. The child is provided with the right to be heard in all matters affecting him or her.[573] As is emphasized in the GCFJ, this

567 Explanatory Memorandum 2011, para. 96.
568 Explanatory Memorandum 2011, para. 94.
569 Explanatory Memorandum 2011, para. 94.
570 Explanatory Memorandum 2011, para. 94.
571 GCFJ, IV(D) 35.
572 Explanatory Memorandum 2011, para. 98.
573 GCFJ, IV(D) 44.

is a right and not a duty of the child.[574] This right to be heard should 'at least' be granted to children 'when they are deemed to have a sufficient understanding of the matter in question'.[575] The GCFJ also explicitly states that the right to be heard should not be denied to children solely on the basis of their age.[576] Although it is not age but 'sufficient understanding' that is relevant in granting the right to be heard, it is not clear what the GCFJ means by the latter. The Explanatory Memorandum only emphasizes that 'irrespective of age, in particular when a child takes the initiative to be heard, a sufficient level of understanding should be presumed'.[577] The 'initiative' of the child is seemingly relevant in the GCFJ, as it is also noted that 'whenever the child takes the initiative to be heard in a case that affect him or her, the judge should not, unless it is in the child's best interests, refuse to hear the child'.[578] This does raise the question of whether it would not be in the child's best interests to be heard, even though they have personally taken the initiative to be heard.

With regard to the manner in which the hearing of the child is to occur, the GCFJ notes that the 'means used' ought to be adapted to the child's individual situation and be determined in consultation with the child.[579] The Explanatory Memorandum states that it will presumably be either by the judge or an appointed expert, noting that although the UNCRC recommends directly hearing the child, children may prefer either of these options.[580]

The right to be heard not only consists of the expression of views, but also includes due weight given to these views.[581] Due weight should be given in accordance with the child's 'age and maturity'.[582] The Explanatory Memorandum provides no further description regarding due weight. Instead, the remark is made that while age should not be determinative for the right to express views, it does 'play a major role in "granting" children their basic right to be heard'.[583] Although the meaning of 'granting' is not directly clear, this appears to refer to the fact that age is a relevant factor in the determination of how much weight will be granted to the child's views. In order to ensure that due weight is given to the child's views, the guidelines require reasoned judgments through which children can understand how their views were taken into account, especially when their views 'have not been followed'.[584]

---

574 GCFJ, IV(D) 46.
575 GCFJ, IV(D) 44.
576 GCFJ, IV(D) 47.
577 Explanatory Memorandum 2011, para. 110.
578 GCFJ, IV(D) 47.
579 GCFJ, IV(D) 44.
580 Explanatory Memorandum 2011, para. 115.
581 GCFJ, IV(D) 45.
582 GCFJ, IV(D) 45.
583 Explanatory Memorandum 2011, para. 110.
584 GCFJ, IV(D) 49.

Finally, with regard to the right to be heard, the Explanatory Memorandum briefly comments on the risk of manipulation. This risk is recognized, but 'all efforts should be made not to let this risk undermine this fundamental right', i.e. the right to be heard.[585] No further guidance is provided.

3.2.5. Representation

Aside from the direct right to be heard, the GCFJ provides for two types of representation. The first type of representation is legal counsel or representation in the child's own name. The right to this type of representation is provided by the GCFJ for proceedings in which there is, or could be, a conflict of interests between the child and his or her parent(s).[586] This representative ought to represent the views of the child, not what he or she considers to be in the best interests of the child.[587] The representative acts as legal counsel and the child should be considered to be a fully-fledged client.[588] In this regard, the guidelines also provide that the lawyer should inform and advise the child and should communicate with the child in an age-appropriate manner, and that the child should have access to free legal aid in the same way as adults.[589] The Explanatory Memorandum clarifies that the legal aid system ought to be effective and that the costs of the lawyer should not be charged to the parents,[590] the reason for this being that it may hinder the independent representation of the child.

The second type of representative afforded to children by the GCFJ is the guardian ad litem or independent representative. This type of representative should be appointed if there is a conflict of interests between the parents and the child.[591] The difference with representation in the child's own name is that the guardian ad litem or independent representative is appointed by and works for the court instead of being client-directed.[592] His or her task is also different. The guardian ad litem or independent representative should bring forward what is in the best interests of the child, while legal counsel should represent the wishes of the child.[593] Whether the guidelines therefore also find that the court should bear the costs of the guardian ad litem or that the cost should be borne by the child or his or her parents is unclear.

585 Explanatory Memorandum 2011, para. 116.
586 GCFJ, IV(D) 37.
587 GCFJ, IV(D) 40; Explanatory Memorandum 2011, para. 104.
588 GCFJ, IV(D) 40.
589 GCFJ, IV(D) 38, 39 and 41.
590 Explanatory Memorandum 2011, paras. 102 and 103.
591 GCFJ, IV(D) 42.
592 Explanatory Memorandum 2011, para. 105.
593 Explanatory Memorandum 2011, paras. 104 and 105.

What is very clear in the Explanatory Memorandum is that the function of representation in the child's own name and representation of the child's interests should not be combined in one person.[594] Both representatives do have the same task following the conclusion of proceedings. According to the GCFJ, they ought to inform and explain to the child the judgment and the available options for appeal or remedies to ensure enforcement.[595]

3.2.6. The Organization of Proceedings

Aside from the rights provided to and throughout the proceedings, child-friendly justice also concerns the organization of proceedings. This entails three features: child-sensitive settings, child-friendly communication and the accompaniment of a trusted adult. Child-sensitive settings concern the places in which children may find themselves (for example, a court). The GCFJ calls for the adaption of these settings if possible – for example, by having judges wear normal clothing instead of gowns. In any case, the child should be familiarized with the setting and those involved.[596] The second feature is communication. Officials involved in the proceedings should communicate to the child in language that is appropriate to their age and level of understanding.[597] In addition, the communication between the officials and the child should occur with respect and sensitivity.[598] This aligns with the fundamental principle of treating children with dignity. Finally, the GCFJ provides that children should be allowed to be accompanied by a trusted adult, unless there is a reasoned decision not to allow this.[599] The trusted adult may be their parent(s) or another adult of choice.

3.2.7. Alternative Dispute Resolution

In addition to the access to court, the right to be heard and representation, the GCFJ also provides for child-friendly justice in alternative dispute resolution (ADR). Specifically, it explains that the rights provided throughout should be guaranteed to the same extent in ADR.[600] This would include the rights of the child to participate. If the available forms of ADR 'may best serve the child's best interests', the GCFJ encourages the use thereof.[601] However, the GCFJ notes that ADR may not form an obstacle to a child's access to justice.

594 Explanatory Memorandum 2011, para. 105.
595 GCFJ, IV(D) 75 and 77.
596 GCFJ, IV(D) 54 and 55; Explanatory Memorandum 2011, paras. 122–123.
597 GCFJ, IV(D) 56.
598 GCFJ, IV(D) 57.
599 GCFJ, IV(D) 58; Explanatory Memorandum 2011, para. 121.
600 GCFJ, IV(B) 26.
601 GCFJ, IV(B) 24.

3.2.8. *Training Professionals*

To provide for smooth sailing through all of the above, the GCFJ emphasizes the importance of training professionals working with and for children. This 'interdisciplinary training' should be about the rights and needs of children, the proceedings available to them, and how to communicate with children of all ages.[602] The Explanatory Memorandum recommends that this training should start in schools and higher education institutes, amongst others in the fields of law, psychology and social work.[603] In addition, special training courses should be set up for those professionals working in the field.

3.3. CONCLUSION

As Liefaard eloquently states, the GCFJ is the 'first instrument to articulate the essential elements of justice systems from a children's right perspective in a comprehensive manner'.[604] In this section, it has become clear that although non-binding, the GCFJ provides extensive guidance with regard to the child's right to participation as a fundamental part of 'child-friendly justice'. It addresses the many elements necessary for participation, including information and feedback, the right to be heard, representation and the organization of proceedings. In that regard, the instrument is certainly comprehensive. However, the GCFJ is at times perhaps too comprehensive. As it addresses civil, criminal and administrative proceedings concerning children, the standards are rather broad and it is not always clear what they entail with regard to family law proceedings (for example, the right to access to court). Notwithstanding the latter, the GCFJ provides a comprehensive overview of elements necessary for child participation and provides inspiration for the practical implementation of standards set in binding instruments.

4. RECOMMENDATION ON THE PARTICIPATION OF CHILDREN

Following the introduction of the GCFJ, the CoE Monaco Strategy on the rights for the rights of the child of 2012–2015 had as one of its objectives, 'promoting child-friendly services and systems'.[605] In this regard, the programme aimed to, amongst other things, support Member States in reviewing and improving their

602 GCFJ, IV(A) 14 and 15.
603 Explanatory Memorandum 2011, para. 65.
604 Liefaard 2017, p. 63.
605 Council of Europe, *Strategy for the Rights of the Child (2012–2015)*, 15 February 2012, p. 9.

laws, policies and practices regarding child-friendly justice.[606] To this end,[607] the Committee of Ministers adopted the Recommendation on the participation of children and young people under the age of 18 in 2012.[608]

4.1. THE NATURE AND SCOPE OF THE RECOMMENDATION

Recommendations are an 'unusual' type of instrument produced by the CoE's Committee of Ministers.[609] They are not legally binding; they do not require signatures or ratifications by Member States. However, this does not mean they are not relevant. Recommendations, such as the one at hand, are directly addressed to the Member States. Member States are expected to, in due time, comply with the standards set out in recommendations.[610]

The standards in the Recommendation on the participation of children apply to a broad scope of subjects. It recommends that Member States ensure that children enjoy the right to be heard and to participate in decision-making in all matters affecting them.[611] The reference to 'all matters' is not taken lightly. From the appendix to the Recommendation, it can be deduced that it includes participation in (all types of) judicial and administrative procedures, healthcare, education, family life, community life and public life. This broad application may explain the general nature of the Recommendation.

4.2. THE CONTENT OF THE RECOMMENDATION

The content of the Recommendation is of a relatively general nature. It is recommended that Member States ensure child participation as is provided by Article 12 UNCRC. Subsequently, the appendix of the Recommendation sets out a definition of participation, principles on participation and measures to protect the right to participate, to promote and inform, and to create spaces for participation.

The Recommendation commences with the following definition of participation:

> 'Participation' is about individuals and groups of individuals having the right, the means, the space, the opportunity and, where necessary, the support to freely express

---

606 Council of Europe, *Strategy for the Rights of the Child (2012–2015)*, 15 February 2012, p. 9.

607 Council of Europe, *Strategy for the Rights of the Child (2012–2015): Implementation Report*, 2016, p. 6.

608 Recommendation CM/Rec(2012)2 of the Committee of Ministers to Member States on the participation of children and young people under the age of 18 (adopted by the Committee of Ministers on 28 March 2012 at the 1138th meeting of the Ministers' Deputies).

609 Lowe 2016, p. 98.

610 Lowe 2016, p. 98.

611 Recommendation CM/Rec(2012)2, no. 1.

> their views, to be heard and to contribute to decision making on matters affecting them, their views being given due weight in accordance with their age and maturity.[612]

This definition reflects the broad scope of the Recommendation. In part, it mirrors Article 12 UNCRC, specifically the second half. The first half is novel, emphasizing not only the right to express views, but also that children should have the space, the opportunity and the support to do so.

In the second section of the Recommendation, ten principles are listed (but not numbered). The first principle emphasizes that no age limit applies to the right to express views freely; all children have the right to be heard. Due weight should be given to the child's views in accordance with his or her age and maturity. Later on, the principles state that 'consideration needs to be given to the notion of evolving capacities'. This is specified as providing an increasing degree of influence to children as they 'acquire more capacities'. The principles also include two concerning non-discrimination; first, participation ought to apply without discrimination on any grounds; and second, particular efforts should be made to enable participation by vulnerable children and those affected by discrimination. Two principles also stress the importance of information. One provides that 'in order to be able to participate meaningfully and genuinely', children should be 'provided with all relevant information' and offered adequate support 'appropriate to their age and circumstances'. This speaks to the opportunity to participate. Subsequently, a second principle addresses the actual participation, as children 'should always be fully informed of the scope of their participation', including on the 'expected and actual outcomes' and limitations of their participation, and on how their views have been taken into consideration. Thus, children should be provided with feedback following their participation. The reference to information in the different phases of participation ties in with the principle that participation 'needs to be understood as a process and not a one-off event'. This principle notes that this is necessary in order for participation to be 'effective, meaningful and sustainable', and that it requires a commitment of time and resources. Also, one principle is dedicated to the protection of children from harm when participating. The final principle explicitly links to the CRC General Comment on Article 12 stating that 'all processes … should be transparent and informative, voluntary, respectful, relevant to children's lives, in child-friendly environments, inclusive (non-discriminatory), supported by training, safe and sensitive to risk, and accountable'. This pushes states to ensure this through legislative or other measures of implementation.

Following the definitions and principles, the third section of the Recommendation lists measures that Member States should carry out to protect the child's right to participate. These measures are listed under three

612 Appendix to Recommendation CM/Rec(2012)2.

headings: 'protecting the right to participate', 'promoting and informing about participation' and 'creating spaces for participation'. Under the first heading, measures such as the provision of 'legal protection' and 'effective redress and remedies' are mentioned, as well as the review and removal of 'restrictions in law and practice' and the allocation of financial resources. With regard to the second heading, public information programmes, professional capacity enhancement and other forms of spreading information are suggested. Finally, a variety of 'spaces for participation' are listed, including within the family, at schools, within the community, and at the public and political levels. Participation spaces within courts or legal proceedings are not specifically mentioned under this heading.

4.3. CONCLUSION

In summary, the Recommendation takes a broad stance on the participation of children. It is broad with regard to the matters which it addresses, the measures recommended and the types of recommendations. As it is non-binding and consists of general recommendations, many of which drawn from other instruments, including the UNCRC, the ECECR and the GCFJ, it does not provide any key additional standards regarding child participation in family law proceedings. However, it again strengthens the calls for CoE Member States to ensure the implementation of child participation.

5. THE CFREU

Alongside the well-known international conventions, including the UNCRC and the ECHR, the EU introduced its own Charter on Fundamental Rights (the CFREU) in 2000.[613] The CFREU explicitly includes children's rights in Article 24, 'The rights of the child'. In the following section, a brief historical introduction of the Charter will be provided, followed by a discussion of the scope and nature of the CFREU, the scope of the participation right included in Article 24, and, finally, the relevant case law from the Court of Justice of the European Union (CJEU).

The CFREU was drafted in 2000 and, by joint proclamation of the European Council, the European Parliament and the European Commission, was adopted in the same year. However, the question of the CFREU's force was left open to future consideration.[614] The CFREU was meant to form a part of the European Constitution of 2004; however, due to the rejection of the European Constitution

[613] Charter of Fundamental Rights of the European Union, 2000/C 364/01.

[614] European Council, *Conclusions of the Presidency*, 7–10 December 2000, Nice, para. 2.

and subsequent lack of ratification, the granting of legal force to the Charter was delayed.[615] It was in 2007 that the Lisbon Treaty granted full legal effect to the CFREU.[616]

5.1. THE NATURE AND SCOPE OF THE CFREU

Since the coming into force of the Lisbon Treaty in 2009, the CFREU has the same legal status as the Treaty on European Union (TEU) and the Treaty on the Functioning of the European Union (TFEU).[617] This means that EU Member States and EU institutions and bodies are directly bound to the CFREU.[618] However, the scope of the Charter is limited. As clarified by Article 51(1), the provisions are addressed 'to the Member States only when they are implementing Union law'.[619]

What does this mean in relation to the children's rights provided under Article 24 CFREU and, more specifically, the right to participate in family law proceedings? The EU has no general competence to promote children's rights as such, and it also lacks competence in domestic family law or child protection.[620] The competence of the EU with regard to topics that touch upon children directly is limited to asylum and migration, cross-border criminal law, and judicial cooperation in civil matters.[621] For the right to participate in family law proceedings, this means that the scope of Article 24 is, in fact, limited to the application and implementation of the Regulation on jurisdiction, the recognition and enforcement of decisions in matrimonial matters, and the matters of parental responsibility, and on international child abduction (Brussels II *bis* and the succeeding Recast)[622] and the Regulation on jurisdiction, applicable law,

---

615 T. Kerikmäe, 'EU Charter: Its Nature, Innovative Character, and Horizontal Effect', in: T. Kerikmäe (ed.), *Protecting Human Rights in the EU*, Berlin Heidelberg: Springer-Verlag 2014, pp. 5–19, p. 7.

616 Treaty of Lisbon amending the Treaty on European Union and the Treaty establishing the European Community (OJ C 306), 13 December 2007, Article 1(8).

617 Article 6(1) TEU.

618 See also H. Stalford & M. Schuurman, 'Are We There Yet?: the Impact of the Lisbon Treaty on the EU Children's Rights Agenda', *International Journal of Children's Rights*, Vol. 19, No. 3, 2011, pp. 381–403, p. 397.

619 See also Explanations relating to the Charter of Fundamental Rights, 2007/C 303/02, p. 32.

620 See R. Lamont, 'Article 24', in: S. Peers et al. (eds.), *The EU Charter of Fundamental Rights: A Commentary*, Oxford: Hart Publishing 2014, pp. 661–691, p. 662.

621 See R. Forastiero, 'The Charter of Fundamental Rights and the Protection of Vulnerable Groups: Children, Elderly People and Persons with Disabilities', in: G. Palmisano (ed.), *Making the Charter of Fundamental Rights a Living Instrument*, Leiden: Brill Nijhoff 2015, pp. 165–198, p. 176; Lamont 2014, p. 663 and Stalford & Schuurman 2011, p. 402.

622 Council Regulation (EC) No 2201/2003 of 27 November 2003 concerning jurisdiction and the recognition and enforcement of judgments in matrimonial matters and the matters of parental responsibility, repealing Regulation (EC) No 1347/2000; and Council Regulation

recognition and enforcement of decisions and cooperation in matters relating to maintenance obligations.[623] According to Article 51(2) CFREU, the CFREU does not extend the competences of the EU, meaning that it does not create new powers for the EU, for example, to legislate or adopt binding legal acts. It should not be used as a 'source of or basis for positive action'.[624] Therefore, Article 24(1) cannot lead the EU to enact legislation on child participation in family law proceedings beyond the cross-border cases.[625]

Aside from the EU's competences to legislate, the rights contained in the Charter are of relevance for the functioning of the EU as such. The provisions of the CFREU are binding on the EU and its institutions and bodies in all of their activities.[626] In that regard, the right to participation in Article 24 provides potential for children's participation within the EU legislative process. For example, Stalford and Schuurman discuss that there may be potential for youth to make use of the Citizen's Initiative introduced by the Treaty of Lisbon, an instrument of direct democracy by which one million citizens residing in at least seven EU Member States can invite the European Commission to submit a legislative proposal within its competence.[627]

5.2. THE CONTENT OF THE CFREU

The CFREU provides a whole range of rights, freedoms and principles, two of which must be considered for the child's right to participate in family law proceedings. The first is Article 24 CFREU, the children's rights article, and the second is Article 7 CFREU, which provides the general right to respect for private and family life.

5.2.1. Article 24 CFREU

There are four rights of the child contained in Article 24 CFREU: the right to protection and care, the right to participate, the child's best interests as a primary

(EU) 2019/1111 of 25 June 2019 on jurisdiction, the recognition and enforcement of decisions in matrimonial matters and the matters of parental responsibility, and on international child abduction (recast).

623 Council Regulation (EC) No 4/2009 of 18 18 December 2008 on jurisdiction, applicable law, recognition and enforcement of decisions and cooperation in matters relating to maintenance obligations.

624 P. Craig & G. de Búrca, *EU Law: Text, Cases, and Materials*, Oxford: Oxford University Press 2020, p. 431.

625 Explanations relating to the Charter of Fundamental Rights, 2007/C 303/02, p. 32. See also Stalford & Schuurman 2011, p. 398.

626 Article 51(1) of the Charter of Fundamental Rights. See also Craig & de Búrca 2020, p. 415.

627 Stalford & Schuurman 2011, p. 389–393; and European Parliament Factsheet on the European Citizens' Initiative, available at: www.europarl.europa.eu/factsheets/en/sheet/149/european-citizens-initiative.

consideration, and the right to maintain contact with parents. The rights provided are familiar as the article was based on four articles of the UNCRC (Articles 3, 9, 12 and 13, according to the explanatory text to the Charter).[628] It is important to note that this article concerns children's rights in all matters and areas, not only children's rights in family law proceedings. The text of Article 24 reads as follows:

1. Children shall have the right to such protection and care as is necessary for their well-being. They may express their views freely. Such views shall be taken into consideration on matters which concern them in accordance with their age and maturity.
2. In all actions relating to children, whether taken by public authorities or private institutions, the child's best interests must be a primary consideration.
3. Every child shall have the right to maintain on a regular basis a personal relationship and direct contact with both his or her parents, unless that is contrary to his or her interests.

It is paragraph 1 of Article 24 which provides for the right to participation. This paragraph starts with a right of children to 'such protection and care as is necessary for their well-being'. This sentence is taken from Article 3(2) UNCRC, although it is reinforced by naming it a 'right' instead of something that should be 'ensured', as it is described in the UNCRC.[629] In the UNCRC, this ensuring of protection and care follows the paragraph that the child's best interests must be a primary consideration, while in the CFREU, the order has been reversed, with the child's best interests as the second paragraph. In putting the right to protection and care in the first paragraph, combined with the right to participation, the article provides what McGlynn calls 'a curious mix' of 'protection rights' and 'autonomy' or 'empowerment' rights.[630] Lamont refers to it as embodying the 'conflict between child welfare and paternalism and child autonomy through participation'.[631] Forastiero argues that this combination has 'imposed' a balancing between the child's right to participation and the child's right to protection.[632] One can assume that the combination of protection and participation and the reversal in reformulating the UNCRC rights to the CFREU was purposeful; however, it is not clear why it was done or why it was considered necessary by the drafters.

---

628 Explanations relating to the Charter of Fundamental Rights, 2007/C 303/02, p. 25.
629 C. McGlynn, 'Rights for Children?: The Potential Impact of the European Union Charter of Fundamental Rights', *European Public Law*, Vol. 8, No. 3, 2002, pp. 387–400, p. 397.
630 McGlynn 2002, p. 398.
631 Lamont 2014, p. 662.
632 Forastiero 2015, p. 174.

Of core importance for the purposes of this discussion are the two sentences of Article 24(1) CFREU which concern participation. The first sentence is short but of great relevance: children 'may express their views freely'. The drafting of the sentence resembles Article 12 UNCRC and the right to participate, albeit that it is drafted in 'less forceful terms', with 'may' being used instead of 'the right to'.[633] The drafting has also amended the condition for expressing views; while Article 12 UNCRC requires a child to be capable of expressing his or her own views, there is no condition included in Article 24 CFREU. The choice to draft it in such a way may be explained in two ways. As McGlynn argues, the absence of a condition in the Charter may be to grant 'greater recognition to the ability and right of children to express their views'.[634] In comparison to the UNCRC, there would be no need to determine whether a child is capable before allowing participation, so 'every' child can express views.[635] Another explanation for the abbreviated drafting may be that is likely that it is this sentence which is also based on Article 13 UNCRC, the right to freedom of expression.[636] It is possible that this sentence is a combination of Articles 12 and 13 UNCRC, as both provide for the expression of views, although their aim and scope is different.

The difference in scope is also reflected in the final sentence of Article 24(1) CFREU. As provided by Article 12 UNCRC, the right to participate includes not only the right to express views, but also for these views to be given due weight. The right to expression of Article 13 UNCRC, on the other hand, provides the right to share any views and ideas in any form, but no consequent right for these views or ideas to be taken into consideration. In Article 24(1) CFREU, children are granted the right for their views 'to be taken into consideration on matters which concern them'. Once again, the drafting differs from that of the UNCRC. The CFREU does not refer to 'due weight', instead requiring that the views be 'taken into consideration'. Whether this change in language is meant to circumvent the discussions on 'due weight' or perhaps to minimize the influence of children's views in decision-making is not clear. Without evidence of the latter, one can expect 'taken into consideration' to, in essence, be very similar in meaning to 'due weight'. In any case, the views should be taken into consideration 'in accordance with their age and maturity'.

To conclude, Article 24(1) CFREU provides children with a right to protection, a right to express views and a right to have their expressed views taken into account. Article 24(1) has brought together a number of children's

---

633 Stalford & Schuurman 2011, p. 396.
634 McGlynn 2002, p. 398.
635 McGlynn 2002, p. 398.
636 See Explanations relating to the Charter of Fundamental Rights, 2007/C 303/02, p. 25.

rights and includes the right to participation in the mix as one of the first to be mentioned in the article. However, the scope and content of Article 24(1) is not yet entirely clear and will require further elaboration in the future – for example, in the case law of the CJEU, as will be discussed in section 5.3 below.

5.2.2. *Article 7 CFREU*

While Article 24 CFREU sets out specific rights of the child, the CFREU also includes a right to respect for private and family life provided in Article 7 CFREU. This article may be of importance for child participation in family law proceedings. Article 7 CFREU corresponds with the rights guaranteed by Article 8 ECHR and must, in accordance with Article 52(3) CFREU, be interpreted as having the same meaning and scope as the right under the ECHR (including the case law of the ECtHR).[637] Does that mean that children's rights to participation which the ECtHR has derived in applying Article 8 ECHR also become binding through the CFREU by virtue of this article? In theory, they should; however, one could argue that it is less relevant as the CFREU provides a *lex specialis* on children's rights with Article 24 CFREU, a *lex specialis* which is not present in the ECHR. In any event, the rights provided by the ECHR and the case law of the ECtHR already apply to the EU Member States directly when they are applying EU law. This means that Article 7 CFREU can be considered of less relevance with regard to the child's right to participation in family law proceedings.

5.3. THE CASE LAW OF THE CJEU

The interpretation of Article 24 CFREU in the case law of the CJEU has been limited. In Curia, the online database of CJEU case law, a search for cases on Article 24 provides a total of 36 results.[638] Using more specific search criteria to split the results per paragraph of Article 24 led to a total of 3 results for Article 24(1), 17 results for Article 24(2) and 6 results for Article 24(3). Some of these results also overlap. In total, 16 cases remained which did not fall under a specific paragraph (see Table 3.2 below for the specific configuration of the search results).

---

637 Explanations relating to the Charter of Fundamental Rights, 2007/C 303/02, pp. 20 and 33.

638 Search conducted on http://curia.europa.eu/juris/ (last search on 18 February 2021). The search form was left blank, except for the option to search 'References to case-law or legislation' with the selection: 'Grounds of judgment' and filling in 'Treaty' > 'Charter of Fundamental Rights of the EU (2007)' > 'Article 24'.

Table 3.2. CJEU case law search results specified

	Searches	Results
Article 24 CFREU	+ Article 24(1) only	1
	+ Article 24(1) + Article 24(2)	2
	+ Article 24(2) only	11
	+ Article 24(2) + Article 24(3)	4
	+ Article 24(3) only	2
	Only	16
	Total	*36*

Source: Compiled by the author.

In order to determine whether any of the case law concerned the right to participation of Article 24(1) CFREU, a quick scan was conducted of the potentially relevant cases: the results under Article 24(1) and those under Article 24 only. Most were not relevant as they only concerned the issue of the child's best interests in various contexts. Only the case of *Aguirre Zarraga* discusses child participation and will therefore be addressed in this section.[639]

Before turning to the judgment, it is necessary to introduce the Brussels II *bis* Regulation. The Brussels II *bis* Regulation is a private international law instrument concerning the jurisdiction, recognition and enforcement of judgments in matrimonial matters and parental responsibility. It provides the rules used to determine in which country cross-border divorce, custody, access and international child abduction proceedings should be dealt with and how decisions made in that regard can be enforced in other EU countries. As an instrument of private international law, Brussels II *bis* does not provide substantive law; however, it does include some procedural rules. In that regard, it includes provisions on the child's right to be heard in these cross-border cases. Through Article 11(2), courts are obliged to hear the child 'unless this appears inappropriate having regard to his or her age or degree of maturity' in international child abduction return proceedings.[640] More broadly, Article 23 allows for the non-recognition of judgments relating to parental responsibilities if a child has not been given the opportunity to be heard. These provisions in Brussels II *bis* further strengthen the right of the child to be heard, without harmonizing domestic laws on child participation.[641]

639 CJEU Judgment of 22 December 2010, *Aguirre Zarraga*, C-491/10 PPU, EU:C:2010:828.

640 See also T. Kruger & L. Samyn, 'Brussels II *bis*: Successes and Suggested Improvements', *Journal of Private International Law*, Vol. 12, No. 1, 2016, pp. 132–168, pp. 156–157. Kruger and Samyn note that this phrasing is stronger than that of Article 12 of the Hague Child Abduction Convention 1980.

641 See T. Kruger & F. Maoli, 'Child Participation in Private International Law: The Hague Conventions and EU Instruments', in: W. Schrama et al. (eds.), *International Handbook on Child Participation in Family Law*, Cambridge: Intersentia 2021, pp. 69–86.

In the *Aguirre Zarraga* judgment, the German Oberlandesgericht Celle requested a preliminary ruling on the interpretation of Brussels II *bis* and the enforcement of return orders in an international child abduction case following an infringement of fundamental rights, specifically Article 24(1) CFREU.[642] The judgment concerns two questions:[643] first, whether courts of the enforcing Member State may exceptionally review the judgment that is to be enforced if there is an infringement of fundamental rights; and, second, whether the court of the enforcing state must enforce a judgment even if the certificate issued by the state of origin contains manifestly inaccurate information. The CJEU's examination of these topics will not be dealt with here, as it concerns the application of Brussels II *bis* and not the scope of the rights provided by the CFREU. Instead, it is relevant to consider the remarks made by the CJEU as to the interpretation of Article 24 CFREU.

The CJEU made various remarks. It started by observing that Article 24 refers to 'having the opportunity to be heard' and not the hearing 'per se', by which the CJEU emphasizes that while a child should have the opportunity to be heard, there may be reasons for the contrary.[644] As is later stated, 'hearing the child cannot constitute an absolute obligation'.[645] The CJEU subsequently focuses on the relation between the right to express views of Article 24(1) and the best interests of the child of Article 24(2). According to the CJEU, the best interests of the child may 'justify a decision not to hear the child'.[646] The opportunity to be heard may not be provided due to the age or maturity of the child, but the CJEU also went further to state that it is for the domestic court 'to assess whether such a hearing is appropriate'. More specifically, a hearing may be 'inappropriate, and even harmful to the psychological health of the child, who is often exposed to such tensions and adversely affected by them'.[647] Again, the CJEU emphasizes the role of the best interests of the child, stating that whether the child should be heard 'must be assessed having regard to what is required in the best interests of the child in each individual case'.[648] Subsequently, the CJEU discusses the discretion that domestic courts have in terms of the manner in which children may express their views to the court. It is said that a 'hearing before the court' is not necessary as long as there are 'legal procedures and conditions' made available to allow the court to obtain the child's views.[649] However, the

[642] CJEU Judgment of 22 December 2010, *Aguirre Zarraga*, C-491/10 PPU, EU:C:2010:828, para. 37.
[643] CJEU Judgment of 22 December 2010, *Aguirre Zarraga*, C-491/10 PPU, EU:C:2010:828, para. 37.
[644] CJEU Judgment of 22 December 2010, *Aguirre Zarraga*, C-491/10 PPU, EU:C:2010:828, para. 62.
[645] CJEU Judgment of 22 December 2010, *Aguirre Zarraga*, C-491/10 PPU, EU:C:2010:828, para. 64.
[646] CJEU Judgment of 22 December 2010, *Aguirre Zarraga*, C-491/10 PPU, EU:C:2010:828, para. 63.
[647] CJEU Judgment of 22 December 2010, *Aguirre Zarraga*, C-491/10 PPU, EU:C:2010:828, para. 64.
[648] CJEU Judgment of 22 December 2010, *Aguirre Zarraga*, C-491/10 PPU, EU:C:2010:828, para. 64.
[649] CJEU Judgment of 22 December 2010, *Aguirre Zarraga*, C-491/10 PPU, EU:C:2010:828, para. 65.

CJEU concluded that although the domestic courts have discretion in terms of whether it is appropriate that the child is heard and how it will occur, Article 24 CFREU in light of Brussels II *bis* does require that when the domestic court decides to hear the child, it must 'take all measures which are appropriate to the arrangement of such a hearing … in order to ensure the effectiveness of those provisions, and to offer to the child a genuine and effective opportunity to express his or her views'.[650]

By balancing the child's right to be heard against his or her best interests, the CJEU seemingly does not depart from the understanding that in principle, it is in the child's best interests to be granted the opportunity to express views. Instead, the CJEU adds a – previously non-existent – ground to justify not giving the child an opportunity to be heard. Whether this is in line with Article 12 UNCRC and the other European standards on the child's right to be heard is a question which will be considered in Chapter 10.

5.4. CONCLUSION

Within the EU, the CFREU has reaffirmed a number of key children's rights in Article 24 and the right to respect for private and family law in Article 7. Neither of these two articles provides novel rights regarding child participation. However, the CFREU strengthen these rights in relation to the EU private international law instruments concerning family law proceedings – most notably Brussels II *bis* and, in the coming years, Brussels II *ter*.[651]

6. CONCLUSION

This chapter commenced with a quote from the Preamble to the ECECR which demonstrates the willingness of European states to further promote children's rights and specifically the child's right to express views in family law proceedings. We have seen that through a myriad of different instruments, the right to participation has been further reinforced within Europe. The diversity of instruments also leads to different (interpretations of) standards within the international and European framework of the child's right to participate in family law proceedings which require alignment to further strengthen the right. This chapter has assisted in determining the European standards.

[650] CJEU Judgment of 22 December 2010, *Aguirre Zarraga*, C-491/10 PPU, EU:C:2010:828, para. 66.

[651] See Kruger & Maoli 2021 with regard to the child's right to be heard in Brussels II *ter*.

Of the CoE instruments, the most explicit in the recognition of child participation in family law proceedings is the ECECR. As a binding regional convention, albeit with a limited ratification record, it sets out a number of procedural participation rights for children. In contrast, the GCFJ is not binding and has a broader scope regarding the types of proceedings addressed. It reaffirms the child's right to participate in family law proceedings and includes more general and practical guidance. Notably, it addresses the importance of providing children with information and feedback, the organization of proceedings, and the training of professionals. The last CoE instrument, the Recommendation on the participation of children, is less extensive and less concrete compared to the other instruments. The strength of the Recommendation is that it provides another call to Member States to effectively implement child participation in all fields, including family law proceedings.

Finally, in the CFREU, the right to participation has been included, and interwoven, with a number of other key children's rights in Article 24. As the scope of application of the CFREU is limited to EU Member States when implementing EU law and the EU institutions themselves, in domestic family law cases, Article 24 will not be of relevance. Yet it does strengthen the participation of children in cross-border family law cases through Brussels II *bis* and, in the future, Brussels II *ter*. This raises the question whether children in domestic cases are provided with less protection for their right to participation than children in cross-border cases. Such an outcome would not be just.

In conclusion, while the impact of the UNCRC on the development of European human rights instruments concerning child participation is already clear from this chapter, the full comparison between the UNCRC, the instruments discussed in this chapter, and the ECHR and ECtHR case law of the following chapters, is explored in Chapter 10.

PART II

THE CHILD'S RIGHT TO PARTICIPATE IN THE CASE LAW OF THE ECtHR

CHAPTER 4

INTRODUCTION TO THE ECHR, THE ECtHR AND THE CASE LAW ANALYSIS

'... the Court finds it important to reiterate that while its case-law requires children's views to be taken into account, those views are not necessarily immutable and their objections, which must be given due weight, are not necessarily sufficient to override the parents' interests ...'

– ECtHR, *K.B. v. Croatia* (2017)[652]

1. INTRODUCTION

At the epicentre of human rights in Europe is the European Convention on Human Rights (ECHR). The Convention is unique, in part due to its binding and expansive nature, but even more so because of the existence of the European Court of Human Rights (ECtHR). The Court provides an international forum where individuals may demand the protection of their rights. The judgments resulting from these applications subsequently set out the status quo of the rights relied upon. The unique nature of the Convention, the Court and its judgments requires further examination. This is even more the case as the ECtHR has introduced standards on child participation in family law proceedings. The quote above is just one example, taken from the comprehensive and innovative case law analysis which will be presented in the following chapters.

The existing literature on child participation in the case law of the ECtHR has left many questions unanswered, prompting the in-depth research in this volume.[653] The aim of this case law analysis is to further clarify whether and

652 ECtHR, *K.B. and others v. Croatia* (Appl. No. 36216/13), 14 March 2017, para. 143. See also ECtHR, *Raw and others v. France* (Appl. No. 10131/11), 7 March 2013, para. 94; ECtHR, *A.V. v. Slovenia* (Appl. No. 878/13), 9 April 2019, para. 72; ECtHR, *Zelikha Magomadova v. Russia* (Appl. No. 58724/14), 8 October 2019, para. 115 and ECtHR, *Pisică v. Republic of Moldova* (Appl. No. 23641/17), 29 October 2019.

653 See Chapter 1, section 1.

how the ECtHR has interpreted the child's right to participate in family law disputes in light of Articles 8 and 6 ECHR. In doing so, the standards imposed by the ECtHR regarding child participation are sought. These standards add to the European human rights framework and prescribe the manner in which European states should provide for child participation in their domestic family law proceedings. In order to evaluate how the international and European human rights framework of the child's right to participate in family law proceedings can be aligned and strengthened, the ECtHR's standards must be considered in addition to those set by the international and European instruments that were studied in Part I. This is even more the case as the case law of the ECtHR provides a unique perspective on the child's right to participate compared to the other instruments: the ECtHR responds to applications concerning specific factual circumstances leading to more applied standards in comparison to those set in instruments such as the UNCRC.

As was briefly discussed in Chapter 1, although the ECHR does not provide any explicit right for children to participate in proceedings, within the scope of Articles 8 and 6 ECHR, the Court has found room to address participation rights. The previous literature has focused on a number of landmark judgments regarding child participation. Thus far, the full scope of case law in which child participation has been raised has not been researched. This gap in the research is something this volume aims to address.

The more innovative feature that distinguishes this case law analysis not only from prior research on child participation, but also from case law analyses in legal scholarship in general is the method used. In this research, the case law of the ECtHR has been subjected to a rigorous qualitative content analysis in order to determine how the child's right to participation in family law disputes has been considered in the case law. The qualitative content analysis method is not frequently employed by legal scholars. The method provides the researcher with the possibility to pick apart the case law into smaller, detailed pieces. Viewing these pieces divided up by topic, reassembling their connections and reconsidering them within the bigger picture of the case provides for new insights. The choice for this specific method as well as the manner in which it has been used will be introduced below.

This chapter will begin with a brief discussion on the nature and scope of the ECHR and the ECtHR (see section 2) before Articles 6 and 8 ECHR are introduced (see section 3). The method used for this case law analysis (see section 4) will then be explained, as well as the structure of the following chapters in which the results of the analysis will be presented (see section 5). Subsequently, two aspects presumed to be relevant throughout the analysis – the applicants (see section 6) and the type of proceedings (see section 7) – will be discussed. Finally, brief remarks on the modes of participation at play in the case law will be given (see section 8).

2. THE NATURE AND SCOPE OF THE ECHR AND THE ECtHR

Before we delve into the case law, it is important to understand the nature and scope of the ECHR and the ECtHR. At its conception in 1950,[654] the ECHR was written with the aim of enforcing the rights provided for by the Universal Declaration of Human Rights (UDHR) at a European level.[655] In following the universal nature of the UDHR, the ECHR consists of civil and political rights for 'everyone' within the jurisdiction of the contracting states (Article 1). In theory, 'everyone' includes children,[656] although in practice, the application to children and their access to the rights can be problematic.[657] These problems arise because the ECHR was not drafted with children in mind. There is no specific mention of children in it (except regarding the detention of a minor)[658] and there is also no explicit restriction regarding the application of the rights to children, except with regard to the right to marry.[659] This raises the question whether children are protected to the same extent as adults by the rights provided in the ECHR. That the drafters did not consider children or children's rights is understandable when considering that international children's rights did not gain traction until the 1970s and 1980s.[660] The ECHR and other human rights documents at that

---

654 Convention for the Protection of Human Rights and Fundamental Freedoms, Rome, 4 November 1950, ETS No. 005.

655 See Preamble to the ECHR.

656 See U. Kilkelly, *The Child and the European Convention on Human Rights*, Aldershot: Ashgate 1999, p. 3; and C. Grabenwarter, *European Convention on Human Rights: Commentary*, Munich: C.H. Beck 2014, p. 3. Some authors take it as a given that children's rights are human rights; see e.g. I. Berro-Lefèvre, 'Improving Children's Access to the European Court of Human Rights', in: Council of Europe, *International Justice for Children*, Strasbourg: Council of Europe Publishing 2008, pp. 69–78, p. 69; and F. Tulkens, 'The European Convention on Human Rights and Children's Rights', in: Council of Europe, *International Justice for Children*, Strasbourg: Council of Europe Publishing 2008, pp. 17–33, p. 18. See also A. Quennerstedt, 'Children, But Not Really Humans? Critical Reflections on the Hampering Effect of the "3 P's"', *International Journal of Children's Rights*, Vol. 18, No. 4, 2010, pp. 619–635, who argues that the conceptualization of children's rights through the language of the 3 p's and thereby as different from human rights is generally problematic, as children are entitled to the same human rights.

657 U. Kilkelly, 'The Best of Both Worlds for Children's Rights? Interpreting the European Convention on Human Rights in the Light of the UN Convention on the Rights of the Child', *Human Rights Quarterly*, Vol. 23, No. 2, 2001, pp. 308–326, p. 314.

658 Article 5(1)(d) ECHR provides when a minor can be deprived of his or her liberty: for the purpose of educational supervision or his or her lawful detention for the purpose of bringing him or her before the competent legal authority.

659 Article 12 limits the right to marry to men and women of 'marriageable age'.

660 The League of Nations Declaration of the Rights of the Child in 1924 only contained five basic principles and the UN General Assembly Declaration on the Rights of the Child of 1959 also consisted solely of ten principles. The drafting of the UNCRC only started in 1979.

time were drafted with the vision of (male) adults as rights-holders.[661] Does this adult-gaze preclude or restrict the application of the ECHR to children? There is no explicit right of the child to participate included in the text of the ECHR, but whether and how it has been read into the Convention is the subject of this analysis.

In order to be able to answer whether and how the ECtHR has introduced a right of the child to participate in family law proceedings under the ECHR, it is appropriate to consider the interpretative leeway available under the Convention. In general, human rights have seen the trends of universalization and proliferation, as a result of which there is a gradual increase of the subjects of rights and the rights themselves.[662] This stretches the scope of treaties such as the ECHR. More specifically, the drafting of the Convention and the existence of the ECtHR provide room for the expansion of rights, including the (potential) recognition of rights for children. With regard to the drafting, the open wording of the articles has led to the understanding that they contain autonomous concepts that are open to interpretation.[663] The existence of the ECtHR provides for an authority to interpret these concepts.

In general, how does the ECtHR interpret the Convention? In the first place, the general interpretation methods as provided for by the Vienna Convention on the Law of Treaties 1969 are used by the Court.[664] Article 31 of the Vienna Convention provides for teleological interpretation in 'good faith in accordance with the ordinary meaning to be given to the terms of the treaty in their context and in the light of its object and purpose'. This is the more classical interpretative method. The ECtHR has also adopted its own interpretative methods. Notably, it has adopted the 'golden rule' of evolutive interpretation,[665] by which it refers to the ECHR as a 'living instrument'.[666] Evolutive interpretation requires interpretation in light of present-day conditions and commonly accepted European (or international) standards.[667] At times, these accepted standards are determined

---

661 See J. Tobin, 'Justifying Children's Rights', *International Journal of Children's Rights*, Vol. 21, No. 3, 2013, pp. 395–441, p. 413, who calls it the 'adult construction dilemma', which led to an understanding of the entitlement to human rights being linked to capacity to reason and autonomy, rather than on the interest theory of rights which he advocates.

662 See Quennerstedt 2010, pp. 625–628.

663 See e.g. Kilkelly 2001, p. 313; and M. Burbergs, 'How the Right to Respect for Private and Family Life, Home and Correspondence Became the Nursery in Which New Rights are Born', in: E. Brems & J. Gerards (eds.), *Shaping Rights in the ECHR: The Role of the European Court of Human Rights in Determining the Scope of Human Rights*, Cambridge: Cambridge University Press 2014, pp. 315–329, p. 322.

664 See e.g. A. Mowbray, 'The Creativity of the European Court of Human Rights', *Human Rights Law Review*, Vol. 5, No. 1, 2005, pp. 57–79, p. 58; and Kilkelly 1999, p. 16.

665 See e.g. Mowbray 2005, p. 64; Burbergs 2014; and Kilkelly 1999.

666 See, ECtHR *Tyrer v. United Kingdom* (Appl. No. 5856/72), 25 April 1978, para. 31.

667 See e.g. Kilkelly 1999, p. 13; Burbergs 2014, pp. 319–320.

in reference to existing (other) European or international instruments, such as the United Nations Convention on the Rights of the Child (UNCRC).[668] Often the Court also considers whether there is a consensus or trend in the approach taken by states parties.[669] The second specific interpretative method used by the Court is the 'practical and effective' application of Convention rights.[670] This interpretative method, specifically the effective application of rights, formed the foundation for the principle of 'positive obligations'.[671] This principle has played a significant role in providing additional human rights protection.[672] Positive obligations require states to actively secure the rights guaranteed by the ECHR, instead of simply refraining from violating rights.

The discussed interpretative methods have played a role in the clarification and expansion of the rights contained in the ECHR. The analogical and case-based argumentation of the ECtHR has also driven the gradual expansion of rights. As one author describes it, the Court at times employs a 'tree-like mode' of reasoning, using previous case law as 'branches' upon which the interpretation in a new case is built.[673] The continual expansion of rights has been the subject of debate and criticism.[674] Gerards has characterized the expansion as a 'prism of fundamental rights'. Each core right in the spectrum is surrounded by a blur of interests which may or may not be considered rights themselves.[675] The clarification and expansion of rights contained in the ECHR is beneficial for the recognition of children's rights: while the ECHR does not speak of the right to participate, Articles 6 and 8 may be interpreted as providing children with the right to participate.

If the ECtHR does set standards as to the child's right to participate in family law proceedings, what legal value do these standards have? Although according to Article 46 ECHR the final judgments of the ECtHR are binding only to the states that were party to the proceedings (i.e. *res judicata*), it is commonly recognized that the case law of the ECtHR has *res interpretata* status. States are bound to ensure compliance with the rights and freedoms guaranteed in the ECHR (Article 1), this includes the interpretation of the ECHR by the ECtHR (Article 19)

668 See e.g. Kilkelly 1999, pp. 14–15; and Kilkelly 2001, p. 313; and M. Woolf, 'Coming of Age? The Principle of "the Best Interests of the Child"', *European Human Rights Law Review*, 2003, pp. 205–221, p. 206.

669 See e.g. Mowbray 2005, p. 69.

670 See e.g. Kilkelly 1999, p. 11; Mowbray 2005, p. 72 and Woolf 2003, p. 206

671 See e.g. Kilkelly 1999, p. 12; and Mowbray 2005, p. 72.

672 M. de Boer-Buquicchio, 'Preface', in: Council of Europe 2008, p. 9; Tulkens 2008, p. 20 and J. Fortin, *Children's Rights and the Developing Law*, Cambridge: Cambridge University Press 2009, pp. 62–63.

673 Burbergs 2014, pp. 325–327.

674 See e.g. the discussion of criticism in J. Gerards, 'The Prism of Fundamental Rights', *European Constitutional Law Review*, Vol. 8, No. 2, 2012, pp. 173–202, pp. 173–177.

675 Gerards 2012, pp. 178–183.

as the case law of the Court 'constitutes the system of the Convention'.[676] The ECtHR not only provides individual relief in the applications brought to it, but also has to 'elucidate, safeguard and develop the rules instituted by the Convention',[677] thereby 'rais[ing] the general standards of protection of human rights'.[678] Therefore, the standards established in the ECtHR's case law must be considered by domestic courts, legislatures and other authorities.[679]

3. INTRODUCING ARTICLES 6 AND 8 ECHR

As the child's right to participation concerns the position of the child within proceedings, the procedural right to a fair trial in Article 6 ECHR is a logical starting point. More specifically, the first paragraph of Article 6 ECHR reads as follows:

> 1. In the determination of his civil rights and obligations or of any criminal charge against him, everyone is entitled to a fair and public hearing within a reasonable time by an independent and impartial tribunal established by law. Judgment shall be pronounced publicly but the press and public may be excluded from all or part of the trial in the interests of morals, public order or national security in a democratic society, where the interests of juveniles or the protection of the private life of the parties so require, or to the extent strictly necessary in the opinion of the court in special circumstances where publicity would prejudice the interests of justice.

In order to determine the relevance of Article 6 ECHR for the child's right to participate in family law proceedings, the material and personal scope must be considered before discussing the substantive rights under which the right to participate may fall: the right to access to court, the right to a fair hearing or the right to effective participation as provided in criminal proceedings.

Although the material scope of Article 6 does include family law proceedings, as they concern disputes over 'civil rights and obligations',[680] it can be questioned whether children fall under the personal scope of Article 6 ECHR in relation to family law proceedings. The text of Article 6 states 'everyone is entitled', so it

---

676 See A. Bodnar, '*Res Interpretata:* Legal Effect of the European Court of Human Rights' Judgments for Other States Than Those Which were Party to the Proceedings', in: Y. Haeck & E. Brems (eds.), *Human Rights and Civil Liberties in the 21st Century*, Dordrecht: Springer 2014, pp. 223–262, p. 226.

677 ECtHR, *Ireland v. United Kingdom* (Appl. No. 5310/71), 18 January 1978, para. 154. See Bodnar 2014, p. 228.

678 ECtHR, *Karner v. Austria* (Appl. No. 40016/98), 24 July 2003, para. 26; and ECtHR, *Rantsev v. Cyprus and Russia* (Appl. No. 25965/04), 7 January 2010, para. 197. See Bodnar 2014, pp. 228–229.

679 See e.g. Bodnar 2014, p. 236.

680 See e.g. ECtHR, *B. v. United Kingdom* (Appl. No. 9840/82), 8 July 1987, para. 78. Regarding the conditions, see further O.J. Settem, *Applications of the 'Fair Hearing' Norm in ECHR Article 6(1)*

could be argued that the wording of the Article does not exclude application to children.[681] If the child is a party to the proceedings, this may be the case, but if the child is not a party – as is common in family law proceedings – Article 6 ECHR may not apply.

Notwithstanding the scope of Article 6 ECHR, there is the question of whether the right to participation would fall under the substance of the right to a fair trial. One aspect of the right to a fair trial is the right to access to court.[682] This right is not absolute; limitations are permitted if they pursue a legitimate aim and are proportionate to that aim.[683] In fact, it is sensible for states to limit the access to court to ensure the proper use of resources through placing conditions on accessibility.[684] One such limit may be the requirement of legal capacity, which will often limit children's access to court. Whether this limitation pursues a legitimate aim and is proportionate to that aim may be debated. However, access to court is a step further than participation.

Article 6 ECHR also provides specific procedural guarantees under the limb of the right to a fair hearing, one of which is the right to be heard.[685] Generally, this means that the person concerned must be given the opportunity to present his or her views on the factual or legal aspects of the case either in person or through legal counsel. However, in civil proceedings, personal participation is not a standard point of departure (although it may be necessary depending on the circumstances of the case).[686] Whether this right also applies to children within family law proceedings to which they are not a party and whether it is similar to the child's right to participate in other instruments is unknown. Nevertheless, Daly has argued that not hearing children in family law proceedings should be a breach of their right to a fair trial under the civil limb of Article 6 ECHR.[687]

Under the criminal limb of Article 6 ECHR, children have been accorded the right to 'effective participation' in their criminal trials.[688] This right to

to Civil Proceedings, Cham: Springer International 2016, p. 53–59; and M. Hazelhorst, *Free Movement of Civil Judgments in the European Union and the Right to a Fair Trial*, The Hague: TMC Asser Press 2017, p. 4.

681 See e.g. S. Choudhry & J. Herring, *European Human Rights and Family Law*, Oxford: Hart Publishing 2010, p. 239.

682 Introduced by the ECtHR in *Golder v. United Kingdom* (Appl. No. 4451/70), 21 February 1975. See also Settem 2016, p. 60; and Grabenwarter 2014, p. 127.

683 ECtHR, *Golder v. United Kingdom* (Appl. No. 4451/70), 21 February 1975, para. 38. See also Settem 2016, p. 63.

684 See Grabenwarter 2014, pp. 127–128.

685 See e.g. Hazelhorst 2017, pp. 138–139.

686 See Grabenwarter 2014, p. 137; Settem 2016, pp. 321 and 326; and Hazelhorst 2017, p. 138.

687 A. Daly, 'The Right of Children to Be Heard in Civil Proceedings and the Emerging Law of the European Court of Human Rights', *International Journal of Human Rights*, Vol. 15, No. 3, 2011, pp. 441–461, p. 445.

688 ECtHR, *T. v. United Kingdom* [GC] (Appl. No. 24724/94), 16 December 1999; ECtHR, *V. v. United Kingdom* [GC] (Appl. No. 24888/94), 16 December 1999 and ECtHR, *S.C. v. United Kingdom* (Appl. No. 60958/00), 15 June 2004. See Kilkelly 1999, p. 123; Kilkelly 2001,

'effective participation' is very different from the right to participation as discussed here. It concerns the participation in criminal proceedings whereby the child is the accused and therefore a party to the proceedings, whereas in family law proceedings, in contrast, the child is generally not a party to the proceedings. In family law proceedings, participation addresses the (voluntary) opportunity available to the child to communicate his or her views to the decision-maker, instead of the rights children have as defendants to effectively participate in their defence. Whether the child's right to participate in family law proceedings has been recognized under the civil limb by the ECtHR has not been further investigated in recent years and must be determined through an analysis of the case law.

In addition to Article 6, the interpretation of the right to respect for private and especially the right to respect for family life in Article 8 ECHR provides potential for the ECtHR to provide for the child's right to participation in family law disputes. The text of Article 8 ECHR reads as follows:

1. Everyone has the right to respect for his private and family life, his home and his correspondence.
2. There shall be no interference by a public authority with the exercise of this right except such as is in accordance with the law and is necessary in a democratic society in the interests of national security, public safety or the economic well-being of the country, for the prevention of disorder or crime, for the protection of health or morals, or for the protection of the rights and freedoms of others.

The potential value of Article 8 ECHR for the child's right to participate is increased by the fact that the ECtHR has read procedural rights into the scope of Article 8.[689] Through this procedural layer, procedural shortcomings at the

pp. 321–324; A. Parkes, *Children and International Human Rights Law: The Right of the Child to Be Heard*, Abingdon: Routledge 2013, pp. 167–171; S. Rap, 'The participation of juvenile defendants in the youth court: A comparative study of juvenile justice procedures in Europe', Ph.D. diss., Utrecht University, 2013, pp. 62–65; Grabenwarter 2014, pp. 155–156 and U. Kilkelly, 'The CRC in Litigation under the ECHR', in: T. Liefaard & J.E. Doek (eds.), *Litigating the Rights of the Child: The UN Convention on the Rights of the Child in Domestic and International Jurisprudence*, Dordrecht: Springer 2015, pp. 193–209, pp. 203–206.

689 See Kilkelly 1999, p. 10; Fortin 2009, p. 61; E. Brems, 'Procedural Protection: An Examination of Procedural Safeguards Read into Substantive Convention Rights', in: E. Brems & J. Gerards (eds.), *Shaping Rights in the ECHR: The Role of the European Court of Human Rights in Determining the Scope of Human Rights*, Cambridge: Cambridge University Press 2013, pp. 137–161, pp. 137–139; Grabenwater 2014, pp. 224–225; Kilkelly 2015, p. 195; T. de Jong, 'Procedurele waarborgen in materiële EVRM-rechten', Ph.D. diss., Leiden University, 2017, p. 150–158 and ECtHR, *Guide on Article 8 of the Convention – Right to Respect for Private and Family Life*, Council of Europe/ECtHR 2020 (available at: www.echr.coe.int/documents/guide_art_8_eng.pdf), para. 319.

national level can be addressed together with (potential) substantive violations, and it may be a way to circumvent the scope restrictions of Article 6.[690] This procedural layer is also relevant in determining the proportionality of the measures or decisions taken by national authorities. In that regard, the margin of appreciation granted to states is also relevant. The margin of appreciation varies depending on the subject matter and circumstances.[691] However, in Article 8 cases concerning the family life of children (and parents) where a best interests decision is made, national courts may be considered to be better placed to decide on the facts of the case.[692] Therefore, states are granted a broader margin of appreciation in both custody and residence proceedings and in care or child protection proceedings, while a more restricted margin of appreciation applies in access or contact proceedings.[693] Where there is a broader margin of appreciation regarding the domestic substantive decision, the procedural rights of all those involved are of extra importance.

With regard to the scope of Article 8 ECHR, it is known that the ECtHR has dealt with child participation in family law proceedings under Article 8 ECHR in its case law. On the basis of the existing literature, it is first and foremost emphasized that in *M. and M. v. Croatia* (2015), the Court recognized the child's right to be heard under the ambit of the child's right to private and family life under Article 8 ECHR.[694] Under prior case law, especially *Sahin v. Germany* (2003), Article 8 ECHR was understood as not 'always requiring the child to be heard in court'.[695] Instead, according to the existing literature, in cases concerning access of a parent without custody, it is for the national courts to

690 Brems 2013, p. 158.

691 See e.g. B. Rainey, E. Wicks & C. Ovey, *The European Convention on Human Rights*, Oxford: Oxford University Press 2014, p. 81.

692 See e.g. de Jong 2017, p. 152; G. Letsas, *A Theory of Interpretation of the European Convention on Human Rights*, Oxford: Oxford University Press 2007, pp. 91–92 and C. Fenton-Glynn, *Children and the European Court of Human Rights*, Oxford: Oxford University Press 2021, p. 8.

693 See e.g. Fenton-Glynn 2021, pp. 264, 272 and 324.

694 ECtHR, *M. and M. v. Croatia* (Appl. No. 10161/13), 3 September 2015, paras. 171 and 181. See E. Merckx, 'Het EHRM over ouderlijk gezag en verblijf in het belang van het kind na relatiebreuk', *Tijdschrift voor Familierecht*, 2017/9, pp. 241–264, p. 245; E. Vertommen, 'Balancing the Right of Parent and Child in Case of Non-compliance with Contact Arrangements: A Case Law Analysis', in: K. Boele-Woelki & D. Martiny (eds.), *Plurality and Diversity of Family Relations in Europe*, Cambridge: Intersentia 2019, pp. 175–201, p. 183; M.R. Bruning et al., *Kind in proces: van communicatie naar effectieve participatie*, Nijmegen: Wolf Legal Publishers 2020, pp. 102–104; ECtHR, *Guide on Article 8 of the Convention – Right to respect for private and family life*, Council of Europe/European Court of Human Rights 2020, para. 322 and E. Merckx, 'The ECtHR on Parental Authority and Contact after Separation: Towards a More Child-Centered Perspective', in: P. Czech et al. (eds.), *European Yearbook on Human Rights 2020*, Cambridge: Intersentia 2020, pp. 97–133, pp. 115–116.

695 ECtHR, *Sahin v. Germany* [GC] (Appl. No. 30943/96), 8 July 2003, para. 73; European Union Agency for Fundamental Rights and Council of Europe, *Handbook on European Law Relating to the Rights of the Child*, Luxembourg: Publications Office of the European Union 2017, p. 42.

determine, taking into account the circumstances of the case and the age and maturity of the child concerned.[696] In *Sahin* and similar cases, the hearing of the child was considered under the procedural rights of the parent in Article 8 – which was criticized by several authors.[697] In addition to the hearing of the child, the literature and the landmark cases referred to above also show that the ECtHR has, at times, recognized the importance of acting in accordance with the child's wishes. Take, for example, the case of *Hokkanen v. Finland* (1994), in which the refusal of the child to have contact with her father was accepted by the ECtHR as being determinative in the contact proceedings and not in violation with the father's rights under Article 8 ECHR.[698] In the later judgment of *C. v. Finland* (2006), the ECtHR has acknowledged that 'courts must take into account the wishes of children' in custody and access proceedings, but that the views could not be held to be determinative without considering other factors.[699] In more recent studies, authors have noted that the weight to be granted to the views of the child regarding contact with a parent will be dependent on the maturity of the child.[700] In light of the previous research, it is clear that within the scope of Article 8 ECHR, the ECtHR has introduced the child's right to participate in family law proceedings. In the case law analysis that follows, the full scope of child participation in the case law of the ECtHR is considered under both Article 8 and Article 6 ECHR.

Bearing the above in mind, it is time to turn to the innovative method used for this case law analysis.

4. METHODOLOGY OF THE CASE LAW ANALYSIS

Legal scholars research case law in many different ways. Cases can be read and considered independently, together as 'landmark' cases or on the basis of another selection. However, many researchers would not describe their approach as a real method. In fact, with regard to legal methodology in general, there is an ongoing debate as to whether legal research is science, what qualifies as doctrinal legal research, which accepted methods of legal research there

---

696 ECtHR, *Sahin v. Germany* [GC] (Appl. No. 30943/96), 8 July 2003, para. 73. See Woolf 2003, pp. 213–214; Choudry & Herring 2010, p. 239; Daly 2011, pp. 447–448; Parkes 2013, p. 112; Kilkelly 2015, p. 200; European Union Agency for Fundamental Rights and Council of Europe 2017, p. 43; Merckx 2017, p. 246 and Bruning et al. 2019, p. 108.

697 See Daly 2011, p. 455; Fenton-Glynn 2013, p. 610; Kilkelly 2015, p. 199 and Merckx 2020, p. 115.

698 ECtHR, *Hokkanen v. Finland* (Appl. No. 19823/92), 23 September 1994. See Kilkelly 1999, p. 117; Woolf 2003, p. 212; Daly 2011, pp. 446 and 450 and Fenton-Glynn 2013, p. 605.

699 ECtHR, *C. v. Finland* (Appl. No. 18249/02), 9 May 2006, para. 57. See Daly 2011, pp. 447 and 451 and Kilkelly 2015, p. 202.

700 See Merckx 2017, p. 246; Vertommen 2019, p. 184 and Merckx 2020, p. 115.

are and how to concretely apply these methods in practice.[701] As of yet in the legal discipline, there is no method of case law analysis laid down in codes or guidelines. It could be argued that there is a shared implicit understanding between legal academics as to how such an analysis should be conducted,[702] but it is unclear what the method is in that regard. Perhaps because it is difficult to pin down legal research and define it beyond 'reading, analyzing and linking' new information to the known body of law'[703] or, as Posner notes 'the messy work product of the judges and legislators requires a good deal of tidying up, of synthesis, analysis, restatement and critique'.[704] Within legal scholarship, there is a trend towards more specifically reasoning the search and selection of cases for an analysis,[705] but an explicit method of analysis is absent. In this research, the method of qualitative content analysis was therefore chosen to fill this gap. What is qualitative content analysis? It is a method originating from the social sciences for the analysis of text by using coding to reduce the data into smaller segments. The specifics of qualitative content analysis (QCA) and the manner in which the method has been employed in this research will be further specified in section 4.2 below. Before we turn to the QCA method, the search and selection of the case law will be described (see section 4.1). The QCA method does not concern itself with data collection, such as the search and selection of case law, as this is a step that precedes the analysis.

In order not to burden the reader with all the methodological technicalities, in the following two sections, the methodology used will be broadly described.

---

701 See e.g. C.J.J.M. Stolker, '"Ja, geléérd zijn jullie wel!" Over de status van de rechtswetenschap', *Nederlands Juristenblad*, No. 15, 2003; G. de Geest, 'Hoe maken we van de rechtswetenschap een volwaardige wetenschap?', *Nederlands Juristenblad*, No. 2, 2004; M. van Hoecke (ed.), *Methodologies of Legal Research: Which Kind of Method for What Kind of Discipline?*, Oxford: Hart Publishing 2011; T. Hutchinson, 'Doctrinal Research: Researching the Jury', in: D. Watkins & M. Burton (eds.), *Research Methods in Law*, Abingdon: Routledge 2013, pp. 7–33; J.M. Smits, *The Mind and Method of the Legal Academic*, Cheltenham: Edward Elgar 2012; M.V.R. Snel, 'Source-Usage within Doctrinal Legal Inquiry: Choices, Problems and Challenges', *Law and Method*, 2014, pp. 1-22; J.M. Smits, 'What is Legal Doctrine? On the Aims and Methods of Legal-Dogmatic Research', in: R. van Gestel, H-W. Micklitz & E.L. Rubin (eds.), *Rethinking Legal Scholarship*, Cambridge: Cambridge University Press 2017, pp. 207–228 and I. Dobinson & F. Johns, 'Legal Research as Qualitative Research', in: M. McConville & W.H. Chui (eds.), *Research Methods for Law*, Edinburgh: Edinburgh University Press 2017, pp. 18–47.

702 See J.B.M. Vranken, *Mr. C. Asser's Handleiding tot de beoefening van het Nederlands Burgerlijk Recht: Algemeen deel****. Een synthese*, Deventer: Kluwer 2014, no. 33 and 87.

703 Hutchinson 2013, p. 13.

704 R.A. Posner, 'In Memoriam: Bernard D. Meltzer (1914–2007)', *University of Chicago Law Review*, Vol. 72, No. 2, 2007, pp. 435–438, p. 437, also cited in Hutchinson 2013, p. 14.

705 Cf. Snel 2014, who writes that in doctrinal legal research, it is not always clear how cases have been selected, whether and why certain 'key' cases are 'key', and whether the cases are representative of a broader group of cases.

4.1. SEARCH AND SELECTION OF CASE LAW

This research aims to ascertain relevant standards and norms concerning child participation in the ECtHR case law on family law proceedings. The case law of the ECtHR is voluminous and although available in the online database HUDOC,[706] it can be difficult to unearth. HUDOC is not straightforward in its use for searching case law and the case law on child participation has not previously been compiled systematically.[707] Therefore, a transparent and reproducible search method was necessary.

There is no standard formulation or terminology used by the ECtHR to refer to child participation. This is due to the lack of a (universal) standard formulation for child participation. Child participation is a broad term and other common terms include, for example, the child's voice, the child's right to be heard and the child's right to express views. As is inherent to this topic, there are also many modes of participation, such as a judge hearing the child, a curator ad litem, a guardian ad litem, etc. With so many potential formulations for the same topic, the choice of search terms was not clear-cut. Therefore, search terms were determined by relying on known relevant case law and related child participation terms. Both English and French search terms were used. No search terms were used to limit the search to family law proceedings because such a limitation was not necessary at this stage.[708] At first, the search was conducted without applying any filters and including both judgments and decisions of the ECtHR.

The use of these search terms resulted in more than 1,000 results – too many for the scope of this research.[709] Therefore, two filter options available in HUDOC were used: a temporal filter[710] and a substantive filter.[711] These two filters sifted out a few hundred cases, but approximately 900 results still remained.

To select only the relevant cases from these results, a number of selection decisions were made. The choice was made to include all Grand Chamber

[706] The HUDOC database is available at: https://hudoc.echr.coe.int/.

[707] For example, there is no factsheet on child participation provided by the Press Office of the ECtHR, although some issues are included in the 'Children's Rights' factsheet of January 2018: www.echr.coe.int/Documents/FS_Childrens_ENG.pdf. While there is some literature in this field (Kilkelly 1999; Daly 2011 and Kilkelly 2015), there has been no systematic comprehensive analysis.

[708] Additionally, ensuring a complete set of search terms for family law proceedings would have brought its own challenges. See also section 6 below.

[709] On the final search on 30 November 2017, 1,355 results appeared.

[710] The temporal filter limited the results to those from 1 November 1998 onwards, the date from which the ECtHR sat as a full-time permanent court as determined by Protocol No. 11 to the ECHR.

[711] The substantive filter limited the results to those cases in which Article 6 and/or Article 8 ECHR were concerned, the two articles under which child participation in family law proceedings may be raised.

judgments because these judgments concern those in which 'a serious question affecting the interpretation of the Convention' is raised or in which 'the resolution of a question [...] might have a result inconsistent with a judgment previously delivered by the Court'.[712] All decisions were removed in which the applications were rendered fully admissible and where judgments and decisions were struck out of the list. Subsequently, in order to make further selection decisions, an approach was devised with search term 'hits' to group the cases in categories of supposed relevance. A random sample of one case per category was then read to determine which categories of judgments and decisions were relevant for the analysis. In doing so, all judgments and decisions in which Article 12 UNCRC was mentioned were included in the selection. Chamber decisions were also included in the selection. Even though decisions address the admissibility of applications and not the merits, the sample read showed that in finding cases inadmissible on grounds of being manifestly ill-founded, the ECtHR does in effect make a (preliminary) decision on the merits.[713]

Altogether, this search and selection method led to a total of 164 selected judgments and decisions in the primary selection at the end of 2017. As time progressed when conducting the analysis, an additional selection of judgments and decisions was included. This additional selection consisted of three sets of cases: (1) five cases which were (repeatedly) mentioned in the analysed case law with regard to child participation; (2) nine cases which were selected following an updated search conducted at the end of 2019[714] and (3) four cases which were added following specific recommendations by fellow researchers at conferences where preliminary results of this analysis were presented.[715] Combined, this led to a final selection of 182 judgments and decisions for the case law analysis.

4.2. QUALITATIVE CONTENT ANALYSIS

As noted above, the aim of this case law analysis is to clarify how the ECtHR has interpreted children's right to participate in family law proceedings in light of Articles 6 and 8 ECHR. In order to fully comprehend the manner in which child participation is dealt with in the 182 judgments and decisions, a high standard

712 See Article 30 ECHR.

713 See also Bodnar 2014, p. 224, specifically fn. 1, in which he notes that: 'Even if the ECtHR does not declare a certain application admissible, the reasoning about the scope of the protected rights under the Convention is important for building the case-law.'

714 The final search was conducted on 18 November 2019 on the basis of the same method as the first search and selection.

715 The author thanks Mariëlle Bruning, Hannele Tolonen and Eva Vertommen in this respect. These four cases were previously excluded from the selection because they did not have 'hits'; therefore, it is possible that a small number of other relevant cases were missed due to the selection on the basis of 'hits'.

of research was aimed at. A systematic and rigorous method was chosen to analyse the case law of the ECHR in order to adhere to the scientific standards of objectivity, falsifiability and transparency.[716] As case law is a form of qualitative data – it is expressed in words and not in numbers – and the aim of this research is to analyse the meaning of the case law, a research method was sought in the literature on qualitative data analysis.[717] The most fitting method proved to be the option of content analysis (CA), which is a method for the 'systematic description of data through coding'.[718] CA is an empirical method which has been previously used for the analysis of case law.[719] The method is best known in its quantitative (classical) form;[720] however, in this research the qualitative method was used. QCA is 'a method for describing the meaning of qualitative material in a systematic way'.[721] Its aim suits this research, as this aim is to systematically describe the data, and in so doing to come to an understanding of the data analysed.

The key difference between QCA and quantitative CA lies in the results of both analyses. Quantitative CA provides precise frequencies and numerical data, and places value on these frequencies. In QCA, the simple presence or absence of a certain concept within the data may be as relevant as the frequencies of occurrence.[722] This distinction is relevant for this research because the aim is to understand which justifications, reasons, arguments, etc. play a role in the case law of the ECtHR regarding child participation; the core aim is not to count or provide statistics on the occurrence of certain issues in the case law.[723] QCA also distinguishes itself by focusing more on the latent meaning of the data, taking a more data-driven and inductive approach, and by being more flexible than quantitative CA. All in all, considering the aim of this research and the

716 See e.g. M.A. Hall & R.F. Wright, 'Systematic Content Analysis of Judicial Opinions', *California Law Review*, Vol. 96, No. 1, 2008, pp. 63–122, pp. 63–66; and U. Kuckartz, *Qualitative Text Analysis: A Guide to Methods, Practice & Using Software*, London: SAGE Publications 2014, pp. 11–13.

717 See e.g. U. Flick (ed.), *The SAGE Handbook of Qualitative Data Analysis*, Los Angeles: SAGE 2014.

718 M. Schreier, 'Qualitative Content Analysis', in: U. Flick (ed.), *The SAGE Handbook of Qualitative Data Analysis*, Los Angeles: SAGE 2014, pp. 170–183, p. 170.

719 See Hall & Wright 2008; E.M.J.M.C. van Wijk-Verhagen, *Redelijkheid en billijkheid in het personen- en familierecht, meer in het bijzonder in het huwelijks- en echtscheidingsvermogensrecht*, The Hague: Boom juridisch 2018; and L. Wijntjens, *Als ik nu sorry zeg, beken ik dan schuld? Over het aanbieden van excuses in de civiele procedure en de medische tuchtprocedure*, The Hague: Boom juridisch 2020.

720 See e.g. K. Krippendorff, *Content Analysis: An Introduction to its Methodology*, London: SAGE Publications 2004; and J. Baxter, 'Content Analysis', in: R. Kitchin & N. Thrift (eds.), *International Encyclopedia of Human Geography*, Oxford: Elsevier 2009, pp. 275–280.

721 Schreier 2012, p. 1.

722 Baxter 2009, p. 278.

723 Cf. the research of van Wijk-Verhagen 2018; and Wijntjens 2020.

differences between QCA and quantitative CA, the QCA method was found to be the most appropriate choice.

It should be noted that in this book, the qualitative analysis has been supplemented by some basic quantitative analysis. This quantitative analysis consisted of counting the number of cases, the types of applicants and proceedings, and the repetition of certain standards. In considering frequencies in addition to the qualitative conclusions, it was further determined how the cases relate to each other, how the standards developed and whether one can speak of a more or less consistent set of standards.

After the choice was made for QCA, the method had to be put into practice. In short, the QCA method consists of four steps.

The first step is the *development of a coding frame*, which is a structured list of codes and their definitions.[724] The coding frame provides the structure by which to interpret the data – namely, the rules by which the data is to be coded.[725] The coding frame was developed through a mixed approach: both inductively, relying on the research questions and prior knowledge; and deductively, relying on a sample of the case law itself. After the development of the various main and subcategories, these categories were defined and checked for unidimensionality, mutual exclusiveness and exhaustiveness.[726]

Following the development of the coding frame, the second step is *testing the coding frame*. The pilot phase provides a chance to test the coding frame for its quality and reliability. The reliability of the coding frame is determined through testing for consistency of coding between persons, also called intersubjectivity.[727] The central question during a pilot phase is whether the coding frame is sufficiently reliable for its application not to be contentious. Through the pilot phase, existing flaws in the developed coding frame were identified and subsequently ironed out. The coding frame was improved throughout the two pilot phases and a final coding frame was adopted.

With the coding frame in hand, the third step is the *main coding phase*. In this phase, the selected cases are read and coded. To assist in the QCA method, the Computer Assisted Qualitative Data Analysis (CAQDAS) software NVivo was used. CAQDAS software, such as NVivo, speeds up and helps in organizing the coding process, but does not replace a methodology or provide for automated content analysis.[728] Throughout the main coding phase, it appeared that a number of the selected ECtHR cases were not relevant for analysis in this research. More specifically, as it had not been possible to select within HUDOC

---

724 Baxter 2009, p. 275.

725 Schreier 2012, p. 61.

726 Schreier 2012, p. 71–77.

727 Schreier 2012, p. 167. Many thanks and gratitude go to Maaike Lelifeld, LL.M. student, for her assistance as second coder.

728 Schreier 2012, pp. 242–243.

for family law proceedings – when reading all the cases a number of irrelevant cases were removed. Therefore, a practical second selection phase took place in which (1) 24 cases in which there was not even a hint of family law, and (2) 11 cases concerning family law, but not concerning minor children were weeded out after being read. Thus, out of the original 182 selected cases, 147 cases were read and coded in the main coding phase.

The fourth and final step is the *analysis and discussion* of the data and results. Following the main coding phase, the researcher was left with a bountiful NVivo file, consisting of the coded cases, a large overview of the attributes of the cases, and a myriad of ways in which to pull up the codes and coded information. This wealth of information also brought with it an abundance of manners in which results could be viewed and subsequently discussed. The choice was therefore made to discuss the data in a structured manner according to theme and then according to the party involved, and to approach and view the data in a multidimensional way. This one choice in fact envelops multiple choices, each of which must be explained. The question of structure will be further discussed in section 5, below. The choice to approach the data in a multidimensional manner will now be explained. The multidimensional approach means that the data collected through coding was viewed in different ways. Trends were studied within the main and subcategories of coding, through so-called 'coding summaries by node'.[729] For example, a coding summary for 'Insufficient participation not justified' within the subcategory of 'ECtHR: Insufficient participation' showed all the quotes from cases in which the ECtHR argues that the participation in the domestic proceeding was insufficient and not justified. Additionally, all the different codes applied were viewed case by case through so-called 'coding summaries by source'.[730] When writing up the results, the coded text was also viewed within the context of the case itself by using NVivo to pull up the PDF of the case and location of the code. Viewing the text surrounding the coded text is meaningful, as the context of the case – for example, other considerations of the ECtHR – help in understanding the coded text. Finally, throughout the following chapters, the analysis is supplemented by relevant quantitative data, such as the frequency in which a complaint is brought, a standard is mentioned or comments are made about a certain topic. As mentioned above, this additional quantitative layer further assists in understanding the qualitative results. In the writing-up of the analysis, another 59 cases revealed themselves to be irrelevant for discussion

729 Coding summaries by node is a report that can be made using the Report Designer in Nvivo. The coding summary lists all the nodes (i.e. code categories) and the files in which they are coded at; any text that is coded is included in the summary.

730 Coding summaries by source is a report which lists all the files (i.e. cases) and the nodes (i.e. code categories) that code them; any text that is coded is included in the summary.

for three different reasons.[731] To conclude, in the following chapters, a total of 88 judgments and decisions are discussed.

5. STRUCTURE OF THE CASE LAW ANALYSIS

In the following five chapters, the results of the case law analysis are presented. As mentioned above, the choice was made to conduct and present the analysis according to theme and then according to the party involved. The structure of the analysis is relevant as it affects the manner in which trends can be seen and conclusions drawn.

A case law analysis can be structured in a number of ways. In legal research, common options are to discuss the results according to case or to discuss the results according to the conclusion reached. In this research, the choice was made to analyse and discuss the results following the structure of the coding frame and thus according to the key theme. The coding frame was developed both inductively and deductively. Therefore, the categories included in it reflect both the aim of this research and the content of the case law. Discussing the case law analysis according to the theme made it possible to bring together a great number of cases and different parties' arguments. This facilitated understanding of how the child's right to participation in family law proceedings has been introduced, interpreted and given substance by the ECtHR. It also streamlined the drawing of conclusions regarding the standards set by the ECtHR. The following chapters therefore each address one of four themes:

- Chapter 5: (In)sufficient participation
- Chapter 6: Weight accorded to the child's views
- Chapter 7: Maturity of the child
- Chapter 8: 'Influence' on the views of the child

The four themes reflect core topics of child participation. In order to illustrate these four themes, an overview of their relationship to the child participation process and their relationship to one another is included in Figure 4.1 below. The first two themes reflect the process of the child's right to participation: the opportunity to participate and the right for the expressed views to be granted due weight. The other two themes tie into both these first themes. The maturity of the child is a factor in whether a child can participate, (potentially) how a

[731] The three reasons were that: (1) no codes applied to the case, because there were no relevant passages; (2) codes applied to the case only concerned the Facts or (International or National) Law section of the case or (3) coded text was not found to be relevant for the analysis upon the discretion of the researcher.

child can participate and to what extent the expressed views are granted weight. The issue of influence is a common counterargument to child participation and is therefore relevant with regard to whether a child should participate and how to weigh his or her views if influenced. These four themes form the main structure of Part II of this book. As the themes are related and overlap to a certain extent, there are multiple cases which will be considered in more than one chapter in Part II.

Figure 4.1. Overview of the child participation process and four themes addressed in case law analysis

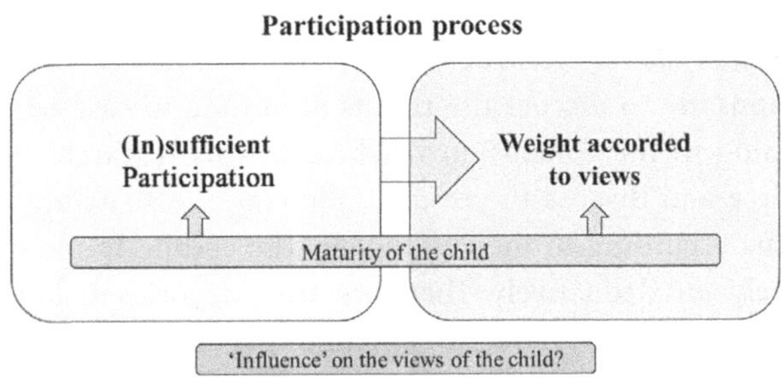

Source: Compiled by the author.

In each of the chapters, the same structure was applied to discuss the results. According to the theme, the applicants' arguments, the governments' comments and the ECtHR's reasoning on the theme are discussed in that order. Subsequently, a concluding analysis is presented which brings together the results of the three sections. Finally, each chapter concludes with a set of standards which have been derived from the analysis. In not only discussing the reasoning of the Court but also including the arguments brought by applicants and comments by governments, this analysis comprehensively shows the developments that have occurred in the ECtHR case law in the past few decades. More importantly, including the applicants' arguments and governments' comments assists in providing an explanation for the standards set by the ECtHR and, in turn, whether the norms are a consistent set of standards. The underlying hypothesis is that who the applicants are and what they complain of together with how the governments respond are relevant determinants for the ECtHR's reasoning on child participation. By themselves, even where there is no complaint by the applicant, the governments' comments on the themes are assumed to be potentially relevant for the ECtHR's reasoning in the cases studied. During the main coding phase, all sections of the case law were also coded, including dissenting and concurring opinions, and third parties' submissions. Where relevant, the dissenting and concurring opinions are discussed under the ECtHR's reasoning. The third parties' submissions are not further discussed in this research as the few third-party interventions present in the case law analysed did not address child participation, with the exception of *Pini and others v. Romania* (2004).[732]

Before we turn to the case law analysis in the following chapters, two aspects presumed to be relevant throughout the analysis must be introduced.

6. APPLICANTS

Without applicants applying to the ECtHR to complain of an alleged violation under the ECHR, there would be no case law to analyse. The first relevant aspect to introduce is therefore the applicants. As there are various possible constellations of applicants to the ECtHR, the applicants are one of the variables considered in the analysis. The underlying hypothesis is that who the applicant is may affect the manner in which the ECtHR addresses the topic of child participation. In other words, one would expect that if a child applies to the ECtHR, the Court will deal with a complaint regarding participation in a different manner from when a parent raises a similar complaint.[733] One would also expect that there may be a difference between a parent complaining on behalf of a child in protracted divorce proceedings or a (more) neutral third person complaining on behalf of a child.

6.1. STANDING OF APPLICANTS

There are various possible options and combinations of applicants in case law concerning child participation. Complaints can be brought by: (1) a parent or parents; (2) a parent or parents also on behalf of their child(ren); (3) a parent or parents together with their child(ren) on their own behalf; (4) a child or children on their own (5) and others, for example, family members or a non-governmental organization (NGO) (potentially also on behalf of the child(ren)). What precisely is the difference between these options and what is possible under the ECHR?

According to Article 34 ECHR, individual applications can be made to the ECtHR by 'any person, non-governmental organization or group of individuals claiming to be the victim of a violation' of ECHR rights by one of the contracting states. Article 34 ECHR does not impose any further requirements as to the person bringing an application. There is no requirement of legal capacity, so children can apply to the court – regardless of their standing in domestic

[732] See also Chapter 7, section 4.4.

[733] See e.g. Fortin 2009.

legal proceedings.[734] Parents, other family members and children can all separately bring a complaint to the ECtHR (see options (1), (4) and (5) above). It is also possible to bring a complaint jointly or as a group. For example, as in option (3), a parent and their child can jointly bring a complaint. The latter is understood as the parent and their child complaining on their own behalf. Both applicants act in their own capacity and in their own interests.

Children bringing complaints on their own behalf without their parents is possible, but not common.[735] In order to apply to the ECtHR, children need to be aware of the option and have the resources, financially and otherwise, to bring a complaint.[736] Lodging an application is complicated; children need to be aware of the possibility to do so and will require legal representation in order to do so successfully. Given that they generally lack legal capacity to start, appear or appeal in domestic proceedings, access to an international court is an even tougher hurdle to clear. Additionally, children may also be hindered by the Court's admissibility requirement of exhausting all domestic remedies in Article 35(1) ECHR.[737] However, when there are no remedies available to children domestically – for example, because children lack legal capacity by law – this will not hinder their application to the ECHR.[738] The practical boundaries children face in accessing the ECtHR are significantly reduced when children complain on their own behalf together with their parent(s), i.e. option (3). It should be noted that it is also not simple for adults to lodge a valid application to the ECtHR; however, children face additional practical boundaries.

Alleged violations of children's rights under the ECHR are not only raised when children bring a complaint on their own behalf (with or without their parents); there is also the option of parents representing their children, thereby bringing complaints on behalf of their children (option (2) above). A parent who is the child's legal guardian and who can represent the child in domestic law can also legally represent and bring a complaint on behalf of their child at

---

734 Directorate of the Jurisconsult, *Practical Guide on Admissibility Criteria*, Strasbourg: Council of Europe/ECtHR, 2019, p. 9.

735 See also Figure 4.2 below.

736 L. Acconciamessa, 'Bringing the Child's Procedural Rights before the ECtHR through Interpretative Tools: Access to Justice, Participation, Representation', in: P. Czech et al. (eds.), *European Yearbook on Human Rights 2020*, Cambridge: Intersentia 2020, pp. 49–77, p. 55. See also Tulkens 2008, p. 19: 'We must avoid the fiction that children and young adults can exercise fundamental rights in the same way as adults.'

737 Berro-Lefèvre 2008, p. 70; and Registry of the ECtHR, 'Access of Children to Justice: Specific Focus on the Access of Children to the ECtHR as well as its Case Law Related to Children's Access to National Jurisdictions', in: Council of Europe, *Compilation of Texts Related to Child-Friendly Justice*, Directorate General of Human Rights and Legal Affairs, 2009, p. 12.

738 Berro-Lefèvre 2008, p. 70; and L. Graziani, 'Access to Justice: A Fundamental Right for All Children', in: T. Liefaard & J. Sloth-Nielsen (eds.), *The United Nations Convention on the Rights of the Child: Taking Stock after 25 Years and Looking Ahead*, Leiden: Brill/Nijhoff 2017, pp. 125–141, p. 130.

the ECtHR.[739] This also means that the parent who has shared custody of the child can bring a complaint on behalf of the child, even if the parent does not have the consent of the other parent.[740] In addition, the ECtHR has held that a natural parent, who is not the legal guardian of the child, can in certain circumstances also represent and bring a complaint on behalf of his or her child.[741] According to the Court, 'whether a natural parent has standing to act on his child's behalf in the proceedings before the Court is dependent on whether the party who opposes the natural parent and is entitled to represent the child under domestic law can be deemed to effectively protect the child's Convention rights'.[742] The Court has found that there is a 'danger' that the child's interests and rights are not effectively protected when it concerns a conflict about the child's interests 'between a natural parent and the person appointed by the authorities to act as the child's guardian'.[743] This means that a parent without custody can complain on behalf of the child with regard to his or her loss of custody, because the decision to withhold custody from that parent can be attributed to the state.[744] On the other hand, if the complaint concerns the child's interests and rights in a conflict about access rights between the natural parent and the parent with custody, then the ECtHR has found that the position as natural parent is not a sufficient basis to represent the child.[745] The admissibility rules for parents representing their children are therefore rather complicated. In that regard, it is interesting to note

739 See ECtHR, *Eberhard and M. v. Slovenia* (Appl. No. 8673/05 and 9733/05) 1 December 2009, para. 88; ECtHR, *Hromadka and Hromadkova v. Russia* (Appl. No. 22909/10), 11 December 2014, para. 119.

740 ECtHR, *Diamante and Pelliccioni v. San Marino* (Appl. No. 32250/08), 27 September 2011, paras. 146–147.

741 Amongst others, in ECtHR, *Scozzari and Giunta v. Italy* [GC] (Appl. Nos. 39221/98 and 41963/98), 13 July 2000. See C. Fenton-Glynn, 'Children, Parents and the European Court of Human Rights', *European Human Rights Law Review*, No. 6, 2019, pp. 643–653; and Merckx 2017.

742 EctHR, *Siebert v. Germany* (dec.) (Appl. No. 59008/00), 9 June 2005.

743 ECtHR, *Scozzari and Giunta v. Italy* [GC] (Appl. Nos. 39221/98 and 41963/98), 13 July 2000, para. 138. Whether the 'person appointed by the authorities to act as the child's guardian' could also be the other parent who by law is automatically the child's guardian is unclear. In the cases included in the selection for this analysis, no example was found in the literature it is briefly mentioned, but there is no reference to case law in which this is the case. It therefore remains unclear whether a natural parent is allowed to represent the child in cases between a natural parent and a parent who is the legal guardian by law when the natural parent has been stripped of custody rights.

744 ECtHR, *Eberhard and M. v. Slovenia* (Appl. No. 8673/05 and 9733/05), 1 December 2009, para. 88. It remains unclear whether the custody being withheld must be attributed to a decision of the state or whether it may also concern custody being withheld without a decision, but on the basis of law.

745 ECtHR, *Eberhard and M. v. Slovenia* (Appl. No. 8673/05 and 9733/05), 1 December 2009, para. 88. See also the discussion on similar cases included in this research: ECtHR, *Wildgruber v. Germany* (dec.) (Appl. No. 32817/02), 16 October 2006; ECtHR, *Moog v. Germany* (Appl. Nos. 23280/08 and 2334/10), 6 October 2016, paras. 41–42 and ECtHR, *K.B. and others v. Croatia* (Appl. No. 36216/13), 14 March 2017, paras. 109–110. See also the three cases discussed in section 6.2 below.

that the Court's 'Practical Guide on Admissibility Criteria' does not provide any information in this regard, while one could assume that it is not a simple task for parents (or their lawyers) to determine their admissibility.[746]

Additionally, a child could be represented by an NGO in an application to the ECtHR (option (5) above). This would certainly be possible if the child's parent or guardian provides the required legal authority for an NGO to represent the child. Additionally, it could be assumed that, as is the case for adults, it is also possible if the child provides written authority and instructions to the NGO.[747] However, in exceptional circumstances, it is also possible for an NGO to act as a de facto representative for a direct victim without the required power of attorney or written authority, as has been determined with regard to adults by the Grand Chamber in *Centre for Legal Resources on Behalf of Valentin Câmpeanu v. Romania* (2014) and recognized for children in *L.R. v. North Macedonia* (2020).[748] The former case concerned the death of a young adult of Roma origin, who was HIV positive with a severe mental disability, in a psychiatric hospital, while the latter concerned a young mentally disabled child who had been abandoned by his parents and subjected to inadequate care and ill-treatment in a state-run institution. The following exceptional circumstances were identified by the Grand Chamber: 'the victim's vulnerability; the nature of the allegations brought before the Court; whether the direct victim has next of kin or a legal guardian likely to lodge an application with the Court; whether there has been contact between the direct victim and the representative; whether the representative was involved in any relevant domestic proceedings and recognized as having standing in those proceedings'.[749] Whether these circumstances would be met in cases concerning child participation in family law proceedings is questionable; as of yet, there are no examples. In general, family law proceedings indicate the existence of next of kin or a legal guardian who can lodge an application to the Court, so the NGO would probably not qualify under the exceptional circumstances.

6.2. APPLICANTS IN THE CASE LAW ANALYSIS

It is clear that applications regarding child participation may be brought to the ECtHR by various constellations of applicants. In that regard, it is interesting

---

746 Directorate of the Jurisconsult, *Practical Guide on Admissibility Criteria*, Council of Europe/ECtHR, 2019.

747 See ECtHR, *L.R. v. North Macedonia* (Appl. No. 38067/15), 23 January 2020, para. 46.

748 ECtHR, *Centre for Legal Resources on Behalf of Valentin Câmpeanu v. Romania* (Appl. No. 47848/08), 17 July 2014, paras. 104–111; and ECtHR, *L.R. v. North Macedonia* (Appl. No. 38067/15), 23 January 2020, para. 47.

749 Phrasing taken from ECtHR, *L.R. v. North Macedonia* (Appl. No. 38067/15), 23 January 2020, para. 47, in reference to ECtHR, *Centre for Legal Resources on Behalf of Valentin Câmpeanu v. Romania* (Appl. No. 47848/08), 17 July 2014, paras. 104–111.

to see the breakdown of the applicants in the cases analysed and discussed in the case law analysis. Two figures are included below to show the different applicants. In Figure 4.2, the applicants are presented according to the manner by which they brought the complaint to the ECtHR. In Figure 4.3, there is a small shift in numbers, as this figure shows the applicants with standing before the ECtHR.

Figure 4.2. Applicants bringing complaints to the ECtHR

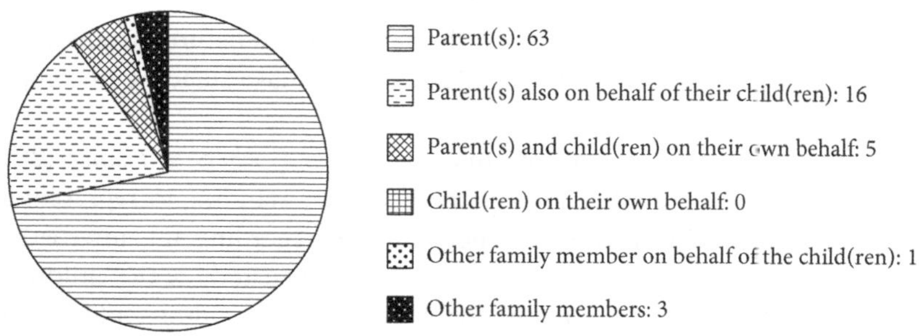

Source: Compiled by the author.

Figure 4.3. Applicants with standing before the ECtHR

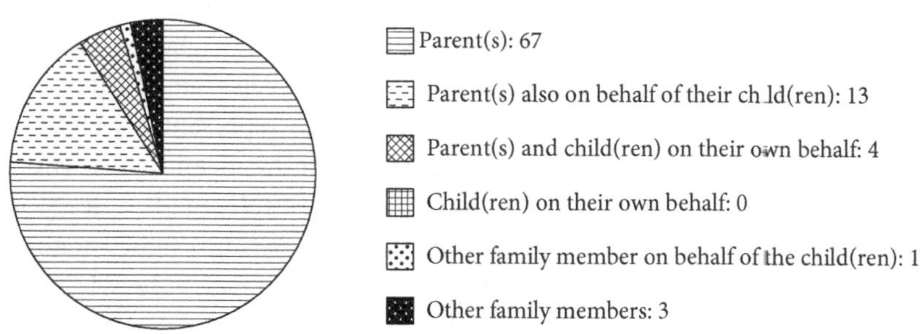

Source: Compiled by the author.

As mentioned above, there is a small difference between the two figures, due to the ECtHR's decisions on the standing of the applicants. Figure 4.3 is important as it shows whose applications the ECtHR actually considered. The difference between the figures concerns cases of children applying on their own behalf with their parent(s) or parents complaining on their behalf. In three cases, the ECtHR found the parent not to have standing to also complain on behalf of their child(ren) and in one case it found the children who complained on their own behalf not to have standing.

Starting with the latter, in *Iglesias Casarrubios and Cantalapiedra Iglesias v. Spain* (2016), a mother and her two children on their own behalf brought an application to the ECtHR, the ECtHR subsequently found the application to be inadmissible regarding the children.[750] It stated that the children were not parties to the divorce proceedings, which was the ground for the complaints.[751] It also noted that there were no grounds for considering the complaints separately from those of the mother; therefore, it found the complaints inadmissible for the children.

In the other three cases, the applicants' complaints on behalf of the children were found to be inadmissible *ratione personae*: the parent was found not to have legal standing to represent the child(ren) in his or her complaint to the ECtHR. In all three cases, the reasoning of the ECtHR was that because the cases concerned access or contact proceedings between the applicant as a natural parent and the other parent with full custody, the applicant did not have standing to complain on behalf of his or her child.[752]

Finally, it is interesting to note that in *Raw and others v. France* (2013), the ECtHR found the mother to have the necessary standing to represent and complain on behalf of all three of her children regarding the international child abduction proceedings because she had shared custody of the children.[753] However, the ECtHR subsequently concluded that the eldest child was not considered to be an applicant. The child had reached the age of majority before the ECtHR ruled on the complaint, so a signed statement was required in which the child stated that he or she wished to remain an applicant, and this had not occurred.[754] It is noteworthy that in the *Khusnutdinov and X v. Russia* (2018) judgment, which concerned residence proceedings between a father deprived of his parental authority and his mother-in-law, who had been granted guardianship by the Uzbek authorities, the father was allowed to represent his child, who remained an applicant, even though the child had in the meantime reached the age of majority, being 20 years old by the time the ECtHR made a decision.[755] The ECtHR did not even delve into the question of requiring a signed statement, as was critiqued in the Joint Partly Dissenting Opinion of Judges Keller and Pastor Vilanova and the Partly Concurring Opinion of Judge Schukking.[756]

Throughout the following chapters, when the attributes of the cases are presented, the applicants shown are those with standing.

---

750 ECtHR, *Iglesias Casarrubios and Cantalapiedra Iglesias v. Spain* (Appl. No. 23298/12), 11 October 2016, para. 27.

751 ECtHR, *Iglesias Casarrubios and Cantalapiedra Iglesias v. Spain* (Appl. No. 23298/12), 11 October 2016, para. 27.

752 ECtHR, *Wildgruber v. Germany* (dec.) (Appl. No. 32817/02), 16 October 2006; ECtHR, *Moog v. Germany* (Appl. Nos. 23280/08 and 2334/10), 6 October 2016, paras. 41–42; and ECtHR, *K.B. and others v. Croatia* (Appl. No. 36216/13), 14 March 2017, paras. 109–110.

753 ECtHR, *Raw and others v. France* (Appl. No. 10131/11), 7 March 2013, para. 52.

754 ECtHR, *Raw and others v. France* (Appl. No. 10131/11), 7 March 2013, para. 53.

755 ECtHR, *Khusnutdinov and X v. Russia* (Appl. No. 76598/12), 18 December 2018.

756 Joint Partly Dissenting Opinion of Judges Keller and Pastor Vilanova and Partly Concurring Opinion of Judge Schukking, ECtHR, *Khusnutdinov and X v. Russia* (Appl. No. 76598/12), 18 December 2018.

Aside from the question of standing, there is an important conclusion to make with regard to the applicants in the analysed cases. The figures show that there are no cases in which a child or children brought a complaint on their own behalf without their parents. Additionally, there are only a meagre three cases in which together with his or her parents, a child complained on their own behalf to the ECtHR. For an analysis on the child's right to participation, this is a shockingly low number. Thankfully, there are still 13 cases in which the ECtHR also considered the topic on the basis of a complaint made by a parent (or other family member) on behalf of the child(ren). However, if we contrast these numbers to the 65 cases in which the complaint has been made solely in name of the parent(s), it is clear that there is a focus on the parental point of view. What this means for the reasoning of the ECtHR regarding child participation will be further reflected upon throughout the following chapters and in Chapter 9 on the conclusions of the case law analysis.

7. TYPES OF PROCEEDINGS

A second aspect considered throughout the case law analysis is the type of proceedings concerned. This is presumed to be a relevant factor in the case law analysis because the types of proceedings may explain or justify different approaches to participation. In that regard, it is important to be able to recognize similar and different types of proceedings. The focus of this research is on the participation of children in family law proceedings, so all analysed cases concern family law. However, within the scope of family law proceedings, there are various types of proceedings. In the following, the terminology used and categorization made throughout Part II for these types of proceedings is explained.

Categories of types of proceedings have been made in order to allow for comparable units in this case law analysis, because the ECtHR does not use autonomous terminology in its case law with regard to family law proceedings.[757] To make these categories and determine which cases belong in which categories, the author had to ascertain the type of proceeding concerned in each case. This task was not as simple as one would expect. The manner in which the ECtHR functions, combined with the differences in the substantive national family law of the 47 European contracting states, leads to an array of different terminology used in the case law examined. The ECtHR also does not categorize or group

757 In contrast, the ECtHR has autonomously interpreted many of the concepts which are included in the text of the ECHR. For example, under the scope of Article 6 ECHR, the concepts 'criminal charge' and 'civil rights and obligations' have been subject to autonomous interpretation, whereby an autonomous distinction is made as to the type of proceeding. See G. Letsas, 'The Truth in Autonomous Concepts: How to Interpret the ECHR', *European Journal of International Law*, Vol. 15, No. 2, 2004, pp. 279–305, pp. 282–382.

case law on the type of proceedings, or use a standard or autonomous set of terminology to refer to the type of family law proceeding in the case law.[758]

Therefore categories of proceedings had to be defined and cases placed in these categories accordingly. All the case law in this analysis concerns family law proceedings. More specifically, all of the proceedings concern the relationship between parents (or guardians) and children. In this area of family law, there are essentially three different categories of proceedings: proceedings concerning the exercise of the rights of a parent (parental authority, custody, residence, access, international child abduction, etc.); parentage proceedings (the establishment of a legal relationship as a parent and child); and public care or child protection proceedings. These general categories are clear, but the more specific subdivision of proceedings is not straightforward. There are a number of manners in which the types of proceedings are phrased in the case law, due to the lack of autonomous terminology for the reasons discussed above. For example, 'access' and 'contact' are used by the ECtHR for similar cases and even interchangeably at times.[759] To allow for a comparison, eight categories of proceedings have been defined. In order to allow for a more precise comparison, these are more specific categories than the three mentioned above. These categorizations are used when presenting the attributes of the cases; within the text of the chapter, the wording given in the case law itself is used in order to provide more detail. The following eight types of proceedings have been used as categories with the corresponding definitions:

- *Custody proceedings*: proceedings concerning the rights and duties to care for the child by a parent or guardian. This category includes proceedings regarding the transfer, withdrawal, exercise and/or enforcement of parental authority and custody rights. Residence proceedings between parents with joint-custody are therefore also included within the scope of custody proceedings. Proceedings concerning the public care of children (e.g. the withdrawal of custody rights as a child protection measures) are not included in this category, but under 'Care proceedings' below.
- *Access proceedings*: proceedings concerning the rights of access to and contact with a child. This category includes proceedings regarding the granting, withdrawal, exercise and/or enforcement of access rights.
- *Custody and access proceedings*: proceedings which concern both custody and access proceedings, within the scope of the definitions provided above.
- *International child abduction proceedings*: proceedings concerning a cross-border wrongful removal or retention of a child. This category concerns return proceedings conducted under the auspices of The Hague Abduction Convention 1980, but also return proceedings to which the Convention was not applicable.

758 For more information, see Appendix.

759 See ECtHR, *Płaza v. Poland* (Appl. No. 18830/07), 25 January 2011, para. 3 compared to para. 8.

- *Care proceedings*: proceedings concerning child protection measures, such as taking children into care, placement in public care, transfer of parental authority to the state (social services, youth office, etc.) or another guardian, and adoption.
- *Care and access proceedings*: proceedings which concern both care and access proceedings, within the scope of the definitions provided above.
- *Parentage proceedings*: proceedings concerning the establishment of a legal relationship between a parent and child, such as paternity proceedings.
- *Adoption proceedings*: proceedings concerning the adoption of a child. In this category, proceedings concerning adoption within the framework of child protection measures are excluded, as they instead included under 'Care proceedings'.

In the Appendix, the method of categorizing the cases is described and tables are included to show under which category the cases have been placed by the author relying on the original phrasing used in the case.

Having placed all 88 cases discussed in this chapter into one of the eight categories, a few comments can be made on the composition of the collection of case law discussed. In Figure 4.4, below, an overview of the case law per category of proceeding is presented.

Figure 4.4. Overview of case law according to the category of proceedings

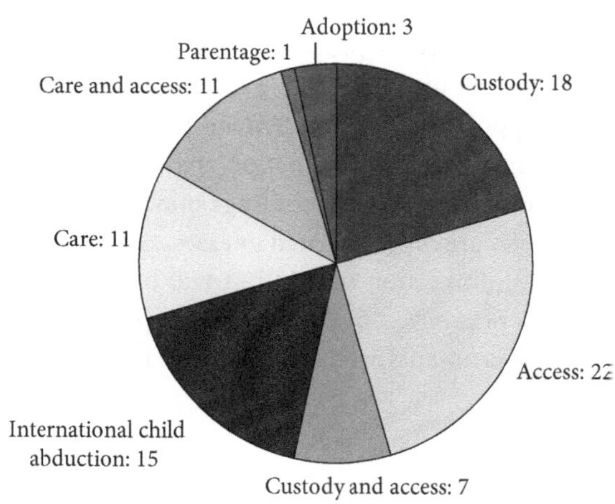

Source: Compiled by the author.

Looking at this figure, it is clear that about half of the cases discussed concern custody, access or custody and access proceedings. This was expected, as it is a common field in which the child's right to participation is addressed and advocated for. As divorce and the separation of parents with minor children is prevalent, custody and access proceedings account for a large proportion of family law proceedings at the domestic level and therefore more applications to the ECtHR. Subsequently, another unsurprising fact is that a fifth of the cases discussed are care proceedings together with care and access proceedings. The involvement of the state in the family through taking children into care or other care measures can very well require the participation of children. More generally, the intrusive nature of these cases understandably leads to applications to the ECtHR when alleged violations occur. More noteworthy is the high percentage of international child abduction proceedings, given the fact that there are domestically far fewer proceedings concerning international child abductions than custody, access or care proceedings. The high number of cases may be explained by the fact that it is a type of proceeding for which, in most jurisdictions, The Hague Abduction Convention provides special procedures to ensure prompt return of the child. More specifically, one of the few exceptions to return in Article 13 of The Hague Abduction Convention concerns the views of the child. The second paragraph of Article 13 provides courts with the discretion not to order the return of the child if the child objects. With parents taking all possible measures to oppose return or to ensure return, a complaint regarding the child's participation at the ECtHR is not far-fetched. In comparison, it may be that parents in other types of proceedings (for example, regarding custody) are less aware of the option of complaining about child participation to achieve their desired outcome. Finally, the small number of parentage and adoption proceedings is also noteworthy. There are a number of possible explanations for this finding. First, parentage proceedings as such are far less common than, for example, custody and access proceedings at the domestic level. Second, one could hypothesize that at the domestic level, it may be that children have fewer participation opportunities in parentage proceedings. This may either be because there are no or little participation rights for children in parentage proceedings, or because parentage proceedings may often concern very young children. However, these are only educated guesses.

Bearing the above information in mind, it will be interesting to see in the analysis how the types of proceedings affect the complaints brought by parents, comments made by governments and, especially, the reasoning of the ECtHR on child participation.

8. MODES OF PARTICIPATION

'Child participation' is an umbrella term under which a variety of modes of participation are understood, as was mentioned in the Introduction to this volume.[760] In the absence of a common terminology for the different modes of

[760] See Chapter 1, section 3.

participation, it is important to comment on the words used in the following chapters.

While in the final coding frame, ten categories of child participation were included as deduced from the 'Facts' sections of the case law, in the reasoning of the ECtHR on participation, only a number of main modes of participation could be distinguished. The following terminology was chosen to refer to these four main modes of participation: direct hearing, representation, use of experts, and litigation on the child's own behalf. The meaning of these four main modes will now be explained.

The most common mode of participation is the direct hearing of a child by a court. This mode of participation consists of the child speaking with one or more judges of a domestic court personally. The term 'direct' or 'directly' clarifies that there is no other party involved between the child expressing his or her views and the court that must attach weight these views. The ECtHR uses phrases such as 'hear a child in court',[761] 'court heard the children in person',[762] 'entendus directement par les tribunaux'[763] and 'audition personelle des enfants'.[764] The phrase 'direct hearing' or 'directly hearing the child' was chosen over terms such as 'testimony', 'interview' or 'questioning', because those terms are often used for witnesses or suspects. It would be undesirable to insinuate that children are either of these, as the intention of child participation is not to provide evidence. In domestic law, it may be that children are heard for the purpose of giving evidence; however, that is not the same as the right to participation in which children are heard for the purpose of being able to express their views on the matter.

A second common mode of participation discussed in the case law is participation through representation. The representation of a child by someone other than their parents or legal guardians is a method of indirect participation, as the child expresses views to the representative, who subsequently conveys these views to the court. There are many different types of representative and their functions can differ greatly. For example, representation can take the form of legal representation, but it is also possible to have best interests representation, or any form in between. The ECtHR's reasoning mentions, amongst other things,

---

761 For example, ECtHR, *Sahin v. Germany* [GC] (Appl. No. 30943/96), 8 July 2003, para. 73.

762 For example, ECtHR, *Wildgruber v. Germany* (dec.) (Appl. Nos. 42402/05 and 42423/05), 29 January 2008.

763 For example, ECtHR, *Havelka and others v. Czech Republic* (Appl. No. 23499/06), 21 June 2007, para. 62.

764 For example, ECtHR, *Gettliffe and Grant v. France* (dec.) (Appl. No. 23547/06), 24 October 2006.

representation by lawyers,[765] guardians ad litem,[766] curators ad litem[767] and representatives generally.[768]

Another indirect mode of participation which appears in the ECtHR's reasoning is the conveyance of views of the child through experts and their reports. Experts such as social workers, psychologists and psychiatrists can speak to children and write up their views in reports, which are subsequently presented to the courts. Whether the use of an expert report to convey views is a credible mode of participation for children will depend in part on the manner in which the expert writes up the report. The manner in which the ECtHR sees this mode of participation will be explored further in Part II of this volume.

Finally, there is the most direct mode of participation, namely the option of a child litigating on his or her own behalf. This mode of participation is very uncommon for children in the field of family law, as is also reflected in the case law analysed, which shows that the procedural autonomy of children remains limited in family law cases.

Understanding the terminology regarding these four modes of participation and the previously discussed attributes of applicants and types of proceedings will enable the reader to comprehend the body of case law analysis which follows.

---

765 For example, ECtHR, *Paulsen-Medalen and Svensson v. Sweden* (dec.) (Appl. No. 47411/99), 30 September 2003.

766 For example, ECtHR, *Moog v. Germany* (Appl. Nos. 23280/08 and 2334/10), 6 October 2016, para. 81.

767 For example, ECtHR, *Paradis and others v. Germany* (dec.) (Appl. No. 4783/03), 15 May 2003.

768 For example, ECtHR, *N.Ts. and others v. Georgia* (Appl. No. 71776/12), 2 February 2016, para. 74.

CHAPTER 5
(IN)SUFFICIENT PARTICIPATION

'The Court is particularly struck by the fact that after four years and three months the [child] has not yet been heard in those proceedings and thus given a chance to express her views ...'

– ECtHR, *M. and M. v. Croatia* (2015)[769]

1. INTRODUCTION

In the landmark judgment of *M. and M. v. Croatia* (2015) quoted above, the European Court of Human Rights (ECtHR) strongly condoned the complete lack of participation by the child in prolonged proceedings on custody. Unsurprisingly, whether the child can (or could) participate in proceedings is a primary question regarding child participation. However, the distinction between sufficient and insufficient participation is not always so clear-cut; it concerns not only whether participation occurred or not, but also the manner in which participation occurred. For example, should a child be able to speak to the judge directly or is a report by an expert sufficient? What about representation – does it matter who the representative is and how they represent the child? In essence, it examines how, when and which children should be able to participate in family law proceedings. This chapter addresses all the complaints, remarks and reasoning on (in)sufficient participation as the first theme in the case law analysis.

The complaints of applicants, arguments of governments and reasoning of the ECtHR on whether the child's participation in the domestic family law proceedings was sufficient or insufficient will be discussed. As was discussed in Chapter 4, this structure allows for a complete understanding of the ECtHR's reasoning on child participation in family law proceedings. Out of the 88 cases analysed in this research, a total of 46 addressed the (in)sufficient participation of the child. These 46 cases are discussed in this chapter. Following the separate analysis of the applicants' complaints (see section 2), governments' arguments (see section 3) and the ECtHR's remarks and reasoning (see section 4), a concluding analysis is presented (see section 5). This chapter closes with a

769 ECtHR, *M. and M. v. Croatia* (Appl. No. 10161/13), 3 September 2015, para. 184.

number of standards derived from the case law analysis for states (see section 6). These standards, the reasoning of the ECtHR and the concluding analysis add to the international and European framework on the child's right to participate.

2. COMPLAINTS BROUGHT BY APPLICANTS

In 26 cases, the applicants complained that there was insufficient participation for the child or children in disputes in the field of family law. This insufficient participation was complained of in two ways: that there was no participation whatsoever (see section 2.1) or that the participation which did take place was insufficient or inadequate (see section 2.2). The latter can be split into six different types of complaints, including, for example, complaints regarding the mode of participation or the lack of an additional hearing.

2.1. LACK OF PARTICIPATION

In seven cases, the applicants complained of a complete lack of participation of the child concerned. Most commonly, they did so by arguing that the children were not heard by the domestic court; at times, the applicants were more specific by referring to another mode of participation. In all these cases, the children had at no point in the proceeding been given the opportunity to express their views. The attributes of these cases are presented below in Table 5.1.

Table 5.1. Attributes of cases with a complaint on the complete lack of participation

Chamber judgments	Type of proceeding	Applicant	Article of complaint
Gajtani v. Switzerland (2014)	International child abduction	Mother	Article 6
Zelikha Magomadova v. Russia (2019)	Custody	Mother	Article 8
Chamber decisions	**Type of proceeding**	**Applicant**	**Article of complaint**
K. and T. v. Finland (1999)	Care	Parents	Article 10
Paulsen-Medalen and Svensson v. Sweden (2003)	Care and access	Parents, also on behalf of child	Article 8
Siebert v. Germany (2005)	Care and access	Father, also on behalf of child	Article 8
Eskinazi and Chelouche v. Turkey (2005)	International child abduction	Mother, also on behalf of child	Article 8
Brillet and Brillet v. Belgium (2014)	Custody	Father and children on own behalf	Article 8

Source: Compiled by the author.

Starting with the Chamber judgments, in *Gajtani v. Switzerland* (2014), the applicant complained that her children had not been heard during the proceeding, which led to the attribution of custody to the other parent.[770] Similarly, in *Zelikha Magomadova v. Russia* (2019), the applicant complained that four of her six children had not been heard, adding that this was in breach of the Russian Family Code for the eldest two of these four children.[771]

In the decisions there are a number of complaints. In *K. and T. v. Finland* (1999), the applicant parents complained that their children were deprived of their freedom of speech, as provided for under Article 10 of the European Convention on Human Rights (ECHR), because their views and opinions were never heard in the proceedings regarding placement in public care.[772] The reliance on Article 10 ECHR instead of Article 6 or 8 is unexpected, but was an original choice as it has never been replicated. More typically, the applicant in *Eskinazi and Chelouche v. Turkey* (2005) complained under Article 8 ECHR that her child had not been heard by the court in the international child abduction proceedings, also referring to Article 13 of The Hague Abduction Convention in that regard.[773] In the other three decisions, the applicants complained of a lack of participation, referring specifically to modes of participation other than direct hearings. For example, the applicant in *Siebert v. Germany* (2005) argued that the domestic courts should have appointed a curator ad litem to represent his child and should have heard the child in person.[774] In *Paulsen-Medalen and Svensson v. Sweden* (2003), the applicants complained that the child did not have standing to institute proceedings on his own until he reached the age of 15.[775] Finally, in *Brillet and Brillet v. Belgium* (2014), the applicants – the children themselves – complained that refusing them an opportunity to participate in the criminal proceedings on the non-execution of custody orders was a breach of the procedural requirements of Article 8 ECHR in combination with Article 12 of the United Nations Convention on the Rights of the Child (UNCRC).[776]

2.2. INSUFFICIENT OR INADEQUATE MODE OF PARTICIPATION

In 19 cases, it was not the complete lack of participation which was complained about, but the fact that the mode of participation used was insufficient or inadequate.

770 ECtHR, *Gajtani v. Switzerland* (Appl. No. 43730/07), 9 September 2014, para. 52.
771 ECtHR, *Zelikha Magomadova v. Russia* (Appl. No. 58724/14), 8 October 2019, para. 88.
772 ECtHR, *K. and T. v. Finland* (dec.) (Appl. No. 25702/94), 8 June 1999.
773 ECtHR, *Eskinazi and Chelouche v. Turkey* (dec.) (Appl. No. 14600/05), 6 December 2005.
774 ECtHR, *Siebert v. Germany* (dec.) (Appl. No. 59008/00), 9 June 2005.
775 ECtHR, *Paulsen-Medalen and Svensson v. Sweden* (dec.) (Appl. No. 47411/99), 30 September 2003.
776 ECtHR, *Brillet and Brillet v. Belgium* (dec.) (Appl. Nos. 14942/11 and 17942/11), 16 December 2014, para. 32.

These complaints can be split into six types of subcomplaints which will be discussed consecutively. In some of the nineteen cases, more than one subcomplaint is raised by applicants. The six subcomplaints can be split into two types of complaints. On the one hand, there are complaints that the children should have been heard directly either: instead of a different participation mode (see section 2.2.1) or again after the passage of time in the proceedings (see section 2.2.2). On the other hand, there are complaints concerning other modes of participation, including: the failure or delay in appointing a representative (see section 2.2.3); complaints on ineffective representation (see section 2.2.4) and complaints on incompetent experts (see section 2.2.5). Finally, there are complaints on insufficient participation which do not fall under any of the above five subcomplaint categories (see section 2.2.6).

2.2.1. *Direct Hearing Instead of Another Participation Mode*

In seven judgments and decisions, the complaint of insufficient participation brought by the applicants was that the child(ren) should have been directly heard by the court instead of through other participation modes. In considering the attributes of these cases (see Table 5.2), we see that most cases concern custody and/or access proceedings, but that the applicants are more diverse.

Table 5.2. Attributes of cases with a complaint on the lack of direct participation

Grand Chamber judgment	**Type of proceeding**	**Applicant**	**Article of complaint**
Sahin v. Germany (2003)	Access	Father	Article 8
Chamber judgments	**Type of proceeding**	**Applicant**	**Article of complaint**
Kajari v. Finland (2007)	Access	Father	Article 8
Kuhlen-Rafsandjani v. Germany (2011)	Custody	Father	Article 8
M. and M. v. Croatia (2015)	Custody	Mother and child on own behalf	Article 8
N.Ts. and others v. Georgia (2016)	Custody	Aunt on behalf of children	Article 8
Iglesias Casarrubios and Cantalapiedra Iglesias v. Spain (2016)	Custody	Mother	Article 6
Chamber decision	**Type of proceeding**	**Applicant**	**Article of complaint**
Gettliffe and Grant v. France (2006)	International child abduction	Mother, also on behalf of children	Article 6

Source: Compiled by the author.

In all these cases, the applicants argued that their child(ren) should have been heard directly in addition to or instead of the other participation modes relied on by the domestic courts. The applicants in *N.Ts. and others v. Georgia* (2016) argued that the children should have been heard directly in addition to the legal representative who was appointed to them.[777] Similar complaints were presented in *Kuhlen-Rafsandjani v. Germany* (2011) and *Gettliffe and Grant v. France* (2006).[778] In *M. and M. v. Croatia* (2015), *Iglesias Casarrubios and Cantalapiedra Iglesias v. Spain* (2016) and *Sahin v. Germany* (2003), the applicants complained that indirect participation by means of psychological expert reports was insufficient and that national courts ought to directly hear the child.[779] A final version of the complaint is expressed by the applicant in *Kajari v. Finland* (2007), who argued that the court should have heard his child directly, 'at least to verify' what the child had expressed to the Social Welfare Board.[780]

2.2.2. *Additional Direct Hearing*

In four cases, the applicants complained that the participation had been inadequate as an additional direct hearing of the children was necessary following the passage of time. The attributes of these cases are shown in Table 5.3 below.

Table 5.3. Attributes of cases with a complaint on the need for an additional direct hearing of the child

Chamber judgments	Type of proceeding	Applicant	Article of complaint
Glesmann v. Germany (2008)	Care and access	Mother	Article 8
Rouiller v. Switzerland (2014)	International child abduction	Mother	Article 8
McIlwrath v. Russia (2017)	International child abduction	Father	Article 8
Chamber decision	**Type of proceeding**	**Applicant**	**Article of complaint**
Wildgruber v. Germany (2008)	Custody	Father	Articles 6 and 8

Source: Compiled by the author.

777 ECtHR, *N.Ts. and others v. Georgia* (Appl. No. 71776/12), 2 February 2016, para. 68.

778 ECtHR, *Gettliffe and Grant v. France* (dec.) (Appl. No. 23547/06), 24 October 2006; ECtHR, *Kuhlen-Rafsandjani v. Germany* (Appl. Nos. 21980/06, 26944/07 and 36948/08), 20 January 2011, para. 94.

779 ECtHR, *Sahin v. Germany* [GC] (Appl. No. 30943/96), 8 July 2003, para. 57; ECtHR, *M. and M. v. Croatia* (Appl. No. 10161/13), 3 September 2015, para. 129 and ECtHR, *Iglesias Casarrubios and Cantalapiedra Iglesias v. Spain* (Appl. No. 23298/12), 11 October 2016, para. 32.

780 ECtHR, *Kajari v. Finland* (Appl. No. 65040/01), 23 October 2007, para. 31.

The applicant in *Rouiller v. Switzerland* (2014) specifically complained about the fact that although the court of first instance had heard the child and drawn up a report of this hearing, the higher courts had not heard her child and had solely relied on the report, which had been acknowledged as being insufficient by these higher courts.[781] The hearing of the children in first instance had taken place in May 2007, with the higher courts considering the case in September and December 2007.

In the other cases, it is more implicit – for example, in *Glesmann v. Germany* (2008), where the applicant argued that the District Court had failed to hear the child (concerning the termination of parental authority in April 2003), while the child had participated at multiple points in the proceedings, being heard directly by the District Court in September 2001 and subsequently having a curator ad litem representing her.[782] In the *Wildgruber v. Germany* (2008) decision, the applicant complained that the Court of Appeal had not heard the child directly during the proceedings running from August 2003 to January 2004 (while the District Court had already done so, hearing one child in March and May 2003).[783] Similarly, in the *McIlwrath v. Russia* (2017) judgment, the failure of the City Court finding out the children's opinions was the subject of the complaint.[784] The facts of the case show that the District Court had heard the children in September 2012 and, seemingly, the City Court had also heard the children in November 2013.[785]

2.2.3. *Failure to Appoint or Delay in Appointing a Representative for the Child*

In a total of seven judgments and decisions, the applicants complained about the failure to appoint or the delay in appointing a special representative for the child (also referred to as guardian ad litem or curator ad litem). The attributes for these cases are presented below in Table 5.4.

Table 5.4. Attributes of cases with a complaint on the failure (or delay) to appoint a special representative

Chamber judgments	Type of proceeding	Applicant	Article of complaint
Glesmann v. Germany (2008)	Care and access	Mother	Article 6
M. and M. v. Croatia (2015)	Custody	Mother and child on own behalf	Article 8
Moog v. Germany (2016)	Access	Father	Article 8

(continued)

781 ECtHR, *Rouiller v. Switzerland* (Appl. No. 3592/08), 22 July 2014, para. 33.
782 ECtHR, *Glesmann v. Germany* (Appl. No. 25706/03), 10 January 2008, para. 96.
783 ECtHR, *Wildgruber v. Germany* (dec.) (Appl. Nos. 42402/05 and 42423/05), 29 January 2008.
784 ECtHR, *McIlwrath v. Russia* (Appl. No. 60393/13), 18 July 2017, para. 115.
785 ECtHR, *McIlwrath v. Russia* (Appl. No. 60393/13), 18 July 2017, paras. 45 and 51.

Table 5.4 *continued*

Chamber decisions	Type of proceeding	Applicant	Article of complaint
Paradis and others v. Germany (2003)	International child abduction	Mother, also on behalf of children	Article 6
Wildgruber v. Germany (2006)	Access	Father	Article 8
Luig v. Germany (2007)	Access	Father	Articles 6 and 8
Wildgruber v. Germany (2008)	Custody	Father	Articles 6 and 8

Source: Compiled by the author.

In a number of these cases, the applicants complained of the delay in appointing a representative for the children. The applicant in *Glesmann v. Germany* (2008) argued that the domestic courts had 'belatedly appointed' a curator ad litem for the child.[786] The applicant noted that the curator ad litem was appointed in October 2001, while the first hearing on the merits had taken place in September 1999.[787] Similarly, in *M. and M. v. Croatia* (2015), the applicants contended that the child's position was 'further exacerbated' by the one-and-a-half year delay in appointing a representative, and this complaint was linked specifically to the requirements of the European Convention on the Exercise of Children's Rights (ECECR).[788] In the *Moog v. Germany* (2016) judgment, the applicant also complained of the domestic courts' 'failure to appoint in due time a guardian ad litem' for the child.[789] Finally, in the *Luig v. Germany* (2007) decision, the applicant complained in light of the length of proceedings that the domestic courts had 'belatedly appointed a curator ad litem'.[790] As per the facts, the proceedings had commenced in February 2000 and a curator ad litem was appointed in July 2001.[791]

In the other three decisions, the applicants complained of the total lack of a representative. In the *Paradis and others v. Germany* (2003) decision, the applicants complained under Article 6 ECHR that there no curator ad litem had been appointed for their children.[792] Similarly, but in light of Article 8 ECHR, the applicant in *Wildgruber v. Germany* (2006) complained that although he had requested it, the domestic courts had refused to appoint a curator ad litem, and the applicant in *Wildgruber v. Germany* (2008) did so under Articles 6 and 8 ECHR.[793]

786 ECtHR, *Glesmann v. Germany* (Appl. No. 25706/03), 10 January 2008, para. 76.
787 ECtHR, *Glesmann v. Germany* (Appl. No. 25706/03), 10 January 2008, para. 76.
788 ECtHR, *M. and M. v. Croatia* (Appl. No. 10161/13), 3 September 2015, para. 129.
789 ECtHR, *Moog v. Germany* (Appl. Nos. 23280/08 and 2334/10), 6 October 2016, para. 43.
790 ECtHR, *Luig v. Germany* (dec.) (Appl. No. 28782/04), 25 September 2007.
791 ECtHR, *Luig v. Germany* (dec.) (Appl. No. 28782/04), 25 September 2007.
792 ECtHR, *Paradis and others v. Germany* (dec.) (Appl. No. 4783/03), 15 May 2003.
793 ECtHR, *Wildgruber v. Germany* (dec.) (Appl. No. 32817/02), 16 October 2006; and ECtHR, *Wildgruber v. Germany* (dec.) (Appl. Nos. 42402/05 and 42423/05), 29 January 2008.

2.2.4. *Ineffective Representative*

A related complaint brought by applicants in three cases was that the special representative appointed for the child was ineffective or insufficient. Table 5.5 shows the attributes of these three judgments and decisions.

Table 5.5. Attributes of cases with a complaint on the ineffectiveness of the special representative appointed for the child

Chamber judgment	Type of proceeding	Applicant	Article of complaint
Havelka and others v. Czech Republic (2007)	Care	Father and children on own behalf	Article 6
Chamber decisions	**Type of proceeding**	**Applicant**	**Article of complaint**
C. v. United Kingdom (2004)	Care	Father	Articles 6 and 8
Wildgruber v. Germany (2006)	Access	Father	Articles 6 and 8

Source: Compiled by the author.

In *Havelka and others v. Czech Republic* (2007), the father and children on their own behalf complained about the combined roles of the social welfare officer in requesting the care measures, while at the same time representing the children in the role of guardian ad litem.[794] The applicants complained that the children were deprived of their procedural rights and argued that the children should have had the opportunity to adopt their own independent position in the proceedings. According to the applicants, this consisted of more than expressing their opinions, but also having the right to propose, submit and challenge evidence. This complaint was brought under Article 6 ECHR and the right to a fair trial.

In two decisions, the complaints related to the limited work of the representatives: in *Wildgruber v. Germany* (2006), the lack of hearing the child in person by the representative; and in *C. v. United Kingdom* (2004), the representative not conducting full assessments.[795]

2.2.5. *Incompetent Expert*

Another shared group of complaints concerned the need for an (additional) expert in relation to the child's participation in the proceedings. Appointing an expert as such is not necessarily a mode of participation, but it can be when the expert is tasked with determining the views or opinion of the child. There are multiple complaints made in which an applicant argued that an expert should

[794] ECtHR, *Havelka and others v. Czech Republic* (Appl. No. 23499/06), 21 June 2007, para. 45.
[795] ECtHR, *C. v. United Kingdom* (dec.) (Appl. No. 14858/03), 14 December 2004, para. 2; and ECtHR, *Wildgruber v. Germany* (dec.) (Appl. No. 32817/02), 16 October 2006.

have been appointed. However, the vast majority of these complaints concerned the question of influence more than the question of participation as such. These complaints, where experts are requested to determine whether the child's views are independent or have been influenced, will not be dealt with in this section, but separately in Chapter 8 on influence. One complaint remains on the need for an expert to hear the child and is discussed here. In the Grand Chamber judgment in *Sahin v. Germany* (2003), the father complained that the expert who had been appointed was biased and that the expert had not asked the child directly about the father, and thus that a competent expert should have been appointed.[796] The attributes of this case are presented in Table 5.6 below.

Table 5.6. Attributes of cases with a complaint on the incompetence of the expert

Grand Chamber judgment	Type of proceeding	Applicant	Article of complaint
Sahin v. Germany (2003)	Access	Father	Article 8

Source: Compiled by the author.

2.2.6. Other Complaints Concerning Insufficient or Inadequate Participation

Lastly, there are two judgments which fall with the category of insufficient or inadequate participation. but not under the above discussed sub-categories. Table 5.7 presents the attributes of these cases.

Table 5.7. Attributes of cases with other complaints on insufficient or ineffective participation

Chamber judgments	Type of proceeding	Applicant	Article of complaint
R. v. Finland (2006)	Care and access	Father	Article 8
Süss v. Germany (2005)	Access	Father	Article 8

Source: Compiled by the author.

In the Chamber judgment in *R. v. Finland* (2006), the father complained under Article 8 ECHR that in the care proceedings, his child had not had a proper opportunity to be heard, as the child had not been heard by an impartial person, but solely by the social welfare authorities who had requested the care measures.[797] Unlike the applicant in *Havelka and others v. Czech Republic* (2007), discussed above, the father did not frame the issue as concerning representation; nevertheless, in substance the complaints are very similar. Finally, in *Süss v. Germany* (2005), the father complained under Article 8 that the child should

796 ECtHR, *Sahin v. Germany* [GC] (Appl. No. 30943/96), 8 July 2003, para. 56.
797 ECtHR, *R. v. Finland* (Appl. No. 34141/96), 30 May 2006, para. 73.

have been present at the hearing, but did not specifically mention whether or not the child should have subsequently been heard at that hearing in front of all parties.[798]

In summary, applicants frequently complained to the ECtHR about a lack of or insufficient participation. The complaints covered the different modes of participation, the competence of representatives or experts, the need for additional participation as proceedings carry on, and the delay in participation.

3. GOVERNMENTS' ARGUMENTS

As applicants complain about insufficient participation, governments maintain that sufficient participation was provided for children. This section considers the arguments raised by the governments with regard to the (in)sufficient participation of children. The reasons adduced by the governments justifying the (in)sufficient participation can be split into four arguments: the children lacked the required age or maturity to participate (see section 3.1); (additional) participation would not be in the child's best interests (see section 3.2); additional participation was not necessary for other reasons (see section 3.3) or another mode of participation was not necessary (see section 3.4). Also, there are the arguments regarding the use of experts, or lack thereof, raised by the governments (see section 3.5). These types of arguments will now be discussed.

3.1. INSUFFICIENT AGE OR MATURITY TO PARTICIPATE

In three cases, the governments argued that the children could not and should not have been able to participate due to their insufficient age or maturity. The attributes of these cases are presented in Table 5.8 below.

Table 5.8. Attributes of cases in which the government argued that the child had insufficient age or maturity to participate

Chamber judgments	Type of proceeding	In response to complaint on
Petrov and X v. Russia (2018)	Custody	Article 8
Zelikha Magomadova v. Russia (2019)	Custody	Article 8
Chamber decision	**Type of proceeding**	**In response to complaint on**
Eskinazi and Chelouche v. Turkey (2005)	International child abduction	Article 8

Source: Compiled by the author.

[798] ECtHR, *Süss v. Germany* (Appl. No. 40324/98), 10 November 2005, para. 77.

The Turkish government in the *Eskinazi and Chelouche v. Turkey* (2005) decision linked the lack of hearing the child to the question of age.[799] The government referred to a Guide to Good Practice on the application of The Hague Convention on International Child Abduction, in which it is recommended to hear children from the age of ten and above.[800] The child in question was aged four to five years old throughout the domestic proceedings. In *Petrov and X v. Russia* (2018), the government submitted that the child was not heard by the domestic courts because he was less than three years old at the time, while the applicable age limit in Russian law was set at ten years.[801] Similarly, in *Zelikha Magomadova v. Russia* (2019), the government responded to the applicant's complaint by referring to the fact that three of the children had not yet reached the age of ten as required by Russian law.[802]

3.2. (ADDITIONAL) PARTICIPATION NOT IN THE CHILD'S BEST INTERESTS

In five cases, the governments argued that the lack of (additional) participation of the child in the national proceedings was argued, in five cases, to be justified by the governments as (additional) participation was not in his or her best interests. These cases are presented with their attributes in Table 5.9 below.

Table 5.9. Attributes of cases in which the government argued that (additional) participation was not in the child's best interests

Grand Chamber judgment	Type of proceeding	In response to complaint on
Sahin v. Germany (2003)	Access	Article 8
Chamber judgments	**Type of proceeding**	**In response to complaint on**
C. v. Finland (2006)	Custody and access	Article 6
Eski v. Austria (2007)	Adoption	Article 8
Rouiller v. Switzerland (2014)	International child abduction	Article 8
Chamber decision	**Type of proceeding**	**In response to complaint on**
Süss v. Germany (2001)	Access	Article 6

Source: Compiled by the author.

The government in the Chamber judgment in *Eski v. Austria* (2007) noted that the applicant had insisted on the child being heard in the presence of the parties 'without caring much about the stress that would inevitably be caused

799 ECtHR, *Eskinazi and Chelouche v. Turkey* (dec.) (Appl. No. 14600/05), 6 December 2005.
800 However, it is unclear which Guide to Good Practice this would or could be.
801 ECtHR, *Petrov and X v. Russia* (Appl. No. 23608/16), 23 October 2018, para. 90.
802 ECtHR, *Zelikha Magomadova v. Russia* (Appl. No. 58724/14), 8 October 2019, para. 92.

to the child'.[803] In all the other cases discussed, the government argued that additional participation would not be in the interests of the child. In *Sahin v. Germany* (2003), the German government argued that 'further questions would have disturbed the child'.[804] Finally, in *Süss v. Germany* (2001), the government argued that the Court of Appeal opted not to hear the child again as it 'would have amounted to danger for her well-being'.[805]

In line with these arguments, albeit more implicit, the government in *C. v. Finland* (2006) stated that the children themselves had protested against further questioning and participation as they were 'fatigued with the procedures'.[806] In *Rouiller v. Switzerland* (2014), the government strengthened its argument that additional participation was not necessary with reference to General Comment No. 12, in which the CRC Committee 'emphasizes that a child should not be interviewed more often than necessary' as it may have a traumatic impact on the child.[807]

3.3. ADDITIONAL PARTICIPATION NOT NECESSARY

Governments not only contended that additional participation was not necessary due to the best interests of the child, but also, in five cases, argued that additional participation was not necessary because the children had been heard previously during the national proceedings. In these cases, the governments did not refer explicitly to the child's best interests – in contrast to those discussed above. In Table 5.10 below, the attributes of these cases are presented, before the specific responses of the governments are discussed.

Table 5.10. Attributes of cases in which the government argued that additional participation was not necessary

Grand Chamber judgment	Type of proceeding	In response to complaint on
Elsholz v. Germany (2000)	Access	Article 6
Chamber judgments	**Type of proceeding**	**In response to complaint on**
Süss v. Germany (2005)	Access	Article 8
Rouiller v. Switzerland (2014)	International child abduction	Article 8
Moog v. Germany (2016)	Access	Article 8
McIlwrath v. Russia (2017)	International child abduction	Article 8

Source: Compiled by the author.

803 ECtHR, *Eski v. Austria* (Appl. No. 21949/03), 25 January 2007, para. 8.
804 ECtHR, *Sahin v. Germany* [GC] (Appl. No. 30943/96), 8 July 2003, para. 61.
805 ECtHR, *Süss v. Germany* (dec.) (Appl. No. 40324/98), 20 September 2001.
806 ECtHR, *C. v. Finland* (Appl. No. 18249/02), 9 May 2006, para. 49.
807 ECtHR, *Rouiller v. Switzerland* (Appl. No. 3592/08), 22 July 2014, para. 51; see also UNCRC General Comment No. 12 2009, para. 24.

In *Elsholz v. Germany* (2000), *Süss v. Germany* (2005) and *Rouiller v. Switzerland* (2014), the governments referred to the existence of written notes or minutes of the previous hearing of the child as the reason why the domestic courts did not consider additional direct participation of the child to be necessary.[808]

In *McIlwrath v. Russia* (2017), the government noted that the authorities had questioned the children several times and that the two eldest children had also submitted written statements to the domestic court.[809] The argument that there were no indications that the child had changed attitude since the last time he had participated enforced the argument of no need for additional participation in *Moog v. Germany* (2016).[810]

3.4. OTHER MODE OF PARTICIPATION NOT NECESSARY

In ten cases, the respective governments argued that an (additional) other mode of participation than the modes of participation employed during the domestic proceedings had not been necessary. The attributes of these cases are given below in Table 5.11.

Table 5.11. Attributes of cases in which the government argued that another mode of participation was not necessary

Grand Chamber judgment	**Type of proceeding**	**In response to complaint on**
Sahin v. Germany (2003)	Access	Article 8
Chamber judgments	**Type of proceeding**	**In response to complaint on**
R. v. Finland (2006)	Care and access	Article 8
Havelka and others v. Czech Republic (2007)	Care	Article 8
Kajari v. Finland (2007)	Access	Article 8
Glesmann v. Germany (2008)	Care and access	Article 6
M. and M. v. Croatia (2015)	Custody	Article 8
N.Ts. and others v. Georgia (2016)	Custody	Article 8
Iglesias Casarrubios and Cantalapiedra Iglesias v. Spain (2016)	Custody	Article 6
Chamber decisions	**Type of proceeding**	**In response to complaint on**
Kajari v. Finland (2006)	Custody and access	Article 8
V.S. v. Germany (2007)	Adoption	Article 8

Source: Compiled by the author.

808 ECtHR, *Elsholz v. Germany* [GC] (Appl. No. 25735/94), 13 July 2000, para. 64; ECtHR, *Süss v. Germany* (Appl. No. 40324/98), 10 November 2005, para. 49; ECtHR, *Rouiller v. Switzerland* (Appl. No. 3592/08), 22 July 2014, para. 49.

809 ECtHR, *McIlwrath v. Russia* (Appl. No. 60393/13), 18 July 2017, para. 112.

810 ECtHR, *Moog v. Germany* (Appl. Nos. 23280/08 and 2334/10), 6 October 2016, para. 66.

When governments contended that another additional mode of participation was not necessary, the arguments raised were at times formulated more generally and at times more specific in reference to the circumstances of the case. In the following, these arguments are all discussed per form of participation which was considered to be unnecessary.

In six cases, *direct participation* was not considered necessary by the governments. In the Grand Chamber judgment in *Sahin v. Germany* (2003), it was argued that there was nothing to show that direct questioning of the child would have been better than the approach taken, as the expert who had heard the child advised against a direct hearing in light of the serious feelings of guilt it might provoke in the child.[811] In *Kajari v. Finland* (2006), the government argued that the child had not been heard by the courts because children 'were in principle not heard in court'.[812] Instead, the child had been interviewed by the Social Welfare Board for its written opinion to the court.[813] In *Kajari v. Finland* (2007), the government reiterated this argument.[814] Similarly, in *R. v. Finland* (2006), it was argued that the social welfare authorities had been responsible for hearing the child and that it was thus within the limits of discretion of the national courts not to hear the child in person.[815] In *N.Ts. and others v. Georgia* (2016), the government asserted that as the eldest child had been provided a representative in the proceedings, direct involvement in the proceedings was not necessary.[816] Also, in *Iglesias Casarrubios and Cantalapiedra Iglesias v. Spain* (2016), the Spanish government argued that children's right to be heard by judicial authorities is not an absolute right in light of Spanish constitutional case law; thus, direct participation was not necessary as the children had been heard by psychosocial teams.[817] The government also argued that direct participation was not necessary as the examination of the children by psychologists was equivalent to an examination by a judge.[818]

In three cases, the governments argued that (additional) *representation* was unnecessary. In *Glesmann v. Germany* (2008), because the child was heard directly by the court, the government argued that it was not necessary to appoint a curator ad litem at an earlier point in the proceedings.[819] In *M. and M. v. Croatia* (2015), the Croatian government argued that neither the ECECR nor domestic law provided an obligation to assign the child an additional special

811 ECtHR, *Sahin v. Germany* [GC] (Appl. No. 30943/96), 8 July 2003, paras. 61–62.
812 ECtHR, *Kajari v. Finland* (dec.) (Appl. No. 65040/01), 14 February 2006.
813 ECtHR, *Kajari v. Finland* (dec.) (Appl. No. 65040/01), 14 February 2006.
814 ECtHR, *Kajari v. Finland* (Appl. No. 65040/01), 23 October 2007, para. 35.
815 ECtHR, *R. v. Finland* (Appl. No. 34141/96), 30 May 2006, para. 102.
816 ECtHR, *N.Ts. and others v. Georgia* (Appl. No. 71776/12), 2 February 2016, para. 64.
817 ECtHR, *Iglesias Casarrubios and Cantalapiedra Iglesias v. Spain* (Appl. No. 23298/12), 11 October 2016, paras. 28–29.
818 ECtHR, *Iglesias Casarrubios and Cantalapiedra Iglesias v. Spain* (Appl. No. 23298/12), 11 October 2016, para. 28.
819 ECtHR, *Glesmann v. Germany* (Appl. No. 25706/03), 10 January 2008, para. 75.

representative in addition to the guardian ad litem who was already appointed to her.[820] Lastly, in the *V.S. v. Germany* (2007) decision, the government argued that the situation in question, concerning the consent of the child for adoption, did not require the assignment of a curator ad litem as giving consent was of a strictly personal nature.[821]

Finally, in the last judgment, *Havelka and others v. Czech Republic* (2007), an *independent procedural position* was argued as not being necessary by the government, with the children's interests being represented by the social authorities in the proceedings.[822] The government considered that Article 6(1) ECHR did not provide children with a right to an independent procedural position in care proceedings.[823]

3.5. ARGUMENTS REGARDING THE USE OF EXPERTS

Governments in two cases considered the use of experts for children's participation in the strict sense, meaning that it concerned the use of an expert as a mode of participation and not arguments with regard to the influence on children's views (these arguments are covered in Chapter 8). Table 5.12 below presents the attributes of these two cases.

Table 5.12. Attributes of cases in which the government presented an argument regarding the use of experts

Grand Chamber judgment	**Type of proceeding**	**In response to complaint on**
Sahin v. Germany (2003)	Access	Article 8
Chamber judgment	**Type of proceeding**	**In response to complaint on**
L. v. Finland (2000)	Care and access	Article 8

Source: Compiled by the author.

In these cases, both governments focused on the value of the expert used in the national proceedings, with the Finnish government in *L. v. Finland* (2000) emphasizing that the child's 'own wishes' were determined in a child psychiatric investigation.[824] In *Sahin v. Germany* (2003), the German government emphasized that there were no doubts about the expertise and experience of the appointed expert.[825]

820 ECtHR, *M. and M. v. Croatia* (Appl. No. 10161/13), 3 September 2015, para. 124.
821 ECtHR, *V.S. v. Germany* (dec.) (Appl. No. 4261/02), 22 May 2007.
822 ECtHR, *Havelka and others v. Czech Republic* (Appl. No. 23499/06), 21 June 2007, para. 38.
823 ECtHR, *Havelka and others v. Czech Republic* (Appl. No. 23499/06), 21 June 2007, para. 38.
824 ECtHR, *L. v. Finland* (Appl. No. 25651/94), 27 April 2000, para. 117.
825 ECtHR, *Sahin v. Germany* [GC] (Appl. No. 30943/96), 8 July 2003, para. 61.

To conclude, governments justified the approach taken by domestic courts regarding child participation on the basis of a variety of arguments. These included the child's age or maturity, the child's best interests, and the fact that the child had been previously afforded the opportunity to express his or her views.

4. THE ECtHR

The ECtHR has considered the question of 'insufficient' participation in a large number of cases, either following the complaint of an applicant or on its own discretion. There are two main categories of findings by the ECtHR: that the 'insufficient' participation was indeed insufficient and not justified; or that the 'insufficient' participation was sufficiently justified. In these two main categories, various reasons were given by the Court. These reasons will be discussed after the general principles are introduced.

4.1. GENERAL PRINCIPLES

A number of general principles have been developed by the ECtHR regarding participation – some are specific and others more general. The starting point is a principle which is common to many areas of the ECtHR's reasoning: 'as a general rule it is for the national courts to assess the evidence before them, including the means used to ascertain the relevant facts'.[826] This general rule is relevant as it clarifies that the ECtHR has a subsidiary position. Within the framework of child participation, this means that the decision as to whether a child can participate and in which way is, in the first instance, one for domestic courts to make. The ECtHR subsequently tests these decisions in light of the procedural obligations and substantive rights protected by Article 8 ECHR (and on rare occasions Article 6 ECHR). In *Eskinazi and Chelouche v. Turkey* (2005), this general rule was supplemented by the Court noting that it is not its task 'to review the interpretation and application of the provisions in international conventions'. In both this judgment and *Maumousseau and Washington v. France* (2007),

[826] ECtHR, *Sahin v. Germany* [GC] (Appl. No. 30943/96), 8 July 2003, para. 73; ECtHR, *Sommerfeld v. Germany* [GC] (Appl. No. 31871/96), 8 July 2003, para. 71; ECtHR, *Gajtani v. Switzerland* (Appl. No. 43730/07), 9 September 2014; ECtHR, *Moog v. Germany* (Appl. Nos. 23280/08 and 2334/10), 6 October 2016, para. 81; ECtHR, *Maumousseau and Washington v. France* (Appl. No. 39388/05), 6 December 2007, para. 79; ECtHR, *Eskinazi and Chelouche v. Turkey* (dec.) (Appl. No. 14600/05), 6 December 2005; ECtHR, *Wildgruber v. Germany* (dec.) (Appl. No. 32817/02), 16 October 2006; ECtHR, *Gettliffe and Grant v. France* (dec.) (Appl. No. 23547/06), 24 October 2006; ECtHR, *Wildgruber v. Germany* (dec.) (Appl. Nos. 42402/05 and 42423/05), 29 January 2008 and ECtHR, *Döring v. Germany* (dec.) (Appl. No. 50216/09), 21 February 2012.

the interpretation and application concerned Article 13 of The Hague Abduction Convention and Article 12 UNCRC.[827]

The explicit recognition of the child's right to sufficient involvement in the decision-making process under the right to family life in Article 8 ECHR was first introduced in *M. and M. v. Croatia* (2015).[828] In that judgment, the ECtHR reiterated the parent's right to sufficient involvement in the decision-making process as an implicit procedural right under Article 8 ECHR.[829] It then went on to determine that, in light of Article 12 UNCRC on the child's right to be heard, this right to sufficient involvement applies *mutatis mutandis* to children in proceedings affecting their rights under the right to family life in Article 8 ECHR. Furthermore, the ECtHR specified that 'in such cases it cannot be said that the children capable of forming their own views were sufficiently involved in the decision-making process if they were not provided with the opportunity to be heard and thus express their views'.[830] This principle has subsequently been reaffirmed and applied in two 2016 judgments: *N.Ts. and others v. Georgia* (2016) and *E.S. v. Romania and Bulgaria* (2016).[831]

In the *M. and M. v. Croatia* (2015) judgment, the ECtHR also discussed the topic of personal autonomy and participation in that regard. According to the Court, the right to personal autonomy, which is contained in the right to personal life of Article 8, has a 'different scope in the case of children' compared to adults.[832] In reference to the UNCRC, the ECtHR noted that children lack the full autonomy of adults. However, the personal autonomy of children 'gradually increases with their evolving maturity, [and] is exercised through their right to be consulted and heard' provided by Article 12 UNCRC.[833] This principle on personal autonomy and the exercise thereof through the right to express views was also reaffirmed as a general principle in the *M.K. v. Greece* (2018) judgment under the right to respect for private life in Article 8 ECHR.[834]

In the *Mustafa and Armağan Akın v. Turkey* (2010) judgment, the ECtHR more generally noted with regard to the right to family life under Article 8 ECHR that in assessing the 'quality of the decision-making process', the Court

827 ECtHR, *Eskinazi and Chelouche v. Turkey* (dec.) (Appl. No. 14600/05), 6 December 2005; and ECtHR, *Maumousseau and Washington v. France* (Appl. No. 39388/05), 6 December 2007, para. 79.

828 ECtHR, *M. and M. v. Croatia* (Appl. No. 10161/13), 3 September 2015.

829 The right to sufficient involvement in the decision-making process for parents as an aspect of Article 8 ECHR has been examined in, amongst others, ECtHR, *Sahin v. Germany* [GC] (Appl. No. 30943/96), 8 July 2003 and ECtHR, *Sommerfeld v. Germany* [GC] (Appl. No. 31871/96), 8 July 2003.

830 ECtHR, *M. and M. v. Croatia* (Appl. No. 10161/13), 3 September 2015, para. 181.

831 ECtHR, *N.Ts. and others v. Georgia* (Appl. No. 71776/12), 2 February 2016, para. 78; and ECtHR, *E.S. v. Romania and Bulgaria* (Appl. No. 60281/11), 19 July 2016, para. 59.

832 ECtHR *M. and M. v. Croatia* (Appl. No. 10161/13), 3 September 2015, para. 171.

833 ECtHR *M. and M. v. Croatia* (Appl. No. 10161/13), 3 September 2015, para. 171.

834 ECtHR, *M.K. v. Greece* (Appl. No. 51312/16), 1 February 2018, para. 74.

must establish whether there was a 'sufficient evidentiary basis' for the domestic decisions and 'whether the interested parties, including the children themselves, were able to express their views'.[835] Similarly, in the *Zelikha Magomadova v. Russia* (2019) judgment, the ECtHR further clarified in its general principles that in assessing whether the reasons justifying the impugned measure were 'relevant and sufficient' for the purposes of the right to family life in Article 8 ECHR, 'the Court will also have regard to whether, where appropriate, the children themselves were able to express their views'.[836]

A general principle of the ECtHR on the direct hearing of children was first expressed in the Grand Chamber judgment of *Sahin v. Germany* (2003): 'it would be going too far to say that domestic courts are always required to hear a child in court on the issue of access to a parent not having custody, but this issue depends on the specific circumstances of each case, having due regard to the age and maturity of the child concerned'.[837] This principle was expressed within the scope of the right to respect for family life in Article 8 ECHR and was reiterated both in the Chamber judgment of *Iglesias Casarrubios and Cantalapiedra Iglesias v. Spain* (2016)[838] (albeit – surprisingly and unexplained – under the gambit of Article 6 ECHR) and the Chamber decision of *Gettliffe and Grant v. France* (2006).[839]

In the Grand Chamber judgment of *Sommerfeld v. Germany* (2003), an affiliated principle was expressed, again in consideration of the right to respect for family life in Article 8 ECHR. The ECtHR held that 'it would be going too far to say that domestic courts are always required to involve a psychological expert on the issue of access to a parent not having custody, but this issue depends on the specific circumstances of each case, having due regard to the age and maturity of the child concerned'.[840] The phrasing is almost identical with the principle expressed in *Sahin v. Germany* (2003), except that it concerned a psychological expert instead of the hearing of the child by a court. This principle was reiterated with reference to *Sommerfeld* in *Moog v. Germany* (2016), *Wildgruber v. Germany* (2006), *Luig v. Germany* (2007) and *Wildgruber v. Germany* (2008).[841]

---

835 ECtHR, *Mustafa and Armağan Akın v. Turkey* (Appl. No. 4694/03), 6 April 2010, para. 22.

836 ECtHR, *Zelikha Magomadova v. Russia* (Appl. No. 58724/14), 8 October 2019, para. 100.

837 ECtHR, *Sahin v. Germany* [GC] (Appl. No. 30943/96), 8 July 2003, para. 73.

838 ECtHR, *Iglesias Casarrubios and Cantalapiedra Iglesias v. Spain* (Appl. No. 23298/12), 11 October 2016, para. 36.

839 ECtHR, *Gettliffe and Grant v. France* (dec.) (Appl. No. 23547/06), 24 October 2006.

840 ECtHR, *Sommerfeld v. Germany* [GC] (Appl. No. 31871/96), 8 July 2003, para. 71.

841 ECtHR, *Moog v. Germany* (Appl. Nos. 23280/08 and 2334/10), 6 October 2016, para. 78; ECtHR, *Wildgruber v. Germany* (dec.) (Appl. No. 32817/02), 16 October 2006; ECtHR, *Luig v. Germany* (dec.) (Appl. No. 28782/04), 25 September 2007 and ECtHR, *Wildgruber v. Germany* (dec.) (Appl. Nos. 42402/05 and 42423/05), 29 January 2008.

It is noteworthy that in the latter decision, the ECtHR reiterated the principle referring to 'questions related to custody', which was seemingly broader than merely issues of access.[842] In the *Wildgruber v. Germany* (2006) decision, the ECtHR found the principle to apply equally to the appointment of a curator ad litem.[843]

The ECtHR presented a separate principle on child participation in the form of an independent right to intervene in criminal proceedings (on the non-execution of custody orders) in the Chamber decision in *Brillet v. Belgium* (2014). According to the Court, the right to respect for private life and family life under Article 8 ECHR cannot be interpreted as requiring domestic courts to recognize a right of children to intervene in proceedings which do not directly affect them, such as criminal proceedings against a parent.[844]

With these general principles in mind, the following two sections cover the specific reasoning of the ECtHR as to whether the (in)sufficient participation in a particular case was justified or not.

4.2. (IN)SUFFICIENT PARTICIPATION WAS NOT JUSTIFIED

In 11 judgments, the ECtHR agreed with the applicants' complaints that the lack of or insufficient mode of participation in the domestic proceedings was not justified. There are two main topics – the lack of directly hearing the child (see section 4.2.1) and the insufficient representation of children (see section 4.2.2) – and these will now be covered. In some cases, both topics were considered.

4.2.1. Lack of Directly Hearing the Child

In ten cases, the ECtHR found the domestic courts' lack of hearing the child directly not to be justified. In doing so, there are three common themes which can be identified in the reasoning: the age and maturity of the child (see section 4.2.1.1), the role of time (see section 4.2.1.2) and the lack of reasoning (see section 4.2.1.3). In Table 5.13 below, the attributes of these ten judgments are presented. In all these judgments, a violation of the respective ECHR article was found to have occurred.

---

842 ECtHR, *Wildgruber v. Germany* (dec.) (Appl. Nos. 42402/05 and 42423/05), 29 January 2008.

843 ECtHR, *Wildgruber v. Germany* (dec.) (Appl. No. 32817/02), 16 October 2006.

844 ECtHR, *Brillet and Brillet v. Belgium* (dec.) (Appl. Nos. 14942/11 and 17942/11), 16 December 2014, para. 37.

Table 5.13. Attributes of cases in which the ECtHR considered 'insufficient' participation not to be justified due to a lack of directly hearing the child

Chamber judgments	Type of proceeding	Conclusion
Sahin v. Germany (2001)	Access	Violation of Article 8
Haase v. Germany (2004)	Care	Violation of Article 8
Havelka and others v. Czech Republic (2007)	Care	Violation of Article 8
Jucius and Juciuvienė v. Lithuania (2008)	Custody	Violation of Article 8
Mustafa and Armağan Akın v. Turkey (2010)	Access	Violation of Article 8
M. and M. v. Croatia (2015)	Custody	Violation of Article 8
N.Ts. and others v. Georgia (2016)	Custody	Violation of Article 8
Moog v. Germany (2016)	Access	Violation of Article 8
Iglesias Casarrubios and Cantalapiedra Iglesias v. Spain (2016)	Custody	Violation of Article 6
Zelikha Magomadova v. Russia (2019)	Custody	Violation of Article 8

Source: Compiled by the author.

4.2.1.1. Age and Maturity of the Child

In five judgments, the lack of a direct hearing was unjustified according to the ECtHR, in part due to the children being of sufficient age and sufficient maturity. In all but one, the ECtHR subsequently found a violation of Article 8 ECHR. In the Chamber judgment in *Sahin v. Germany* (2001), the ECtHR noted that the child had 'at no stage in the proceedings' been heard directly by the courts.[845] The Court reflected that the domestic court had not done so as an expert had concluded that hearing the five-year-old child would have 'amounted to psychological strain'.[846] The Court found that the failure to hear the child revealed 'insufficient involvement' of the father in the access proceedings; the domestic court should have had 'direct contact with the child' and should have considered the possibility of hearing the child with special arrangements due to her young age.[847] In *Havelka and others v. Czech Republic* (2007), the Court found it regrettable that the children – who were 13, 12 and 11 years old – had not been heard directly by the domestic courts.[848] Similarly, in *Iglesias Casarrubios and Cantalapiedra Iglesias v. Spain* (2016), the Court saw no reason as to why the eldest child, who was 12 years old at the relevant time, had not been directly heard by the court of first instance, especially seeing as the domestic law

845 ECtHR, *Sahin v. Germany* (Appl. No. 30943/96), 11 October 2001, para. 46.
846 ECtHR, *Sahin v. Germany* (Appl. No. 30943/96), 11 October 2001, para. 46.
847 ECtHR, *Sahin v. Germany* (Appl. No. 30943/96), 11 October 2001, para. 47.
848 ECtHR, *Havelka and others v. Czech Republic* (Appl. No. 23499/06), 21 June 2007, para. 62.

required it.[849] The ECtHR subsequently concluded that the applicant mother had been unduly deprived of her right to have her children heard directly by the court without having a remedy available to contest the lack thereof, thus leading to a violation of the right to fair trial under Article 6 ECHR.[850]

In *M. and M. v. Croatia* (2015), the ECtHR was struck by the fact that the child had not yet been heard and that there was a delay in doing so because her maturity had to be assessed, even though, according to the Court, 'there was nothing to call into question the presumption that the first applicant – who was at the time twelve years old – was capable of forming her own views and expressing them', referencing in this regard General Comment No. 12 of the UNCRC.[851] Finally, the ECtHR concluded in *Zelikha Magomadova v. Russia* (2019) that the lack of hearing two of the children – who were 13 and 11 years old at the time – had been 'in breach of the relevant requirements of domestic law' requiring children aged 10 and over to be heard.[852] Additionally, the ECtHR criticized the failure of the domestic courts to seek an expert opinion as to whether the two other children could have been heard in court, even though they were younger than the legal age requirement.[853]

4.2.1.2. The Role of Time

A second theme raised by the ECtHR in its reasoning on finding the lack of a (additional) direct hearing of the children not to be justified concerns the role of time. The Court stressed the delays in *M. and M. v. Croatia* (2015), which led to the child not having been heard in the proceedings for more than four years, the delay of 19 months before steps were taken to determine whether the child had sufficient maturity to participate (as discussed above) and especially the fact that the situation was not resolved more quickly once the child had started exhibiting self-harming behaviour.[854] In *Moog v. Germany* (2016), the ECtHR noted that it was of the opinion that hearing the child again, obtaining new statements from a guardian ad litem or other options of ascertaining the views of the child would have produced relevant information for the child's present attitude, given that the previous declaration of the child, used by the domestic courts was made 16 months earlier.[855] The ECtHR thus concluded that the domestic

849 ECtHR, *Iglesias Casarrubios and Cantalapiedra Iglesias v. Spain* (Appl. No. 23298/12), 11 October 2016, para. 42.
850 ECtHR, *Iglesias Casarrubios and Cantalapiedra Iglesias v. Spain* (Appl. No. 23298/12), 11 October 2016, paras. 42–43.
851 ECtHR, *M. and M. v. Croatia* (Appl. No. 10161/13), 3 September 2015, para. 184.
852 ECtHR, *Zelikha Magomadova v. Russia* (Appl. No. 58724/14), 8 October 2019, para. 116.
853 ECtHR, *Zelikha Magomadova v. Russia* (Appl. No. 58724/14), 8 October 2019, para. 116.
854 ECtHR, *M. and M. v. Croatia* (Appl. No. 10161/13), 3 September 2015, para. 184.
855 ECtHR, *Moog v. Germany* (Appl. Nos. 23280/08 and 2334/10), 6 October 2016, para. 81.

court 'overstepped its margin of appreciation in reaching its decision without obtaining fresh statements by the parties involved'.[856]

4.2.1.3. Lack of Reasoning

In three of the judgments, the ECtHR concentrated not only on the lack of directly hearing the child, but also on the lack of reasoning given by the domestic courts for not allowing this mode of participation by the children involved. This theme is perhaps of a different nature, which is more procedural than the above two more substantive themes, but in these cases proves to be relevant.

The ECtHR noted in *Haase v. Germany* (2004) that the domestic courts provided no reasons to justify the urgency taken in the proceedings which led to the children not being heard.[857] Similarly, in *Iglesias Casarrubios and Cantalapiedra Iglesias v. Spain* (2016), the Court did not comprehend why the domestic court could not have given a reasoned decision when dismissing the request for the children to be heard directly.[858] Considering the domestic provision on the expression of the child's views and with reference to a variety of international standards on child participation – including the UNCRC and the guidelines on child-friendly justice – and the *M. and M. v. Croatia* (2015) case, the ECtHR in *N.Ts. and others v. Georgia* (2016) most clearly formulated this argument: 'the Court does not understand why the domestic courts failed both to give any consideration to the possibility of directly involving the older boy in the proceedings and to give reasons for not hearing him'.[859]

Not all ten cases in which the ECtHR criticized the lack of direct hearing fall under the three themes discussed here. In *Jucius and Juciuvienė v. Lithuania* (2008), the Court held that it was 'essential to the fairness of the proceedings' that the children (and their aunt and uncle – the applicants) were afforded an opportunity to be heard and fully participate so that their best interests could be ensured.[860] It is noteworthy that in this case, the applicants had not complained about insufficient participation; instead, they had focused their complaint on the weight granted to the expressed views of the eldest child, noting that the domestic courts had 'ignored her wishes', while domestic law had required these wishes to be taken into account.[861] Finally, in *Mustafa and Armağan Akın v. Turkey* (2010), the ECtHR found a violation of Article 8 ECHR because the domestic courts had 'failed to have due regard to the best interests of the family', amongst

---

856 ECtHR, *Moog v. Germany* (Appl. Nos. 23280/08 and 2334/10), 6 October 2016, para. 81.

857 ECtHR, *Haase v. Germany* (Appl. No. 11057/02), 8 April 2004, para. 97.

858 ECtHR, *Iglesias Casarrubios and Cantalapiedra Iglesias v. Spain* (Appl. No. 23298/12), 11 October 2016, para. 42.

859 ECtHR, *N.Ts. and others v. Georgia* (Appl. No. 71776/12), 2 February 2016, para. 80.

860 ECtHR, *Jucius and Juciuvienė v. Lithuania* (Appl. No. 14414/03), 25 November 2008, para. 31.

861 ECtHR, *Jucius and Juciuvienė v. Lithuania* (Appl. No. 14414/03), 25 November 2008, para. 24.

other things because the domestic court 'did not only fail to seek the opinion of the children but also failed to base its decision on any evidence' regarding the psychological problems caused by the siblings not seeing each other.[862] As in the previous judgment, there was no specific complaint by the applicants regarding insufficient participation.

4.2.2. *Insufficient Representation*

Four judgments in which the ECtHR found the insufficient participation no to be justified concerned the representative appointed to the children or the lack thereof. In Table 5.14 below, the attributes of these four judgments are presented. In all three judgments, a violation of Article 8 ECHR was found.

Table 5.14. Attributes of cases in which the ECtHR considered 'insufficient' participation not to be justified due to insufficient representation

Chamber judgments	Type of proceeding	Conclusion
Havelka and others v. Czech Republic (2007)	Care	Violation of Article 8
Nanning v. Germany (2007)	Custody and access	Violation of Article 8
N.Ts. and others v. Georgia (2016)	Custody	Violation of Article 8
Moog v. Germany (2016)	Access	Violation of Article 8

Source: Compiled by the author.

In *Havelka and others v. Czech Republic* (2007), the Court agreed with the applicants' complaint regarding the social welfare authorities who were wearing two hats, being the children's guardian ad litem and requesting the care measures at the same time.[863] The ECtHR found it regrettable that social welfare authorities were tasked with the conflicting role of being the children's guardian ad litem[864] – all the more so as the children were not given the opportunity to express their views directly.[865]

In *Nanning v. Germany* (2007), the ECtHR agreed with the German Constitutional Court in its criticism of the representation of the child before the lower domestic courts.[866] According to both, the child had 'not been properly represented by an independent curator ad litem', according to the facts because there had been no representative appointed at all.[867] In combination with the lack of a direct hearing of the child by the Regional Court, the ECtHR was not

---

862 ECtHR, *Mustafa and Armağan Akın v. Turkey* (Appl. No. 4694/03), 6 April 2010, para. 27.
863 ECtHR, *Havelka and others v. Czech Republic* (Appl. No. 23499/06), 21 June 2007, para. 62.
864 ECtHR, *Havelka and others v. Czech Republic* (Appl. No. 23499/06), 21 June 2007, para. 62.
865 ECtHR, *Havelka and others v. Czech Republic* (Appl. No. 23499/06), 21 June 2007, para. 62.
866 ECtHR, *Nanning v. Germany* (Appl. No. 39741/02), 12 July 2007, para. 75.
867 ECtHR, *Nanning v. Germany* (Appl. No. 39741/02), 12 July 2007, paras. 27 and 75.

convinced by the domestic courts' reasoning to exclude access and therefore found a violation of Article 8 ECHR.[868]

In *N.Ts. and others v. Georgia* (2016), the ECtHR examined the role and competences of the appointed representative at length. It began by noting that it had 'certain reservations' as to the role of the appointed representative for the children in the domestic proceedings.[869] The reservations were twofold. Firstly, the ECtHR remarked that the representative only became formally involved at the appeal stage, playing no role at first instance 'for unknown reasons'.[870] It then noted that the representative had 'the status of an "interested party"', a status which is not provided for in the Georgian Code of Civil Procedure.[871] Therefore, the ECtHR questioned how the children's interests could be 'effectively represented' if the representative had no 'formal procedural role' or procedural rights in the domestic proceedings.[872] Secondly, although the representatives were designated on the basis of an article in the Georgian Civil Code, the ECtHR found it 'ambiguous' as to what type of representation the legislation implied, in addition to it not being clear what the functions and powers of the representative were.[873] Considering the facts of the case, the Court noted that during the two years of the domestic proceedings, there were various persons from the Social Services Agency acting as representatives, meeting the children only a few times and only drafting reports on the situation of the children.[874] Referring to the international standards of the ECECR and the Guidelines on Child-Friendly Justice (GCFJ), the ECtHR concluded that the representation in practice could not be considered 'adequate and meaningful representation'.[875] Thus, this form of representation was considered to be insufficient participation.

Finally, in *Moog v. Germany* (2016), as discussed above, the ECtHR held that as 16 months had passed since the declarations of the child, obtaining new statements from a guardian ad litem or any other mode of participation would have been desirable.[876]

4.3. (IN)SUFFICIENT PARTICIPATION WAS JUSTIFIED

On the flipside of the argument that 'insufficient' participation was not justified are the ECtHR's conclusions in a range of judgments and decisions that the

---

868 ECtHR, *Nanning v. Germany* (Appl. No. 39741/02), 12 July 2007, paras. 74–78.
869 ECtHR, *N.Ts. and others v. Georgia* (Appl. No. 71776/12), 2 February 2016, para. 74.
870 ECtHR, *N.Ts. and others v. Georgia* (Appl. No. 71776/12), 2 February 2016, para. 74.
871 ECtHR, *N.Ts. and others v. Georgia* (Appl. No. 71776/12), 2 February 2016, para. 74.
872 ECtHR, *N.Ts. and others v. Georgia* (Appl. No. 71776/12), 2 February 2016, para. 74.
873 ECtHR, *N.Ts. and others v. Georgia* (Appl. No. 71776/12), 2 February 2016, para. 75.
874 ECtHR, *N.Ts. and others v. Georgia* (Appl. No. 71776/12), 2 February 2016, para. 75.
875 ECtHR, *N.Ts. and others v. Georgia* (Appl. No. 71776/12), 2 February 2016, para. 76.
876 ECtHR, *Moog v. Germany* (Appl. Nos. 23280/08 and 2334/10), 6 October 2016, para. 81.

(potentially) complained of 'insufficiency' was justified. In these 17 cases, the ECtHR concluded that there was no need for (additional) participation. With the general principles discussed above in mind, the ECtHR considered the facts of the case to determine whether participation should have taken place or should have taken place in a different manner. There are four ways in which the ECtHR concluded that the (lack of) participation in the domestic proceedings was sufficient and justified: the lack of directly hearing the child was justified (see section 4.3.1); no additional participation was required (see section 4.3.2); the child was sufficiently represented (see section 4.3.3); and a competent expert was used (see section 4.3.4).

4.3.1. The Lack of Directly Hearing the Child was Justified

In four cases, the ECtHR found the lack of a direct hearing to be justified. In Table 5.15 below, the type of proceedings and conclusions of the ECtHR in these four cases are presented. In all four, the ECtHR considered the complaint under the scope of Article 8 ECHR, finding no violation or the complaint to be manifestly ill-founded.

Table 5.15. Attributes of cases in which the ECtHR considered that 'insufficient' participation was sufficiently justified for the lack of directly hearing the child

Chamber judgment	Type of proceeding	Conclusion
Gajtani v. Switzerland (2014)	International child abduction	No violation of Article 8
Chamber decisions	**Type of proceeding**	**Conclusion**
Siebert v. Germany (2005)	Care and access	Article 8 complaint manifestly ill-founded
Eskinazi and Chelouche v. Turkey (2005)	International child abduction	Article 8 complaint manifestly ill-founded
Colombo and others v. Italy and Germany (2016)	International child abduction	Article 8 complaint manifestly ill-founded

Source: Compiled by the author.

In three of these cases, the lack of directly hearing the child was found to be justified because of the young age of the children. In *Eskinazi and Chelouche v. Turkey* (2005), the ECtHR found that the concerned child was too young at five years old to require direct participation in the domestic proceedings.[877] In *Siebert v. Germany* (2005), the Court agreed with the reason given by the domestic courts for not hearing the child due to her 'rather young age' of three

[877] ECtHR, *Eskinazi and Chelouche v. Turkey* (dec.) (Appl. No. 14600/05), 6 December 2005.

to four during the proceedings.[878] Similarly, in *Gajtani v. Switzerland* (2014), the Court found that the lack of directly hearing the younger child – who was aged five at the time of the proceedings – was not unreasonable, referring back to *Eskinazi and Chelouche v. Turkey* (2005).[879]

In the fourth case, the ECtHR found the lack of directly hearing the children to be justified, as the reason for the lack of a direct hearing did not lie with the domestic courts. In *Colombo and others v. Italy and Germany* (2016), the Court noted that the reason why the children had not been heard directly lay with the applicant mother herself, as she had obstructed the courts from obtaining the children's views.[880] In the domestic proceedings, the children had been represented through a curator ad litem.[881]

4.3.2. No Additional Participation was Required

The ECtHR in ten cases argued that sufficient participation has taken place and that no additional participation was necessary. This translates into two conclusions: either that an additional direct hearing was not necessary (see section 4.3.2.1) or that there was no need for a representative for the child because previous participation had occurred (see section 4.3.2.2). In Table 5.16 below, the type of proceedings and conclusions of the ECtHR in these ten cases are presented. In all judgments and decisions, the ECtHR found no violation of Article 8 ECHR or considered the Article 8 complaint to be manifestly ill-founded.

Table 5.16. Attributes of cases in which the ECtHR considered that 'insufficient' participation was sufficiently justified as no additional participation was required

Chamber judgments	Type of proceeding	Conclusion
Süss v. Germany (2005)	Access	No violation of Article 8
Kajari v. Finland (2007)	Access	No violation of Article 8
Maumousseau and Washington v. France (2007)	International child abduction	No violation of Article 8
Rouiller v. Switzerland (2014)	International child abduction	No violation of Article 8
Gajtani v. Switzerland (2014)	International child abduction	No violation of Article 8

(continued)

[878] ECtHR, *Siebert v. Germany* (dec.) (Appl. No. 59008/00), 9 June 2005.
[879] ECtHR, *Gajtani v. Switzerland* (Appl. No. 43730/07), 9 September 2014, para. 112.
[880] ECtHR, *Colombo and others v. Italy and Germany* (dec.) (Appl. No. 73708/10), 4 October 2016, para. 79.
[881] ECtHR, *Colombo and others v. Italy and Germany* (dec.) (Appl. No. 73708/10), 4 October 2016, para. 12.

Table 5.16 *continued*

Chamber decisions	Type of proceeding	Conclusion
Paradis and others v. Germany (2003)	International child abduction	Article 8 complaint manifestly ill-founded
Siebert v. Germany (2005)	Care and access	Article 8 complaint manifestly ill-founded
Wildgruber v. Germany (2006)	Access	Article 8 complaint manifestly ill-founded
Wildgruber v. Germany (2008)	Custody	Article 8 complaint manifestly ill-founded
Döring v. Germany (2012)	Custody	Article 8 in conjunction with 14 complaint manifestly ill-founded

Source: Compiled by the author.

4.3.2.1. An Additional Direct Hearing was not Necessary

The first conclusion of the ECtHR – that no additional direct hearing was necessary – was found in eight cases. In *Süss v. Germany* (2005), the ECtHR found the Court of Appeal's decision not to hear the child again to be justified, as the child had 'repeatedly expressed her will … in an unequivocal manner' and because not doing so would have subjected the child to 'the strains of another hearing'.[882] In the *Kajari v. Finland* (2007) judgment, the ECtHR responded to the applicant's 'grievance' regarding the lack of a direct hearing of the child by the domestic court by noting that the views of the child had previously been recorded in a report by the Social Welfare Board and shared with the domestic courts.[883] Similarly, in three Chamber decisions – *Wildgruber v. Germany* (2006), *Wildgruber v. Germany* (2008) and *Döring v. Germany* (2012) – the Court found that the domestic courts made reasonable decisions in opting not to hear the children again, either because a court in an earlier instance had already done so or because a guardian ad litem had done so not long before the decision.[884] The ECtHR specifically considered the children's interests not only in *Süss v. Germany* (2005), but also in *Rouiller v. Switzerland* (2014) and *Gajtani v. Switzerland* (2014), where it found that the national courts had sufficiently justified not hearing the children (in *Gajtani*, the elder child) as it would have had traumatic

882 ECtHR, *Süss v. Germany* (Appl. No. 40324/98), 10 November 2005, para. 97.
883 ECtHR, *Kajari v. Finland* (Appl. No. 65040/01), 23 October 2007, para. 43
884 ECtHR, *Wildgruber v. Germany* (dec.) (Appl. No. 32817/02), 16 October 2006; ECtHR, *Wildgruber v. Germany* (dec.) (Appl. Nos. 42402/05 and 42423/05), 29 January 2008 and ECtHR, *Döring v. Germany* (dec.) (Appl. No. 50216/09), 21 February 2012

consequences for them.[885] Finally, in *Maumousseau and Washington v. France* (2007), the lack of direct testimony from the child was not considered a violation of Article 8 ECHR because the child had been interviewed by experts previously and because 'in view of the child's age', taking direct testimony would have been 'non-decisive', the child being three to five years old during the proceedings.[886]

4.3.2.2. No Need for a Representative

In four decisions, the ECtHR saw no need for the appointment of a representative for the child, as the child had already been represented or heard in the proceedings. In *Paradis and others v. Germany* (2003), the Court found that there was 'no indication that appointing a curator ad litem was necessary in order to safeguard the children's procedural rights'.[887] This was after the ECtHR noted that the children were heard during the proceedings and their views assessed by an expert. It also noted the 'benefit of direct contact' between the domestic court and the children in *Wildgruber v. Germany* (2006), and thus found the decision not to consult a psychological expert and/or curator ad litem to be reasonable.[888] In *Wildgruber v. Germany* (2008), the Court also did not see the need for a guardian ad litem to 'assess the children's best interests and thus to safeguard the applicant's procedural rights under Article 8'.[889] Again, the ECtHR had mentioned the direct hearing of the children by the domestic court before coming to this conclusion. Subsequently, it also noted that as the applicant (father) and the mother had also been able to submit arguments on behalf of their children in the domestic proceedings, a guardian ad litem would not 'raise further issues not yet raised by the parties'.[890] This may also explain the connection to the applicant's procedural rights. In *Siebert v. Germany* (2005), the ECtHR found that the domestic courts' decision not to appoint a curator ad litem for the child did not reveal 'an insufficient involvement of [the applicant] in the decision-making process'.[891] Again, the procedural rights of the applicant parent were those concerned for the question of participation through a representative instead of those of the child herself. The ECtHR concluded that the failure to appoint a curator ad litem was not unreasonable, given that the Youth Office was heard throughout the proceedings as a guardian of the child.[892]

---

885 ECtHR, *Rouiller v. Switzerland* (Appl. No. 3592/08), 22 July 2014, para. 72; and ECtHR, *Gajtani v. Switzerland* (Appl. No. 43730/07), 9 September 2014, para. 111.

886 ECtHR, *Maumousseau and Washington v. France* (Appl. No. 39388/05), 6 December 2007, para. 80.

887 ECtHR, *Paradis and others v. Germany* (dec.) (Appl. No. 4783/03), 15 May 2003.

888 ECtHR, *Wildgruber v. Germany* (dec.) (Appl. No. 32817/02), 16 October 2006.

889 ECtHR, *Wildgruber v. Germany* (dec.) (Appl. Nos. 42402/05 and 42423/05), 29 January 2008.

890 ECtHR, *Wildgruber v. Germany* (dec.) (Appl. Nos. 42402/05 and 42423/05), 29 January 2008.

891 ECtHR, *Siebert v. Germany* (dec.) (Appl. No. 59008/00), 9 June 2005.

892 ECtHR, *Siebert v. Germany* (dec.) (Appl. No. 59008/00), 9 June 2005.

4.3.3. *Sufficient Representation of the Child*

In three judgments and decisions, the ECtHR found the domestic courts' approach to be justified with regard to the participation of the child because the child was sufficiently represented. In Table 5.17, the attributes of these three cases are shown. In all three cases, the ECtHR found no violation of the respective article or considered the complaint to be manifestly ill-founded.

Table 5.17. Attributes of cases in which the ECtHR considered 'insufficient' participation was sufficiently justified due to sufficient representation of the child

Chamber judgment	**Type of proceeding**	**Conclusion**
Glesmann v. Germany (2008)	Care and access	No violation Article 6
Chamber decisions	**Type of proceeding**	**Conclusion**
Paulsen-Medalen and Svensson v. Sweden (2003)	Care and access	Article 8 complaint manifestly ill-founded
Gettliffe and Grant v. France (2006)	International child abduction	Articles 6 and 8 complaints manifestly ill-founded

Source: Compiled by the author.

In two cases, the ECtHR noted that a representative for the child was appointed. In *Paulsen-Medalen and Svensson v. Sweden* (2003), it responded to the applicant's complaint that the child could not institute proceedings himself until he was 15 years old by referring to the representation of the child by a lawyer.[893] According to the Court, the views and interests of the child were adequately heard in the domestic proceedings in this regard. Subsequently, the Court noted that the child did not feel 'aggrieved by the existence of such procedural limitations';[894] therefore, it found the complaint to be manifestly ill-founded. In the *Glesmann v. Germany* (2008) judgment, the ECtHR, within the ambit of Article 6 ECHR, noted that the applicant's request for a 'curator ad litem to represent the child's interests' was fulfilled by the domestic court.[895]

A separate comment on the sufficient nature of representation was made in the *Gettliffe and Grant v. France* (2006) decision. The ECtHR again saw no reason to doubt the appointment of a lawyer for the child to express the child's views, nor did it doubt the professional competences of the lawyer.[896]

---

893 ECtHR, *Paulsen-Medalen and Svensson v. Sweden* (dec.) (Appl. No. 47411/99), 30 September 2003.

894 ECtHR, *Paulsen-Medalen and Svensson v. Sweden* (dec.) (Appl. No. 47411/99), 30 September 2003.

895 ECtHR, *Glesmann v. Germany* (Appl. No. 25706/03), 10 January 2008, para. 83.

896 ECtHR, *Gettliffe and Grant v. France* (dec.) (Appl. No. 23547/06), 24 October 2006.

4.3.4. *Use of a Competent Expert*

Finally, there are two cases in which the ECtHR commented positively on the competence of an expert appointed to determine the views of the child. The attributes of these cases are given in Table 5.18.

Table 5.18. Attributes of cases in which the ECtHR considered 'insufficient' participation was sufficiently justified due to the competence of the expert

Grand Chamber judgment	Type of proceeding	Conclusion
Sahin v. Germany (2003)	Access	No violation of Article 8
Chamber judgment	**Type of proceeding**	**Conclusion**
A.V. v. Slovenia (2019)	Access	Violation of Article 8

Source: Compiled by the author.

In the Grand Chamber judgment in *Sahin v. Germany* (2003), the ECtHR found no cause to doubt the competence of the appointed expert, which was disputed by the applicant, or the methods of the expert in interviewing the child.[897] In conjunction with the other relevant elements, it subsequently found no violation of Article 8 ECHR. In *A.V. v. Slovenia* (2019), the ECtHR agreed with the domestic courts that there was no need for an additional expert psychologist report, as there had been an expert psychiatrist report based on an interview with the children.[898] In this judgment, the Court did find a violation of Article 8 ECHR, but not concerning the child's participation as such.

4.4. DISSENTING OPINIONS

In a number of judgments, ECtHR judges delivered separate opinions discussing, amongst other things, the question of participation. Two of these dissenting opinions were attached to judgments previously discussed in this section – the Chamber judgment in *Sahin v. Germany* (2001) and the subsequent Grand Chamber judgment in *Sahin v. Germany* (2003)[899] – while two other dissenting opinions covered participation without the topic having played a role in the core judgment.

In the *Sahin* judgments, the dissenting opinions are diametrically opposed, just as the judgments themselves are diametrically opposed. In the Chamber

897 ECtHR, *Sahin v. Germany* [GC] (Appl. No. 30943/96), 8 July 2003, paras. 75–76.

898 ECtHR, *A.V. v. Slovenia* (Appl. No. 878/13), 9 April 2019, para. 85.

899 ECtHR, *Sahin v. Germany* (Appl. No. 30943/96), 11 October 2001; and ECtHR, *Sahin v. Germany* [GC] (Appl. No. 30943/96), 8 July 2003.

judgment, *Sahin v. Germany* (2001), the ECtHR held that there was a violation of Article 8 ECHR, as the lack of hearing the child led to the applicant's 'insufficient involvement', especially because the appointed expert had not questioned the child about the applicant.[900] However, Judge Pellonpää and Judge Vajić dissented, arguing *inter alia* that the domestic court had 'very correctly' asked for the expert's opinion on whether or not to hear the child again in light of potential psychological strain and subsequently deciding not to do so.[901] In the Grand Chamber judgment in *Sahin v. Germany* (2003), the ECtHR disagreed with the Chamber judgment and held that there was no violation of Article 8 ECHR. Two partly dissenting opinions were joined to the judgment. Judge Rozakis joined by Judge Tulkens partly dissented, disagreeing with the majority's decision not to find a violation of Article 8 ECHR. Judge Rozakis noted that the domestic courts' decisions 'were based on mere hypothesis', reaching conclusions 'without hearing the child at all' and without balancing all the interests at stake.[902] In the partly dissenting opinion of Judge Ress joined by Judges Pastor Ridruejo and Türmen, the judges also concluded that a violation of Article 8 ECHR should have been found. They considered that the applicant father was 'not sufficiently involved in the decision-making process' because the applicant's child had not been 'heard personally'.[903] Subsequently, the judges agreed with the Chamber judgment and underlined the conclusions made therein, noting that 'even if the will and the wishes of a 5-year-old girl cannot be decisive for the question of access, it would nevertheless have been important to know the child's answer to the question whether she would like to see her father in order for the expert to ascertain the child's true wishes'.[904] All in all, it can be concluded that the *Sahin* case left the ECtHR to some extent divided as to the need for direct participation by a young child. As we have seen above (see section 4.3.1) and will further consider in Chapter 7, in later judgments and decisions, the ECtHR has held that it was justified not to (directly) hear young children.

Two other dissenting opinions remarked on (the lack of) participation, even though the issue had not been raised by the applicant(s), the government or the ECtHR in the judgment. In *Kijowski v. Poland* (2011), Judge De Gaetano dissented, finding that there was a violation of Article 8 ECHR due to the lack of expeditious proceedings in the child custody case. Regarding the issue of

---

900 ECtHR, *Sahin v. Germany* (Appl. No. 30943/96), 11 October 2001, para. 47–49.

901 Dissenting opinion of Judge Pellonpää joined by Judge Vajić, ECtHR, *Sahin v. Germany* (Appl. No. 30943/96), 11 October 2001.

902 Partly dissenting opinion of Judge Rozakis joined by Judge Tulkens, ECtHR *Sahin v. Germany* [GC] (Appl. No. 30943/96), 8 July 2003, para. 1.

903 Partly dissenting opinion of Judge Ress joined by Judges Pastor Ridruejo and Türmen, ECtHR, *Sahin v. Germany* [GC] (Appl. No. 30943/96), 8 July 2003, para. 3.

904 Partly dissenting opinion of Judge Ress joined by Judges Pastor Ridruejo and Türmen, ECtHR *Sahin v. Germany* [GC] (Appl. No. 30943/96), 8 July 2003, para. 4.

participation, he noted that the case was 'almost surreal as to the length of time' that it took between the application in April 2008, the hearing of the child in court in April 2009 and the commissioning of an expert opinion in August 2009.[905] In this case, (in)sufficient participation was not raised, but the issues of due weight and age and maturity were, as will be discussed in the following sections. The second dissenting opinion is that of Judges Laffranque and Turković in *R.L. and others v. Denmark* (2017), who also noted the lack of participation by the children in light of the best interests of the children as not being parties to the proceedings and because the children's views were not discussed in the domestic court judgment. In doing so, they reiterated the ECtHR's repeated emphasis on the 'importance of the right of children to be heard and the need to take their views into consideration on matters which concern them in accordance with their age and maturity'.[906]

4.5. CONCLUSIONS ON THE ECTHR'S REASONING

All in all, a number of conclusions can be drawn from the ECtHR's reasoning on child participation. The first overarching conclusion is that child participation is accepted as a right of the child under Article 8 by the ECtHR – more specifically, under the scope of the right to respect for family life more so than the right to respect for private life, albeit that in *M. and M. v. Croatia* (2015), the ECtHR did recognize the child's right to participation as key to the child's right to personal autonomy and thus the right to respect for private life.[907] Article 6 ECHR has on occasion been the scope under which the ECtHR has considered (in)sufficient participation of the child, but this is not often the case.[908]

The general principles given at the start of this section show the ECtHR's recognition of the children's right to express their views in family law proceedings affecting them. The principles also clarify that the right to participate is not absolute; it depends on the circumstances of the case as well as the capability or maturity of the child. Therefore, when domestic courts decide not to grant children the opportunity to express views, their decisions should be properly reasoned.

---

905 Dissenting opinion of Judge De Gaetano, ECtHR *Kijowski v. Poland* (Appl. No. 33829/07), 5 April 2011, para. 4.

906 Dissenting opinion of Judges Laffranque and Turković, ECtHR, *R.L. and others v. Denmark* (Appl. No. 52629/11), 7 March 2017, para. 12.

907 ECtHR, *M. and M. v. Croatia* (Appl. No. 10161/13), 3 September 2015, para. 171, as later reaffirmed in ECtHR, *M.K. v. Greece* (Appl. No. 51312/16), 1 February 2018, para. 74.

908 See ECtHR, *Iglesias Casarrubios and Cantalapiedra Iglesias v. Spain* (Appl. No. 23298/12), 11 October 2016; and ECtHR, *Glesmann v. Germany* (Appl. No. 25706/03), 10 January 2008.

In the application to the facts, the ECtHR has held true to these principles. In the majority of the cases, it has agreed that children should have the opportunity – at least at one point in the proceedings – whether directly or otherwise, to express their views on the matter. This is exhibited clearly in the cases where the Court found the lack of participation to be unjustified and argued for participation when none had taken place. Also, when the ECtHR agreed with the domestic approach and found no violation regarding insufficient participation, most of the children concerned had been given an opportunity to express their views in the majority of cases. Only in three cases – *Eskinazi and Chelouche v. Turkey* (2005), *Siebert v. Germany* (2005) and *Gajtani v. Switzerland* (2014) – did the ECtHR accept that the child had no occasion to express his or her views. According to the Court, in these three cases, the very young age of the children justified the lack of participation.

Turning from participation as such to the modes of participation, the ECtHR seemingly accepted all the different modes – from direct hearings, to representation, to the use of an expert or other third party in conveying the views of the child. In many cases, the Court found no reason why the domestic courts should have employed other additional modes of participation than the mode of participation used in the proceedings. However, in a number of cases, the Court has been critical about the choices made by domestic courts as to which mode of participation to rely on or about the functioning of representatives. This signifies that at the outset, the ECtHR respects the discretion that domestic courts have in relation to child participation and the mode of participation used. Still, the Court will examine whether the participation has been sufficient in light of its own principles set out under Article 8 ECHR.

5. CONCLUDING ANALYSIS

Having considered the applicants' complaints, the governments' arguments and the ECtHR's reasoning on (in)sufficient child participation now brings us to the concluding analysis. Here the three sections are brought together in order to seek overall conclusions. After starting with the conclusions in numbers, we will delve into substantive conclusions. The following will be discussed: how to understand 'participation' as a right in the case law, how (in)sufficient participation can be determined and the factors that may play a role in that determination, and whether there is a relationship with the types of proceedings. Finally, the question of why the ECtHR does not always consider the topic, even when it is raised by applicants, is considered. These substantive aspects are relevant to determining and better understanding the standards set by the ECtHR (see section 6), as well as for the comparison with the other international and European instruments and the evaluation of how to align and strengthen the framework on the child's right to participate.

5.1. UNDERSTANDING 'PARTICIPATION'

The child's right to participation is not explicitly present in the text of the ECHR, yet the topic has been covered thoroughly in the case law. This calls for a consideration of what is understood as 'participation' by the ECtHR.

The general principles expressed by the Court consistently elucidate that the child's right to participate in family law proceedings is protected by Article 8 ECHR. Why it falls under the scope of Article 8 and not Article 6 ECHR is dealt with later on. The right to participation is protected by Article 8 ECHR through a number of approaches. To start with, the right of the child to express his or her views is covered by the right to family life under Article 8 ECHR as the right to sufficient involvement in the decision-making process in proceedings affecting a child's rights.[909] Additionally, the right to be heard is a key aspect of the child's right to personal autonomy according to the ECtHR and is covered by the right to private life.[910] Recently, the Court has clarified that in reviewing whether disputed domestic measures were 'relevant and sufficient' with regard to the right to family life under Article 8 ECHR, the question of whether children were able to express views should to be considered.[911] As a result, it can be argued that the right to participation has not been introduced in the case law as an independent right of the child; instead, it seeped into the rulings of the ECtHR when the Court reframed existing parental rights to also apply to children, including the right to express their views. In this regard, the child's right to participate provided by Article 12 UNCRC has played a role, being referenced in four of the five judgments in which these principles were expressed.[912]

This leads us to consider the fact that these general principles are drawn from cases adjudicated from 2015 onwards, while a large number of cases before this time also reviewed the topic of participation. In those earlier judgments and decisions, the ECtHR addressed the issue of child participation within the scope of the parents' rights. Taking the judgments in which the ECtHR found the insufficient participation not to be justified, there is an equal split between judgments from before 2015 and after. In two of those earlier judgments, *Sahin v. Germany* (2001) and *Haase v. Germany* (2004), the Court found the violation of Article 8 because the applicants – respectively the father and the

---

909 ECtHR, *M. and M. v. Croatia* (Appl. No. 10161/13), 3 September 2015, para. 181. See also ECtHR, *N.Ts. and others v. Georgia* (Appl. No. 71776/12), 2 February 2016, para. 78; and ECtHR, *E.S. v. Romania and Bulgaria* (Appl. No. 60281/11), 19 July 2016, para. 59.

910 ECtHR, *M. and M. v. Croatia* (Appl. No. 10161/13), 3 September 2015, para. 171. See also ECtHR, *M.K. v. Greece* (Appl. No. 51312/16), 1 February 2018, para. 74.

911 ECtHR, *Zelikha Magomadova v. Russia* (Appl. No. 58724/14), 8 October 2019, para. 100.

912 See ECtHR, *M. and M. v. Croatia* (Appl. No. 10161/13), 3 September 2015, para. 181; ECtHR, *N.Ts. and others v. Georgia* (Appl. No. 71776/12), 2 February 2016, para. 78; ECtHR, *E.S. v. Romania and Bulgaria* (Appl. No. 60281/11), 19 July 2016, para. 59 and ECtHR, *M.K. v. Greece* (Appl. No. 51312/16), 1 February 2018, para. 74.

parents – were not involved in the decision-making process to a sufficient degree.[913] This is clearly the original parental version of the right to sufficient involvement protected under Article 8 ECHR, which was later also recognized as a child's right in *M. and M. v. Croatia* (2015). Additionally, in both *Havelka and others v. Czech Republic* (2007) and *Nanning v. Germany* (2007), the ECtHR found a violation of Article 8 because the reasons adduced by the domestic courts were insufficient to justify the measures which interfered with the applicants' family life.[914] The children's lack of participation in both cases fed into the deficiency of the reasoning, again being of more concern to the interference of parents' rights than to the independent right of the children to express views or their independent right to family life. Since the *M. and M. v. Croatia* (2015) judgment, the focus has to a greater extent been shifted to the child's right. However, this has not meant that the child's lack of participation has no longer been considered in light of parents' rights. Take, for example, *Iglesias Casarrubios and Cantalapiedra Iglesias v. Spain* (2016), in which the ECtHR concluded that the applicant mother had been unduly deprived of her right to have her children heard directly by the domestic court without having a remedy available to contest the lack thereof, therefore leading to a violation of Article 6 and the right to a fair trial.[915] The ECtHR's recognition of the child's right to participation has therefore not yet been consistently adopted by the Court in its own case law. In part, this may be due to the fact that the complaints regarding insufficient participation are overwhelmingly brought by parents, a few times also on behalf of their children, and rarely also by children on their own behalf. This has likely skewed the reasoning of the ECtHR towards parents' rights, as it is their rights which must be evaluated. The subsequent twists and turns made by the ECtHR to address participation within the framework of the parents' rights, such as in *Iglesias Casarrubios and Cantalapiedra Iglesias v. Spain* (2016), has led to remarkable conclusions. Does the ECtHR really mean to say that it is a parent's right to have his or her child heard? If so, then the child may become a pawn in the game, unwillingly drawn into a conflict between parents. This is problematic, as the child should voluntarily be able to choose whether or not to express his or her views in proceedings. One would hope that the ECtHR actually means to say that a child's right to be heard can be protected within a parent's right to family life as an ancillary means of protection.

In order to fully understand the child's right to participation in the case law of the ECtHR, a remark must be made about the ECHR articles concerned. The general principles directly place the right of the child to express his or

[913] ECtHR, *Sahin v. Germany* (Appl. No. 30943/96), 11 October 2001, para. 46-47; and ECtHR, *Haase v. Germany* (Appl. No. 11057/02), 8 April 2004, para. 98.

[914] ECtHR, *Havelka and others v. Czech Republic* (Appl. No. 23499/06), 21 June 2007, para. 63; and ECtHR, *Nanning v. Germany* (Appl. No. 39741/02), 12 July 2007, para. 77.

[915] ECtHR, *Iglesias Casarrubios and Cantalapiedra Iglesias v. Spain* (Appl. No. 23298/12), 11 October 2016, paras. 42–43.

her views under the ambit of Article 8 ECHR, both with regard to the right to respect for family life and to the right to respect for private life. Additionally, the topic of participation has been discussed under the scope of the right to respect for family life of Article 8 ECHR in the majority of the judgments and decisions. It could be said that this is not an obvious choice. The right to a fair trial provided by Article 6 ECHR would appear, at first sight, to be more suitable in terms of providing the right to participate (or the parent's right to sufficient involvement for that matter) as it is in essence a procedural right. However, there are only three cases in which the ECtHR discussed child participation under Article 6 ECHR and there are no general principles tying the right to Article 6 ECHR. This is intriguing, but not completely unexpected, for two reasons. First, as the scope of Article 8 ECHR is constantly increasing, the inclusion of the child's right to participation under Article 8 ECHR follows this general trend of including procedural rights and protection within the substantive rights to family life and private life.[916] This leads to the second reason, namely that the topic of child participation is highly intertwined with the substantive topics in the case law of the ECtHR on family law proceedings. The question of a lack of child participation is rarely raised as an independent human rights breach, but is instead raised as a procedural shortcoming occurring simultaneously with the infringement of a substantive right – for example, a restriction of contact rights. This is largely because parents are most often the applicants raising child participation as a subcomplaint. Having the child's right to participation protected as an embedded procedural right under Article 8 ECHR instead of as an independent right under Article 6 ECHR is problematic to a certain extent, as it could make the violation of a lack of child participation dependent on the existence of a substantive violation. This diminishes the value of the child's right to participation as a right of the child. However, viewed from a pragmatic perspective, the child's right to participation as an embedded right under Article 8 ECHR does allow for more control by the ECtHR. Independent complaints by children focused solely on their lack of participation seem unlikely – or, in any case are likely to be rare – in the coming years.[917] Therefore, having the ECtHR address participation through Article 8 can be seen as a positive development, as it progressively strengthens the child's right to express views within family law proceedings, even where children are not the applicants.

Finally, in attempting to fully understand participation and the child's right to participate as provided by the ECHR, it must be considered on what children are asked to express their views. More specifically, are children asked to express a wish or preference as to the outcome of the proceedings or are they asked about the situation more broadly, including their views on their lives and relationships?

916 See e.g. Brems 2013, p. 138.

917 See also Chapter 4, section 6.2 on applicants in the case law analysis.

This question is not addressed in the case law, even though it should be, as it concerns the scope of participation. In addition, what children are asked when participating is relevant for the issue of the weight to be accorded to their views. Too little attention is given by the ECtHR to *what* children were given the opportunity to or asked to express views on– in future case law, this should be considered.

5.2. CONCLUSION IN NUMBERS

The topic of (in)sufficient child participation is a popular one for applicants, governments and the ECtHR itself. In 46 judgments and decisions out of the 88 analysed, the topic was raised and discussed. In Table 5.20, which is given at the end of this section, an overview is given of all the cases and in which section they have been discussed. This table shows that there have been different combinations. Taking a glance at Table 5.19 below, we see that in almost a quarter of the cases, the applicant, the government and the ECtHR reflected on the question of child participation, but that similarly, in another quarter of the cases, the applicants and governments (whether only one of the two or both) commented on participation without a response from the ECtHR. At the same time, there are 12 cases in which the ECtHR provided reasoning on the (in)sufficiency of participation without any impetus from either the applicant or the government.

Table 5.19. Number of cases in which the topic of (in)sufficient participation was discussed

Discussed by:	
Applicant only	3
Government only	8
Applicant and government	2
Applicant, government and ECtHR	12
Applicant and ECtHR	9
Government and ECtHR	0
ECtHR only	12
Total	46

Source: Compiled by the author.

What do these numbers show? Starting with the applicants, there are a significant number of complaints, especially compared to the other themes in the following chapters.[918] In 26 out of the 46 cases, the applicants complained that there was either a complete lack of child participation or that the participation which

[918] See Chapter 6, section 5.1; Chapter 7, section 5.1 and Chapter 8, section 5.1.

had occurred in the domestic proceedings was insufficient. The governments provided either a response to the complaint or their own comments on participation in 22 cases. This number is high, likely due to the amount of complaints, but also because of the general trend of granting attention to the question of participation.[919] Finally, in 33 judgments and decisions, the ECtHR concentrated on child participation in its reasoning. It is noteworthy that in 12 cases, this occurred without any complaint on the part of the applicant. This may indicate that child participation has become embedded in the independent review of the ECtHR when Article 8 ECHR is complained of more generally with regard to domestic proceedings. Why the ECtHR did not go into the complaints of applicants in six cases will be discussed at the end of this concluding analysis.

5.3. DETERMINING (IN)SUFFICIENT PARTICIPATION

The ECtHR recognizing the child's right to participation is significant, but it gives rise to the subsequent questions of when children ought to participate and how. In essence, where has the ECtHR placed the line between sufficient and insufficient participation in the examined case law and why? In section 4 on the ECtHR's reasoning we have seen that the Court found a violation with regard to the child's lack of or insufficient participation in ten cases. In contrast, it agreed with the domestic approach to participation in 16 cases. These numbers show that although not in the majority of cases, the ECtHR was relatively often in disagreement with the domestic courts' handling of participation, both with regard to the subsidiary role of the ECtHR as well as in comparison to the issue of the weight to be granted to the views of the child (see Chapter 6).[920] This may signify that the issue of child participation is judged more critically than the other topics covered in Part II in this volume, although a conclusion in that regard remains to be determined. There are four aspects of relevance that were identified in the ECtHR's reasoning in determining the issue of (in)sufficient participation, which will now be discussed.

5.3.1. Modes of Participation

The concept of participation is an umbrella for a range of modes through which children can express their views in proceedings concerning them. In the case law, a number of modes have been recognized: direct hearing, representation, the use of reports by experts (for example, psychologists or social workers), and litigation by the child. Before discussing these modes separately, some general conclusions should be made.

[919] See also Chapter 1, section 1.

[920] See also Chapter 6, section 5.2.

The most important general conclusion is that in its case law, the ECtHR does not appear to show any favouritism towards a certain mode of participation. There is no ranking of participation modes by the Court. While applicants frequently argued that a direct hearing should have occurred instead of other participation modes, the ECtHR does not as a rule place direct hearings above other modes of participation. Only in a number of cases did the Court find that a direct hearing specifically should have occurred, amongst other things because domestic law required it (e.g. *Iglesias Casarrubios and Cantalapiedra Iglesias v. Spain* (2016) and *Zelikha Magomadova v. Russia* (2019)). The lack of a ranking between the modes of participation proves the discretion afforded to domestic laws and domestic courts and the subsidiary position of the ECtHR. It also shows a pragmatic approach to participation. It is not so much a question of how to participate, but that a mode and opportunity to express views must have been present. This permissive stance of the ECtHR is constructive, as it allows states to develop their own practices regarding child participation within the minimum standards set by the Court.

This does not mean that the modes of participation are unrestricted with regard to how children can express their views. It is necessary that the mode of participation does actually allow for the child to express his or her views. Especially with regard to representatives, the ECtHR has detailed certain base requirements to ensure that the representative can effectively and meaningfully represent the children, especially in *N.Ts. and others v. Georgia* (2016). The representative ought to have a formal procedural role in the domestic proceedings with explicit functions and powers corresponding to its task. The ECtHR considers that representatives should preferably be one and the same person instead of various persons, and should maintain 'regular or frequent contact' with the children.[921] As per the ECtHR in *Havelka and others v. Czech Republic* (2007), in care proceedings it is key that the appointed representative is not the social welfare authority who is applying for the care measures.[922] This conflict of interests is not accepted. Additionally, the ECtHR has reiterated that representatives and experts are valid modes of participation insofar as they are competent, i.e. professional. Whether representatives or experts must meet other requirements, such as having an independent position or being qualified in a certain way, is not addressed by the ECtHR and has not been raised by any applicants.

5.3.2. *The Role of Time*

Another relevant aspect is the role of time, especially with regard to the question of additional participation. Additional participation concerns two aspects: whether

921 ECtHR, *N.Ts. and others v. Georgia* (Appl. No. 71776/12), 2 February 2016, para. 75.
922 ECtHR, *Havelka and others v. Czech Republic* (Appl. No. 23499/06), 21 June 2007, para. 62.

a different mode of participation was necessary (as discussed above) or whether in protracted proceedings children should be able to participate again.[923] The latter concerns the role of time and length of proceedings. Considering the cases regarding additional participation, the time between participation and potential additional participation appears to be relevant in the ECtHR's reasoning. In *Moog v. Germany* (2016), the child had not been heard again during the proceedings before the Court of Appeal.[924] This meant that a decision was made based in part on the child's views expressed 16 months earlier. According to the ECtHR, an additional hearing of the child was necessary in this case. In contrast, there are also a number of cases in which the ECtHR did not find an additional hearing to be called for. In these cases, the Court reasoned that previous participation had occurred, at times supplemented by the conclusion that an additional hearing would have been stressful for the child. In these cases, the length of time between previous participation and the point at which additional participation could have occurred was much shorter than in *Moog v. Germany* (2016). For example, in *Wildgruber v. Germany* (2006), less than five months had passed, as noted by the ECtHR.[925] In the six other cases, the range of time was between one month and 11 months, as could be (approximately) calculated from the facts of the case.[926] In all these cases, the views of the children had been ascertained within at least the last year – while in *Moog v. Germany* (2016), more than a year had passed. Therefore, it can very tentatively be said that although the ECtHR does not find it necessary for domestic courts to hear the child at all instances throughout the proceedings, if more than a year has passed, domestic courts should not rely on previously expressed views of the child and should arrange an additional hearing.

5.3.3. *Age and Maturity*

In all the case law of the ECtHR, the only accepted exception for an absolute lack of participation in domestic proceedings is the young age of the children involved. This makes age and maturity a very relevant factor with regard to participation. This topic will be extensively discussed in Chapter 7, but a few comments will also be made here.

---

923 For the applicants' complaints regarding the first aspect, see section 2.2.1, and for the second aspect, see section 2.2.2.

924 ECtHR, *Moog v. Germany* (Appl. Nos. 23280/08 and 2334/10), 6 October 2016, para. 81.

925 ECtHR, *Wildgruber v. Germany* (dec.) (Appl. No. 32817/02), 16 October 2006.

926 ECtHR, *Süss v. Germany* (Appl. No. 40324/98), 10 November 2005 (approx. two months); ECtHR, *Kajari v. Finland* (Appl. No. 65040/01), 23 October 2007 (approx. two months); ECtHR, *Wildgruber v. Germany* (dec.) (Appl. Nos. 42402/05 and 42423/05), 29 January 2008 (approx. 11 months); ECtHR, *Döring v. Germany* (dec.) (Appl. No. 50216/09), 21 February 2012 (approx. one month); ECtHR, *Rouiller v. Switzerland* (Appl. No. 3592/08), 22 July 2014 (approx. seven months) and ECtHR, *Gajtani v. Switzerland* (Appl. No. 43730/07), 9 September 2014 (approx. six months).

In the general principles on participation, the maturity or age of children is repeatedly noted as a condition for participation. The right to sufficient involvement for children is for those who are 'capable of forming their own views' and the right to personal autonomy – exercised by children through expressing views – 'gradually increases with their evolving maturity'.[927] Additionally, the question of whether domestic courts should directly hear the child or should appoint an expert to do so depends in part on 'the age and maturity of the child concerned'.[928] Besides the 'circumstances of the case', the age and maturity of the child is the only condition contained in these general principles. This condition did not materialize out of thin air – it is clearly taken from the phrasing of Article 12 UNCRC on the right to child participation.

The condition presents itself not only in the general principles, but also in the ECtHR's application of the principles to the case. On the one hand, the ECtHR has in a number of cases explicated that the domestic courts should have heard children because they fulfilled the condition of sufficient age and maturity. On the other hand, in some cases, the ECtHR accepted the domestic court's motivation for not hearing the child because of the young age of the children in question. The dividing line between sufficient and insufficient maturity will be further explored in Chapter 7. Nonetheless, the ECtHR's approach is to assume that a child should participate, and therefore domestic courts should always consider the possibility of hearing a child. Only when this is not feasible due to the young age of the child can it be justified not to do so. This is also emphasized in the *Zelikha Magomadova v. Russia* (2019) judgment, where the ECtHR stated that the domestic courts should have sought to find out if the young children could have been heard.[929]

5.3.4. *Reasoning and Justification*

In all the above three aspects and the case law on (in)sufficient participation, a common theme is the importance of adequate reasoning and justification by the domestic court as to why (additional) participation was not required.

In three judgments where insufficient participation was not accepted by the ECtHR, the Court explicitly criticizes domestic courts for insufficiently justifying the decision not to hear children.[930] With regard to the cases in which the insufficient participation was justified according to the ECtHR, there is no explicit discussion by the Court on the reasoning of domestic courts as such. However, in all those judgments and decisions, the ECtHR did follow the

[927] ECtHR, *M. and M. v. Croatia* (Appl. No. 10161/13), 3 September 2015, paras. 181 and 171.

[928] See, amongst others, ECtHR, *Sahin v. Germany* [GC] (Appl. No. 30943/96), 8 July 2003, para. 73 and ECtHR, *Sommerfeld v. Germany* [GC] (Appl. No. 31871/96), 8 July 2003, para. 71.

[929] ECtHR, *Zelikha Magomadova v. Russia* (Appl. No. 58724/14), 8 October 2019, para. 116.

[930] ECtHR, *Haase v. Germany* (Appl. No. 11057/02), 8 April 2004, para. 97; ECtHR, *Iglesias Casarrubios and Cantalapiedra Iglesias v. Spain* (Appl. No. 23298/12), 11 October 2016, para. 42 and ECtHR, *N.Ts. and others v. Georgia* (Appl. No. 71776/12), 2 February 2016, para. 80.

domestic courts' reasoning for the insufficient participation. In so doing and considered in combination with the three judgments mentioned above, it can be concluded that the motivation and justification for no (further) participation is relevant in the ECtHR's reasoning. The ECtHR requires domestic courts to at least consider additional or other modes of participation explicitly, but will often accept the domestic courts' decisions on the matter. This also demonstrates the subsidiary role of the ECtHR and the discretion afforded to domestic courts.

5.4. (IN)SUFFICIENT PARTICIPATION AND THE TYPES OF PROCEEDINGS

The cases analysed with regard to (in)sufficient participation have concerned all types of family law proceedings. The topics of the domestic proceedings range from custody and access to international child abduction and care proceedings. In the general principle regarding the child's right to sufficient involvement, the ECtHR speaks of proceedings 'affecting a child's rights under Article 8 ECHR'.[931] It does not further specify what types of proceedings these are, but following this analysis there do not appear to be any limitations with regard to family law proceedings.

Although a differentiation between the child's participation rights in different proceedings may have been expected, the analysis shows no distinction between any of the types of proceedings. In all family law proceedings, the child's right to participation is relevant and may be provided through any of the modes of participation. With regard to the aspects discussed above, there are also no significant differences between the types of proceedings. On the one hand, this is a positive conclusion because it ensures that at the level of the ECtHR's reasoning, there is no unfounded differentiation made between types of proceedings. On the other hand, justified distinctions may be warranted at the domestic level. For example, it could be argued that the nature of care proceedings in which parents and children are confronted with state measures which may separate them may require additional or other types of child participation than traditional family law proceedings such as custody and access proceedings.

5.5. NO PARTICIPATION DISCUSSION BY THE ECtHR

In five cases, there was no discussion regarding participation by the ECtHR, even though the applicants complained about (in)sufficient participation. In this section, the reason for the lack of response by the ECtHR is sought.

[931] ECtHR, *M. and M. v. Croatia* (Appl. No. 10161/13), 3 September 2015, para. 181. See also ECtHR, *N.Ts. and others v. Georgia* (Appl. No. 71776/12), 2 February 2016, para. 78; and ECtHR, *E.S. v. Romania and Bulgaria* (Appl. No. 60281/11), 19 July 2016, para. 59.

At times, the reason is straightforward and related to procedure. For example, in *Kuhlen-Rafsandjani v. Germany* (2011), the reason lay with the applicant, who opted to withdraw his complaint relating to the lack of participation of the children.[932] In *C. v. United Kingdom* (2004), the applicant had complained about the representative, but the ECtHR in the decision did not comment further on this complaint, as it was found to be admissible.[933] A subsequent substantive judgment never came, as the case was struck from the list due to a friendly settlement between the parties.[934]

The reason why the ECtHR does not discuss participation can also be substantive in nature. In *K. and T. v. Finland* (1999), the ECtHR did examine the complaint on the lack of hearing the children, as the applicants brought their complaint under Article 10 ECHR. This article concerns the right to freedom of speech, but that is a different form of speech from that meant by the parents, who should have brought the complaint under Article 8 ECHR if they had wanted a chance that the ECtHR would find their complaint admissible.[935]

Finally, in two judgments, *R. v. Finland* (2006) and *McIlwrath v. Russia* (2017), the applicants complained and the governments even responded to the complaints on participation.[936] And yet the ECtHR still did not respond. Why was this? There was no good reason for the Court not to do so. In *R. v. Finland* (2006), the ECtHR did not respond to the complaint as it fell under the topic of 'Access restrictions' and the ECtHR found a violation of Article 8 ECHR under the complaints on the reunification of the family, thus finding it unnecessary to examine 'as a possible separate source of violation' the other complaints.[937] The fact that the case was decided in 2006 could add to the explanation why the ECtHR did not find it necessary to separately address the complaints on participation. This is a shame, as the Court could have discussed the discretion available to domestic courts to hear a child directly or not. Similarly, in *McIlwrath v. Russia* (2017), the ECtHR found a violation of Article 8 ECHR as 'the Russian authorities failed in their duty to assist the applicant in addressing the claims he was making and thus to comply with their positive obligation under Article 8 of the Convention'.[938] Many aspects of the proceedings were discussed in that regard, but not the question of participation – seemingly, the ECtHR did not find it necessary to do so.

---

932 ECtHR, *Kuhlen-Rafsandjani v. Germany* (Appl. Nos. 21980/06, 26944/07 and 36948/08), 20 January 2011, para. 95.

933 ECtHR, *C. v. United Kingdom* (dec.) (Appl. No. 14858/03), 14 December 2004.

934 ECtHR, *C. v. United Kingdom* (Appl. No. 14858/03), 10 May 2007.

935 ECtHR, *K. and T. v. Finland* (dec.) (Appl. No. 25702/94), 8 June 1999.

936 ECtHR, *R. v. Finland* (Appl. No. 34141/96), 30 May 2006; and ECtHR, *McIlwrath v. Russia* (Appl. No. 60393/13), 18 July 2017.

937 ECtHR, *R. v. Finland* (Appl. No. 34141/96), 30 May 2006, para. 94.

938 ECtHR, *McIlwrath v. Russia* (Appl. No. 60393/13), 18 July 2017, para. 137.

Table 5.20. Combined overview for (in)sufficient participation

		Applicants' complaint:			Governments' argument:						ECtHR:								
												Not justified		Justified					
		Lack of participation	Insufficient or inadequate participation	No complaint	Insufficient age or maturity to participate	(Additional) participation not in best interests of child	Additional participation not necessary	Other mode of participation not necessary	Use of expert	No argument	General principles	Lack of directly hearing the child	Insufficient representation	Lack of directly hearing the child	No additional participation required	Sufficient representation	Competent expert	No discussion
GC judgments	*Elsholz v. Germany (2000)*	-	-	X	-	-	X	-	-	-	-	-	-	-	-	-	-	X
	Sahin v. Germany (2003)	-	X	-	-	X	-	X	X	-	X	-	-	-	-	-	X	-
	Sommerfeld v. Germany (2003)	-	-	X	-	-	-	-	-	X	X	-	-	-	-	-	-	-

Chamber judgments	*L. v. Finland* (2000)	-	-	X	-	-	-	-	X	-	-	-	-	-	-	-	-	X
	Sahin v. Germany (2001)	-	-	X	-	-	-	-	-	X	-	X	-	-	-	-	-	-
	Haase v. Germany (2004)	-	-	X	-	-	-	-	-	X	-	X	-	-	-	-	-	-
	Süss v. Germany (2005)	-	X	-	-	-	X	-	-	-	-	-	-	-	X	-	-	-
	C. v. Finland (2006)	-	-	X	-	X	-	-	-	-	-	-	-	-	-	-	-	X
	R. v. Finland (2006)	-	X	-	-	-	-	X	-	-	-	-	-	-	-	-	-	X
	Eski v. Austria (2007)	-	-	X	-	X	-	-	-	-	-	-	-	-	-	-	-	X
	Havelka and others v. Czech Republic (2007)	-	X	-	-	-	-	X	-	-	-	X	-	-	-	-	-	-
	Nanning v. Germany (2007)	-	-	X	-	-	-	-	-	X	-	-	X	-	-	-	-	-
	Kajari v. Finland (2007)	-	X	-	-	-	-	X	-	-	-	-	-	-	X	-	-	-
	Maumousseau and Washington v. France (2007)	-	-	X	-	-	-	-	-	X	X	-	-	-	X	-	-	-
	Glesmann v. Germany (2008)	-	X	-	-	-	-	X	-	-	-	-	-	-	-	X	-	-
	Jucius and Juciuvienė v. Lithuania (2008)	-	-	X	-	-	-	-	-	X	-	X	-	-	-	-	-	-
	Mustafa and Armağan Akın v. Turkey (2010)	-	-	X	-	-	-	-	-	X	X	X	-	-	-	-	-	-
	Kuhlen-Rafsandjani v. Germany (2011)	-	X	-	-	-	-	-	-	X	-	-	-	-	-	-	-	X
	Rouiller v. Switzerland (2014)	-	X	-	-	X	X	-	-	-	-	-	-	-	X	-	-	-
	Gajtani v. Switzerland (2014)	X	-	-	-	-	-	-	-	X	-	-	-	X	X	-	-	-
	M. and M. v. Croatia (2015)	-	X	-	-	-	-	X	-	-	X	X	-	-	-	-	-	-
	N.Ts. v. Georgia (2016)	-	X	-	-	-	-	X	-	-	X	X	X	-	-	-	-	-
	E.S. v. Romania and Bulgaria (2016)	-	-	X	-	-	-	-	-	X	X	-	-	-	-	-	-	-
	Moog v. Germany (2016)	-	X	-	-	-	X	-	-	-	X	X	X	-	-	-	-	-
	Iglesias Casarrubios and Cantalapiedra Iglesias v. Spain (2016)	-	X	-	-	-	-	X	-	-	X	X	-	-	-	-	-	-
	McIlwrath v. Russia (2017)	-	X	-	-	-	X	-	-	-	-	-	-	-	-	-	-	X
	M.K. v. Greece (2018)	-	-	X	-	-	-	-	-	X	X	-	-	-	-	-	-	-
	Petrov and X v. Russia (2018)	-	-	X	X	-	-	-	-	-	-	-	-	-	-	-	-	X
	A.V. v. Slovenia (2019)	-	-	X	-	-	-	-	-	X	-	-	-	-	-	-	X	-
	Zelikha Magomadova v. Russia (2019)	X	-	-	X	-	-	-	-	-	X	X	-	-	-	-	-	-

(continued)

Table 5.20 *continued*

		Applicants' complaint:			Governments' argument:						ECtHR:							
												Not justified		Justified				
		Lack of participation	Insufficient or inadequate participation	No complaint	Insufficient age or maturity to participate	(Additional) participation not in best interests of child	Additional participation not necessary	Other mode of participation not necessary	Use of expert	No argument	General principles	Lack of directly hearing the child	Insufficient representation	Lack of directly hearing the child	No additional participation required	Sufficient representation	Competent expert	No discussion
Chamber decisions	*K. and T. v. Finland* (1999)	X	-	-	-	-	-	-	-	X	-	-	-	-	-	-	-	X
	Süss v. Germany (2001)	-	-	X	-	X	-	-	-	-	-	-	-	-	-	-	-	X
	Paradis and others v. Germany (2003)	-	X	-	-	-	-	-	-	N	-	-	-	-	X	-	-	-
	Paulsen-Medalen and Svensson v. Sweden (2003)	X	-	-	-	-	-	-	-	N	-	-	-	-	-	X	-	-
	C. v. United Kingdom (2004)	-	X	-	-	-	-	-	-	X	-	-	-	-	-	-	-	X
	Siebert v. Germany (2005)	X	-	-	-	-	-	-	-	X	-	-	-	X	X	-	-	-
	Eskinazi and Chelouche v. Turkey (2005)	X	-	-	X	-	-	-	-	-	X	-	-	X	-	-	-	-
	Kajari v. Finland (2006)	-	-	X	-	-	-	X	-	-	-	-	-	-	-	-	-	X

Chamber decisions	*Wildgruber v. Germany* (2006)	-	X	-	-	-	-	-	-	N	X	-	-	-	X	-	-	-
	Gettliffe and Grant v. France (2006)	-	X	-	-	-	-	-	-	N	X	-	-	-	-	X	-	-
	V.S. v. Germany (2007)	-	-	X	-	-	-	X	-	-	-	-	-	-	-	-	-	X
	Luig v. Germany (2007)	-	X	-	-	-	-	-	-	N	X	-	-	-	-	-	-	-
	Wildgruber v. Germany (2008)	-	X	-	-	-	-	-	-	N	X	-	-	-	X	-	-	-
	Döring v. Germany (2012)	-	-	X	-	-	-	-	-	N	-	-	-	-	X	-	-	-
	Brillet and Brillet v. Belgium (2014)	X	-	-	-	-	-	-	-	N	X	-	-	-	-	-	-	-
	Colombo and others v. Italy and Germany (2016)	-	-	X	-	-	-	-	-	N	-	-	-	X	-	-	-	-

N = no arguments provided at all by the government because the complaint was not communicated to the contracting party, as is only required when the Chamber does not immediately declare the application inadmissible (see Rule 54 of the Rules of Court).

6. CONCLUSION: STANDARDS

The case law analysis on children's participation has brought to light various features of child participation. Building on this analysis and the themes recognized therein together with the general principles expressed by the ECtHR, a number of standards can be explicated for children's participation. These are the first set of standards provided in Part II of this volume and are labelled using 'P' to clarify that these standards concern participation.

> P.1 The child has the right to express his or her views in family law proceedings under Article 8 ECHR through the right to sufficient involvement in the decision-making process and the right to personal autonomy.

This first standard is based on the general principles expressed by the ECtHR in *M. and M. v. Croatia* (2015), explicitly reaffirmed in *N.Ts. and others v. Georgia* (2016), *E.S. v. Romania and Bulgaria* (2016) and *M.K. v. Greece* (2018).[939] In this case law, the child's right to express his or her views in family law proceedings has been recognized as falling under the scope and protection of Article 8 ECHR. On the one hand, the right to family life includes the right to sufficient involvement in the decision-making process for children themselves in addition to their parents. On the other hand, under the right to private life, the different scope of children's right to personal autonomy contains the child's right to express his or her views. These aspects combined and the factual consideration of the ECtHR in the absolute majority of cases clarifies that the child's right to participation is protected by Article 8 ECHR. More specifically, the ECtHR in most cases considers the participation of children under the scope of Article 8 ECHR's right to family life. The case law analysis has also shown that this right concerns all family law proceedings affecting the child's rights under Article 8 ECHR without distinction.

> P.2 The child has the right to express views, but this right is not absolute. Whether domestic courts are required to hear a child, appoint a representative or involve another expert in family law proceedings depends on the specific circumstances of each case, having due regard to the age and maturity of the child concerned.

This standard contains various facets and therefore also draws on multiple aspects from the analysis. First, the standard specifies that the child has the right to express his or her views – as also clarified in the first standard – but that this is not an absolute right. The case law has shown that the starting point is that a

---

[939] ECtHR, *M. and M. v. Croatia* (Appl. No. 10161/13), 3 September 2015, paras. 171 and 181; ECtHR, *N.Ts. and others v. Georgia* (Appl. No. 71776/12), 2 February 2016, para. 78; ECtHR, *E.S. v. Romania and Bulgaria* (Appl. No. 60281/11), 19 July 2016, para. 59 and ECtHR, *M.K. v. Greece* (Appl. No. 51312/16), 1 February 2018, para. 74.

child should be able to express his or her views in the proceedings one way or another. However, the right is not absolute as the age and maturity of the child or other circumstances may give domestic courts a reason not to offer a child the opportunity to express his or her views.

The second sentence of the standard has been expressed in similar but varying phrases by the ECtHR. In *Sahin v. Germany* (2003), it was stated with regard to hearing children in court for access proceedings – later reiterated in *Iglesias Casarrubios and Cantalapiedra Iglesias v. Spain* (2016) and *Gettliffe and Grant v. France* (2006).[940] In *Sommerfeld v. Germany* (2003), the principle was expressed regarding the use of a psychological expert in access proceedings, later reaffirmed and broadened to include custody proceedings more broadly in *Moog v. Germany* (2016), *Wildgruber v. Germany* (2006), *Luig v. Germany* (2007) and *Wildgruber v. Germany* (2008).[941] Finally, in *Wildgruber v. Germany* (2006), the principle was also expressed regarding representation by a curator ad litem.[942] Taking all these cases and considering the facts of other cases considered by the ECtHR, this standard has been phrased as including all modes of participation and all types of family law proceedings.

The standard concludes with a reference to the age and maturity of the child. This is drawn from the above principles, but is also seen more broadly in the case law as the single exception accepted by the ECtHR for a complete lack of participation by the child. This factor will therefore also be further discussed in Chapter 7.

> P.3 In deciding on the participation of the child, domestic courts should adequately reason and justify their decisions.

The third standard emphasizes the importance for the domestic courts to reason and justify their decisions when they decide against giving a child an (additional) opportunity to participate in proceedings or decide against a certain mode of participation. The standard is tied to the previous standard, as it requires domestic courts to clarify the relevant circumstances and the age and maturity of the child when opting not to provide him or her with an opportunity to express his or her views. A lack of reasoning can lead to criticism from the ECtHR, as was the case in *Haase v. Germany* (2004), *Iglesias Casarrubios and*

---

940 ECtHR, *Sahin v. Germany* [GC] (Appl. No. 30943/96), 8 July 2003, para. 73; ECtHR, *Iglesias Casarrubios and Cantalapiedra Iglesias v. Spain* (Appl. No. 23298/12), 11 October 2016, para. 36 and ECtHR, *Gettliffe and Grant v. France* (dec.) (Appl. No. 23547/06), 24 October 2006.

941 ECtHR, *Sommerfeld v. Germany* [GC] (Appl. No. 31871/96), 8 July 2003, para. 71; ECtHR, *Moog v. Germany* (Appl. Nos. 23280/08 and 2334/10), 6 October 2016, para. 78; ECtHR, *Wildgruber v. Germany* (dec.) (Appl. No. 32817/02), 16 October 2006; ECtHR, *Luig v. Germany* (dec.) (Appl. No. 28782/04), 25 September 2007 and ECtHR, *Wildgruber v. Germany* (dec.) (Appl. Nos. 42402/05 and 42423/05), 29 January 2008.

942 ECtHR, *Wildgruber v. Germany* (dec.) (Appl. No. 32817/02), 16 October 2006.

Cantalapiedra Iglesias v. Spain (2016) and *N.Ts. and others v. Georgia* (2016). As the ECtHR has a subsidiary role, if domestic courts adequately justify their decision, the ECtHR is more likely to accept the decision as falling within their discretion.

P.4 In general, a child has no right to repeatedly participate in domestic proceedings unless the duration of domestic proceedings are drawn-out, then additional participation should be considered by the domestic courts.

The fourth standard concerns the question of additional participation in proceedings that are lengthy. In the case law, the ECtHR considered whether additional and repeated participation was required in proceedings that lasted a longer period of time and different court instances. An extended period of time, such as the 16 months between a decision and the previous hearing of the child in *Moog v. Germany* (2016), can require additional participation of the child.[943] However, this is dependent on the circumstances of the case, both in terms of the length of time concerned and the interests of the child, as the ECtHR has also agreed with domestic courts that it may not be in the interests of the child to have to express his or her views again.

P.5 If a representative is appointed to the child, the representation should be adequate and meaningful. The representative should have an unambiguous procedural role.

The final standard specifically addresses representation as a mode of participation. The standard is based on *N.Ts. and others v. Georgia* (2016), in which the ECtHR was critical of the status, function, task and powers of the representative appointed to the children.[944] The ECtHR clarified that adequate and meaningful representation should have been the goal. The representative should have a formal procedural role and procedural rights in the proceedings. Additionally, the task, function and powers of the representative should be clear, with sufficient communication between the representative and the children. In care proceedings, the representative should not pursue conflicting interests, as was the case in *Havelka and others v. Czech Republic* (2007), where the social welfare authority requested the care measures and was tasked with representing the children.[945] In the earlier decision of *Gettliffe and Grant v. France* (2006), the professional competence of a lawyer as a representative was accepted by the ECtHR as providing a sufficient opportunity to the child to express his or her views.[946]

---

943 ECtHR, *Moog v. Germany* (Appl. Nos. 23280/08 and 2334/10), 6 October 2016, para. 81.
944 ECtHR, *N.Ts. and others v. Georgia* (Appl. No. 71776/12), 2 February 2016, paras. 74–75.
945 ECtHR, *Havelka and others v. Czech Republic* (Appl. No. 23499/06), 21 June 2007, para. 62.
946 ECtHR, *Gettliffe and Grant v. France* (dec.) (Appl. No. 23547/06), 24 October 2006.

CHAPTER 6
WEIGHT ACCORDED TO THE CHILD'S VIEWS

'The right of a child to express his or her own views should not be interpreted as effectively giving an unconditional veto power to children ...'

– ECtHR, *K.B. and others v. Croatia* (2017)[947]

1. INTRODUCTION

Once a child has been given the opportunity to express his or her views in a family law proceeding, a court is tasked with deciding on the matter and, in doing so, must take into account the views of the children. In the process of child participation, giving due weight to the views of the child is the second step following the child's participation or, more precisely, expression of views. The topic of according weight to the child's views is equally important as the topic of (in)sufficient participation addressed in the previous chapter, even though it is a subsequent step. Without participation, according weight is not possible, but without according weight to the views of the child, participation is simply the expression of views, not being 'heard'. As stipulated by Article 12 of the United Nations Convention on the Rights of the Child (UNCRC), due weight has to be given to the child's views.[948]

What is meant by 'due weight' and how should weight be accorded to a child's views in family law proceedings? This chapter examines these questions within the European Court of Human Rights (ECtHR) case law. Various perspectives are addressed: the complaints applicants raise with regard to the weight granted to the child's views; the manner in which governments stand by the decisions taken domestically; and the reasoning of the ECtHR regarding the weight accorded to children's views. The latter is especially important in answering the question of whether and how due weight should be accorded to a child's views in family law proceedings. Bundling together the ECtHR's consideration of various cases, each

[947] ECtHR, *K.B. and others v. Croatia* (Appl. No. 36216/13), 14 March 2017, para. 143.
[948] See also Chapter 2, section 3.1.1.5.

with differing circumstances, provides the necessary information to determine the standards set by the Court. These standards will add to the international and European framework, and a clear and comprehensive understanding of them will assist in aligning and strengthening this framework. The quote above is a first example of this, as it shows the ECtHR unequivocally stating that the child's right to participate does not mean that children are granted a veto power. If a child's views are not to be granted unconditional decisive weight, then the question is how much weight is *due* weight.

In this chapter, the complaints by applicants, remarks by governments and conclusions by the ECtHR on the amount of weight accorded to the views of the children will be discussed. In total, 59 judgments and decisions are discussed in the following section. By considering the complaints and the governments' responses in addition to the ECtHR's reasoning, this analysis provides an insight into possible factors relevant for due weight. As we will see, the topics of maturity and influence, which will be addressed in the next two chapters, are also relevant factors for due weight. Equally, the relationship between due weight and participation, as introduced above, will be considered in this chapter. At the end of the chapter, conclusions will be drawn in relation to the existing standards and an overview table will be given.

2. COMPLAINTS BROUGHT BY APPLICANTS

In 17 cases, applicants alleging a violation of Article 6 or 8 of the European Convention on Human Rights (ECHR) made a complaint regarding the weight accorded by domestic authorities to the views of the child. Applicants complain in one of two ways: either that too much weight was accorded to the child's views or that more weight should have been accorded.

2.1. TOO MUCH WEIGHT ACCORDED TO THE CHILD'S VIEWS

There are ten judgments and decisions in which the applicants complained that too much weight was accorded to the views of the child. These complaints can be further split into two types of complaints. The first type are general, with applicants noting that too much weight was accorded to the views of the child. The second type also concern too much weight, but the applicants were explicit in arguing that *exclusive* weight should not have been given to the views of the child. This is one step further than too much weight, as the applicants noted that the decisions were based exclusively on the child's views. The attributes of these ten cases are presented in Table 6.1 below. Notably, there were more fathers complaining about an unreasonable weight accorded to the child's views, which presumably reflects the gender dimension present in custody and access cases.

Table 6.1. Attributes of cases in which the applicant complained of unreasonable weight being accorded to the child's views

Grand Chamber judgment	**Type of proceeding**	**Applicant**	**Article of complaint**
Elsholz v. Germany (2000)	Access	Father	Article 8
Chamber judgments	**Type of proceeding**	**Applicant**	**Article of complaint**
Kosmopoulou v. Greece (2004)	Access	Mother	Article 8
Süss v. Germany (2005)	Access	Father	Article 6(1)
C. v. Finland (2006)	Custody and access	Father	Article 8
R. v. Finland (2006)	Care and access	Father	Article 8
Płaza v. Poland (2011)	Access	Father	Article 8
Blaga v. Romania (2014)	International child abduction	Father	Articles 6, 8, 14, 17 and 18, Article 1, Protocol No. 12, and Article 5, Protocol No. 7
G.B. v. Lithuania (2016)	Custody	Mother	Article 8
Khusnutdinov and X v. Russia (2018)	Custody	Father, also on behalf of child	Article 8
Chamber decision	**Type of proceeding**	**Applicant**	**Article of complaint**
W.F. v. Italy (2001)	Care	Father	Article 8

Source: Compiled by the author.

2.1.1. Too Much Weight

There are four cases in which the applicants complained more generally that too much weight was granted to the views of the child. In the Grand Chamber judgment in *Elsholz v. Germany* (2000), the applicant contested that the German courts of appeal 'attached considerable importance to the will of a child of this age' and thus that the courts were not likely to grant the applicant access when it was against the child's will.[949] The applicant further tied this to the question of influence over the child's views. In a similar vein, in *W.F. v. Italy* (2001), the applicant father argued that the child was manipulated and that even if the views expressed had been the child's own strong wishes, the authorities should not have given weight to these wishes.[950] Likewise, the applicant in *Süss v. Germany* (2005) alleged that the court of appeal was biased because of the importance placed on the views of the child, even though the applicant asserted that the child was influenced by her mother.[951] In *Płaza v. Poland* (2011), the applicant found the weight granted to the child's refusals to be inconsistent with the 'obligation

[949] ECtHR, *Elsholz v. Germany* [GC] (Appl. No. 25735/94), 13 July 2000, para. 31.
[950] ECtHR, *W.F. v. Italy* (Appl. No. 34803/97), 5 April 2001.
[951] ECtHR, *Süss v. Germany* (Appl. No. 40324/98), 10 November 2005, para. 108.

of the authorities to execute judicial decisions and judgments', which according to the applicant was a denial of the rule of law.[952]

2.1.2. Exclusive Weight

In the following six judgments, the applicants also complained of too much weight being granted to the child's views and specifically alleged that the child's views were given exclusive weight as the sole factor in the domestic decisions. In *Kosmopoulou v. Greece* (2004), the applicant recognized that the child's wishes had been thoroughly examined and taken into account, but argued that 'those views should not have been decisive' in determining whether to enforce her visiting rights.[953] The child's views had already been considered in the substantive proceedings, so the applicant argued that they should not have been reconsidered at the point of enforcement.[954] In *C. v. Finland* (2006), the applicant explicitly complained both that 'the court accorded an unreasonable weight to the opinion and age of the children' and that 'while the child's views had to be taken into account, they did not have to be regarded as decisive'.[955] As in *Elsholz* and *Süss*, this applicant also raised the issue of influence in this regard.[956] Another Finnish case, *R. v. Finland* (2006), saw the applicant complain about the fact that the restrictions to his access rights while the child was in care were 'entirely based' on the child's views, additionally noting that these views 'had not been properly and reliably examined'.[957] The applicant in *Blaga v. Romania* (2014) brought the complaint of the national courts 'exclusively' relying on the children's views under a great number of Articles (6, 8, 14, 17 and 18 and Article 1, Protocol No. 12 and Article 1, Protocol No. 7).[958] In *G.B. v. Lithuania* (2016), the applicant argued that 'although a child's opinion was very important, it was not a determining factor'.[959] The applicant submitted that 'a child's wishes could not be considered when they were against his or her best interests' and that the domestic courts should have given more weight to the psychological state of the children, arguing that the children had developed parental alienation syndrome.[960] Finally, in *Khusnutdinov and X v. Russia* (2018), the applicants

---

952 ECtHR, *Płaza v. Poland* (Appl. No. 18830/07), 25 January 2011, para. 69.
953 ECtHR, *Kosmopoulou v. Greece* (Appl. No. 60457/00), 5 February 2004, para. 36.
954 ECtHR, *Kosmopoulou v. Greece* (Appl. No. 60457/00), 5 February 2004, para. 36.
955 ECtHR, *C. v. Finland* (Appl. No. 18249/02), 9 May 2006, para. 43.
956 ECtHR, *C. v. Finland* (Appl. No. 18249/02), 9 May 2006, para. 43.
957 ECtHR, *R. v. Finland* (Appl. No. 34141/96), 30 May 2006, para. 69.
958 ECtHR, *Blaga v. Romania* (Appl. No. 54443/10), 1 July 2014, para. 55. The ECtHR characterized the complaint as falling under Article 8 ECHR; see para. 56.
959 ECtHR, *G.B. v. Lithuania* (Appl. No. 36137/13), 19 January 2016, para. 74.
960 ECtHR, *G.B. v. Lithuania* (Appl. No. 36137/13), 19 January 2016, para. 74.

complained that the domestic courts 'should not have established [child]'s best interests on the basis of her opinion alone'.[961] The applicants referred to other relevant factors which were disregarded when determining the child's best interests, such as the influence of the grandparents.[962]

2.2. TOO LITTLE WEIGHT ACCORDED TO THE CHILD'S VIEWS

Contrary to the complaints described above, there are also applicants who complained that the domestic authorities either failed to take into account or insufficiently took into account the child's views. In these five Chamber judgments and two decisions, the applicants argued that more weight should have been accorded to the child's views. The attributes of these cases are presented in Table 6.2 below.

Table 6.2. Attributes of cases in which the applicant complained that the child's views were accorded too little weight

Chamber judgments	**Type of proceeding**	**Applicant**	**Article of complaint**
Jucius and Juciuvienė v. Lithuania (2008)	Custody	Aunt and uncle	Article 8
Z.J. v. Lithuania (2014)	Custody	Father	Article 8
Rouiller v. Switzerland (2014)	International child abduction	Mother	Article 8
Gajtani v. Switzerland (2014)	International child abduction	Mother	Article 8
N.Ts. and others v. Georgia (2016)	Custody	Aunt on behalf of children	Article 8
Chamber decisions	**Type of proceeding**	**Applicant**	**Article of complaint**
Tiemann v. France and Germany (2000)	International child abduction	Father	Article 8
Brede v. Germany (2009)	Care	Mother	Article 8

Source: Compiled by the author.

In the Chamber judgment in *Jucius and Juciuvienė v. Lithuania* (2008), the applicants complained that the domestic district court had awarded custody to the grandparents without reason, contending that the child had 'expressed her clear wish to stay with the applicants', but that these wishes had been 'ignored'.[963]

961 ECtHR, *Khusnutdinov and X v. Russia* (Appl. No. 76598/12), 18 December 2018, para. 70.
962 ECtHR, *Khusnutdinov and X v. Russia* (Appl. No. 76598/12), 18 December 2018, para. 70.
963 ECtHR, *Jucius and Juciuvienė v. Lithuania* (Appl. No. 14414/03), 25 November 2008, para. 24.

The applicants also emphasized that this was contrary to the domestic legislation, which required that 'particular attention should be paid to the wishes of the child'.[964] In *Z.J. v. Lithuania* (2014) and *Rouiller v. Switzerland* (2014), the applicants complained that the wishes of the children were not sufficiently taken into account by the courts because they 'disregarded the experts' finding' on the views or because the child's clear wishes had not been correctly reflected in the report.[965] The weight granted to the children's views in light of the Article 13(2) exception of The Hague Abduction Convention was complained about by the applicant in *Gajtani v. Switzerland* (2014),[966] who contended that the domestic court should have considered the views of the child as opposition to return.[967] In *N.Ts. and others v. Georgia* (2016), the applicant contended, on behalf of the children, that the domestic courts had 'disregarded' the categorical opposition of the children to living with their father and that more attention should have been paid to these views rather than focusing on the living conditions of the father.[968] More specifically, the applicants tied the lack of weight accorded to the children's views with the child's best interests principle, contending that the 'superficial assessment of the situation concerning the boys, in combination with the disregard for their own opinions, had led the domestic courts to adopt a decision that was contrary to their best interests'.[969] Finally, in both Chamber decisions, *Tiemann v. France and Germany* (2000) and *Brede v. Germany* (2009), the applicants complained that the children's wishes were not taken into account by the domestic courts.[970]

3. GOVERNMENTS' ARGUMENTS

In numerous cases, the governments referenced the weight granted to the views of the children. At times, this occurred in response to an applicant's complaint, but governments also referred to the weight granted on their own instigation. The governments always agreed with the weight granted to the views by the domestic courts, regardless of the complaint made by the applicants. This explains why the next sections have a different structure compared to the above section on the applicants' complaints. The following remarks and arguments by governments will be discussed: arguments that the child's views were taken into account, arguments that the child's views were not given weight, but that the

964 ECtHR, *Jucius and Juciuvienė v. Lithuania* (Appl. No. 14414/03), 25 November 2008, para. 24.

965 ECtHR, *Z.J. v. Lithuania* (Appl. No. 60092/12), 29 April 2014, para. 84 and ECtHR, *Rouiller v. Switzerland* (Appl. No. 3592/08), 22 July 2014, para. 44.

966 ECtHR, *Gajtani v. Switzerland* (Appl. No. 43730/07), 9 September 2014, para. 90.

967 ECtHR, *Gajtani v. Switzerland* (Appl. No. 43730/07), 9 September 2014, para. 90.

968 ECtHR, *N.Ts. and others v. Georgia* (Appl. No. 71776/12), 2 February 2016, para. 66.

969 ECtHR, *N.Ts. and others v. Georgia* (Appl. No. 71776/12), 2 February 2016, para. 69.

970 ECtHR, *Tiemann v. France and Germany* (dec.) (Appl. Nos. 47457/99 and 47458/99), 27 April 2000; and ECtHR, *Brede v. Germany* (dec.) (Appl. No. 35198/05), 3 February 2009.

domestic authorities were correct in doing so, and neutral remarks in which the child's views were mentioned as a factor taken into account without specific reference to due weight.

3.1. THE CHILD'S VIEWS ACCORDED DUE WEIGHT

The most common argument made by governments is that the child's views were accorded due weight by having an impact on the final decision or that the views were taken into account by being listed as part of the evidence or information relied on. The attributes of the 20 judgments and decisions in which this was argued by governments are shown in Table 6.3.

Table 6.3. Attributes of cases in which the government in question argued that the views of children were accorded due weight

Chamber judgments	**Type of proceeding**	**In response to complaint on**
L. v. Finland (2000)	Care and access	Article 8
Hansen v. Turkey (2003)	Access	Article 8
Kosmopoulou v. Greece (2004)	Access	Article 8
Süss v. Germany (2005)	Access	Article 8
C. v. Finland (2006)	Custody and access	Article 8
Nanning v. Germany (2007)	Custody and access	Article 8
Glesmann v. Germany (2008)	Care and access	Article 8
Jucius and Juciuvienė v. Lithuania (2008)	Custody	Article 8
Płaza v. Poland (2011)	Access	Article 8
Y.C. v. United Kingdom (2012)	Care	Article 8
Gobec v. Slovenia (2013)	Access	Article 8
G.B. v. Lithuania (2016)	Custody	Article 8
Buchleither v. Germany (2016)	Access	Article 8
Iglesias Casarrubios and Cantalapiedra Iglesias v. Spain (2016)	Custody	Article 6
M.K. v. Greece (2018)	International child abduction	Article 8
Khusnutdinov and X v. Russia (2018)	Custody	Article 8
A.V. v. Slovenia (2019)	Access	Article 8
Milovanović v. Serbia (2019)	Custody	Article 8
Chamber decisions	**Type of proceeding**	**In response to complaint on**
G.H.B. v. United Kingdom (2000)	Care	Article 8
Süss v. Germany (2001)	Access	Article 8

Source: Compiled by the author.

The argument that the views were influential on the final decision and thus were given due weight was used by governments in these 20 cases. The argument was made in reference to various factors and will be discussed according to the relevant factor. In some cases, more than one factor was raised by the government; these cases will therefore reappear under various subheadings.

3.1.1. *Balancing Views and Interests*

In seven cases, the governments argued that the children's views were accorded due weight as they were included in the balancing exercise between all interests involved. In *Süss v. Germany* (2001), the government submitted that the domestic court of appeal balanced the competing interests, 'considering the child's firm will not to see her father', thereby concluding that suspension of access was in the child's best interests.[971] Another reference to the balance of interests and the child's best interests prevailing was made by the government in *Płaza v. Poland* (2011), where it argued that 'a balance needed to be struck between the interests of all members of the family, and when those interests were at variance, the interests of the child should prevail', before moving on to refer to the child's views, which 'had been given due consideration'.[972] Similarly, in *G.B. v. Lithuania* (2016), the government stated that the domestic courts had balanced the interests in the case, with the children's interests overriding others as due regard had been given to these views.[973] According to the government in *Buchleither v. Germany* (2016), the domestic court of appeal's decision on contact was based on detailed reasoning focusing on the child's wishes and the 'parents' agnostic relationship' and on 'thoroughly investigated facts', including an expert report and oral hearings of the parties, the child and the guardian ad litem.[974] In *Iglesias Casarrubios and Cantalapiedra Iglesias v. Spain* (2016), the government reiterated that the domestic courts both at first instance and on appeal took into consideration the views of the children, noting specifically that the youngest daughter's views were also expressly taken into account.[975] The government in *M.K. v. Greece* (2018) noted that throughout the domestic proceedings, at every decision the domestic courts exercised their discretionary power in evaluating the interests of the child taking into account the child's wishes, amongst other factors.[976] In *Khusnutdinov and X v. Russia* (2018), the government noted that the domestic courts had 'taken into account' the

971 ECtHR, *Süss v. Germany* (dec.) (Appl. No. 40324/98), 20 September 2001.
972 ECtHR, *Płaza v. Poland* (Appl. No. 18830/07), 25 January 2011, paras. 63–64.
973 ECtHR, *G.B. v. Lithuania* (Appl. No. 36137/13), 19 January 2016, paras. 83–84.
974 ECtHR, *Buchleither v. Germany* (Appl. No. 20106/13), 28 April 2016, para. 35.
975 ECtHR, *Iglesias Casarrubios and Cantalapiedra Iglesias v. Spain* (Appl. No. 23298/12), 11 October 2016, para. 30.
976 ECtHR, *M.K. v. Greece* (Appl. No. 51312/16), 1 February 2018, para. 71.

child's wishes.[977] In *Y.C. v. United Kingdom* (2012), the government contended that the child's views were taken into account as part of all the relevant considerations – even if they were not followed – and that there was nothing to 'indicate that the judge had left the [child]'s wishes out of account in reaching its decision'.[978]

3.1.2. *Legal Obligation to Provide Due Weight*

In two cases, the governments affirmed the obligation to give due weight to a child's expressed views. In *Hansen v. Turkey* (2003), the government noted that 'the authorities were also under an obligation under Article 8 of the Convention to protect the interests of the children who were mature enough to have their views taken into account'.[979] In light of this obligation, the government was not at fault for the failure to enforce access rights because it was a result of 'the children's refusal'.[980] In *C. v. Finland* (2006), the Finnish government referred to domestic law which 'required that children's wishes and opinions be taken into account', as well as other ECtHR cases in which children's views were taken into account, including *Sommerfeld v. Germany* (2003), when referring to the children's views.[981] In *A.V. v. Slovenia* (2019), referring to Article 12 UNCRC, the Slovenian government argued that it was the domestic court's duty to give due weight to the children's views.[982]

3.1.3. *Child-Specific Factors*

Governments repeatedly raise factors regarding due weight which concern the child as such. These factors refer specifically to the child concerned instead of, for example, the circumstances of the case. There are three child-specific factors which recur in the cases: the consistency and strength of the child's views, his or her best interests, and his or her age and maturity.

The first child-specific factor repeatedly raised by governments when arguing that children's views were accorded due weight is the consistency and strength of the child's views. In *A.V. v. Slovenia* (2019) concerning access proceedings, the government noted that the children had 'categorically refused' and had continuously and clearly expressed their wishes.[983] In addition, according to the government, the children could not be 'forced against their will'.[984]

---

977 ECtHR, *Khusnutdinov and X v. Russia* (Appl. No. 76598/12), 18 December 2018, para. 70.
978 ECtHR, *Y.C. v. United Kingdom* (Appl. No. 4547/10), 13 March 2012, paras. 127–128.
979 ECtHR, *Hansen v. Turkey* (Appl. No. 36141/97), 23 September 2003, para. 93.
980 ECtHR, *Hansen v. Turkey* (Appl. No. 36141/97), 23 September 2003, para. 93.
981 ECtHR, *C. v. Finland* (Appl. No. 18249/02), 9 May 2006, para. 47.
982 ECtHR, *A.V. v. Slovenia* (Appl. No. 878/13), 9 April 2019, para. 59.
983 ECtHR, *A.V. v. Slovenia* (Appl. No. 878/13), 9 April 2019, paras. 58–59.
984 ECtHR, *A.V. v. Slovenia* (Appl. No. 878/13), 9 April 2019, para. 59.

The consistent refusal of the child was also referred to in *Gobec v. Slovenia* (2013), with the government adding that the 'strength of feeling … had only deepened with time', and therefore it was fitting to give due weight to the child's views.[985] In other cases, the governments either mentioned the consistency or the strength of the child's views. As mentioned above, in *Süss v. Germany* (2001), the 'child's firm will' was relevant in deciding to suspend access. In *Milovanović v. Serbia* (2019), the government argued that the children's views were taken into account and that 'coercion would have been unacceptable' in enforcing the custody judgment, therefore implicitly acknowledging the strength of the children's views.[986] In *Nanning v. Germany* (2007), the government referred twice to the child's consistent wishes before arguing that it was within the margin of appreciation of the domestic courts to base 'their decisions primarily on the [child]'s clearly expressed wishes'.[987] Similarly, in *Glesmann v. Germany* (2008), the government argued the applicant's right to family life had not been violated and noted that the domestic court of appeal had based its decision on the withdrawal of parental authority both on the 'child's consistent refusal' and on expert opinion.[988]

The second child-specific factor is the child's interests. In *G.H.B. v. United Kingdom* (2000), the government submitted that the adoption order was in the best interests of the child and that it complied with the child's own wishes and the opinion of the expert witness.[989] The government in *Kosmopoulou v. Greece* (2004) even went so far as to state that it had been 'necessary' to respect the child's wishes in order to protect her mental health.[990]

The third and final child-specific factor is the age or maturity of the child. This was only mentioned once by a government in these cases. In the earliest judgment, *L. v. Finland* (2000), the government emphasized that taking into account the child's age (14), 'her wishes should be respected as far as possible' for the access restrictions and that this was done by the domestic authorities accordingly.[991]

3.1.4. *The Role of Experts*

A final factor seen in the argumentation of governments regarding due weight is the role of experts. The reliance on the child's views and an expert's opinion on these views was sufficient to tip the balance of competing interests in favour

---

985 ECtHR, *Gobec v. Slovenia* (Appl. No. 7233/04), 3 October 2013, para. 124.
986 ECtHR, *Milovanović v. Serbia* (Appl. No. 56065/10), 8 October 2019, para. 112.
987 ECtHR, *Nanning v. Germany* (Appl. No. 39741/02), 12 July 2007, paras. 57–58.
988 ECtHR, *Glesmann v. Germany* (Appl. No. 25706/03), 10 January 2008, para. 98.
989 ECtHR, *G.H.B. v. United Kingdom* (dec.) (Appl. No. 42455/98), 4 May 2000.
990 ECtHR, *Kosmopoulou v. Greece* (Appl. No. 60457/00), 5 February 2004, para. 40.
991 ECtHR, *L. v. Finland* (Appl. No. 25651/94), 27 April 2000, para. 124.

of the child's interests, according to the government in the Chamber judgment in *Süss v. Germany* (2005).[992] Additionally, in *Glesmann v. Germany* (2008), as mentioned above, the government argued that both the child's views and the expert opinion tipped the scales towards withdrawal of parental authority.[993]

3.1.5. Other Reasoning

Finally, there is one case in which the government's argument differed from the rest due to the course of events following the application to the ECtHR. The government in *Jucius and Juciuvienė v. Lithuania* (2008) raised the fact that the children's views had been – since the applicants had lodged a complaint at the ECtHR – given due weight, thus arguing that the complaint was inadmissible because it was found to be manifestly ill-founded.[994]

3.2. VIEWS NOT GIVEN EXCLUSIVE WEIGHT

In one judgment, *Rouiller v. Switzerland* (2014), the government explicitly and fully agreed with the domestic court, which argued that Article 13(2) of The Hague Abduction Convention does not confer on children the possibility to freely choose where they want to live, and that the wishes of the child in the case were not sufficient to apply the exception of the article for non-return.[995]

3.3. NEUTRAL REMARK ON WEIGHT ACCORDED

In three Chamber judgments and one Grand Chamber judgment, the governments made a neutral remark on the weight granted to the views of the children. This is qualified as neutral in the sense that the child's views were mentioned as one factor in a list of factors taken into account by the domestic courts. In *Haase v. Germany* (2004), the government noted that the domestic court had 'relied on all available information at its disposal', including hearing the children and the assessment of a curator ad litem.[996] In *Havelka and others v. Czech Republic* (2007), in light of the question of whether the children ought to have been heard directly, the government noted that the domestic courts had taken into account the opinions of the children indirectly established through

---

992 ECtHR, *Süss v. Germany* (Appl. No. 40324/98), 10 November 2005, para. 79.

993 ECtHR, *Glesmann v. Germany* (Appl. No. 25706/03), 10 January 2008, para. 98.

994 ECtHR, *Jucius and Juciuvienė v. Lithuania* (Appl. No. 14414/03), 25 November 2008, para. 23.

995 ECtHR, *Rouiller v. Switzerland* (Appl. No. 3592/08), 22 July 2014, para. 48.

996 ECtHR, *Haase v. Germany* (Appl. No. 11057/02), 8 April 2004, para. 78.

the psychological reports.[997] The government in *Blaga v. Romania* (2014) noted that the domestic courts had 'relied on all the evidence adduced', including the children's statements.[998] In the Grand Chamber judgment in *Elsholz v. Germany* (2000), the government pointed out that the domestic court had 'relied upon its personal impressions after having heard the child' in making its conclusion.[999] The attributes of these four cases are presented in Table 6.4 below.

Table 6.4. Attributes of cases in which the government provided a neutral remark on weight accorded

Grand Chamber judgment	Type of proceeding	In response to complaint on
Elsholz v. Germany (2000)	Access	Article 8
Chamber judgments	**Type of proceeding**	**In response to complaint on**
Haase v. Germany (2004)	Care	Article 8
Havelka and others v. Czech Republic (2007)	Care	Article 8
Blaga v. Romania (2014)	International child abduction	Article 8

Source: Compiled by the author.

4. THE ECtHR

Whether in response to an applicant's complaint, a remark by the government or on its own initiative, the ECtHR has in many cases considered the question of how much weight should have been or has been accorded to a child's views by domestic courts. As we will see below, the ECtHR has commented on due weight in more cases than those in which it has been complained about. This means that it is not possible to discuss the reasoning according to the structure used in the previous sections. Instead, the ECtHR has three types of reasoning concerning the weight accorded to the views of the child, which are covered below in separate sections. These are: a negative response to the weight granted, a positive response to the weight granted and a neutral response to the weight granted. Additionally, the topic of exclusive weight will be discussed separately, because the question of whether domestic courts can give exclusive weight to the views of the child is one which the ECtHR has explicitly covered, especially with regard to international child abduction cases. Before discussing these types of reasoning, this section will begin with examining general principles on due weight formulated by the ECtHR.

997 ECtHR, *Havelka and others v. Czech Republic* (Appl. No. 23499/06), 21 June 2007, para. 39.
998 ECtHR, *Blaga v. Romania* (Appl. No. 54443/10), 1 July 2014, para. 62.
999 ECtHR, *Elsholz v. Germany* [GC] (Appl. No. 25735/94), 13 July 2000, para. 39.

4.1. GENERAL PRINCIPLES

A number of general principles have been formulated by the ECtHR throughout its case law. The first general principle was introduced in *Płaza v. Poland* (2011). The ECtHR, in providing its relevant principles under Article 8, clarified that 'as children mature and become, with the passage of time, able to formulate their own opinion on their contact with the parents, domestic courts should give due weight also to their views and feelings as well as to their right to respect for their private life'.[1000] This principle has been reiterated in the subsequent judgments in *Gobec v. Slovenia* (2013), *Petrov and X v. Russia* (2018), *Khusnutdinov and X v. Russia* (2018) and *Zelikha Magomadova v. Russia* (2019).[1001] In the latter three, the ECtHR did not use the phrase 'on their contact with the parents', thereby signalling a broader application to other types of proceedings concerning children. Specifically, these judgments concerned parental authority, residence and access proceedings.

With regard to the amount of weight to be granted, the ECtHR first bundled its doctrine as general principles for custody and access proceedings in *K.B. and others v. Croatia* (2017) under the scope of Article 8 ECHR. Referring to its case law, specifically *Raw and others v. France* (2013), the Court noted that while it is required that a child's views are taken into account, 'those views are not necessarily immutable and their objections, which must be given due weight, are not necessarily sufficient to override the parents' interests, especially in having regular contact with their child'.[1002] The Court then referred to *C. v. Finland* (2006), a judgment that will be discussed in the next section, stating that 'the right of a child to express his or her own views should not be interpreted as effectively giving an unconditional veto power to children', without considering other factors or examining the child's best interests.[1003] The combination of these two principles was reiterated by the ECtHR in *A.V. v. Slovenia* (2019) and *Pisică v. Republic of Moldova* (2019) under the header 'General principles' and in *Zelikha Magomadova v. Russia* (2019) – all in light of Article 8 ECHR.[1004] Additionally, in *K.B. and others v. Croatia* (2017), the ECtHR concluded its principles, stating that 'if a court would base a decision on the views of children who are palpably unable to form and articulate an opinion as to their wishes – for example, because of a loyalty conflict and/or their exposure to the alienating

---

[1000] ECtHR, *Płaza v. Poland* (Appl. No. 18830/07), 25 January 2011, para. 71.

[1001] ECtHR, *Gobec v. Slovenia* (Appl. No. 7233/04), 3 October 2013, para. 133; ECtHR, *Petrov and X v. Russia* (Appl. No. 23608/16), 23 October 2018, para. 108; ECtHR, *Khusnutdinov and X v. Russia* (Appl. No. 76598/12), 18 December 2018, para. 86 and ECtHR, *Zelikha Magomadova v. Russia* (Appl. No. 58724/14), 8 October 2019, para. 115.

[1002] ECtHR, *K.B. and others v. Croatia* (Appl. No. 36216/13), 14 March 2017, para. 143.

[1003] ECtHR *K.B. and others v. Croatia* (Appl. No. 36216/13), 14 March 2017, para. 143.

[1004] ECtHR, *A.V. v. Slovenia* (Appl. No. 878/13), 9 April 2019, para. 72 ECtHR, *Zelikha Magomadova v. Russia* (Appl. No. 58724/14), 8 October 2019, para. 115 and ECtHR, *Pisică v. Republic of Moldova* (Appl. No. 23641/17), 29 October 2019, para. 65.

behaviour of one parent – such a decision could run contrary to Article 8 of the Convention'.[1005]

More specifically with regard to care proceedings, in *Y.C. v. United Kingdom* (2012), the ECtHR noted in the 'General principles' section that in assessing the child's best interests, domestic courts must 'weigh a number of factors in the balance'. In particular, with regard to placement proceedings for adoption, the domestic courts must have regard to the child's 'ascertained wishes'.[1006] This principle was reiterated in *J. and others v. Finland* (2013) and *A.E.L. v. Finland* (2013), with the ECtHR stating that 'in seeking to identify the best interests of a child and in assessing the necessity of any proposed measure in the context of proceedings concerning taking into public care, placement, contact restrictions and reunion', the domestic courts must have regard to 'the age, maturity and ascertained wishes of the child'.[1007]

4.2. EXCLUSIVE WEIGHT

In five judgments and one decision, the ECtHR commented on the granting of decisive and *exclusive* weight to the views of the child by the domestic courts. These six cases have been set out in Table 6.5 below, which shows that the issue was dealt with under Article 8 in all cases and that most of these cases concerned international child abductions. The relationship between international child abduction proceedings and the issue of exclusive weight will therefore be dealt with specifically below after considering the odd one out.

Table 6.5. Attributes of cases with ECtHR reasoning on decisive weight

Chamber judgments	Type of proceeding	Applicant(s)	Reasoning under
C. v. Finland (2006)	Custody and access	Father	Article 8
Raw and others v. France (2013)	International child abduction	Mother, also on behalf of child	Article 8
Blaga v. Romania (2014)	International child abduction	Father	Article 8
Rouiller v. Switzerland (2014)	International child abduction	Mother	Article 8
Gajtani v. Switzerland (2014)	International child abduction	Mother	Article 8

(continued)

1005 ECtHR, *K.B. and others v. Croatia* (Appl. No. 36216/13), 14 March 2017, para. 143.
1006 ECtHR, *Y.C. v. United Kingdom* (Appl. No. 4547/10), 13 March 2012, para. 135.
1007 ECtHR, *J. and others v. Finland* (dec.) (Appl. No. 51555/09), 12 February 2013, para. 81; and ECtHR, *A.E.L. v. Finland* (dec.) (Appl. No. 59435/10), 10 December 2013, para. 61.

Table 6.5 *continued*

Chamber decision	Type of proceeding	Applicant(s)	Reasoning under
Paradis and others v. Germany (2003)	International child abduction	Mother, also on behalf of her four children	Article 8

Source: Compiled by the author.

In *C. v. Finland* (2006), the Finnish Supreme Court had granted decisive weight to the views of the children in the custody proceedings. The children wished to continue living with their deceased mother's partner and not with their father (the applicant).[1008] According to the ECtHR, the children had been given an 'unconditional veto power' by the Supreme Court, as it had not considered factors other than the children's views.[1009] These other factors were, in particular, the applicant's rights as a father, but also included the children's best interests.[1010] Thus, the ECtHR reasoned, the domestic courts had failed to strike a proper balance between the interests involved, which was a violation of Article 8 ECHR.[1011]

In five cases on international child abduction – four judgments from 2013 and 2014 and one earlier decision – the ECtHR commented on whether the views of children can or should be exclusively decisive in light of the exception to return in Article 13(2) of The Hague Abduction Convention. The key principle in this regard was introduced in *Raw and others v. France* (2013), where the ECtHR clarified that a child's opposition to return was not necessarily an obstacle to a return order in the framework of The Hague Abduction Convention and Brussels II Regulation (EC) No 1347/2000 (Brussels II *bis*).[1012] The exception of Article 13(2) The Hague Abduction Convention is not absolute.

This has been reaffirmed in the other three judgments. In *Blaga v. Romania* (2014), the ECtHR noted that the children's views had been decisive in the return proceedings.[1013] The Court interpreted Article 13(2) of The Hague Abduction Convention as not providing children with a veto to return and reiterated that 'while the Convention recognizes that the objecting child should have a voice, it does not consider that voice to amount to a veto in the process of deciding whether he or she will be returned'.[1014] The domestic courts should also consider other relevant circumstances.[1015] Although the Romanian courts had done so, the ECtHR was not convinced that all interests – those of the applicants, other

1008 ECtHR, *C. v. Finland* (Appl. No. 18249/02), 9 May 2006, para. 33.
1009 ECtHR, *C. v. Finland* (Appl. No. 18249/02), 9 May 2006, paras. 57 and 58.
1010 ECtHR, *C. v. Finland* (Appl. No. 18249/02), 9 May 2006, paras. 57 and 58.
1011 ECtHR, *C. v. Finland* (Appl. No. 18249/02), 9 May 2006, para. 59.
1012 ECtHR, *Raw and others v. France* (Appl. No. 10131/11), 7 March 2013, para. 94.
1013 ECtHR, *Blaga v. Romania* (Appl. No. 54443/10), 1 July 2014, para. 79.
1014 ECtHR, *Blaga v. Romania* (Appl. No. 54443/10), 1 July 2014, para. 80.
1015 ECtHR, *Blaga v. Romania* (Appl. No. 54443/10), 1 July 2014, para. 81.

parties and the children – were sufficiently balanced.[1016] In combination with the delays throughout the proceedings and the effects of those delays, the ECtHR concluded that there was a violation of the applicant's right to respect for his family life under Article 8.[1017]

In the other two judgments, the ECtHR did not find a violation of Article 8 ECHR, but did reaffirm the principle. In *Rouiller v. Switzerland* (2014), the ECtHR agreed with the domestic courts in appeal that Article 13(2) does not confer on children the possibility to freely choose where to live.[1018] Thus, the Court agreed with the finding of the domestic courts that the child's expressed preference was insufficient for the exception to apply.[1019] A few months later, in *Gajtani v. Switzerland* (2014), the ECtHR again noted in interpreting Article 13(2) that a child's opposition does not lead to an obligation for the domestic courts to not order the return of the child.[1020] The weight to be given to a child's views was a decision for the domestic courts within their margin of appreciation.[1021] The Court therefore did not find a violation of Article 8 ECHR as the return order was not disproportionate.

Finally, it is relevant to note that in *Paradis and others v. Germany* (2003), the ECtHR already (ten years before *Raw and others*) agreed with the domestic courts in not exclusively attaching decisive weight to the children's views in the decision to return. Considering the young age of the children, they could not 'decide for themselves what was in their best interests', so it was not arbitrary for the domestic courts not to attach exclusive weight to the children's objections to return.[1022]

In all these cases on international child abduction proceedings, it is clear that the views of the child are not by themselves decisive in preventing return. The exception to return in Article 13(2) of The Hague Abduction Convention is not immutable. Other interests may prevail, such as ensuring a prompt return and the interests of the left-behind parent. More generally, also considering *C. v. Finland* (2006), it can be concluded from these cases that the ECtHR agreed with 'due weight', but not 'exclusive weight' being accorded to children's views.

4.3. NEGATIVE RESPONSE TO THE AMOUNT OF WEIGHT ACCORDED TO VIEWS

The ECtHR has rarely disagreed with the amount of weight accorded to the children's views at the national level. Only in the above-discussed

1016 ECtHR, *Blaga v. Romania* (Appl. No. 54443/10), 1 July 2014, para. 81.
1017 ECtHR, *Blaga v. Romania* (Appl. No. 54443/10), 1 July 2014, paras. 79–90.
1018 ECtHR, *Rouiller v. Switzerland* (Appl. No. 3592/08), 22 July 2014, para. 73.
1019 ECtHR, *Rouiller v. Switzerland* (Appl. No. 3592/08), 22 July 2014, para. 73.
1020 ECtHR, *Gajtani v. Switzerland* (Appl. No. 43730/07), 9 September 2014, para. 108.
1021 ECtHR, *Gajtani v. Switzerland* (Appl. No. 43730/07), 9 September 2014, para. 108.
1022 ECtHR, *Paradis and others v. Germany* (dec.) (Appl. No. 4783/03), 15 May 2003.

judgments – *C. v. Finland* (2006) and *Blaga v. Romania* (2014) on exclusive weight granted to the child's views and *M. and M. v. Croatia* (2015) and *N.Ts. and others v. Georgia* (2016) – has the ECtHR disagreed with the weight accorded. The attributes of these four judgments are included in Table 6.6 below.

Table 6.6. Attributes of cases in which the ECtHR responds negatively to weight accorded to views

Chamber judgments	Type of proceeding	Applicant(s)	Reasoning under
C. v. Finland (2006)	Custody and access	Father	Article 8
Blaga v. Romania (2014)	International child abduction	Father	Article 8
M. and M. v. Croatia (2015)	Custody	Mother and child on own behalf	Article 8
N.Ts. and others v. Georgia (2016)	Custody	Aunt on behalf of children	Article 8

Source: Compiled by the author.

In *M. and M. v. Croatia* (2015), the ECtHR held that there had been an infringement of the child's right to respect for her private and family life, and thus a violation of her rights under Article 8 ECHR, as the domestic courts had not respected her wishes regarding with which parent she wanted to live – with her mother instead of her father.[1023] The ECtHR also relied on domestic Croatian case law when finding this infringement, according to which 'in situations where both parents are equally fit to take care of the child, and the child is, having regard to his or her age and maturity, capable of forming his or her own views and expressing them, the child's wishes as regards which parent to live with must be respected'.[1024] The ECtHR stated that it must endorse this line of reasoning because 'otherwise the rule that the views of the child must be given due weight would be rendered meaningless'.[1025]

In *N.Ts. and others v. Georgia* (2016), the ECtHR did not explicitly refer to due weight or the wishes of the child. However, in finding a violation of Article 8 ECHR due to the insufficient participation of the children, it noted that the violation was 'exacerbated by inadequate and one-sided consideration of the boys' best interests, in which their emotional state of mind was simply ignored'.[1026] It found that the domestic courts had failed to consider

[1023] ECtHR, *M. and M. v. Croatia* (Appl. No. 10161/13), 3 September 2015, paras. 186 and 187.
[1024] ECtHR, *M. and M. v. Croatia* (Appl. No. 10161/13), 3 September 2015, para. 185.
[1025] ECtHR, *M. and M. v. Croatia* (Appl. No. 10161/13), 3 September 2015, para. 185.
[1026] ECtHR, *N.Ts. and others v. Georgia* (Appl. No. 71776/12), 2 February 2016, para. 85.

'one important fact: the boys did not want to be reunited with their father'.[1027] Labelled the 'emotional state' of the children, this can be considered to refer to the children's wishes – which had not been able to be determined as such due to the flaws in participation – combined with the attitudes determined by expert reports.[1028]

4.4. POSITIVE RESPONSE TO WEIGHT ACCORDED TO VIEWS

The overwhelming reasoning of the ECtHR on the weight accorded to children's views has been positive, with the Court agreeing with the weight granted by the domestic courts in 23 judgments and decisions. These cases are introduced in Table 6.7 below. It is clear that they mostly address family law proceedings concerning custody, access, adoption or care and that the ECtHR reasoning on due weight has been considered consistently in light of Article 8 ECHR.

Table 6.7. Attributes of cases in which the ECtHR responds positively to weight accorded to views

Grand Chamber judgments	**Type of proceeding**	**Applicant(s)**	**Reasoning under**
Elsholz v. Germany (2000)	Access	Father	Article 8
Sommerfeld v. Germany (2003)	Access	Father	Article 8
Chamber judgments	**Type of proceeding**	**Applicant(s)**	**Reasoning under**
Gnahoré v. France (2000)	Care and access	Father	Article 8
Mihailova v. Bulgaria (2006)	Custody	Mother	Article 8
Eski v. Austria (2007)	Adoption	Father	Article 8
Gineitienė v. Lithuania (2010)	Custody	Mother	Article 8 in conjunction with 14
Płaza v. Poland (2011)	Access	Father	Article 8
Cristescu v. Romania (2012)	Access	Father	Article 8
Gobec v. Slovenia (2013)	Access	Father	Article 8
G.B. v. Lithuania (2016)	Custody	Mother	Article 8
Buchleither v. Germany (2016)	Access	Father	Article 8
M.K. v. Greece (2018)	International child abduction	Mother	Article 8
Khusnutdinov and X v. Russia (2018)	Custody	Father, also on behalf of child	Article 8

(continued)

[1027] ECtHR, *N.Ts. and others v. Georgia* (Appl. No. 71776/12), 2 February 2016, para. 81.
[1028] ECtHR, *N.Ts. and others v. Georgia* (Appl. No. 71776/12), 2 February 2016, paras. 80–83.

Table 6.7 *continued*

Chamber decisions	Type of proceeding	Applicant(s)	Reasoning under
Tiemann v. France and Germany (2000)	International child abduction	Father	Article 8
G.H.B. v. United Kingdom (2000)	Care	Grandparent	Article 8
W.F. v. Italy (2001)	Care	Father	Article 8
Johansen v. Norway (2002)	Care and access	Mother	Article 8
Miffek v. Czech Republic (2003)	Custody	Father	Article 8
Paulsen-Medalen and Svensson v. Sweden (2003)	Care and access	Father and mother, also on behalf of their son	Article 8
Petersen v. Germany (2006)	Custody and access	Father	Article 8
Brede v. Germany (2009)	Care	Mother	Article 8
Döring v. Germany (2012)	Custody	Father	Article 8
T.S. and J.J. v. Norway (2016)	Care and access	Father	Article 8

Source: Compiled by the author.

The ECtHR agreed with the domestic courts on the weight given in various ways and to different degrees of specificity, as we will now see.

4.4.1. *Explicit Positive Response to the Weight Accorded to the Child's Views*

There are nine cases in which the ECtHR was explicitly positive and in agreement with the domestic courts regarding the weight granted to the views of the child. For example, in three decisions – *G.H.B. v. United Kingdom* (2000), *Paulsen-Medalen and Svensson v. Sweden* (2003) and *T.S. and J.J. v. Norway* (2016) – the ECtHR found that the domestic courts were 'justified in giving weight to the child's own views'[1029] or even 'justified in placing the emphasis'[1030] on the child's views. In *Paulsen-Medalen and Svensson v. Sweden* (2003), the ECtHR referred to Article 12 UNCRC in this regard,[1031] while in *T.S. and J.J. v. Norway* (2016), the Court referred back to the *G.H.B.* decision.[1032] In both of these cases, the children did not wish to have more contact with their parents. In the earlier *G.H.B. v. United Kingdom* (2000)

[1029] ECtHR, *G.H.B. v. United Kingdom* (dec.) (Appl. No. 42455/98), 4 May 2000; ECtHR, *T.S. and J.J. v. Norway* (dec.) (Appl. No. 15633/15), 11 October 2016, para. 29.

[1030] ECtHR, *Paulsen-Medalen and Svensson v. Sweden* (dec.) (Appl. No. 47411/99), 30 September 2003.

[1031] EctHR, *Paulsen-Medalen and Svensson v. Sweden* (dec.) (Appl. No. 47411/99), 30 September 2003.

[1032] ECtHR, *T.S. and J.J. v. Norway* (dec.) (Appl. No. 15633/15), 11 October 2016, para. 29.

decision, the ECtHR emphasized the importance of giving weight to the child's views in contact proceedings, noting that if the domestic court had gone against the wishes of the child, it would have 'constituted a failure to properly respect the child's own rights under Article 8'.[1033] The child wished not to have contact with her grandparent or family. In the fourth decision, *W.F. v. Italy* (2001), the ECtHR found that the domestic courts did not exceed their margin of appreciation in deciding not to return the child to the care of his father for a number of reasons. It concluded by attaching particular importance on the child's best interests, noting that the child was almost 17 and had always firmly expressed the wish not to return to his father in Germany.[1034] More recently, in *G.B. v. Lithuania* (2016), the ECtHR considered that the children were heard by the domestic court and that 'the need to respect the views of the child' was underlined by the CRC Committee.[1035] In this case, which concerned custody proceedings, the children had expressed their preference of living with their father instead of with their mother (the applicant).[1036] The ECtHR found no violation of the procedural requirements implicit in Article 8 ECHR, as the applicant (the mother) had been involved in the decision-making process.[1037] Also, with regard to the other complaints raised by the applicant, no violation of Article 8 ECHR was found.

The ECtHR expanded on this topic in the chamber judgment in *Płaza v. Poland* (2011). First, it reiterated its general principles on due weight, as discussed above. In applying these principles to the case, it found that the domestic courts' approach of taking the child's psychological situation and her wishes into consideration, as it was of the 'greatest relevance', as not 'open to criticism'.[1038] It found that the decision fell within the margin of appreciation afforded to domestic authorities regarding parental authority.[1039] The case concerned access proceedings and the child did not want to see her father (the applicant).[1040]

In *M.K. v. Greece* (2018), the ECtHR also spent several paragraphs on the topic. It started by noting that the domestic reports showed that the child had repeatedly and clearly reiterated his wish to remain in Greece and not to return to France.[1041] Subsequently, the Court pointed out that the child at that time had

---

1033 ECtHR, *G.H.B. v. United Kingdom* (dec.) (Appl. No. 42455/98), 4 May 2000.
1034 ECtHR, *W.F. v. Italy* (Appl. No. 34803/97), 5 April 2001.
1035 ECtHR, *G.B. v. Lithuania* (Appl. No. 36137/13), 19 January 2016, para. 105.
1036 ECtHR, *G.B. v. Lithuania* (Appl. No. 36137/13), 19 January 2016, para. 84.
1037 ECtHR, *G.B. v. Lithuania* (Appl. No. 36137/13), 19 January 2016, para. 105.
1038 ECtHR, *Płaza v. Poland* (Appl. No. 18830/07), 25 January 2011, para. 86.
1039 ECtHR, *Płaza v. Poland* (Appl. No. 18830/07), 25 January 2011, para. 86.
1040 ECtHR, *Płaza v. Poland* (Appl. No. 18830/07), 25 January 2011, paras. 21, 22 and 25.
1041 ECtHR, *M.K. v. Greece* (Appl. No. 51312/16), 1 February 2018, para. 87.

reached the age of discernment and that his clearly expressed wishes could only weigh heavily on the domestic authorities' decision.[1042] According to the Court, the very firm wishes of the child could not be ignored in the assessment, also taking into account the family situation, the best interests of the child and the changes over time.[1043] Finally, it concluded its reasoning with reference to the international legal instruments which require courts to give due weight to views expressed by children: the UNCRC, the European Convention on the Exercise of Children's Rights (ECECR), the Charter of Fundamental Rights of the European Union (CFREU) and The Hague Abduction Convention.[1044]

In *Khusnutdinov and X v. Russia* (2018), the ECtHR considered that the domestic courts had taken into account the child's expressed 'clear wish' to keep living with her grandparents, subsequently referring to the general principle from *Płaza v. Poland* (2011).[1045] Furthermore, it found that the decision to follow the child's wishes could be considered as having been 'made in the interests of the child', also considering additional factors.[1046] It concluded that overall, the decision-making process was fair – in part also because the child's views were heard and taken into account.[1047]

Finally, in *Gobec v. Slovenia* (2013), the ECtHR noted that the child's 'persistent refusal of contact with the applicant' was of great importance in the domestic proceedings, subsequently noting that the child 'categorically' expressed negative views which remained unchanged throughout the proceedings.[1048] The Court concluded that domestic courts 'struck a fair balance' between the applicant's contact rights and the child's best interests – allowing her interests to be given priority.[1049]

4.4.2. The Weight Accorded to Child's Views as Part of the Evidentiary Basis

At times, the ECtHR has been positive without being overly explicit, noting that the views have been weighed in the decision-making process alongside other interests and factors. For example, the granting of weight to the children's views was seen as forming part of the 'sufficient evidentiary basis' of a domestic court's decision in *Cristescu v. Romania* (2012).[1050] The statements by witnesses, psychological and other expert reports, and the parties' wishes completed this evidentiary basis. In this case, the children expressed a preference towards

---

1042 ECtHR, *M.K. v. Greece* (Appl. No. 51312/16), 1 February 2018, para. 88.
1043 ECtHR, *M.K. v. Greece* (Appl. No. 51312/16), 1 February 2018, para. 90.
1044 ECtHR, *M.K. v. Greece* (Appl. No. 51312/16), 1 February 2018, paras. 91–92.
1045 ECtHR, *Khusnutdinov and X v. Russia* (Appl. No. 76598/12), 18 December 2018, para. 86.
1046 ECtHR, *Khusnutdinov and X v. Russia* (Appl. No. 76598/12), 18 December 2018, para. 91.
1047 ECtHR, *Khusnutdinov and X v. Russia* (Appl. No. 76598/12), 18 December 2018, para. 93.
1048 ECtHR, *Gobec v. Slovenia* (Appl. No. 7233/04), 3 October 2013, paras. 135 and 137.
1049 ECtHR, *Gobec v. Slovenia* (Appl. No. 7233/04), 3 October 2013, para. 139
1050 ECtHR, *Cristescu v. Romania* (Appl. No. 13589/07), 10 January 2012, para. 62.

residing with their mother. In *Gnahoré v. France* (2000), the Court found that the decision to renew the care order was not unreasonable within the margin of appreciation, noting that the judge had not only considered the experts' proposals but had also, amongst other things, 'listened to the views of the child', who wished to stay in his foster home.[1051] The views of the child formed part of the consideration; however, the focus was on the father's inability to care for the child's educational or material needs and the best interests of the child.[1052] Similarly, in *Eski v. Austria* (2007), the ECtHR found that the domestic courts struck a fair balance between the interests involved when granting the adoption, 'after having heard evidence from the child, her adoptive father and the child's mother'.[1053] It recognized that the domestic courts had focused on the best interests of the child and the limited relationship with the applicant (the father) and had weighed this against the adverse effects for the father.[1054] Another example is *Buchleither v. Germany* (2016), in which the ECtHR noted that the domestic courts relied on 'detailed extensive information', including the views of the child (who had the 'firm wish' not to have contact with her father), the applicant father, the mother and an expert.[1055] This satisfied the Court that the interests involved were afforded respect.[1056]

4.4.3. *Weight Granted as Part of the 'Relevant and Sufficient Reasons'*

A third category of positive responses has been the recurring conclusion of the ECtHR that with the amount of weight given to children's views, the domestic courts had made a decision based on 'relevant and sufficient reasons'. This phrase did not materialize out of thin air. In determining whether there has been a violation of Article 8 ECHR, the ECtHR examines whether the interference of the applicant's right to respect for private or family life is 'in accordance with the law' has a 'legitimate aim' and is 'necessary in a democratic society'. Under that final condition, the ECtHR considers, amongst other things, whether the reasons provided by the domestic authorities to interfere in the applicant's rights were 'relevant and sufficient'.[1057] This general evaluative criterion has been commonly relied upon by the Court in the case law concerning family law proceedings, mostly brought by parents, under Article 8 ECHR – including in

1051 ECtHR, *Gnahoré v. France* (Appl. No. 40031/98), 19 September 2000, paras. 57–58.
1052 ECtHR, *Gnahoré v. France* (Appl. No. 40031/98), 19 September 2000, para. 57.
1053 ECtHR, *Eski v. Austria* (Appl. No. 21949/03), 25 January 2007, paras. 40 and 42.
1054 ECtHR, *Eski v. Austria* (Appl. No. 21949/03), 25 January 2007, para. 42.
1055 ECtHR, *Buchleither v. Germany* (Appl. No. 20106/13), 28 April 2016, para. 47.
1056 ECtHR, *Buchleither v. Germany* (Appl. No. 20106/13), 28 April 2016, para. 47.
1057 Directorate of the Jurisconsult, *Guide on Article 8 of the European Convention on Human Right*, Strasbourg: Council of Europe/European Court of Human Rights 2018, p. 11.

most of the cases discussed in the previous two categories.[1058] However, in two Grand Chamber judgments, three Chamber judgments and six decisions, the ECtHR specifically linked the weight given to the child's views to the 'relevant and sufficient' reasons. These will now be discussed.

In the six decisions – *Tiemann v. France and Germany* (2000), *Johansen v. Norway* (2002), *Miffek v. Czech Republic* (2003), *Paulsen-Medalen and Svensson v. Sweden* (2003), *Petersen v. Germany* (2006) and *Döring v. Germany* (2012) – the ECtHR found the domestic courts to have adduced 'relevant and sufficient reasons' whether granting no weight, great weight or some amount in between to the views of the child.[1059] For example, the Court found the domestic courts in *Johansen v. Norway* (2002) to have 'understandably attached great weight' to the child's views, who did not wish to meet her mother, given that the child was 11 years old at the time.[1060] In balancing these views together with the child's 'need for a secure and calm foster family environment', the ECtHR found the complaint to be manifestly ill-founded as the domestic courts provided 'relevant and sufficient reasons' for the adoption.[1061] In *Miffek v. Czech Republic* (2003), the reasoning not to change the custody was based on the children's expressed views of wanting to live with their mother, supplemented by the strained relations between the parents and the potential for harm to the development of the children.[1062] In *Petersen v. Germany* (2006), the impossibility of enforcing the potential access rights in another country and the best interests of the child, together with the wish of the child not to see his father, formed relevant and sufficient reasoning by the domestic courts.[1063]

In the first Chamber judgment, *Gineitienė v. Lithuania* (2010), the ECtHR was 'particularly struck by the Supreme Court's emphasis on the views of the children, who had, at all stages of the proceedings, voiced a strong desire to live with their father'.[1064] In deciding on the best interests of the children, the wishes

---

1058 ECtHR, *G.H.B. v. United Kingdom* (dec.) (Appl. No. 42455/98), 4 May 2000; ECtHR, *Gnahoré v. France* (Appl. No. 40031/98), 19 September 2000, para. 54; ECtHR, *Płaza v. Poland* (Appl. No. 18830/07), 25 January 2011, para. 72; ECtHR, *Gobec v. Slovenia* (Appl. No. 7233/04), 3 October 2013, para. 132; ECtHR, *G.B. v. Lithuania* (Appl. No. 36137/13), 19 January 2016, para. 94; ECtHR, *Buchleither v. Germany* (Appl. No. 20106/13), 28 April 2016, para. 42 and ECtHR, *T.S. and J.J. v. Norway* (dec.) (Appl. No. 15633/15), 11 October 2016, para. 27.

1059 ECtHR, *Tiemann v. France and Germany* (dec.) (Appl. Nos. 47457/99 and 47458/99), 27 April 2000; ECtHR, *Johansen v. Norway* (dec.) (Appl. No. 12750/02), 10 October 2002; ECtHR, *Miffek v. Czech Republic* (dec.) (Appl. No. 55069/00), 27 January 2003; ECtHR, *Paulsen-Medalen and Svensson v. Sweden* (dec.) (Appl. No. 47411/99), 30 September 2003; ECtHR, *Petersen v. Germany* (dec.) (Appl. Nos. 38282/97 and 68891/01), 12 January 2006 and ECtHR, *Döring v. Germany* (dec.) (Appl. No. 50216/09), 21 February 2012.

1060 ECtHR, *Johansen v. Norway* (dec.) (Appl. No. 12750/02), 10 October 2002.

1061 ECtHR, *Johansen v. Norway* (dec.) (Appl. No. 12750/02), 10 October 2002.

1062 ECtHR, *Miffek v. Czech Republic* (dec.) (Appl. No. 55069/00), 27 January 2003.

1063 ECtHR, *Petersen v. Germany* (dec.) (Appl. Nos. 38282/97 and 68891/01), 12 January 2006.

1064 ECtHR, *Gineitienė v. Lithuania* (Appl. No. 20739/05), 27 July 2010, para. 38.

were balanced together with the fact that the living conditions with their mother were 'unsafe' and that a change in residence may have caused a separation of the siblings.[1065] Subsequently, the ECtHR concluded that the reasoning was relevant and sufficient, as it was clear that the interests of the children were considered paramount.[1066] In the second Chamber judgment, *Mihailova v. Bulgaria* (2006), the ECtHR found the decision to revise custody measures to be based on relevant and sufficient grounds. These grounds included that the 'child had formed an opinion in favour of staying with him' (the father), but also the child's development, living conditions and the animosity between the parents.[1067] Finally, in *Khusnutdinov and X v. Russia* (2018), a judgment also considered in the first category, the ECtHR concluded that having taken into account the child's views 'as much as possible', the 'reasons advanced by the domestic courts were relevant and sufficient'.[1068]

In both Grand Chamber judgments, *Elsholz v. Germany* (2000) and *Sommerfeld v. Germany* (2003), the ECtHR held that the domestic courts had adduced relevant reasons relying on the statements of the children concerned, both of whom did not want to have contact with their father.[1069] In *Elsholz v. Germany* (2000), the views of the child were weighed together with the strained relationship of the parents and the negative effects of further contact. In both judgments, the ECtHR subsequently delved separately into the question of whether the reasoning was 'sufficient', noting that it had to be determined whether the decision-making process, seen as a whole, provided the applicant with the requisite protection of interests.[1070] Thus, the weight granted to the views of the child was considered by the ECtHR to be relevant, but other factors ended up determining whether or not a violation of Article 8 had occurred.

4.4.4. *Positive Response to No Weight Granted*

Finally, it is relevant to draw attention to the fact that the ECtHR has at times agreed with the domestic courts' approach to *not* grant any weight. In *Döring v. Germany* (2012), the child had at first expressed a wish to 'stay with each of his parents on an alternating weekly basis'; later on in the proceedings, this changed to a wish to live with his father (instead of his mother) and only to visit his mother.[1071] The ECtHR agreed with the domestic decision not to

1065 ECtHR, *Gineitienė v. Lithuania* (Appl. No. 20739/05), 27 July 2010, para. 38.
1066 ECtHR, *Gineitienė v. Lithuania* (Appl. No. 20739/05), 27 July 2010, para. 39.
1067 ECtHR, *Mihailova v. Bulgaria* (Appl. No. 35978/02), 12 January 2006, para. 100.
1068 ECtHR, *Khusnutdinov and X v. Russia* (Appl. No. 76598/12), 18 December 2018, para. 93.
1069 ECtHR, *Elsholz v. Germany* [GC] (Appl. No. 25735/94), 13 July 2000, paras. 51–52; and ECtHR, *Sommerfeld v. Germany* [GC] (Appl. No. 31871/96), 8 July 2003, para. 65.
1070 ECtHR, *Elsholz v. Germany* [GC] (Appl. No. 25735/94), 13 July 2000, paras. 52–53; and ECtHR, *Sommerfeld v. Germany* [GC] (Appl. No. 31871/96), 8 July 2003, paras. 66–74.
1071 ECtHR, *Döring v. Germany* (dec.) (Appl. No. 50216/09), 21 February 2012.

give weight to the child's wishes in a decision on the attribution of parental authority.[1072] According to the Court, the child lacked the necessary age or maturity to 'appreciate the consequences' of the decision to be made (see also Chapter 7).[1073] In *Brede v. Germany* (2009), the ECtHR found that the domestic courts had provided sufficient reasoning to go against the wishes of the children to remain with their parents.[1074] In the decision on the transfer of parental authority to the Youth Office, the domestic courts had balanced these views against the children's development and the mother's ability to care for her children.[1075]

4.5. NEUTRAL RESPONSE TO WEIGHT ACCORDED TO VIEWS

Finally, there are a number of cases in which the ECtHR's reasoning on the weight granted has been neutral. The Court took note of the weight granted to the views of the child, but did not attach a positive or negative conclusion to it. It did so in nine judgments and decisions, the attributes of which are shown in Table 6.8 below.

Table 6.8. Attributes of cases with the ECtHR being neutral in response to the weight accorded to the child's views

Chamber judgments	Type of proceeding	Applicant(s)	Reasoning under
Süss v. Germany (2005)	Access	Father	Article 8
Glesmann v. Germany (2008)	Care and access	Mother	Article 8
Aune v. Norway (2010)	Care	Mother	Article 8
Kijowski v. Poland (2011)	Custody and access	Father	Article 8
A.V. v. Slovenia (2019)	Access	Father	Article 8
Stankūnaitė v. Lithuania (2019)	Care	Mother	Article 8
Chamber decisions	**Type of proceeding**	**Applicant(s)**	**Reasoning under**
Luig v. Germany (2007)	Access	Father	Article 8
Wildgruber v. Germany (2008)	Custody	Father	Article 8
Colombo and others v. Italy and Germany (2016)	International child abduction	Mother, also on behalf of child, and grandmother	Article 8

Source: Compiled by the author.

1072 ECtHR, *Döring v. Germany* (dec.) (Appl. No. 50216/09), 21 February 2012.
1073 ECtHR, *Döring v. Germany* (dec.) (Appl. No. 50216/09), 21 February 2012.
1074 ECtHR, *Brede v. Germany* (dec.) (Appl. No. 35198/05), 3 February 2009.
1075 ECtHR, *Brede v. Germany* (dec.) (Appl. No. 35198/05), 3 February 2009.

In the *Luig v. Germany* (2007), *Wildgruber v. Germany* (2008) and *Colombo and others v. Italy and Germany* (2016) decisions and the Chamber judgments in *Süss v. Germany* (2005), *Glesmann v. Germany* (2008), the ECtHR noted that the domestic courts or authorities relied on the child's views, but attached no further opinion to these views.[1076] In *Colombo and others v. Italy and Germany* (2016), the ECtHR was very brief in noting that the domestic courts relied on the children's statements.[1077] The focus of the ECtHR's reasoning was on a variety of other aspects of the international child abduction and subsequent custody and access proceedings – for example, the children's schooling. In both *A.V. v. Slovenia* (2019) and *Stankūnaitė v. Lithuania* (2019), the ECtHR also remained neutral as to the weight granted to the children's views. In *Stankūnaitė v. Lithuania* (2019), the Court noted that the child had been heard by investigators and experts and referred back to the *G.B. v. Lithuania* (2016) and *N.Ts. and others v. Georgia* (2016) judgments, reaffirming that the 'need to respect the views of the child' is highlighted by the CRC Committee as well as by the ECECR.[1078] In *A.V. v. Slovenia* (2019), the ECtHR simply 'observed' that the children's views – specifically, their refusal to have contact with their father – were considered in the first set of proceedings, but were not deemed sufficient to decide in favour of discontinuing contact.[1079] Subsequently, the ECtHR considered how the children kept refusing contact by leaving the contact sessions and discussed whether the authorities had taken sufficient measures to reunite the father with his children.

A stronger message was made by the ECtHR in *Aune v. Norway* (2010), namely that there was 'no reason to doubt that the impugned measures corresponded to [the child]'s wishes'.[1080] However, the Court provided no positive or negative response to that statement. It found there to be no violation of Article 8 in this case, because the measures taken to deprive the parents of parental authority and to authorize the adoption of the child were proportionate to the legitimate aim of protecting the child's best interests – the views of the child playing a marginal role in this.[1081] The main considerations were that the child had been in foster care for most of her life, there was no attachment to the biological parents and she had a need for security.[1082]

[1076] ECtHR, *Luig v. Germany* (dec.) (Appl. No. 28782/04), 25 September 2007; ECtHR, *Wildgruber v. Germany* (dec.) (Appl. Nos. 42402/05 and 42423/05), 29 January 2008; ECtHR, *Colombo and others v. Italy and Germany* (dec.) (Appl. No. 73708/10), 4 October 2016; ECtHR, *Süss v. Germany* (Appl. No. 40324/98), 10 November 2005, paras. 95 and 98 and ECtHR, *Glesmann v. Germany* (Appl. No. 25706/03), 10 January 2008, para. 107.

[1077] ECtHR, *Colombo and others v. Italy and Germany* (dec.) (Appl. No. 73708/10), 4 October 2016.

[1078] ECtHR, *Stankūnaitė v. Lithuania* (Appl. No. 67068/11), 29 October 2019, para. 128.

[1079] ECtHR, *A.V. v. Slovenia* (Appl. No. 878/13), 9 April 2019, para. 76.

[1080] ECtHR, *Aune v. Norway* (Appl. No. 52502/07), 28 October 2010, para. 72.

[1081] ECtHR, *Aune v. Norway* (Appl. No. 52502/07), 28 October 2010, para. 79.

[1082] ECtHR, *Aune v. Norway* (Appl. No. 52502/07), 28 October 2010, paras. 69–71.

In *Kijowski v. Poland* (2011), the ECtHR referred to the domestic courts having to take into account the child's wishes as a factor in the complex proceedings on the residence of the child, offering no further view on the weight attached.[1083] The Court remarked that the complexity was caused by the conflict between the parents and because the father (the applicant) had acted in breach of the law by keeping the child with him.[1084] The wishes of the child had to be taken into account in light of his age and that he 'clearly wished to live with the applicant'.[1085]

4.6. CONCLUSIONS ON THE ECtHR'S REASONING

In this section, the reasoning of the ECtHR with regard to the weight accorded to a child's views has been discussed. Before we move on to the concluding analysis, a brief conclusion of the Court's reasoning is required. Most significantly, this section has shown that the ECtHR has recognized that due weight must be given to a child's views under the scope of Article 8 ECHR – more specifically, the applicant parent's right to family life. This does not mean that the child's views are to be considered decisive by themselves exclusively, but instead that they must be weighed together with other factors in determining the child's best interests and with other interests, such as those of parents. In considering the facts of the different cases, the ECtHR has relied on these general principles and in the vast majority of the case law has agreed with the weight granted by domestic courts to children's views. In the concluding analysis, we will further examine how due weight is to be determined and which factors have been relied upon by the ECtHR, as well as by the applicants and governments. But before we do so, it is important to make a final remark with regard to the views of the children in the analysed case law. It is noteworthy that in most cases, the children's views consisted of a clear wish or preference – for example, that he or she no longer wants to see a parent or that he or she prefers to reside with one of the two parents. Generally, one would assume that in family law proceedings, children do not immediately have such a clear preference between parents.[1086] In *Döring v. Germany* (2012),

1083 ECtHR, *Kijowski v. Poland* (Appl. No. 33829/07), 5 April 2011, para. 58.

1084 ECtHR, *Kijowski v. Poland* (Appl. No. 33829/07), 5 April 2011, para. 58.

1085 ECtHR, *Kijowski v. Poland* (Appl. No. 33829/07), 5 April 2011, para. 58.

1086 See e.g. J. Cashmore & P. Parkinson, 'Children's and Parents' Perceptions on Children's Participation in Decision Making after Parental Separation and Divorce', *Family Court Review*, Vol. 46, No. 1, 2008, pp. 91–104, pp. 66 and 68–69. Parkinson and Cashmore note that there is a difference between children in contested versus non-contested matters, with the children in non-contested matters more likely to wish to have a 'voice', but not a 'choice'.

for example, the facts show that the child had initially expressed a wish to 'stay with each of his parents on an alternating weekly basis';[1087] only later in the proceedings did the child further develop a clear wish in favour of his father. That so many children in this analysis do have a clear wish as to the outcome of the decision may be explained by the fact that the cases brought to the ECtHR often concern highly contested proceedings which have spanned a longer period of time. In this sense, the case law of the ECtHR may present a distorted picture in comparison to domestic child participation. For example, as in *Döring v. Germany* (2012), drawn-out proceedings may lead to a child's views becoming more fixed. Finally, it is not clear from the case law what children were asked when they were given the opportunity to express their views, and therefore whether the questions asked may have led to the expression of clear wishes and preferences rather than more general views.

5. CONCLUDING ANALYSIS

In taking together the complaints of applicants, the arguments made by governments and the considerations of the ECtHR, a number of conclusions can be made. In the existing literature on the topic, the analysis has not gone further than discussing participation as such. Therefore, this qualitative content analysis provides innovative insights into the ECtHR's reasoning on due weight. These insights will be discussed as the core conclusions of this section. To start with, a numerical analysis will be provided of the cases discussed in this section, as this provides an overarching picture of how due weight plays a role in the case law of the ECtHR. Subsequently, to ascertain the ECtHR standards regarding due weight for the comparison and the evaluation of the international and European framework of the child's right to participate, section 5.2 addresses how due weight is to be determined according to the case law of the ECtHR. This is followed by a section on the relationship between due weight and participation. Finally, attention is paid to the cases in which there was no discussion by the ECtHR on the subject of due weight, even though it was raised by applicants or governments, as this provides some insights into the position of due weight within the case law.

5.1. CONCLUSION IN NUMBERS

Before diving into the deep end, let us dip our toes into the water with the overall numbers of this section. In 59 judgments and decisions, the amount of weight

[1087] ECtHR, *Döring v. Germany* (dec.) (Appl. No. 50216/09), 21 February 2012.

granted to the child(ren)'s expressed views is discussed. The breakdown of these cases are presented in Table 6.9 below.

Table 6.9. Number of cases in which the topic of due weight is discussed

Discussed by:	
Applicant only	2
Government only	8
Applicant and government	2
Applicant, government and ECtHR	8
Applicant and ECtHR	5
Government and ECtHR	7
ECtHR only	27
Total	59

Source: Compiled by the author.

Starting with the applicants, the complaints go both ways: too much weight was given to the children's views or not enough. Seeing as the majority of applicants were the parents themselves, the facts of the case determined the complaint. If the child was negative about the applicant parent and if this played a role in the decision-making process, then the complaint was that too much weight was given to the child's views. If the child had spoken positively about the applicant parent, but the final decision was not in favour of the applicant, then the complaint was that more weight should have been granted to the child's views. What this means is that most complaints on due weight stem from parents using it as an argument to achieve the desired substantive result in their case. Instrumentalizing children's rights for parents' own gain can be problematic if the subsequent consideration by the ECtHR is not child-centred. Although one would rather have parents raise the issue of due weight in furtherance of their children's rights, even when it is raised for the parents' gain, it allows the ECtHR to consider the topic of due weight. If parents were not to raise the question of due weight at all, would we still have the same amount of reasoning? Perhaps not.

Governments explained why due weight was granted or why it was not necessary to grant any weight to the views. It is notable that in 15 cases, governments also raised due weight without a complaint, whereby in half of these cases, the ECtHR also addressed due weight, but did not do so in the other half. The governments were positive, or in some instances neutral, as to the weight granted to the child's views by the domestic courts, with or without a complaint made by an applicant regarding due weight.

The ECtHR at times agreed with the applicants, but generally sided with the governments or domestic courts on the issue. It is interesting to note that the topic of due weight was overwhelmingly discussed or mentioned by the ECtHR itself – in 47 judgments and decisions, it was included in the Court's reasoning. That the ECtHR discussed the issue of due weight in 27 judgments and decisions without any impetus from an applicant's complaint or comment by the government is unexpected. One would expect the ECtHR to focus its reasoning on the complaints presented to it. One reason for this discrepancy is that it concerns nine decisions in which the ECtHR discussed due weight without any government remark, because the governments provided no arguments in the cases at all as the cases in question were (most likely) not communicated to them. This is possible under Rule 54 of the Rules of Court, which only requires complaints to be communicated to contracting parties when the Chamber does not immediately declare the application inadmissible. In the other 16 judgments and two decisions, it can be seen as a positive development that the ECtHR has delved into due weight without outside impetus. It may signify that the child's right to express views and have these views given due weight is becoming ingrained in the Court's case law as a topic of importance.

5.2. DETERMINING DUE WEIGHT

At the domestic level, in reaching a decision in family law proceedings, courts may attach weight to the expressed views of the child to various degrees. There is a spectrum ranging from the views of children not being considered at all, to views being considered by the courts but granted no weight, to views being considered and given weight together with other interests, to views being granted decisive weight in relation to other interests, and finally to views being given exclusive decisive weight. All of these options are possible; however, the ECtHR has determined that due weight should not be interpreted as exclusive weight in the form of a 'veto power'. In essence, due weight is a balancing exercise. The views of children should be weighed against and alongside other factors and interests, and the resulting decision may be in line with the child's views or not, depending on the circumstances.

The ECtHR focuses on the scales in which the children's views must be placed. In these scales, the child's views are weighted depending on child-specific factors and are balanced together with and against other interests and rights – both their own and those of other concerned parties. The ECtHR has been overwhelmingly positive about the balancing exercise conducted by the domestic courts. In 23 cases, the Court agreed with the domestic courts, in contrast to the four judgments in which it disagreed with the weight granted by these courts. This can be explained by the subsidiary position of the ECtHR and the margin of appreciation granted to states. The ECtHR abides by the principle that it is for the national courts to assess the evidence before them and that it 'cannot substitute itself for the domestic authorities' in making decision on custody, access or care.[1088] This means that the ECtHR will generally not weigh the views of the child against other interests and factors itself, but will only review the decisions taken at the domestic level in light of Articles 6 and 8 ECHR. This broader review is what occurs in most cases, even when the applicants complained of too much or too little weight granted. Take, for example, *G.B. v. Lithuania* (2016), in which the applicant complained that too much weight had been placed on the child's views, but the ECtHR found that the domestic courts had properly heard and respected the views of the child.[1089] In light of the ECtHR's subsidiary position, the reasoning of domestic courts is important. As was discussed in section 4.4.3 above, the ECtHR, in determining whether there is a violation of Article 8 ECHR, examined, amongst other things, whether there were relevant and sufficient reasons for the interference of the applicant's right to family life (or private life). In reaching a decision, the domestic courts should consider the views of the child, and in their reasoning of the balancing exercise, it is therefore important that the issue of what weight has been attached to the child's views is clarified.

The judgments in which the ECtHR disagreed with the amount of weight granted to the child's views can be qualified as uncommon, accounting for only four out of the 36 cases in which the Court commented on due weight. In two of these judgments – *C. v. Finland* (2006) and *Blaga v. Romania* (2014) – the ECtHR disagreed with the views of the children being exclusively decisive in the domestic proceedings. The Court did not conduct a balancing exercise of the interests and views itself, but concluded that the domestic courts should have done so. In the *M. and M. v. Croatia* (2015) judgment, the ECtHR deviated from the restrained review. Instead, it concluded that the child's views on residence should have been respected because otherwise due weight would be 'rendered meaningless'.[1090] However, this rather resolute conclusion must be understood in light of the Croatian case law, according to which the child's views are determinative in residence decisions, having regard to the child's age and maturity, if both parents are 'equally fit' to care for the child.[1091] In *N.Ts. and others v. Georgia* (2016), the ECtHR was not as explicit, but did emphasize that in determining children's best interests, their 'emotional state', which can be understood to include their views, are key to the assessment.[1092]

1088 See e.g. ECtHR, *C. v. Finland* (Appl. No. 18249/02), 9 May 2006, para. 52; and ECtHR, *Płaza v. Poland* (Appl. No. 18830/07), 25 January 2011, para. 86.

1089 ECtHR, *G.B. v. Lithuania* (Appl. No. 36137/13), 19 January 2016, para. 105.

1090 ECtHR, *M. and M. v. Croatia* (Appl. No. 10161/13), 3 September 2015, para. 185.

1091 ECtHR, *M. and M. v. Croatia* (Appl. No. 10161/13), 3 September 2015, para. 185.

1092 ECtHR, *N.Ts. and others v. Georgia* (Appl. No. 71776/12), 2 February 2016, para. 84.

To conclude, in order for the ECtHR to disapprove of the domestic courts' weighing exercise, the domestic courts either have to have completely foregone a weighing exercise or, in light of their own domestic laws, to have undeniably given the wrong weight to the views of the child.

It is important to note that in all the cases analysed here, the topic of due weight was in the ECtHR's reasoning always considered under Article 8 ECHR; it was at no point discussed under the ambit of Article 6 ECHR. It can be concluded that the right for a child's expressed views to be given due weight in family law proceedings is protected under the scope of Article 8 ECHR. However, the question is whether this is protected as the child's right under Article 8 ECHR or as the parent's right. In the vast majority of cases where due weight was considered by the ECtHR, the applicants were the parents. The topic of due weight is addressed within the scope of a potential violation of the parents' right to family life under Article 8 ECHR. In the general principles formulated regarding due weight, the ECtHR did not explicitly recognize the granting of due weight to the child's views as a right of the child under Article 8 ECHR. In the general principle introduced in *Płaza v. Poland* (2011), the ECtHR spoke of the child's right to respect for their private life, but as a factor that domestic courts must consider in addition to the child's views and feelings.[1093] Only in *G.H.B. v. United Kingdom* (2000) did the ECtHR hint at a child's right to have their wishes taken into account. The Court noted that had the domestic courts ordered contact against the wishes of the child, it would have 'constituted a failure to properly respect the child's own rights under Article 8'.[1094] To conclude, giving due weight to the views of the child falls under the scope of the right to family life in Article 8 ECHR, but the ECtHR did not consistently explicitly recognize it as a right of children and not their parents.

Another significant aspect with regard to the consistent deliberation of weight granted to children's views under Article 8 ECHR is that the balancing exercise and the question of determining due weight often concern competing Article 8 ECHR interests under the right to family life – the competing interests, for example, being those between two parents or between a child and his or her parent(s). It is therefore necessary to have a multidimensional understanding of Article 8 ECHR in relation to due weight. Article 8 in these cases not only concerns the substantive rights of family members (e.g. a parent's right to contact with his or her child and the child's right to family life), but also concerns the procedural rights of children and, in fact, of the parents themselves. This can cloud the understanding of Article 8 ECHR and requires the ECtHR to very

1093 ECtHR, *Płaza v. Poland* (Appl. No. 18830/07), 25 January 2011, para. 133.
1094 ECtHR, *G.H.B. v. United Kingdom* (dec.) (Appl. No. 42455/98), 4 May 2000.

carefully emphasize whose Article 8 rights are considered and why these may be given more weight than those of the other parties involved.

In order to better understand how due weight should be attributed to the expressed views of children, the following two sections will delve into the identified factors impacting due weight: first, the child-specific factors are addressed, followed by circumstance-specific factors, and finally the relevance of the type of proceedings.

5.2.1. Child-Specific Factors Impacting Due Weight

With the core conclusion of due weight as a balancing exercise, it is relevant to consider which factors may impact the amount of weight granted to the expressed views of the child. In this analysis, two child-specific factors were inferred: consistency and strength of views, and age and maturity.

The first recurring child-specific factor mentioned as a reason for placing more weight on the children's views is the consistency and strength of views expressed. The governments in *Nanning v. Germany* (2007), *Glesmann v. Germany* (2008) and *Gobec v. Slovenia* (2013) referred to the children's consistent, clear and strong views when arguing that the domestic courts were correct in giving weight to these views.[1095] The ECtHR also invoked the consistency and strength of children's views when agreeing with the domestic courts' decisions on the weight given. For example, in *W.F. v. Italy* (2001), the child had firm views, and in *Paulsen-Medalen and Svensson v. Sweden* (2003), it was noted that the child had 'very clear views'.[1096] In the *Gobec v. Slovenia* (2013) judgment, the ECtHR agreed with the government that the 'persistent refusal' and 'categorically' expressed views which did not change over time were of great importance for the domestic courts' decision.[1097] Subsequently, in *M.K. v. Greece* (2018), the Court also referred to the repeated, firm and clearly expressed wishes of the child, while in *Khusnutdinov and X v. Russia* (2018), the clear wishes of the child were emphasized.[1098]

The reference to the consistency of a child's view means that there were multiple points in time during the domestic proceedings at which the views of the child were ascertained. It may not be common in domestic proceedings to

---

1095 ECtHR, *Nanning v. Germany* (Appl. No. 39741/02), 12 July 2007, paras. 57–58; ECtHR, *Glesmann v. Germany* (Appl. No. 25706/03), 10 January 2008, para. 98 and ECtHR, *Gobec v. Slovenia* (Appl. No. 7233/04), 3 October 2013, para. 124.

1096 ECtHR, *W.F. v. Italy* (Appl. No. 34803/97), 5 April 2001; ECtHR, *Paulsen-Medalen and Svensson v. Sweden* (dec.) (Appl. No. 47411/99), 30 September 2003.

1097 ECtHR, *Gobec v. Slovenia* (Appl. No. 7233/04), 3 October 2013, paras. 135 and 137.

1098 ECtHR, *M.K. v. Greece* (Appl. No. 51312/16), 1 February 2018, paras. 87 and 90; and ECtHR, *Khusnutdinov and X v. Russia* (Appl. No. 76598/12), 18 December 2018, para. 86.

have the child participate more than once; however, in lengthy proceedings or proceedings which go to appeal and further (e.g. to the ECtHR itself), this may occur. In drawn-out proceedings, it may even be advisable for domestic courts to reaffirm whether the child's views have changed or remain consistent.[1099]

The second child-specific factor is the age and maturity of the child. Take, for example, *Döring v. Germany* (2012), in which the ECtHR accepted the insufficient maturity as a reason not to grant any weight to the views of the child. Other examples are *W.F. v. Italy* (2001) and *Johansen v. Norway* (2002), where we have seen that the ECtHR did the opposite: the age and maturity of the child was a relevant aspect in relation to the weight granted to the views of the child. As will be further discussed in Chapter 7 on the relevance of the child's maturity for participation and due weight, the ECtHR recognized in 15 judgments and decisions that the children were of sufficient age and maturity to grant weight to their views and in two decisions focused on the children's lack of maturity in terms of not applying due weight to their views.[1100] One can therefore say that age and maturity are relevant in the process of according due weight to the child's views.

5.2.2. Circumstance-Specific Factors Impacting Due Weight

In addition to child-specific factors, there are also circumstance-specific factors which may impact the weighing exercise. These are factors that relate to the circumstances of the case, but do not concern the children themselves. One factor has been derived from the case law of the ECtHR: the potential influence on the child's views.

This circumstance-specific factor relates to the relationship between the parents and the child. One of the parents may influence the child's views. In the general principles formulated by the ECtHR on due weight, an indication has already been given on the relevance of (allegedly) influenced views of the child to the weight to be granted to these views. The impact and relevance of (allegedly) influenced views on due weight has not been considered in this chapter, but is discussed at length in Chapter 8. To a certain extent, influence can be seen as a counterpart to the factor of consistent and strong views – this is also discussed more extensively in Chapter 8.

5.2.3. Types of Proceedings and Due Weight

In addition to the factors discussed above, there is a relevant variable in the determination of due weight: the type of proceedings concerned. In the analysis,

1099 See also Chapter 5, section 5.3.2.
1100 See Chapter 7, sections 4.2.2 and 4.3.2.

it has become apparent that the type of proceeding may lead to a different weighting of views. Although they are all family law proceedings and thus in essence concern the relations between children, parents and potentially the state, the type of proceedings does have an impact on the question of weight. This can be explained by the fact that the type of proceedings may affect the (competing) interests that are to be considered in coming to a decision. Another possible explanation may be the manner or extent to which the type of proceeding impacts the child.

Starting with custody and access proceedings, it can be said that in general, the balancing of interests and the views of the child are at the centre of the ECtHR's conclusions on due weight.

Considering the cases on custody proceedings, a number of interests have been raised by the ECtHR as relevant in the balancing exercise. Most importantly, according to the Court, the rights and interests of the parents and child generally have to be considered. Notably, in *C. v. Finland* (2006), the children's views should have been weighed together with the rights of the father in the custody and contact case, and the children's best interests, including consideration of the potential harm to the children's welfare.[1101] Additionally, for example, in *Miffek v. Czech Republic* (2003), *Mihailova v. Bulgaria* (2006), *Kijowski v. Poland* (2011) and *Döring v. Germany* (2012), the strained relations or conflicts between parents were relevant in addition to the children's development, well-being or living conditions.[1102] Similarly, in *Gineitienė v. Lithuania* (2010), the relevant considerations were that the children's living conditions were rendered 'unsafe' and the potential separation of siblings.[1103] These interests – the child's and those of others – may warrant a decision contrary to the child's explicit wishes or may strengthen the need to follow the child's wishes. As we saw in the *M. and M. v. Croatia* (2015) judgment, if the situation for the child's best interests is similar – the parents are equally fit to care for the child – then the child's views should be respected.[1104]

Turning to access proceedings, a specific argument is repeatedly referred to by the ECtHR when justifying the views of the child being granted additional weight. Generally, the ECtHR has found that the best interests of the child 'normally dictate that the child's ties with its family must be maintained, except in cases where this would harm the child's health and development', as mentioned in *K.B. and others v. Croatia* (2017).[1105] However, in the case law of

---

1101 ECtHR, *C. v. Finland* (Appl. No. 18249/02), 9 May 2006, para. 58.

1102 ECtHR, *Miffek v. Czech Republic* (dec.) (Appl. No. 55069/00), 27 January 2003; ECtHR, *Mihailova v. Bulgaria* (Appl. No. 35978/02), 12 January 2006, para. 100; ECtHR, *Kijowski v. Poland* (Appl. No. 33829/07), 5 April 2011, para. 58 and ECtHR, *Döring v. Germany* (dec.) (Appl. No. 50216/09), 21 February 2012.

1103 ECtHR, *Gineitienė v. Lithuania* (Appl. No. 20739/05), 27 July 2010, para. 38.

1104 ECtHR, *M. and M. v. Croatia* (Appl. No. 10161/13), 3 September 2015, para. 185.

1105 ECtHR, *K.B. and others v. Croatia* (Appl. No. 36216/13), 14 March 2017, para. 143.

the ECtHR, a trend has developed in which the Court has accepted children's resistance to access as being of decisive weight when balanced against other interests. The Court emphasized in *G.H.B. v. United Kingdom* (2000) that considering the child's age and future potential for contact, ordering the child to remain in contact with her grandfather would have been an infringement of her Article 8 rights.[1106] In this case, as well as in *Glesmann v. Germany* (2008) and *T.S. and J.J. v. Norway* (2016), the potential for future contact was a reason for allowing the child's wishes to be determinative. The ECtHR argued in the latter case that 'there will be nothing to prevent him from taking the initiative to increase contact at any time in the future if he so desires'.[1107] More explicitly, the Court recognized in *C. v. Finland* (2006) that 'there may also come a stage where it becomes pointless, if not counter-productive and harmful, to attempt to force a child to conform to a situation which, for whatever reasons, he or she resists'.[1108] This appears to reflect the direct impact of the decision on the life of the child. However, in this judgment and others, the ECtHR did emphasize that the wishes of the child should not be a veto power. Restricting access prompted by the child's wishes may be a decision that can be taken by a domestic court, but only after all the relevant interests have been considered. For example, in *Płaza v. Poland* (2011), the ECtHR referred to the father's rights to contact and the psychological situation as relevant weighting factors.[1109]

Turning our attention to care proceedings, the domestic courts are again expected to balance interests. Additional aspects of relevance were the inability to protect or care for the child, or the child's need for a secure and calm foster family in *Gnahoré v. France* (2000), *Johansen v. Norway* (2002) and *Brede v. Germany* (2009).[1110] More specifically in judgments concerning adoption, such as *Eski v. Austria* (2007) and *Aune v. Norway* (2010), the balance had to be struck between the child's interests in granting adoption, the wishes of the child and the adverse effects for the child's biological parents.[1111]

Finally, there are international child abduction cases which occupy a special position in the due weight discussion due to the exception in Article 13(2)

1106 ECtHR, *G.H.B. v. United Kingdom* (dec.) (Appl. No. 42455/98), 4 May 2000.

1107 ECtHR, *T.S. and J.J. v. Norway* (dec.) (Appl. No. 15633/15), 11 October 2016, para. 29; see also ECtHR *G.H.B. v. United Kingdom* (dec.) (Appl. No. 42455/98), 4 May 2000 and ECtHR, *Glesmann v. Germany* (Appl. No. 25706/03), 10 January 2008, para. 111.

1108 ECtHR, *C. v. Finland* (Appl. No. 18249/02), 9 May 2006, para. 57.

1109 ECtHR, *Płaza v. Poland* (Appl. No. 18830/07), 25 January 2011, para. 86.

1110 ECtHR, *Gnahoré v. France* (Appl. No. 40031/98), 19 September 2000, para. 57; ECtHR, *Johansen v. Norway* (dec.) (Appl. No. 12750/02), 10 October 2002 and ECtHR, *Brede v. Germany* (dec.) (Appl. No. 35198/05), 3 February 2009.

1111 ECtHR, *Eski v. Austria* (Appl. No. 21949/03), 25 January 2007, paras. 40 and 42; and ECtHR, *Aune v. Norway* (Appl. No. 52502/07), 28 October 2010, paras. 69–72.

of The Hague Abduction Convention. We have seen that the ECtHR has emphasized that this exception remains within the discretion of domestic courts. Children should not be given a veto power through the exception. Instead, the domestic courts should consider the various interests at stake and balance them against the application of the exception, as clarified in, for example, *Blaga v. Romania* (2014).[1112] Thus, it can be concluded that although The Hague Abduction Convention appears to grant children a stronger position in terms of the weight attached to their views, it in fact remains a balancing exercise of due weight, as in the other types of proceedings.

To conclude, there are differences between the types of proceedings, but also a great deal of similarity. In all types of family law proceedings, according to the ECtHR, due weight requires a balance to be struck between the views of the child, other factors concerning their best interests, and the interests of the other parties – mainly their parents. Regardless of the type of proceeding, this balance remains. However, the balancing exercise itself may differ slightly depending on the type of proceeding. In custody proceedings, the children's best interests remain crucial – the views of the child may either correspond with these interests or have to be weighed against them – together with the interests of both parents. In access proceedings, this is to a great extent similar, with one important distinction. The ECtHR accepts that the child's refusal to have contact with a parent may be decisive for the decision to restrict access in the child's best interests, as attempting to force a child may be harmful and the potential for future access remains. The rather straightforward reasoning that a child may re-establish contact once time has passed can be questioned and will be further discussed in Chapter 7 and in the conclusions in Chapter 9. The overall balancing of different interests together with the child's views is also seen in care proceedings and in proceedings on international child abduction. The latter, although taken separately, are of course closely related to custody proceedings regarding the residence of the child. Notwithstanding the international aspect of such cases, it is therefore just to take a similar balancing exercise. It is not unexpected that in care proceedings, the child's interests in relation to their protection and safety are of extra importance. However, it is again befitting of the ECtHR to find the general balance of all interests necessary in these cases – including the views of the child. This shows that the ECtHR considers, respects and safeguards the interests of all those involved in family law proceedings, including persons other than the applicant, such as the child or the other parent.

[1112] ECtHR, *Blaga v. Romania* (Appl. No. 54443/10), 1 July 2014, paras. 80–81.

5.3. DUE WEIGHT AND PARTICIPATION

Due weight can only be given to a child's views once these have been expressed. Therefore, due weight is a step that follows the right to participation. This has also been spelled out by the ECtHR in the *M. and M. v. Croatia* (2015) judgment. This judgment is noteworthy because although the applicant's complaint focused on the child's lack of participation, the ECtHR went further and introduced the question of due weight. In finding a violation of Article 8 ECHR, the Court not only relied on the lack of hearing the child in the domestic proceedings, but also found that the domestic courts had unjustly not respected her wishes regarding with which parent she wanted to live.[1113] The ECtHR thereby endorsed the understanding of Article 12 UNCRC as providing a two-step right: first participation and then due weight.

The ECtHR recognizing due weight as the second step, following participation, helps explain a number of cases in which the Court did not pay much (or any) attention to due weight. In these cases, it focused on participation in its judgment instead of on the question of due weight.

Consider the following four cases – first, the Grand Chamber judgment in *Elsholz v. Germany* (2000), in which the applicant father had contested the amount of weight accorded to the child's views. Although the ECtHR found a violation of Article 8 ECHR, the weight accorded to the views of the child played no role in the violation. Instead, the ECtHR focused on the need for an independent psychological report and a hearing before the Regional Court, leading to the insufficient involvement of the applicant in the decision-making process.[1114] In the Chamber judgment in *Süss v. Germany* (2005), the applicant raised a variety of complaints regarding the proceedings leading to the suspension of access. Amongst those complaints were: the complaint that the child's views had been accorded too much weight, but also complaints regarding the need for an expert and that the child's views had been influenced by the other parent. The ECtHR was neutral with regard to the weight accorded to the child's views, focusing in its reasoning on the question of influence and finding no violation of Article 8 in regard to any of the complaints.[1115] In *Nanning v. Germany* (2007), *Havelka and others v. Czech Republic* (2007) and *Iglesias Casarrubios and Cantalapiedra Iglesias v. Spain* (2016), although the governments commented on due weight, the applicants did not raise the issue and the ECtHR did not comment on it

1113 ECtHR, *M. and M. v. Croatia* (Appl. No. 10161/13), 3 September 2015, paras. 186 and 187.
1114 ECtHR, *Elsholz v. Germany* [GC] (Appl. No. 25735/94), 13 July 2000, paras. 52–53.
1115 ECtHR, *Süss v. Germany* (Appl. No. 40324/98), 10 November 2005.

either, because the core issue was the insufficient participation of the children. In all three judgments, the ECtHR held that the domestic courts should have directly heard the children involved or ensured proper representation; not doing so led to a violation of Article 6 in the latter case and of Article 8 in the former two.[1116] These cases are clear examples in which the ECtHR focused on the first step: if there was insufficient participation, the issue of due weight could be placed on the backburner. One could argue that due weight cannot be achieved without a sufficient expression of views in the first place.

Additionally, there are two cases in which the ECtHR remarked on the issue of weight granted, even though there had been no complaint by the applicant or any remarks by the government on that point. In both, the issue of insufficient participation was of greater relevance in the ECtHR's reasoning than the issue of due weight. In the Grand Chamber judgment in *Sommerfeld v. Germany* (2003), the applicant's complaint concerned the influence on the child's views, not the weight attached to those views per se.[1117] However, besides discussing the issue of influence, the ECtHR also considered the need for a psychological expert for participation, as seen in the previous section, and made a brief remark on the issue of due weight. This brief remark was no more than to find that the domestic courts had adduced relevant reasons for their decision by including the views of the child. A lengthier remark was also not called for, as there had been no complaint addressing due weight. In *Wildgruber v. Germany* (2008), the ECtHR made a neutral remark as to due weight, noting the reliance on the child's views without attaching any judgment to it.[1118] Again, the Court was not called upon to judge the issue of due weight, as the applicant's complaints focused on the need for additional participation, the use of an expert and the issue of influence – not so much the question of weight. It would have been interesting to see how the ECtHR would have responded had the applicant decided to also raise the question of weight.

It is perhaps legitimate for due weight to take a backseat in the reasoning of the ECtHR when there are already complications regarding participation as such. The problems with child participation may require solutions before due weight can be considered. However, this should not lead the ECtHR to fully disregard due weight if a violation regarding participation is already found. Especially where the violation regarding participation addresses insufficient

---

1116 ECtHR, *Nanning v. Germany* (Appl. No. 39741/02), 12 July 2007, paras. 74–75; ECtHR, *Havelka and others v. Czech Republic* (Appl. No. 23499/06), 21 June 2007, paras. 62–63 and ECtHR, *Iglesias Casarrubios and Cantalapiedra Iglesias v. Spain* (Appl. No. 23298/12), 11 October 2016, paras. 42–43.

1117 ECtHR, *Sommerfeld v. Germany* [GC] (Appl. No. 31871/96), 8 July 2003.

1118 ECtHR, *Wildgruber v. Germany* (dec.) (Appl. Nos. 42402/05 and 42423/05), 29 January 2008.

participation and not a complete lack of participation, cases in which the applicants specifically raised due weight call for a response by the ECtHR – even if it is minimal. It is therefore also good to see that the ECtHR has at times been willing to discuss the issue of due weight on its own initiative without any complaints or comments. In doing so, it has reaffirmed the two-step right of child participation: first, sufficient participation and then due weight.

5.4. NO DUE WEIGHT DISCUSSION BY THE ECtHR

There are nine judgments and decisions which have been named and discussed under the applicant's complaints and governments responses that have not been discussed yet in this conclusion. The reason for this is that the ECtHR did not discuss the issue of weight granted in any of these judgments or decisions.

In four judgments, the applicants had contested the weight granted to the views of the child. In *Kosmopoulou v. Greece* (2004), the applicant's complaint that too much weight had been granted to her daughter's wishes did not play a role in the ECtHR finding a violation of Article 8 (the applicant's right to family life). The violation concerned the procedural approach of domestic courts in deciding on the question of access between the mother and her child. Instead of the issue of due weight, the applicant's lack of hearings in front of the domestic courts which decided to provisionally suspend her visiting rights, which had detrimental consequences to the relation between the applicant and the child, formed the key to the ECtHR's finding.[1119] In another case concerning access restrictions, *R. v. Finland* (2006), the applicant also complained about the strong weight placed on the child's views. Both the government and the ECtHR overlooked this issue. The ECtHR found a violation of Article 8 ECtHR due to the authorities' failure to take sufficient steps to reunite the applicant with his child following care measures, which in fact directed towards non-reunification by restricting access.[1120] In *Jucius and Juciuvienė v. Lithuania* (2008), the ECtHR zoomed in on the effect that time had on the custody proceedings when finding a violation of Article 8, disregarding the applicants' complaint that the views of the child were ignored. This is perhaps because, as the government also pointed out, after the complaint was lodged, the children's views had been given due weight in domestic proceedings.[1121] In *Z.J. v. Lithuania* (2014), although the

[1119] ECtHR, *Kosmopoulou v. Greece* (Appl. No. 60457/00), 5 February 2004, para. 49.

[1120] ECtHR, *R. v. Finland* (Appl. No. 34141/96), 30 May 2006, paras. 92–94.

[1121] ECtHR, *Jucius and Juciuvienė v. Lithuania* (Appl. No. 14414/03), 25 November 2008, paras. 23–24.

applicant complained that the courts had 'disregarded the experts' finding' on the child's views, the ECtHR did not consider the issue of due weight. Instead, the Court looked at the situation as a whole and found that the domestic authorities fulfilled their responsibility and positive obligations to return the children to applicant, and thus found no violation of Article 8.[1122] In these four judgments, the weighting attached to the children's views did not form a core part of the complaint; instead, it was one ingredient in the cocktail of complaints. This may explain why the ECtHR ignored the issue in its reasoning, as it could instead focus on other concerns raised by the applicants.

In five other judgments and decisions, the applicants themselves did not even complain about the weight granted to the views of the children, but the governments did comment on the issue. Again, the ECtHR did not discuss the weight granted to views in its reasoning. In *Hansen v. Turkey* (2003), *Milovanović v. Serbia* (2019) and *Haase v. Germany* (2004), the ECtHR instead found a violation of Article 8 due to the failure to enforce access or custody rights with regard to the first two judgments, and a violation of Article 8 for the unjustified decision-making process leading to the taking of a newborn into care in the latter.[1123] In *L. v. Finland* (2000), the ECtHR held that there was no violation of Article 8 because the applicant had been able to continue having contact and the decisions on restricting access were justifiable.[1124] Finally, in *Süss v. Germany* (2001), the government noted that due weight was granted to the views of the child, but the ECtHR did not respond substantively as it declared the complaint of the applicant under Article 8 ECHR to be admissible.[1125] The lack of complaints from applicants on the issue of due weight in these cases may explain why the ECtHR did not discuss the issue further in its reasoning.

In rounding off this concluding analysis, a final remark should be made that in Table 6.10 below, a combined overview is included of all the judgments and decisions discussed in this section and the corresponding relevance regarding the weight accorded to the child's views. This table not only provides a useful overview when reading the conclusions set out above, but glancing at it also offers some final insights. Most clearly, it shows the increased relevance of due weight in the 2010s. The ECtHR's increased reasoning in the past decade is noteworthy.

1122 ECtHR, *Z.J. v. Lithuania* (Appl. No. 60092/12), 29 April 2014, paras. 105–106.

1123 ECtHR, *Hansen v. Turkey* (Appl. No. 36141/97), 23 September 2003, para. 108; ECtHR, *Milovanović v. Serbia* (Appl. No. 56065/10), 8 October 2019, para. 136 and ECtHR, *Haase v. Germany* (Appl. No. 11057/02), 8 April 2004, para. 104.

1124 ECtHR, *L. v. Finland* (Appl. No. 25651/94), 27 April 2000, paras. 127–128.

1125 ECtHR, *Süss v. Germany* (dec.) (Appl. No. 40324/98), 20 September 2001.

Table 6.10. Combined overview for weight accorded to the child's views

		Applicants' complaint			Governments' argument				ECtHR					
		Unreasonable amount of weight	Views accorded too little weight	No complaint	Views accorded due weight	Neutral remark on weight	Views not given exclusive weight	No argument	General principles	Exclusive weight	Positive on the amount of weight granted	Negative on the amount of weight granted	Neutral	No discussion
GC judgments	*Elsholz v. Germany* (2000)	X	-	-	-	X	-	-	-	-	X	-	-	-
	Sommerfeld v. Germany (2003)	-	-	X	-	-	-	X	-	-	X	-	-	-

Chamber judgments	*L. v. Finland* (2000)	-	-	X	X	-	-	-	-	-	-	-	-	X
	Gnahoré v. France (2000)	-	-	X	-	-	-	X	-	-	X	-	-	-
	Hansen v. Turkey (2003)	-	-	X	X	-	-	-	-	-	-	-	-	X
	Kosmopoulou v. Greece (2004)	X	-	-	X	-	-	-	-	-	-	-	-	X
	Haase v. Germany (2004)	-	-	X	-	X	-	-	-	-	-	-	-	X
	Süss v. Germany (2005)	X	-	-	X	-	-	-	-	-	-	-	X	-
	Mihailova v. Bulgaria (2006)	-	-	X	-	-	-	X	-	-	X	-	-	-
	C. v. Finland (2006)	X	-	-	X	-	-	-	-	X	-	X	-	-
	R. v. Finland (2006)	X	-	-	-	-	-	X	-	-	-	-	-	X
	Eski v. Austria (2007)	-	-	X	-	-	-	X	-	-	X	-	-	-
	Havelka and others v. Czech Republic (2007)	-	-	X	-	X	-	-	-	-	-	-	-	X
	Nanning v. Germany (2007)	-	-	X	X	-	-	-	-	-	-	-	-	X
	Glesmann v. Germany (2008)	-	-	X	X	-	-	-	-	-	-	-	X	-
	Jucius and Juciuvienė v. Lithuania (2008)	-	X	-	X	-	-	-	-	-	-	-	-	X
	Gineitienė v. Lithuania (2010)	-	-	X	-	-	-	X	-	-	X	-	-	-
	Aune v. Norway (2010)	-	-	X	-	-	-	X	-	-	-	-	X	-
	Płaza v. Poland (2011)	X	-	-	X	-	-	-	X	-	X	-	-	-
	Kijowski v. Poland (2011)	-	-	X	-	-	-	X	-	-	-	-	X	-
	Cristescu v. Romania (2012)	-	-	X	-	-	-	X	-	-	X			
	Y.C. v. United Kingdom (2012)	-	-	X	X	-	-	-	X	-	-	-	-	-
	Raw and others v. France (2013)	-	-	X	-	-	-	X	-	X	-	-	-	-
	Gobec v. Slovenia (2013)	-	-	X	X	-	-	-	X	-	X	-	-	-

(continued)

Table 6.10 *continued*

		Applicants' complaint			Governments' argument				ECtHR					
		Unreasonable amount of weight	Views accorded too little weight	No complaint	Views accorded due weight	Neutral remark on weight	Views not given exclusive weight	No argument	General principles	Exclusive weight	Positive on the amount of weight granted	Negative on the amount of weight granted	Neutral	No discussion
Chamber judgments	*Z.J. v. Lithuania* (2014)	-	X	-	-	-	-	X	-	-	-	-	-	X
	Blaga v. Romania (2014)	X	-	-	-	X	-	-	-	X	-	X	-	-
	Rouiller v. Switzerland (2014)	-	X	-	-	-	X	-	-	X	-	-	-	-
	Gajtani v. Switzerland (2014)	-	X	-	-	-	-	X	-	X	-	-	-	-
	M. and M. v. Croatia (2015)	-	-	X	-	-	-	X	-	-	-	X	-	-
	G.B. v. Lithuania (2016)	X	-	-	X	-	-	-	-	-	X	-	-	-
	N.Ts. and others v. Georgia (2016)	-	X	-	-	-	-	X	-	-	-	X	-	-
	Buchleither v. Germany (2016)	-	-	X	X	-	-	-	-	-	X	-	-	-
	Iglesias Casarrubios and Cantalapiedra Iglesias v. Spain (2016	-	-	X	X	-	-	-	-	-	-	-	-	X

Chamber judgments	*K.B. and others v. Croatia* (2017)	-	-	X	-	-	-	X	X	-	-	-	-	-
	M.K. v. Greece (2018)	-	-	X	X	-	-	-	-	-	X	-	-	-
	Petrov and X v. Russia (2018)	-	-	X	-	-	-	X	X	-	-	-	-	-
	Khusnutdinov and X v. Russia (2018)	X	-	-	X	-	-	-	X	-	X	-	-	-
	A.V. v. Slovenia (2019)	-	-	X	X	-	-	-	X	-	-	-	X	-
	Milovanović v. Serbia (2019)	-	-	X	X	-	-	-	-	-	-	-	-	X
	Pisică v. Republic of Moldova (2019)	-	-	X	-	-	-	X	X	-	-	-	-	-
	Zelikha Magomadova v. Russia (2019)	-	-	X	-	-	-	X	X	-	-	-	-	-
	Stankūnaitė v. Lithuania (2019)	-	-	X	-	-	-	X	-	-	-	-	X	-
Chamber decisions	*Tiemann v. France and Germany* (2000)	-	X	-	-	-	-	N	-	-	X	-	-	-
	G.H.B. v. United Kingdom (2000)	-	-	X	X	-	-	-	-	-	X	-	-	-
	W.F. v. Italy (2001)	X	-	-	-	-	-	X	-	-	X	-	-	-
	Süss v. Germany (2001)	-	-	X	X	-	-	-	-	-	-	-	-	X
	Johansen v. Norway (2002)	-	-	X	-	-	-	N	-	-	X	-	-	-
	Miffek v. Czech Republic (2003)	-	-	X	-	-	-	N	-	-	X	-	-	-
	Paradis and others v. Germany (2003)	-	-	X	-	-	-	N	-	X	-	-	-	-

(continued)

Table 6.10 *continued*

		Applicants' complaint			Governments' argument				ECtHR					
		Unreasonable amount of weight	Views accorded too little weight	No complaint	Views accorded due weight	Neutral remark on weight	Views not given exclusive weight	No argument	General principles	Exclusive weight	Positive on the amount of weight granted	Negative on the amount of weight granted	Neutral	No discussion
Chamber decisions	*Paulsen-Medalen and Svensson v. Sweden* (2003)	-	-	X	-	-	-	N	-	-	X	-	-	-
	Petersen v. Germany (2006)	-	-	X	-	-	-	N	-	-	X	-	-	-
	Luig v. Germany (2007)	-	-	X	-	-	-	N	-	-	-	-	X	-
	Wildgruber v. Germany (2008)	-	-	X	-	-	-	N	-	-	-	-	X	-
	Brede v. Germany (2009)	-	X	-	-	-	-	N	-	-	X	-	-	-
	Döring v. Germany (2012)	-	-	X	-	-	-	N	-	-	X	-	-	-
	J. and others v. Finland (2013)	-	-	X	-	-	-	X	X	-	-	-	-	-
	A.E.L. v. Finland (2013)	-	-	X	-	-	-	X	X	-	-	-	-	-
	Colombo and others v. Italy and Germany (2016)	-	-	X	-	-	-	N	-	-	-	-	X	-
	T.S. and J.J. v. Norway (2016)	-	-	X	-	-	-	N	-	-	X	-	-	-

N = no arguments provided at all by the government because the complaint was not communicated to the contracting party, as is only required when the Chamber does not immediately declare the application inadmissible (see Rule 54 of the Rules of Court).

Source: Compiled by the author.

6. CONCLUSION: STANDARDS

Due weight has proven to be an important but puzzling feature of child participation in this analysis. The complaints brought by applicants, the arguments put forward by governments and the ECtHR's reasoning have been studied both separately and collectively in the concluding analysis. The time has now come to determine what standards can be drawn from the case law regarding due weight. In total, five explicit standards can be identified which are relevant for the international and European framework of the child's right to participate. These standards are labelled using a 'W' to signal that they concern 'Weight'.

> W.1 Courts should give due weight to a child's expressed views in family law proceedings.

This standard reflects the common understanding that children's views should be given due weight. It is based on the general principle introduced by the ECtHR in *Płaza v. Poland* (2011) and reiterated in *Gobec v. Slovenia* (2013), *Petrov and X v. Russia* (2018), *Khusnutdinov and X v. Russia* (2018) and *Zelikha Magomadova v. Russia* (2019) explicitly. The standard reproduces the fundamental aspects of this general principle concerning due weight. It can be understood as falling under the scope of Article 8 ECHR, although the ECtHR has not yet consistently referred to it as part of the child's right to family life.

> W.2 Determining due weight is a balancing exercise: the child's views have to be weighed together with his or her best interests and other interests. A child's views are not necessarily immutable and are not necessarily sufficient to override other interests.

This second standard answers the question of what due weight is. This standard mirrors the ECtHR's understanding of due weight as a balancing exercise. Children's views should be given due weight, but not a veto power. This standard is a combination of the general principles expressed in *K.B. and others v. Croatia* (2017), based on *C. v. Finland* (2006) and *Raw and others v. France* (2013), and reiterated explicitly in *A.V. v. Slovenia* (2019), *Pisică v. Republic of Moldova* (2019) and *Zelikha Magomadova v. Russia* (2019). As the concluding analysis has shown, in family law proceedings – whether those concerning custody, access or care – the child's views have to be weighed together with and against the other interests of the children themselves and all other parties involved. The reasoning of the domestic courts is relevant in that respect.

W.3 In determining the weight to be granted to the views of the child, it is relevant to take into account child-specific factors (the consistency and strength of his or her views, and his or her age and maturity) and circumstance-specific factors (inter alia, influence).

Based on the concluding analysis, three factors were identified which can impact on the amount of weight given to the child's views. These factors are split between child-specific factors, which relate to the child and his or her expressed views as such, and circumstance-specific factors, which concern the relationship between the child and their parents, such as potential influence. These factors may push the scale in the balancing exercise of due weight, but, as always, in relation to the other interests involved in the proceedings.

W.4 In international child abduction proceedings, the exception of Article 13(2) of The Hague Abduction Convention is not absolute; the child's objection to return should form part of the balancing exercise together with other interests.

The ECtHR has repeatedly deliberated on the specific question of due weight or decisive weight in international child abduction cases in light of the exception in The Hague Abduction Convention. The standard has consistently been that the child's objection to return should not amount to a veto power. As in other types of proceedings, the views of the child must be weighed against other interests and circumstances.

W.5 Due weight is the required second step following participation. Participation alone is not sufficient; due weight must be given to the child's views. However, if there is insufficient participation, the issue of due weight may be of less importance.

Due weight is closely associated with participation. This principle permeates the entire analysis of due weight in this section. More explicitly, the ECtHR has clarified that a child's participation as such is not sufficient if there no due weight is granted to the child's views – see, for example, *M. and M. v. Croatia* (2015). However, what has also become clear in the concluding analysis is that if participation is lacking – either completely or in part – the ECtHR will generally focus on this first step and overlook the complaints on due weight, although the latter is not advised.

CHAPTER 7
MATURITY OF THE CHILD

'As children mature and, with the passage of time, become able to formulate their own opinion, the court should give due weight also to their views and feelings ...'

– ECtHR, *Petrov and X v. Russia*[1126]

1. INTRODUCTION

As the fountain of youth remains a myth, every person on the planet grows older with the passage of time. Someone's age cannot be halted; the passing days add up to months and years. Adults grow old and children grow up. Growing up is the process through which children gradually achieve physical and mental maturity. As the European Court of Human Rights (ECtHR) eloquently phrased it in the quote above, as children mature, they become able to formulate their own opinions and, in family law proceedings, the courts should give due weight to their views and opinions. In the previous two chapters on (in)sufficient participation and the weight granted to children's views, the child's maturity has surfaced as a relevant factor. The importance of the child's maturity also stems from the fact that it is the most common condition applied in international law and domestic law for child participation.[1127] It was therefore included in the coding framework for this analysis and rightfully so, as it is a common point of discussion in the case law studied.

1126 ECtHR, *Petrov and X v. Russia* (Appl. No. 23608/16), 23 October 2018, para. 108. This principle was originally introduced in ECtHR, *Płaza v. Poland* (Appl. No. 18830/07), 25 January 2011, para. 71, but was limited to contact proceedings. It was subsequently reaffirmed in ECtHR, *Gobec v. Slovenia* (Appl. No. 7233/04), 3 October 2013, para. 133; ECtHR, *Khusnutdinov and X v. Russia* (Appl. No. 76598/12), 18 December 2018, para. 86 and ECtHR, *Zelikha Magomadova v. Russia* (Appl. No. 58724/14), 8 October 2019, para. 115. See also section 4.1 below.

1127 See e.g. M.R. Bruning & C.R. Mol, 'Child Participation in International and Regional Human Rights Instruments', in: W.M. Schrama et al. (eds.), *International Handbook on Child Participation in Family Law*, Cambridge: Intersentia 2021, pp. 13–40, p. 39; and C.R. Mol, 'Child Participation in Family Law Proceedings Compared', in: W.M. Schrama et al. (eds.), *International Handbook on Child Participation in Family Law*, Cambridge: Intersentia 2021a, pp. 335–358, pp. 351–352.

In this chapter, the maturity of the child will be discussed both in relation to participation as well as for the weight to be attached to the child's views. As shown in Figure 4.1 in Chapter 4, the theme of maturity overlaps with these two central themes. Whereas in Chapters 5 and 6 the focus was on the (in) sufficient participation and the weight accorded to a child's views respectively, in this chapter the focus is on how the child's maturity is considered as such, and how it functions as a factor in participation and due weight. In that sense, while some of the case law discussed has been included in the preceding chapters, this chapter also includes other case law and draws new conclusions and inferences.

The topic of the child's maturity will be discussed in the following sections on the complaints brought by applicants, the governments' arguments and the ECtHR's considerations. In each of these sections, comments and considerations have been split between those on insufficient maturity and those on sufficient maturity. By considering the complaints and the governments' responses in addition to the ECtHR's reasoning, this analysis provides for an insight into all the possible factors that may explain the standards drawn by the ECtHR. Conclusions will be drawn that tie all of the above together and an overview table is included. At the very end of this chapter, the standards drawn from the ECtHR's case law on the maturity of the child are presented, which are relevant for the comparison in Chapter 10 and the evaluation of the international and European framework in Chapter 11.

2. COMPLAINTS BROUGHT BY APPLICANTS

The maturity of children was not a common focus of applicants' complaints, appearing in the complaints of only five cases. The relevant attributes of these cases are presented in Table 7.1 below. The complaints concerned the child's maturity for participation, the child's maturity for due weight and the manner in which maturity was determined.

Table 7.1. Attributes of cases in which the applicant complained regarding the maturity of the child

Chamber judgments	Type of proceeding	Applicant	Article of complaint
C. v. Finland (2006)	Custody and access	Father	Article 8
Blaga v. Romania (2014)	International child abduction	Father	Article 8
M. and M. v. Croatia (2015)	Custody	Mother and child on own behalf	Article 8
Zelikha Magomadova v. Russia (2019)	Custody	Mother	Article 8

(continued)

Table 7.1 *continued*

Chamber decision	Type of proceeding	Applicant	Article of complaint
Eskinazi and Chelouche v. Turkey (2005)	International child abduction	Mother, also on behalf of child	Article 8

Source: Compiled by the author.

In two judgments, the applicants complained that the children had sufficient maturity to participate, but had not been afforded the opportunity to do so. The applicants in *M. and M. v. Croatia* (2015) complained that the child (one of the applicants) had not been heard, even though 'her age and maturity so permitted'.[1128] At the time of the domestic proceedings, the child was 9–12 years old. More specifically, the applicants noted that the 'forensic experts regarded her as being of above-average intellectual capacities' and that she had repeatedly unequivocally expressed her wishes.[1129] Similarly, in *Zelikha Magomadova v. Russia* (2019), the applicant complained that four of her children had not been heard, although they 'had been mature enough' being 13, 11, 9, and 7 years old respectively.[1130] In raising this complaint with regard to the two eldest children, the applicant referred to domestic Russian law, which requires that the views of children over ten years old should be taken into account.[1131]

In a third judgment, the complaint concerned the question of due weight. The applicant in *Blaga v. Romania* (2014) alleged that the children had insufficient maturity to have their views granted exclusive and decisive weight in The Hague return proceedings.[1132] The children were 11, 9 and 9 years old at the time.

Finally, the two other complaints concerned how the child's maturity ought to be established. In *C. v. Finland* (2006), the applicant complained that the Supreme Court had 'applied the criteria of age automatically without regard to issues of maturity or voluntariness of the views expressed.[1133] The facts of this case disclose that the Finnish Supreme Court decided to give weight to the views expressed by the children, who were at that point in time 14 and 12 years old.[1134] In the Chamber decision in *Eskinazi and Chelouche v. Turkey* (2005), the applicants argued that it should not have been at the sole discretion of the judge to decide that the child lacked the necessary maturity to be heard in the proceedings, but that it should have been determined by someone with scientific expertise.[1135] The child concerned was four years old at that time.

1128 ECtHR, *M. and M. v. Croatia* (Appl. No. 10161/13), 3 September 2015, para. 129.
1129 ECtHR, *M. and M. v. Croatia* (Appl. No. 10161/13), 3 September 2015, para. 129.
1130 ECtHR, *Zelikha Magomadova v. Russia* (Appl. No. 58724/14), 8 October 2019, para. 88.
1131 ECtHR, *Zelikha Magomadova v. Russia* (Appl. No. 58724/14), 8 October 2019, para. 88.
1132 ECtHR, *Blaga v. Romania* (Appl. No. 54443/10), 1 July 2014, para. 60.
1133 ECtHR, *C. v. Finland* (Appl. No. 18249/02), 9 May 2006, para. 43.
1134 ECtHR, *C. v. Finland* (Appl. No. 18249/02), 9 May 2006, paras. 33–34.
1135 ECtHR, *Eskinazi and Chelouche v. Turkey* (dec.) (Appl. No. 14600/05), 6 December 2005.

3. GOVERNMENTS' ARGUMENTS

Governments also addressed the topic of a child's maturity in relation to the participation process. The issue was brought up by governments in one of two ways: either the child concerned was sufficiently mature to participate or to have their views taken into account, or the child did not have the required maturity. Whichever way the governments argued, in all 16 judgments and decisions discussed below, the governments justified the decisions made by domestic courts, doing so either in response to a complaint brought by the applicant or on their own initiative.

3.1. INSUFFICIENT MATURITY

The lack of required maturity was argued four times by the governments, either regarding the maturity required to participate or for the question of due weight. The attributes of these four cases are provided in Table 7.2.

Table 7.2. Attributes of cases in which the government argued that the child had insufficient age or maturity

Chamber judgments	Type of proceeding	In response to complaint on
Gajtani v. Switzerland (2014)	International child abduction	Article 8
Petrov and X v. Russia (2018)	Custody	Article 8
Zelikha Magomadova v. Russia (2019)	Custody	Article 8
Chamber decision	**Type of proceeding**	**In response to complaint on**
Eskinazi and Chelouche v. Turkey (2005)	International child abduction	Article 8

Source: Compiled by the author.

In three cases the insufficient age or maturity of the child was argued in relation to participation. The first case involved the Turkish government in *Eskinazi and Chelouche v. Turkey* (2005), which justified the domestic court not hearing the child by referring to a practical guide that recommended hearing the child in international child abduction cases aged ten and above.[1136] The child in this case was four to five years old during the proceedings, so far below this age suggestion. The Russian government argued that children were only required to be heard from the age of ten upwards on the grounds of domestic law in two judgments: *Petrov and X v. Russia* (2018)

[1136] ECtHR, *Eskinazi and Chelouche v. Turkey* (dec.) (Appl. No. 14600/05), 6 December 2005.

and *Zelikha Magomadova v. Russia* (2019).[1137] Therefore the children concerned, who were younger than ten, were not required to be heard.

In the final case, the insufficient maturity concerned due weight. In Chamber judgment in *Gajtani v. Switzerland* (2014), the Swiss government recalled that the decision of the Court of Appeal not to take the views of the child into account was reasonable as it found the child to be at the lower boundary of capacity at the age of 11 and a half years old.[1138]

3.2. SUFFICIENT MATURITY

In 12 cases, the respective governments commented on the relevance of the child having sufficient maturity. These governments either found the child to have sufficient maturity to participate (see section 3.2.1) or sufficient maturity for the views of the child to be given the weight they were given in the domestic proceedings (see section 3.2.2). For all these cases, the attributes are presented in Table 7.3 below.

Table 7.3. Attributes of cases in which the government argued that the child had sufficient age or maturity

Grand Chamber judgment	**Type of proceeding**	**In response to complaint on**
Sommerfeld v. Germany (2003)	Access	Article 8
Chamber judgments	**Type of proceeding**	**In response to complaint on**
L. v. Finland (2000)	Care and access	Article 8
K.A. v. Finland (2003)	Care	Article 8
Hansen v. Turkey (2003)	Access	Article 8
C. v. Finland (2006)	Custody and access	Article 8
R. v. Finland (2006)	Care and access	Article 8
Nanning v. Germany (2007)	Custody and access	Article 8
Płaza v. Poland (2011)	Access	Article 8
Gobec v. Slovenia (2013)	Access	Article 8
Ónodi v. Hungary (2017)	Access	Article 8
Milovanović v. Serbia (2019)	Custody	Article 8
Chamber decision	**Type of proceeding**	**In response to complaint on**
Petersen v. Germany (2006)	Custody and access	Article 8

Source: Compiled by the author.

[1137] ECtHR, *Petrov and X v. Russia* (Appl. No. 23608/16), 23 October 2018, para. 90; and ECtHR, *Zelikha Magomadova v. Russia* (Appl. No. 58724/14), 8 October 2019, para. 92.

[1138] ECtHR, *Gajtani v. Switzerland* (Appl. No. 43730/07), 9 September 2014, paras. 96–97.

3.2.1. *Sufficient Maturity to Participate*

With regard to whether the child had sufficient maturity to participate, there were three cases in which the government argued that the children did. The government in *R. v. Finland* (2006) argued in response to the question of whether the child had been given an opportunity to be heard that, as the child had grown older, 'it had been possible to have more discussions with a view to finding out his views and wishes'.[1139] The child was five years old at the start of the proceedings and ten years old at the end. The 'discussions' of the welfare officers with the child started once he had been placed in a substitute family at the age of eight.[1140] Additionally, in one decision – *Petersen v. Germany* (2006) – the German government indicated that the child had been heard by the domestic courts at the age of nine and ten,[1141] and in Chamber judgment in *L. v. Finland* (2000), the government referred to the fact that the eight-year-old child had been heard in the domestic proceedings.[1142]

3.2.2. *Sufficient Maturity to Give Weight to Views*

In ten judgments, the governments argued that the children had sufficient maturity to give due weight to their views. The most telling comment with respect to children's maturity and the weight given to their views was made by the Turkish government in *Hansen v. Turkey* (2003): 'in such circumstances the authorities were also under an obligation under Article 8 of the Convention to protect the interests of the children who were mature enough to have their views taken into account'.[1143] The circumstances referred to were the repeated expressed reluctance of the children to see their mother and the fact that the two children were 11 and 10 years old when first heard and 17 and 16 years old when the proceedings were at final instance. In *Gobec v. Slovenia* (2013), the government 'pointed to the requirement to give due weight to the wishes of a child who was capable of understanding the meaning and implications of the proceedings'.[1144] However, the source of this requirement is unclear. The government argued that the prohibition of contact was sufficiently reasoned because of the findings of a number of psychologists that the child was 'mature for her age', in combination with the fact that she consistently refused and was resolute with her views.[1145] The findings referred to appear to concern the

---

1139 ECtHR, *R. v. Finland* (Appl. No. 34141/96), 30 May 2006, para. 78.
1140 ECtHR, *R. v. Finland* (Appl. No. 34141/96), 30 May 2006, para. 78.
1141 ECtHR, *Petersen v. Germany* (dec.) (Appl. Nos. 38282/97 and 68891/01), 12 January 2006.
1142 ECtHR, *L. v. Finland* (Appl. No. 25651/94), 27 April 2000, para. 126.
1143 ECtHR, *Hansen v. Turkey* (Appl. No. 36141/97), 23 September 2003, para. 93.
1144 ECtHR, *Gobec v. Slovenia* (Appl. No. 7233/04), 3 October 2013, para. 124.
1145 ECtHR, *Gobec v. Slovenia* (Appl. No. 7233/04), 3 October 2013, para. 124.

child when she was aged 12–13.[1146] In *L. v. Finland* (2000), the government argued that the wishes of one of the children 'should be respected as far as possible', taking into account the age of child, who at the time was 14 years old.[1147] In *Płaza v. Poland* (2011), the child's 'views had been given due consideration' because the experts had found the child to be 'very mature for her age as well as articulate and able to express her views and feelings in a clear manner'.[1148] At the time of these domestic proceedings, the child was 7–18 years old – the child was granted the opportunity to express views from the age of 11 onwards.[1149] The maturity of the child was also referred to in *Ónodi v. Hungary* (2017), where the government concluded its reply to the applicant's complaint that the authorities had failed to enforce his contact with his child by stating that the child 'had had full capacity to understand the situation' and opposed contact.[1150] The domestic proceedings ran from when the child was 12 until she was 17 years old. Similarly, in *Milovanović v. Serbia* (2019), the government argued that it was not possible to coerce the children to reside with their father at the age of 12 when 'their opinions had to be taken into account', or later when they reached the age of 15 and they could 'legally decide' on their residence.[1151]

In three other judgments, the governments referred to the age of the children with regard to giving weight to their views. In *C. v. Finland* (2006), the children were 14 and 12 years old respectively when the Finnish Supreme Court took their wishes and opinions into account,[1152] and in *K.A. v. Finland* (2003), the children were 13 and 12 years old.[1153] The German government noted the 'child's increasing age' in combination with the child's consistent refusal as grounds for the decision to deny access rights when the child was 17 years old in *Nanning v. Germany* (2007).[1154]

One argument was raised that was something of an odd one out: in the Grand Chamber judgment in *Sommerfeld v. Germany* (2003), the government noted that the domestic courts could rely on the age of the child, who was 13 years old at the time, in addition to the 'broad factual basis' of repeated refusal by the child throughout the years – therefore not requiring an additional expert opinion.[1155]

1146 ECtHR, *Gobec v. Slovenia* (Appl. No. 7233/04), 3 October 2013, para. 59.
1147 ECtHR, *L. v. Finland* (Appl. No. 25651/94), 27 April 2000, para. 125.
1148 ECtHR, *Płaza v. Poland* (Appl. No. 18830/07), 25 January 2011, para. 64.
1149 ECtHR, *Płaza v. Poland* (Appl. No. 18830/07), 25 January 2011, para. 30.
1150 ECtHR, *Ónodi v. Hungary* (Appl. No. 38647/09), 30 May 2017, para. 28.
1151 ECtHR, *Milovanović v. Serbia* (Appl. No. 56065/10), 8 October 2019, paras. 112–113.
1152 ECtHR, *C. v. Finland* (Appl. No. 18249/02), 9 May 2006, para. 47.
1153 ECtHR, *K.A. v. Finland* (Appl. No. 27751/95), 14 January 2003, para. 133.
1154 ECtHR, *Nanning v. Germany* (Appl. No. 39741/02), 12 July 2007, para. 58.
1155 ECtHR, *Sommerfeld v. Germany* [GC] (Appl. No. 31871/96), 8 July 2003, para. 58.

4. THE ECtHR

In cases on child participation at the ECtHR, the maturity and age of children are often discussed by the Court. Generally, this occurs in the application of the principles to the case when considering the factual circumstances. The Court remarks on whether the maturity of the children was sufficient or insufficient and the way in which this was taken into account by the domestic courts. It may do so in response to complaints by the applicants, or comments made by the governments or *ex officio*, as will be further discussed below. Before the considerations on sufficient versus insufficient maturity are discussed, it is relevant to observe the general principles set out by the Court with regard to age and maturity.

4.1. GENERAL PRINCIPLES ON MATURITY

The ECtHR has over time construed a number of general principles *in abstracto* regarding maturity and child participation. As was observed previously in Chapter 5 on (in)sufficient participation,[1156] it has held since *Sahin v. Germany* (2003) and *Sommerfeld v. Germany* (2003) that domestic courts are not always required to hear a child in court, but that 'this issue depends on the specific circumstances of each case, having due regard to the *age and maturity* of the child concerned'.[1157] The age and maturity of the child can thus be determinative for the question whether the child should be heard. In extension, in *Płaza v. Poland* (2011), the Court specified that 'as children mature and become, with the passage of time, able to formulate their own opinion on their contact with the parents, the courts should give due weight also to their views and feelings as well as to their right to respect for their private life'.[1158] This was reaffirmed in *Gobec v. Slovenia* (2013), *Petrov and X v. Russia* (2018), *Khusnutdinov and X v. Russia* (2018) and *Zelikha Magomadova v. Russia* (2019).[1159] In the latter three of these judgments, the ECtHR omitted the phrase 'on their contact with the parents', thereby signalling a broader application to other types of proceedings concerning children. The age and maturity of a child play a role in terms of whether he or she ought to be heard and, subsequently, in the amount of weight given to his or her views.

1156 See Chapter 5, section 4.1.

1157 ECtHR, *Sahin v. Germany* [GC] (Appl. No. 30943/96), 8 July 2003, para. 73; and ECtHR, *Sommerfeld v. Germany* [GC] (Appl. No. 31871/96), 8 July 2003, para. 71. Emphasis added.

1158 ECtHR, *Płaza v. Poland* (Appl. No. 18830/07), 25 January 2011, para. 71.

1159 ECtHR, *Gobec v. Slovenia* (Appl. No. 7233/04), 3 October 2013, para. 133; ECtHR, *Petrov and X v. Russia* (Appl. No. 23608/16), 23 October 2018, para. 108; ECtHR, *Khusnutdinov and X v. Russia* (Appl. No. 76598/12), 18 December 2018, para. 86 and ECtHR, *Zelikha Magomadova v. Russia* (Appl. No. 58724/14), 8 October 2019, para. 115.

Article 12 of the United Nations Convention on the Rights of the Child (UNCRC) is relevant in this regard, as it determines that the child 'capable of forming his or her own views' has the right to express these views and that due weight should be given to him or her 'in accordance with the age and maturity of the child'.[1160] A child's capacity or maturity is thus relevant both for the 'capability' of expressing views as to the weight given to his or her views. More specifically, the CRC Committee stipulated that:

> States parties should presume that a child has the capacity to form his or her own views and recognize that she or he has the right to express them; it is not up to the child to first prove her or his capacity.[1161]

This presumption of capacity was explicitly affirmed by the ECtHR in *M. and M. v. Croatia* (2015), referencing the General Comment.[1162] This signalled a clear commitment of the ECtHR to adhere to the standard of Article 12 UNCRC and the mindset that children have capacity to participate unless proven otherwise. The relevance of Article 12 UNCRC and other international standards was emphasized in the judgment of *M.K. v. Greece* (2018), in which the ECtHR noted that wishes expressed by a child with sufficient '*discernement*' is a key element to be taken into account in proceedings concerning him or her.[1163] The ECtHR referred to the *M. and M. v. Croatia* (2015) judgment, Article 12 UNCRC, Articles 3 and 6 of the European Convention on the Exercise of Children's Rights (ECECR), the 2012 Recommendation of the Council of Europe and Article 24 of the Charter of Fundamental Rights of the European Union (CFREU) in that regard.[1164] How the Court defines maturity in specific cases – for example, through reference to age or other factors – will be discussed in the following section, starting with insufficient maturity, before moving on to sufficient maturity.

4.2. INSUFFICIENT MATURITY

In nine cases, the ECtHR observed that children had insufficient maturity. The Court did not provide a specific list of criteria for immaturity, but more generally remarked that it was reasonable that children 'taking into account their age' had not been granted the opportunity to participate or that their expressed views were not granted decisive weight.

1160 See also Chapter 2, sections 3.1.1.2, 3.1.1.6 and 3.2.2.2.
1161 UNCRC General Comment No. 12 2009, para. 20.
1162 ECtHR, *M. and M. v. Croatia* (Appl. No. 10161/13), 3 September 2015, para. 184.
1163 ECtHR, *M.K. v. Greece* (Appl. No. 51312/16), 1 February 2018, para. 91.
1164 ECtHR, *M.K. v. Greece* (Appl. No. 51312/16), 1 February 2018, para. 91.

4.2.1. *Insufficient Maturity to Participate*

In two Grand Chamber judgments, three Chamber judgments and two decisions, the insufficient maturity of the child was linked to the question of whether he or she ought to have participated in the domestic proceedings. These seven cases are presented in Table 7.4 below.

Table 7.4. Attributes of cases in which the ECtHR considered children to have insufficient maturity to participate

Grand Chamber judgments	Type of proceeding	Reasoning under	Age of children
Sahin v. Germany (2003)	Access	Article 8	3–5
X. v. Latvia (2013)	International child abduction	Article 8	4–5
Chamber judgments	**Type of proceeding**	**Reasoning under**	**Age of children**
Maumousseau and Washington v. France (2007)	International child abduction	Article 8	3–5
X. v. Latvia (2011)	International child abduction	Article 8	4–5
Gajtani v. Switzerland (2014)	International child abduction	Article 8	5
Chamber decisions	**Type of proceeding**	**Reasoning under**	**Age of children**
Siebert v. Germany (2005)	Care and access	Article 8	3–4
Eskinazi and Chelouche v. Turkey (2005)	International child abduction	Article 8	4–5

Source: Compiled by the author.

In *Sahin v. Germany* (2003), taking into account the general principle reiterated above, the ECtHR noted that the child was three years and ten months old at the start of the appeal proceedings, and five years and two months old at the end. Thus, the conclusion by the expert and subsequently the Regional Court that the child was too young to hear the child in court without putting her at risk was reasonable.[1165] In the *X. v. Latvia* judgments, at the Chamber in *X. v. Latvia* (2011) and the Grand Chamber in *X. v. Latvia* (2013), the young age of the child – four years at the start and five years at the end of the domestic proceedings – was mentioned by the Court in both judgments as having prevented her from being heard in court.[1166] This consideration in the

1165 ECtHR, *Sahin v. Germany* [GC] (Appl. No. 30943/96), 8 July 2003, paras. 73–75.

1166 ECtHR, *X. v. Latvia* [GC] (Appl. No. 27853/09), 26 November 2013, para. 112; and ECtHR, *X. v. Latvia* (Appl. No. 27853/09), 13 December 2011, para. 71.

Grand Chamber judgment in *X. v. Latvia* was also referred to by the ECtHR in *Gajtani v. Switzerland* (2014) – where the youngest child had not been heard when she was five years old – as endorsing the decision of domestic authorities that children aged four are too young to validly express a preference on residence in domestic proceedings.[1167]

The lack of hearing the child in *Maumousseau and Washington v. France* (2007) did not entail a violation of Article 8 ECHR, especially considering that the hearing would have been non-decisive as the child was between the ages of three and five throughout the proceedings.[1168] Lastly, in two decisions, the ECtHR found it reasonable that the young children were not heard. In *Siebert v. Germany* (2005), the Court was satisfied with the domestic courts' decision and reasons for not hearing the child due to her 'rather young age' of three to four during the proceedings.[1169] In the *Eskinazi and Chelouche v. Turkey* (2005) decision, the ECtHR 'considers it plausible' that the hearing of the child would be unnecessary, taking into account the young age of the child – again, around four at the start and five at the end of the domestic proceedings.[1170]

These judgments and decisions show that the ECtHR has repeatedly held children under the age of six to be of insufficient maturity to participate – or, at least, to be heard directly by courts – in domestic proceedings (see also Table 7.4 above). It is interesting to note that five out of seven of these cases concerned international child abduction proceedings. This may be explained by the fact that in this type of proceedings, Article 13 of The Hague Abduction Convention provides discretion not to order the return of the child if the child objects. With parents taking all possible measures to oppose return, a complaint on the lack of participation even for very young children at the ECtHR cannot excluded. In comparison, it may be that parents in other types of proceedings – for example, regarding custody – do not expect children of such a young age to participate and thus do not complain over a lack of such participation at the ECtHR. Whether the conclusion would be similar in other types of proceedings cannot be said with any certainty. However, it could be hypothesized that it would likely be the same. In various jurisdictions,[1171] it is already the case that children are

---

1167 ECtHR, *Gajtani v. Switzerland* (Appl. No. 43730/07), 9 September 2014, para. 112.

1168 ECtHR, *Maumousseau and Washington v. France* (Appl. No. 39388/05), 6 December 2007, paras. 79–80.

1169 ECtHR, *Siebert v. Germany* (dec.) (Appl. No. 59008/00), 9 June 2005.

1170 ECtHR, *Eskinazi and Chelouche v. Turkey* (dec.) (Appl. No. 14600/05), 6 December 2005.

1171 See, for example, the Netherlands and England and Wales, where children from the age of six are invited to express their views directly or indirectly. See M.R. Bruning & W.M. Schrama, 'The Netherlands', in: W.M. Schrama et al. (eds.), *International Handbook on Child Participation in Family Law*, Cambridge: Intersentia 2021, pp. 231–244, p. 240; M. Freeman & N. Lowe, 'England and Wales', in: W.M. Schrama et al. (eds.), *International Handbook on Child Participation in Family Law*, Cambridge: Intersentia 2021, pp. 171–183, p. 174-175; and Mol 2021a, p. 349.

heard at a younger age in child abduction proceedings compared to other types of family law proceedings. However, the reasoning of the ECtHR in other types of proceedings regarding sufficient maturity may provide more insight in this matter.

4.2.2. *Insufficient Maturity to Attach Weight to Views*

In two Chamber decisions, the children were considered insufficiently mature for a certain amount of weight to be attached to their views. See Table 7.5 below for the attributes of these two cases.

Table 7.5. Attributes of cases in which the ECtHR considered children to have insufficient maturity for the weight attributed to their views

Chamber decisions	Type of proceeding	Reasoning under	Age of children
Paradis and others v. Germany (2003)	International child abduction	Article 8	9 and 9
Döring v. Germany (2012)	Custody	Article 8 in conjunction with 14	11

Source: Compiled by the author.

It is relevant to remember that due weight itself is a balancing exercise, as has been discussed in Chapter 6. In this section, the focus is not so much on the precise balancing, but on how the consideration of maturity plays a role in the assessment of weight granted to the views of the child.

First, in *Paradis and others v. Germany* (2003), the children had been heard by the domestic courts and their maturity played a decisive role in the weight granted to their views. The domestic Court of Appeal found that the children, both aged nine, had not 'reached an age and degree of maturity … to decide for themselves what was in their best interest' and thus that decisive weight could not be attached to their views.[1172] In the decision, the ECtHR did not find this assessment arbitrary, thereby agreeing with the German courts' assessment regarding maturity.[1173] In *Döring v. Germany* (2012), the Court considered that the child's statement 'could not lead to a different assessment of the situation', because of the child's youth. It accepted that the domestic courts followed the expert's assessment 'that given the child's young age the latter was incapable of appreciating the consequences' of the custody decision.[1174] Of relevance in this regard was that sole custody could only be transferred to the father (applicant)

[1172] ECtHR, *Paradis and others v. Germany* (dec.) (Appl. No. 4783/03), 15 May 2003.
[1173] ECtHR, *Paradis and others v. Germany* (dec.) (Appl. No. 4783/03), 15 May 2003.
[1174] ECtHR, *Döring v. Germany* (dec.) (Appl. No. 50216/09), 21 February 2012.

if the well-being of the child was jeopardized and there was nothing pointing in that direction; in fact, the domestic courts had found that the transfer of sole custody would be against the child's interests.[1175] The ECtHR noted that the child's views were taken into account, but the child's youth was reason not to give more or even decisive weight to his views.

As there were only two decisions on insufficient maturity and the weight granted to children's views, it is not possible to make general conclusions regarding maturity. However, it is relevant to emphasize that in neither of these two cases did the ECtHR say that there should be *no* weight granted to the views of the children because they were too young. Instead, it agreed with the domestic courts that the children's maturity did not provide a reason to give *more* weight to their views.

4.3. SUFFICIENT MATURITY

Contrary to the judgments and decisions discussed above, there are 18 judgments and decisions in which the ECtHR considered the maturity of the children sufficient for their participation (see section 4.3.1) and for weight to be given to their views (see section 4.3.2).

4.3.1. Sufficient Maturity to Participate

There are four Chamber judgments and one decision in which the ECtHR referred to the maturity of the children as relevant in relation to their ability to participate in the domestic proceedings. These five cases are presented with the relevant attributes in Table 7.6.

In *Havelka and others v. Czech Republic* (2007), the reference to the children's sufficient maturity for participation occurred in a negative connotation. The ECtHR considered it regrettable that the three children were not heard directly by the domestic courts, although at the time they were 13, 12 and 11 years old.[1176] Similarly, in *Iglesias Casarrubios and Cantalapiedra Iglesias v. Spain* (2016), the ECtHR observed that the eldest daughter was 14 and the youngest was 11 at the time of the divorce judgment, and the children were 15 and 12 around the time of the appeal.[1177] Subsequently, it noted that the domestic court's rejection, without motivation, of the mother's requests to hear the

[1175] ECtHR, *Döring v. Germany* (dec.) (Appl. No. 50216/09), 21 February 2012.
[1176] ECtHR, *Havelka and others v. Czech Republic* (Appl. No. 23499/06), 21 June 2007, para. 62.
[1177] ECtHR, *Iglesias Casarrubios and Cantalapiedra Iglesias v. Spain* (Appl. No. 23298/12), 11 October 2016, para. 41.

children directly unduly deprived the mother of a fair trial.[1178] It also noted that at a minimum, the eldest daughter, who was aged over 12, could have been heard as this was also required by domestic law.[1179] In *M. and M. v. Croatia* (2015), the ECtHR doubled down on the domestic courts that had not provided the child an opportunity to participate. The domestic courts had held off hearing the child while awaiting the assessment of the child's capability. The ECtHR referred to the presumption of maturity as discussed above and strongly stated that there was 'nothing to call into question the presumption', as the child was 12 years old at the time.[1180] According to the Court, steps should have been taken to provide the child with an opportunity to express her opinion. The ECtHR was also critical in *Zelikha Magomadova v. Russia* (2019), finding that the failure to hear two of the children was in breach of domestic law as they were both older than ten.[1181]

In *Luig v. Germany* (2007), the ECtHR had no reason to be critical, noting simply that the child 'was already fourteen years old' when heard in court.[1182]

Table 7.6. Attributes of cases in which the ECtHR considered children to be sufficiently mature to participate

Chamber judgments	Type of proceeding	Reasoning under	Age of children
Havelka and others v. Czech Republic (2007)	Care	Article 8	13, 12 and 11
M. and M. v. Croatia (2015)	Custody	Article 8	9–12 (13 at ECtHR)
Iglesias Casarrubios and Cantalapiedra Iglesias v. Spain (2016)	Custody	Article 6	11–12 and 14–15
Zelikha Magomadova v. Russia (2019)	Custody	Article 8	13 and 11
Chamber decision	**Type of proceeding**	**Reasoning under**	**Age of children**
Luig v. Germany (2007)	Access	Article 8	14

Source: Compiled by the author.

Considering these five cases, it appears that the ECtHR (generally) finds children aged 11–12 sufficiently mature to participate (specifically, to be heard by the courts) in domestic proceedings in the sphere of general family law proceedings on custody, access and care (see Table 7.6 above).

1178 ECtHR, *Iglesias Casarrubios and Cantalapiedra Iglesias v. Spain* (Appl. No. 23298/12), 11 October 2016, paras. 42–43.

1179 ECtHR, *Iglesias Casarrubios and Cantalapiedra Iglesias v. Spain* (Appl. No. 23298/12), 11 October 2016, para. 42.

1180 ECtHR, *M. and M. v. Croatia* (Appl. No. 10161/13), 3 September 2015, para. 184.

1181 ECtHR, *Zelikha Magomadova v. Russia* (Appl. No. 58724/14), 8 October 2019, para. 116.

1182 ECtHR, *Luig v. Germany* (dec.) (Appl. No. 28782/04), 25 September 2007.

4.3.2. *Sufficient Maturity to Attach Weight to Views*

In 15 Chamber judgments and decisions, the ECtHR remarked that the children involved had sufficient maturity to attach weight to their views. In one judgment, the Court disagreed with the domestic courts, while in the other 14 it agreed with the decision of the domestic courts. It should be recalled that the balancing aspect of due weight will not be dealt with further in this section, but has been explicitly covered in Chapter 6. Table 7.7 below gives the attributes of the 15 cases discussed in this section.

Table 7.7. Attributes of cases in which the ECtHR considered children to be sufficiently mature to attach weight to their views

Chamber judgments	Type of proceeding	Reasoning under	Age of children
C. v. Finland (2006)	Custody and access	Article 8	14 and 12
Glesmann v. Germany (2008)	Care and access	Article 8	13
Płaza v. Poland (2011)	Access	Article 8	14
Kijowski v. Poland (2011)	Custody and access	Article 8	13
Gobec v. Slovenia (2013)	Access	Article 8	13
Blaga v. Romania (2014)	International child abduction	Article 8	11, 9 and 9
M. and M. v. Croatia (2015)	Custody	Article 8	9–12 (13 at ECtHR)
M.K. v. Greece (2018)	International child abduction	Article 8	13
Khusnutdinov and X v. Russia (2018)	Custody	Article 8	13
Chamber decisions	**Type of proceeding**	**Reasoning under**	**Age of children**
G.H.B. v. United Kingdom (2000)	Care	Article 8	12
W.F. v. Italy (2001)	Care	Article 8	9–15 (17 at ECtHR)
Johansen v. Norway (2002)	Care and access	Article 8	11
Paulsen-Medalen and Svensson v. Sweden (2003)	Care and access	Article 8	12
Luig v. Germany (2007)	Access	Article 8	14
T.S. and J.J. v. Norway (2016)	Care and access	Article 8	12

Source: Compiled by the author.

Let us start with the sole judgment in which the ECtHR disagreed with the domestic courts' approach. The *M. and M. v. Croatia* (2015) judgment, in addition to the issue of reasoning on a child's maturity for participation, also provides the ECtHR's standpoint on the relevance of maturity for the weight to be given to the child's views. The Court observed that the child was nine and a half years old at the start of the domestic proceedings, and 13 and a half by the time of the ECtHR's judgment – when the proceedings were again pending domestically.[1183] The Court also noted the child's educational success and 'good or even above average intellectual capacities'.[1184] Taking that into account, it found that the child was capable of forming her own views and expressing them freely, and thus 'finds that not respecting her wishes as regards the issue of which parent to live with would, in the specific circumstances of the present case, constitute an infringement of her right to respect for private and family life'.[1185] Therefore, it found that substantial weight should have been given to the child's views, taking into account the Croatian case law, which provides that a child's view can be decisive regarding residence when both parents are found to be equally fit.[1186]

In eight Chamber judgments and six decisions, the ECtHR found the weight given to the views of the child by the domestic courts to be appropriate or reasonable, given the maturity or age of the child.

Six of these cases concerned domestic proceedings on access. In all six cases, the children did not wish to have contact with the respective (grand)parent who applied to the ECtHR. In *Płaza v. Poland* (2011), the child had 'consistently refused' to see her father – as was noted by the domestic court when she was 14 years old.[1187] The ECtHR concluded that the child had matured throughout the domestic proceedings and 'was able to take her own decisions in respect of her contact with her father'.[1188] Thus, in reviewing the approach of the domestic courts and authorities, it did not find them to have exceeded their margin of appreciation under Article 8 ECHR. The consistent refusal was also noted by the Court with regard to the views expressed by the 12-year-old child in *Glesmann v. Germany* (2008).[1189] In this judgment and in the other two decisions on access, the ECtHR connected the maturity of the children (aged 13, 12 and 12) to the fact that the children could increase contact with the (grand)parent in the future if they wished to.[1190] It agreed with the government in *Gobec v. Slovenia* (2013) that the child, who was 13 years old and 'an adolescent', was 'able to express her opinion and wishes regarding contact and to understand their consequences'.[1191]

1183 ECtHR, *M. and M. v. Croatia* (Appl. No. 10161/13), 3 September 2015, para. 186.
1184 ECtHR, *M. and M. v. Croatia* (Appl. No. 10161/13), 3 September 2015, para. 186.
1185 ECtHR, *M. and M. v. Croatia* (Appl. No. 10161/13), 3 September 2015, para. 186.
1186 ECtHR, *M. and M. v. Croatia* (Appl. No. 10161/13), 3 September 2015, para. 185.
1187 ECtHR, *Płaza v. Poland* (Appl. No. 18830/07), 25 January 2011, para. 86.
1188 ECtHR, *Płaza v. Poland* (Appl. No. 18830/07), 25 January 2011, para. 86.
1189 ECtHR, *Glesmann v. Germany* (Appl. No. 25706/03), 10 January 2008, para. 110.
1190 ECtHR, *Glesmann v. Germany* (Appl. No. 25706/03), 10 January 2008, para. 111; ECtHR, *G.H.B. v. United Kingdom* (dec.) (Appl. No. 42455/98), 4 May 2000; ECtHR, *T.S. and J.J. v. Norway* (dec.) (Appl. No. 15633/15), 11 October 2016, para. 29.
1191 ECtHR, *Gobec v. Slovenia* (Appl. No. 7233/04), 3 October 2013, paras. 137–138.

The domestic authorities took the child's wishes as a core reason to suspend access and the ECtHR agreed that the decision was justified by relevant and sufficient reasons.[1192]

In *Luig v. Germany* (2007), the ECtHR noted that the domestic courts reached a reasoned decision in deciding to suspend access so as not to force the child to have contact, in view of the child's views considering her 'age and her stage of development'[1193] (the child in question was 14 years old at the time). Finally, in two decisions – *G.H.B. v. United Kingdom* (2000) and *T.S. and J.J. v. Norway* (2016) – the ECtHR found the domestic courts 'justified in giving weight to the child's own views', given the age of the children.[1194] In both cases, the children concerned were 12 years old. More explicitly, in *G.H.B. v. United Kingdom* (2000), the Court considered that ordering the child to remain in contact with her grandfather would have been a failure to respect the child's own rights under Article 8 ECHR.[1195]

The other judgments and decisions did not concern access proceedings. In the Chamber judgment in *Kijowski v. Poland* (2011), the ECtHR remarked that domestic authorities 'had to take into account the wishes' of the child 'who had reached the age of thirteen' and had a clear wish to live with the applicant in the residence proceedings.[1196] The ECtHR also used strong words in the *M.K. v. Greece* (2018) judgment. It pointed out that the child had reached the age of 'discernment', being 13 years of age at the time, and thus his firmly expressed views could only weigh heavily on the decision of the domestic authorities and could not be ignored.[1197] The child in *Khusnutdinov and X v. Russia* (2018) was also 13 years old and therefore the ECtHR concluded that she was 'able to form her own opinion on the matter and to understand its consequences', thus agreeing with the domestic courts on the weight granted to her views.[1198]

In two of the Chamber decisions primarily concerning care proceedings rather than access – *Johansen v. Norway* (2002) and *Paulsen-Medalen and Svensson v. Sweden* (2003) – the ECtHR also recognized either that the domestic courts had been justified in placing emphasis on the children's views or that it had been understandable, considering the fact that the children were 11 and 12 years old in these cases.[1199] In the *Paulsen-Medalen and*

1192 ECtHR, *Gobec v. Slovenia* (Appl. No. 7233/04), 3 October 2013, paras. 137–138.
1193 ECtHR, *Luig v. Germany* (dec.) (Appl. No. 28782/04), 25 September 2007.
1194 ECtHR, *G.H.B. v. United Kingdom* (dec.) (Appl. No. 42455/98), 4 May 2000; ECtHR, *T.S. and J.J. v. Norway* (dec.) (Appl. No. 15633/15), 11 October 2016, para. 29.
1195 ECtHR, *G.H.B. v. United Kingdom* (dec.) (Appl. No. 42455/98), 4 May 2000.
1196 ECtHR, *Kijowski v. Poland* (Appl. No. 33829/07), 5 April 2011, para. 58.
1197 ECtHR, *M.K. v. Greece* (Appl. No. 51312/16), 1 February 2018, paras. 88 and 90.
1198 ECtHR, *Khusnutdinov and X v. Russia* (Appl. No. 76598/12), 18 December 2018, para. 86.
1199 ECtHR, *Johansen v. Norway* (dec.) (Appl. No. 12750/02), 10 October 2002; ECtHR, *Paulsen-Medalen and Svensson v. Sweden* (dec.) (Appl. No. 47411/99), 30 September 2003.

Svensson v. Sweden (2003) decision, the Court referred to Article 12 UNCRC in this regard.[1200] In the final decision, *W.F. v. Italy* (2001), it attached particular importance on the best interests of the child, specifically the strong views of the child who at the time of the ECtHR decision was already 17 years old.[1201]

Finally, in the Chamber judgment in *Blaga v. Romania* (2014), the ECtHR examined the role which the children's objection to return played in the domestic international child abduction proceedings. With regard to the maturity of the children, the Court made two remarks. The first was a concerned remark on the participation as such: the ECtHR noted that only one of the three children had been over ten years old at the time of the hearing by the domestic courts. This meant that only one of the children 'met the minimum lawful age requirement for her opinion to be heard by the domestic courts'.[1202] This concern is surprising, as the domestic law in question did not have a 'minimum lawful age requirement' – it has a mandatory requirement to hear children who are ten years and older, but a discretionary option for courts to hear younger children if they consider this to be necessary.[1203] However, the ECtHR accepted that the domestic courts could take into account the children's views, remarking that 'they had been considered by the judicial authorities to be sufficiently mature'.[1204] It can be concluded that the ECtHR questioned whether children aged nine were sufficiently mature to participate in light of national law, but found that they were sufficiently mature to give weight to their views, accepting the domestic courts' judgment in this regard.

In one judgment, *C. v. Finland* (2006), the ECtHR found the children sufficiently mature – both were over 12 years old – for their wishes to be taken into account, but concluded that granting decisive weight to their views without considering any other factors or providing any options for the applicant father to respond at an oral hearing was a violation of Article 8 ECHR, as the decision-making procedure failed to strike a proper balance of interests.[1205]

In sum, looking at Table 7.7 above, the age ranges of the children – from nine to 18 years old – immediately catches the eye. It could be argued that the line at which the ECtHR considered children sufficiently mature for domestic courts to attach weight to their views could very carefully be drawn at around nine, ten or eleven years old.

1200 ECtHR, *Paulsen-Medalen and Svensson v. Sweden* (dec.) (Appl. No. 47411/99), 30 September 2003.

1201 ECtHR, *W.F. v. Italy* (dec.) (Appl. No. 34803/97), 5 April 2001.

1202 ECtHR, *Blaga v. Romania* (Appl. No. 54443/10), 1 July 2014, para. 78.

1203 ECtHR, *Blaga v. Romania* (Appl. No. 54443/10), 1 July 2014, para. 50.

1204 ECtHR, *Blaga v. Romania* (Appl. No. 54443/10), 1 July 2014, para. 78.

1205 ECtHR, *C. v. Finland* (Appl. No. 18249/02), 9 May 2006, paras. 57–59.

4.4. OTHER ISSUES CONCERNING MATURITY

In addition to the judgments and decisions described above, there are four judgments which must be considered separately because they concern side-issues. The first is the Grand Chamber judgment in *Sommerfeld v. Germany* (2003). The maturity of the child was discussed by the ECtHR in light of the question as to whether the domestic courts should have ordered a psychological report to determine if the child's views were not influenced by the other parent. The ECtHR noted that the child had been heard at the ages of 10, 11 and 13 by the same judge in the two sets of proceedings.[1206] The domestic court could thus reasonably rely on the views of the child, without obtaining an additional expert opinion.[1207] The second judgment specifically concerned the consent of a child for adoption. Consent is a step further than due weight, as it requires the child to actively decide. In *Pini and others v. Romania* (2004), the age of the two children who were to be adopted was discussed by the ECtHR in relation to their views and the issue of a child's consent for adoption.[1208] As third party interveners, the two children had raised the fact that 'they were now more than eleven years old' and their views and wishes should be respected.[1209] With regard to the children's consent for adoption, the ECtHR noted that it had not been obtained by the domestic courts, but that this was not required as the children had been under the age at which consent was compulsory according to domestic legislation.[1210] The children were nine and a half years old at the time of adoption, and Romanian legislation required consent from the age of ten and above.[1211] However, the children were considered by the ECtHR to have 'reached an age at which it could reasonably be considered that their personality was sufficiently formed and they had attained the necessary maturity to express their opinion as to the surroundings in which they wished to be brought up'.[1212] Thus, the children's opposition to the adoption and, according to the Court, their consistent refusal (even after reaching the age of ten) to join their adoptive parents carried a certain weight.[1213]

1206 ECtHR, *Sommerfeld v. Germany* [GC] (Appl. No. 31871/96), 8 July 2003, para. 72.
1207 ECtHR, *Sommerfeld v. Germany* [GC] (Appl. No. 31871/96), 8 July 2003, para. 72.
1208 ECtHR, *Pini and others v. Romania* (Appl. Nos. 78028/01 and 78030/01), 22 June 2004.
1209 ECtHR, *Pini and others v. Romania* (Appl. Nos. 78028/01 and 78030/01), 22 June 2004, paras. 134–135.
1210 ECtHR, *Pini and others v. Romania* (Appl. Nos. 78028/01 and 78030/01), 22 June 2004, para. 145.
1211 ECtHR, *Pini and others v. Romania* (Appl. Nos. 78028/01 and 78030/01), 22 June 2004, para. 102.
1212 ECtHR, *Pini and others v. Romania* (Appl. Nos. 78028/01 and 78030/01), 22 June 2004, para. 157.
1213 ECtHR, *Pini and others v. Romania* (Appl. Nos. 78028/01 and 78030/01), 22 June 2004, paras. 159 and 164.

Therefore, the domestic authorities' decision not to enforce the adoption did not violate Article 8 ECHR.

In the final two judgments, the ECtHR discussed whether children's maturity to participate ought to have been explored. In *Petrov and X v. Russia* (2018), the Court commented on the situation concerning 'very young children who are still unable to form or express their wishes'.[1214] In this case, the child concerned was two to three years old during the domestic residence and contact proceedings. In comparison to the *Sahin v. Germany* (2003) judgment, the ECtHR noted that an expert opinion was never sought to determine, amongst other things, 'whether it was possible, given the [child]'s age and maturity, to interview him in court, if need be with the assistance of a specialist in child psychology'.[1215] The latter was reiterated in *Zelikha Magomadova v. Russia* (2019) with regard to two younger children who were nine and seven years old at the time of the domestic parental authority proceedings.[1216]

4.5. CONCLUSIONS ON THE ECtHR'S REASONING

Bringing together all the statements made by the ECtHR regarding children's maturity, the following remarks can be made. The first important conclusion is that the ECtHR differentiates between the maturity or age necessary for participation and the maturity or age relevant for due weight. This distinction is drawn in the general principles, but is also consistently visible in the ECtHR's application of these principles to the circumstances in the cases. Second, the conclusions on sufficient and insufficient maturity can be combined. Figure 7.1 illustrates the – very rough – age ranges around which the ECtHR considered children sufficiently or insufficiently mature to either participate (at the top) or to attach (more) weight to their views (at the bottom).

Figure 7.1. The ECtHR's age ranges for child maturity

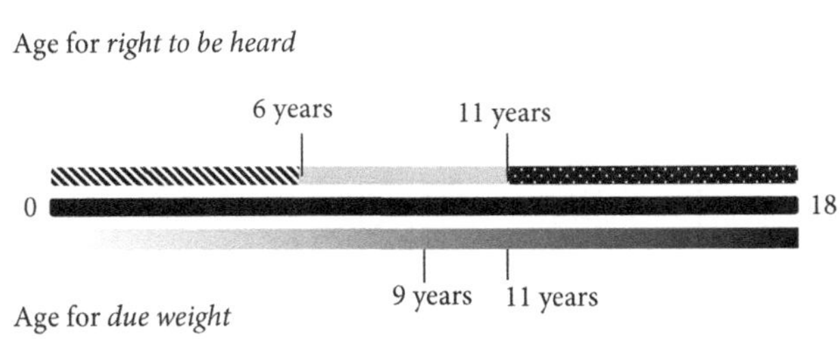

Source: Compiled by the author.

1214 ECtHR, *Petrov and X v. Russia* (Appl. No. 23608/16), 23 October 2018, para. 108.
1215 ECtHR, *Petrov and X v. Russia* (Appl. No. 23608/16), 23 October 2018, para. 108.
1216 ECtHR, *Zelikha Magomadova v. Russia* (Appl. No. 58724/14), 8 October 2019, para. 116.

In relation to participation, it is noteworthy that the case law provides a quite clear age under which children were seen as not having the required maturity (6 years and younger). However, whether they are mature from that age remains unclear from the studied case law. Thus, a grey area remains between the ages of 6 and 11 with regard to participation. Children over the age of 11 have been consistently held to be sufficiently mature in the studied judgments and decisions.

Determining age ranges for due weight is more difficult – if not impossible. This is not only due to the fact that there were only two decisions in which the ECtHR agreed with the domestic courts that the children were of insufficient maturity for significant weight to be attached to their views. The difficulty lies mostly in the relative nature of due weight. As was previously concluded in Chapter 6, due weight is a balancing exercise. Therefore, it is not possible to speak of an age or 'amount' of maturity from which one must give a certain amount of weight; it will always depend on the circumstances of the case. However, it is possible to conclude that maturity is a relevant factor in determining the amount of weight to give to a child's views. There were 15 judgments and decisions in which the ECtHR did find the children sufficiently mature for weight to be attached to the child's views. Thereby, in the majority of cases, the Court agreed with the weight granted by domestic courts to the views of the children concerned (14 times). In these cases, most of the children were aged 11 or 12 and over, although there were also some judgments in which the children were younger (e.g. nine years old). In the two decisions on insufficient maturity, the ECtHR also agreed with the domestic courts: granting less weight to the views of the child was reasonable because the children were too young. To conclude, there is no threshold under which the views of a child should not be given *due* weight. However, the child's maturity may make it reasonable for the domestic courts to grant *less* weight to the views of younger children and *more* weight to the views of older or more mature children. To symbolize this, the choice was made in Figure 7.1 to represent due weight as a sliding greyscale.

These age ranges must be viewed with caution, not only because grey zones remain, but also because the judgments and decisions of the ECtHR are casuistic and dependent on the complaints brought to them. Additionally, the ECtHR must approach the question of maturity from a distance due to the 'subsidiary nature of the supervisory mechanism'[1217] provided by the ECtHR and the margin of appreciation afforded to national authorities. The Court does not determine the maturity of a child before it, as domestic courts do, but must review whether the domestic courts took reasonable decisions in this regard in

---

1217 Brussels Declaration, adopted at the High-Level Conference on the Future of the European Court of Human Rights, 27 March 2015.

accordance with domestic law and the ECHR.[1218] According to the ECtHR, it is not its task 'to substitute its own assessment of the facts and the evidence for that of the [domestic] courts regarding the adequacy of such a delicate process or to review the interpretation and application of the provisions of international conventions (in the present case Article 13 of the Hague Abduction Convention and Article 12 §1 of the Convention on the Rights of the Child), other than in cases of an arbitrary decision'.[1219] This helps explain why in the judgments and decisions discussed, the ECtHR rarely deviated from the conclusions of the domestic courts regarding the maturity of children and their participation in family law proceedings.[1220] Only in *Havelka and others v. Czech Republic* (2007), *M. and M. v. Croatia* (2015), *Iglesias Casarrubios and Cantalapiedra Iglesias v. Spain* (2016) and *Zelikha Magomadova v. Russia* (2019) did the Court disagree with the domestic courts' determination of maturity for participation (and due weight in the case of *M. and M. v. Croatia* (2015)). Thus, the age ranges presented reflect to a great extent the – likely shared – European national understandings of maturity for child participation in family law proceedings.[1221] In the concluding analysis (see the next section), this will also become more visible when the complaints, governments' arguments and the conclusions drawn by the ECtHR are seen together. The differences between types of family law proceedings will also be explicated.

The primary relevance of age instead of other factors in determining maturity is a separate conclusion that must be drawn. In the majority of judgments and decisions the ECtHR referred to the age of the children when determining maturity. This may be explained by the subsidiary nature of the ECtHR and if age was a leading factor at the domestic level, it is relatively effortless for the ECtHR to also focus on age. That does not preclude the ECtHR from opting to involve further factors to determine maturity. However, it may be more difficult to do so if the information is not available in the application or does not become apparent throughout the proceedings before the ECtHR. In all the cases discussed above, only three other factors for the determination of a child's maturity became apparent and only in a small selection of cases (six total). One was the intellectual

1218 See also C.R. Mol, 'Maturity and the Child's Right to Be Heard in Family Law Proceedings: Article 12 UNCRC and Case Law of the ECtHR Compared', in: K. Boele-Woelki & D. Martiny (eds.), *Plurality and Diversity of Family Relations in Europe*, Cambridge: Intersentia 2019a, pp. 237–254, p. 250.

1219 ECtHR, *Eskinazi and Chelouche v. Turkey* (dec.) (Appl. No. 14600/05), 6 December 2005; confirmed in ECtHR, *Maumousseau and Washington v. France* (Appl. No. 39388/05), 6 December 2007, para. 79 and ECtHR, *Gajtani v. Switzerland* (Appl. No. 43730/07), 9 September 2014, para. 112.

1220 See also Mol 2019a, p. 250.

1221 See also Mol 2019a, p. 250.

capacities of a child, as in *M. and M. v. Croatia* (2015), where the Court referred to the child's educational success and intellectual capacities.[1222] Another factor was the consistency of the child's views over time, as was noted in both *Glesmann v. Germany* (2008) and *Płaza v. Poland* (2011).[1223] The final factor apparent in *Döring v. Germany* (2012), *Gobec v. Slovenia* (2013) and *Khusnutdinov and X v. Russia* (2018) was the ability to 'appreciate' or 'understand' the consequences of the decision.[1224]

It is noteworthy that in the recent judgments of *Petrov and X v. Russia* (2018) and *Zelikha Magomadova v. Russia* (2019), the ECtHR challenged the lack of an expert opinion to determine whether (very) young children could be heard by a court with or without assistance of a specialist in child psychology. The fact that both cases concerned domestic family law proceedings, for which there was no national requirement for hearing young children, and no international child abductions proceedings, in which hearing younger children has become more routine, makes the reasoning of the ECtHR even more remarkable. The ECtHR appears to be heading in a new direction with regard to young children – the question remains how that will develop in the coming years.

5. CONCLUDING ANALYSIS

The maturity or age of children is undoubtedly important in the participation process. Both for the opportunity to express views and for the weighing of these views, the child's maturity is a relevant factor. In taking together the complaints of applicants, the arguments made by governments and the considerations of the ECtHR, a number of conclusions can be made. Some core conclusions in this chapter have already been addressed in section 4.5 in which the ECtHR's reasoning on age and maturity was brought together. These conclusions will not be repeated here. Instead, we will consider additional conclusions, such as the relationship between maturity and the modes of participation or the types of proceedings. These conclusions are relevant to ultimately determining the international and European framework of child participation, and to consider how it can be aligned and strengthened.

1222 ECtHR, *M. and M. v. Croatia* (Appl. No. 10161/13), 3 September 2015, para. 186.

1223 ECtHR, *Płaza v. Poland* (Appl. No. 18830/07), 25 January 2011, para. 86; and ECtHR, *Glesmann v. Germany* (Appl. No. 25706/03), 10 January 2008, para. 110.

1224 ECtHR, *Döring v. Germany* (dec.) (Appl. No. 50216/09), 21 February 2012; ECtHR, *Gobec v. Slovenia* (Appl. No. 7233/04), 3 October 2013, paras. 137–138 and ECtHR, *Khusnutdinov and X v. Russia* (Appl. No. 76598/12), 18 December 2018, para. 86.

5.1. CONCLUSION IN NUMBERS

Let us start by looking at the numbers. A total of 38 judgments and decisions were discussed. In Table 7.8, the numbers of these cases are split according to the actor who commented on age and maturity.

Table 7.8. Amount of cases in which the topic of age and maturity was discussed

Discussed by:	
Applicant only	0
Government only	8
Applicant and government	0
Applicant, government and ECtHR	3
Applicant and ECtHR	2
Government and ECtHR	5
ECtHR only	20
Total	38

Source: Compiled by the author.

In the 38 cases discussed in this section, age and maturity is by and large addressed in the reasoning of the ECtHR. There are five cases in which the applicants' complaints related to age and maturity, and 16 cases in which the governments commented on age and maturity in their response, while the ECtHR discussed it in 30 judgments and decisions. This signifies that age and maturity for participation and due weight is a topic which is often discussed *ex officio* by the Court or in response to governments' arguments. A possible explanation for this can be found in the complaints that the applicants do make in these cases. In the judgments and decision in which the applicants did not complain about age and maturity, but the ECtHR did so in its reasoning, the applicants sometimes complained about the more pressing participation issues. For example, the applicants complained either about participation (as discussed in section 2 above) or due weight (as discussed in section 3 above). The response of the ECtHR then incorporates the age and maturity of the child to justify or critique the (lack of) participation and due weight.[1225] It is very reasonable that

[1225] This occurs in ECtHR, *W.F. v. Italy* (dec.) (Appl. No. 34803/97), 5 April 2001; ECtHR, *Sahin v. Germany* [GC] (Appl. No. 30943/96), 8 July 2003; ECtHR, *Siebert v. Germany* (dec.) (Appl. No. 59008/00), 9 June 2005; ECtHR, *Luig v. Germany* (dec.) (Appl. No. 28782/04), 25 September 2007; ECtHR, *Havelka and others v. Czech Republic* (Appl. No. 23499/06), 21 June 2007; ECtHR, *Płaza v. Poland* (Appl. No. 18830/07), 25 January 2011; ECtHR, *Gajtani v. Switzerland* (Appl. No. 43730/07), 9 September 2014; ECtHR, *Iglesias Casarrubios and Cantalapiedra Iglesias v. Spain* (Appl. No. 23298/12), 11 October 2016; ECtHR, *Khusnutdinov and X v. Russia* (Appl. No. 76598/12), 18 December 2018.

the ECtHR did so, as age and maturity are relevant factors for the questions of participation and due weight. This is also visible in the analysis in Chapters 5 and 6. In that sense, the ECtHR did not stray far from its subsidiary nature in assessing whether decisions taken domestically have violated either Article 6 or Article 8 ECHR.

5.2. DETERMINING MATURITY

Returning to the substance, a relevant question is how the determination of maturity has been approached. This question was raised by two applicants. In *C. v. Finland* (2006), the use of age as the sole criteria without considering maturity or the 'voluntariness of the views' was complained about in *Eskinazi and Chelouche v. Turkey* (2005), in which the applicants argued that the maturity should have been determined by an expert, not by the judge.[1226] Governments generally offer no response as to how maturity should be determined. However, it is interesting to note that in justifying the sufficient or insufficient age and maturity of children, the governments refer not only to age, but at times also state that the child is 'mature',[1227] has 'full capacity'[1228] or is at the 'lower boundary of capacity'.[1229] Only in *Gobec v. Slovenia* (2013) did the government further specify that the determination was made by relying on the findings of psychologists that the child was 'mature for her age'.[1230] However, in the majority of objections, the governments did not clarify how maturity was determined.

The ECtHR, as we have seen above, mostly referred to the age of the children. Only in six cases was this supplemented by other factors, as discussed above. In *M. and M. v. Croatia* (2015), the ECtHR referred to the child's educational success and intellectual capacities,[1231] and, in five other cases, to the two factors of the consistency of views and the capacity to understand the consequences of the decision. The ECtHR did not respond in any way to the applicants' complaints as to how maturity is determined in *C. v. Finland* (2006) or *Eskinazi and Chelouche v. Turkey* (2005). This lack of response could be interpreted as the ECtHR disagreeing with the applicants' complaints.

1226 ECtHR, *C. v. Finland* (Appl. No. 18249/02), 9 May 2006, para. 43; and ECtHR, *Eskinazi and Chelouche v. Turkey* (dec.) (Appl. No. 14600/05), 6 December 2005.

1227 ECtHR, *Hansen v. Turkey* (Appl. No. 36141/97), 23 September 2003, para 93; ECtHR, *Płaza v. Poland* (Appl. No. 18830/07), 25 January 2011, para. 64 and ECtHR, *Gobec v. Slovenia* (Appl. No. 7233/04), 3 October 2013, para. 124.

1228 ECtHR, *Ónodi v. Hungary* (Appl. No. 38647/09), 30 May 2017, para. 28.

1229 ECtHR, *Gajtani v. Switzerland* (Appl. No. 43730/07), 9 September 2014, paras. 96–97.

1230 ECtHR, *Gobec v. Slovenia* (Appl. No. 7233/04), 3 October 2013, para. 124.

1231 ECtHR, *M. and M. v. Croatia* (Appl. No. 10161/13), 3 September 2015, para. 186.

This would mean that the ECtHR did not require more to determine maturity than age and did not require an expert to determine maturity. This interpretation is strengthened by the fact that the ECtHR did include the issue of age and maturity in its reasoning in both cases. However, it may also be that the Court did not wish to encroach on the national approaches to determining maturity and therefore did not respond to the complaints. Overall, in the case law analysed, the Court did not discuss whether age should be supplemented with additional criteria, such as maturity. Only recently has the ECtHR changed course and discussed whether an additional expert is necessary to determine the maturity of a young child. In *Petrov and X v. Russia* (2018) and *Zelikha Magomadova v. Russia* (2019), the Court appeared to suggest that an expert opinion could or should be used to determine whether (very) young children can be heard by a court with or without the assistance of, for example, a specialist in child psychology.[1232] If this recent development were to become a new standard in the case law of the ECtHR, it would be good for the Court to signal whether an expert opinion should be acquired for all (very) young children or if this is an exception that should only be employed in certain circumstances. Ideally, the ECtHR will reiterate the presumption of capacity instead, taking into account the potential burden on domestic courts if expert opinions are required.

A final relevant conclusion to draw with regard to the determination of maturity is the inherent dynamic nature of maturity. Unlike the endless youth of Peter Pan, the age and maturity of children continually advances with time. This means that in lengthy legal proceedings, the age and maturity of the children also increases steadily. With regard to the reasoning of the ECtHR on maturity, this translates into a check of maturity not only at the start of the contested domestic proceedings, but specifically at the determinative stages. For example, in *Płaza v. Poland* (2011), domestic proceedings ran from 1997 to 2008. The ECtHR specifically noted that in the course of proceedings, the child had matured and was subsequently able to make decisions in relation to the contact arrangements with her father.[1233] As lengthy proceedings are not uncommon – for example, with regard to high-conflict separations – this is an important conclusion. As was previously discussed in Chapter 5, drawn-out proceedings may require additional participation,[1234] so the maturity of the child should in those situations be reassessed at the determinative stages.

1232 ECtHR, *Petrov and X v. Russia* (Appl. No. 23608/16), 23 October 2018, para. 108; and ECtHR, *Zelikha Magomadova v. Russia* (Appl. No. 58724/14), 8 October 2019, para. 116.

1233 ECtHR, *Płaza v. Poland* (Appl. No. 18830/07), 25 January 2011, para. 86.

1234 See also Chapter 5, section 5.3.2.

Two other considerations that should be made in bringing together all the aspects of the analysis on age and maturity is whether there is a difference depending on the mode of participation (see section 5.3) or the type of proceedings (see section 5.4). It can be hypothesized that either or both of these factors may have an impact on the required age and maturity for participation or the due weight to be given.

5.3. MATURITY AND THE MODES OF PARTICIPATION

As we have seen in Chapter 5, there are different modes of participation available to children in family law proceedings. The most common is the option of a direct hearing by a court, but it is also possible that children are represented (e.g. through a curator or guardian ad litem) or that an expert interviews the children and brings a report of their views to the attention of the court. When we consider the ages accepted or critiqued by the ECtHR in relation to participation, all the remarks concern the mode of direct hearing.[1235] Most notably, in *Havelka and others v. Czech Republic* (2007), the ECtHR found that the children were of a sufficient age to have been heard directly by the court, and reprimanded the domestic courts in this regard, even though the children had been able to participate, albeit via a guardian ad litem.[1236] Although in all of the case law there are no conclusions drawn by the ECtHR on the required maturity for other modes of participation, within the discussed cases on maturity for due weight, there are cases in which the children had not been heard directly, but indirectly. This occurred through a representative in *Paulsen-Medalen and Svensson v. Sweden* (2003), *C. v. Finland* (2006) and *T.S. and J.J. v. Norway* (2016), where the ECtHR considered the children to be of sufficient maturity to have due weight attached to their views, and in *Döring v. Germany* (2012), where the child was

1235 See ECtHR, *Sahin v. Germany* [GC] (Appl. No. 30943/96), 8 July 2003, paras. 73–75; ECtHR, *Siebert v. Germany* (dec.) (Appl. No. 59008/00), 9 June 2005; ECtHR, *Eskinazi and Chelouche v. Turkey* (dec.) (Appl. No. 14600/05), 6 December 2005; ECtHR, *Havelka and others v. Czech Republic* (Appl. No. 23499/06), 21 June 2007, para. 62; ECtHR, *Luig v. Germany* (dec.) (Appl. No. 28782/04), 25 September 2007; ECtHR, *Maumousseau and Washington v. France* (Appl. No. 39388/05), 6 December 2007, paras. 79–80; ECtHR, *X. v. Latvia* (Appl. No. 27853/09), 13 December 2011, para. 71; ECtHR, *X. v. Latvia* [GC] (Appl. No. 27853/09), 26 November 2013, para. 112; ECtHR, *Gajtani v. Switzerland* (Appl. No. 43730/07), 9 September 2014, para. 112; ECtHR, *M. and M. v. Croatia* (Appl. No. 10161/13), 3 September 2015, para. 184; ECtHR, *Iglesias Casarrubios and Cantalapiedra Iglesias v. Spain* (Appl. No. 23298/12), 11 October 2016, paras. 42–43 and ECtHR, *Zelikha Magomadova v. Russia* (Appl. No. 58724/14), 8 October 2019, para. 116.

1236 ECtHR, *Havelka and others v. Czech Republic* (Appl. No. 23499/06), 21 June 2007, para. 62.

considered insufficiently mature for due weight to be given to his views.[1237] Additionally, in *Gobec v. Slovenia* (2013), the child was heard indirectly through social workers and a psychologist, and was considered sufficiently mature by the ECtHR for due weight to be afforded to her views.[1238] In none of these five cases did the ECtHR comment as to the required maturity for the views to be heard indirectly through a representative or other expert. It only considered the maturity for due weight, which may in part be because of the lack of complaints regarding the maturity for participation itself. Additionally, it may be explained by the fact that in all these five cases, the children were 11 years or older, thereby also aligning with the ECtHR's understanding of sufficient maturity for participation through direct hearing.

More generally, while there are examples of judgments and decisions in which the ECtHR of its own accord delved into the maturity for participation with regard to direct participation, it is interesting to note that this is not the case for other modes of participation. It may be wondered why the question of maturity for these other modes of participation has never arisen. A straightforward answer cannot be presented, but we can speculate. The reason may lie with the domestic situation seeping through into the reasoning of the ECtHR. With regard to the other modes of participation, whether a representative or an expert ascertaining views, it may be that domestic laws do not provide for age limits. This may be because these modes could also be considered to be suitable for younger children. Representatives and experts are in all likelihood expected and trusted to have sufficient expertise in determining the maturity of the children who they speak with, and to subsequently make appropriate decisions in qualifying and reporting these views to the courts. Another reason could be that more commonly within the topic of participation, the focus is on direct modes of participation. This subsequently means that the condition of the age and maturity of the child is also more often discussed than the potential conditions applicable to other modes of participation. That may then place this issue at the forefront of the ECtHR's reasoning, instead of the relevance of age and maturity for other modes of participation. Perhaps the ECtHR has not yet considered that the conditions in Article 12 apply not only to a direct hearing, but also the hearing through a representative. Of course, all these speculations may be incorrect; it may just as well be pure chance that the question of maturity for other modes of participation has not yet been raised. Let this be an invitation for future applicants to raise the question.

1237 ECtHR, *Paulsen-Medalen and Svensson v. Sweden* (dec.) (Appl. No. 47411/99), 30 September 2003; ECtHR, *C. v. Finland* (Appl. No. 18249/02), 9 May 2006, para. 57; ECtHR, *Döring v. Germany* (dec.) (Appl. No. 50216/09), 21 February 2012; ECtHR, *T.S. and J.J. v. Norway* (dec.) (Appl. No. 15633/15), 11 October 2016, para. 29.

1238 ECtHR, *Gobec v. Slovenia* (Appl. No. 7233/04), 3 October 2013, paras. 137–138.

5.4. MATURITY AND THE TYPES OF PROCEEDINGS

Turning from the modes of participation to the type of proceedings, it can immediately be concluded that there is more diversity in the decisions and judgments discussed. Care, access, custody, international child abduction and even adoption proceedings are covered, as was visible in the multiple tables included throughout the chapter. If we group the decisions and judgments on maturity according to the type of proceeding, the following becomes apparent. The ECtHR conclusions on insufficient maturity (for both participation and due weight) were concentrated in the international child abduction cases. Six of the nine decisions and judgments in which the ECtHR found the maturity of the children to be insufficient concerned international child abduction proceedings.[1239] As a result, in all the other types of proceedings (access, custody, care and adoption), the ECtHR overwhelmingly found the children to be of sufficient maturity for participation or due weight to be given to their views, or did not remark on the maturity of the children. This split between types of proceedings signals that international child abduction cases are different from other proceedings. As previously noted in section 4.3.1 above, the application of the international The Hague Abduction Convention, with one of its limited exceptions to return being the child's objection, may explain this difference. With the abducting parents grasping at every straw to oppose return, a complaint that their very young children were not heard or that their views were not granted due weight could be anticipated. In comparison, parents in all the other types of proceedings may complain about a wider variety of issues and may not even consider raising the right of a (very) young child to be heard. This is especially the case as in the other areas of family law proceedings, and specifically proceedings relating to custody and access, there are no international conventions providing uniform law, in contrast to The Hague Abduction Convention. This has the potential to create an imbalance in the child's right to be heard between domestic family law proceedings and international child abduction proceedings, where there are extra safeguards in place. Arguably, this imbalance may be problematic as children are far more likely to be confronted with domestic family law proceedings on custody or access. The choice not to hear younger children in domestic family law proceedings as often as in international child abduction cases should be an explicit one with supplementary reasons, beyond the fact that they are not cross-border cases.

1239 These are: ECtHR, *Paradis and others v. Germany* (dec.) (Appl. No. 4783/03), 15 May 2003; ECtHR, *Eskinazi and Chelouche v. Turkey* (dec.) (Appl. No. 14600/05), 6 December 2005; ECtHR, *Maumousseau and Washington v. France* (Appl. No. 39388/05), 6 December 2007; ECtHR, *X. v. Latvia* (Appl. No. 27853/09), 13 December 2011; ECtHR, *X. v. Latvia* [GC] (Appl. No. 27853/09), 26 November 2013 and ECtHR, *Gajtani v. Switzerland* (Appl. No. 43730/07), 9 September 2014.

A separate conclusion can be reached regarding the types of proceedings when we zoom into the access decisions. Almost half of the cases in which the ECtHR found the children to have been sufficiently mature to attach a certain amount of weight to their views concerned access proceedings. More notably, in all these six judgments and decisions, the ECtHR accepted the domestic courts giving decisive weight to the views of the children in restricting or suspending access (see also Chapter 6 in this regard). Additionally, the ECtHR referred to the increasing maturity of children in access proceedings as providing the potential for future (increased) contact with the (grand)parents, whose access had been suspended or restricted at the contested point of time. On the one hand, the potential for future contact may indeed justify the weight placed on children's views in these cases; on the other hand, it is remarkable, as the refusal of access is a major decision which may in fact impact the future potential of (restored) contact. The distinction made regarding access proceedings is critically examined in more depth in section 5.3 of Chapter 9 on the overall conclusions of the case law analysis.

In rounding off this concluding analysis, a final remark should be made that in Table 7.9 below, a combined overview is included of all the judgments and decisions discussed in this section and the corresponding relevance regarding the maturity of the child.

Table 7.9. Combined overview for maturity of the child

		Applicants' complaint				Governments' argument					ECtHR						
						Insufficient maturity		Sufficient maturity				Insufficient maturity		Sufficient maturity			
		Determination of maturity	Insufficient maturity for weight to views	Sufficient maturity for participation	No complaint	Participation	Weight to views	Participation	Weight to views	No argument	General principles	Participation	Weight to views	Participation	Weight to views	Other	No discussion
GC judgments	*Sahin v. Germany* (2003)	-	-	-	X	-	-	-	-	X	X	X	-	-	-	-	-
	Sommerfeld v. Germany (2003)	-	-	-	X	-	-	-	X	-	X	-	-	-	-	X	-
	X. v. Latvia (2013)	-	-	-	X	-	-	-	-	X	-	X	-	-	-	-	-

(continued)

Table 7.9 *continued*

		Applicants' complaint				Governments' argument					ECtHR						
						Insufficient maturity		Sufficient maturity				Insufficient maturity		Sufficient maturity			
		Determination of maturity	Insufficient maturity for weight to views	Sufficient maturity for participation	No complaint	Participation	Weight to views	Participation	Weight to views	No argument	General principles	Participation	Weight to views	Participation	Weight to views	Other	No discussion
Chamber judgments	*L. v. Finland* (2000)	-	-	-	X	-	-	X	X	-	-	-	-	-	-	-	X
	K.A. v. Finland (2003)	-	-	-	X	-	-	-	X	-	-	-	-	-	-	-	X
	Hansen v. Turkey (2003)	-	-	-	X	-	-	-	X	-	-	-	-	-	-	-	X
	Pini and others v. Romania (2004)	-	-	-	X	-	-	-	-	X	-	-	-	-	-	X	-
	C. v. Finland (2006)	X	-	-	-	-	-	-	X	-	-	-	-	-	X	-	-
	R. v. Finland (2006)	-	-	-	X	-	-	X	-	-	-	-	-	-	-	-	X
	Havelka and others v. Czech Republic (2007)	-	-	-	X	-	-	-	-	X	-	-	-	X	-	-	-
	Nanning v. Germany (2007)	-	-	-	X	-	-	-	X	-	-	-	-	-	-	-	X
	Maumousseau and Washington v. France (2007)	-	-	-	X	-	-	-	-	X	-	X	-	-	-	-	-
	Glesmann v. Germany (2008)	-	-	-	X	-	-	-	-	X	-	-	-	-	X	-	-
	Płaza v. Poland (2011)	-	-	-	X	-	-	-	X	-	X	-	-	-	X	-	-
	Kijowski v. Poland (2011)	-	-	-	X	-	-	-	-	X	-	-	-	-	X	-	-

Chamber judgments	*X. v. Latvia* (2011)	-	-	-	X	-	-	-	-	X	-	X	-	-	-	-	-
	Gobec v. Slovenia (2013)	-	-	-	X	-	-	-	X	-	X	-	-	-	X	-	-
	Blaga v. Romania (2014)	-	X	-	-	-	-	-	-	X	-	-	-	-	X	-	-
	Gajtani v. Switzerland (2014)	-	-	-	X	-	X	-	-	-	-	X	-	-	-	-	-
	M. and M. v. Croatia (2015)	-	-	X	-	-	-	-	-	X	X	-	-	X	X	-	-
	Iglesias Casarrubios and Cantalapiedra Iglesias v. Spain (2016)	-	-	-	X	-	-	-	-	X	-	-	-	X	-	-	-
	Ónodi v. Hungary (2017)	-	-	-	X	-	-	-	X	-	-	-	-	-	-	-	X
	M.K. v. Greece (2018)	-	-	-	X	-	-	-	-	X	X	-	-	-	X	-	-
	Petrov and X v. Russia (2018)	-	-	-	X	X	-	-	-	-	X	-	-	-	-	X	-
	Khusnutdinov and X v. Russia (2018)	-	-	-	X	-	-	-	-	X	X	-	-	-	X	-	-
	Milovanović v. Serbia (2019)	-	-	-	X	-	-	-	X	-	-	-	-	-	-	-	X
	Zelikha Magomadova v. Russia (2019)	-	-	X	-	X	-	-	-	-	X	-	-	X	-	X	-
Chamber decisions	*G.H.B. v. United Kingdom* (2000)	-	-	-	X	-	-	-	-	X	-	-	-	-	X	-	-
	W.F. v. Italy (2001)	-	-	-	X	-	-	-	-	X	-	-	-	-	X	-	-
	Johansen v. Norway (2002)	-	-	-	X	-	-	-	-	N	-	-	-	-	X	-	-
	Paradis and others v. Germany (2003)	-	-	-	X	-	-	-	-	N	-	-	X	-	-	-	-
	Paulsen-Medalen and Svensson v. Sweden (2003)	-	-	-	X	-	-	-	-	N	-	-	-	-	X	-	-
	Siebert v. Germany (2005)	-	-	-	X	-	-	-	-	X	-	X	-	-	-	-	-
	Eskinazi and Chelouche v. Turkey (2005)	X	-	-	-	X	-	-	-	-	-	X	-	-	-	-	-
	Petersen v. Germany (2006)	-	-	-	X	-	-	X	-	-	-	-	-	-	-	-	X
	Luig v. Germany (2007)		-	-	X	-	-	-	-	N	-	-	-	X	X	-	-
	Döring v. Germany (2012)	-	-	-	X	-	-	-	-	N	-	-	X	-	-	-	-
	T.S. and J.J. v. Norway (2016)	-	-	-	X	-	-	-	-	N	-	-	-	-	X	-	-

N = no arguments provided at all by the government because the complaint was not communicated to the contracting party, as is only required when the Chamber does not immediately declare the application inadmissible (see Rule 54 of the Rules of Court).

Source: Compiled by the author.

6. CONCLUSION: STANDARDS

The above analysis has led us through a great deal of data on the maturity of the child in the case law on participation. We have considered the complaints brought by applicants, the governments' arguments and the ECtHR's reasoning both separately and collectively in the concluding analysis. The time has now come to determine what standards can be drawn from the case law regarding maturity. On the basis of all of the above, four standards can be identified. These standards are labelled using an 'M' to signal that they concern 'Maturity'.

Participation

The first set of standards applies to the question of participation itself, but they are limited to the mode of direct participation as discussed above.

> M.1 Whether a court should directly hear a child in family law proceedings depends on the age and maturity of the child concerned and the specific circumstances of the case.

This first standard is drawn from the general principles on maturity as defined by the ECtHR in *Sahin v. Germany* (2003) and *Sommerfeld v. Germany* (2003). It is further confirmed by the ECtHR's repeated consideration of maturity when determining whether a child should have been heard or not. This standard corresponds in part to Standard P.2 in Chapter 5, where the specific circumstances of the case – such as previous participation, the length of proceedings and the interests of the child – have also been addressed.

> M.2 A child is presumed to be of sufficient maturity to be heard directly in family law proceedings from the age of 11 years and older. A child younger than 11 years old may also be sufficiently mature, but a child younger than six years old may lack the required maturity.

The second standard is drawn from the analysis of the ECtHR's reasoning in the judgments and decisions. It is a standard drafted as a presumption, as maturity should not depend solely on the age of the child, but should be determined based on multiple factors. However, a cautious presumption of maturity from a certain age can be inferred from the analysis. It is important to note that a presumption can always be disproven and this can be done in favour of a younger child. More specifically, for (very) young children, it may be necessary for domestic courts to request an expert opinion as to whether a young child can be heard and, if so, whether additional expertise is needed in that regard, as follows from *Petrov and X v. Russia* (2018) and *Zelikha Magomadova v. Russia* (2019). However, the latter is too recent a development to justify a separate standard, especially as it was only raised by the ECtHR in two cases, both of which concerned Russia.

Due weight

The third standard relates to the step following participation – the question as to how much weight should be given to the expressed views of the child.

> M.3 In family law proceedings, due weight should be accorded to the child's views irrespective of his or her age or maturity. However, the child's maturity may impact the weighing of his or her views. Depending on the circumstances of the case, it may be reasonable to give less weight to the views of a younger child or more significant weight to the views of an older or more mature child.

The analysis of the ECtHR's reasoning has shown that due weight is not dependent on the child's maturity, but that the child's age and maturity may function as a factor. The ECtHR has at no point said that *no* weight should be granted to the views of younger child, but it may be reasonable for domestic courts to give *less* weight to these views. Similarly, the views of more mature or older children – i.e. aged 12 or older – may be given *more* significant weight. It is important to remember that granting due weight to a child's views is part of a balancing exercise, so there may be more flexibility with regard to maturity and the amount of weight granted than the relationship between maturity and the participation of the child.

Determining maturity

The final standard addresses potential factors recognized by the ECtHR which may assist in determining the maturity of the child concerned.

> M.4 In addition to the age of the child, three other factors may assist domestic courts in determining the maturity of the child: the child's intellectual capacities, the consistency of the child's views over time, and the child's ability to understand the consequences of the decision.

The fourth standard is drawn from a small batch of cases in which the ECtHR names other factors in addition to age when discussing the maturity of the child. The first factor, the intellectual capacities of the child is drawn from *M. and M. v. Croatia* (2015), the second factor, the consistency of the child's views over time from *Glesmann v. Germany* (2008) and *Płaza v. Poland* (2011), and the final factor on understanding the consequences from *Döring v. Germany* (2012), *Gobec v. Slovenia* (2013) and *Khusnutdinov and X v. Russia* (2018).

CHAPTER 8
'INFLUENCE' ON THE VIEWS OF THE CHILD

'[The applicant] claimed that [the child] had been manipulated by her mother and, as she had hardly had any contacts with him for years, she had not been able to express her own view on access.'

– Applicant in *Luig v. Germany* (2007)[1240]

1. INTRODUCTION

A common concern with regard to child participation in family law proceedings is that children may be unduly influenced. In disputes following the separation or divorce of parents the worry exists that children, when asked to express their views, may get caught in the middle and be pressured by their parents to pick a side. In that regard, reference is made to a conflict of loyalties or even parental alienation syndrome. The existence of parental alienation syndrome is a contested topic in the field,[1241] but 'parental alienation' is a term used to refer broadly to 'a child who has been influenced to reject one parent'.[1242] More nuanced, in the literature parental alienation is mentioned as a phenomenon by which 'the child becomes hostile to one parent while strongly allying with the other parent, with alienation implying that the aligned parent intentionally

1240 ECtHR, *Luig v. Germany* (dec.) (Appl. No. 28782/04), 25 September 2007.

1241 See e.g., J.B. Kelly & J.R. Johnston, 'The Alienated Child: A Reformulation of Parental Alienation Syndrome', *Family and Conciliation Courts Review*, Vol 39, No. 3, 2001, pp. 249–266; M. Saini et al., 'Empirical Studies of Alienation', in: L. Drozd, M. Saini & N. Olsesen (eds.), *Parenting Plan Evaluations: Applied Research for the Family Court*, Oxford: Oxford University Press 2016, pp. 374–430, p. 433; J.J. Harman, D.A. Hines & E. Kruk, 'Parental Alienating Behaviors: An Unacknowledged Form of Family Violence', *Psychological Bulletin*, Vol. 144, No. 12, 2018, pp. 1275–1299 and M.V. Antokolskaia et al., *Naleving van contact-/omgangsafspraken na scheiding: een rechtsvergelijkend en sociaalwetenschappelijk perspectief*, The Hague: Boom Juridische Uitgevers 2019, pp. 122–125.

1242 Saini et al. 2016, p. 399.

created a wedge between the child and her or his other parent'.[1243] Parental alienation, in that sense, may be seen as an extreme form of influence.

The question of 'influenced' views is one that appears in the case law. The quote above shows one example in which a parent who did not benefit from the child's participation in the proceedings claimed that the child's views were influenced or 'manipulated' by the other parent. This applicant does not stand alone, as we will see in this chapter, and governments and the European Court of Human Rights (ECtHR) also discuss influence. In that regard, the topics of loyalty conflicts and parental alienation are also raised – by parents, governments and the ECtHR. It is important to note the relationship between the topic of influence and the topics that were at the centre of the previous chapters. As was mentioned in Chapter 4, all four topics addressed in the case law analysis are interrelated. The topic of influence stands alone, but is also raised both in light of (in)sufficient participation and the weight to be granted to the child's views.

This chapter will first examine the complaints raised by applicants regarding potential influence before addressing how governments consider influence and what the ECtHR makes of the issue of 'influence'. As in the previous chapters, a concluding analysis joins together all three sections, and standards are derived from the analysis.

2. COMPLAINTS BROUGHT BY APPLICANTS

Nineteen applicants complained about influence of the child's views in light of alleged violations of Article 6 or 8 of the European Convention on Human Rights (ECHR). These complaints can be split into two categories, the most common being that the views of the child were influenced and the other rare complaint being that they were not influenced, and the conflict of loyalties should not have been used to set aside the children's views.

2.1. INFLUENCED VIEWS

In 18 cases, the applicants brought a complaint alleging that the concerned children were influenced and that this should have elicited a different response by the domestic courts – either regarding participation or due weight. These complaints were brought explicitly referring to 'influence' or 'manipulation',

1243 M.K. Pruett & R. Barker, 'Children of Divorce: New Trends and Ongoing Dilemmas', in: J.H. Bray & M. Stanton (eds.), *The Wiley-Blackwell Handbook of Family Psychology*, Malden, MA: Blackwell. 2009, pp. 463–474, p. 469.

but also by referring to the lack of 'voluntariness' of views or 'genuine' views. The attributes of the cases can be found in Table 8.1 below, which shows that these complaints are brought almost exclusively in proceedings on custody and access, and by a parent only on his or her own behalf. Notably, the majority of the applicants are fathers, which may suggest a gender dimension with regard to influence or, more likely, a gender dimension with regard to custody and access proceedings.

Table 8.1. Attributes of cases in which the applicant complained of influenced views of the child

Grand Chamber judgments	**Type of proceeding**	**Applicant**	**Article of complaint**
Elsholz v. Germany (2000)	Access	Father	Article 8
Scozzari and Giunta v. Italy (2000)	Care and access	Mother, also on behalf of children	Article 8
Sommerfeld v. Germany (2003)	Access	Father	Article 8
Chamber judgments	**Type of proceeding**	**Applicant**	**Article of complaint**
Kosmopoulou v. Greece (2004)	Access	Mother	Article 8
Süss v. Germany (2005)	Access	Father	Article 8
C. v. Finland (2006)	Custody and access	Father	Articles 6 and 8
Fiala v. Czech Republic (2006)	Access	Father	Article 8
Cristescu v. Romania (2012)	Access	Father	Article 8
G.B. v. Lithuania (2016)	Custody	Mother	Article 8
Zdravković v. Serbia (2016)	Custody and access	Mother	Article 8
Moog v. Germany (2016)	Access	Father	Article 8
Ónodi v. Hungary (2017)	Access	Father	Article 8
Khusnutdinov and X v. Russia (2018)	Custody	Father, also on behalf of child	Article 8
Chamber decisions	**Type of proceeding**	**Applicant**	**Article of complaint**
W.F. v. Italy (2001)	Care	Father	Article 8
Vámosi v. Hungary (2004)	Custody	Father	Article 8
Petersen v. Germany (2006)	Custody and access	Father	Article 8
Luig v. Germany (2007)	Access	Father	Articles 6 and 8
Wildgruber v. Germany (2008)	Custody	Father	Articles 6 and 8

Source: Compiled by the author.

In some cases, the applicants simply briefly refer to the influence. In *Cristescu v. Romania* (2012), the father reiterated that the mother had 'negatively influenced' their child so that the child would 'have a bad impression of him'.[1244] Similarly, in *Ónodi v. Hungary* (2017), the applicant father argued that the child had been 'manipulated' by her mother,[1245] and in *Zdravković v. Serbia* (2016), the applicant mother went further, saying that the child had been 'systematically manipulated' by the father into refusing to see her.[1246] Finally, in *Scozzari and Giunta v. Italy* (2000), the applicant mother alleged that the social services had 'strongly' influenced her child into adopting a position of hostility towards her.[1247]

In a number of complaints, the issue of influence is associated with the role of time, specifically the length of proceedings or lack of enforcement. In *Vámosi v. Hungary* (2004), the applicant father submitted that the lack of enforcement of his custody rights for years had 'enabled the mother to manipulate the child against him'.[1248] Subsequently, the applicant argued that the passing of time and manipulation had led to the wishes of the child being key in the national Supreme Court's decision to grant custody to the mother.[1249] The applicant father in *Sommerfeld v. Germany* (2003) also complained of the passage of time which led to influenced views and subsequently to a refusal of access for the applicant.[1250] The father argued that taking into account the five years that the child lived with the mother, there was at least a 'subliminal influence' or 'suspicion' of influence by the mother on the child's views and attitude.[1251] Similar concerns were expressed vividly by the applicant father in *Fiala v. Czech Republic* (2006), who argued that questioning children after they had for a long period been under the exclusive influence of the mother amounted to 'torture'.[1252]

It is interesting to note that at times the applicants recognized the importance of giving due weight to children's views, but disagreed in their particular case with the weight given due to influence or manipulation. The applicant mother in *Kosmopoulou v. Greece* (2004) argued in this manner, stating that she 'entirely respected her daughter's wishes', but that the child's reluctance 'should be genuine and the child's will free from manipulation'.[1253] Similarly, in *G.B. v. Lithuania* (2016), the applicant mother noted the importance of the children's wishes, but argued that they should not be determinative, especially when these wishes were contrary to the

1244 ECtHR, *Cristescu v. Romania* (Appl. No. 13589/07), 10 January 2012, para. 53.
1245 ECtHR, *Ónodi v. Hungary* (Appl. No. 38647/09), 30 May 2017, para. 24.
1246 ECtHR, *Zdravković v. Serbia* (Appl. No. 28181/11), 20 September 2016, para. 59.
1247 ECtHR, *Scozzari and Giunta v. Italy* [GC] (Appl. Nos. 39221/98 and 41963/98), 13 July 2000, para. 154.
1248 ECtHR, *Vámosi v. Hungary* (dec.) (Appl. No. 71657/01), 23 March 2004.
1249 ECtHR, *Vámosi v. Hungary* (dec.) (Appl. No. 71657/01), 23 March 2004.
1250 ECtHR, *Sommerfeld v. Germany* [GC] (Appl. No. 31871/96), 8 July 2003, paras. 51 and 53.
1251 ECtHR, *Sommerfeld v. Germany* [GC] (Appl. No. 31871/96), 8 July 2003, paras. 51 and 53
1252 ECtHR, *Fiala v. Czech Republic* (Appl. No. 26141/03), 18 July 2006, para. 90.
1253 ECtHR, *Kosmopoulou v. Greece* (Appl. No. 60457/00), 5 February 2004, para. 34.

children's best interests, as the daughters 'had developed parental alienation syndrome'.[1254] On the contrary, in *W.F. v. Italy* (2001), the applicant father argued that the child was manipulated, but even if it had been the child's own strong wishes, the authorities should not have given weight to those wishes.[1255] These three judgments and decisions show that the issue of 'influence' has been raised by parents who disagreed with giving weight to the views of children, but also by parents who recognized the importance of children's wishes.

In four judgments and three decisions, the applicants went further than those discussed above by not only raising the issue of influence or manipulation, but also by addressing their complaint to national courts who ought to have examined and addressed this influence.

The first applicant to do so was the father in *Elsholz v. Germany* (2000).[1256] The refusal of access to his son led the applicant to allege a violation of Article 8 ECHR. In that regard, the applicant noted that his child had become alienated from him due to the passage of time and the mother's influencing of the child against him.[1257] The applicant referred to American research on parental alienation syndrome and argued that the German courts could have reached a different decision if they had taken into account the child's alienation or should have at the very least have 'appointed a competent expert'.[1258]

The applicant father in *Süss v. Germany* (2005) alleged a violation of Article 8 ECHR because the suspension of access should not have been based on the wishes of the child, as they were 'manipulated in the course of the lengthy proceedings'.[1259] The applicant furthermore argued that 'the expert had notably ignored that [the child]'s negative statements resulted from the parental-alienation-syndrome she suffered from as a result of [the mother]'s influence'.[1260] The complaint addressed to the national courts was that the courts ought to have considered the 'findings of modern psychology according to which a child did not have an independent will'.[1261] Additionally, the applicant complained that the expert appointed by the domestic courts had not been sufficiently qualified, so another expert should have been appointed, especially as the expert had ignored the possibility of parental alienation syndrome.[1262]

In *C. v. Finland* (2006), the applicant father alleged a violation of Articles 6 and 8 ECHR.[1263] Influence was raised under both these complaints. With regard

[1254] ECtHR, *G.B. v. Lithuania* (Appl. No. 36137/13), 19 January 2016, para. 74.
[1255] ECtHR, *W.F. v. Italy* (dec.) (Appl. No. 34803/97), 5 April 2001.
[1256] ECtHR, *Elsholz v. Germany* [GC] (Appl. No. 25735/94), 13 July 2000.
[1257] ECtHR, *Elsholz v. Germany* [GC] (Appl. No. 25735/94), 13 July 2000, paras. 31 and 33.
[1258] ECtHR, *Elsholz v. Germany* [GC] (Appl. No. 25735/94), 13 July 2000, para. 35.
[1259] ECtHR, *Süss v. Germany* (Appl. No. 40324/98), 10 November 2005, para. 75.
[1260] ECtHR, *Süss v. Germany* (Appl. No. 40324/98), 10 November 2005, para. 76.
[1261] ECtHR, *Süss v. Germany* (Appl. No. 40324/98), 10 November 2005, para. 75.
[1262] ECtHR, *Süss v. Germany* (Appl. No. 40324/98), 10 November 2005, para. 76.
[1263] ECtHR, *C. v. Finland* (Appl. No. 18249/02), 9 May 2006.

to Article 8 ECHR, the applicant argued that the national Supreme Court had accorded an unreasonable weight to the views of his children, views which had been influenced and manipulated by the female partner of their mother.[1264] The applicant complained that the Supreme Court 'did not order any examination of the substance or voluntariness of their views', nor had it made any reference to the findings that they had been influenced.[1265] Moreover, the applicant alleged a violation of Article 6 because the Supreme Court had not held an oral hearing.[1266] He submitted that the Supreme Court should not have granted such weight to the children's views, as they 'had not been independently formed', without having examined the 'reliability of their expressed wishes' by experts.[1267] It is interesting to note that this was the only applicant who raised the issue of influence as an alleged violation of Article 6 ECHR; all other applicants complained of influence or manipulation under Article 8 ECHR.

In *Luig v. Germany* (2007), the applicant contended that the domestic courts had 'failed to give relevant and sufficient reasons' as to why they did not consult a psychological expert to determine the child's 'true will'.[1268] According to the applicant, the child had been 'manipulated' by her mother and thus had 'not been able to express her own view on access'. Similarly, in *Petersen v. Germany* (2006), the applicant complained that an expert opinion on the child's 'true wishes' had been necessary and should have occurred.[1269] In *Wildgruber v. Germany* (2008), the applicant again argued that the domestic courts' decision-making process had been 'defective', as they had 'failed to consult an expert psychologist on the children's true wishes'.[1270] The lack of appointing an expert was also raised in the complaint of the applicant in the *Moog v. Germany* (2016) judgment. The applicant complained that the courts had failed to order an expert opinion for 'the question of whether the refusal to see his father had been genuine'.[1271]

In the more recent *Khusnutdinov and X v. Russia* (2018) judgment, the applicant argued that too much weight had been placed on the views of the child, especially considering that the child had been influenced by her grandparents during the separation from the applicant 'for a long time'.[1272] Additionally, the applicant complained that the child had been heard by the court 'in the

1264 ECtHR, *C. v. Finland* (Appl. No. 18249/02), 9 May 2006, para. 43.
1265 ECtHR, *C. v. Finland* (Appl. No. 18249/02), 9 May 2006, para. 43.
1266 ECtHR, *C. v. Finland* (Appl. No. 18249/02), 9 May 2006, para. 63.
1267 ECtHR, *C. v. Finland* (Appl. No. 18249/02), 9 May 2006, para. 65.
1268 ECtHR, *Luig v. Germany* (dec.) (Appl. No. 28782/04), 25 September 2007.
1269 ECtHR, *Petersen v. Germany* (dec.) (Appl. Nos. 38282/97 and 68891/01), 12 January 2006.
1270 ECtHR, *Wildgruber v. Germany* (dec.) (Appl. Nos. 42402/05 and 42423/05), 29 January 2008.
1271 ECtHR, *Moog v. Germany* (Appl. Nos. 23280/08 and 2334/10), 6 October 2016, para. 65.
1272 ECtHR, *Khusnutdinov and X v. Russia* (Appl. No. 76598/12), 18 December 2018, para. 70.

presence of her grandmother, who could have influenced her statements'.[1273] According to the applicant, the fact that the child responded to the questions with 'monosyllabic' answers made it 'impossible' for the court to determine whether her views were given 'freely and after a thorough reflection'.[1274] The applicant argued that the domestic courts should have appointed an expert to determine whether the child had been 'subjected to psychological influence'.[1275]

2.2. UNJUSTIFIED RELIANCE ON INFLUENCE

Only in one case did the applicant complain that the domestic courts had incorrectly dealt with influence, in the sense that influence had been wrongly taken into account: *Gajtani v. Switzerland* (2014).[1276] Contrary to the complaints on influence discussed above, the applicant mother alleged that the Swiss court should have given due weight to the views of the children, allowing them to form an exception to return under Article 13(2) of The Hague Abduction Convention, instead of having set the views aside under the assumption that the children were stuck in a conflict of loyalties.[1277] The applicant brought this complaint under Article 8 ECHR.

3. GOVERNMENTS' ARGUMENTS

The 'influence' of the child's views or lack thereof is brought up in governments' arguments in two different ways. Governments may either argue that children were influenced or argue that children were not influenced, but had independent views. These two positions will now be discussed, with a final separate category for other types of remarks regarding influence.

3.1. INFLUENCED VIEWS

In three cases, governments remarked that children were influenced or might be influenced. These three cases, all in response to an Article 8 ECHR complaint, are introduced with their attributes in Table 8.2 below.

1273 ECtHR, *Khusnutdinov and X v. Russia* (Appl. No. 76598/12), 18 December 2018, para. 70.
1274 ECtHR, *Khusnutdinov and X v. Russia* (Appl. No. 76598/12), 18 December 2018, para. 70.
1275 ECtHR, *Khusnutdinov and X v. Russia* (Appl. No. 76598/12), 18 December 2018, para. 70.
1276 ECtHR, *Gajtani v. Switzerland* (Appl. No. 43730/07), 9 September 2014.
1277 ECtHR, *Gajtani v. Switzerland* (Appl. No. 43730/07), 9 September 2014, para. 90.

Table 8.2. Attributes of cases in which the government argued that the views of children were influenced

Chamber judgments	Type of proceeding	In response to complaint on
Rouiller v. Switzerland (2014)	International child abduction	Article 8
Gajtani v. Switzerland (2014)	International child abduction	Article 8
Chamber decision	**Type of proceeding**	**In response to complaint on**
Vámosi v. Hungary (2004)	Custody	Article 8

Source: Compiled by the author.

In the *Gajtani v. Switzerland* (2014) judgment, the government noted that children were influenced when arguing in favour of the domestic courts granting no weight to the views of the children. The government linked the issue of influence to maturity, noting that one of the children was young (11 years old) and thus his maturity was insufficient for his views to be considered sufficiently independent ('suffisamment autonome').[1278] It also stated that the child was caught in a conflict of loyalties between the parents.[1279] In the *Vámosi v. Hungary* (2004) decision, the government noted that the applicant father had contributed to the child's alienation from him 'to a great extent',[1280] while the applicant had complained of the mother's manipulation. In a final judgment, *Rouiller v. Switzerland* (2014), the government did not argue that the children were influenced, but that they might be. In relation to the applicant's complaint that the eldest child had not been heard again, the Swiss government argued that if the child had been heard again she might have felt pressured and would have been subjected to more influence than the first time when she had been able to express her views.[1281]

3.2. INDEPENDENT VIEWS

In six cases, the governments either explicitly remarked that the views of the children were their own independent views or more implicitly argued that the consistency and strength of these views argued against suggestions of influence. In Table 8.3 below, the attributes of these cases are presented. It is interesting to see that most of these cases concerned access proceedings and this point will be further explored in the concluding analysis.

1278 ECtHR, *Gajtani v. Switzerland* (Appl. No. 43730/07), 9 September 2014, para. 97.
1279 ECtHR, *Gajtani v. Switzerland* (Appl. No. 43730/07), 9 September 2014, para. 97.
1280 ECtHR, *Vámosi v. Hungary* (dec.) (Appl. No. 71657/01), 23 March 2004.
1281 ECtHR, *Rouiller v. Switzerland* (Appl. No. 3592/08), 22 July 2014, para. 51.

Table 8.3. Attributes of cases in which the government argued that the views of children were independent

Grand Chamber judgment	Type of proceeding	In response to complaint on:
Sommerfeld v. Germany (2003)	Access	Article 8
Chamber judgments	**Type of proceeding**	**In response to complaint on:**
Kosmopoulou v. Greece (2004)	Access	Article 8
C. v. Finland (2006)	Custody and access	Articles 6 and 8
Cristescu v. Romania (2012)	Access	Article 8
Gobec v. Slovenia (2013)	Access	Article 8
K.B. and others v. Croatia (2017)	Access	Article 8

Source: Compiled by the author.

The government in *Sommerfeld v. Germany* (2003) pointed out that its courts 'acted on the understanding that the child's wishes were only relevant to the extent that they were the expression of her own free will', therefore considering influence within the ambit of due weight.[1282] According to the government, it was not necessary to obtain an expert opinion with regard to the wishes of the child as the domestic courts were able to rely on the views expressed by the child, who was already 13 at the time and had expressed these views for several years.[1283] Combined with the 'repeated refusal' of the child, there was in this case no reason to doubt that the views expressed were her 'own free will'.[1284] In *C. v. Finland* (2006), the government backed its Supreme Court, which had determined on the basis of evidence that the children's wishes were 'their own and independent opinion[s]'.[1285] In this regard, the 'repeated and thorough' examination of these wishes was emphasized by the government by experts with expertise in social welfare, child psychiatry and psychology.[1286] Additionally, in response to a separate complaint under Article 6, the Finnish government added that the consistently expressed wishes of the children were a relevant reason not to have further expert evidence on the views of the children.[1287] Similarly, in *Gobec v. Slovenia* (2013), the government, in considering the question of weight granted to the child's views, clarified that two experts had assessed the child's views as 'genuine and not the result of external manipulation'.[1288] In addition, the government also pointed out that

1282 ECtHR, *Sommerfeld v. Germany* [GC] (Appl. No. 31871/96), 8 July 2003, para. 57.
1283 ECtHR, *Sommerfeld v. Germany* [GC] (Appl. No. 31871/96), 8 July 2003, para. 58.
1284 ECtHR, *Sommerfeld v. Germany* [GC] (Appl. No. 31871/96), 8 July 2003, para. 58.
1285 ECtHR, *C. v. Finland* (Appl. No. 18249/02), 9 May 2006, para. 48.
1286 ECtHR, *C. v. Finland* (Appl. No. 18249/02), 9 May 2006, paras. 48–49.
1287 ECtHR, *C. v. Finland* (Appl. No. 18249/02), 9 May 2006, para. 66.
1288 ECtHR, *Gobec v. Slovenia* (Appl. No. 7233/04), 3 October 2013, para. 124.

the wishes of the child were consistent with a 'strength of feeling' that had 'only deepened with time'.[1289] Finally, in *K.B. and others v. Croatia* (2017), the government was more concise, noting that there was 'no indication' of influence by the mother (the applicant).[1290]

Without explicitly referring to influenced views or independent views, some governments responded to applicants' complaints of influence by emphasizing the consistency and strength of children's views. In both *Kosmopoulou v. Greece* (2004) and *Cristescu v. Romania* (2012), the governments referred to the 'persistent refusal'[1291] or 'consistent refusal'[1292] of the children.

3.3. OTHER REMARKS

In *Fiala v. Czech Republic* (2006), the government did not argue that the children were or were not influenced. Instead, the government stated only that the competent authorities had taken all necessary steps, including warning the mother of the danger of manipulating her children.[1293]

4. THE ECTHR

Influence, manipulation or parental alienation – these are all reflected upon by the ECtHR. The Court does not generally determine whether the children were influenced when expressing their views, but it does review the manner in which domestic courts have dealt with the issue of (potential) influence. In this section, the reasoning on influence will be discussed according to the manner in which influence was of relevance in the domestic proceedings: first, influence in relation to participation as such is discussed and then in relation to weight granted to views. Finally, cases which do not fall under these themes are presented.

4.1. INFLUENCE AND PARTICIPATION

In six cases, the ECtHR discussed 'influence' in the light of questions of participation. These six cases have been set out in Table 8.4 below. The table shows that this topic is always considered under the scope of the right to respect for family life of Article 8 ECHR of the applicants, i.e. in most cases the parent.

1289 ECtHR, *Gobec v. Slovenia* (Appl. No. 7233/04), 3 October 2013, para. 124.
1290 ECtHR, *K.B. and others v. Croatia* (Appl. No. 36216/13), 14 March 2017, para. 143.
1291 ECtHR, *Kosmopoulou v. Greece* (Appl. No. 60457/00), 5 February 2004, para. 41.
1292 ECtHR, *Cristescu v. Romania* (Appl. No. 13589/07), 10 January 2012, para. 54.
1293 ECtHR, *Fiala v. Czech Republic* (Appl. No. 26141/03), 18 July 2006, para. 85.

The types of proceedings concerned custody, access and international child abduction.

Table 8.4. Attributes of cases in which the ECtHR provided reasoning on influence and participation

Grand Chamber judgments	**Type of proceeding**	**Applicant(s)**	**Reasoning under**
Elsholz v. Germany (2000)	Access	Father	Article 8
Sommerfeld v. Germany (2003)	Access	Father	Article 8
Chamber judgments	**Type of proceeding**	**Applicant(s)**	**Reasoning under**
Sommerfeld v. Germany (2001)	Access	Father	Article 8
Gajtani v. Switzerland (2014)	International child abduction	Mother	Article 8
Khusnutdinov and X v. Russia (2018)	Custody	Father, also on behalf of child	Article 8
Chamber decisions	**Type of proceeding**	**Applicant(s)**	**Reasoning under**
Luig v. Germany (2007)	Access	Father	Article 8
Wildgruber v. Germany (2008)	Custody	Father	Article 8

Source: Compiled by the author.

In the majority of these cases, the question of influence was raised with regard to how the children should have participated and, specifically, whether a (psychological) expert should have been used in determining the child's views. Mostly, the ECtHR was in agreement with the domestic courts' decisions, except in *Elsholz v. Germany* (2000). In the Grand Chamber judgment in *Elsholz v. Germany* (2000), the ECtHR noted that the German District Court had referred to 'the mother's objections to the applicant which she imparted to the child' and found that the national court should have arranged an expert opinion 'to explore the true wishes' of the child.[1294] The Court found that the reasoning of the domestic court of first instance was insufficient to explain why no expert advice was arranged and that the domestic court of appeal 'should not have been satisfied' with not having the psychological expert evidence to evaluate the child's statements.[1295] The refusal to have ordered an independent psychological report together with the absence of a hearing for the applicant in appeal led to a violation of Article 8 ECHR because of the applicant's insufficient involvement in the decision-making process.[1296] The absence of a hearing made sense in that regard; how the lack of a psychological report for the child fed into

[1294] ECtHR, *Elsholz v. Germany* [GC] (Appl. No. 25735/94), 13 July 2000, para. 52.
[1295] ECtHR, *Elsholz v. Germany* [GC] (Appl. No. 25735/94), 13 July 2000, para. 52.
[1296] ECtHR, *Elsholz v. Germany* [GC] (Appl. No. 25735/94), 13 July 2000, para. 53.

insufficient involvement of the father was less straightforward. Subsequently, in the *Sommerfeld v. Germany* (2001) judgment, the ECtHR did not agree with the government's argument that a psychological expert was not necessary, as the domestic courts had been able to hear the child directly. It stated that the domestic court of appeal 'should not have been satisfied with hearing only the child as to her wishes on the matter without having at its disposal psychological expert evidence to evaluate the child's seemingly firm wishes'.[1297] The Court referred to three factors in this regard: the 'superficial submissions' given by the psychologist in first instance, the lapse of time (two years between instances) and 'what was at stake in the proceedings, namely, the relations between a father and his child'.[1298] However, the Grand Chamber disagreed with this reasoning, as will be discussed below.

In the other four judgments and decisions, the ECtHR did not see any need for an expert. Not all judges agreed in the Grand Chamber judgment in *Sommerfeld v. Germany* (2003). In this judgment, the ECtHR departed from the judgment by the Chamber discussed above regarding the involvement of a psychological expert to evaluate the child's wishes.[1299] The Grand Chamber found the national court well placed to determine whether the child's wishes were her own or not.[1300] It spent no further words on the issue of influence or parental alienation. This was contested by Judges Ress, Pastor Ridruejo and Türmen in their partly dissenting opinion. The Judges argued that it should be a procedural requirement to have psychological expert evidence as an 'indispensable prerequisite for establishing the child's true wishes' and to strike a fair balance between all interests at stake in access proceedings.[1301] The Judges referred to research on parental alienation syndrome and further stated that national courts should 'address the question whether parental alienation syndrome is present and what specific consequences such a syndrome could have on the child's development and – as the Chamber put it – on the establishment of "a child's true wishes"'.[1302]

In the *Luig v. Germany* (2007) decision, the ECtHR made various comments regarding influence.[1303] First, the Court noted that the domestic courts based their decision on the views of the child, which were 'firmly and consistently expressed'. The domestic courts found that the child 'vigorously refused' to have contact with her father and decided not to force the child to have contact, even

[1297] ECtHR, *Sommerfeld v. Germany* (Appl. No. 31871/96), 11 October 2001, para. 43.
[1298] ECtHR, *Sommerfeld v. Germany* (Appl. No. 31871/96), 11 October 2001, para. 43.
[1299] ECtHR, *Sommerfeld v. Germany* [GC] (Appl. No. 31871/96), 8 July 2003, para. 67.
[1300] ECtHR, *Sommerfeld v. Germany* [GC] (Appl. No. 31871/96), 8 July 2003, para. 72.
[1301] Partly dissenting opinion of Judge Ress joined by Judges Pastor Ridruejo and Türmen in ECtHR, *Sommerfeld v. Germany* [GC] (Appl. No. 31871/96), 8 July 2003, para. 3.
[1302] Partly dissenting opinion of Judge Ress joined by Judges Pastor Ridruejo and Türmen in ECtHR, *Sommerfeld v. Germany* [GC] (Appl. No. 31871/96), 8 July 2003, para. 3.
[1303] ECtHR, *Luig v. Germany* (dec.) (Appl. No. 28782/04), 25 September 2007.

if she 'could have been influenced' by the mother. The ECtHR concluded that the domestic courts were well placed to evaluate the child's statements and 'to establish whether or not she was able to make up her own mind'. Therefore, it found that the decision of the domestic courts not to seek expert advice was reasonable and found the complaint to be inadmissible.[1304]

In *Wildgruber v. Germany* (2008), the ECtHR found the statements of the children to have been 'reasonably interpreted' by the national courts, as they were sufficiently clear and the national courts had 'no reason to doubt that they reflected the child's true wishes'.[1305] Additionally, the ECtHR observed that the domestic courts had examined and rejected the allegations of manipulation. Taking these factors together, it found that the domestic courts could reasonably draw conclusions without recourse to an expert.[1306]

In the *Khusnutdinov and X v. Russia* (2018) judgment, the ECtHR first reaffirmed the general principle that national courts are to 'assess the evidence before them, including the means to ascertain the relevant facts'.[1307] The Court then turned to the question of requiring a psychological expert to determine whether views were influenced. It reiterated the principle that it is not always required to involve an expert, as it depends on the circumstances. In this case, the circumstances – that the applicant never requested an expert during the proceedings, combined with the fact that the child was 13 years old when heard and assisted by a specialist – meant that the ECtHR concluded that the domestic courts could reasonably find that the child's statements 'reflected her true wishes' and so did not require an expert's opinion.[1308]

Finally, another type of consideration was made regarding participation in *Gajtani v. Switzerland* (2014). The ECtHR considered that it was reasonable of the national courts not to hear the children again because of the conflict of loyalties they were facing, taking into account the margin of appreciation and the general rule that it is for the national courts to assess the evidence before them.[1309] Thus, the ECtHR agreed with the domestic courts that influence provided sufficient reason not to have children participate once again.

4.2. INFLUENCE AND DUE WEIGHT

The topic of influence was discussed in eight cases with regard to the question of weight to be attributed to children's expressed views. The attributes of these judgments and decisions are presented in Table 8.5 below. The table clarifies

1304 ECtHR, *Luig v. Germany* (dec.) (Appl. No. 28782/04), 25 September 2007

1305 ECtHR, *Wildgruber v. Germany* (dec.) (Appl. Nos. 42402/05 and 42423/05), 29 January 2008.

1306 ECtHR, *Wildgruber v. Germany* (dec.) (Appl. Nos. 42402/05 and 42423/05), 29 January 2008.

1307 ECtHR, *Khusnutdinov and X v. Russia* (Appl. No. 76598/12), 18 December 2018, para. 87.

1308 ECtHR, *Khusnutdinov and X v. Russia* (Appl. No. 76598/12), 18 December 2018, para. 87.

1309 ECtHR, *Gajtani v. Switzerland* (Appl. No. 43730/07), 9 September 2014, para. 111.

that it is a topic discussed solely in the light of Article 8 ECHR and mostly in custody and access proceedings. More specifically, the reasoning was conducted in light of the parents' right to respect for family life, the exceptions being *N.Ts. and others v. Georgia* (2016), where the reasoning concerned the children's right to respect for private and family life.

Table 8.5. Attributes of cases in which the ECtHR provided reasoning on influence and due weight

Chamber judgments	Type of proceeding	Applicant(s)	Reasoning under
Süss v. Germany (2005)	Access	Father	Article 8
C. v. Finland (2006)	Custody and access	Father	Article 8
Fiala v. Czech Republic (2006)	Access	Father	Article 8
Gobec v. Slovenia (2013)	Access	Father	Article 8
N.Ts. and others v. Georgia (2016)	Custody	Aunt on behalf of children	Article 8
K.B. and others v. Croatia (2017)	Access	Mother	Article 8
Zelikha Magomadova v. Russia (2019)	Custody	Mother	Article 8
Chamber decision	**Type of proceeding**	**Applicant(s)**	**Reasoning under**
Paradis and others v. Germany (2003)	International child abduction	Mother, also on behalf of children	Article 8

Source: Compiled by the author.

To start with, it is relevant to consider a principle that has been expressed by the ECtHR in two cases, without the Court applying these principles to the facts. In the *K.B. and others v. Croatia* (2017) judgment, the ECtHR was very explicit as to influence and due weight: 'if a court would base a decision on the views of children who are palpably unable to form and articulate an opinion as to their wishes – for example, because of a loyalty conflict and/or their exposure to the alienating behaviour of one parent – such a decision could run contrary to Article 8 of the Convention'.[1310] This statement is made with a reference to *Laylle v. Germany*, an unreported Commission decision from 1996.[1311] It is unclear why the ECtHR decides to be so explicit with this opinion on the basis of a decision from 20 years earlier, without discussing the more recent judgments in which parental alienation or a conflict of loyalties was present. In any event, the ECtHR reaffirmed this statement in the *Zelikha Magomadova v. Russia* (2019) judgment without further application in that case.[1312]

1310 ECtHR, *K.B. and others v. Croatia* (Appl. No. 36216/13), 14 March 2017, para. 143.

1311 *Laylle v. Germany* (Appl. No. 26376/95), Commission decision of 4 September 1996, unreported.

1312 ECtHR, *Zelikha Magomadova v. Russia* (Appl. No. 58724/14), 8 October 2019, para. 115.

If we look at the other cases, there are different ways in which the ECtHR considers influence in relation to due weight.

First, there are cases in which there was presumably influence. Take *Fiala v. Czech Republic* (2006), in which the ECtHR was critical of the approach of the domestic courts. The Court held that it should not be overlooked that the children had been under the exclusive influence of their mother for some time.[1313] Therefore, the ECtHR denounced the following the children's views and not enforcing the access arrangements, even though it would have been in their best interests.[1314] Another judgment in which the ECtHR was critical, although for very different reasons, was *N.Ts. and others v. Georgia* (2016). In this judgment, the ECtHR found that the domestic courts had not adequately given weight to the children's wish not to be reunited with their father. According to the Court, 'whatever the manipulative role played by the maternal family', the children had an 'unambiguous' 'hostile attitude' towards their father.[1315] Additionally, the ECtHR mentioned the conclusion of the social workers that there was 'severe alienation of the children from their father'.[1316] Taking all this into account, it found that it would be contrary to the best interests of the children to reunite them with their father without any preparatory measures.[1317] Thus, the Court calls for weight to be granted to the children's views, even if they are potentially manipulated. Similarly, in *Süss v. Germany* (2005), the ECtHR agreed with the applicant and the domestic courts that the child's negative views towards her father 'was presumably partly caused by [mother]'s influence', but it was nevertheless the 'child's firm wish'.[1318] The Court subsequently found the domestic court's conclusion to be reasonable – that even if the views were partly caused by influence, it had been the child's clear wishes and not the reasons for those wishes which were decisive in the balancing of the child's best interests.[1319]

There are also cases in which it was concluded that there was no influence on the children's views. In *Paradis and others v. Germany* (2003), the ECtHR found that the German Court of Appeal had not made an 'arbitrary' assessment in the weighing of the children's views or in following the appointed expert's finding that the children's objections came from their experiences with their father, not the influence of their mother.[1320] Similarly, the ECtHR in *Gobec v. Slovenia* (2013) found that the domestic courts struck a fair balance in the contact proceedings relying in part on the child's views. The Court noted, in

1313 ECtHR, *Fiala v. Czech Republic* (Appl. No. 26141/03), 18 July 2006, para. 103.
1314 ECtHR, *Fiala v. Czech Republic* (Appl. No. 26141/03), 18 July 2006, para. 103.
1315 ECtHR, *N.Ts. and others v. Georgia* (Appl. No. 71776/12), 2 February 2016, para. 82.
1316 ECtHR, *N.Ts. and others v. Georgia* (Appl. No. 71776/12), 2 February 2016, para. 82.
1317 ECtHR, *N.Ts. and others v. Georgia* (Appl. No. 71776/12), 2 February 2016, para. 83.
1318 ECtHR, *Süss v. Germany* (Appl. No. 40324/98), 10 November 2005, para. 91.
1319 ECtHR, *Süss v. Germany* (Appl. No. 40324/98), 10 November 2005, para. 95.
1320 ECtHR, *Paradis and others v. Germany* (dec.) (Appl. No. 4783/03), 15 May 2003.

that regard, that two psychologists had assessed the child's wishes as not being caused by the mother's influence.[1321]

Lastly, in *C. v. Finland* (2006), the ECtHR remarked that 'all court instances essentially agreed as to the consistency and strength of the child's views' and that it was therefore relevant for the domestic court to rely on their views.[1322] However, it was critical as to the decisive weight placed on these views without recourse to other interests or facts, noting that this 'understandably left the applicant with the impression that L., the mother's partner, had been allowed to manipulate the children and the court system to deprive him unjustifiably of his parental role'.[1323] Granting children veto power is not approved, but it is even less acceptable when the children appear to be manipulated.

4.3. OTHER REASONING ON INFLUENCE

There are four cases in which the ECtHR discussed the issue of influence, but where the reasoning did not concern the question of participation or due weight. These attributes of these cases are presented in Table 8.6 below – again showing similar case attributes, with reasoning under the parents' right to respect for family life in Article 8 and the cases mostly concerning custody and access.

Table 8.6. Attributes of cases in which the ECtHR provides reasoning on other issues of influence

Grand Chamber judgment	Type of proceeding	Applicant(s)	Reasoning under
Scozzari and Giunta v. Italy (2000)	Care and access	Mother, also on behalf of children	Article 8
Chamber judgments	**Type of proceeding**	**Applicant(s)**	**Reasoning under**
Cristescu v. Romania (2012)	Access	Father	Article 8
G.B. v. Lithuania (2016)	Custody	Mother	Article 8
M.K. v. Greece (2018)	International child abduction	Mother	Dissenting opinions

Source: Compiled by the author.

In the Grand Chamber judgment in *Scozzari and Giunta v. Italy* (2000), the ECtHR stated that it 'cannot express any view as to the genuineness of the assertions' made by the child in a letter; however, it did find the changes in attitude by the children 'worrying'.[1324]

1321 ECtHR, *Gobec v. Slovenia* (Appl. No. 7233/04), 3 October 2013, para. 138.
1322 ECtHR, *C. v. Finland* (Appl. No. 18249/02), 9 May 2006, para. 57.
1323 ECtHR, *C. v. Finland* (Appl. No. 18249/02), 9 May 2006, para. 58.
1324 ECtHR, *Scozzari and Giunta v. Italy* [GC] (Appl. Nos. 39221/98 and 41963/98), 13 July 2000, para. 210.

In *Cristescu v. Romania* (2012), the topic of influence was relevant in relation to the enforcement of the access decisions. The ECtHR agreed with the manner in which the domestic courts had taken the applicant father's assertions that the mother had negatively influenced the child into consideration.[1325] The domestic courts did not accept the assertion of sole influence, instead repeatedly finding that it was the 'responsibility of both parents to improve the family relationship'.[1326]

In *G.B. v. Lithuania* (2016), the issue of influence arose in light of the enforcement of an order in a residence dispute. The ECtHR started by noting that the applicant 'has put much emphasis on parental alienation syndrome', but did not follow her line of reasoning.[1327] Instead, the Court stated that 'without refuting the finding by the psychologists' (that the children suffered from parental alienation syndrome and alienated from their mother),[1328] it 'takes notice of' the national court's conclusion that the children staying with the father for only seven days was too short for the children to 'cardinally' change their views towards their mother.[1329] The ECtHR did not take a stance on parental alienation syndrome, accepting both the findings of the psychologists as well as the decision taken by the national courts. This was also criticized in the dissenting opinion of Judges Sajó and Motoc, who argued that the ECtHR ought to have considered the issue more carefully, as parental alienation syndrome 'has been considered as relevant and important by the Court in at least a dozen cases'.[1330] The dissenting judges exaggerated the amount of existing case law on parental alienation syndrome. The dissenting Judges argued that national courts ought to address the question of whether the children suffered from parental alienation syndrome and what consequences it could have on their development.[1331]

Finally, *M.K. v. Greece* (2018) should be mentioned here. Although the ECtHR did not discuss the issue of influence in its judgment, instead focusing positively on the weight attached to the child's views, it was debated in the two dissenting opinions. Judge Wojtyczek was very critical of the majority in his dissenting opinion, specifically regarding the issue of influence. According to him, the majority ignored the fact that a child is always strongly influenced by the parent with custody, as this parent often manipulates the child and trains them against the other parent.[1332] He argued that the passage of time increases

1325 ECtHR, *Cristescu v. Romania* (Appl. No. 13589/07), 10 January 2012, para. 66.
1326 ECtHR, *Cristescu v. Romania* (Appl. No. 13589/07), 10 January 2012, para. 66.
1327 ECtHR, *G.B. v. Lithuania* (Appl. No. 36137/13), 19 January 2016, para. 95.
1328 ECtHR, *G.B. v. Lithuania* (Appl. No. 36137/13), 19 January 2016, paras. 25 and 30.
1329 ECtHR, *G.B. v. Lithuania* (Appl. No. 36137/13), 19 January 2016, para. 95.
1330 Dissenting opinion of Judges Sajó and Motoc in ECtHR, *G.B. v. Lithuania* (Appl. No. 36137/13), 19 January 2016.
1331 Dissenting opinion of Judges Sajó and Motoc in ECtHR, *G.B. v. Lithuania* (Appl. No. 36137/13), 19 January 2016.
1332 Dissenting opinion of Judge Wojtyczek in ECtHR, *M.K. v. Greece* (Appl. No. 51312/16), 1 February 2018, para. 3.

this influence and therefore the lack of execution of the custody decision could be used to achieve a fait accompli.[1333] In the second dissenting opinion, Judge Koskelo did not reach such radical conclusions as Wojtyczek; instead, he noted the potential risk of putting great emphasis on the views of the child when these views have been given following a passage of time during which an initial decision was not executed.[1334] Koskelo remarked that the views might have been 'influenced by the passage of time' and that it was necessary to conduct a hearing in a timely manner in order to 'establish the genuine views and wishes of a child'.[1335]

4.4. CONCLUSIONS ON THE ECtHR'S REASONING

Tying together all of the ECtHR's reasoning on influence, a few conclusions can be made. The first is that the ECtHR has a subsidiary role with regard to influence. The Court itself does not determine whether children were influenced or not, but instead reviews the way in which domestic courts have addressed the issue of (alleged) influence. A subsequent conclusion is that influence is generally a topic on which the ECtHR agreed with the domestic courts' decisions. Of the 18 judgments and decisions in this area, the ECtHR only reprimanded the domestic approach in three judgments. Notwithstanding the general acceptance by the ECtHR, the (potential) influence applied on children and the manner in which to deal with this influence – either at the phase of participation or when giving weight to the views of the children – led to discussion within the ECtHR. This is clear from the dissenting opinions in which certain judges criticized the way in which influence was considered by the Court.

Despite the internal debates on influence, the following can be said about the role of influence with regard to participation and due weight. In most circumstances, the ECtHR found domestic courts to be well placed to evaluate children's statements and views. In determining whether the child's views are influenced or not, the domestic courts can rely on their own impression if they have heard the child directly, and can consider the other evidence available to them. Without any direct complaints from applicants, it will therefore not be necessary to take any additional measures. However, if one of the parents does

1333 Dissenting opinion of Judge Wojtyczek in ECtHR, *M.K. v. Greece* (Appl. No. 51312/16), 1 February 2018, para. 3.

1334 Dissenting opinion of Judge Koskelo in ECtHR, *M.K. v. Greece* (Appl. No. 51312/16), 1 February 2018, para. 19 and 34.

1335 Dissenting opinion of Judge Koskelo in ECtHR, *M.K. v. Greece* (Appl. No. 51312/16), 1 February 2018, para. 34.

explicitly call into question the potential impact of influence by the other parent, it may be necessary for an expert to assist in evaluating the children's views. It is important to emphasize that this is not always required by the ECtHR, as we will see in section 5.2.3 below.

In relation to the weight to be placed on the expressed wishes, the ECtHR's reasoning has been inconsistent. On the one hand, in *K.B. and others v. Croatia* (2017) and *Zelikha Magomadova v. Russia* (2019), the ECtHR was very explicit that relying on a child's clearly influenced views might lead to a violation of Article 8 ECHR. Presumably, the Court referred here to the parent's right to respect for family life under Article 8 and not the child's right. On the other hand, in a number of judgments concerning access or custody proceedings, the ECtHR has held that if the child's wishes are firm, it may be in their best interests to rely on these wishes, even if they are presumably influenced or manipulated. The Court therefore accepts that children do not have to present some kind of 'objective truth', but that their views are relevant as is, whether or not these are the product of influence. This is an approach which appears to focus on the empowerment and autonomy of children, and thereby the child's right to participate. Accepting potential influence as impacting the child's views, but still emphasizing the child's wishes and interests reduces the power of the parental disagreements. By zooming out of the question of influence, the ECtHR has made it a less viable tool for parents to use in family law disputes.

5. CONCLUDING ANALYSIS

The views of a child being 'influenced' or 'manipulated' is a recurring topic in the analysed case law from the ECtHR. In the concluding analysis of this chapter, the complaints from applicants, responses from governments and reasoning from the Court are taken together. We will once again start with the numbers before turning to the core issue: how to determine and deal with influence. This is meaningful for determining the ECtHR's input in the international and European framework. Finally, the potential relationship between influence and the types of proceedings and applicants is considered. This adds more flesh to the understanding of the standards set and may prove relevant for the comparison and evaluation of international and European standards.

5.1. CONCLUSION IN NUMBERS

Before we turn to the substantive conclusions, a brief qualitative overview is in order. There were a total of 27 judgments and decisions in which influence was addressed. In Table 8.7 below, an overview in numbers is presented of how the topic of influence appears in these cases.

Table 8.7. Number of cases in which the topic of influence is discussed

Discussed by:	
Applicant	5
Government	1
Applicant and government	2
Applicant, government and ECtHR	5
Applicant and ECtHR	7
Government and ECtHR	2
ECtHR only	5
Total	27

Source: Compiled by the author.

The topic of influence is the last one covered in this chapter with the most limited presence. This is not due to the complaints of the applicants, with 19 complaints made regarding influence. Influence is a topic commonly relied on by a parent in the role of applicant as a means to accomplish his or her own rights to custody or access. This means that it is not so much a topic raised for the realization of their child's procedural rights as a tool instrumentalized to strengthen the parent's substantive position in a parental dispute. Although one might expect more complaints on influence, it is relevant to understand that a parent will only do so if the child has participated at the domestic level and expressed themselves negatively towards the applicant. This will explain why there are more complaints on the other topics of 'insufficient' participation and due weight than on influence.

The low overall number of cases in which influence was discussed can be explained by the response of the ECtHR. The topic of influence is mostly considered by the ECtHR when there is a complaint by an applicant concerning influence (12 out of the 19 cases in which the ECtHR commented on influence). Only in a limited number of cases did the ECtHR discuss the issue of influence on its own initiative. This may signify that the Court sees the topic of influence as too complex in the discussion on child participation compared to the question of participation and due weight itself. More likely, however, the reason that the ECtHR rarely addressed influence on its own initiative is that the topics of participation and due weight are more visible in the facts of the case and can therefore be more easily referred to, even if the complaint does not address it. Additionally, whether or not a child has participated, whether or not the domestic courts have considered their views and what the child's age was can be established more objectively on the basis of the facts of the case.

5.2. DETERMINING AND DEALING WITH INFLUENCE ON VIEWS

With the participation of children in proceedings and the potential weight given to their views, influence is a contested topic. Applicants to the ECtHR repeatedly challenge the manner in which domestic courts respond to the assertion that children were influenced when expressing views. Governments, of course, stand by their domestic courts and disagree with the applicants. The ECtHR was then faced with the question of how influence can or should be determined and, if it is found, how to deal with influenced views in proceedings. The conclusions in the previous section on the reasoning on the Court already provide some initial answers as to influence and participation, and influence and due weight. But what can we also conclude from the analysis to answer those questions? There is no clear-cut answer, but there are a number of overarching facets to consider: consistency and strength of views, the role of time, the use of experts and parental alienation syndrome. Notably, the topic of maturity is not listed. The ECtHR did not refer to or rely on the maturity of the child in relation to influence, even though the government in *Gajtani v. Switzerland* (2014) linked the topics together.

5.2.1. *Consistency and Strength of Views*

A common response by the governments to the applicants' complaints that the views of their children were influenced was that this was not the case, as proven by the consistency and strength of the children's views. The governments used the consistency and strength of views as the sole argument that the child's views are their own in *Kosmopoulou v. Greece* (2004) and *Cristescu v. Romania* (2012)[1336] or as an additional justification in *Sommerfeld v. Germany* (2003), *C. v. Finland* (2006) and *Gobec v. Slovenia* (2013).[1337] The ECtHR has at

---

1336 ECtHR, *Kosmopoulou v. Greece* (Appl. No. 60457/00), 5 February 2004, para. 41; and ECtHR, *Cristescu v. Romania* (Appl. No. 13589/07), 10 January 2012, para. 54.

1337 ECtHR, *Sommerfeld v. Germany* [GC] (Appl. No. 31871/96), 8 July 2003, para. 58; ECtHR, *C. v. Finland* (Appl. No. 18249/02), 9 May 2006, para. 66 and ECtHR, *Gobec v. Slovenia* (Appl. No. 7233/04), 3 October 2013, para. 124.

times similarly referenced the consistency and strength of children's views as confirmation that the children's views are free of influence – for example, in *Luig v. Germany* (2007) with regard to the question of needing an expert.[1338] However, the ECtHR also accepts that children can have a consistent and firm wish while being (presumably) influenced. Consider *Süss v. Germany* (2005) or *N.Ts. and others v. Georgia* (2016), in which the ECtHR found that it was likely that the children were manipulated, but that their views were nonetheless strong and unambiguous.[1339]

Therefore, the ECtHR rightfully accepts that the consistency and strength of children's views does not in itself amount to a lack of influence. It will depend on the situation whether the consistency signals independent views or whether it shows the continued influence exerted over a child's views or the internalized effect of influence or conflict. The fact that the factor 'consistency and strength' can go both ways, signalling independent views *or* influenced views, makes it difficult – if not impossible – to use as a counterargument to a claim of influence; while governments have often done so, it may not be appropriate. It is important for all parties to consider whether a child's repeated views are influenced views or not and to consider whether it is even possible to determine the presence of influence on the basis of consistency and strength.

5.2.2. The Role of Time

The relevance of consistency leads us to our next facet: the role of time. The passage of time can have an impact on influence in a number of ways. It may allow children to repeatedly express consistent views or it may allow for the opposite, with children maturing to have different views over time. The passage of time may also increase influence because it may lead to a longer period of time during which the child only sees one parent. It may also allow for children to realize the influence that has been exerted over them. A number of applicants specifically raised the former issue in their complaints. For example, in *Vámosi v. Hungary* (2004), the applicant alleged that the lack of enforcement of his custody rights for years resulted in influenced views relied on by the Supreme Court ten years later.[1340] Governments do not emphasize the impact of passing time on the potential for influence. This is not a surprise, as common reasons for the passage of time are the length of domestic proceedings and lack of enforcement

1338 ECtHR, *Luig v. Germany* (dec.) (Appl. No. 28782/04), 25 September 2007.

1339 ECtHR, *Süss v. Germany* (Appl. No. 40324/98), 10 November 2005, para. 91; and ECtHR, *N.Ts. and others v. Georgia* (Appl. No. 71776/12), 2 February 2016, para. 82.

1340 ECtHR, *Vámosi v. Hungary* (dec.) (Appl. No. 71657/01), 23 March 2004.

by domestic authorities. These are not facts which the governments wish to emphasize. The ECtHR, on the other hand, did refer to the role of time in four judgments. In *Fiala v. Czech Republic* (2006), the Court noted that the children were under the exclusive influence of their mother for some time and found that this should not have been overlooked by the domestic courts.[1341] Similarly, in *Gajtani v. Switzerland* (2014), it found that the domestic courts' decision not to hear the children again because of the conflict of loyalties they were by then facing was reasonable.[1342] On the other side of the spectrum is *G.B. v. Lithuania* (2016), in which the ECtHR agreed with the domestic court that seven days with the father was too short a time for the children to be influenced and to completely change their views towards their mother.[1343] Additionally, Judge Wojtyczek in his dissenting opinion in *M.K. v. Greece* (2018) drew attention to the role of time, arguing that the passage of time increases a parent's influence over his or her child and therefore the non-execution of custody decisions could be used to achieve a fait accompli.[1344]

The applicants and the ECtHR stressed the role of time in potentially increasing the influence of one parent on the views of the child towards another parent. In doing so, the Court raised a compelling reason why states should ensure that the length of family law proceedings is not excessive and that enforcement is effective. While this is certainly commendable, the question of whether the passage of time will increase the influence of a parent on the child's views is one that would benefit from more research.

5.2.3. *The Use of Experts*

A third facet which repeatedly appears throughout the complaints and subsequently in the ECtHR's reasoning is the use of experts to assess the child's 'true' wishes. In seven cases, the applicants either complained that the expert used in the domestic proceedings was insufficiently competent or qualified with regard to determining the child's wishes and the question of influence, or that an expert should have been appointed when none had been in the domestic proceedings. In six cases, the ECtHR provided a response to these kinds of complaints. The common trend is that the Court did not find that domestic courts are required to have an expert in order to determine whether the views of the child are his or her own or are in some way influenced.

1341 ECtHR, *Fiala v. Czech Republic* (Appl. No. 26141/03), 18 July 2006, para. 103.
1342 ECtHR, *Gajtani v. Switzerland* (Appl. No. 43730/07), 9 September 2014, para. 111.
1343 ECtHR, *G.B. v. Lithuania* (Appl. No. 36137/13), 19 January 2016, para. 95.
1344 Dissenting opinion of Judge Wojtyczek in ECtHR, *M.K. v. Greece* (Appl. No. 51312/16), 1 February 2018, para. 3.

It will depend on the circumstances of the case, but generally the ECtHR has found that domestic courts are well placed to evaluate the child's views and whether an expert is needed themselves. This was the opinion of the Court in *Sommerfeld v. Germany* (2003), *Luig v. Germany* (2007), *Wildgruber v. Germany* (2008) and *Khusnutdinov and X v. Russia* (2018). Only in *Elsholz v. Germany* (2000) did the ECtHR find that the domestic court should have appointed an expert, specifically mentioning that the domestic court's reasoning as to why they did not involve an expert was insufficient. It can therefore be concluded that an expert is certainly not a necessity when questions of influence are raised, but that the domestic courts must consider the circumstances and properly justify their decision as to whether they are themselves capable of evaluating the child's views or whether an expert is required.

5.2.4. Parental Alienation Syndrome

In considering influence, a discussion on the frequently cited question of parental alienation syndrome cannot be omitted. The applicants in the following three judgments complained of this: *Elsholz v. Germany* (2000), *Süss v. Germany* (2005) and *G.B. v. Lithuania* (2016). The governments did not discuss parental alienation syndrome, but the ECtHR did so in a number of cases either in its reasoning or through judges in their dissenting opinions. In the judgments from the early 2000s – *Elsholz v. Germany* (2000), *Sommerfeld v. Germany* (2003) and *Süss v. Germany* (2005) – the ECtHR preferred to sidestep the issue of parental alienation syndrome. However, this was criticized by Judges Ress, Pastor Ridruejo and Türmen in their dissenting opinion to *Sommerfeld v. Germany* (2003). In the later judgments – *G.B. v. Lithuania* (2016), *K.B. and others v. Croatia* (2017) and *Zelikha Magomadova v. Russia* (2019) – the ECtHR itself referred to parental alienation, although not as a syndrome in the latter two. In *K.B. and others v. Croatia* (2017) and *Zelikha Magomadova v. Russia* (2019), the Court provided a general principle with reference to a conclusion on parental alienation from the early 1990s. In *G.B. v. Lithuania* (2016), the ECtHR did not take a clear stance on parental alienation syndrome, which was again criticized in a dissenting opinion, this time by Judges Sajó and Motoc, who called for more careful consideration on parental alienation syndrome and the potential consequences to children. In conclusion, it can be argued that the ECtHR has been inconsistent and has not yet formed a set opinion on parental alienation syndrome and its role in relation to children's expressed views. Given that parental alienation syndrome is a controversial topic in the legal sphere, but especially in child psychology, it may be praiseworthy that the ECtHR has not adopted a strict approach to the issue. By refraining from putting emphasis on parental alienation syndrome, the Court has not provided additional ammunition to parents in high-conflict proceedings.

5.3. INFLUENCE AND THE TYPES OF PROCEEDINGS AND APPLICANTS

Of the 24 cases discussed in this chapter, the overwhelming majority concerned custody or access proceedings. Only three cases concerned international child abduction proceedings and one concerned care (and access) proceedings.

This overrepresentation of custody and access proceedings is tied to another clear majority in the attributes of the cases in which applicants complained of influence. In 15 out of the 16 cases in which applicants complained, the applicant was a parent only complaining on his or her own behalf. In the reasoning of the ECtHR, the focus also appears to be placed on the parents and not so much the children when considering influence and participation. The consideration as to whether or not domestic courts should have brought in an expert to determine a child's true wishes is not so much about the child's rights, but more about the right of the parent to have courts only give weight to children's views when these views are completely free of influence. However, the ECtHR did place more focus on the children in its judgments where, although the child might have been influenced, their views were given priority in assessing their best interests. The general focus on parents' rights instead of children's rights is especially visible in relation to influence, but is not uncommon in relation to child participation in family law proceedings. This is problematic insofar as the ECtHR's principles on children's rights are muddied by the rights of parents – especially with regard to the child's procedural rights. The ECtHR does not consider the issue of influence on a child's views in isolation; the topic is continually framed within the scope of a parent's breached substantive right. This means that we have no 'clean' opinion of the Court on influence. It would be interesting to see what the ECtHR would say if the topic could be considered in a test lab – free from circumstances relating to parents.

With most cases concerning custody and access proceedings, the link between influence and the passage of time, as described above, is perhaps even more relevant. In custody and access proceedings, preventing delays and ensuring timely enforcement may assist in decreasing influence (insofar as the passage of time has an impact on the influence exerted over a child's views). Ensuring that children remain in contact with both parents will likely lessen the assertions of influence. Applicants may also bring fewer complaints regarding influence if the ECtHR continues to assert that, in light of the child's best interests, their views are given weight regardless of the alleged influence.

Table 8.8. Combined overview for the 'influence' on the views of the child

		Applicants' complaint					Governments' argument						ECtHR				
		Influence or manipulation	Examine and address influence	PAS or conflict of loyalties	Unjustified reliance on influence	No complaint	Influenced views	PAS or conflict of loyalties	Independent views	Consistency and strength of views	Other	No mention	Influence and participation	Influence and due weight	Other reasoning influence	Dissenting opinions	Not discussed
GC judgments	*Elsholz v. Germany* (2000)	-	X	X	-	-	-	-	-	-	-	X	X	-	-	-	-
	Scozzari and Giunta v. Italy (2000)	X	-	-	-	-	-	-	-	-	-	X	-	-	X	-	-
	Sommerfeld v. Germany (2003)	X	-	-	-	-	-	-	X	X	-	-	X	-	-	X	-

Chamber judgments	*Sommerfeld v. Germany* (2001)	-	-	-	-	X	-	-	-	-	-	X	X	-	-	-	-
	Kosmopoulou v. Greece (2004)	X	-	-	-	-	-	-	-	X	-	-	-	-	-	-	X
	Süss v. Germany (2005)	-	X	X	-	-	-	-	-	-	-	X	-	X	-	-	-
	C. v. Finland (2006)	-	X	-	-	-	-	-	X	X	-	-	-	X	-	-	-
	Fiala v. Czech Republic (2006)	X	-	-	-	-	-	-	-	-	X	-	-	X	-	-	-
	Cristescu v. Romania (2012)	X	-	-	-	-	-	-	-	X	-	-	-	-	X	-	-
	Gobec v. Slovenia (2013)	-	-	-	-	X	-	-	X	X	-	-	-	X	-	-	-
	Rouiller v. Switzerland (2014)	-	-	-	-	X	X	-	-	-	-	-	-	-	-	-	X
	Gajtani v. Switzerland (2014)	-	-	-	X	-	X	X	-	-	-	-	X	-	-	-	-
	G.B. v. Lithuania (2016)	X	-	X	-	-	-	-	-	-	-	X	-	-	X	X	-
	N.Ts. and others v. Georgia (2016)	-	-	-	-	X	-	-	-	-	-	X	-	X	-	-	-
	Zdravković v. Serbia (2016)	X	-	-	-	-	-	-	-	-	-	X	-	-	-	-	X
	Moog v. Germany (2016)	-	X	-	-	-	-	-	-	-	-	X	-	-	-	-	X
	K.B. and others v. Croatia (2017)	-	-	-	-	X	-	-	X	-	-	-	-	X	-	-	-
	Ónodi v. Hungary (2017)	X	-	-	-	-	-	-	-	-	-	X	-	-	-	-	X
	M.K. v. Greece (2018)	-	-	-	-	X	-	-	-	-	-	X	-	-	-	X	-
	Khusnutdinov and X v. Russia (2018)	X	X	-	-	-	-	-	-	-	-	X	X	-	-	-	-
	Zelikha Magomadova v. Russia (2019)	-	-	-	-	X	-	-	-	-	-	X	-	X	-	-	-

(continued)

Table 8.8 *continued*

		Applicants' complaint					Governments' argument						ECtHR				
		Influence or manipulation	Examine and address influence	PAS or conflict of loyalties	Unjustified reliance on influence	No complaint	Influenced views	PAS or conflict of loyalties	Independent views	Consistency and strength of views	Other	No mention	Influence and participation	Influence and due weight	Other reasoning influence	Dissenting opinions	Not discussed
Decisions	*W.F. v. Italy* (2001)	X	-	-	-	-	-	-	-	-	-	X	-	-	-	-	X
	Paradis and others v. Germany (2003)	-	-	-	-	X	-	-	-	-	-	N	-	X	-	-	-
	Vámosi v. Hungary (2004)	X	-	-	-	-	-	X	-	-	-	-	-	-	-	-	X
	Petersen v. Germany (2006)	-	X	-	-	-	-	-	-	-	-	X	-	-	-	-	X
	Luig v. Germany (2007)	-	X	-	-	-	-	-	-	-	-	N	X	-	-	-	-
	Wildgruber v. Germany (2008)	-	X	-	-	-	-	-	-	-	-	N	X	-	-	-	-

N = no arguments provided at all by the government because the complaint was not communicated to the contracting party, as is only required when the Chamber does not immediately declare the application inadmissible (see Rule 54 of the Rules of Court).

Source: Compiled by the author.

6. CONCLUSION: STANDARDS

In drawing this discussion to a close, it is time to consider which standards can be derived from the above analysis. Influence may be difficult to pinpoint, but it still calls for a response by domestic courts when children participate in proceedings and in giving the expressed views weight. The following three standards have been identified. As in the previous chapters in Part II, the standards are labelled with a letter to indicate the topic they address: 'I' is used to indicate that the standards concern influence.

> I.1 Courts should address assertions of influence, but are well placed to examine and evaluate whether children's expressed views are their own. An expert opinion to evaluate the child's wishes may be used to determine the existence of influence, but this is not always required.

Taking into account the general rule that it is for the domestic courts to assess the evidence before them and the fact that the ECtHR has a subsidiary role, the first standard mirrors the general response of the ECtHR in terms of accepting how domestic courts have addressed claims of influence. Domestic courts should examine and evaluate the statements and evidence available to them in considering whether or not children's views are influenced. The second sentence draws on the ECtHR's reasoning in *Elsholz v. Germany* (2000), where the Court found that the circumstances required an expert opinion. However, it is also based on the ECtHR's conclusions in *Sommerfeld v. Germany* (2003), *Luig v. Germany* (2007), *Wildgruber v. Germany* (2008) and *Khusnutdinov and X v. Russia* (2018). These cases show that it will depend on the circumstances of the case as to whether an expert opinion is necessary, it can be sufficient for the domestic courts to examine and evaluate the expressed wishes of the child themselves. For the ECtHR, it is important that the domestic courts properly justify their decision whether or not to appoint an expert to assess (alleged) potential influence.

> I.2 Basing a decision on the views of children who are palpably unable to form and articulate an opinion as to their wishes – because of a loyalty conflict and/or their exposure to the alienating behaviour of one parent – may give rise to a violation of the parent's rights under Article 8 ECHR. However, giving weight to the views of a (potentially) influenced child is accepted insofar as it is in the child's best interests.

This second standard is twofold and concerns the weight to be given to a child's views if these are potentially influenced. The first part of the standard is directly taken from *K.B. and others v. Croatia* (2017) and *Zelikha Magomadova v. Russia* (2019), in which the ECtHR was very explicit on this issue. The second part of the standard is derived from *Süss v. Germany* (2005), *Fiala v. Czech Republic*

(2006) and *N.Ts. and others v. Georgia* (2016). These judgments show that the ECtHR did agree that the children's views should be given due weight, even when they were influenced, if doing so was in the child's best interests. Therefore, influenced views do not directly lead to the conclusion of no weight; it remains a balancing exercise.

> I.3 Courts should realize that the passage of time may impact the amount of influence on a child's views.

The final standard draws on the concluding analysis in which the passage of time is seen as a relevant factor to child's views being influenced. Specifically, in custody and access proceedings, it is important that domestic courts realize the impact which time can have in influencing a child's views. This does not mean that influence will always increase with the passage of time, but it is certainly possible. Therefore, it is suggested to give due consideration to the length of proceedings and the enforcement of decisions.

CHAPTER 9

CONCLUSIONS OF THE CASE LAW ANALYSIS

'The Court reiterates that children are entitled to be consulted and heard on matters affecting them.'

– ECtHR, *Petrov and X v. Russia* (2018)[1345]

1. INTRODUCTION

In Part II of this book, the breadth of the European Court of Human Rights (ECtHR) case law analysis on child participation has been presented. At the start, the aim of the analysis was disclosed: to see which standards on child participation can be distilled from the ECtHR's case law within the scope of Articles 8 and 6 of the European Convention on Human Rights (ECHR). This aim has undeniably been achieved as each of the four chapters concluded with a set of standards. These standards strengthen the European human rights framework concerning child participation in family law proceedings. In addition to the standards set, the case law analysis has shown the development of child participation as a topic within the Court's case law. The comprehensive and systematic analysis, also considering how applicants and governments raise the topic, has provided further substance to these standards. The developments and standards have been explained and the internal alignment between case law has been sought. In this conclusion, the key findings from the chapters included in Part II will be brought together.

The conclusions are based on those drawn in each of the four chapters: (in)sufficient participation (Chapter 5), the weight accorded to the child's views (Chapter 6), the maturity of the child (Chapter 7) and 'influence' on the views of the child (Chapter 8). These four chapters have addressed four key themes with regard to child participation. The first two – (in)sufficient participation and weight accorded to the child's views – concern the two steps of child participation: the question of whether and how a child can participate, and

[1345] ECtHR, *Petrov and X v. Russia* (Appl. No. 23608/16), 23 October 2018, para. 108.

subsequently how the views expressed are given weight. The latter two themes concern factors which could impact child participation – either in the question of participation itself or in the granting of weight. The maturity of the child and the 'influence' on children's views therefore arise in the first two themes, but also warrant a separate analysis.

In this chapter, a number of overarching conclusions can be drawn. By means of an introduction, we start with a conclusion in numbers to provide a quantitative overview of the cases discussed in Part II (see section 2). Subsequently, conclusions are drawn regarding child participation in the broader sense, encompassing all four chapters. First, conclusions on child participation as a topic, regarding the themes and factors it consists of and how they are interrelated (see section 3) and secondly, on child participation as a right under the ECHR (see section 4). The latter is of crucial importance to understand how the standards set in the case law relate to the ECHR, in which child participation is not mentioned. Then core factors and variables tested and deduced throughout this case law analysis will be presented (see section 5). The core factors are those which have been shown to impact decisions on participation and due weight and are split into two types: the child-specific factors (see section 5.1) and the circumstance-specific factors (see section 5.2). The variables discussed are aspects which were presumed to be relevant for differences between the standards applied, these include the types of proceedings (see section 5.3), modes of participation (see section 5.4) and applicants (see section 5.5). Following the factors and variables, the role of international standards, such as Article 12 of the United Nations Convention on the Rights of the Child (UNCRC), within the analysed case law of the ECtHR will be set out (see section 6). This provides preliminary insights on the alignment of the case law of the ECtHR with the other international and European instruments. Subsequently, an overview is presented of the standards distilled in the analysis (see section 7). This is a single-page visual answer to the core aim of Part II of this research and is of value for European states, future applicants and the ECtHR. The conclusions then turn towards the functioning of the ECtHR itself, with procedural and practical suggestions (see section 8). Finally, Part II will come to a real end with some concluding remarks (see section 9).

2. OVERARCHING CONCLUSION IN NUMBERS

Until now, each conclusion per chapter has included a conclusion in numbers; in this final conclusion of Part II, this pattern is upheld. Throughout Part II, a total of 88 cases have been discussed. At the end of this conclusion, Table 9.4 is included, providing an overview of all the cases discussed in Part II and showing in which chapter they have been discussed. From this overview and the conclusion in numbers per chapter, a number of remarks can be made.

To start with, it is no surprise that the chapters in which most cases were covered were (in)sufficient participation (Chapter 5) and weight accorded to views (Chapter 6), as Table 9.1 below shows. These two sections concerned the core topics of child participation, with both maturity and influence closely related – as we will see in the following section.

Table 9.1. Number of cases discussed per chapter

Chapter	Number of cases
5: (In)sufficient participation	46
6: Weight accorded to the child's views	59
7: Maturity of the child	38
8: 'Influence' on the views of the child	27

Source: Compiled by the author.

The numbers in Table 9.1 clearly add up to more than 88, the total amount of cases discussed in the case law analysis of Part II. This means that a large number of cases are discussed in more than one section. Using Table 9.4 (see the end of this section), it is possible to break down how many cases appear in multiple sections and in which combination of sections they appear. To save the reader some time, the results of doing so are presented in Table 9.2 below. What does this show? As expected from the previous numbers, in over half of the cases, more than one topic regarding participation is discussed. Seven cases appeared in all four chapters, and 22 cases appeared in three chapters. The 'key' cases on child participation – e.g. those in which the ECtHR has set out general principles – are mainly to be found among these 28 cases. The table also shows that there are 37 cases (quite a large number) which are covered only in one chapter. This does not make them less relevant; on the contrary, in these cases, subtopics of child participation are discussed as extensively as in other cases. It does show that while in some cases the topic is multifaceted, issues surrounding child participation may also be complained of and addressed in relation to the subtopic alone.

Table 9.2. Number of cases discussed according to the combination of topics

Combination of topics	Number of cases
All four topics:	**7**
– (In)sufficient participation, Weight accorded to the child's views, Maturity of the child, and 'Influence' on the views of the child	7
Three topics:	**21**
– (In)sufficient participation, Weight accorded to the child's views, and Maturity of the child	11

(continued)

Table 9.2 *continued*

Combination of topics	Number of cases
– (In)sufficient participation, Weight accorded to the child's views, and 'Influence' on the views of the child	6
– (In)sufficient participation, Maturity of the child and 'Influence' on the views of the child	0
– Weight accorded to the child's views, Maturity of the child, and 'Influence' on the views of the child	4
Two topics:	23
– (In)sufficient participation and Weight accorded to the child's views	7
– (In)sufficient participation and Maturity of the child	4
– (In)sufficient participation and 'Influence' on the views of the child	1
– Weight accorded to the child's views and Maturity of the child	7
– Weight accorded to the child's views and 'Influence' on the views of the child	3
– Maturity of the child and 'Influence' on the views of the child	1
One topic:	37
– (In)sufficient participation	14
– Weight accorded to the child's views	14
– Maturity of the child	4
– 'Influence' on the views of the child	5

Source: Compiled by the author.

In each of the separate chapters, the conclusion in numbers also considered who raised the topic: the applicant, the government and/or the ECtHR. In Table 9.3 below, a comparison is made by chapter between those cases in which the topic is raised by the applicant and reflected upon by the ECtHR (with or without comments by the governments) and those cases in which the ECtHR addresses the topic on its own accord, without any complaint by the applicant or comments by the governments. What stands out is that the ECtHR has not shied away from raising or referring to the various topics of child participation by itself. What is striking in Table 9.3 is that this is especially the case with regard to the weight accorded to the views of the child and the maturity of the child. This does not always mean that the ECtHR goes beyond its mandate; in many cases the topic was raised by the ECtHR within its response to the applicant's complaint on other issues or aspects of participation. This is especially the case regarding the weight accorded to a child's views and the child's maturity, as these are procedural aspects which can be drawn from the facts of the case – even where it is not included in the complaint – which may have impacted the substantive conclusions drawn by the domestic courts. For example, the ECtHR may note that the domestic court's decision, which led to the interference of the applicant's right to family life, was justified amongst other things because the child's views were given due weight. Notably, the ECtHR is much less inclined to address potential influence on the child's views on its own volition. Perhaps this is because influence, unless it has been raised explicitly, is not as visible in the facts of the case. Another likely reason is that there is currently no clear line in the ECtHR's reasoning as to how to deal with influenced views and due weight, which may explain why the ECtHR is more reluctant to address influence.

Table 9.3. Number of cases discussed in each chapter according to the combination of actors

	Topic discussed by:	
Chapter	**Applicant and ECtHR**	**ECtHR only**
5: (In)sufficient participation	21	12
6: Weight accorded to the child's views	13	27
7: Maturity of the child	5	20
8: 'Influence' on the views of the child	12	5

Source: Compiled by the author.

3. CHILD PARTICIPATION AS A TOPIC: THE RELATIONSHIPS BETWEEN THEMES AND FACTORS

If the case law selected was a prism, then the analysis was a ray of light shining through to reveal a full rainbow of child participation. The topic consists of as many different subtopics and relevant factors as there are colours in the rainbow. At the same time, it is a highly fragmented topic, often appearing in cases as one piece in the larger puzzle of family law conflicts. What this has meant for the analysis will now be discussed.

The rainbow of subtopics has shown itself in all four themes discussed in Part II. The analysis covers how, when and which children should be able to participate in relation to (in)sufficient participation as well as the subsequent step of due weight, the relevance of their maturity and the issue of (alleged) influence. Throughout the analysis, it becomes clear that these four themes often overlap, just as the colours of the rainbow do. In Chapter 4, which provided the introduction to this case law analysis, the relationship between the four themes addressed in the case law analysis was hypothesized. In doing so, Figure 4.1 was presented (this is reproduced below).

Figure 4.1. Overview of the child participation process and four themes addressed in case law analysis

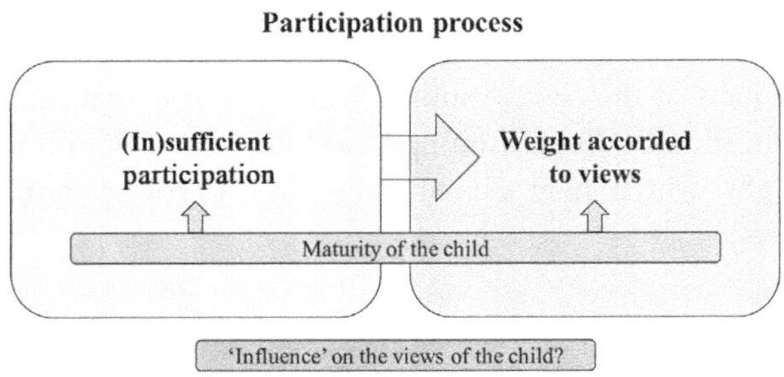

Source: Compiled by the author.

Following the preceding four chapters and the analysis presented, it has become clear that Figure 4.1 is too simple a representation of the participation process as understood by the ECtHR. As noted above, the topic has proven to be a rainbow of overlapping subtopics which interrelate and impact each other in various ways. In light of this, Figure 4.1 has been revised and Figure 9.1 below presents the overview of the child participation process as understood by the ECtHR. It includes not only the four themes addressed in the chapters, but also other factors which have repeatedly emerged in the analysis. The arrows included in Figure 9.1 present the relationship between each of the topics and factors.

Figure 9.1. Overview of the child participation process and themes and factors addressed in the case law analysis

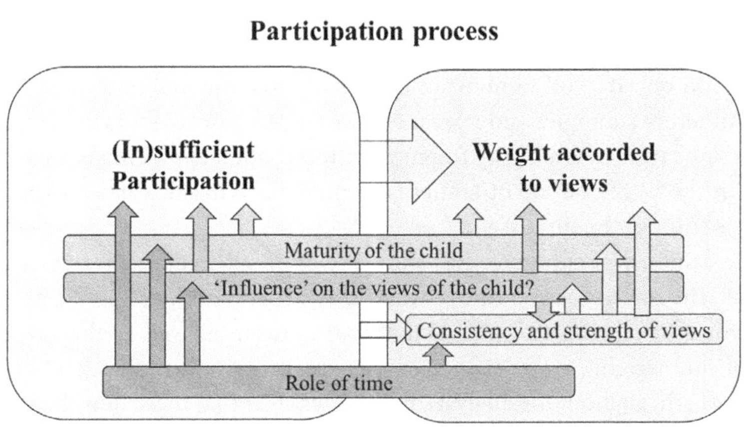

Source: Compiled by the author.

Figure 9.1 shows that the topic of (in)sufficient participation is the first key theme. Following participation, the process is continued by the according of weight to the views of the child. As mentioned throughout Part II in this volume, the two steps of child participation are again visible in this figure. The realization of both of these steps relies on various factors. Two of these were topics addressed in separate chapters: the maturity of the child and the 'influence' on the views of the child. Both of these topics concern the question of how to determine maturity or influence, as well as the impact these topics have as a factor in the question of participation and the weight attached to the child's views. Figure 9.1 also includes two new factors which appeared in the case law analysis: the role of time, and the consistency and strength of views (which can only be determined following repeated participation). Both factors impact, albeit to different extents, the two key themes (participation and weight) and the two factors (maturity and influence). They also relate to each other, as the passage of time can require repeated participation which can lead to the expression of consistent and strong views. In contrast to maturity and influence, these two factors are less susceptible to interpretation, so the determination of these factors is not a point of contention for applicants. It is apparent from Figure 9.1 and the case law analysis as a whole that when discussing child participation, there is a diversity of subtopics involved and, moreover, that the manner in which they relate to each other is not straightforward. This will also be further discussed in section 5 below on the different factors.

Child participation is not only a diverse topic of itself, but also a topic which is often discussed in a fragmented manner and within the context of larger themes. In the majority of cases, issues of child participation were not the core complaint and did not play a key role in the reasoning of the ECtHR; instead, it was often just one piece in the puzzle. In relation to the applicants, the topic was often part of a broader complaint. More specifically, as the overwhelming majority of applicants were parents, their complaints focused on the violations of their own rights. Participation complaints were included as a means to plump up their key complaint – for example, the lack of access with their child. In doing so, children's rights are to some extent instrumentalized by parents in order to achieve their own goals. This was, for example, clearly visible with regard to due weight and influence.[1346] From the point of view of an applicant and his or her lawyer, it is a logical move; for example, complaining about the influence on his or her child's views in addition to a central complaint on the lack of access rights can help achieve a judgment in his or her favour. Viewed from the children's rights perspective, it is not directly desirable as this brings with it the risk of having the ECtHR consider children's rights without a child-centred approach. The child's right to participate can in that way become muddled with parents' rights and interests (see also section 4 below). If child participation is not considered from the perspective of the child and his or her rights and interests, but instead in

[1346] See Chapter 6, section 5.1 and Chapter 8, section 5.1.

relation to (one of) his or her parents' complaints, then there is a risk that the ECtHR's reasoning is tainted by the complaint made by the parent, especially if the complaint is part of a larger substantive alleged violation. When the ECtHR departs from the parent's complaint in its examination of whether there has been a violation in relation to child participation, then the child's perspective on the matter may be lost. On the other hand, having parents increasingly raise child participation issues, even if it is not the main complaint, has ensured that the ECtHR has had to tackle these issues. If we had to wait for children to bring their own complaints, then there would certainly not have been as much reasoning on the themes as we have seen in the preceding four chapters. The piecemeal inclusion of child participation in complaints has therefore assisted in the development of the ECtHR's reasoning on child participation. In combination with a number of key cases, such as *M. and M. v. Croatia* (2015), the ECtHR has now embraced the child's right to participation in family law proceedings within the scope of Article 8. This has subsequently led to more and more cases in which the Court has discussed themes of participation without a complaint being made by the applicants (see also Table 9.3 above).[1347]

4. CHILD PARTICIPATION AS A RIGHT UNDER THE ECHR

The key conclusion of this analysis is that children have the right to participate in family law proceedings protected by Article 8 ECHR. This right cannot be found in the written text of the Convention, but it has been read into the scope of Article 8 ECHR by the ECtHR and in a very limited manner also under Article 6 ECHR.[1348] That the right to express views as well as the right to have views given due weight are both incorporated into the scope of Article 8 ECHR is noteworthy. One would have expected that Article 6 ECHR would have played a larger role, as child participation is a procedural right at its core and Article 6 ECHR provides the right to a fair trial and associated procedural rights. However, the ECtHR consistently discusses the topic of participation – from the general principles on participation and on due weight to the reasoning on the facts regarding all four themes – under Article 8 ECHR.[1349] There are only three cases out of the 70[1350] in which the ECtHR's discussion

[1347] See Chapter 5, section 5.1 and Chapter 6, section 5.1.

[1348] See Chapter 5, section 5.2 and Chapter 6, section 5.2.

[1349] See Chapter 5, section 5.2 and Chapter 6, section 5.2.

[1350] These 70 cases are those in which the ECtHR addressed child participation in its reasoning. Out of the total of 88 cases, there are 18 cases in which the ECtHR did not address child participation – only the applicants and/or governments did.

on participation took place under the scope of Article 6 ECHR (two solely under (in)sufficient participation and one under (in)sufficient participation and maturity).[1351] The role of Article 6 is therefore extremely limited and addressing child participation in family law proceedings under Article 6 ECHR is an exception.

As was discussed in Chapter 5, there are two explanations as to why Article 8 ECHR is of great importance regarding child participation and Article 6 ECHR only plays a limited role in this. The first explanation is the so-called 'procedural turn' of the ECtHR, which includes the general trend by which the Court increasingly reads procedural obligations into substantive Convention rights.[1352] The scope of Article 8 ECHR has in that way been stretched to include procedural obligations, including child participation.[1353] The second explanation ties into what has been said in the previous section – the highly fragmented nature of the topic of child participation within the case law of the ECtHR. With child participation discussed in a great number of cases as one puzzle piece within a broader complaint on violations of the applicant's right to family life, the topic has become highly intertwined with the substantive topics addressed. Complaints as to child participation – including insufficient participation and the weight granted to the child's views – are rarely brought forward as an independent violation, but instead as one component of a violation (e.g. a restriction of contact rights). This is even more the case because most applicants are parents. If complaints were brought by children individually and addressing their right to participate explicitly, then it may have been more logical to address the child's procedural rights under Article 6 ECHR.

1351 ECtHR, *Iglesias Casarrubios and Cantalapiedra Iglesias v. Spain* (Appl. No. 23298/12), 11 October 2016 (Chapters 5 and 7); ECtHR, *Gajtani v. Switzerland* (Appl. No. 43730/07), 9 September 2014 (Chapter 5); ECtHR, *Gettliffe and Grant v. France* (dec.) (Appl. No. 23547/06), 24 October 2006 (Chapter 5).

1352 J. Gerards, 'Procedural Review by the ECtHR: A Typology', in: J. Gerards & E. Brems (eds.), *Procedural Review in European Fundamental Rights Cases*, Cambridge: Cambridge University Press 2017, pp. 127–160, p. 129; and O.M. Arnardóttir, 'The "Procedural Turn" under the European Convention on Human Rights and Presumptions of Convention Compliance', *International Journal of Constitutional Law*, Vol. 15, No. 1, 2017, pp. 9–35, p. 13. See also E. Brems, 'Procedural Protection: An Examination of Procedural Safeguards Read into Substantive Convention Rights', in: E. Brems & J. Gerards (eds.), *Shaping Rights in the ECHR: The Role of the European Court of Human Rights in Determining the Scope of Human Rights*, Cambridge: Cambridge University Press 2013, pp. 137–161, pp. 137–161.

1353 See Brems 2013, p. 138; E. Brems & L. Lavrysen, 'Procedural Justice in Human Rights Adjudication: The European Court of Human Rights', *Human Rights Quarterly*, Vol. 35, No. 1, 2013, pp. 176–200, p. 191; T. de Jong, 'Procedurele waarborgen in materiële EVRM-rechten', Ph.D. diss., Leiden University, 2017, pp. 390–391 and J. Gerards, 'Procedural Review by the ECtHR: A Typology', in: J. Gerards & E. Brems (eds.), *Procedural Review in European Fundamental Rights Cases*, Cambridge: Cambridge University Press 2017, pp. 127–160, p. 136.

Knowing that child participation rights are protected under Article 8 ECHR is relevant for applicants and lawyers in preparing their complaints. It also helps to define the right and in that regard there are four further issues of qualification to be addressed. The first two are considered together: whether it is recognized as the child's right or as the parent's right and whether it falls under the right to respect for family life or the right to respect for private life. Third, does the right concern a substantive or procedural right and, finally, is the right to participation (and all it entails) a negative or positive obligation?

4.1. CHILD'S OR PARENT'S RIGHT AND THE RIGHT TO RESPECT FOR FAMILY LIFE OR PRIVATE LIFE

Whether the rights provided under Article 8 ECHR by the ECtHR regarding child participation concern the child's rights or the parent's rights and their right to family life or their private life is not as simple as it seems. To start with, it depends on the topic concerned – in the following, a distinction is made between the right to (sufficient) participation, the right to have due weight accorded to the child's views and the topic of influence. The topic of maturity is not discussed, as the topic itself does not introduce rights as such, instead falling under the rights to participation and the according of due weight. For each of the topics, the determination will first be made as to whether it is a child's right or the parent's right and, if so, whether it falls under the right to family life or the right to private life.

With regard to (in)sufficient participation, as was discussed in Chapter 5, there is a clear distinction between the case law prior to 2015 and the developments following *M. and M. v. Croatia* (2015).[1354] In the older case law, the question of (in)sufficient participation was addressed within the scope of the applicants' (i.e. parents') right to family life. Since 2015, the ECtHR's reasoning has shifted towards children's rights, although it continues to be addressed in a number of cases under the Article 8 rights of parents. The ambiguity presented by those cases in which the ECtHR discussed the topic of (in)sufficient participation within the scope of parents' rights, thereby seemingly accepting child participation as a right of the parent, is troubling. However, it is understandable as most cases are brought by parents. When discussing (in)sufficient participation on the basis of a parent's complaint, the ECtHR should ensure that the child's right to express views is protected as the child's right, even when it is discussed within the scope of the parent's right to family life. In the *M. and M. v. Croatia* (2015) judgment, the ECtHR recognized the child's right to participate as both the right to sufficient involvement under the scope of the right to respect for family life and the right to personal autonomy under the child's right to respect for private life.

[1354] See Chapter 5, section 5.2.

Let us now move from (in)sufficient participation to the weight to be accorded to a child's views. It is unclear whether the obligation placed upon courts to give due weight falls under the child's Article 8 rights or that of the parents, or both. However, the analysis does show that the obligation placed upon courts to give due weight unmistakably falls under the right to respect for family life.[1355] As was discussed in the concluding analysis of Chapter 6, the ECtHR considers due weight within the scope of parents' right to family life and has, to date, only once explicitly recognized the obligation as pertaining to children's rights.[1356] One would hope that the Court has the chance to more consistently tie the obligation to give due weight to a child's views to children's rights in future case law on the topic, recognizing that the general principle in *Płaza v. Poland* (2011) stems from Article 12 UNCRC, the child's right to participate. In fact, the ECtHR could or – it could even be argued – should recognize that giving due weight to a child's views falls under his or her right to respect for private life as it concerns children's autonomy in decision-making.

Lastly, with regard to the topic of (alleged) influence on a child's views, the ECtHR recognizes a potential violation with regard to parents' rights on the one hand and a potential violation of children's rights on the other. The Court is explicit in noting that basing a decision on an influenced child's views may give rise to a violation of a parent's right to respect for family life under Article 8 ECHR.[1357] At the same time, it recognizes that if the child holds a firm wish, it may be contrary to his or her best interests to decide against his or her wishes.[1358] In that regard, the ECtHR seemingly finds influence to be a reason not to accord (more) weight to a child's views as a potential hazard to the his or her right to have a decision made in his or her best interests. The latter has been considered in at least one case as relevant to the children's right to private and family life.[1359]

To conclude, the classification of the right to participation in the broad sense – including due weight and the topic of influence – as a right of the child is not as simple as it seems. The ECtHR, faced with parents and not children as applicants, has introduced children's rights under the umbrella of parents' rights through interpretation and the expansion of rights. The development since 2015, whereby the Court has increasingly recognized the right to participation as the child's right, will hopefully also persist with regard to the consist recognition of the child's right to have his or her views given due weight. For both influence and maturity, it is not necessary for the ECtHR to recognize any rights of the child. These two topics are highly intertwined with the child's right to participation

---

1355 See Chapter 6, section 5.2.

1356 See Chapter 6, section 5.2.

1357 See Chapter 8, section 4.2.

1358 See Chapter 8, section 4.2.

1359 See Chapter 8, section 4.2 and specifically ECtHR, *N.Ts. and others v. Georgia* (Appl. No. 71776/12), 2 February 2016, para. 84.

and due weight, and if these are recognized as children's rights under the ECHR, then standards on maturity and influence may fall under this umbrella.

4.2. PROCEDURAL OR SUBSTANTIVE RIGHTS

The second qualification considered is whether the rights are procedural or substantive in nature, as this may affect how the right is reviewed by the ECtHR, especially when the applicant is the parent and not the child. With regard to this aspect, it is important to distinguish between the right to (sufficient) participation and the obligation of courts to give due weight to the child's views.

The child's right to participate, specifically to express views, is protected under the scope of Article 8 as part of the right to sufficient involvement in the decision-making process and as part of the right to personal autonomy.[1360] The child's right to sufficient involvement echoes the parent's right to sufficient involvement. As that right is an implicit procedural element of the right to respect for family life under Article 8 ECHR, it can be assumed the same applies to the child's right.[1361] As part of the child's right to personal autonomy, child participation is also protected by the right to private life under Article 8 ECHR. The right to personal autonomy is seemingly less procedural and more substantive in nature. However, the expression of views could be seen as a procedural right which assists in the fulfilment of the substantive right to personal autonomy. In addition to the specific recognition of the right to express views under these two rights in Article 8 ECHR, the Court repeatedly found a violation of Article 8 on the grounds of insufficient reasons to justify an interference in the applicants' (mostly parents') family life. In these cases, the lack of child participation led to the ECtHR concluding that the domestic courts' reasoning was deficient. The child's lack of participation was then perceived not so much as a breach of the child's procedural right as a breach of the parent's substantive right. The child's right to participation becomes interdependent on his or her parents' rights. This is a trend throughout the case law on insufficient participation, as mentioned previously.

If we turn to the granting of due weight to the views expressed by the child, the relationship between the procedural nature of the right often becomes muddied with the substantive rights of both the child themselves as well as of their parents.[1362] For example, various rights have been considered by the ECtHR

1360 See Chapter 5, sections 4.1 and 5.2.

1361 See Chapter 5, sections 4.1 and 5.2.

1362 See Chapter 6, section 5.2.

in cases where the parent's right to contact has been interfered with: the parent's substantive right to contact, his or her procedural rights as to how the decision to suspend contact was made, the child's substantive right to contact, and his or her procedural rights in the form of participation and due weight. Granting a child's views due weight safeguards his or her procedural rights, as well as, to a certain extent, his or her parent's procedural rights. However, it is possible that there is a conflict between the child's views and his or her parent's substantive rights, or even the child's own substantive right. Thus, it is unlikely that all substantive and procedural rights can simultaneously be provided. When there is a conflict between rights, it is important that any interference with substantive rights is sufficiently justified – in this regard, procedural rights are of great importance.

In conclusion, although the topic of child participation is very often raised within the context of a breach of a substantive right to family life, the rights and obligations regarding child participation (e.g. the right to express views and have these views given due weight) are procedural in nature. In light of all the above, the ECtHR should further ensure that the participation rights are considered from the perspective of the child as his or her procedural right. The participation rights could thereby be further disconnected from who the applicant is and from the substantive violation of family life. Considering that child participation is meant to empower children, it allows for the consideration of a violation of a child's right regardless of the substantive outcome of a family law conflict.

4.3. POSITIVE OR NEGATIVE OBLIGATIONS

The third issue is the classification of the right as a positive or negative obligation for the state. This classification is relevant as it tells us how states have to protect the right. Negative obligations are those where the state must not arbitrarily interfere with the exercise of a right.[1363] These are the traditional rights and the 'should nots' – for example, the state should not separate a child from his or her parents without legitimate reasons. Positive obligations are those where the state should take measures to ensure the effective protection of rights.[1364] The 'shoulds' include a state's obligation to ensure an 'effective 'respect' for family life'.[1365] Although the ECtHR has not explicitly qualified children's participation

1363 J. Gerards, *General Principles of the European Convention on Human Rights*, Cambridge: Cambridge University Press 2019, p. 108.

1364 Gerards 2019, pp. 108–110. See also ECtHR, *Marckx v. Belgium* (Appl. No. 6833/74), 13 June 1979, para. 31.

1365 ECtHR, *Marckx v. Belgium* (Appl. No. 6833/74), 13 June 1979, para. 31.

rights, it can be deduced from the case law that these are not negative obligations, but positive obligations. The analysis shows that the ECtHR requires states to actively provide children with an opportunity to participate in domestic proceedings and to guarantee that children's views are granted due weight. States cannot simply lean back, but must consider their domestic laws and practices – with regard to courts and other state institutions – in light of the standards laid down by the ECtHR.

4.4. THE AIM OF CHILD PARTICIPATION

In addition to qualifying the right to participation within the framework of the ECHR as an Article 8 right, of the children (and parents) and a (mostly) procedural positive obligation, one final topic remains: the aim or rationale of child participation. In principle, following Article 12 UNCRC, the aim of the right to participation is for children to be able to express their views in proceedings affecting them and for their expressed views to be granted due weight. The intention is to provide an opportunity for children to communicate their views and to be and feel heard as their views are taken into account, even when they are not determinative. However, this is not always how the right to participation is considered by applicants, governments or the ECtHR. At times, the participation of children is seen (solely) as the collection of evidence. For example, with regard to the topic of due weight, the views of the children are at times simply listed as part of the evidence or available information.[1366] Viewing child participation as a form of evidence instead of as a procedural right undermines the position of children as participants in a proceeding with an independent right. In essence, it undermines their (circumscribed) autonomy. Instead, it reinforces the position of child participation as part of the right of parents to a reasonable decision. Of course, the views expressed by children – like those expressed by the parties (e.g. parents) – form part of the information which judges must consider; however, as with the views expressed by the parties, it cannot be seen as simple evidence.

5. CORE FACTORS AND VARIABLES IN THE CASE LAW ANALYSIS

Throughout the case law analysis, there are a number of factors which reappear in numerous chapters and thereby prove to be the core factors impacting participation.

1366 See Chapter 6, section 4.5.

These factors not only assist in determining whether or not a child should be able to participate, but also in the subsequent issue of due weight. There are four factors which fall into two categories: (1) the age and maturity of the child and (2) the consistency and strength of his or her views are considered as child-specific factors (see section 5.1); and (3) the role of time and (4) influence are considered as circumstance-specific factors (see section 5.2). Additionally, there are three variables which must be considered: the types of proceedings (see section 5.3), the modes of participation (see section 5.4) and the applicants (see section 5.5).

5.1. CHILD-SPECIFIC FACTORS

Throughout the analysis, there are two child-specific factors which reappear: the age and maturity of the child, and the consistency and strength of his or her expressed views.

The *age and maturity of the child* is a factor which was anticipated and included as subcategory in the coding frame. It is factor which appears under (in)sufficient participation and due weight, but which is also thoroughly covered separately in Chapter 7 on maturity. The key conclusion is that the age and maturity of the child is highly relevant in deciding whether he or she may participate and, subsequently, how to balance his or her views with other factors and interests. With regard to the question of participation, the analysis has shown that age and maturity is the core condition for participation, and that the only accepted exception by the ECtHR for an absolute lack of participation in the domestic proceedings was the young age of the child involved. The analysis in Chapter 7 provided additional insights into how the age and maturity of the child is and should be assessed. With regard to participation, the ECtHR consistently found that children from the age of 11 and above should have the opportunity to be heard directly, while children under the age of six do not need to be heard directly as they can generally be considered too young. With regard to due weight, the Court has repeatedly found the age and maturity of the child to be a factor in the balancing exercise. More specifically, from the analysis in Chapter 7 on maturity, it could carefully be concluded that the expressed views of children over the age of 11 had to be given serious consideration, while the weight granted to the views of younger children would be more dependent on the circumstances of the case. More generally, whether considered for participation or due weight, the factor is mostly determined through the age of the children by the ECtHR, but the maturity of the child is not only determined by his or her age. The ECtHR itself recognized three other factors which help determine the maturity of the child: (1) the intellectual capacities of the child; (2) the consistency of the child's views over time and (3) the child's ability to appreciate or understand the consequences of the decision to be taken in the proceedings. The manner in which maturity is determined is explicated to a certain extent by these three factors, although they are also subject to further discussion.

The first factor, intellectual capabilities, can reinforce the determination that a child is sufficiently mature – but should intellect, as such, be a determining factor for maturity? In light of Article 12 UNCRC (as will be further discussed in Chapter 10), intellect should not be determinative as this would mean that children with lower intellectual capabilities are thereby hindered from the opportunity to express their views. The second factor of consistency would benefit from extra consideration – does a consistently held view unequivocally signal more maturity or could the opposite also hold true? Developing and changing one's views over time may also indicate increased maturity. The third factor referred to by the ECtHR is the ability to understand or appreciate the consequences of the decision, by which the Court appears to mean whether the child is able to understand what it means if his or her views on the matter are determinative – for example, the consequence of no longer having contact with one of their parents – and not so much what the legal decision means.

All in all, even if it is wishful thinking, it would be beneficial to receive clear guidance by the ECtHR as to whether these are the only factors and how these factors relate to the age of the child (on which the focus commonly lies). This need for more guidance and clarity from the ECtHR is especially relevant, considering the tentative nature of the age ranges deduced from the case law of the ECtHR and noting the caution expressed in the conclusions on the ECtHR's reasoning in Chapter 7 on maturity.[1367] The repeated relevance of age and maturity as a factor for participation and due weight strengthens this call for more attention towards the determination of children's maturity and, perhaps, at the domestic level, a reconsideration of the current requirements both in law and as applied in practice.

The second child-specific factor is the *consistency and strength of the child's views*. This factor is of importance for: (1) the due weight to be attached to the child's views, (2) the question of influence – both to show for influenced and for independent views and (3) the determination of the child's maturity with regard to due weight. Figure 9.2 below illustrates the recurrent relevance of views considered to be consistent and strong (following repeated participation). It also shows how the consistency and strength of the child's views seeps through to the question of due weight in different manners (through maturity, directly and influence).

[1367] See Chapter 7, section 4.5.

Figure 9.2. The relevance of consistent and strong views within the framework of participation

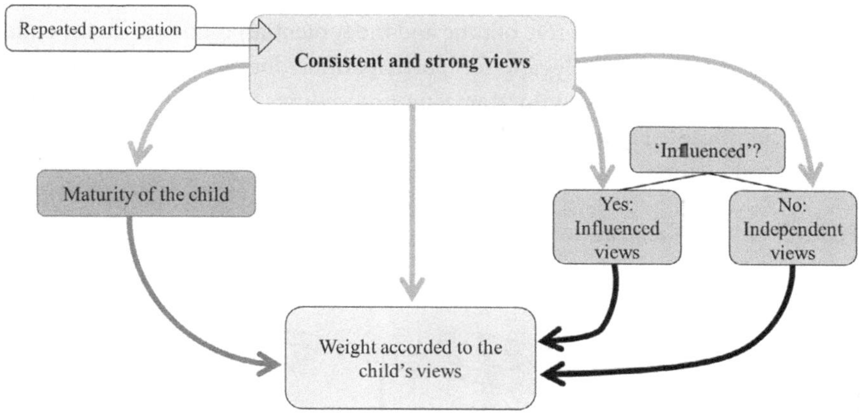

Source: Compiled by the author.

The analysis has shown that when a child's views are strong and consistent over time, the ECtHR accepts that (more) weight has been given to those views. In the case of potential influence, the consistency and strength of the child's views can act as proof that the child's views are his or her own and are free of influence, but the ECtHR has similarly accepted that influenced children can also have strong and consistent views. The factor is therefore relevant, but is not a clear-cut signal for the lack or existence of influence. Domestic courts are advised to reason and justify their decision regarding due weight not only by relying on the consistency and strength of the child's views, but also considering other factors and circumstances. In some cases, the consistency and strength of views may plead in favour of more weight – for example, because not doing so may be detrimental to the child in the short or long term. In other cases, the long-term interests of the child and the rights of others, such as parents, may outweigh the consistency and strength of the child's views. If there is any suggestion of influence, domestic courts cannot infer only from the consistency and strength of the child's views whether he or she has been influenced; additional factors will have to be considered. The concluding suggestion for applicants – whether parents or children – who raise the consistency and strength of views in their favour is to supplement this factor with other arguments for (dis)proving influence or to ensure that more weight is attached to the child's views. The consistency and strength of views works as a factor to strengthen the argumentation, but not as an argument on its own.

5.2. CIRCUMSTANCE-SPECIFIC FACTORS

At various points throughout the analysis, there are two circumstance-specific factors which reappear: the role of time and the (potential) influence on the child.

The *role of time* is relevant for participation, due weight, maturity and influence. Especially in lengthy domestic proceedings, the role of time can be highly significant. Figure 9.3 below illustrates the role of time for each of the themes and factors.

Figure 9.3. The role of time within the framework of participation

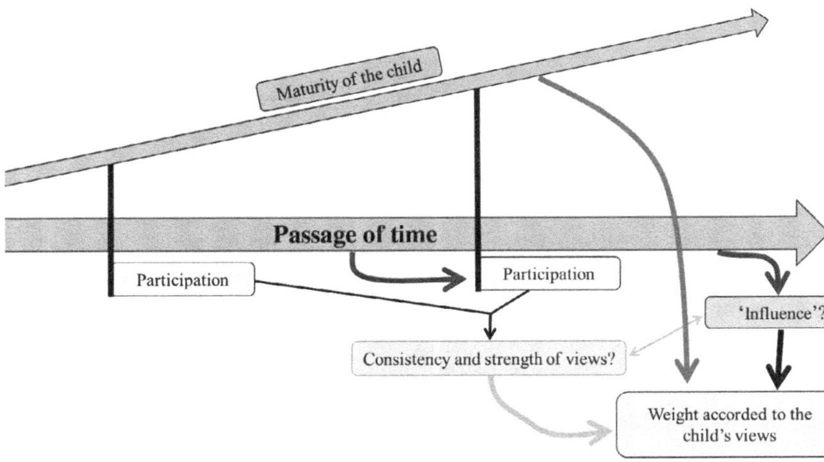

Source: Compiled by the author.

With regard to participation as such, protracted proceedings may require additional participation of the child according to the ECtHR. When additional participation occurs, it will also be possible to determine whether a child's views are consistent over time – one of the relevant child-specific factors for due weight. The passing of time is also relevant with regard to the age and maturity of a child, as this increases automatically over time. In domestic proceedings, it is therefore relevant to acknowledge the dynamic nature of age and maturity, and to reconsider its impact on participation or due weight throughout the various stages of proceedings. The views of a child may stay consistent over time or the views may change. In light of this, it is also a relevant factor regarding (potential) influence. It is possible that the passage of time may increase one parent's influence over the child and that must be considered by domestic courts. As the passage of time may impact the need for additional participation as well as potential influence, it is strongly encouraged that states prevent excessively lengthy proceedings. This applies notwithstanding the many other negative consequences of drawn-out proceedings, such as additional stress, conflict and costs.

Influence, as such, is the second circumstance-specific factor. In Chapter 8, this factor was considered separately as a relatively common point of contention with regard to child participation. However, it is a factor which only briefly arises in the other chapters. With regard to due weight, influence is a potential factor. As was discussed in Chapter 8, the ECtHR does not have a fixed approach regarding the impact of influenced views on due weight. On the one hand, the Court has held that relying on a child's influenced views may lead to a violation of Article 8 ECHR, while on the other hand, in a number of cases the ECtHR has accepted and even called for weight to be given to children's views, even if they had been potentially manipulated.

It is important to note that there is also a relationship between the factors of influence and the consistency and strength of views. As was discussed previously, this relationship is not straightforward. At times, consistency and strength of views is considered to prove that the child has not been influenced, while at other times it is considered to be a sign of influence. All things considered, influence is a serious factor to consider when there are indications of it, but it is not as relevant a factor as some may have expected it to be. The inconsistency in the case law in terms of addressing influence in child participation may explain why the topic has had less impact. Instead, influence remains to be addressed by domestic courts themselves. What is apparent is that (potential) influence is not a valid blanket argument against child participation in family law proceedings.

5.3. TYPES OF PROCEEDINGS

In addition to the specific factors discussed above, the type of proceeding is a variable which is common to all the case law analysed here. All of the case law concerned family law proceedings, as that is the focus of this research. However, within the scope of family law proceedings, there are various types of proceedings (as introduced in Chapter 4).[1368] At the start of this research, a hypothesis was that the type of proceedings might impact various aspects of the right to participation – e.g. whether and how participation should take place, and how to attach weight to the views of the child. This hypothesis proved to be correct in some parts of the analysis, but certainly not all.

With regard to the question of participation as such, there was no key distinction between the types of proceedings. In all types of proceedings, the ECtHR recognized the child's right to participation. There was also no distinction made by the Court regarding the modes of participation between the different types of proceedings. This was unexpected, but is positive, as it

---

1368 See Chapter 4, section 7.

shows that the ECtHR does not constrain child participation on the broad basis of a type of proceeding. The Court recognizes that participation is not an absolute right, allowing domestic courts a margin of discretion on the basis of the specific circumstances of the case and the age and maturity of the child. This provides for a more subjective approach than objectively limiting participation per types of proceedings. Although at a minimum there should be an opportunity for child participation regardless of the type of proceeding, there are certain types of proceedings which may warrant additional child participation requirements. It could be argued that this may be appropriate – for example, for proceedings in which there is a higher level of state interference, such as care proceedings.

However, the hypothesis did hold true with regard to due weight. While the core conclusion is that giving due weight to the views of the child is a balancing exercise regardless of the type of proceeding, what goes into the balancing scales can be affected by the type of proceedings.[1369] For example, in care proceedings, the child's interests for protection and safety are of extra importance. With regard to access proceedings, the ECtHR repeatedly found that although the ties between children and their family should in principle be maintained, the child's resistance to access can be of decisive weight when balanced against other interests. The prevalent reason given by the ECtHR for this is the potential for future contact when the child is older. It can be questioned which harm is greater: the lack of access between a child and his or her parent in his or her younger years or the overruling of the child's resistance and ordering access. In this regard, recourse to empirical and interdisciplinary research is necessary.[1370] Further critical reflection on the difference between the 'future potential' in access proceedings and the 'future potential' in proceedings regarding custody may also raise new insights on the arguments raised in favour or against giving determinative weight to a child's wishes.

In any case, the child does not have a veto power, either in access proceedings or in any of the other types of proceedings. This is a conclusion which is specifically relevant with regard to international child abductions, where the specific exception of Article 13(2) of The Hague Abduction Convention might seem to say otherwise. The ECtHR repeatedly clarified that the exception requires the child's views to be seriously considered, but that domestic courts retain the discretion whether or not to order return.

With regard to the chapters on maturity and influence, the hypothesis did not hold up. In both chapters, there is no distinction present between the types of proceedings. However, it is interesting that the cases in which influence was discussed all concerned custody and access proceedings, or – albeit less often –

1369 See Chapter 6, section 5.2.3.

1370 See e.g. B.J. Fidler & N. Bala, 'Children Resisting Postseparation Contact with a Parent: Concepts, Controversies, and Conundrums', *Family Court Review*, Vol. 48, No. 1, 2010, pp. 10–47.

international child abduction proceedings. This could have been expected, perhaps because it is in these cases that parents oppose one another and are therefore more likely to argue that the other has influenced the child.[1371]

All in all, the impact of the different types of family law proceedings was not as great as expected within the ECtHR's reasoning on child participation. Differences are only found with regard to due weight, where the particular interests at play in certain types of proceedings must be taken into account in the balancing scale alongside the child's views. Whether (more) distinction should or should not be made between the types of proceedings will be reflected upon further in the final conclusions (see Chapter 11).

Lastly, it is important to again emphasize that this research focuses solely on family law proceedings. Whether the ECtHR would provide similar reasoning in other fields of law has not been explored in this research, but one can speculate that there will be some similarities and differences, for example between participation in family law proceedings versus criminal law proceedings or asylum proceedings regarding children. As the rights and obligations concerning child participation have been introduced by the ECtHR for the most part within the scope of the right to family life in Article 8 ECHR and the reasoning is very much linked to the substantive complaints regarding family life, the question becomes to what extent the other types of proceedings interfere with the right to family life and whether the substantive differences in types of proceedings would affect the child's right to participation according to the ECtHR under Article 8 ECHR. Or perhaps the ECtHR has introduced similar rights within the scope of Article 6 ECHR or other substantive rights in the Convention for proceedings concerning different fields of law. This is a comparison worthy of further research.

5.4. MODES OF PARTICIPATION

Another variable considered throughout the analysis was whether any differences were made regarding the modes of participation (to be) used. In Chapter 4, section 8, the four main modes of participation were introduced; in the analysis, the modes at times proved relevant, at other times less so.

A noteworthy conclusion with regard to (in)sufficient participation is that there has been no favouritism expressed by the ECtHR towards a certain mode of participation. It remains within the discretion of the domestic laws and courts to decide which mode of participation is most suited to the case in question.

1371 Children could potentially also be influenced by other people than their parents – for example, foster parents or other adults in care proceedings. However, this argument was not made in the case law studied and is also probably less common at the domestic level.

The choice is left completely open to domestic courts, as the ECtHR also does not provide any factors as to when one mode or another would be more fitting. This permissive stance of the Court reflects the subsidiary nature of its supervisory mechanism; states are offered the discretion to develop their own practices regarding child participation within the (minimum) standards set out by the ECtHR. In that regard, the ECtHR does emphasize that the chosen mode of participation must ensure that the child can express his or her views.[1372] This is especially relevant if indirect modes of participation are used – for example, a representative.

While there is no preference between modes of participation expressed with regard to participation as such, it is noteworthy that all the remarks made regarding the age and maturity of the child in Chapter 7 only concerned the mode of direct hearing. This raises questions, such as whether age and maturity is not a relevant factor for other modes of participation.[1373] One would expect it to be equally relevant for other modes of participation, but there are not complaints by applicants, arguments by governments or comments by the ECtHR in that direction. Another possible explanation for the lack of consideration may be the potential absence of age and maturity requirements for other modes of participation in the domestic laws and practices.[1374] Or perhaps other modes of participation are considered more suitable for younger children, instead of directly hearing the child, and therefore no complaints or remarks are made. In any case, it is a topic to keep in mind and which would benefit from further (comparative) research.

Where the focus in relation to maturity lay with direct hearing, in Chapter 8 on influence, the question of the use of experts was highly relevant. The use of experts can be seen as a mode of indirect participation when they speak to children and convey their expressed views to domestic courts. However, experts can also play more of an evidentiary role in which they help the domestic court to assess the maturity of the child or whether a child has been influenced or not. The potential hybrid role of an expert is tricky and if an expert is used as a mode of participation, then his or her role in conveying the child's views must be guaranteed. The supplementary position of an expert in assessing the views of a child who was also heard directly, as is mostly the case when complaints of influence were raised, is less contentious. However, even then, the ECtHR has established that it is not required – domestic courts are sufficiently well placed to evaluate a child's statements.

1372 See Chapter 5, section 5.3.1.

1373 See also Chapter 7, section 5.3.

1374 See e.g. C.R. Mol, 'Child Participation in Family Law Proceedings Compared', in: W.M. Schrama et al. (eds.), *International Handbook on Child Participation in Family Law*, Cambridge: Intersentia 2021a, pp. 335–358, p. 352.

5.5. APPLICANTS

A final variable considered throughout the analysis is the applicant or applicants (the parent, the child or both) who brought the complaint to the ECtHR. As mentioned in Chapter 4, a hypothesis was that who the applicant was might affect the manner in which the ECtHR addressed the topic of child participation. The expectation was that there would be a difference in the handling of applications brought by children on their own behalf versus parents, parents also on behalf of their children or solely on their own behalf, etc. This hypothesis can be considered largely disproven on the level of the cases themselves. There is no clear distinction regarding the applicants and the Court's reasoning regarding the weight accorded to a child's views, the maturity of the child or any influence over a child's views. This may be explained by the fact that the vast majority of the applicants were parents on their own. As discussed in Chapter 4, the overwhelming majority of applicants were parents, in approximately 76% of the cases on their own, in 14% also on behalf of their child(ren), and in only 5% together with their child as an applicant on their own behalf.[1375]

This composition of applicants in the cases analysed here was relevant with regard to the ECtHR's understanding of the right to participation. At first instance, this led to a parent-focused approach of the ECtHR towards the right to participation. In the conclusions of Chapter 5 on (in)sufficient participation, the effects of this were revealed.[1376] In essence, the ECtHR in the earlier judgments discussed the issue of child participation within the scope of parents' rights. In these judgments, the insufficiency of the child's participation either led to a violation due to the parents' insufficient involvement in the decision-making process or because the measures which interfered with the parents' family life were insufficiently justified. The latter has a clear focus on the substantive rights of the parents and has the insufficient child participation form a part of the reason why the measures were not justified, while the other does focus on procedural rights, but on those of the parents instead of those of the child. In 2015, a shift occurred with the *M. and M. v. Croatia* (2015) judgment, in which the applicants were a mother and daughter acting on her own behalf. The ECtHR then recognized the child's right to express views as a right under Article 8 ECHR of the child and not as part of a parent's right to family life. Since then, the Court has increasingly addressed participation as a child's right, even when the complaint is not brought on behalf of or by the child. However, especially

1375 See Chapter 4, section 6.2.

1376 See Chapter 5, section 5.2.

in the cases where parents are the sole applicants, the parent-focused consideration of the right to participate remains.

With regard to the topic of weight accorded to the child's views, the applicants' complaints show that parents instrumentalize children's rights for their own gain, complaining either of too much weight or insufficient weight, depending on the desired substantive result in their case.[1377] As the ECtHR subsequently does not clearly pronounce whether granting due weight to the child's views is a right of the child or a right of the parent, the instrumentalization by parents is not discouraged. Children's right to participation should not become a token right used by parents to achieve their own outcome. The ECtHR may counteract this result by continually (re)focusing the considerations on child participation towards the child and his or her rights under Article 8 ECHR even if the parent is the applicant (see also section 4 above). The role of the parent as applicant – whether on behalf of his or her child or not – remains important because it ensures that complaints regarding child participation reach the ECtHR which otherwise might never be addressed. More child-focused case law would be more attainable if there are more cases brought by children on their own behalf (with or without their parents). Further suggestions in that regard will be made in section 8 below.

6. INTERNATIONAL STANDARDS AND THE ECtHR

Aside from the ECHR and the case law of the ECtHR, there are a number of other international and European human rights instruments which cover the child's right to participation. These instruments were discussed separately in Chapters 2 and 3 in Part I. A number of these instruments, especially the UNCRC, are referred to in the case law and in this section of the conclusion, the impact of these instruments on the Court's reasoning is discussed. Considering whether and how the other international standards played a role in the case law of the ECtHR is relevant. The following discussion provides preliminary insights as to the alignment of the ECtHR's standards with the other international and European instruments.

In all the ECtHR's cases, a section is included entitled 'Relevant Law', in which domestic and/or international law relevant to the case is cited. It is in this section where other international instruments and standards on child participation are included in certain cases. More specifically, in 16 cases, Article 12 UNCRC

[1377] See Chapter 6, section 5.1.

is included,[1378] on three occasions, reference is made to General Comment No. 12 regarding Article 12 UNCRC,[1379] and twice only, other relevant General Comments regarding participation are included.[1380] Additionally, the European Convention on the Exercise of Children's Rights (ECECR) is referenced in five cases,[1381] the Guidelines on Child-Friendly Justice (GCFJ) in five cases[1382] and the EU Charter in two.[1383] Notably, these references are only made in a total of 19 cases from 2005 to 2019. There are a number of cases in which multiple sources are cited; these are also some of the key cases throughout this analysis, such as *M. and M. v. Croatia* (2015), *N.Ts. and others v. Georgia* (2016), and *M.K. v. Greece* (2018).

Citing the international instruments under 'Relevant Law' is one thing, but the ECtHR actually referencing and relying on the instruments in its reasoning is another. A noteworthy conclusion, by itself, is that the ECtHR has relied on the international instruments with regard to three of the themes in this analysis:

1378 ECtHR, *Eskinazi and Chelouche v. Turkey* (dec.) (Appl. No. 14600/05), 6 December 2005; ECtHR, *Gettliffe and Grant v. France* (dec.) (Appl. No. 23547/06), 24 October 2006; ECtHR, *Havelka and others v. Czech Republic* (Appl. No. 23499/06), 21 June 2007, para. 31; ECtHR, *Maumousseau and Washington v. France* (Appl. No. 39388/05), 6 December 2007, para. 45; ECtHR, *Gineitienė v. Lithuania* (Appl. No. 20739/05), 27 July 2010, para. 29; ECtHR, *Płaza v. Poland* (Appl. No. 18830/07), 25 January 2011, para. 44; ECtHR, *Raw and others v. France* (Appl. No. 10131/11), 7 March 2013, para. 46; ECtHR, *Brillet and Brillet v. Belgium* (dec.) (Appl. Nos. 14942/11 and 17942/11), 16 December 2014, para. 29; ECtHR, *Rouiller v. Switzerland* (Appl. No. 3592/08), 22 July 2014, para. 24; ECtHR, *M. and M. v. Croatia* (Appl. No. 10161/13), 3 September 2015, para. 94; ECtHR, *Iglesias Casarrubios and Cantalapiedra Iglesias v. Spain* (Appl. No. 23298/12), 11 October 2016, para. 21; ECtHR, *N.Ts. and others v. Georgia* (Appl. No. 71776/12), 2 February 2016, para. 40; ECtHR, *T.S. and J.J. v. Norway* (dec.) (Appl. No. 15633/15), 11 October 2016, para. 18; ECtHR, *McIlwrath v. Russia* (Appl. No. 60393/13), 18 July 2017, para. 62; ECtHR, *M.K. v. Greece* (Appl. No. 51312/16), 1 February 2018, para. 45; ECtHR, *A.V. v. Slovenia* (Appl. No. 878/13), 9 April 2019, para. 48.

1379 ECtHR, *Rouiller v. Switzerland* (Appl. No. 3592/08), 22 July 2014, para. 25; ECtHR, *M. and M. v. Croatia* (Appl. No. 10161/13), 3 September 2015, para. 97; ECtHR, *N.Ts. and others v. Georgia* (Appl. No. 71776/12), 2 February 2016, para. 42.

1380 ECtHR, *Maumousseau and Washington v. France* (Appl. No. 39388/05), 6 December 2007, para. 46; ECtHR, *A.V. v. Slovenia* (Appl. No. 878/13), 9 April 2019, para. 49.

1381 ECtHR, *Z.J. v. Lithuania* (Appl. No. 60092/12), 29 April 2014, para. 72; ECtHR, *M. and M. v. Croatia* (Appl. No. 10161/13), 3 September 2015, para. 98; ECtHR, *N.Ts. and others v. Georgia* (Appl. No. 71776/12), 2 February 2016, para. 44; ECtHR, *M.K. v. Greece* (Appl. No. 51312/16), 1 February 2018, para. 46; ECtHR, *Stankūnaitė v. Lithuania* (Appl. No. 67068/11), 29 October 2019, para. 88.

1382 ECtHR, *Z.J. v. Lithuania* (Appl. No. 60092/12), 29 April 2014, para. 73; ECtHR, *M. and M. v. Croatia* (Appl. No. 10161/13), 3 September 2015, para. 102; ECtHR, *N.Ts. and others v. Georgia* (Appl. No. 71776/12), 2 February 2016, para. 43; ECtHR, *A.V. v. Slovenia* (Appl. No. 878/13), 9 April 2019, para. 50; ECtHR, *Stankūnaitė v. Lithuania* (Appl. No. 67068/11), 29 October 2019, para. 89.

1383 ECtHR, *X. v. Latvia* [GC] (Appl. No. 27853/09), 26 November 2013, para. 41; ECtHR, *M.K. v. Greece* (Appl. No. 51312/16), 1 February 2018, para. 49.

(in)sufficient participation, the weight accorded to a child's views and the maturity of the child.

The ECtHR refers to international instruments in the development of general principles and the application thereof with regard to the right to participation and the topic of maturity. In *M. and M. v. Croatia* (2015), the introduction of the core principle of the child's right to express views through the right to sufficient involvement and the right to personal autonomy expressed was inspired by Article 12 UNCRC.[1384] In *N.Ts. and others v. Georgia* (2016), the ECECR and the GCFJ acted as sources for the ECtHR's reasoning on representation as a mode of participation.[1385] Additionally, in the same case, the ECtHR referred to Article 12 UNCRC and the GCFJ with regard to the opportunity for children to be heard by judicial authorities.[1386] The impact of the international instruments is also perceivable with regard to the general principles regarding maturity – Article 12 UNCRC and the matching General Comment most notably, as the presumption of capacity formulated by the CRC Committee was affirmed by the ECtHR in *M. and M. v. Croatia* (2015).[1387] In addition to the UNCRC, the ECECR, the Charter of Fundamental Rights of the European Union (CFREU) and The Hague Abduction Convention are also mentioned in *M.K. v. Greece* (2018) when the ECtHR noted that the wishes expressed by a child with sufficient '*discernement*' must be given due weight.[1388] More implicitly, it is likely that the key principle expressed in *Płaza v. Poland* (2011) that the views of children should be given due weight as they mature is based on Article 12 UNCRC, which was included in the 'Relevant Law' section of the case.[1389] Aside from the general principle, with regard to the weight given to a child's expressed views, the international standards also visibly influenced the ECtHR's reasoning in a select number of cases. Take, for example, *M.K. v. Greece* (2018), in which the ECtHR referred to a whole list of instruments – the UNCRC, the ECECR, the CFREU and the Council of Ministers Recommendation – in order to emphasize the importance of granting due weight to a child's views.[1390]

1384 See Chapter 5, section 4.1 and Norm P.1.
1385 See Chapter 5, section 4.2.2 and Norm P.5.
1386 See Chapter 5, section 4.2.1.3.
1387 See Chapter 7, section 4.1.
1388 See Chapter 7, section 4.1.
1389 See Chapter 6, section 4.1 and Norm W.1.
1390 See Chapter 6, section 4.4.1.

With respect to the reference to other human rights instruments, it is especially notable that the ECtHR has included the ECECR in cases where the state involved has not even ratified the Convention. This first occurred in *Z.J. v. Lithuania* (2014), where the ECtHR also admitted that Lithuania had not ratified the ECECR.[1391] Later, the similar situation occurred in *N.Ts. and others v. Georgia* (2016), where the ECECR also played a significant role in the ECtHR's reasoning on representatives. The Court recognized that the ECECR was not ratified by Georgia, but called it a 'useful tool for the interpretation of relevant principles'.[1392] This 'useful tool' was again used in *Stankūnaitė v. Lithuania* (2019), with Lithuania in the meantime still having not ratified the ECECR.[1393] Relying on the ECECR even for states that are legally not bound by it contravenes the general principles of international law. However, the ECtHR seemingly prefers the interpretative value of the ECECR over a strict application of legal standards.[1394] In using the ECECR in that way, the Court has created binding standards for the non-ratifying states by means of its case law and the inferred principles created under the scope of Article 8 ECHR.

Overall, the other international and European human rights instruments are perhaps not cited explicitly in the case law as often as one would expect (in only 19 out of 88 cases). However, where they have been cited, they have evidently had an impact in the formulation of certain general principles by the ECtHR. Examples are the recognition of child participation as a right under the scope of Article 8 ECHR in *M. and M. v. Croatia* (2015) and the giving of due weight to the views of the child in *Płaza v. Poland* (2011). Additionally, even when the instruments are not quoted explicitly, they seemingly have had a latent impact – for example, in cases where reference was made to principles from other cases in which the instruments were explicitly cited. The standards from the other instruments seep into the ECtHR's principles and in that manner impact future cases.

In addition to international standards, the case law of the ECtHR is of course also shaped by the domestic laws on child participation. At various

1391 ECtHR, *Z.J. v. Lithuania* (Appl. No. 60092/12), 29 April 2014, paras. 105–106, para. 72.

1392 ECtHR, *N.Ts. and others v. Georgia* (Appl. No. 71776/12), 2 February 2016, para. 76.

1393 ECtHR, *Stankūnaitė v. Lithuania* (Appl. No. 67068/11), 29 October 2019, para. 128.

1394 See ECtHR, *Demir and Bayakara v. Turkey* [GC] (Appl. No. 34503/97), 12 November 2008, para. 78, in which the ECtHR noted that 'in searching for common ground among the norms of international law it has never distinguished between sources of law according to whether or not they have been signed or ratified by the respondent State'. See also A. Nussberger, *The European Court of Human Rights*, Oxford: Oxford University Press 2020, pp. 143–144.

points in the case law analysis, applicants, governments and the ECtHR have explicitly referred to relevant domestic laws on child participation.[1395] This goes both ways. For example, the lack of a legal obligation in domestic laws to hear children under 10 years of age was relied on by the Russian government in two cases.[1396] The ECtHR referred to the same Russian law in *Zelikha Magomadova v. Russia* (2019) when concluding that the children aged 13 and 11 should have been heard.[1397] Considering the subsidiary nature of the ECtHR, the reliance on domestic laws is not surprising.

7. KEY CONCLUSIONS FOR STATES

Each of the chapters in Part II has concluded with a set of standards derived from the case law analysis. These standards are the key conclusions for states. The domestic courts and legislators have to take these standards on child participation into account, as not doing so may lead to a violation of Article 8 ECHR. In Figure 9.4 below, an overview has been given of all the standards defined in the four chapters of Part II. It is in that sense a roadmap for domestic courts and legislators, as well as for lawyers, children, parents and other interested parties, if not also the ECtHR itself. Following each of the standards in Figure 9.4, brackets are included with reference back to the standard in the relevant chapter: P.# for (in)sufficient participation, W.# for weight accorded to the views of the child, M.# for the maturity of the child and I.# for influence.

1395 See with regard to the applicants ECtHR, *Jucius and Juciuvienė v. Lithuania* (Appl. No. 14414/03), 25 November 2008, para. 24, in which the applicants argued that domestic legislation required the views of the child to be given due weight (see Chapter 6, section 2.2). See with regard to governments, for example, ECtHR, *C. v. Finland* (Appl. No. 18249/02), 9 May 2006, para. 47, in which Finland noted that domestic law requires the views of the child to be given due weight (see Chapter 6, section 3.1.2), or ECtHR, *M. and M. v. Croatia* (Appl. No. 10161/13), 3 September 2015, para. 124, in which the Croatian government argues that there is no domestic obligation to assign an additional special representative for the child (Chapter 5, section 5.4). With regard to the ECtHR, see ECtHR, *M. and M. v. Croatia* (Appl. No. 10161/13), 3 September 2015, para. 185, in which the ECtHR referred to Croatian case law which called for the child's wishes to be respected in residence proceedings where both parents are equally fit to care for the child, as discussed in Chapter 6, section 4.3.

1396 See ECtHR, *Petrov and X v. Russia* (Appl. No. 23608/16), 23 October 2018, para. 90; and ECtHR, *Zelikha Magomadova v. Russia* (Appl. No. 58724/14), 8 October 2019, para. 92, as discussed in Chapter 7, section 3.1.

1397 ECtHR, *Zelikha Magomadova v. Russia* (Appl. No. 58724/14), 8 October 2019, para. 116 as discussed in Chapter 5, section 4.2.1.1. See in that Section also ECtHR, *Iglesias Casarrubios and Cantalapiedra Iglesias v. Spain* (Appl. No. 23298/12), 11 October 2016, para. 42.

Figure 9.4. Overview of all standards on child participation

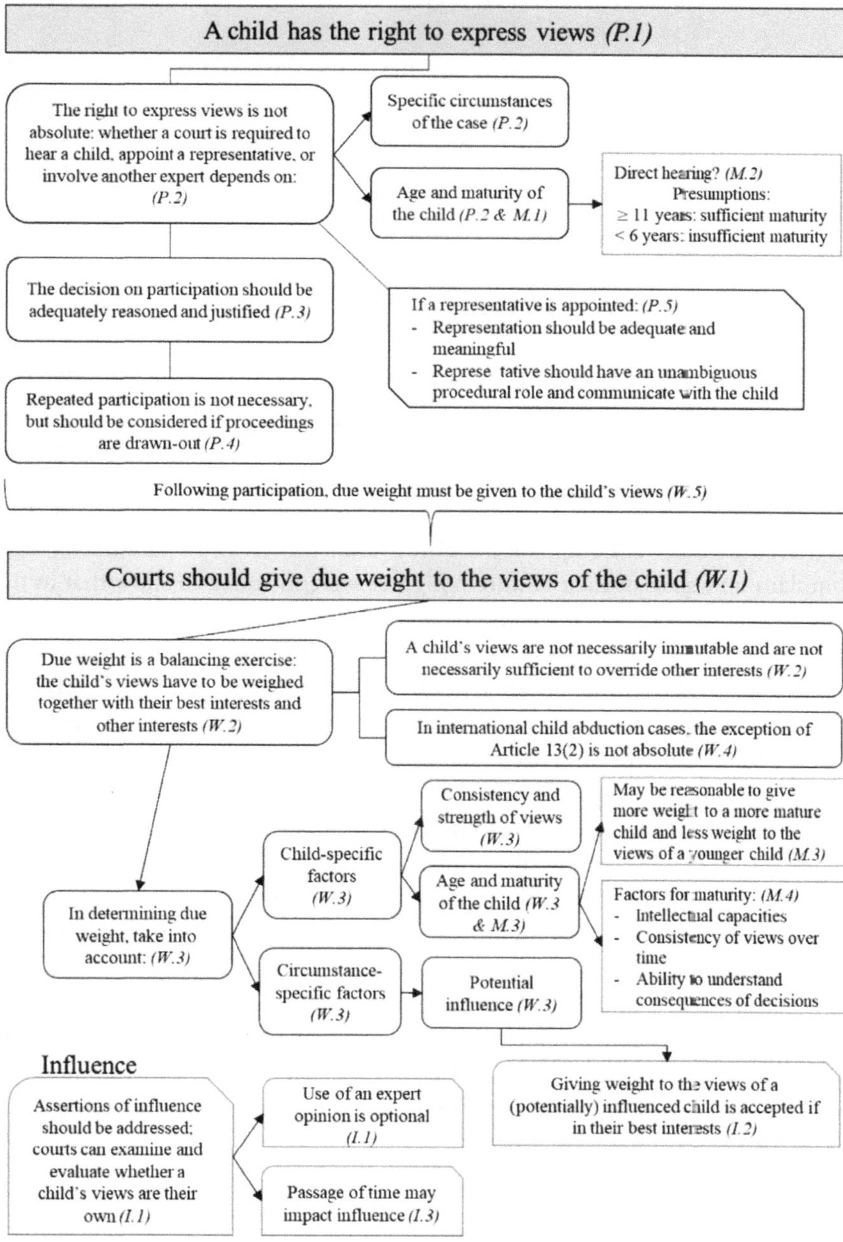

Source: Compiled by the author.

8. PROCEDURAL AND PRACTICAL SUGGESTIONS FOR THE ECtHR AND HUDOC

The manner in which applicants, governments and the ECtHR address the topic of child participation has been discussed throughout this analysis. Up to this point, the key conclusions in that regard have been dealt with. In this section, some additional procedural and practical conclusions and suggestions will be made.

8.1. SUGGESTIONS FOR THE ECtHR

The first issue to be discussed is who can apply to the ECtHR and the obstacles children face in this regard. In Chapter 4, the introduction to the case law analysis, the possible applicants and the admissibility criteria applicable to them were set out. Article 34 ECHR and supplementary case law dictate that parents and children may bring complaints on their own behalf and that in certain situations – although it is not always clear which ones – parents may also complain on behalf of their children. Figures were included to show that in the present analysis, in the overwhelming majority of discussed cases, the applicants were the parents acting solely on their own behalf. In addition, in 13 cases, parents also had standing to complain on behalf of their child(ren). Only in a mere four cases did a parent complain together with his or her child(ren) on his or her own behalf and in no cases did a child complained by himself or herself on his or her own behalf.[1398] Why is it relevant to rehash here what was said in the introduction? Because there is visibly room for improvement.

To start with, explaining the admissibility criteria for parents on behalf of their children is not an easy task. There is no explanation in the Court's 'Practical Guide on Admissibility Criteria', so parents – and the lawyers assisting them – are seemingly left to search for answers themselves.[1399] If the parent is the child's legal guardian, it is straightforward; if not, then it becomes more complicated. The natural parent can also in certain circumstances apply on behalf of his or her child, as set out in *Scozzari and Giunta v. Italy* (2000) and *Eberhard and M. v. Slovenia* (2005), but some questions regarding this option remain.[1400]

[1398] See Chapter 4, section 6.2. The four cases were ECtHR, *Havelka and others v. Czech Republic* (Appl. No. 23499/06), 21 June 2007; ECtHR, *Mustafa and Armağan Akın v. Turkey* (Appl. No. 4694/03), 6 April 2010; ECtHR, *Brillet and Brillet v. Belgium* (dec.) (Appl. Nos. 14942/11 and 17942/11), 16 December 2014 and ECtHR, *M. and M. v. Croatia* (Appl. No. 10161/13), 3 September 2015.

[1399] See Chapter 4, section 6.1.

[1400] See Chapter 4, section 6.1 and footnotes 750 and 751.

Two recommendations can therefore be made. First, it is recommended that the Directorate of the Jurisconsult, which is responsible for the preparation of the Practical Guide, include a paragraph in the Practical Guide setting out the admissibility criteria for parents complaining on behalf of their child. Second, if the ECtHR is given the opportunity to do so, it would be advisable to further specify the admissibility criteria regarding natural parents. For example, can a natural parent complain about the lack of the child's participation on behalf of the child in a conflict between the natural parent stripped of his or her custody rights and a parent who is the new legal guardian?

Aside from the opportunity of parents representing the child in applications to the ECtHR, what about the position of children as applicants themselves? Although legally children have the unequivocal right to bring an application regardless of their age or their legal standing in domestic proceedings, in practice it is not so simple to apply to the Court as a child alone. For example, in this analysis, there were no cases brought by children on their own behalf without their parents. This raises the question as to whether children's access to the ECtHR should be and, if so, can be improved. The answer to the first half of that question – the 'should' – will depend on the interests considered. From a children's rights perspective, it would be beneficial to have more cases brought by children regarding violations of their rights. It would alert all involved to the violations which most affect children and would likely result in more case law addressing violations from the perspective of children. From the ECtHR's perspective, this may be less desirable as the Court is faced with a heavy workload, with many applications pending.[1401] However, taking into account the current practice in domestic states, it is unlikely that children would start applying to the ECtHR in droves. In addition to more opportunities for children to apply to the ECtHR, states should also ensure (more) domestic opportunities to address children's complaints. Should the decision fall in the direction of making applications to the ECtHR more accessible for children, then the question is whether that can be done and by whom. It would likely require practical measures, such as the provision of independent representation or legal assistance (preferably without costs to the child, but with safeguards to ensure that there is no misuse of these provisions by parents) and, crucially, more information directed towards and provided to children. As such, it is a topic for further consideration.

Stepping back from children applying on their own behalf and alone, a final remark needs to be made regarding complaints brought by parents on behalf

1401 See e.g. Public Relations Unit, *The European Court of Human Rights in Facts & Figures 2019*, European Court of Human Rights 2020, available at: https://echr.coe.int/Documents/Facts_Figures_2019_ENG.pdf, p. 3.

of children. In light of the child's right to participation it is striking that it is not required for the child to confirm his or her intention to be represented as an applicant to the ECtHR.[1402] In fact, it is unclear whether the child is even informed of his or her parent's complaint in his or her name. It would be fitting for the ECtHR to at least ensure that the child has been informed of the application lodged on his or her behalf when he or she is sufficiently mature. Similarly, following a decision or judgment, the ECtHR should inform the child what was decided on his or her behalf. The question also arises as to what the ECtHR ought to do when a parent brings a complaint solely on behalf of the child and there is a clear conflict of interests between them.[1403] In domestic courts, this (at times) leads to the appointment of an impartial representative – would something similar be possible at the ECtHR? In this regard, the proposition of Acconciamessa, whereby a distinction is made between the power to apply on behalf of a child and the power to represent him or her in the initiated proceeding, should be considered.[1404]

8.2. SUGGESTIONS FOR HUDOC

These conclusions and suggestions concern the start of a procedure at the ECtHR, but what happens after a case has been decided: the judgment or decision is entered into HUDOC, the Court's online database. For the search and selection of cases in this case law analysis, HUDOC played a key role. Both in the process of searching and selecting cases and during the analysis itself, a number of conclusions arose regarding the functioning of HUDOC. As was mentioned in Chapter 4 and in this chapter,[1405] the case law on child participation is scattered and diffused within case law on family law matters. There is no standard formulation used by the ECtHR to refer to child participation and therefore finding the relevant cases required more effort with a systematic multistep approach (which will be further examined in Chapter 11).[1406] This not only complicates the search and selection of cases for academic purposes, but also

1402 See ECtHR, *Hromadka and Hromadkova v. Russia* (Appl. No. 22909/10), 11 December 2014, para. 117; and extensively on this topic: Joint partly dissenting opinion of Judges Keller and Pastor Vilanova and Partly Concurring Opinion of Judge Schukking, ECtHR, *Khusnutdinov and X v. Russia* (Appl. No. 76598/12), 18 December 2018.

1403 See also Concurring Opinion of Judge Koskelo, ECtHR, *C v. Croatia* (Appl. No. 80117/17), 8 October 2020.

1404 L. Acconciamessa, 'Bringing the Child's Procedural Rights before the ECtHR through Interpretative Tools: Access to Justice, Participation, Representation', in: P. Czech et al. (eds.), *European Yearbook on Human Rights 2020*, Cambridge: Intersentia 2020, pp. 49–77, p. 60.

1405 See Chapter 4, section 4.1 on the methodology for the search and selection of case law.

1406 See Chapter 11, section 4.

makes it more difficult for states to observe the development of principles and standards on child participation by the ECtHR in its case law. The latter is of great importance, as states (and domestic courts) must abide by the interpretation and the standards set by the ECtHR within the scope of the Convention. For states, judges, scholars and others alike, the search for case law on child participation in family law proceedings could be easier if the terminology used for child participation was more consistent and if HUDOC would categorize case law by type of proceeding.

First, the use of a standard formulation by the ECtHR to refer to child participation in its case law could reduce the amount of search terms which (at present) need to be used. The growing set of general principles on participation and due weight may assist in future searches, as the phrasing used in these principles provides new search terms or phrases.

Second, it would be useful if HUDOC included a filter for the type of proceeding concerned. At present, there is no categorization made as to the type of proceeding, nor is a standard or autonomous set of terminology used to refer to the type of family law proceeding in the cases (as was discussed in Chapter 4).[1407] Only under the keywords pertaining to Article 6 ECHR is it possible to choose between, amongst others, 'administrative proceedings', 'civil proceedings', 'constitutional proceedings' and 'criminal proceedings'. This is likely due to the autonomous interpretation developed by the ECtHR to define 'criminal charges' and 'civil rights and obligations'.[1408] The ECHR does not speak of family law proceedings per se, but instead of 'private life' and 'family life' – an autonomous distinction between specific types of family law proceedings has not occurred. Aside from the distinction between proceedings as keywords under Article 6 ECHR, it would be of great help if it were possible to distinguish between broad categories of proceedings irrespective of the Convention right concerned. HUDOC could, for example, include a filter for civil proceedings, criminal law proceedings, asylum and immigration proceedings, and – most importantly for this research – family law proceedings. It may be too difficult to differentiate between such broad categories, but it would be a great help in the search of case law. Of course, it would be wishful thinking to retag all previous cases, but introducing this option for new cases would be valuable.

To conclude, although they may be too idealistic, these are the procedural and practical conclusions which could be addressed by the ECtHR and HUDOC.

1407 See Chapter 4, section 7.

1408 See G. Letsas, 'The Truth in Autonomous Concepts: How to Interpret the ECHR', *European Journal of International Law*, Vol. 15, No. 2, 2004, pp. 279–305, pp. 282–382.

9. CONCLUSION

Evidently, a lot can be said about child participation in the case law of the ECtHR – that much is clear from the chapters included in Part II of this volume. The ECtHR has over time developed standards for child participation through a case-by-case application and interpretation of Article 8, and to a very small degree Article 6 ECHR. The cases brought concerning child participation in family law – whether as a key complaint or as a secondary complaint – have allowed for further crystallization of the right. This case law analysis has also helped answer what the standards for the child's right to participate in family law proceedings are according to the ECHR and the ECtHR. Not only has the ECtHR addressed the core question of (in)sufficient participation, but it has also delved into the weight granted to the child's views and specific aspects such as the maturity of the child or potential influence. Child participation is a topic with many dimensions, which this qualitative content analysis of the case law has helped to uncover. Throughout the analysis, the standards set by the ECtHR for each of these dimensions were evaluated as to their consistency and coherency – e.g. how do these standards align within the framework of the ECHR? In that regard, preliminary steps have been taken to answer how the framework of standards in the international and European human rights instruments can be aligned and strengthened. To fully answer this question, it is time to turn to Part III of this volume, the synthesis, in which the standards are compared and recommendations are made on how to align and strengthen the framework.

Table 9.4. Overview of all cases with sections in which they were discussed

		(In)sufficient participation				Due Weight				Age and maturity				Influence			
		Applicant	Government	ECtHR	None	Applicant	Government	ECtHR	None	Applicant	Government	ECtHR	None	Applicant	Government	ECtHR	None
GC judgments	*Elsholz v. Germany* (2000)	-	X	-	-	X	X	X	-	-	-	-	X	X	-	X	-
	Scozzari and Giunta v. Italy (2000)	-	-	-	X	-	-	-	X	-	-	-	X	X	-	X	-
	Sahin v. Germany (2003)	X	X	X	-	-	-	-	X	-	-	X	-	-	-	-	X
	Sommerfeld v. Germany (2003)	-	-	X	-	-	-	X	-	-	X	X	-	X	X	X	-
	X. v. Latvia (2013)	-	-	-	X	-	-	-	X	-	-	X	-	-	-	-	X
Chamber judgments	*L. v. Finland* (2000)	-	X	-	-	-	X	-	-	-	X	-	-	-	-	-	X
	Gnahoré v. France (2000)	-	-	-	X	-	-	X		-	-	-	X	-	-	-	X
	Sahin v. Germany (2001)	-	-	X	-	-	-	-	X	-	-	-	X	-	-	-	X
	Sommerfeld v. Germany (2001)	-	-	-	X	-	-	-	X	-	-	-	X	-	-	X	-
	K.A. v. Finland (2003)	-	-	-	X	-	-	-	X	-	X	-	-	-	-	-	X
	Hansen v. Turkey (2003)	-	-	-	X	-	X	-	-	-	X	-	-	-	-	-	X
	Kosmopoulou v. Greece (2004)	-	-	-	X	X	X	-	-	-	-	-	X	X	X	-	-
	Haase v. Germany (2004)	-	-	X	-	-	X	-	-	-	-	-	X	-	-	-	X
	Pini and others v. Romania (2004)	-	-	-	X	-		-	X	-	-	X	-	-	-	-	X
	Süss v. Germany (2005)	X	X	X	-	X	X	X	-	-	-	-	X	X	-	X	-
	Mihailova v. Bulgaria (2006)	-	-	-	X	-	-	X	-	-	-	-	X	-	-	-	X
	C. v. Finland (2006)	-	X	-	-	X	X	X	-	X	X	X	-	X	X	X	-
	R. v. Finland (2006)	X	X	-	-	X	-	-	-	-	X	-	-	-	-	-	X
	Fiala v. Czech Republic (2006)	-	-	-	X	-	-	-	X	-	-	-	X	X	X	X	-
	Eski v. Austria (2007)	-	X	-	-	-	-	X	-	-	-	-	X	-	-	-	X
	Havelka and others v. Czech Republic (2007)	X	X	X	-	-	X	-	-	-		X	-	-	-	-	X

(continued)

Table 9.4 *continued*

		(In)sufficient participation				Due Weight				Age and maturity				Influence			
		Applicant	Government	ECtHR	None	Applicant	Government	ECtHR	None	Applicant	Government	ECtHR	None	Applicant	Government	ECtHR	None
Chamber judgments	*Nanning v. Germany* (2007)	-	-	X	-	-	X	-	-	-	X	-	-	-	-	-	X
	Kajari v. Finland (2007)	X	X	X	-	-	-	-	X	-	-	-	X	-	-	-	X
	Maumousseau and Washington v. France (2007)	-	-	X	-	-	-	-	X	-	-	X	-	-	-	-	X
	Glesmann v. Germany (2008)	X	X	X	-	-	X	X	-	-	-	X	-	-	-	-	X
	Jucius and Juciuvienė v. Lithuania (2008)	-	-	X	-	X	X	-	-	-	-	-	X	-	-	-	X
	Mustafa and Armağan Akın v. Turkey (2010)	-	-	X	-	-	-	-	X	-	-	-	X	-	-	-	X
	Gineitienė v. Lithuania (2010)	-	-	-	X	-	-	X	-	-	-	-	X	-	-	-	X
	Aune v. Norway (2010)	-	-	-	X	-	-	X	-	-	-	-	X	-	-	-	X
	Kuhlen-Rafsandjani v. Germany (2011)	X	-	-	-	-	-	-	X	-	-	-	X	-	-	-	X
	Płaza v. Poland (2011)	-	-	-	X	X	X	X	-	-	X	X	-	-	-	-	X
	Kijowski v. Poland (2011)	-	-	DO	-	-	-	X	-	-	-	X	-	-	-	-	X
	X. v. Latvia (2011)	-	-	-	X	-	-	-	X	-	-	X	-	-	-	-	X
	Cristescu v. Romania (2012)	-	-	-	X	-	-	X	-	-	-	-	X	X	X	X	-
	Y.C. v. United Kingdom (2012)	-	-	-	X	-	X	X	-	-	-	-	X	-	-	-	X
	Raw and others v. France (2013)	-	-	-	X	-	-	X	-	-	-	-	X	-	-	-	X
	Gobec v. Slovenia (2013)	-	-	-	X	-	X	X	-	-	X	X	-	-	X	X	-
	Z.J. v. Lithuania (2014)	-	-	-	X	X	-	-	-	-	-	-	X	-	-	-	X
	Blaga v. Romania (2014)	-	-	-	X	X	X	X	-	X	-	X	-	-	-	-	X
	Rouiller v. Switzerland (2014)	X	X	X	-	X	X	X	-	-	-	-	X	-	X	-	-
	Gajtani v. Switzerland (2014)	X	-	X	-	X	-	X	-	-	X	X	-	X	X	X	-

(continued)

Table 9.4 ***continued***

		(In)sufficient participation				Due Weight				Age and maturity				Influence			
		Applicant	Government	ECtHR	None	Applicant	Government	ECtHR	None	Applicant	Government	ECtHR	None	Applicant	Government	ECtHR	None
Chamber judgments	*M. and M. v. Croatia* (2015)	X	X	X	-	-	-	X	-	X	-	X	-	-	-	-	X
	G.B. v. Lithuania (2016)	-	-	-	X	X	X	X	-	-	-	-	X	X	-	X	-
	N.Ts. and others v. Georgia (2016)	X	X	X	-	X	-	X	-	-	-	-	X	-	-	X	-
	Buchleither v. Germany (2016)	-	-	-	X	-	X	X	-	-	-	-	X	-	-	-	X
	E.S. v. Romania and Bulgaria (2016)	-	-	X	-	-	-	-	X	-	-	-	X	-	-	-	X
	Zdravković v. Serbia (2016)	-	-	-	X	-	-	-	X	-	-	-	X	X	-	-	-
	Moog v. Germany (2016)	X	X	X	-	-	-	-	X	-	-	-	X	X	-	-	-
	Iglesias Casarrubios and Cantalapiedra Iglesias v. Spain (2016)	X	X	X	-	-	X	-	-	-	-	X	-	-	-	-	X
	R.L. and others v. Denmark (2017)	-	-	DO	-	-	-	-	X	-	-	-	X	-	-	-	X
	K.B. and others v. Croatia (2017)	-	-	-	X	-	-	X	-	-	-	-	X	-	X	X	-
	Ónodi v. Hungary (2017)	-	-	-	X	-	-	-	X	-	X	-	-	X	-	-	-
	McIlwrath v. Russia (2017)	X	X	-	-	-	-	-	X	-	-	-	X	-	-	-	X
	M.K. v. Greece (2018)	-	-	X	-	-	X	X	-	-	-	X	-	-	-	X	
	Petrov and X v. Russia (2018)	-	X	-	-	-	-	-	X	-	X	X	-	-	-	-	X
	Khusnutdinov and X v. Russia (2018)	-	-	-	X	X	X	X	-	-	-	X	-	X	-	X	-
	A.V. v. Slovenia (2019)	-	-	X	-	-	X	X	-	-	-	-	X	-	-	-	X
	Milovanović v. Serbia (2019)	-	-	-	X	-	X	-	-	-	X	-	-	-	-	-	X
	Pisică v. Republic of Moldova (2019)	-	-	-	X	-	-	X	-	-	-	-	X	-	-	-	X
	Zelikha Magomadova v. Russia (2019)	X	X	X	-	-	-	X	-	X	X	X	-	-	-	X	-
	Stankūnaitė v. Lithuania (2019)	-	-	-	X	-	-	X	-	-	-	-	X	-	-	-	X

(continued)

Table 9.4 *continued*

		(In)sufficient participation				Due Weight				Age and maturity				Influence			
		Applicant	Government	ECtHR	None	Applicant	Government	ECtHR	None	Applicant	Government	ECtHR	None	Applicant	Government	ECtHR	None
Chamber decisions	*K. and T. v. Finland* (1999)	X	-	-	-	-	-	-	X	-	-	-	X	-	-	-	X
	Tiemann v. France and Germany (2000)	-	-	-	X	X	*	X	-	-	-	-	X	-	-	-	X
	G.H.B. v. United Kingdom (2000)	-	-	-	X	-	X	X	-	-	-	X	-	-	-	-	X
	W.F. v. Italy (2001)	-	-	-	X	X	-	X	-	-	-	X	-	X	-	-	-
	Süss v. Germany (2001)	-	X	-	-	-	X	-	-	-	-	-	X	-	-	-	X
	Johansen v. Norway (2002)	-	-	-	X	-	*	X	-	-	*	X	-	-	-	-	X
	Miffek v. Czech Republic (2003)	-	-	-	X	-	*	X	-	-	-	-	X	-	-	-	X
	Paradis and others v. Germany (2003)	X	*	X	-	-	*	X	-	-	*	X	-	-	*	X	-
	Paulsen-Medalen and Svensson v. Sweden (2003)	X	*	X	-	-	*	X	-	-	*	X	-	-	-	-	X
	Vámosi v. Hungary (2004)	-	-	-	X	-	-	-	X	-	-	-	X	X	X	-	-
	C. v. United Kingdom (2004)	X	-	-	-	-	-	-	X	-	-	-	X	-	-	-	X
	Siebert v. Germany (2005)	X	-	X	-	-	-	-	X	-	-	X	-	-	-	-	X
	Eskinazi and Chelouche v. Turkey (2005)	X	X	X	-	-	-	-	X	X	X	X	-	-	-	-	X
	Petersen v. Germany (2006)	-	-	-	X	-	*	X	-	-	X	-	-	X	*	-	
	Kajari v. Finland (2006)	-	X	-	-	-	-	-	X	-	-	-	X	-	-	-	X
	Wildgruber v. Germany (2006)	X	*	X	-	-	-	-	X	-	-	-	X	-	-	-	X
	Gettliffe and Grant v. France (2006)	X	*	X	-	-	-	-	X	-	-	-	X	-	-	-	X
	V.S. v. Germany (2007)	-	X	-	-	-	-	-	X	-	-	-	X	-	-	-	X
	Luig v. Germany (2007)	X	*	X	-	-	*	X	-	-	*	X	-	X	*	X	-

(continued)

Table 9.4 *continued*

		(In)sufficient participation				Due Weight				Age and maturity				Influence			
		Applicant	Government	ECtHR	None	Applicant	Government	ECtHR	None	Applicant	Government	ECtHR	None	Applicant	Government	ECtHR	None
Chamber decisions	*Wildgruber v. Germany* (2008)	X	*	X	-	-	*	X	-	-	-	-	X	X	*	X	-
	Brede v. Germany (2009)	-	-	-	X	X	*	X	-	-	-	-	X	-	-	-	X
	Döring v. Germany (2012)	-	*	X	-	-	*	X	-	-	*	X	-	-	-	-	X
	J. and others v. Finland (2013)	-	-	-	X	-	-	X	-	-	-	-	X	-	-	-	X
	A.E.L. v. Finland (2013)	-	-	-	X	-	-	X	-	-	-	-	X	-	-	-	X
	Brillet and Brillet v. Belgium (2014)	X	*	X	-	-	-	-	X	-	-	-	X	-	-	-	X
	Colombo and others v. Italy and Germany (2016)	-	*	X	-	-	*	X	-	-	-	-	X	-	-	-	X
	T.S. and J.J. v. Norway (2016)	-	-	-	X	-	*	X	-	-	*	X	-	-	-	-	X

*DO = dissenting opinions | * = no arguments provided by the government because the complaint was not communicated to the contracting party.*

Source: Compiled by the author.

PART III

COMPARATIVE REMARKS AND CONCLUSIONS

CHAPTER 10

COMPARISON OF THE INTERNATIONAL AND EUROPEAN STANDARDS

'Le droit d'un enfant d'être entendu et de participer à la prise de décision dans une procédure familiale qui l'affecte en premier lieu est garanti par plusieurs instruments juridiques internationaux.'

– ECtHR, *M.K. v. Greece* (2018)[1409]

1. INTRODUCTION

The child's right to participate in family law proceedings is provided by multiple international and European human rights sources, as also recognized by the European Court of Human Rights (ECtHR) in the quote above. The cradle of the right to participate was the UN Convention on the Rights of the Child (UNCRC); subsequently in the European legal realm, the child's right was mirrored in new binding instruments (the European Convention on the Exercise of Children's Rights (ECECR) and the Charter of Fundamental Rights of the European Union (CFREU)) and soft law instruments (the Guidelines on Child-Friendly Justice (GCFJ) and the Recommendation on the participation of children). More interestingly, as Part II of this volume has shown, the child's right to participation has also 'come of age' as a right under Article 8 of the European Convention of Human Rights (ECHR) through the case law of the ECtHR. These developments regarding the child's right to participation over the past 30 years are an example of the 'widening' and 'thickening' of human rights.[1410] The adoption of new instruments, such as the ECECR and the CFREU, and the recognition of the right to participation in the case law of the ECtHR led to the 'widening' of the

1409 ECtHR, *M.K. v. Greece* (Appl. No. 51312/16), 1 February 2018, para. 91: 'The right of a child to be heard and to participate in the decision-making in family proceedings that primarily affect him or her is guaranteed by several international legal instruments' [Author's translation].

1410 V. Blaker Strand, 'Interpreting the ECHR in its Normative Environment: Interaction between the ECHR, the UN Convention on the Elimination of All Forms of Discrimination against Women and the UN Convention on the Rights of the Child', *International Journal of Human Rights*, Vol. 24, No. 7, 2020, pp. 979–992, p. 979.

right at the international and regional levels. Through the widening, the right also thickens, as European states are now bound to provide for the child's right to participation under multiple instruments. In other words, the accumulation of international and European human rights instruments addressing the child's right to participate in family law proceedings has strengthened the right, but has also led to diverging interpretations of the right. The latter makes the comparison of these instruments an exciting endeavour.

In this chapter, the standards on child participation in the international and European instruments studied in this research are compared. The comparison aims to determine similarities and differences between the standards set in the different instruments. In doing so, the comparison critically examines how the framework of the child's right to participate in family law proceedings can be aligned and strengthened. In comparing the standards, they are evaluated as to their coherence and consistency – in relation to each other and in relation to the aim of child participation. Where differences or inconsistent interpretations are found in this comparison, suggestions are made to align and strengthen the international and European framework. Alignment is sought through coherence and consistency, whereas suggestions for strengthening the framework are made in light of the aim of child participation: the empowerment of children and, following this, the improvement of the decision-making process. In that regard, practical benefits are considered, as are the rights of others. These primary suggestions are subsequently further considered in Chapter 11.

Five themes of child participation are addressed in this chapter. To start with, the four themes that formed the skeleton of the case law analysis in Part II: participation (see section 2), due weight accorded to a child's views (see section 3), maturity of the child (see section 4) and 'influence' on the child's views (see section 5). These four themes are supplemented by a fifth topic, the relevance of which has been shown in the analysis of the UNCRC and other European sources: the information to be provided to a child regarding child participation and practical affairs relevant for effective participation (see section 6). This chapter will not regurgitate the detailed analysis contained in Part I or Part II; instead, according to section or theme, the key similarities and differences are discussed between each of the instruments analysed: the UNCRC, the case law of the ECtHR, the ECECR, the GCFJ, the Recommendation and the CFREU. The last section concludes with some final reflections on the comparison, including overarching explanations for the similarities and differences.

Before we turn to the first section, a few remarks must be made concerning the nature and scope of the instruments compared. As this research focuses on family law proceedings, the selection of sources leads to one key – and obvious – similarity: all of the instruments provide children with a right to participation in family law proceedings. Aside from this, the instruments differ greatly in their nature and scope. The UNCRC is a binding international convention with a specific focus on children's rights, with a committee, but no court, whereas the

ECHR is a broad regional human rights instrument with no explicit reference to children's rights, but an active court with great interpretative powers creating case law in response to specific complaints. Similar to the ECHR, the CFREU is a broad regional instrument, but its binding nature is limited to EU Member States only when they are implementing EU law. The other sources are more specific: the ECECR is a niche convention on the right to participate in family law proceedings and binding, but not for all European states, whereas the GCFJ and the Recommendation are not binding – the GCFJ addresses child participation in legal proceedings at length and the Recommendation more generally restates the right to participation in all matters. These differences make the instruments, as units of comparison, unequal to a certain extent. However, although the comparability of the instruments may be questioned, a comparison remains meaningful and relevant as the subject matter of the standards coincide: all provide human rights standards on the child's right to participate applicable to European jurisdictions.

Let us now turn to the comparison of these standards, starting with the topic of participation itself: the right to express views.

2. PARTICIPATION: THE RIGHT TO EXPRESS VIEWS

The first theme addressed in Part II and in this comparison is the question of participation itself. In this section, the right to participation is first discussed, followed by three relevant topics: the modes of participation, the conditions for participation, and the proceedings in which children can participate.

The child's right to participation is provided by all six sources studied in this volume. This is not a surprise as the aim was to dissect the international and European sources of human rights regarding the child's right to participation in family law proceedings. The right was introduced in Article 12 UNCRC and was phrased as the 'right to express views' or, specifically for legal proceedings, the 'opportunity to be heard'.[1411] In the ECECR, the GCFJ, the Recommendation and the CFREU, it is provided as the right to express views.[1412] In the ECHR, this right is not included in the text of the Convention, but has been introduced by the ECtHR as a child's right under the right to respect for private life and family life of Article 8 ECHR.[1413] That participation is a right of the child and not a duty is emphasized in Article 12 UNCRC and by the UN Committee on the Rights of the Child (CRC Committee) as well as in other sources.[1414] In the case law of

1411 See Chapter 2, sections 3.1.1.3 and 3.1.2.1.

1412 See Chapter 3, sections 2.2, 3.2.1, 4.2 and 5.2.1.

1413 See Chapter 5, section 4.5.

1414 See Chapter 2, sections 3.1.13 and 3.1.2.1, and Chapter 3, sections 3.2, 3.2.4, 4.2 and 5.2.1.

the ECtHR, this is not made explicit, but as participation has been introduced as a right of the child, it can also be understood not to be a duty, but a choice for the child. However, the ECtHR's consideration of child participation as a right of the (applicant) parent can cloud this understanding. When the Court finds a violation of the parent's rights because a child has not been heard, it raises the question of whether a child could be required to express his or her views instead of being given the opportunity to express his or her views, with the option not to.[1415] In this regard, it is important that the ECtHR continues to clarify that it is the child's right to participate protected through the parent's rights instead of a parent's right.

For the implementation of this right to participate, the following three topics are relevant: the modes of participation that should be available to children (see section 2.1), the conditions for participation (see section 2.2) and the type of proceedings in which children can participate (see section 2.3). The standards set by the different human rights sources will now be compared for these three topics.

2.1. MODES OF PARTICIPATION

Child participation can take many different forms, as was indicated in Chapter 1 and throughout the subsequent chapters. In essence, there are four modes of participation which can be ascertained throughout the different sources: direct hearing, representation, indirect hearing, and litigation or party status. These four modes of participation are not all included in each of the instruments, as we will see below. In addition, both the CFREU and the Recommendation do not distinguish modes of participation; therefore, they are not discussed in the following.

2.1.1. Direct Hearing

The first mode of participation is the child being heard directly. This is also the first of the three modes of participation mentioned in the second paragraph of Article 12 UNCRC. A direct hearing is when the child can communicate his or her views to the decision-maker directly, without the involvement or intervention of others. In the case law of the ECtHR, the direct hearing of the child is the mode of participation most commonly raised by applicants and discussed by the court, with multiple applicants specifically complaining that the children should have been directly heard by the domestic court instead of through other modes of participation.[1416] In *Sahin v. Germany* (2003), the ECtHR has expressed the

[1415] See Chapter 5, section 5.2.

[1416] See the complaints in Chapter 5, section 2 and specifically section 2.2.1.

general principle regarding the direct hearing of children, finding that domestic courts are not always required to hear a child in court, but that this 'depends on the specific circumstances of each case, having due regard to the age and maturity of the child concerned'.[1417] As in Article 12 UNCRC and the ECtHR case law, the ECECR and the GCFJ also provide that children should be able to directly express their views to the decision-maker.[1418]

2.1.2. *Representation*

Another common mode of participation is representation of the child. As with the direct hearing, this mode of participation is also explicitly mentioned in Article 12(2) UNCRC and appears in the case law of the ECtHR.[1419] In various forms, representation is also included in the ECECR and the GCFJ.[1420] As a mode of participation, representation refers to the presence of a representative who speaks and/or acts on behalf of the child. Between the UNCRC, the case law of the ECtHR, the ECECR and the GCFJ, there are differences as to who these representatives can be and what their key task or aim should be. There is also a proliferation of terms to refer to different (and similar) kinds of representatives – in addition to 'representative', options include 'curator ad litem', 'guardian ad litem', 'special representative', 'separate representative', 'legal counsel', 'independent representative', 'representative in the child's own name' and 'own representative'. What type of representation is meant by each term is not always clear.[1421] In that regard, it would be beneficial to have – at the human rights level – shared terminology to categorize different forms of representation.

There are various options as to who can be appointed to represent a child. A representative can be a specific person or an appointed body. In all four sources, the option of an appointed lawyer is present.[1422] Within the framework of legal proceedings, this is an expected option. The CRC Committee also mentions the option of another (lay)person as appointed representative, an alternative that is not explicitly mentioned in the other sources, but that is also not excluded. In contrast, in the ECECR, the option of a body appointed as a representative is mentioned.[1423] In the case law of the ECtHR, this is also visible – for example, the Youth Office in *Siebert v. Germany* (2005). However, this option should be used with caution as the ECtHR in *Havelka and others v. Czech Republic* (2007)

[1417] See Chapter 5, section 4.1.
[1418] See Article 3(b) ECECR, which speaks of 'consultation' (Chapter 3, section 2.2) and Guideline IV(D) 44 (Chapter 3, section 3.2.4).
[1419] See Chapter 2, section 3.1.2.3 and Chapter 5, sections 4.2.2 and 4.3.3.
[1420] See Chapter 3, sections 2.2 and 3.2.5.
[1421] See Chapter 3, section 2.2.
[1422] See Chapter 2, section 3.1.2.3, Chapter 3, sections 2.2 and 3.2.5 and Chapter 5, section 4.3.3.
[1423] See Article 2(c) ECECR, Chapter 3, section 2.2.

condemned the appointment of the social welfare authority as the children's guardian ad litem because of the authority's dual role, both requesting the care measures and representing the children.[1424] The CRC Committee does not refer to the appointment of a body as a representative – as this option is considered separately in the text of Article 12 UNCRC. A final option is having the child's parent(s) represent him or her. In general, as the holders of parental responsibility or parental authority, parents are tasked with the legal representation of the child. In the context of Article 12, the CRC Committee notes that while a parent or parents jointly can represent the child, vigilance should be exercised due to the risk of a conflict of interests between the child and the parent(s) or amongst the parents.[1425] In the case law of the ECtHR, representation by the child's parents as a form of participation was only considered once in passing by the Court.[1426] The explanatory report to the ECECR recognizes that while parents typically represent their children, this does not fulfil the task and duties of a representative as described in the ECECR, noting that this is only so when the parent has been specifically appointed as such.[1427] In contrast, parents are not recognized as potential representatives under the GCFJ.

To sum up, the most suitable persons to be appointed representatives for children, according to these sources, appear to be legal professionals or other third persons, not parents, as a conflict of interests is a serious risk in family law proceedings. Public authorities with a conflict of interests in the proceeding, such as social welfare authorities who apply for the care measures, are also less suitable, as was noted in the ECtHR case law.[1428] Whether legal professionals, other professionals or other third persons are the most suitable representatives in practice will depend on the task of the representative and requires (further) empirical research.

Aside from the question of *who* is appointed as representative, the more important question arises as to what the representative's task should be. In a nutshell, there are three options. The representative can: (1) represent the child's views and wishes; (2) represent the child's best interests (as determined by the representative); or (3) represent both the child's views and his or her best interests. With regard to representation as provided by Article 12 UNCRC, the task of the representative should be to correctly transmit the views of the child to the decision-maker. The representative's task is not to determine the child's best interests – as protected under Article 3 UNCRC – but to represent the child's views, i.e. the first option in the above list.[1429] The ECtHR has not directly

1424 See Chapter 5, section 4.2.2.
1425 See Chapter 2, section 3.1.2.3.
1426 See *Wildgruber v. Germany* (2008), as discussed in Chapter 5, section 4.3.2.2.
1427 See Chapter 3, section 2.2.
1428 See Chapter 5, sections 4.2.2 and 5.3.1.
1429 See Chapter 2, section 3.1.2.3.

considered the task of representatives as representing child's views, best interests or both. However, in the case law analysis, it can be inferred that representation is viewed by the ECtHR as either the first or third option. In a number of cases, the Court has held that there was no need for a representative in domestic proceedings where the child had been heard directly or indirectly through other modes.[1430] In that regard, the Court sees representation as a method of transmitting the child's views. From the *N.Ts. and others v. Georgia* (2015) judgment, a key takeaway regarding the representative's task is that it must be clear, with a formal procedural role and unambiguous functions and powers.[1431] The ECtHR does not specify what the task should be, except noting in reference to the GCFJ that the child's views and interests should be represented.[1432] This leans towards the third option of representing both the child's wishes and his or her best interests, although the ECtHR appears to emphasize the former when speaking critically of the representatives drafting reports on the children's situation instead of about his or her views. Similarly, in the ECECR, the focus of the representatives appears to be on representing the child's views (i.e. the first option), although the explanatory report opens the door for the third option in noting that the representative may also give his or her 'own views' on the child's best interests.[1433] In contrast to all the above, the GCFJ introduces two different types of representative, each with his or her own task, and very clearly notes that these two tasks cannot be combined in one person.[1434] The legal counsel or representation in the child's own name should solely raise the child's views (i.e. option one), while the guardian ad litem or independent representative should raise what is in the best interests of the child (i.e. option two).[1435]

To conclude, there are clear differences between the different sources as to what the task of a representative should be. From the perspective of child participation as aiming to give children the opportunity to express their views, representation with the task of transmitting the child's views (i.e. option one) is most suitable. This does not mean that the second option is no good. There are likely to be situations in which a best interests representative is a valuable addition to legal proceedings; however, such a representative does not provide the child with the autonomy to share his or her views with the decision-maker without the interference of a third party. In that sense, it does not meet the core aim of child participation – the empowerment of children – and this should

1430 See Chapter 5, section 4.3.2.2.

1431 See Chapter 5, section 4.2.2.

1432 ECtHR, *N.Ts. and others v. Georgia* (Appl. No. 71776/12), 2 February 2016, para. 76. See Chapter 5, section 4.2.2.

1433 See Chapter 3, section 2.2.

1434 See Chapter 3, section 3.2.5.

1435 See Chapter 3, section 3.2.5.

be recognized.[1436] It should be noted in this regard that the child's views as to what is in his or her best interests should fall under the first option as it is the child's views, in contrast to a representative's views as to what is in the child's best interests (i.e. the second option).

2.1.3. *Indirect Hearing*

Now turning to the third mode of participation ascertained in the various sources and formulated in this volume as the indirect hearing of the child. This refers to the opportunities by which children can express their views to a person or body other than the decision-maker who will communicate the views to the decision-maker, but who does not represent the child (this distinction is further assessed in Chapter 11).[1437] The mode of indirectly hearing the child is not recognized as such in the text of Article 12 UNCRC; this will be further discussed after considering the ECtHR's case law in which indirectly hearing the child was prevalent. The indirect hearing of children by means of expert reports has been a common phenomenon in the case law of the ECtHR.[1438] However, aside from the question of the competence of the experts, it is unclear whether the ECtHR accepts expert reports as a mode of participation. It is noteworthy in this regard that in both *M. and M. v. Croatia* (2015) and *Iglesias Casarrubios and Cantalapiedra Iglesias v. Spain* (2016), the ECtHR found that the children should have been heard directly in the domestic proceedings following the applicants complaining that, amongst other things, the indirect participation of the children via psychological reports was insufficient participation.[1439] However, the need for a direct hearing was reasoned by the ECtHR in relation to the age and maturity of the children and the passage of time rather than because the expert reports were considered insufficient participation.[1440] Turning back to the UNCRC, while the CRC Committee has noted that an adult involved (e.g. a social worker) or a specialist (e.g. a child psychologist) may hear the child, it is not clarified under which mode of participation this is understood. Is it a direct hearing? No, because the expert or social worker is not the decision-maker. It may be understood as the hearing through an appropriate body – the mode for which the CRC Committee has provided no guidance – but in the literature, that is understood to mean the representation by an institution rather than an

---

1436 Take, for example, the Dutch *bijzondere curator*, as discussed in C.R. Mol, 'Kinderparticipatie in Nederland: Wat kunnen we leren van het IVRK en het EVRM?', in: J. Tigchelaar (ed.), *Actuele ontwikkelingen in het familierecht: Vijftiende UCERF symposium*, Nijmegen: Ars Aequi 2021b, pp. 59–76, p. 72.

1437 See Chapter 11, section 2.1.

1438 See Chapter 5, sections 4.3.2.2 and 4.3.4.

1439 See Chapter 5, section 2.2.1.

1440 See Chapter 5, sections 4.2.1.1 and 4.2.1.2.

individual.[1441] Perhaps the indirect hearing of a child through a report drafted by an expert is considered a mode of representation by the CRC Committee. That may be fitting at times, but it is possible to delegate the hearing of the child without expecting the individual to also represent the child. This appears to be the manner in which the ECECR and the GCFJ also view an indirect hearing. The ECECR provides for 'consultation' by the judge in person (i.e. a direct hearing) or through other persons or bodies.[1442] The latter can be understood to refer to an indirect hearing. The GCFJ also refers to the option of an appointed expert in addition to the judge hearing the child, again without making a clear distinction between the two.[1443] As the indirect hearing of children is common, as is visible in the ECtHR's case law and comparative research,[1444] it would be fitting that the CRC Committee provides further guidance on the possibility of indirectly hearing the child in the future.

2.1.4. Litigation or Party Status

With regard to the last mode of participation, we can be brief. Neither the UNCRC nor the case law of the ECtHR accords the child the right to initiate, litigate or intervene in family law proceedings on his or her own behalf.[1445] In contrast, the ECECR and the GCFJ do include reference to the possibility of granting children party status or the right to initiate proceedings or have access to court. However, both do not strongly call for this: the ECECR includes it as an optional procedural right and as per the explanatory report of the GCFJ, the child's access to court is not unconditional and is meant for situations in which the child's legal representative does not act on behalf of the child or where there is a conflict of interests between the legal representative and the child.[1446] The possibility for a child to litigate on his or her own behalf in family law proceedings is not provided in so many words by the GCFJ.[1447] That both the ECECR and the GCFJ go beyond participation as the expression of views into the territory of the initiation of proceedings can be explained by the nature of the sources, as the ECECR provides ratifying states the option to pick and choose further procedural rights and the GCFJ is soft law. Both sources can therefore go further than the binding sources such as Article 12 UNCRC and

1441 See Chapter 2, section 3.1.2.3.
1442 See Chapter 3, section 2.2.
1443 See Chapter 3, section 3.2.4.
1444 See C.R. Mol, 'Child Participation in Family Law Proceedings Compared', in: W.M. Schrama et al. (eds.), *International Handbook on Child Participation in Family Law*, Cambridge: Intersentia 2021a, pp. 335–358, pp. 344–345.
1445 See Chapter 2, section 3.1.2.3 and Chapter 5, section 4.1.
1446 See Chapter 3, sections 2.2 and 3.2.3.
1447 See Chapter 3, section 3.2.3.

provide possibilities to those states that wish to provide extensive procedural rights to children. Party status in the field of family law proceedings is not commonly accepted for children and it remains to be seen whether it soon will be, in contrast to participation.[1448]

A final topic to be considered regarding the modes of participation is whether a ranking or preference exists between them. The CRC Committee has expressed a preference for children to be heard directly over other modes of participation. This preference is recognized by the GCFJ. The ECECR does not rank the modes of participation. However, through the distinction between mandatory and optional rights, the direct hearing and representation modes of participation are more strongly anchored in the ECECR than the others. In contrast, the ECtHR has not ranked the modes of participation. This reflects the subsidiary nature of the Court as it provides discretion to domestic courts and legislators to determine the mode of participation used.

2.2. CONDITIONS FOR PARTICIPATION

The child's right to participate in family law proceedings is not unconditional. In the international and European human rights sources, there are several conditions for participation. The most common condition is the maturity (or age) of the child. In Article 12 UNCRC, this is the sole condition set, although it is phrased as a capability requirement. This condition will be further discussed and compared in section 4 below. In the case law of the ECtHR, age and maturity is supplemented by the condition of the 'specific circumstances of each case'.[1449] This condition is not further specified, but in the case law analysis, two circumstances do appear. The first is the length of proceedings. Additional participation, in the sense of granting the child the opportunity to again express his or her views, may be necessary when proceedings are drawn out over a long period of time.[1450] With respect to potential additional participation, the second circumstance can be distinguished: the interests of the child. An additional direct hearing was considered unnecessary in three cases due to the 'strains' or 'traumatic' effect of another hearing.[1451] Although the ECtHR has noted that the specific circumstances of the case are relevant for the question as to whether a child should be heard directly, represented or heard by an expert, the two circumstances found in the case law only address additional participation. This is noteworthy; in that regard, the ECtHR follows the UNCRC in only applying

1448 See Mol 2021a, pp. 346–348.

1449 See Chapter 5, section 4.1.

1450 See Chapter 5, section 5.3.2 and Norm P.4.

1451 See Chapter 5, section 4.3.2.1.

a condition of maturity to the right to express views in family law proceedings. If we turn back to the UNCRC, it is striking that the CRC Committee does not discuss the role of time in relation to the need for additional participation. It is important that both the CRC Committee as well as states ensure that children are afforded the opportunity to participate more than once in (excessively) lengthy proceedings, especially considering Article 5 UNCRC and the 'evolving capacities' of children.

A separate condition applied to the appointment of representatives is included in the ECECR and the GCFJ, namely the presence of a conflict of interests, or potential thereof, between the child and his or her parents.[1452] In the General Comment regarding Article 12 UNCRC, this is not considered a condition for the appointment of a representative, but the CRC Committee does note that a conflict of interests may provide a reason to appoint a representative who is not the child's parent.[1453] In the cases analysed, the ECtHR has not been asked to consider the appointment of representatives in light of a conflict of interests or a lack thereof by the applicants. However, since the completion of the case law analysis, in the *C. v. Croatia* (2020) judgment, the ECtHR reasoned that a representative should have been appointed for the child in light of the domestic legislation and international standards (the ECECR and the GCFJ) which allow for the appointment of a representative where a conflict of interests is present.[1454] The condition has therefore seeped into the case law of the ECtHR as a reason in favour of representation by means of the Court's interpretation in line with international legal standards.

One might have expected that one of the conditions for participation would be that it is in the child's best interests to do so; although this is not a condition according to the international and European instruments, it is imperative that we touch upon the relationship between participation and the child's best interests (as protected by Article 3 UNCRC). As was discussed at length in Chapter 2, while there is a potential for tension between the child's right to express views and his or her best interests, this tension should be limited to exceptional circumstances.[1455] The right to participate is in the child's interests and the right is voluntary, as it is for children to decide whether to participate. In the case law, this perspective is seemingly adopted by the ECtHR, as the interests of the children were only considered to justify withholding additional participation in three cases. It would be interesting to see whether the ECtHR would accept the child's best interests as a justification for the lack of any participation whatsoever. If domestic courts in Europe use such reasoning, it

---

1452 See Chapter 3, sections 2.2 and 3.2.5.

1453 See Chapter 2, section 3.1.2.3.

1454 ECtHR, *C. v. Croatia* (Appl. No. 80117/17), 8 October 2020, paras. 76–77.

1455 See Chapter 2, section 4.2.1.

would make for an interesting application to the ECtHR and, similarly, for an individual communication to the CRC Committee. The CRC Committee also let the opportunity pass to explicitly remark on the topic when finding the *Y. and Z. v. Finland* (2019) communication to be inadmissible instead of responding to the state's argument that the children could not be interviewed as it would have been contrary to their best interests.[1456]

2.3. TYPES OF PROCEEDINGS

Knowing that a child has the right to participate, the existence and acceptance of different modes of participation, and the conditions for participation leaves one final topic to be addressed in this comparison: the types of proceedings in which a child has the right to participate. The comparison can be very brief, as in all international and European instruments studied, the child is provided with the right to participate in all family law proceedings. In most instruments – the UNCRC, the ECECR, the GCFJ and the Recommendation – this explicitly includes both judicial and administrative proceedings.[1457] Although not explicitly mentioned in the CFREU or the case law of the ECtHR, there are no signs that this is not also true for these two instruments. There are differences between the sources as to which other proceedings or matters the rights address: with Article 12 UNCRC on the far end, as it concerns 'all matters affecting the child', and the ECECR and the CFREU with the most restricted scope, the former only addressing family law proceedings and allowing ratifying states to pick which proceedings specifically, and the latter only concerning those proceedings in the implementation of EU law. While the scope affects the elaboration and interpretation of the child's right to participate, it does not detract from the fact that all sources provide for the right to participate in family law proceedings.

3. DUE WEIGHT ACCORDED TO A CHILD'S VIEWS

The child's right to participate is not solely the right to express views, but is completed by the decision-maker giving due weight to the child's views. This is what differentiates children's participation rights from the right to freedom of expression, i.e. the difference between Article 12 and Article 13 UNCRC.[1458] The child's right to have due weight accorded to his or her views brings purpose to the right to participation. In all the human rights sources studied here, the

---

1456 See Chapter 2, section 5.2.1.

1457 See Chapter 2, section 3.1.2.2, and Chapter 3, sections 2.1, 3.1 and 4.1.

1458 See Chapter 2, section 4.6.

child's right to participation includes the right to have due weight accorded to his or her views, although it is phrased as views being 'taken into consideration' in the CFREU.[1459] This right is indisputable; the subsequent question is what is meant by 'due' weight and how to determine what is 'due'? This question is addressed by the CRC Committee for the UNCRC and by the ECtHR in its case law, while the ECECR, the GCFJ, the Recommendation and the CFREU give little guidance and will therefore not be discussed any further.

3.1. VIEWS OR WISHES

Before we turn to the meaning of due weight and the determination thereof, it is important to reflect on a question that is often overlooked in the discussion on participation and due weight: what do we ask children when they participate? There is a significant difference between asking children with whom they would rather reside (with their mother or with their father) and asking children what their life currently looks like and what they would like their life to look like in the future.[1460] The CRC Committee does not address this question explicitly beyond noting that the hearing of the child should not be a one-sided examination, but a talk.[1461] However, the drafting history of Article 12 shows that the choice was made to use the word 'views' instead of 'wishes' to reflect the fact that participation encompasses all views, not only wishes or opinions.[1462] In the case law of the ECtHR, the distinction between views and wishes has not been discussed. However, as mentioned in the analysis, in most cases the children's views consisted of a clear wish or preference, which may be explained by the fact that applications to the ECtHR often concern highly contested proceedings.[1463] The hypothesis is that children in lengthy family law proceedings are more likely to develop a preference or wish in favour of one outcome over the other. One would assume that this provides a distorted picture, as many children will not want to express a preference between their parents. Therefore, it is important to emphasize that when children participate in family law proceedings, the questions should be open-ended and should address children's views and feelings more broadly than the decision that must be taken. In light of providing children with the opportunity to express their views and thereby more autonomy (i.e. the aim of child participation), this is more fitting than questioning children as to

1459 See Chapter 2, section 3.1.1.5, Chapter 3, sections 2.2, 3.2.1, 4.2 and 5.2.1 and Chapter 6, section 4.1.

1460 See also P. Parkinson & J. Cashmore, *The Voice of a Child in Family Law Disputes*, Oxford: Oxford University Press 2008, p. 18.

1461 See Chapter 2, section 3.2.2.1.

1462 See Chapter 2, section 3.1.1.3.

1463 See Chapter 6, section 4.6.

what their preference is. Additionally, decision-makers may also benefit from having a broader and better picture of the child's views.

3.2. WHAT IS 'DUE WEIGHT'?

There is no definition of 'due weight' given by the CRC Committee in the General Comment on Article 12 and nor does the ECtHR define 'due weight' in its case law. In light of the normal meaning of the term, due weight can be understood as meaning that proper or just relative importance is accorded.[1464] As concluded in Chapter 6, the ECtHR's case law shows that due weight is a balancing exercise.[1465] A definition of due weight cannot provide a magic formula for decision-makers who must provide due weight to a child's views because of the relative and open nature of the concept. Due weight cannot be determined *in abstracto*, as it depends on the circumstances of each individual case.[1466] However, what is indisputable, both for the UNCRC and in the ECtHR's case law, is that due weight means that the child has a right to participation, not a right to self-determination.[1467] The views of children can be decisive in the balancing exercise, but the children's views should not have 'unconditional veto power' or be given exclusive weight without consideration of other interests and factors.

3.3. FACTORS FOR ACCORDING DUE WEIGHT

This leads us to consider which factors are relevant in the weighing of a child's views. The common factor is the age and maturity of the child, as it is included in the text of Article 12 UNCRC, the case law of the ECtHR, the GCFJ, the Recommendation and the CFREU.[1468] This key factor for determining the weight to be attributed to a child's views will be discussed in depth in the section 4.2. Notably, the ECECR does not refer to the child's maturity as a factor for due weight and nor does it mention any other factors for according due weight.[1469]

In the case law analysis, two other factors impacting the weight granted to a child's views were identified as being relied upon by the ECtHR. The first is the consistency and strength of the child's views, whereby more consistent and

1464 See Chapter 2, section 3.1.1.5.
1465 See Chapter 6, section 5.2.
1466 See Chapter 2, section 3.1.1.5.
1467 See Chapter 2, section 3.1.1.5, and Chapter 6, sections 4.1 and 4.2.
1468 See Chapter 2, sections 3.1.1.5 and 3.1.1.6, Chapter 3, sections 3.2.1, 4.2 and 5.2.1 and Chapter 6, sections 4.1 and 5.2.1.
1469 See Chapter 3, section 2.2.

strong views are seen as a reason to give more weight to the child's views.[1470] The second is the influence on a child's views, where the ECtHR finds that relying on a child's palpably influenced views could violate Article 8 ECHR.[1471] The topic of influence will be discussed further below in section 5, but it is important to note that as a factor in due weight, the ECtHR does accept that a child's views can be given weight even if these have (potentially) been influenced insofar, as doing so is in the child's best interests.[1472] These two factors relied on in the ECtHR's case law are not mentioned in the other instruments, but do overlap with factors suggested in the literature. Specifically, Willow has included the strength of the child's views as a factor, and Daly has referred to the strength and duration of the child's views as well as the validity of the child's views (which refers in part to whether they were the child's 'own' views).[1473]

Article 12 UNCRC does not further specify any other factors to be considered. However, in the General Comment analysis of Article 12(1), one further factor can be discerned: the impact of the matter on the child.[1474] This factor has not been identified as such in the case law of the ECtHR. This is noteworthy, but can be explained by the fact that the analysis concerned case law on family law proceedings. All family law proceedings can be said to have a serious impact on the child's life, as they determine with whom the child has legal ties, resides with or has contact with. In contrast, Article 12 UNCRC – especially the first paragraph – concerns all matters affecting the child. This is much broader and includes participation beyond legal proceedings, at school, in public debates, etc.[1475] In that regard, it makes more sense to differentiate between the impact of the specific matter on the individual child for the question of due weight, not the type of family law proceeding. As all family law proceedings have a great impact on children's lives, the aim of child participation calls for a careful balance to be sought between autonomy and protection. In the case law analysis, which solely concerned family law proceedings, the types of proceedings were considered as a variable for the weight to be accorded, but there was no explicit difference made as to the impact that the types of family law proceedings have on the child.[1476] As will be discussed below, when distinguishing between the type of proceedings, one might discern that this is (implicitly) due to the impact of the matter on the child. What is, or should be, the relevance of the impact of proceedings as a factor for due weight within family law proceedings specifically? It is clear that all types of family law proceedings concerning children have a serious impact on

[1470] See Chapter 6, section 5.2.1.
[1471] See Chapter 6, section 5.2.2.
[1472] See Chapter 8, section 4.4.
[1473] See Chapter 2, section 3.1.1.5.
[1474] See Chapter 2, section 3.1.1.5.
[1475] See Chapter 2, section 3.1.1.4.
[1476] See Chapter 6, section 5.2.3.

the child on various fronts, including on their rights, legal status, relationships, living arrangements, etc. The question arises as to whether there may be distinctions between family law proceedings as to the impact and subsequently the weight to be given to a child's views. This requires a definition of impact and weighing between different types of impact – for example, between the short-term versus long-term impact, and the impact on legal rights or on the concrete situation. It is difficult to distinguish which family law proceedings have more impact than others, as this will depend on the definition of 'impact' chosen.

In addition to these factors, in the case law analysis, the significance of the types of proceedings for the determination of due weight has been examined. The subject matter of the proceeding is not mentioned by the CRC Committee with regard to due weight, but the ECtHR's case law shows that it impacts the interests to be considered by the decision-maker. In all types of family law proceedings, a balance must be struck between the child's views, other factors determining the child's interests, and the interests of other parties – in most proceedings, those of the parent(s).[1477] Subsequently, the balancing exercise varies only slightly between the types of proceedings and remains dependent on the circumstances of the specific case. The key differences are visible with respect to access proceedings and care proceedings. In the latter, the child's interests for protection and safety are of extra importance.[1478] In access proceedings, the difference is most notable as to the weight accorded to a child's views. The ECtHR has accepted that a child's refusal to have contact can be given more weight because of the potential for future contact and because it is considered 'pointless', 'counterproductive' or even 'harmful' to force a child to have contact against his or her wishes.[1479] This development in allowing the child's wishes against contact to be a decisive factor in the restriction of access shows the increased acceptance of his or her views. However, the question remains whether the distinction for access proceedings is fitting – in comparison, for example, to custody proceedings – if we consider the impact of the proceedings on the child's future and the rights of parents, and the potential for future developments. Does the ECtHR accept decisive weight with regard to access because it considers it to have less impact on the child's life compared to care or custody decisions, or does it do so because it considers the impact on the child's life to be so great that his or her wishes can be decisive?

All in all, how courts are to give *due* weight to a child's views in family law proceedings is not set in stone by any of the human rights sources. The CRC Committee and the case law do provide relevant factors which must be considered, including: the child's maturity, the impact of the proceedings,

[1477] See Chapter 6, section 5.2.3.
[1478] See Chapter 6, section 5.2.3.
[1479] See Chapter 6, section 5.2.3.

the consistency and strength of the child's views, the influence on the child's views and the types of proceedings. In that regard, the child's views, his or her best interests and the interests of others, such as parents, must be placed in the scale and the subsequent balancing act must be properly motivated by decision-makers. Child participation calls for conscientious balancing, whereby the autonomy of children is respected even where considering the protection of children.

3.4. DUE WEIGHT AND THE CHILD'S BEST INTERESTS

In coming to a decision in family law proceedings, the child's best interests should be at the forefront of the courts' decision. Therefore, the balancing exercise we speak of regarding the child's views occurs within the assessment of the child's best interests. In Chapter 2, the relationship between the child's best interests principle (as provided by Article 3 UNCRC) and due weight following child participation (provided by Article 12 UNCRC) has been discussed at length.[1480] Following the CRC Committee's interpretation, the key takeaway is that the child's views should be a fundamental component in the assessment of the child's best interests. In determining the child's best interests, the child's views are one element to be considered together with others – such as the child's identity, the child's safety or the maintenance of family relations. The child's views do not compete with the child's best interests, but should help shape the decision – providing nuance or a pivoting weight. Like the CRC Committee, the ECtHR considers the child's views as a factor in the best interests determination. In several cases, this is recognized – for example, in *Y.C. v. United Kingdom* (2012),[1481] *Gineitienė v. Lithuania* (2010)[1482] and *N.Ts. and others v. Georgia* (2016).[1483] Even in those cases where the ECtHR found that the child's best interests gave reason not to decide in keeping with the child's wishes, this was because other factors in determining the child's interests outweighed the child's views.[1484] The symbiotic relationship between the child's best interests and participation and due weight is emphasized by the CRC Committee and is visible in the ECtHR's case law. This symbiosis deserves continued attention, including more explicit recognition in the ECtHR's case law, to reinforce this understanding also at the national level.

1480 See Chapter 2, section 4.2.2.

1481 See Chapter 6, section 4.2 regarding *Y.C. v. United Kingdom* (2012), *J. and others v. Finland* (2013) and *A.E.L. v. Finland* (2013).

1482 See Chapter 6, section 4.4.3.

1483 See Chapter 6, section 4.3.

1484 See Chapter 6, section 4.4.4.

4. MATURITY OF THE CHILD

Legally, a child is a child and not an adult by virtue of his or her age. Age is not only a numerical value, but also symbolizes the development of a child from baby to adult. In addition to ageing, as a result of which the body grows, children mature over time as they learn new things and gain experiences, i.e. as their brains develop. A child's age and maturity has been shown to be a relevant factor for the child's right to participation in family law proceedings. In the various international and European sources studied here, there are many different phrases used to refer to a child's maturity, including: age and maturity, being capable of forming his or her own views, having sufficient understanding or his or her discernment. Maturity – through various phrases – is raised both as a condition for the right to express views and as a factor for due weight. It is therefore relevant for the two stages of participation. This does not mean that there is only one criteria of maturity, which subsequently determines both the right to express views and due weight. Both in Article 12 UNCRC and the ECtHR's case law, there is a distinction made between sufficient maturity for participation and the subsequent consideration of maturity for due weight.[1485] At each point, maturity must be considered separately. In the subsequent comparison, we will follow this division considering maturity and participation first, followed by maturity and due weight.

4.1. MATURITY AND PARTICIPATION

The child's right to participate in family law proceedings is not unconditional in Article 12 UNCRC, the case law of the ECtHR, the ECECR or the GCFJ. The maturity condition for the right to express views is phrased differently: as 'capable of forming his or her own views' in the UNCRC, 'age and maturity' in the case law of the ECtHR, and as 'sufficient understanding' in the ECECR and GCFJ.[1486] The conditions differ not only in their phrasing, but also in their interpretation, mostly because of the nature of the instruments, as we will see below. There are no maturity conditions for child participation in the Recommendation or the CFREU. Following the discussion of the maturity conditions in the other instruments, an explanation will be sought for this absence.

To start with, in the case law of the ECtHR, there is no general guidance provided as to how the ECtHR understands maturity as a condition for participation. In contrast, as Article 12 UNCRC has been further explained by the CRC Committee in the General Comment, the following interpretative

---

1485 See Chapter 2, section 3.2.2.2, and Chapter 7, section 4.5.

1486 See Chapter 2, section 3.1.1.2, Chapter 3, sections 2.1 and 3.2.4, and Chapter 7, section 4.1.

comments have been made. First, the CRC Committee has clarified that there should be no age limits in law or in practice for the right to be heard, but instead a presumption of capacity should apply.[1487] Subsequently, young children can also be capable of forming views, even when they are not yet verbal.[1488] Instead of relying on age limits, capability should be determined in other ways. The CRC Committee does not provide much clarity beyond elaborating that 'sufficient understanding' is required, but 'comprehensive knowledge' of the matter is not, and that it should be assessed whether the child can form an 'autonomous opinion', without explaining what that means, or how. Thus, while there is an explanation of the maturity condition, it remains a vague explanation. This vagueness can be explained by the broad nature of the condition – Article 12 provides the right to participate in all matters, not just family law proceedings – and by the nature of international treaties, whereby a compromise must be reached when drafting them. Similarly, the condition of 'sufficient understanding' in the ECECR is left open to states' interpretation: states can define their own criteria to determine whether children are 'capable' of expressing views and the use of age as a presumption is suggested.[1489] Using the same condition of 'sufficient understanding', the GCFJ disapproves of age as a sole criterion without providing further interpretation or criteria for 'sufficient understanding' besides a presumption of understanding where a child takes the initiative to be heard.[1490]

In contrast to these drafted conditions, the ECtHR's approach to maturity has developed through the case law by means of a case-by-case consideration of the facts. In considering maturity for the participation in family law proceedings specifically, the ECtHR does not adhere to the guidance of the CRC Committee. Although the Court has acknowledged the presumption of capacity as formulated by the CRC Committee,[1491] it relies exclusively on the ages of children to determine whether they should have been heard by the domestic courts.[1492] From the case law analysed, age ranges emerge whereby the ECtHR has consistently found children over the age of 11 to be sufficiently mature to be heard and children under the age of 6 too young to be heard.[1493] In between these ages, a grey zone remains, as the ECtHR has not considered the maturity needed for participation in any cases where the children were between the ages of 6 and 11. In future applications and case law, this grey zone will hopefully be addressed. The subsidiary supervisory nature of the ECtHR explains why the Court relies on age instead of other criteria for maturity. The ECtHR reviews the

1487 See Chapter 2, section 3.1.1.2.
1488 See Chapter 2, section 3.1.1.2.
1489 See Chapter 3, section 2.1.
1490 See Chapter 3, section 3.2.4.
1491 See Chapter 7, section 4.1.
1492 See Chapter 7, sections 4.2.1 and 4.3.1.
1493 See Chapter 7, section 4.5.

decisions made regarding the child's maturity for participation in the domestic proceedings relying on the facts presented to it; it does not assess the child's maturity itself.[1494] It is worth noting with regard to the ECtHR's case law that maturity as a condition for participation was only addressed in relation to the direct hearing of the child by the domestic court and not in relation to other modes of participation such as representation or the indirect hearing of the child.

It is notable that neither the CFREU nor the Recommendation includes a maturity condition for the child's right to participate. The reason for this omission in Article 24(1) CFREU is not included in the Explanations for the Charter and nor is this reason self-explanatory. As was discussed in Chapter 3, it may be because the CFREU wishes to go further than the UNCRC in recognizing that all children can express their views or it may be because Article 24 consolidated various UNCRC articles, so the short sentence may combine both Article 12 and Article 13 UNCRC.[1495] The Recommendation emphasizes that there should be no age limit for child participation and therefore that all children have the right to be heard – without any other maturity condition.[1496] It is likely that the general and non-binding nature of the Recommendation, combined with the broad scope concerning all matters affecting the child, is why the Recommendation does not include any other maturity condition for the expression of views. As we will see below, maturity is mentioned in relation to due weight.

In light of the above, four points deserve additional attention: (1) the use of age limits; (2) the potential of hearing (very) young children; (3) the modes of participation and maturity; and (4) the dynamic nature of maturity.

Use of age limits

With regard to the first topic, it is clear that the UNCRC and ECtHR take different approaches as to the use of age limits. The ECtHR's reliance on the child's age to determine the child's maturity for participation clashes with the approach advanced by the CRC Committee that the right to participation is not limited by age limits. The GCFJ follows in the footsteps of the CRC Committee in this regard, while the Explanatory Report to the ECECR recognizes that states can rely on the child's age, as the ECtHR does, at least in the form of a presumption.[1497] The two conflicting approaches can be categorized as idealistic (no age limits, but an individual assessment per child) versus pragmatic (age as a presumption to simplify the determination of maturity). Individually assessing

1494 See Chapter 7, section 4.5.
1495 See Chapter 3, section 5.2.1.
1496 See Chapter 3, section 4.2.
1497 See Chapter 3, sections 2.1 and 3.2.4.

children in legal proceedings comes with a price tag and it needs to be considered whether this is the best use of funds by states.

Hearing (very) young children

The difference regarding age limits is also closely related to the second point: whether (very) young children should be able to participate. While the CRC Committee notes that even children who are not yet verbal are capable of forming views, the ECtHR agrees with domestic courts that very young children need not be heard in family law proceedings. Again, one can speak of an idealistic versus a pragmatic interpretation. The difference may be explained by the fact that the right in Article 12 UNCRC applies more broadly than legal proceedings, while the ECtHR and the ECECR specifically address family law proceedings, and the ECtHR only discusses maturity for participation through a direct hearing (see below). In implementing Article 12 within the home setting where the parents are the decision-makers for day-to-day decisions, it is suitable to note that very young children's views should also be considered. In legal proceedings, it is questionable whether the participation of very young children is practical, advisable or desired. It is worth noting the ECtHR's reasoning in two recent judgments, whereby it appears to require domestic courts to obtain an expert opinion as to whether (very) young children can be heard by a court, with or without the assistance of a specialist in child psychology.[1498] It will be interesting to see whether the ECtHR continues this trend of reasoning and whether this may lead to violations where very young children are not heard in future case law in specific circumstances or more generally.[1499] Obtaining an expert opinion for all young children will very likely increase the cost of child participation in legal proceedings, present new logistical issues, and may lead to undesirable delays, as was the case in *M. and M. v. Croatia* (2015).[1500] This can subsequently hinder child participation, which runs counter to the aim of child participation, which is to empower children by providing an accessible and effective opportunity to express their views. In addition, insisting on the unconditional participation of young children or the assessment of all young children may reduce support for the implementation of the child's right to participation among national institutions and professionals (for example, judges). To conclude, while the CRC Committee's recommendation to do away with age limits and to give very young children the opportunity to participate is commendable from a child's rights perspective, pragmatically, the reliance on age as a presumption for maturity to participate may allow for more effective and efficient implementation of the

1498 See Chapter 7, sections 4.4 and 4.5.
1499 See Chapter 7, section 5.2.
1500 See Chapter 5, section 4.2.1.1.

child's right to participation. Especially if these age presumptions are not set too high, it may encourage states and courts to diligently provide the opportunity to participate to all children of that age and above.

Modes of participation and maturity

Aside from age and youth, it is remarkable that the ECtHR has only discussed maturity for participation in relation to the direct hearing of the child and never for representation or the indirect hearing. Likewise, the ECECR and the GCFJ only attach a maturity condition to the direct hearing and not to any of the representation modes.[1501] In contrast, neither the UNCRC nor the CRC Committee makes any distinction between modes of participation. This raises the question of whether there ought to be a distinction between the maturity conditions for the different modes of participation. In the case law of the ECtHR, the absence of maturity consideration for representation or indirect hearings likely reflects the lack of age conditions in the national laws.[1502] But are certain modes of participation more suitable for certain age cohorts of children? The answer to this question requires further – empirical and interdisciplinary – research, and will depend on the specific tasks and practical functioning of the different modes of participation.

The dynamic nature of maturity

The final point to consider is the dynamic nature of maturity, i.e. the fact that maturity changes over time. In the UNCRC, this is recognized by the concept of 'evolving capacities' in Article 5: children progressively mature with the passage of time. However, the capability condition in Article 12 UNCRC is more static than the concept of evolving capacities. A child is either capable of expressing views or not and can therefore exercise his or her right to participation or not – there is no sliding scale. In contrast, Article 5 concerns the continually shifting equilibrium of responsibility and autonomy between parents and children. In the setting of family law proceedings, the determination of capability is static because it concerns whether a child can express his or her views at that particular moment in time. In that regard, the use of flexible age limits (i.e. presumptions based on age) is more fitting for participation in family law proceedings than the child's evolving capacities. However, the evolving capacities (i.e. the growing independence and autonomy of children) must be taken into account. In the *M. and M. v. Croatia* (2015) judgment, the ECtHR recognized that a child's personal autonomy 'gradually increases with their evolving maturity' and confirmed the importance of the right to be heard in that regard.[1503] In the

1501 See Chapter 3, sections 2.1 and 3.2.4.
1502 See Chapter 7, section 5.3. See also Mol 2021a, p. 352.
1503 See Chapter 5, section 4.1.

Court's reasoning, the dynamic nature of maturity is especially visible in case law on lengthy proceedings – e.g. those on high-conflict separations. In these situations, the ECtHR has recognized the need to reassess maturity in order to provide opportunities to participate as the proceedings continue.[1504]

4.2. MATURITY AND DUE WEIGHT

Once the child has had the opportunity to express his or her views, the decision-maker is faced with the task of according due weight to these views when coming to a decision. As mentioned above, the age and maturity of the child is the key factor for the determination of due weight as per the UNCRC and is an important factor in the case law of the ECtHR. Similarly, in the GCFJ, the Recommendation and the CFREU, the 'age and maturity' of the child is the sole factor mentioned for the granting of due weight, with the GCFJ noting specifically that age plays a major role in determining due weight.[1505] These three instruments provide no further guidance as to how age and maturity will impact due weight. In contrast, both the CRC Committee and the ECtHR emphasize that as children mature, their views should be given increasing weight in the balancing scales or the assessment of their best interests.[1506]

In determining the maturity with regard to due weight, the CRC Committee emphasizes the dual nature of the criterion in Article 12: age *and* maturity. Age by itself cannot be relied on, but must be supplemented by the determination of maturity, for which the CRC Committee refers to factors such as the information available to the child, the child's experience, social and cultural expectations, and levels of support.[1507] The ECtHR relies mostly on age, but has considered three other aspects in a number of cases: the consistency and strength of the child's views, the child's capacity to understand the consequences of his or her decisions, and the child's educational success or intellectual capacities.[1508] There is a disconnect between the factors used by the ECtHR and those listed by the CRC Committee, as they do not match up. As mentioned in the previous section, this can be explained by the subsidiary nature of the ECtHR and its reliance on the information presented by the applicants and governments. While the ECtHR could rely on the factors set out by the CRC Committee, the Court is dependent on developments at the domestic level. If children or other applicants feel that

---

1504 See Chapter 7, section 5.2.

1505 See Chapter 3, sections 3.2.4, 4.2 and 5.2.1. In contrast, as mentioned above, the ECECR does not refer to the child's maturity in determining due weight and does not include any other factors in the Explanatory Report either, see Chapter 3, section 2.2.

1506 See Chapter 2, section 4.4.2, and Chapter 7, section 4.1.

1507 See Chapter 2, section 3.1.1.6.

1508 See Chapter 7, section 5.2.

the CRC Committee's factors are more appropriate or telling in relation to the question of maturity, then these should be included in their applications to the ECtHR so that the Court can consider them. When it comes to the ECtHR's reliance on age, it is important to note that, unlike for participation, it is not possible to determine age ranges because of the relative nature of due weight. The case law shows that the ECtHR agrees with the weight domestic courts grant to children from the age of nine years and above. At the same time, the ECtHR accepted that less weight should be given to children because of their youth in two cases where the children were 9 and 11 years old. There is no threshold under which the ECtHR finds that child's views should be given *any* due weight, but instead the Court has accepted that domestic courts may give *less* weight to the views of younger children and *more* weight to older or more mature children.

Before we conclude the discussion on due weight and maturity, it is relevant to again emphasize the dynamic nature of maturity. As is the case with regard to participation, a child's age and maturity increase over time, and this must be taken into account. Both the UNCRC – through the relationship between Article 3, Article 12 and 'evolving capacities' in Article 5 – and the ECtHR recognize that as the child matures, more weight should be accorded to his or her views. Within the context of lengthy proceedings, the ECtHR has also noted that the child's views may be increasingly decisive.[1509] Therefore, the passage of time and the child's evolving capacities must be taken into account in the due weight determination process.

5. 'INFLUENCE' ON THE CHILD'S VIEWS

A different theme which intersects both participation and due weight is the potential influence over a child and his or her views. It is an important theme in the context of family law proceedings specifically, as these proceedings concern the child–parent relationship and children are, typically, very attached to their parents. Disputes between parents can leave children caught in the middle, potentially subject to pressure, manipulation or a conflict of loyalties. Therefore, in the context of child participation, the concern that a child has been influenced by one of his or her parents is common. In domestic proceedings, especially high-conflict separations, allegations of influence are raised by parents to argue against participation or the weight granted to a child's views, as we can see in the case law of the ECtHR and in an individual communication to the CRC Committee.[1510]

1509 See Chapter 7, section 5.2.

1510 See Chapter 2, section 5.2.1, and Chapter 8, section 2.1.

How is the topic of influence addressed by the sources studied here? For a complete comparison, the topic must be split into three steps: first, what is influence and how can or should it be determined?; second, what does influence mean for the right to express views? and, finally, what is the impact of influence on the question of due weight?

5.1. DETERMINING INFLUENCE

A child – or any other person for that matter – is influenced when his or her behaviour, belief or opinion is affected or changed by someone else. We are all influenced on a day-to-day basis by the people we speak to or, for example, the media. Influence as such is a standard part of life, there is no person – whether child or adult – who is not subject to influence. The matter at hand is not this 'standard' level of influence, but the manipulation or undue influence on a child's views, i.e. when a parent's power or authority is used to influence the child.

How can this influence be determined according to the sources studied? The ECECR, the Recommendation, the CFREU and the GCFJ offer no guidance in this respect. Article 12 UNCRC provides children the right to express their 'own' views 'freely'. The term 'freely' refers both to the voluntary nature of participation – a child has the choice to participate – and to the absence of undue influence or pressure on the child when expressing his or her views.[1511] This is emphasized by the CRC Committee, as the child has the right to express his or her own views, not the views of others. In the General Comment on Article 12, the CRC Committee also notes, in relation to the capability condition, that states should assess the child's capacity to form an 'autonomous opinion'.[1512] This phrase is not further specified, but one can assume it means that the child must be able to form an opinion free from undue influence at a minimum, perhaps an 'autonomous opinion' must be free from all influence – but this is not specified.[1513]

The General Comment does not provide any insight as to how influence could or should be determined; in contrast, the ECtHR's case law has dealt more extensively with the question of how (undue) influence should be determined and the following has been discerned from the analysis. The ECtHR has held that domestic courts themselves are well placed to examine and evaluate whether a child's views are his or her own or have been influenced, obtaining an expert opinion is not required, but may be used.[1514] In examining whether there is influence, the ECtHR has recognized that the consistency and strength of a child's

1511 See Chapter 2, section 3.1.1.3.
1512 See Chapter 2, section 3.1.1.2.
1513 See Chapter 2, section 3.1.1.2.
1514 See Chapter 8, section 5.2.3.

views may be a sign that the views are his or her own, but can similarly be proof of influence – it will depend on the other circumstances of the case.[1515] In that regard, the passage of time is also relevant, as it may lead to increased influence, but also allows for the opportunity to hear the child at multiple points in time and to determine whether his or her views are consistent or not and his or her own views or not.[1516] However, whether the consistency and strength of views can be used to determine the presence of influence is questionable, especially when the ECtHR has recognized that it can go both ways.[1517] Finally, the ECtHR has had to consider the controversial subject of parental alienation (syndrome), but has to date not yet taken a clear stance on the issue.[1518] Although the issue of how to determine influence has not been addressed in the General Comment, in one individual communication the CRC Committee has been asked to consider the topic. Although the CRC Committee has found the communication to be inadmissible, it has inadvertently conveyed that an expert report can be of use for domestic courts in determining whether a child's views were his or her own or not.[1519] This is not much, but does match the ECtHR's perspective on the matter.

5.2. INFLUENCE AND PARTICIPATION

Following the determination of influence, let us now turn to what influence means for the right to express views, i.e. the first step of participation. The emphasis on the child's own or autonomous views in the CRC Committee's General Comment raises the question of what the consequence of influence – once determined – on the child should be in relation to participation. It is of course preferable that children are not subject to influence and states should ensure this to the furthest possible extent,[1520] but what if a child is (already) influenced – does that mean a child should not be afforded the opportunity to express his or her views? In other words, are the child's autonomous, own or freely formed views a condition for the right to participate? The current General Comment appears to lean that way, but that imposes a new threshold on the right to participation and it should therefore be further considered by the CRC Committee, particularly as it would thwart the aim of providing children with the opportunity to express their views, and it may be questioned whether it is possible to determine whether a child is influenced prior to hearing his or her views. While in the case law of the

---

1515 See Chapter 8, section 5.2.1.

1516 See Chapter 8, section 5.2.2.

1517 See Chapter 8, section 5.2.1.

1518 See Chapter 8, section 5.2.4.

1519 See Chapter 2, section 5.2.1.

1520 See also UNCRC General Comment No. 12 (2009), para. 132.

ECtHR, influence is discussed at length, the question of whether influence can form a reason to withhold the option of participation has not been discussed. While the ECECR, the Recommendation and the CFREU all do not address influence, the explanatory memorandum to the GCFJ does briefly mention the risk of manipulation, emphasizing that all efforts should be taken not to let this undermine the right to be heard.[1521] This appears to be similar to the remarks made by the CRC Committee, being different only in that the GCFJ appears to state that the right to express views should not be hampered, whereas the CRC Committee's remarks can be understood in that way.

5.3. INFLUENCE AND DUE WEIGHT

Last, but certainly not least, if a child's views have been influenced, what does that mean for the due weight to be accorded to those views? The CRC Committee, the ECECR, the CFREU, the GCFJ and the Recommendation all remain silent on what it means for due weight if a child's views are found to have been influenced. In contrast, as applicants have over the years complained about the weight granted to a child's allegedly influenced views,[1522] the ECtHR has dealt with this question in its case law. In doing so, the Court has taken two – to a certain extent opposed – approaches. On the one hand, it has held that if children are 'palpably unable to form' their own opinion because of undue influence by means of a loyalty conflict or alienating behaviour, granting these views considerable weight could lead to a violation of the parent's right to family life under Article 8 ECHR.[1523] On the other hand, the ECtHR has accepted that even though the child's wishes were subject to influence, his or her views should be given due weight and can be decisive in the assessment of his or her best interests.[1524] In this regard, the Court makes a valid distinction between the child's wishes and the reasons for those wishes. With child participation in family law proceedings, the aim is not to find the objective truth, but to allow a child to express his or her views and feelings on the matter. When a child is – partially or wholly – influenced by a parent, this might change his or her views, opinions or wishes regarding the other parent, but it does not mean that these new views and emotions are not true to the child at that point in time. It can be argued that this second approach by the ECtHR most respects the child's autonomy and thereby the aim of child participation: the ECtHR condones manipulation and undue influence, but accepts that once it has occurred, the child's views

1521 See Chapter 3, section 3.2.4.
1522 See Chapter 8, section 2.1.
1523 See Chapter 8, section 4.2.
1524 See Chapter 8, section 4.2.

are his or her views, whether they were formed with or without influence. This second approach also simplifies the situation for domestic courts to a certain extent, as the determination of influence is less relevant when influence does not disqualify the child's views from being given due weight.

6. INFORMATION AND PRACTICAL AFFAIRS

The right to participation does not come to full fruition when children do not know they have the right to express their views in a proceeding or are not informed how their views have been given due weight. Information is an essential element for the implementation of the child's right to participation in family law proceedings. This has been emphasized by the CRC Committee, which has set out the need for the child to be informed prior to the hearing and afterwards in the General Comment's five steps for effective implementation.[1525] The CRC Committee distinguishes six pieces of information which must be provided to children: prior to the hearing (1) their right to express their views; (2) the impact their views will have; (3) the participation modes available to them; and (4) the practical arrangements of the hearing; and following the decision (5) the outcome of the proceeding and (6) how their views were considered.[1526] The CRC Committee places the responsibility to inform the child with the decision-maker or, in relation to the child's role in the proceedings, the person responsible for hearing the child.[1527] In the GCFJ, the child's right to information is included throughout as one of the general elements of child-friendly justice.[1528] The GCFJ recommends informing the child before, during and after judicial proceedings in a manner which he or she can understand, preferably directly and not (only) through his or her parents.[1529] The ECECR and the Recommendation also stress that the child should be informed to ensure meaningful participation.[1530] In the ECECR, the judicial authority specifically has the obligation to ensure that the child has been informed.

In relation to the provision of information, the ECtHR really is the odd one out. At no point in the case law analysis did the Court consider whether the concerned children received any information as to their right to participate, the process of participation or the outcome of proceedings. The topic of information was not raised by any of the applicants or governments either, which is noteworthy

1525 See Chapter 2, section 3.2.
1526 See Chapter 2, sections 3.2.1 and 3.2.3.
1527 See Chapter 2, sections 3.2.2.1 and 3.2.3.
1528 See Chapter 3, section 3.2.2.
1529 See Chapter 3, section 3.2.2.
1530 See Chapter 3, sections 2.2 and 4.2.

of itself. That there were no applications brought by children alone and on their own behalf and only four cases in which children complained on their own behalf together with a parent may partially explain why this topic was not raised. It is interesting to note that in the recent *C. v. Croatia* (2020) judgment, the lack of information provided to the child as to his right to participate was raised by the applicant (the child, not on his own behalf, but represented by his mother).[1531] The ECtHR did not directly address the complaint regarding information, but in the context of finding that a 'special guardian ad litem' should have been appointed, the Court did refer to the ECECR and the GCFJ, which find that the task of a representative includes keeping the child informed.[1532] It would not be surprising if the provision of information to the child is the subject of more applications in the future, and in keeping with the other sources the ECtHR will need to consider the relevance of information for the child's effective right to participation.

In addition to informing the child, there are a number of other practical affairs relevant for the implementation of child participation. The CRC Committee refers to a number of these affairs when discussing the five steps to effective implementation of Article 12 UNCRC.[1533] According to the CRC Committee, the 'context' of the hearing should be enabling and encouraging, and children should preferably be heard under conditions of confidentiality instead of in open court. Additionally, the CRC Committee notes that participation should be 'child-friendly' through ensuring that the environment of the hearing is adapted to the child and it should be inclusive respectful, safe and sensitive to risk. Finally, the CRC Committee notes that in order to meet these standards of implementation, training may be needed for those involved. In the GCFJ, these practical affairs are included and further fleshed out. With regard to the organization of proceedings, the GCFJ notes three aspects: (1) the environment, such as the court, should be child-sensitive and adapted to the child; (2) the communication with the child should match the child's age and level of understanding and be respectful and sensitive and (3) the child should be allowed to be accompanied by a trusted adult.[1534] The latter is guidance specific to the GCFJ; none of the other instruments provide for accompaniment. In line with the CRC Committee, the GCFJ also emphasize that the (interdisciplinary) training of professionals in the field is necessary.[1535] The Recommendation also mirrors the GCFJ and the CRC Committee's steps to effective implementation in very broad terms, as it notes that participation processes should be respectful, in

1531 ECtHR, *C. v. Croatia* (Appl. No. 80117/17), 8 October 2020, para. 65.
1532 ECtHR, *C. v. Croatia* (Appl. No. 80117/17), 8 October 2020, paras. 76–77.
1533 See Chapter 2, section 3.2.2.1.
1534 See Chapter 3, section 3.2.6.
1535 See Chapter 3, section 3.2.8.

child-friendly environments, inclusive, supported by training, safe and sensitive to risk.[1536] The ECECR, the CFREU and the case law of the ECtHR all do not go into the practical affairs of implementation. However, one can presume that the practical affairs are considered equally important by these instruments. It would not be surprising if in future applications the ECtHR is presented with alleged violations of child participation because of deficiencies in the practical implementation of participation.

7. CONCLUSION

Having considered how the five themes of child participation are dealt with by the different sources studied, the final section of this chapter provides an overview of the key similarities and differences, and provides a number of underlying explanations. In Parts I and II of this volume, the international and European instruments of human rights, or children's rights specifically, were analysed in detail. In this chapter, the framework of the child's right to participate in family law proceedings according to international and European human rights law has been discussed and preliminary reflections and recommendations have been made to align and strengthen the framework where the standards or interpretation thereof have differed. While the final reflections and recommendations will be given in the conclusions in Chapter 11, it is relevant here to consider explanations for similarities and differences between the instruments.

Considering the big picture, there are many similarities between the international and European instruments for the right to participation and they share much of the same terminology and phrasing. These similarities are logical as the norms on child participation in the ECECR, the GCFJ, the Recommendation and the CFREU were developed in response to Article 12 UNCRC and build upon the UNCRC and each other over time.[1537] With regard to the ECtHR's case law, the similarities with Article 12 UNCRC and other European instruments can be explained by the increased reception of international law by the ECtHR. As described previously, the Court's formulation of general principles on child participation and due weight since 2015 has especially and explicitly been influenced by Article 12 UNCRC, the ECECR and the other European instruments.[1538] This follows a general trend of the ECtHR relying on external

[1536] See Chapter 3, section 4.2.

[1537] See Chapter 3, sections 2, 3, 4 (specifically 4.2) and 6.2.1. See also L. Lixinski, 'Comparative International Human Rights Law: An Analysis of the Right to Private and Family Life across Human Rights "Jurisdictions"', *Nordic Journal of Human Rights*, Vol. 32, No. 2, 2014, pp. 99–117, p. 99.

[1538] See Chapter 9, section 6.

sources of international law, as the ECtHR itself has said that the ECHR 'cannot be interpreted in a vacuum'.[1539] Forowicz has identified various factors which can explain this trend.[1540] The ECtHR interprets the provisions of the ECHR in accordance with international human rights law, especially in the field of children's rights as the Convention does not provide any explicit rights to children.[1541] The ECtHR can rely on the UNCRC in that regard. Additionally, as the UNCRC has been ratified almost universally – including by all Council of Europe states – it provides the Court's with reasoning greater authority and assists the Court in maintaining its institutional credibility.[1542] The references to the ECECR and the GCFJ in the ECtHR's case law can be explained by the fact that these instruments offer more specific guidelines for child participation (especially for representation) not only in comparison to the ECHR, but also compared to the UNCRC.[1543] Even when the ECECR and the GCFJ are not binding on the state concerned, the ECtHR relies on these instruments for their interpretative value.[1544] The inclusion in the ECtHR's case law subsequently strengthens and consolidates these European instruments and – to a more limited extent – Article 12 UNCRC.

There would have been no need for a comparison, if all of the instruments provided for identical rights to participation. In the previous sections, differences between the instruments have been identified. Differences include the conditions for participation and the factors for determining due weight, the discouraging of age limits versus the use of age as a key factor, the classification of indirect hearing, and the discussion or lack thereof of influence and information. The nature and scope of the instruments provide explanations for the differences in

---

1539 See e.g., ECtHR, *Al-Adsani v. United Kingdom* [GC] (Appl. No. 35763/97), 21 November 2001, para. 55. See R. Nordeide, 'The ECHR and its Normative Environment: Difficulties Arising from a Regional Human Rights Court's Approach to Systematic Integration', in: O.K. Fauchald & A. Nollkaemper (eds.), *The Practice of International and National Courts and the (De-)Fragmentation of International Law*, Oxford: Hart Publishing 2012, pp. 117–138, p. 121; G. Ulfstein, 'Evolutive Interpretation in the Light of Other International Instruments: Law and Legitimacy', in: A. van Aaken & I. Motoc (eds.), *The European Convention on Human Rights and General International Law*, Oxford: Oxford University Press 2018, pp. 83–94, p. 89; Blaker Strand 2020, p. 980 and A. Nussberger, *The European Court of Human Rights*, Oxford: Oxford University Press 2020, p. 136.

1540 M. Forowicz, 'Factors Influencing the Reception of International Law in the ECtHR's Case Law: An Overview', in: M. Andenas & E. Bjorge (eds.), *A Farewell to Fragmentation: Reassertion and Convergence in International Law*, Cambridge: Cambridge University Press 2015, pp. 191–217.

1541 U. Kilkelly, *The Child and the European Convention on Human Rights*, Aldershot: Ashgate 1999, p. 15; Forowicz 2015, pp. 194–195; and Blaker Strand 2020, p. 988. In relation to the UNCRC, see also ECtHR, *Maire v. Portugal* (Appl. No. 48206/99), 26 June 2003, para. 72.

1542 Forowicz 2015, p. 209.

1543 See also Forowicz 2015, pp. 201–202.

1544 See Chapter 9, section 6.

the depth of which a topic is discussed, the discretion offered to states and the idealistic versus practical approach.

To start with, the depth and level of detail in which the different instruments set standards and provide guidance differs due to the interplay between the legal nature of the instruments, the territorial application and the scope of matters addressed in them. Take, for example, the GCFJ, which provides extensive standards on participation specifically in legal proceedings. This is possible because it is a non-binding regional instrument drafted by the Council of Europe states as a tool for the implementation of the existing standards rather than as an additional binding instrument to raise the standards for child participation. The ECECR as a binding convention – although also regional and specific to family law proceedings – is less extensive and provides great liberty to its ratifying states that choose the proceedings to which it applies and can opt-in to the optional representation and litigation rights for children.

In contrast, the UNCRC is an international binding convention on the whole spectrum of children's rights. As an international convention, it applies to states in all corners of the world, with different cultural, social and legal practices and expectations. In order to be able to achieve universal agreement on children's rights, the drafted rights are general so as to allow for the cultural, social and legal differences between states. Article 12 is just a single article in this Convention, even though it has been promoted as one of the four general principles. The right to participation is therefore formulated in only two sentences: the first addresses child participation in the broad sense, not just in family law proceedings, while the second offers an additional sentence as to participation in legal proceedings. This all explains why, even though the CRC Committee has provided further interpretation in the General Comment, there remain open ends as to the understanding of child participation in family law proceedings.

Compared to the UNCRC, the ECHR is an even more general binding convention on human rights, as it was drafted more than 70 years ago in response to the Second World War and was inspired by the Universal Declaration of Human Rights. Therefore, it does not even include children's rights in its text; however, the work of the ECtHR has led to more specific standards on child participation in family law proceedings. This is because, as a court, the ECtHR has considered the functioning of child participation within specific family law disputes, with different situations and subjects. The Court has had to go into the details and could not refrain from applying its general principles to specific situations. In addition, as a regional court, the ECtHR can depart from a shared European culture to the extent that it is present, whereby the other Council of Europe (CoE) instruments also add to a similar understanding on child participation. Of course, as a subsidiary court, the ECtHR does leave some room for the discretion of domestic states and courts, but within the scope of the standards set by the Court. The differences between European states are thereby more limited than differences internationally.

In addition to these four instruments which provide standards for the child's right to participation in family law proceedings, there are the two regional instruments which provide less additional guidance: the Recommendation and the CFREU. Due to its general nature and broad scope, the Recommendation does not offer any new insights on child participation in family law proceedings that were not already included in the existing instruments – including the GCFJ. The CFREU, in leaning heavily on the UNCRC and the ECHR with the accompanying ECtHR case law, also does not offer new insights. In addition, the broad nature of the Charter and its limited scope of application make it less relevant for states and domestic courts when giving form to child participation in family law proceedings. Its potential value lies elsewhere – for example, with regard to child participation within the EU legislative process.

A final key difference which must be highlighted is the idealistic nature and approach of the UNCRC and the CRC Committee versus the pragmatic approach of the ECtHR in its case law. As discussed previously, some differences between the interpretation of the CRC Committee and that of the ECtHR can be traced back to the idealistic children's rights focus of the UNCRC and Committee, and the subsidiary more overarching consideration of the right to family life by the ECtHR. The UNCRC and subsequently the CRC Committee set out broad aims which depart from the perspective of children's rights; this has led – at times – to standards which may be considered too idealistic, such as the hearing of very young children. In contrast, the applications which the ECtHR must consider show the messy reality of family law proceedings in which there are often conflicting human rights. Therefore, the ECtHR does not consider the child's right to participation in a vacuum, but within the framework of domestic proceedings and in relation to the matter of the dispute, parents' rights and other rights of the child. This provides for a more realistic application of the child's right to participate in certain respects, recognizing that there are justified limits to child participation, but also explicating factors for determining due weight and dealing with complaints of influence.

To conclude, the international and European human rights instruments addressing child participation uphold common core aspects of the right, but differ in terms of the depth of standards and in certain details. The accumulation of instruments has strengthened or 'thickened' the child's right to participation, but at the same time has 'widened' the right and led to differences in the understanding of participation. These differences complicate the matter, but from a positive point of view, it can be said that the widening also provides new perspectives and the impetus to further develop the child's right to participation. As Lixinski so eloquently notes, 'fragmentation from above is only pluralism from below'.[1545]

[1545] Lixinski 2014, p. 112.

CHAPTER 11
CONCLUSIONS

'I believe that as young people, innocent to the situation we have been put into, it is our thoughts, our wishes, and our feelings that are most important, and first priority in our family cases. What happens at the court affects our lives dramatically, and we can do very little than explain how we feel and hope that this is taken into consideration when a final judgement is taking place.'

– Laura, 15 years old[1546]

1. INTRODUCTION

In the past few decades, child participation has developed at a significant rate. Children's right to step out of the silence and use their voice to express their views has, since the introduction of the United Nations Convention on the Rights of the Child (UNCRC), found its way into multiple European human rights instruments and the case law of the European Court of Human Rights (ECtHR). Increasingly society has accepted the Dr Seuss saying 'a person's a person, no matter how small!' Children's rights have made their way to the centre stage and European states have actively pursued the ratification of children's rights instruments concerning child participation. The increased attention for the child's right to participate in family law proceedings has led to the proliferation of instruments addressing this right.

In this volume, the widening and thickening of the child's right to participate has been addressed. The aim has been to study the standards of child participation in family law proceedings applicable to European states and to determine how the framework can be aligned and strengthened. Through legal doctrinal work in Part I, the UNCRC, the European Convention on the Exercise of Children's Rights (ECECR), the Guidelines on Child-Friendly Justice (GCFJ), the 2012 Recommendation on the participation of children (Recommendation) and the Charter of Fundamental Rights of the European Union (CFREU)

1546 As quoted in J.E. McIntosh, 'Four Young People Speak about Children's Involvement in Family Court Matters', *Journal of Family Studies*, Vol. 15, No. 1, 2009, pp. 98–103, p. 100.

were analysed and in Part II, by means of the innovative method of qualitative content analysis (QCA), the case law of the ECtHR has been meticulously studied. In Chapter 10, the wealth of standards on child participation in family law proceedings in these instruments have been compared, whereby a first set of conclusions have been drawn. It is now time to conclude with final reflections on these standards and with recommendations on how to align and strengthen the framework for the right of children to participate in family law proceedings. In doing so, it must be recognized that presently there remains a gap between the standards and their practical implementation.[1547] While it is likely in part due to the inconsistencies of the standards set and the uncertainty as to best practices, it is mostly because it is easier to say you support children's rights than to implement them: states are talking the talk, but not walking the walk.

This conclusion consists of four sections. First, final reflections and recommendations are made regarding the standards for child participation in family law proceedings (see section 2). Here the possibilities for aligning and strengthening the standards as such are discussed substantively. Subsequently, it is asked what needs to occur in order to allow for the aligning and strengthening of the child's right to participate (see section 3). What does this research mean for the instruments studied and the institutions and actors involved? Do we need a new European instrument on child participation? Should we abolish any of the existing instruments or are there other options to strengthen the existing standards? One of the pioneering aspects of this volume has been the use of the QCA method to study the case law of the ECtHR (the use of QCA and other methodological choices will be evaluated in section 4). The advantages and disadvantages of QCA are discussed and recommendations are presented for legal researchers. Finally, this chapter concludes with some reflections as to the future of child participation in family law proceedings (see section 5).

1547 See e.g. S. Aras Kramar & I. Milas Klarić, 'The Main Challenges of Implementing the Procedural Rights of the Child in the Family Justice Systems of Some Southeast European Countries', in: T. Liefaard & J. Sloth-Nielsen (eds.), *The United Nations Convention on the Rights of the Child: Taking Stock after 25 Years and Looking Ahead*, Leiden: Brill/Nijhoff 2017, pp. 247–271; A. Daly & S. Rap, 'Children's Participation in the Justice System', in: U. Kilkelly & T. Liefaard (eds.), *International Human Rights of Children*, Singapore: Springer 2019, pp. 299–319, p. 310; M.R. Bruning et al., *Kind in proces: van communicatie naar effectieve participatie*, Nijmegen: Wolf Legal Publishers 2020; I. Boone, C. Declerck & E. Vertommen, 'Belgium', in: W.M. Schrama et al. (eds.), *International Handbook on Child Participation in Family Law*, Cambridge: Intersentia 2021, pp. 103–120; E. Di Napoli & F. Maoli, 'Italy', in: W.M. Schrama et al. (eds.), *International Handbook on Child Participation in Family Law*, Cambridge: Intersentia 2021, pp. 219–229 and E.K.M. Tisdall, 'Scotland', in: W.M. Schrama et al. (eds.), *International Handbook on Child Participation in Family Law*, Cambridge: Intersentia 2021, pp. 287–301.

2. FINAL REFLECTIONS: CHILD PARTICIPATION IN FAMILY LAW PROCEEDINGS

Building upon the in-depth analysis of standards set in the international and European instruments for the child's right to participate in family law proceedings, in this section final recommendations are made on how to align and strengthen the framework. As mentioned in Chapter 1, child participation is important for the empowerment of children and their autonomy, and it likely provides for better decision-making and outcomes in family law proceedings. Given these premises and considering the similarities and differences between the standards as discussed in the comparison, what can be improved and how? In the previous chapter, initial conclusions and recommendations have already been made as to the five themes of child participation. In the following discussion, final recommendations will be made for each of them: participation (see section 2.1), due weight (see section 2.2), maturity (see section 2.3), influence (see section 2.4) and information and practical affairs (see section 2.5).

2.1. PARTICIPATION

The starting point for child participation – that the child has the right to participate in family law proceedings – is provided by all instruments studied. Beyond a shadow of a doubt, the child has the right to express his or her views in family law proceedings. This is a right and not a duty of the child; children may opt not to express their views. It is also critically the child's right, not a right of the parent, which is perhaps self-explanatory as it originates from the UNCRC, but which must continue to be emphasized in the case law of the ECtHR, where through applications of parents, the right has at times been recognized under the scope of the parent's right under Article 8 ECHR instead of the child's right.

2.1.1. Conditions for Participation

The right of the child to express views is not an absolute right in family law proceedings;[1548] most notably, participation will depend on the maturity or age of the child, as will be further discussed below (see section 2.3). In the instruments studied, other conditions for participation have also been relied upon. However, these conditions do not hinder the child's right to participate as such. Instead, the conditions of the length of proceedings (or passing of time) and the interests of the child both concern the question of *additional* participation in the case law

[1548] See also Standard P.2 in Chapter 5.

of the ECtHR. Therefore, these conditions are relevant only when considering if the child should be able to express his or her views again, after having already done so previously in the proceedings. For the appointment of a representative, an additional condition is also expressed: the conflict of interests between a child and his or her parent(s). This condition is only raised for the appointment of a representative specifically; it does not apply for the child's right to express views.

An important conclusion is that the best interests of the child do not form a condition for children to be able to express their views. Children must have the opportunity to express their views and they may themselves decide against it if they do not wish to participate. In essence, child participation as such is deemed to be in the best interests of the child. It is not for adults to decide in advance whether child participation would be too 'difficult' or 'harmful' for a child and therefore not in the child's best interests. This does not mean that the process of participation should not be adapted to children; it simply means that participation cannot be restricted through the simple reference to the child's best interests. In the light of this, it is important that domestic courts adequately motivate their decisions on participation when they decide not to provide children with the opportunity to be heard or in deciding between different modes of participation, as considered in the case law of the ECtHR.[1549]

In light of the aim of child participation, it is encouraging to note the absence of further conditions for child participation beyond the child's maturity. In the balance between protection and empowerment, the recognition that children ought to have the opportunity to express views regardless of the circumstances or their presumed best interests further strengthens the autonomy of children. This is especially so when it provides children with the choice whether they wish to express their views in the matter.

2.1.2. Modes of Participation

We now turn from the conditions for child participation to the modes of participation. The comparison made in this volume has discussed, in depth, the different standards and interpretations given to the various modes of participation.[1550] In this conclusion, several overarching topics need to be further addressed to align and strengthen the existing framework. We will start with the terminology for the modes of participation before turning to two specific modes of participation.

Let us begin with the need to define and use common terminology for the different modes of participation at the international and European level. This is important for the alignment of the international and European framework.

[1549] See also Standard P.3 in Chapter 5.

[1550] See Chapter 10, section 2.1.

The lack of a shared terminology not only complicates the understanding, implementation and application of human rights, but also stands in the way of critically thinking and discussing what is needed to implement the child's right to participate, as well as making comparative research on child participation in national laws more difficult.[1551] In this research, a distinction was made between four modes of participation (direct hearing, indirect hearing, representation and party status). This is not a common categorization of the modes of participation in the international and European human rights instruments – for example, the ECECR and the GCFJ do not seemingly distinguish between a hearing in person by the judge or having a hearing delegated to other persons or bodies. However, the distinction between the four modes of participation is preferable as it recognizes the differences between the indirect hearing and the direct hearing or representation (see below). A clear and uniform distinction can contribute to the better realization of the child's right to participate. In that regard, to strengthen the framework, more guidance on the position of the indirect hearing should be provided by the UN Committee on the Rights of the Child (CRC Committee) and the ECtHR, especially as comparative research indicates that it is the most common mode of participation in some states (although it is not recognized as a mode of participation in others).[1552]

Turning now to the specific modes of participation, with regard to the modes of representation available to children, there is a proliferation of terms and simultaneously different tasks delegated to these representatives. Terminology needs to be established which clearly delineates between the key types of representatives. This would simplify the discussion on representation and provide more clarity as to the type of participation meant and the applicable standards. In delineating between the types of representatives, the GCFJ most clearly provides for two distinctive types of representatives with their own respective tasks: (1) 'representation in the child's own name' or 'legal counsel', with the task of representing the child's own views; and (2) the 'guardian ad litem' or 'independent representative', with the task of representing the child's best interests. Before we further discuss the role representatives should have, if we depart from these two types of representation, which terms are fitting? The terms used in the GCFJ are not the most suitable for the type of participation they symbolize. Regarding the first type of representation, 'legal counsel' is not the best term as it need not be through legal representation. 'Representation in the child's own name' is more fitting in that regard, but is a phrase instead of a clear term. Instead, it is suggested to use the term of the child's 'own representative' as coined in the ECECR. This is a better option as it reflects that

[1551] See C.R. Mol, 'Child Participation in Family Law Proceedings Compared, in: Schrama et al. 2021a, pp. 335–358, pp. 337 and 356.

[1552] See Mol 2021a, p. 345.

the representative acts on and voices the child's own views and wishes. With regard to the second type of representation, both the terms 'guardian ad litem' and 'independent representative' do not immediately clarify that the child's best interests are represented and not his or her own views on the matter, or his or her own views on his or her best interests for that matter. A more straightforward option – although not used in any of the instruments – is the term 'best interests representative'.

Notwithstanding the issue of terminology, it is crucial that the role of representatives is clear. As discussed in the comparison, the most suitable type of representation to empower children is the child's own representative, who transmits the child's views and therefore speaks and acts on behalf of the child.[1553] Whereas the scales in the balance between protection and empowerment lean towards protection with a best interests representative, the scales lean towards empowerment with an 'own representative' as the expression of the child's views is placed front and centre.

With this role of representatives in mind, one may wonder whether the 'own representative' is not the same as an indirect hearing, whereby someone other than the decision-maker (often an expert, such as a child psychologist) hears the child and reports back to the decision-maker. Although representation is also an indirect mode of participation, there is a difference between reports drafted to convey the child's view to the decision-maker and representatives who both communicate these views and have a procedural function representing the child throughout the process and in legal proceedings. The difference may at times appear minimal, but is present. Where the representative should act and speak on behalf of the child, a person or body appointed to hear the child indirectly solely acts on behalf of the decision-maker or any other party who has instructed them to do so. An indirect hearing falls somewhere between the direct hearing and a representative as it is the delegated hearing of the child. To strengthen the framework of child participation, it is important to recognize the distinction between representation and an indirect hearing as well as between a direct hearing and indirect hearing. The differences between these three modes of participation will call for other standards, practical measures and/or safeguards. For example, additional requirements are defined for representation by the CRC Committee and the ECtHR, such as the existence of codes of conducts, the representative having clear functions, powers and a formal procedural role, and there being no conflict of interests as to the role of the representative in the proceedings.[1554] It would make sense that the person responsible for the indirect hearing is also subject to codes of conduct and should have no conflict of interest, even if this person does not have a formal procedural role.

1553 See Chapter 10, section 2.1.

1554 See Chapter 2, section 3.1.2.3, and Chapter 5, section 4.2.2.

Finally, although the international and European instruments do not commonly provide for a child's right to be granted party status or to initiate family law proceedings,[1555] this fourth mode of participation must be considered. Party status and especially the initiation of proceedings is a form of participation plus – it allows for the child's participation in the legal proceedings, but also goes further in granting a procedural status and procedural rights to the child. In this sense, it provides additional autonomy to children. Whereas participation grants the child a circumscribed autonomy in the process of the proceedings, party status may provide the child with the autonomy to initiate proceedings and increased autonomy throughout the proceedings.[1556] Although not currently required by human rights standards in family law proceedings and not a widespread practice domestically, this is an area for further consideration, especially as certain states have already introduced party status or the right to initiate proceedings, although often limited and under specific circumstances.[1557]

In light of the distinction between the four modes of participation, the question arises as to whether children have a choice between modes of participation or whether there ought to be a preferred mode of participation in general or, for example, according to the type of proceeding. As was discussed in Chapter 2, Article 12 UNCRC may be understood as providing children with a choice for a specific mode of participation, but in light of the aim of child participation, the first crucial step is that children are offered an opportunity to effectively express their views.[1558] The GCFJ reflect the stance of the CRC Committee in a limited manner, noting that the child should be consulted as to whether they wish to be heard directly or indirectly.[1559] In contrast, the other instruments – most notably the ECECR and the case law of the ECtHR – do not grant children a choice between participation modes. Of crucial importance is effective participation. Once child participation is implemented to a sufficient degree domestically, whereby all (or most) children are afforded the opportunity to participate, should the step be made towards providing children with a choice between multiple modes of participation if this is shown to improve the child's abilities to express views or to improve the decision-making process.

In this regard, to strengthen the framework of child participation, it may be beneficial to determine a preferred mode of participation. As noted in the comparison, the CRC Committee and the GCFJ express a general preference for the direct hearing of children.[1560] This preference can be endorsed for a number

1555 See Chapter 10, section 2.1.
1556 See Figure 2.1 in Chapter 2, section 6.
1557 See Mol 2021a, pp. 346–348.
1558 See Chapter 2, section 3.1.2.3.
1559 See Chapter 3, section 3.2.4.
1560 See Chapter 10, section 2.1.

of reasons. In this participation mode, the views of the child are communicated directly to the decision-maker, which should prevent any unnecessary or faulty paraphrasing, interpretation or modifications made to the views of the child. Considering the aim of participation to empower children, it can be argued that the direct hearing most clearly recognizes and respects the child's autonomy. It also allows children to feel heard as they meet with the decision-maker themselves.[1561] The child benefits, but so does the decision-maker, as he or she has the opportunity to meet the child and to form a picture of the child beyond what has been or can ever be communicated in reports. This can assist the decision-making and may lead to better decisions, especially when the decision-maker has also been able to meet with and speak to the other parties involved, i.e. the parents. Additionally, the direct hearing may be the most budget-friendly mode of participation – although this requires further research.

The preference for direct hearing is also supported by a number of existing empirical studies in which children have expressed their preference for direct hearings.[1562] There has also been some research on the perspectives of judges, lawyers, other actors and parents on the direct hearing of the child,[1563] but further research comparing participation through a direct hearing, indirect hearing, representation and party status from the perspective of children and the perspective of other actors would be beneficial. It would be interesting to see what the actual impact on decision-making would be if in similar cases, the child would participate through different modes.

Although it could be argued that the type of family law proceeding or the maturity of the child may function as a factor for the preferred mode of participation, it is noteworthy that none of the human rights instruments or the case law of the ECtHR distinguishes between types of family law proceedings and the participation rights children have in these proceedings. This is not

1561 See e.g. P. Parkinson, J. Cashmore & J. Single, 'Parents' and Children's Views on Talking to Judges in Parenting Disputes in Australia', *International Journal of Law, Policy and the Family*, Vol. 21, No. 1, 2007, pp. 84–107.

1562 See e.g. Parkinson, Cashmore & Single 2007; U. Kilkelly, *Listening to Children about Justice: Report of the Council of Europe Consultation with Children on Child-Friendly Justice*, CJ-S-CH(2010) 14 rev., Strasbourg, 5 October 2010; R. Birnbaum & M. Saini, 'A Scoping Review of Qualitative Studies about Children Experiencing Parental Separation', *Childhood*, Vol. 20, No. 2, 2012, pp. 260–282 and Bruning et al. 2020, p. 175.

1563 See e.g. N. Bala, R. Birnbaum & F. Cyr, 'Judicial Interviews of Children in Canada's Family Courts: Growing Acceptance But Still Controversial', in: T. Gal & B. Duramy (eds.), *International Perspectives and Empirical Findings on Child Participation: From Social Exclusion to Child-Inclusive Policies*, Oxford: Oxford University Press 2015, pp. 135–156; T. Morag & Y. Sorek, 'Children's Participation in Israeli Family Courts: An Account of an Ongoing Learning Process', in: T. Gal & B. Duramy (eds.), *International Perspectives and Empirical Findings on Child Participation: From Social Exclusion to Child-Inclusive Policies*, Oxford: Oxford University Press 2015, pp. 157–179 and Bruning et al. 2020.

always the case domestically, where the modes of participation can be dependent on the types of proceedings and other factors, such as the child's maturity.[1564]

It can be questioned which approach is better. Making no distinction between types of proceedings – i.e. a uniform mode of participation in all family law proceedings – ensures consistency. Not having a patchwork of participation rights simplifies the child's right to participation, making it simpler and more straightforward for children to understand their rights and adding to legal certainty. A uniform mode of participation should also simplify the implementation process for states. However, there may also be valid and justifiable reasons to differentiate between types of proceedings. For example, it could be argued that specific modes of child participation are warranted in proceedings where there is a higher level of state involvement (for example, care proceedings) or where the outcome of the decision has a greater impact on the child (although questions could be raised as to how this could or should be determined).

In the same vein, it may be questioned whether certain modes of participation are more suitable for young(er) children. In the case law of the ECtHR, the maturity of the child has been solely considered for the direct hearing mode of participation and not for other modes. It is unclear whether this is meant to signal that those other modes of participation are more suitable for younger children or whether the lack of addressing the topic finds its origins elsewhere.[1565]

To strengthen child participation domestically, it is advised that, at a minimum, a uniform mode of participation should be available to children without distinction in all family law proceedings. Once that has been achieved, other additional modes of participation dependent on the type of proceeding or the child's maturity could be considered. Differentiating between additional modes of participation for different types of proceedings, children with different levels maturity, children with special circumstances or otherwise is a step that can be made once the implementation and realization of child participation is further advanced. To determine whether specific modes of participation are suitable in certain types of proceedings or more suitable for certain children, existing empirical studies must be considered, and further empirical, interdisciplinary and comparative research could assist in this respect.

2.2. DUE WEIGHT

Moving on from participation to due weight, while all instruments recognize that the views of the child must be given due weight, how decision-makers ought

---

1564 See e.g. Aras Kramar & Milas Klarić 2017, p. 261; and Mol 2021a, pp. 336–337.

1565 See Chapter 9, section 5.4.

to do so is only discussed at some length in the UNCRC and the ECtHR's case law, as noted in Chapter 10. This is remarkable as due weight is a central aspect of the child's right to participate and is what distinguishes participation from the freedom of expression. In the comparison, the meaning of due weight, relevant factors according to the CRC Committee and the ECtHR, the differences between types of proceedings, and the relationship between due weight and the child's best interests have already been touched upon. The comparison has also emphasized the difference between views and wishes, reflecting on the lack of information as to what children are asked and noting the relevance of open and broad questions. In this conclusion, there are two final aspects which deserve extra attention: considering the aligning and strengthening of child participation.

To start with, it is critical to emphasize the symbiotic relationship between children's best interests and giving due weight to the child's views as also expressed by the CRC Committee. In family law proceedings, the child's best interests must be a primary consideration. Following the international and European instruments, this should not mean that children's views can be simply disregarded by the decision-maker in reference to their best interests; instead, the relationship must be nurtured. In that regard, it is advisable that when children are given the opportunity to express their views, they should be asked about their views and feelings in relation to the matter at hand and what they consider to be in their best interests, both in the short term and the long term. Subsequently, the decision-maker should weigh the child's views as a fundamental component in the assessment of his or her best interests pursuant to the relationship between Article 3 and Article 12 UNCRC. In the balance between protection and autonomy and with the aim of child participation in mind, it is of great importance that the child's views are not set aside because of his or her presumed best interests, but instead form a central component to determining what is in his or her best interests. This amplifies children's autonomy, even if a tension may remain with the protection of a child or the interests of others. In their reasoning, decision-makers should clearly motivate how the balancing exercise of the child's views, the other interests of the child, and the rights and interests of others has led to the decision taken. Making the weighing process explicit, beyond a formulaic expression that the views were given due weight, can strengthen the position of a child's views within the balancing process. Explicit reasoning allows for further review and debate as to the balancing of a child's views, their interests, and the interests of parents and others in certain types of proceedings. It may also push decision-makers to further consider or even depart from the child's views.

The second topic is the question of whether due weight is sufficient for effective child participation. At present, children have a voice, but not a choice. Should they have a choice? Daly strongly argues for a departure from due weight towards outcome autonomy for children in best interests proceedings.[1566] As was discussed in Chapter 2, Daly's proposal of outcome autonomy would mean that the child has the choice to determine the outcome of the proceedings if he or she wishes, whereby the child's choice may only be departed from if it is likely that this will cause 'significant harm' to him or her.[1567] This proposed children's autonomy principle goes beyond the child's right to participate in the UNCRC, the case law of the ECtHR and the other European human rights instruments. On the basis of the present research, it can be argued that this new principle is not necessary. If a child has clear wishes, then due weight can mean that these wishes are decisive for the assessment of his or her best interests, which, in turn, is a primary consideration in family law proceedings. Consider, for example, the case law of the ECtHR, where the child's wishes not to have contact with a parent are, in a number of proceedings, decisive in the balancing exercise. Daly's children's autonomy principle calls for a shift of perspective: consider the child's views and wishes first and then address whether these would lead to significant harm. However, this perspective is already present in the symbiotic relationship between the child's views and his or her best interests as advocated by the UNCRC. The decision-maker should depart from the understanding that the child's views form a crucial factor for the determination of his or her interests instead of departing from the supposed decision in the best interests of the child and assessing whether his or her views can change this decision. Seen in this way, if due weight is correctly implemented, it can be argued that it provides sufficient room for children's autonomy. This circumscribed autonomy is fitting in light of the aim of child participation. The difference between Daly's proposal and due weight is that the principle of due weight does not discount the other interests of the child (including the protection of children) or the interests of parents and other parties, nor does it place the pressure of deciding on children. This is especially relevant in family law proceedings, where the impact of the decisions is significant not only on the lives of children but also of their parents. In proceedings concerning a child's personal status and identity, such as proceedings to change his or her name or gender, the rights and interests of others are arguably less relevant. In these types of proceedings, it could be argued that children are deserving of more outcome autonomy.

2.3. MATURITY FOR PARTICIPATION AND DUE WEIGHT

Both in respect of participation and due weight, the age and maturity of the child is a factor. In following all that has been said in the comparison made here, it is

---

1566 A. Daly, *Children, Autonomy and the Courts: Beyond the Right to Be Heard*, Leiden: Brill 2018a.

1567 See Daly 2018a, p. 10.

relevant to address potential areas for further alignment of the international and European framework, and options to strengthen the child's right to participate.

Regarding child participation, the two main points of contention are whether (very) young children should be offered the opportunity to participate and whether it is acceptable to rely on age as a condition for participation. These two points are closely related, as the use of age limits leads to the exclusion of younger children. However, as the use of an open maturity condition will likely also lead to the exclusion of younger children, the two points should also be considered separately. For both, there is an idealistic approach (most clearly advanced by the UNCRC) and a pragmatic approach (visible in the case law of the ECtHR).

Before turning to the question of (very) young children, let us start with the issue of age as a condition for participation. Although idealistically, the use of open maturity criteria may be best – as it allows for an individual case-by-case assessment of the child – it has various disadvantages. Open criteria are difficult to define and subjective; those tasked with assessing the child will need clear guidance.[1568] Additionally, relying on subjective criteria in addition to or instead of objective criteria brings with it the risk for inequality because of differences between assessors and biases. Furthermore, a case-by-case assessment of the maturity of the child is time-consuming and costly.[1569] In that regard, one can argue in favour of age as a presumption of maturity. More specifically, a flexible age limit – i.e., a presumption whereby children from a certain age are given the opportunity to express their views, while it remains possible to give younger children the opportunity to participate where fitting – has multiple benefits. Age is an objective criterion which offers legal certainty, is easy to implement and does not require costly or time-consuming assessments. A disadvantage is that it is likely that children below the age limit will rarely be granted the opportunity to express their views. This must be taken into consideration when posing the subsequent question: at which age should the presumption be set?

This leads us to the discussion of whether (very) young children should be able to express their views in family law proceedings. If we consider the rationale of child participation – the empowerment of children on the one hand and the improvement of decision-making processes on the other – it can be argued that the most profit to be made is with the effective participation of children who are

---

[1568] See e.g. C.M.M. van Leeuwen, 'Het hoorrecht in het civiele jeugdrecht gaat over grenzen: Over de functie en de waarde van de leeftijdsgrens in het hoorrecht in het civiele jeugdrecht', *Tijdschrift voor Familie- en Jeugdrecht*, No. 10, 2017, pp. 260–265, p. 264.

[1569] See e.g. A. Parkes, *Children and International Human Rights Law: The Right of the Child to be Heard*, Abingdon: Routledge 2013, p. 115; and M.R. Bruning & J. Peper, 'Giving Children a Voice in Court? Age Boundaries for Involvement of Children in Civil Proceedings and the Relevance of Neuropsychological Insights', *Erasmus Law Review*, No. 1, 2020, pp. 31–44, p. 44.

able to express themselves verbally and have some understanding of the dispute. The ECtHR's pragmatic approach in agreeing with domestic courts that children under the age of six were not heard by the courts can be supported in that regard. It can be questioned how much can be gained through having children under the age of six express their views in family law proceedings directly or through other modes of participation. To be able to determine a fitting age presumption, one must rely on interdisciplinary and empirical research, such as the recent interdisciplinary literature review wherein authors concluded that children from the age of eight are competent to express their views to judges.[1570] Further research would be beneficial on the possibility and value of hearing very young children directly or otherwise in light of the aim of child participation, both for children themselves and the decision-makers, as well as regarding the costs, both in terms of money and time.

In determining the weight to be given to a child's expressed views, the child's maturity is a relevant factor in all the instruments, except for the ECECR. The factors which are relevant to determine this maturity beyond relying on the age of the child differ between the CRC Committee and the ECtHR. The factors mentioned by the ECtHR (consistency and strength of the child's views, his or her understanding of the consequences, and his or her intellectual capacity) are more straightforward in their implementation than those of the CRC Committee (information available to the child, his or her experience, social and cultural expectations, and the level of support). However, the factors of the CRC Committee better reflect the reality that children are not a homogeneous group – differences between children may impact the weight given to their views, but should not disqualify certain children from the right to have their expressed views given due weight. In considering the child's maturity for due weight, domestic courts can rely on the factors mentioned by both the ECtHR and the UNCRC – these factors are not exhaustive and will likely be used in different combinations depending on the circumstances of the case. These factors for considering the child's maturity for determining due weight can therefore be added to a more general checklist on factors for due weight. The central principle regarding the child's maturity and due weight should be that (generally *more*) weight should be given to the views of older or more mature children, because as they approach adulthood, their autonomy increases in light of their evolving capacities. This reflects the viewpoint of the UNCRC and the ECtHR.

1570 Bruning & Peper 2020; and Bruning et al. 2020, pp. 123–160; as also discussed in D.J.H. Smeets & S. Rap, 'Child Participation in Family Law Proceedings: Pedagogical Insights on Why and How to Involve Children', in: W.M. Schrama et al. (eds.), *International Handbook on Child Participation in Family Law*, Cambridge: Intersentia 2021, pp. 41–66, p. 56.

2.4. INFLUENCE

The fourth theme, influence, is one which is of specific relevance for child participation in family law proceedings. As allegations of influence are especially common in high-conflict divorces or separations and the number of high-conflict separations show no signs of slowing down, the topic is increasingly relevant. At the same time, what is meant with influence and what to do with child participation and due weight if influence is exerted over a child and their views are questions which are insufficiently addressed in the international and European human rights instruments. As mentioned in the comparison, the distinction between 'standard' influence to which we are all subject and undue influence or manipulation is key. To date, in the discussion on the determination and impact of influence on child participation, this distinction has not been adequately addressed. Perhaps it is taken for granted, but the distinction between influence and undue influence needs to be made explicit in future discussions concerning child participation. In those discussions, interdisciplinary research on determining and defining influence must be considered.[1571] There is limited empirical and interdisciplinary research on what (undue) influence means for child participation in family law proceedings,[1572] and further research is necessary, especially on the opinion and lived experiences of children in this regard. Bearing that in mind, the CRC Committee, the ECtHR and legal scholars generally need to further consider how undue influence can be determined – with or without experts, relying on the consistency and strength of a child's views or not – and how an acceptable level of influence can be distinguished from undue influence.

Provided that undue influence should be prevented so far as possible, the question remains as to whether the presence of *undue* influence should impact the right to express views and/or the weight to be accorded to these views needs to be clarified. With regard to participation, it would be unfavourable if (alleged) undue influence would prevent the child from having the opportunity to express his or her views. Undue influence should not function as a threshold for child

---

1571 See e.g. G. Mantle et al., 'Whose Wishes and Feelings? Children's Autonomy and Parental Influence in Family Court Enquiries', *British Journal of Social Work*, Vol. 37, No. 5, 2007, pp. 785–805; M. Saini et al., 'Empirical Studies of Alienation', in: L. Drozd, M. Saini & N. Olsesen (eds.), *Parenting Plan Evaluations: Applied Research for the Family Court*, Oxford: Oxford University Press 2016, pp. 374–430.

1572 See F. Bell, 'Barriers to Empowering Children in Private Family Law Proceedings', *International Journal of Law, Policy and the Family*, Vol. 30, No. 3, 2016, pp. 225–247, pp. 233–235; F. Morrison, E.K.M. Tisdall & J.E.M. Callaghan, 'Manipulation and Domestic Abuse in Contested Contact: Threats to Children's Participation Rights', *Family Court Review*, Vol. 58, No. 2, 2020, pp. 403–416 and E.K.M. Tisdall, F. Morrison & J. Warburton, 'Challenging Undue Influence? Rethinking Children's Participation in Contested Child Contact', *Journal of Social Welfare and Family Law*, Vol. 43, No. 1, 2021, pp. 8–22.

participation. If undue influence should be relevant in child participation at all, it should be at the stage of due weight. However, even there, it can be questioned if it is fitting to give undue influence great leverage. From the perspective of strengthening child participation and the aim of providing children autonomy, the ECtHR's approach that children's views can be given due weight even if these have presumably been influenced in the assessment of their best interests is compelling. It respects children's views as their own, regardless of the reason for these views. This may provide an incentive for parents to manipulate and exert undue influence on their children, but opting not to give children's views any weight to prevent parents or others from exerting influence disproportionately intrudes on a child's right to participate. If domestic courts find there to be undue influence, this may require a response and may impact the balancing of interests, but the child's views should still be given due weight. As mentioned above, further research on (undue) influence, especially from the perspective of children, is needed to assist in finding the fitting response to undue influence.

2.5. INFORMATION AND PRACTICAL AFFAIRS

The final theme to be considered are the circumstances which allow for effective participation: the information provided to the child and practical affairs.

To start with, children need to be informed of their right to participate, the process of participation and what has been decided following their participation. As discussed in the comparison, the CRC Committee, the GCFJ, the ECECR and the Recommendation all emphasize the importance of informing the child. While the ECtHR has not yet considered the issue, it will likely need to, especially if the topic is raised by applicants in the future. Acknowledging the importance of information, the follow-up question is how and by whom should the child be informed? On the basis of the international and European instruments, it is preferred that the child is informed directly – through the decision-maker, the person responsible for hearing the child and/or a representative – instead of by his or her parents. However, there is no explicit preference as to how the child should be informed. In practice, this is an area which has been developing in the past few years – for example, with the drafting of child-friendly invitations to participate and judgments.[1573] These are positive developments and should be pursued further.

In addition to the provision of information, there are a number of practical affairs which can ensure that the process of participation is child-friendly and

[1573] See e.g. J.H. Lieber, 'De rechter en de taal van het kind', *Tijdschrift voor Familie- en Jeugdrecht*, No. 6, 2018, pp. 172–179; H. Stalford & K. Hollingworth, '"This Case is about You and Your Future": Towards Judgments for Children', *Modern Law Review*, Vol. 83, No. 5, 2020, pp. 1030–1058 and Boone, Declerck & Vertommen 2021.

effective. These include, amongst other things, the use of child-sensitive settings – e.g. safe, less formal and comfortable rooms, appropriate communication for the child's level of understanding, and the training of professionals to work with and for children.[1574] As children do not form a homogeneous group, the diversity between children must be taken into account. In the implementation of child participation, children from different backgrounds, with disabilities or with different support networks may benefit from practical measures which have considered the diversity of children. While the guidance from the international and European instruments is limited – with the exception of the GCFJ – for the implementation of the child's right to participate in family law proceedings, these practical affairs are important and therefore deserve continued attention.

3. ALIGNING AND STRENGTHENING THE INTERNATIONAL AND EUROPEAN INSTRUMENTS

In this volume, the question was posed how the international and European human rights framework on the child's right to participate in family law proceedings could be aligned and strengthened. The answer lies not only in the comparison and analysis of standards, as reflected upon above, but also in the relationship between the instruments, the functioning of the instruments themselves, and the institutions and actors involved. In this section, the manner in which the international and European framework can be aligned and strengthened through the instruments, institutions and actors involved is reflected upon.

At the start of this chapter, the following questions were posed: do we need a new European instrument on child participation? Should we abolish any of the existing instruments? Are there other options to strengthen the existing standards? After having considered, compared and evaluated the standards set in the existing instruments, it can be concluded that there is no need for a new international or European instrument on child participation in family law proceedings. At present, there is enough to work with in the existing instruments. This is especially because of the open and general phrasing of Article 12 UNCRC and the interpretative powers of the ECtHR. To align and strengthen the standards of the child's right to participate, the interpretation and use of the existing instruments and framework can be improved without abolishing or replacing existing instruments or adding new instruments to the framework. The drafting of a new international or European human rights instrument would require time and money better spent elsewhere. European states should focus

1574 For further research on these aspects, see e.g. Smeets & Rap 2021.

on the domestic implementation of the child's right to participate on the basis of the existing instruments, as this is where children have the most to gain. International and European human rights instruments are important to ascertain and stimulate the child's right to participate, but children are often not aware of these instruments. In their lives, when in the throes of divorce, separation or other family law proceedings, the human rights instruments cannot provide children with the opportunity to participate, but domestic laws, policies and practice can. Children are aided most by accessible and effective opportunities to participate in the domestic family law proceedings.

In order for states to be able to successfully implement the child's right to participate, the existing framework must be clear, and this research has assisted in clarifying the applicable standards. Throughout the analysis and comparison, many standards have been determined, but existing gaps and differences have also been brought to light. What can be done to align the standards and to close the gaps and thereby strengthen the framework?

At the international level, it would be advisable for the CRC Committee to update its General Comment on Article 12 UNCRC. It has been more than ten years since the current General Comment was drafted and in that time our understanding of the child's right to participate in family law proceedings, and in other matters, has advanced. If the CRC Committee were to draft an updated General Comment, then – on the basis of this research – the following should be considered. First, the CRC Committee should clarify if and where the standards set in the General Comment differ due to the matter at hand, and more specifically if and where the standards may differ because it concerns child participation in family law proceedings, in contrast to other legal proceedings or in other matters and settings (participation at school, within the family, etc.).[1575] Second, as discussed previously, it would be beneficial if the CRC Committee could provide further guidance on a number of topics, including the indirect hearing as a mode of participation and the issue of undue influence in family law proceedings.[1576] In doing so, the CRC Committee could draw on the standards developed in Europe, as studied, compared and reported in this volume. The standards developed in the case law of the ECtHR in particular could function as a model for, amongst other things, the topic of influence. However, the CRC Committee must be mindful that the UNCRC is a universal convention which must address different cultures and traditions,[1577] even if no

1575 See also Chapter 2, section 6.

1576 See Chapter 10, sections 2.1 and 5, and section 2 in this chapter above.

1577 See e.g. L. Lixinski, 'Comparative International Human Rights Law: An Analysis of the Right to Private and Family Life across Human Rights "Jurisdictions"', *Nordic Journal of Human Rights*, Vol. 32, No. 2, 2014, pp. 99–117, p. 101, noting that reliance on the European standards may mean simply perpetuating the notion that human rights is an European and colonial export.

reservations to Article 12 UNCRC were made by ratifying states.[1578] Standards and practices developed outside of Europe should therefore also be considered. If an updated General Comment is drafted, then the CRC Committee should allow for children's participation in that process.[1579] Finally, as the existing body of legal, empirical and interdisciplinary research on child participation in family law proceedings has developed in the past few years, it would be recommended that the CRC Committee considers and refers to this body of research to provide evidence-based guidance.

Within Europe, at the level of the European Court of Human Rights, there are recommendations which can be made to further align and strengthen the child's right to participate in family law proceedings with the other European sources and the UNCRC. In the ECtHR's case law, the recognition of and standards for the child's right to participate in family law proceedings have developed in leaps and bounds. This development can be ascribed in part to the reliance on the other international and European instruments, but more importantly the ECtHR has developed its own standards and has in many cases included child participation in its reasoning *ex officio*. The developments in the case law of the ECtHR are promising for the future. In order to further align and strengthen the child's right to participate, the following recommendations can be made for the consideration of the ECtHR. An important recommendation is that while the topic of child participation is fragmented within the case law of the ECtHR, the Court should approach the child's right to participate in family law proceedings from an overarching perspective.[1580] The results of the case law analysis presented in this volume provide insights – also for the ECtHR itself – on the standards set in all types of family law proceedings. In future case law, the ECtHR should build upon the standards set and continue developing the child's right to participation in a coherent manner. In that regard, there have been multiple specific recommendations made for the ECtHR, both in Part II of this volume and in the comparison (see Chapter 10). Of central importance in these recommendations is that the ECtHR should continue to address the topic of child participation from the perspective of the child's rights – even where children are not the applicants.[1581] In that regard, it would be convenient if in its reasoning, the ECtHR would be (more) explicit as to whose rights are being considered and under which part of Article 8 ECHR: the right to private life or the right to family life.[1582] The latter is relevant as it may distinguish whether the

---

1578 See Chapter 2, section 3.1.1.1.

1579 See e.g. the large-scale consultation with children for the drafting of the GCFJ, as mentioned in Chapter 3, section 3; Kilkelly 2010.

1580 See also Chapter 9, section 3.

1581 See Chapter 9, sections 4.1 and 5.5.

1582 See Chapter 9, section 4.1.

child's right to participate is conditional on the child's position within the family or whether it is an aspect of the child's autonomy, i.e. their right to private life. Finally, there are numerous areas in which the ECtHR should, and hopefully will be able to, further clarify the child's right to participate, including the role of representatives, the child's right to information and more. It will be exciting to see how the ECtHR's case law continues to develop in this field.

If we turn now from the responsibilities of the international and European institutions to the European states, there is one very obvious and two additional recommendations to be made. The core recommendation is that states need to ensure the implementation of the standards set by the international and European instruments. The framework of the child's right to participate has been elaborately outlined in this book. It is now clearer what is required, what is allowed and what is recommended for child participation in family law proceedings. Considering the framework, states should evaluate their national practices and continue to ensure and improve the realization of child participation in family law proceedings. In developing new laws, policies or practices, states should consult children to gain their views and perspectives.

At the international level, it is highly recommended that states that have not yet done so should ratify the third optional protocol to the UNCRC on the individual communications procedure in light of children's access to justice where their rights – including the right to participate in family law proceedings – have been violated. With regard to the ECtHR, children's access to justice, through bringing complaints on their own behalf, and children's participation in ECtHR proceedings commenced by parents that are also brought on their behalf require further consideration.[1583] The ECtHR should ensure that children have been or are informed of applications brought to the Court on their behalf and judgments made regarding their lives.[1584] In addition to these international options, at the domestic and even the local levels, it should be possible for children to have access to justice (including complaint mechanisms, etc.) where their opportunity to participate in family law proceedings has been hindered. This may further empower children in effectuating their rights and can assist in holding states accountable to the participation rights they are obliged to provide. In addition to the responsibility of states, there may be a role for non-governmental organizations (NGOs), national children's ombudsmen and other civil society actors in assisting children in effectuating their participation rights and, where this is not possible, accessing justice.

In addition to the ratification of the third optional protocol to the UNCRC, European states that have not yet ratified the ECECR should consider doing so. However, this need not be a priority, as the ECECR does not set higher

[1583] See Chapter 9, section 8.
[1584] See further Chapter 9, section 8.

standards than those provided by the UNCRC or the other instruments. This is in part due to the distinction between mandatory and optional rights provided in the ECECR. Ratification of the ECECR may provide a new incentive for European states to evaluate their practices as to child participation in family law proceedings and the possibility of the optional rights, such as the right to party status. In that regard, it would be interesting if further research was conducted on the implementation of the ECECR in those states that have ratified it – for example, if it has led to the introduction of the optional rights. Even if states have not ratified the ECECR and will not do so in the future, the standards set as to representation remain relevant part of the European framework as they have been incorporated into the case law of the ECtHR.[1585]

To conclude, in order for the alignment and strengthening of the child's right to participate in the international and European human rights framework, it is key that the existing instruments are interpreted and applied in such a manner as to achieve consistency and an improved realization of child participation. The CRC Committee and the ECtHR have the opportunity to play a central role in aligning and strengthening the right to participate in family law proceedings at the level of human rights. A consistent and clear framework should subsequently assist European states in the (improved) implementation of the child's right to participate. The implementation is not only conditional on the international and European framework, but also on the willingness, efforts and means of domestic states and authorities. Similarly, legal professionals and civil society, in the form of NGOs and ombudsmen for children, can play a part in raising awareness, educating, encouraging, advocating for and monitoring the child's right to participate in family law proceedings both domestically and internationally.[1586]

To assist all of these actors in (advocating for) the improved implementation of the child's right to participate, the human rights framework and conclusions of this volume must be disseminated in an abridged form. The standards and conclusions provide recommendations for legislators and the judiciary, whose decisions must comply with the human rights framework. At the national level, further research on the implications of the human rights framework on the current domestic practice of child participation in family law proceedings could provide more specific guidance. Dissemination of this research to legal professionals, both those working for parents as those working for or with children, can assist in the realization of child participation. It may provide input for professionals to rely on these standards in domestic legal proceedings and, potentially, in bringing complaints to the ECtHR or the CRC Committee. Finally, it is important that the child's right to participate in family law proceedings becomes common knowledge. It would be beneficial if adults (especially

1585 See Chapter 9, section 6.
1586 Consider, for example, the option of a third party intervention before the ECtHR.

parents) know, accept and can potentially advocate for or assist children with their participation in family law proceedings. More importantly, the human rights framework and this research is for and about children, so it needs to be made and shared with them. Accessible and understandable information must be provided on their rights in domestic family law proceedings and their rights to apply to the ECtHR or the CRC Committee if their right to participate has been violated.

4. METHODOLOGICAL CONCLUSIONS

For legal researchers, a case law analysis is nothing new, but the method of qualitative content analysis is. The choice to use this method for a legal analysis was made with the aim of achieving insights in the case law of the ECtHR, which would have not been possible otherwise. At the conclusion of this volume, it is time to reflect on whether and, if so, how the use of the QCA method has impacted the results of this research. Subsequently, the advantages and disadvantages of the QCA method, and search and selection methods used in this volume will be discussed and recommendations will be made for legal researchers.

In this volume, the structured search and selection of case law and the QCA method provided more data, objectivity and valid results, in part because of the large selection of case law, but also due to a more systematic analysis. What does that mean for the results? If the conventional approach had been taken and the landmark cases on child participation had been analysed, then for a number of the general principles, there would likely have been no big difference.[1587] However, many of the conclusions that have been drawn in this book would not have been possible. Take, for example, the overarching conclusions in Chapter 9 on the position of child participation as a right under the ECHR.[1588] Chapter 6 on determining due weight was also dependent on the broad range of cases, including those with brief remarks as to the weight of a child's views. Many of the conclusions could not have been drawn on a limited sample – for example, the determination of child-specific and circumstance-specific factors for due weight.[1589] Similarly, the conclusions drawn concerning the maturity of the child could not have been drawn without recourse to the entire range of case law, as a trend (e.g. regarding age ranges) can only be defined when all (or at least

1587 See, for example, those regarding (in)sufficient participation (Chapter 5, section 4.1) set out in ECtHR, *Sahin v. Germany* [GC] (Appl. No. 30943/96), 8 July 2003; ECtHR, *Sommerfeld v. Germany* [GC] (Appl. No. 31871/96), 8 July 2003 and ECtHR, *M. and M. v. Croatia* (Appl. No. 10161/13), 3 September 2015.

1588 See Chapter 9, sections 6.2 and 6.3.

1589 See Chapter 6.

multiple) cases have been considered.[1590] If this research had only relied on the key cases, then a distorted reality of the ECtHR reasoning on child participation would have been presented. The more nuanced reality – in which the ECtHR at times opts not to respond to complaints on child participation or where the child's rights are seen as being conditional on parents' rights – would have been lost. In addition, the large-scale case law analysis showed the development of the themes analysed over time. It includes the in-between cases where small steps were taken by the Court before the landmark cases were delivered. It also shows that although the international norms, such as Article 12 UNCRC, are relevant in the landmark cases, they are not referred to explicitly in the whole selection of cases. This shows that the ECtHR has been able to build upon its own case law with regard to child participation. In short, there is a lot that this volume has been able to conclude which would have otherwise not been possible. However, what this book does not provide, and which a conventional method likely would have, is a case-by-case discussion. If one wants to read how the ECtHR dealt with the facts of a certain case, this is not the book for you; instead, a theme based critical analysis has been presented.

Aside from the substantive benefits, what are the methodological and practical advantages and disadvantages of the methodology used in this research, and what recommendations can be made for other legal researchers?

With regard to the *search and selection of cases*, it is advisable – regardless of the methods used – that legal researchers explicate their selection of cases. Choices in the search and selection of cases may colour the outcomes of the research, and although the researcher may have taken this into account, the reader should also be allowed to consider the effects of the selection. In this research, a systematic search and selection approach was taken and, in relation to the research question posed, this made the research more valid as the selected cases almost certainly represent the whole population of cases on the topic.[1591] With regard to the analysis of ECtHR case law and the jurisprudence of the CRC Committee, this volume has also shown that – depending on the aim of the research – the inclusion of inadmissibility decisions can be advised. When applications are found inadmissible on the criteria of being 'manifestly ill-founded' or 'insufficiently substantiated', there is a *prima facie* assessment made of the merits of the case which provides insights on the understanding of the rights considered.[1592] If researchers are confronted with very many cases after searching and their research topic is fragmented, such as child participation was,

[1590] See Chapter 7, section 4.5.

[1591] See Chapter 4, section 4.1.

[1592] See also J. Gerards, 'Inadmissibility Decisions of the European Court of Human Rights: A Critique of the Lack of Reasoning', *Human Rights Law Review*, Vol. 14, No. 1, 2014, pp. 148–158, p. 155.

then the use of the hits method used here is suggested.[1593] This method is less time-consuming than reading or scanning every case and at the same time it is more precise when a topic is fragmented.[1594] This method should be supplemented by including cases through the snowball method or following suggestions of other researchers, as it is possible that a number of relevant cases could slip through the net when using hits.[1595] A potential drawback to a structured and explicit search and selection method is that it may be more time-consuming – although trying to find all the relevant case law on child participation without a method would have likely taken days and cases would have been missed. Accounting for the method used will also require additional time and words in subsequent publications; however, legal academia will hopefully increasingly appreciate the transparency of methods and reserve space either in print or elsewhere for researchers to explicate their search and selection methods.

When analysing the case law using the *QCA method*, there was a clear step-by-step process for the creation and testing of a coding frame and for the coding of the case law itself. The coding was supported by using NVivo software, which allowed for a very thorough and systematic collection of data, and assisted in the safe storage and retrieval of cases throughout the analysis. When using the QCA method, the coding frame is used consistently to code all cases equally, with no difference being made between 'landmark' cases and other cases, which allows for a more objective analysis. It also means that the QCA method produces more data, including data which might have otherwise been missed. Combined, the above makes the QCA method more reproducible and reliable than the conventional method of case law research. With regard to how time-consuming the QCA method is, it is certainly true that the development and testing of the coding frame will be more time-consuming than starting the research without a coding frame. However, quoting Miguel de Cervantes, 'to be prepared is half the victory'.[1596] The subsequent coding of case law using NVivo will be less time-consuming compared to the conventional legal method, where notes have to be made or Excel sheets filled in manually. It may even be questioned whether it would have been possible to conduct a case law analysis with a similar number of cases without using a method such as QCA.

In the *presentation and writing down of the results* from the analysis, the use of the QCA method has one important distinction compared to the conventional legal method: it leads to a vast amount of fragmented data. The benefit is that

1593 For more information, see Chapter 4, section 4.1.

1594 In this research, the hit method was not used on the Grand Chamber Judgments. Looking back, it would have been advisable to do so as the reading of these judgments in the coding phase took up more time and most judgments were subsequently removed from the selection.

1595 See also Chapter 4, section 4.1, where the inclusion of additional cases in this research is explained.

1596 Quote from *Don Quixote*.

viewing and analysing the coded text per topic (e.g. per code) offers a different perspective on the case law, therefore providing new insights. However, the consequence is that there is the risk of losing sight of the context of the case: the combination between different arguments or topics raised in a single case is sometimes lost. Using NVivo allows the researcher to see the coded text within the text of the entire case, but it remains more difficult to see the context for each individual case when fragments are being compared and analysed. In this volume, the topic of child participation lent itself to an analysis by topic as it is a fragmented topic in the case law itself. However, this will not be the case for all legal case law analyses. Due to the fragmented data and the wealth of data generated, writing the analysis after the use of the QCA method is laborious, but that is in part because more *can* be written on the topic. However, a benefit is that the structured approach and use of NVivo allows for quick access to the relevant cases and the relevant sections within the case law.

A lot can be said regarding the methodology used in the research for this volume, but what does this mean for future legal researchers? Should QCA be the new gold standard? No, that is not necessarily the conclusion. The methods used in this volume have proven to be worthwhile for legal case law analyses and bring with them many benefits. For legal researchers, using structured search and selection methods and making them explicit strengthens the quality of the research without needing to be much more time-consuming. Whether QCA is a fitting method for legal research will depend on the research question and aim of the research. If the aim is to discuss a select small group of key cases, then QCA may not be a good fit due to the fragmentation of the data and the time it takes. The more cases considered in a case law analysis, the more beneficial a structured method such as QCA. QCA is a good option if the research aims to draw qualitative conclusions, which is a common aim in legal research. Aside from the research question and aim, practical factors will also play a role in whether QCA is suitable. Consider the amount of time a researcher has, the available funding, whether one works alone or in a team, etc. Finally, with regard to the recording of the results, a knowledgeable researcher is of as much importance for the QCA method as it is for a conventional case law analysis. The analysis by means of the QCA method is neutral and objective, but the conclusions drawn in presenting the analysis will depend to a certain extent on the perspective of the researcher. This is common to the work of the legal researcher. Legal research requires more than adding up the data – it needs interpretation, understanding and out-of-the-box thinking. As Smits says, 'legal science is the discipline of conflicting arguments', as it 'consists of identifying the relevant arguments for and against' rules and outcomes and questioning these rules and outcomes.[1597]

[1597] J.M. Smits, *The Mind and Method of the Legal Academic*, Cheltenham: Edward Elgar 2012, pp. 58–59.

In this regard, there is no need to stray from legal research as we know it. Legal research as a normative science remains undoubtedly valuable.

5. VISIONS FOR THE FUTURE OF CHILD PARTICIPATION

With the final conclusions and recommendations made as to the substance of this book and the methodology used in it, it is time to draw to a close with some final visions for the future of child participation. There is no sign that the development and further implementation of child participation in family law proceedings will slow down in the coming years. In fact, it can be assumed that child participation will continue to be a topic of debate at the international, European and national levels. The ECtHR will be faced with continued – if not increased – applications regarding child participation in family law proceedings and, likewise, the CRC Committee will presumably receive individual communications about violations of Article 12 UNCRC. This all should hopefully lead to improved implementation of the child's right to participate and a more aligned and strengthened right to participate at the European level. This will be important in all family law proceedings, but especially in relation to high-conflict separation or divorce cases. In these cases, there is a risk of the child's right to participate being instrumentalized by parents to achieve their preferred outcome, and this requires special consideration as to the child's position, his or her rights and the length of proceedings. The question of undue influence will likely also play a larger role in these types of proceedings. As clear guidance on influence and the child's right to participate at the human rights level is lacking, there needs to be more awareness, research and solutions provided for this topic.

With regard to child participation in family law disputes, two final remarks merit attention. This volume has focused on the child's right to participate in family law proceedings, but not all family law disputes reach the courts. Taking into account the developments in the field of family law in Europe, especially the increasing popularity of alternative dispute resolution, it is important to emphasize that child participation is equally relevant in other settings.[1598] In addition to the child's right to participation in judicial and administrative

[1598] Other relevant trends which may impact child participation rights include the increasing amount of informal relationships in which children are born and where the separation of parents may not be subject to the same jurisdiction as the divorce or separation of formal relationships (see e.g. K. Boele-Woelki et al., *Principles of European Family Law Regarding Property, Maintenance and Succession Rights of Couples in De Facto Unions*, Cambridge: Intersentia 2019, pp. 25–26 and pp. 231–233) and the trend towards non-judicial divorces.

proceedings, the child's right to participate must be provided in ADR processes.[1599] More fundamentally, it would be desirable if the empowerment and autonomy of children improves from the ground up. Child participation should start with the child being afforded the opportunity to express his or her views and be taken seriously by his or her parents and within the family environment.[1600] To achieve this, parents and society at large will need to be (further) informed and made aware of child participation and its benefits.

Looking into the crystal ball, with the increased technological possibilities available to us, the new General Comment on children's rights in the digital environment,[1601] and the digital agility and innovation prompted by the COVID-19 pandemic, digital child participation in family law proceedings is a potential solution for some of the hurdles and costs of physical participation, but most of all is a topic that needs to be considered and further researched. Finally, although this volume pleads for the implementation and realization of effective child participation first, the independent access to court, the right to initiate proceedings and access to justice for children will likely be the next big developments in the field of children's rights.[1602]

In Chapter 1, we began with a quote by Rachel Cusk on the invisibility of children, who are silenced until divorce proceedings start, after which their vote is sought by both parents. Having now come to the very end, this volume has shown how mistaken the novel's characters' understanding is of children's rights in family law proceedings. It is time for this common misunderstanding in society to be replaced with awareness of the child's right to participate in family law disputes to the extent that it is familiar and normal practice. To answer the question posed in the title of this volume, children should no longer be silenced, but should be represented and heard, or preferably heard directly. To achieve this, the child's right to participate and the human rights framework must be straightforward: the standards have to be consistent, clear and accessible. It is advised that states focus on implementing a strong foundation of child participation, starting with realistic standards before building towards the idealistic goals, to achieve an effective right to participation for children in the near future.

1599 See the GCFJ on ADR in Chapter 3, section 3.2.7.

1600 See also Parkes 2013, pp. 71–87.

1601 See UN Committee on the Rights of the Child, *General Comment No. 25 (2021) on Children's Rights in Relation to the Digital Environment*, 2 March 2021, CRC/C/GC/25.

1602 This was previously a step too far – for example, for the Committee of Experts on Family Law, which drafted the ECECR and discussed consent or veto rights for certain proceedings, but did not include them; see Chapter 3, section 2.

APPENDIX

Categorization of Cases Per Type of Proceeding

In this volume, eight types of proceedings have been defined: (1) custody proceedings; (2) access proceedings; (3) custody and access proceedings; (4) international child abduction proceedings; (5) care proceedings; (6) care and access proceedings; (7) parentage proceedings and (8) adoption proceedings. Each of the cases has been categorized into one of these types of proceedings, as shown below.

Custody proceedings	
Miffek v. Czech Republic (2003) (dec.)	'Custody proceedings'
Vámosi v. Hungary (2004) (dec.)	'Enforcement of custody rights and transfer of custody'
Mihailova v. Bulgaria (2006)	'Enforcement of custody' (para. 76)
Jucius and Juciuvienė v. Lithuania (2008)	'Custody proceedings' (para. 20)
Wildgruber v. Germany (2008) (dec.)	'Custody proceedings'
Gineitienė v. Lithuania (2010)	'Proceedings on place of residence' (para. 30)
Kuhlen-Rafsandjani v. Germany (2011)	'Custody proceedings' (para. 63)
Döring v. Germany (2012) (dec.)	'Custody proceedings'
Brillet and Brillet v. Belgium (2014) (dec.)	'Procédure pénale de non-présentation d'enfant et de nonassistance à personne en danger' (para. 16) and 'Procédure civile de non-présentation d'enfant' (para. 12)
Z.J. v. Lithuania (2014)	'Deprivation of parental right to live with children' (para. 74)
M. and M. v. Croatia (2015)	'Custody proceedings' (para. 127) and 'Prosecution for child abuse' (para. 126)
G.B. v. Lithuania (2016)	'Custody proceedings' (para. 67)
Iglesias Casarrubios and Cantalapiedra Iglesias v. Spain (2016)	'Procédure de divorce' (para. 22); 'l'attribution de la garde' (para. 12)
N.Ts. and others v. Georgia (2016)	'Return to father' (para. 62)
Petrov and X v. Russia (2018)	'Granting of residence order' (para. 30)
Khusnutdinov and X v. Russia (2018)	'Return from grandparents to parent' (para. 52)
Milovanović v. Serbia (2019)	'Enforcement of child custody-related decisions' (para. 91)
Zelikha Magomadova v. Russia (2019)	'Deprivation of parental authority' (para. 76)

Access proceedings	
Elsholz v. Germany (2000) [GC]	'Access proceedings' (para. 29)
Sahin v. Germany (2001)	'Dismissal of access' (para. 31)
Sommerfeld v. Germany (2001)	'Dismissal of access' (para. 29)
Süss v. Germany (2001) (dec.)	'Suspension of access'
Hansen v. Turkey (2003)	'Enforcement of access' (para. 91)
Sahin v. Germany (2003) [GC]	'Access proceedings' (para. 47)
Sommerfeld v. Germany (2003) [GC]	'Access proceedings' (para. 42)
Kosmopoulou v. Greece (2004)	'Visiting rights' (para. 33)
Süss v. Germany (2005)	'Suspension of access' (para. 74)
Fiala v. Czech Republic (2006)	'Non-exécution du droit de visite' (para. 81)
Wildgruber v. Germany (2006) (dec.)	'Contact proceedings'
Kajari v. Finland (2007)	'Restriction of access rights' (para. 31)
Luig v. Germany (2007) (dec.)	'Suspension of access'
Mustafa and Armağan Akın v. Turkey (2010)	'Access arrangements' (para. 12)
Płaza v. Poland (2011)	'Enforcement of contact' (para. 52)
Cristescu v. Romania (2012)	'Enforcement of contact' (para. 49)
Gobec v. Slovenia (2013)	'Restriction, suspension and non-enforcement of contact rights' (para. 105)
Buchleither v. Germany (2016)	'Suspension of contact' (para. 28)
Moog v. Germany (2016)	'Contact proceedings' (para. 43)
K.B. and others v. Croatia (2017)	'Contact proceedings' (para. 111)
Ónodi v. Hungary (2017)	'Enforcement of contact' (para. 22)
A.V. v. Slovenia (2019)	'Discontinuation of contact' (para. 52)

Custody and access proceedings	
C. v. Finland (2006)	'Refusal of custody' and 'contact' (para. 42)
Kajari v. Finland (2006) (dec.)	'Custody proceedings' and 'access proceedings'
Petersen v. Germany (2006) (dec.)	'Access' and 'withdrawal of custody'
Nanning v. Germany (2007)	'Partial withdrawal of custody rights' (para. 57) and 'denial of access' (para. 56)
Kijowski v. Poland (2011)	'Change of residence' and 'contact' (para. 42)
Zdravković v. Serbia (2016)	'Non-enforcement of interim custody and access orders' and 'custody proceedings' (para. 50)
Pisică v. Republic of Moldova (2019)	'Enforcement of custody' (para. 58) and 'enforcement of access' (para. 3)

International child abduction proceedings	
Tiemann v. France and Germany (2000) (dec.)	'Le retour des enfants'
Paradis and others v. Germany (2003) (dec.)	'Decision to return'
Eskinazi and Chelouche v. Turkey (2005) (dec.)	'Le renvoi de sa fille'
Gettliffe and Grant v. France (2006) (dec.)	'Le retour de ses enfants'
Maumousseau and Washington v. France (2007)	'Return proceedings' (para. 48)
X. v. Latvia (2011)	'Return proceedings' (para. 46)
Raw and others v. France (2013)	'Le retour des enfants' (para. 54)
X. v. Latvia (2013) [GC]	'Return proceedings' (para. 52)
Blaga v. Romania (2014)	'Return proceedings' (para. 55)
Gajtani v. Switzerland (2014)	'Le déplacement coercitif des enfants' (para. 78) and 'L'attribution de la garde' (para. 52)
Rouiller v. Switzerland (2014)	'Le retour de ses enfants' (para. 33)
Colombo and others v. Italy and Germany (2016) (dec.)	'Procédure de retour' (para. 63)
E.S. v. Romania and Bulgaria (2016)	'Return proceedings' and 'custody proceedings' (para. 49)
McIlwrath v. Russia (2017)	'Failure to assist in reuniting children following international abduction' (para. 80)
M.K. v. Greece (2018)	'Enlèvement d'enfant' and 'la garde d'enfant' (para. 51)

Care proceedings	
K. and T. v. Finland (1999) (dec.)	'Placement of children in public care'
G.H.B. v. United Kingdom (2000) (dec.)	'Adoption order' and 'contact'
W.F. v. Italy (2001) (dec.)	'Interdisant à son enfant de quitter le territoire italien et ayant confié la garde de celui-ci aux services sociaux'
K.A. v. Finland (2003)	'Children's placement in public care' (para. 74)
C. v. United Kingdom (2004) (dec.)	'Care orders' and 'freeing for adoption'
Haase v. Germany (2004)	'Parental rights withdrawn and children taken into public care' (para. 73)
Havelka and others v. Czech Republic (2007)	'La prise en charge des enfants de l'Etat' (para. 34)
Brede v. Germany (2009) (dec.)	'Transfer of parental authority to the Youth Office'
Aune v. Norway (2010)	'Deprivation of parental responsibilities and consent to being adopted' (para. 46)
Y.C. v. United Kingdom (2012)	'Placement order' (para. 115)
Stankūnaitė v. Lithuania (2019)	'Taking of child into temporary care' (para. 90)

Care and access proceedings	
Gnahoré v. France (2000)	'Removal of child, put in the care of child-welfare service and placed with foster parents' and 'limited contact' (para. 43)
L. v. Finland (2000)	'Taking of children into public care' and 'access prohibitions' (para. 98)
Scozzari and Giunta v. Italy (2000) [GC]	'Parental rights suspended and children taken into care' and 'contact visits' (para. 130)
Johansen v. Norway (2002) (dec.)	'Care', 'right of access' and 'authorisation for adoption'
Paulsen-Medalen and Svensson v. Sweden (2003) (dec.)	'Care order' and 'right of access'
Siebert v. Germany (2005) (dec.)	'Guardianship proceedings' and 'access proceedings'
R. v. Finland (2006)	'Public care and restriction of access' (para. 65)
Glesmann v. Germany (2008)	'Child's placement in foster family and access' (para. 95)
A.E.L. v. Finland (2013) (dec.)	'Public care' and 'contact rights' (para. 46)
J. and others v. Finland (2013) (dec.)	'Public care' and 'no contact' (para. 65)
T.S. and J.J. v. Norway (2016) (dec.)	'Contact rights' and 'exercise of public care'

Parentage proceedings	
R.L. and others v. Denmark (2017)	'Refusal to reopen paternity cases' (para. 32)

Adoption proceedings	
Pini and others v. Romania (2004)	'Failure to execute adoption' (para. 105)
Eski v. Austria (2007)	'Permission to adopt without consent' (para. 29)
V.S. v. Germany (2007) (dec.)	'Consentement d'adoption'

Source: Compiled by the author.

BIBLIOGRAPHY

L. Acconciamessa, 'Bringing the Child's Procedural Rights before the ECtHR through Interpretative Tools: Access to Justice, Participation, Representation', in: P. Czech et al. (eds.), *European Yearbook on Human Rights 2020*, Cambridge: Intersentia 2020, pp. 49–77.

P. Alderson, 'Giving Children's Views "Due Weight" in Medical Law', *International Journal of Children's Rights*, Vol. 26, No. 1, 2018, pp. 16–37.

P. Alston, 'The Historical Origins of the Concept of "General Comments" in Human Rights Law', in: L. Boisson de Chazournes & V. Gowlland-Debas, *The International Legal System in Quest of Equity and Universality: Liber Amoricum Georges Abi-Saab*, The Hague: Martinus Nijhoff 2001, pp. 763–776.

P. Alston, N. Cantwell & J. Tobin, 'Art. 21 Adoption', in: J. Tobin (ed.), *The UN Convention on the Rights of the Child: A Commentary*, Oxford: Oxford University Press 2019, pp. 759–816.

P. Alston & J. Tobin, *Laying the Foundations for Children's Rights: An Independent Study of some Key Legal and Institutional Aspects of the Impact of the Convention on the Rights of the Child*, Florence: United Nations Children's Fund 2005.

F. Ang et al., 'Participation Rights in the UN Convention on the Rights of the Child', in: F. Ang et al. (eds.), *Participation Rights of Children*, Antwerp: Intersentia 2006, pp. 9–26.

M.V. Antokolskaia et al., *Naleving van contact-/omgangsafspraken na scheiding: een rechtsvergelijkend en sociaalwetenschappelijk perspectief*, The Hague: Boom Juridische Uitgevers 2019.

S. Aras Kramar & I. Milas Klarić, 'The Main Challenges of Implementing the Procedural Rights of the Child in the Family Justice Systems of Some Southeast European Countries', in: T. Liefaard & J. Sloth-Nielsen (eds.), *The United Nations Convention on the Rights of the Child: Taking Stock after 25 Years and Looking Ahead*, Leiden: Brill/Nijhoff 2017, pp. 247–271.

D. Archard & M. Skivenes, 'Balancing a Child's Best Interests and a Child's Views', *International Journal of Children's Rights*, Vol. 17, No. 1, 2009, pp. 1–21.

O.M. Arnardóttir, 'The "Procedural Turn" under the European Convention on Human Rights and Presumptions of Convention Compliance', *International Journal of Constitutional Law*, Vol. 15, No. 1, 2017, pp. 9–35.

N. Bala, R. Birnbaum & F. Cyr, 'Judicial Interviews of Children in Canada's Family Courts: Growing Acceptance But Still Controversial', in: T. Gal & B. Duramy (eds.), *International Perspectives and Empirical Findings on Child Participation: From Social Exclusion to Child-Inclusive Policies*, Oxford: Oxford University Press 2015, pp. 135–156.

R.H. Ballard et al., 'Hearing the Voice of the Child in Divorce', in: M.K. Miller, J. Chamberlain & T. Wingrove (eds.), *Psychology, Law, and the Wellbeing of Children*, Oxford: Oxford University Press 2014, pp. 122–135.

J. Baxter, 'Content Analysis', in: R. Kitchin & N. Thrift (eds.), *International Encyclopedia of Human Geography*, Oxford: Elsevier 2009, pp. 275–280.

F. Bell, 'Barriers to Empowering Children in Private Family Law Proceedings', *International Journal of Law, Policy and the Family*, Vol. 30, No. 3, 2016, pp. 225–247.

I. Berro-Lefèvre, 'Improving Children's Access to the European Court of Human Rights', in: Council of Europe, *International Justice for Children*, Strasbourg: Council of Europe Publishing 2008, pp. 69–78.

S. Bessel, 'Participation in Decision-Making in Out-of-Home Care in Australia: What Do Young People Say?', *Children and Youth Services Review*, Vol. 33, No. 4, 2011, pp. 497–501.

S. Besson & E. Kleber, 'Art. 2 The Right to Non-discrimination', in: J. Tobin (ed.), *The UN Convention on the Rights of the Child: A Commentary*, Oxford: Oxford University Press 2019, pp. 41–72.

R. Birnbaum & M. Saini, 'A Scoping Review of Qualitative Studies about Children Experiencing Parental Separation', *Childhood*, Vol. 20, No. 2, 2012, pp. 260–282.

V. Blaker Strand, 'Interpreting the ECHR in its Normative Environment: Interaction between the ECHR, the UN Convention on the Elimination of All Forms of Discrimination against Women and the UN Convention on the Rights of the Child', *International Journal of Human Rights*, Vol. 24, No. 7, 2020, pp. 979–992.

A. Bodnar, '*Res Interpretata:* Legal Effect of the European Court of Human Rights' Judgments for Other States Than Those Which were Party to the Proceedings', in: Y. Haeck & E. Brems (eds.), *Human Rights and Civil Liberties in the 21st Century*, Dordrecht: Springer 2014, pp. 223–262.

K. Boele-Woelki et al., *Principles of European Family Law Regarding Parental Responsibilities,* Antwerp: Intersentia 2007.

——, *Principles of European Family Law Regarding Property, Maintenance and Succession Rights of Couples in De Facto Unions,* Cambridge: Intersentia 2019.

I. Boone, C. Declerck & E. Vertommen, 'Belgium', in: W.M. Schrama et al. (eds.), *International Handbook on Child Participation in Family Law*, Cambridge: Intersentia 2021, pp. 103–120.

J. Brannan, 'Translation of Judgments: European Court of Human Rights (ECtHR)', in: *Max Planck Encyclopedia of International Procedural Law*, Oxford: Oxford University Press 2015, nr. 23.

E. Brems, 'Procedural Protection: An Examination of Procedural Safeguards Read into Substantive Convention Rights', in: E. Brems & J. Gerards (eds.), *Shaping Rights in the ECHR: The Role of the European Court of Human Rights in Determining the Scope of Human Rights*, Cambridge: Cambridge University Press 2013, pp. 137–161.

E. Brems & L. Lavrysen, 'Procedural Justice in Human Rights Adjudication: The European Court of Human Rights', *Human Rights Quarterly*, Vol. 35, No. 1, 2013, pp. 176–200.

H. Brighouse, 'How Should Children Be Heard?', *Arizona Law Review*, Vol. 45, No. 3, 2003, pp. 691–711.

M.R. Bruning & C.R. Mol, 'Child Participation in International and Regional Human Rights Instruments', in: W.M. Schrama et al. (eds.), *International Handbook on Child Participation in Family Law*, Cambridge: Intersentia 2021, pp. 13–40.

M.R. Bruning et al., *Kind in proces: van communicatie naar effectieve participatie,* Nijmegen: Wolf Legal Publishers 2020.

——, 'Conclusion', in: W.M. Schrama et al. (eds.), *International Handbook on Child Participation in Family Law*, Cambridge: Intersentia 2021, pp. 359–367.

M.R. Bruning & J. Peper, 'Giving Children a Voice in Court? Age Boundaries for Involvement of Children in Civil Proceedings and the Relevance of Neuropsychological Insights', *Erasmus Law Review*, No. 1, 2020, pp. 31–44.

M.R. Bruning & W.M. Schrama, 'The Netherlands', in: W.M. Schrama et al. (eds.), *International Handbook on Child Participation in Family Law*, Cambridge: Intersentia 2021, pp. 231–244.

M. Burbergs, 'How the Right to Respect for Private and Family Life, Home and Correspondence Became the Nursery in Which New Rights are Born', in: E. Brems & J. Gerards (eds.), *Shaping Rights in the ECHR: The Role of the European Court of Human Rights in Determining the Scope of Human Rights*, Cambridge: Cambridge University Press 2014, pp. 315–329.

N. Cantwell, 'Are Children's Rights Still Human?', in: A. Invernizzi & J. Williams (eds.), *The Human Rights of Children: From Visions to Implementation*, Abingdon: Routledge 2011, pp. 51–70.

J. Cardona Llorens, 'The Legal Value of the Views and Interim Measures Adopted by United Nations Treaty Bodies', *Spanish Yearbook of International Law*, Vol. 23, 2019, pp. 146–165.

J. Cashmore, 'Children's Participation in Family Law Decision-Making: Theoretical Approaches to Understanding Children's Views', *Children and Youth Services Review*, Vol. 33, No. 4, 2011, pp. 515–520.

J. Cashmore & P. Parkinson, 'Children's and Parents' Perceptions on Children's Participation in Decision Making after Parental Separation and Divorce', *Family Court Review*, Vol. 46, No. 1, 2008, pp. 91–104.

S. Choudhry & J. Herring, *European Human Rights and Family Law*, Oxford: Hart Publishing 2010.

P. Craig & G. de Búrca, *EU Law: Text, Cases, and Materials*, Oxford University Press: Oxford 2020.

A. Daly, 'The Right of Children to Be Heard in Civil Proceedings and the Emerging Law of the European Court of Human Rights', *International Journal of Human Rights*, Vol. 15, No. 3, 2011, pp. 441–461.

——, *Children, Autonomy and the Courts: Beyond the Right to Be Heard*, Leiden: Brill 2018a.

——, 'No Weight for "Due Weight"? A Children's Autonomy Principle in Best Interest Proceedings', *International Journal of Children's Rights*, Vol. 26, No. 1, 2018b, pp. 61–92.

A. Daly & S. Rap, 'Children's Participation in the Justice System', in: U. Kilkelly & T. Liefaard (eds.), *International Human Rights of Children*, Singapore: Springer 2019, pp. 299–319.

M. de Boer-Buquicchio, 'Preface', in: Council of Europe, *International Justice for Children*, Strasbourg: Council of Europe Publishing 2008, pp. 9–13.

G. de Geest, 'Hoe maken we van de rechtswetenschap een volwaardige wetenschap?', *Nederlands Juristenblad*, No. 2, 2004, pp. 58–66.

T. de Jong, 'Procedurele waarborgen in materiële EVRM-rechten', Ph.D. diss., Leiden University, 2017.

E. di Napoli & F. Maoli, 'Italy', in: W.M. Schrama et al. (eds.), *International Handbook on Child Participation in Family Law*, Cambridge: Intersentia 2021, pp. 219–229.

I. Dobinson & F. Johns, 'Legal Research as Qualitative Research', in: M. McConville & W.H. Chui (eds.), *Research Methods for Law*, Edinburgh: Edinburgh University Press 2017, pp. 18–47.

J.E. Doek, 'Article 8: The Right to Preservation of Identity, and Article 9: The Right Not to Be Separated from His or Her Parents', in: A. Alen et al. (eds.), *A Commentary on the United Nations Convention on the Rights of the Child*, Leiden: Martinus Nijhoff 2006a.

——, 'What Does the Children's Convention Require?', *Emory International Law Review*, Vol. 20, No. 1, 2006b, pp. 199–208.

J. Eekelaar, 'The Interests of the Child and the Child's Wishes: The Role of Dynamic Self-Determinism', *International Journal of Law and the Family*, Vol. 8, No. 2, 1994, pp. 42–61.

J. Eekelaar & J. Tobin, 'Art. 3 The Best Interests of the Child', in: J. Tobin (ed.), *The UN Convention on the Rights of the Child: A Commentary*, Oxford: Oxford University Press 2019, pp. 73–107.

European Union Agency for Fundamental Rights and Council of Europe, *Handbook on European Law Relating to the Rights of the Child*, Luxembourg: Publications Office of the European Union 2017.

European Union Fundamental Rights Agency, *Child-Friendly Justice. Perspectives and Experiences of Children Involved in Judicial Proceedings as Victims, Witnesses or Parties in Nine EU Member States*, Luxembourg: Publications Office of the European Union 2017.

C. Fenton-Glynn, 'The Child's Voice in Adoption Proceedings: A European Perspective', *International Journal of Children's Rights*, Vol. 21, No. 4, 2013, pp. 590–615.

——, 'Children, Parents and the European Court of Human Rights', *European Human Rights Law Review*, No. 6, 2019, pp. 643–653.

——, *Children and the European Court of Human Rights*, Oxford: Oxford University Press 2021.

S. Ferreira, 'It is My Adoption, But is Anyone Listening to Me?', *New Zealand Law Review*, Vol. 26, No. 3, 2013, pp. 335–355.

B.J. Fidler & N. Bala, 'Children Resisting Postseparation Contact with a Parent: Concepts, Controversies, and Conundrums', *Family Court Review*, Vol. 48, No. 1, 2010, pp. 10–47.

K. Filali, 'Algeria: Experiences in Algeria with the Use of the CRC in Legal Proceedings', in: T. Liefaard & J.E. Doek (eds.), *Litigating the Rights of the Child: The UN Convention on the Rights of the Child in Domestic and International Jurisprudence*, Dordrecht: Springer 2015, pp. 157–175.

R. Fitzgerald & A. Graham, '"Something Amazing I Guess": Children's Views on Having a Say about Supervised Contact', *Australian Social Work*, Vol. 64, No. 4, 2011, pp. 487–501.

U. Flick (ed.), *The SAGE Handbook of Qualitative Data Analysis*, Los Angeles: SAGE 2014.

R. Forastiero, 'The Charter of Fundamental Rights and the Protection of Vulnerable Groups: Children, Elderly People and Persons with Disabilities', in: G. Palmisano (ed.), *Making the Charter of Fundamental Rights a Living Instrument*, Leiden: Brill Nijhoff 2015, pp. 165–198.

M. Forowicz, 'Factors Influencing the Reception of International Law in the ECtHR's Case Law: An Overview', in: M. Andenas & E. Bjorge (eds.), *A Farewell to Fragmentation: Reassertion and Convergence in International Law*, Cambridge: Cambridge University Press 2015, pp. 191–217.

J. Fortin, *Children's Rights and the Developing Law*, Cambridge: Cambridge University Press 2009.

D. Fottrell, 'One Step Forward or Two Steps Sideways? Assessing the First Decade of the Children's Convention on the Righs of the Child', in: D. Fottrell (ed.), *Revisiting Children's Rights: 10 Years of the UN Convention on the Rights of the Child*, The Hague: Kluwer Law International 2000, pp. 1–14.

M. Freeman, 'Towards a Sociology of Children's Rights', in: M. Freeman (ed.), *Law and Childhood Studies*, Oxford: Oxford University Press 2012, pp. 29–38.

M. Freeman & N. Lowe, 'England and Wales', in: W.M. Schrama et al. (eds.), *International Handbook on Child Participation in Family Law*, Cambridge: Intersentia 2021, pp. 171–183.

J. Gerards, 'The Prism of Fundamental Rights', *European Constitutional Law Review*, Vol. 8, No. 2, 2012, pp. 173–202.

——, 'Inadmissibility Decisions of the European Court of Human Rights: A Critique of the Lack of Reasoning', *Human Rights Law Review*, Vol. 14, No. 1, 2014, pp. 148–158.

——, 'Procedural Review by the ECtHR: A Typology', in: J. Gerards & E. Brems (eds.), *Procedural Review in European Fundamental Rights Cases*, Cambridge: Cambridge University Press 2017, pp. 127–160.

——, *General Principles of the European Convention on Human Rights*, Cambridge: Cambridge University Press 2019.

C. Grabenwarter, *European Convention on Human Rights: Commentary*, Munich: C.H. Beck/Hart/Nomos/Helbing Lichtenhahn 2014.

L. Graziani, 'Access to Justice: A Fundamental Right for All Children', in: T. Liefaard & J. Sloth-Nielsen (eds.), *The United Nations Convention on the Rights of the Child: Taking Stock after 25 Years and Looking Ahead*, Leiden: Brill/Nijhoff 2017, pp. 125–141.

M.A. Hall & R.F. Wright, 'Systematic Content Analysis of Judicial Opinions', *California Law Review*, Vol. 96, No. 1, 2008, pp. 63–122.

K. Hanson & L. Lundy, 'Does Exactly What it Says on the Tin? A Critical Analysis and Alternative Conceptualisation of the So-Called "General Principles" of the Convention on the Rights of the Child', *International Journal of Children's Rights*, Vol. 25, No. 2, 2017, pp. 285–306.

J.J. Harman, D.A. Hines & E. Kruk, 'Parental Alienating Behaviors: An Unacknowledged Form of Family Violence', *Psychological Bulletin*, Vol. 144, No. 12, 2018, pp. 1275–1299.

R.A. Hart, *Children's Participation: From Tokenism to Citizenship*, Florence: UNICEF International Child Development Centre 1992.

M. Hazelhorst, *Free Movement of Civil Judgments in the European Union and the Right to a Fair Trial*, The Hague: TMC Asser Press 2017.

K. Herbots, 'Het nieuwe Europees Verdrag inzake de uitoefening van de rechten van het kind en de situatie in België', *Tijdschrift voor Privaatrecht*, 1997, pp. 1763–1823.

K. Herbots & J. Put, 'The Participation Disc: A Conceptual Analysis of (a) Child('s Right to) Participation', *International Journal of Children's Rights*, Vol. 23, No. 1, 2015, pp. 154–188.

R. Hodgkin & P. Newell, *Implementation Handbook for the Convention on the Rights of the Child*, New York: UNICEF 2007.

T. Hutchinson, 'Doctrinal Research: Researching the Jury', in: D. Watkins & M. Burton (eds.), *Research Methods in Law*, Abingdon: Routledge 2013, pp. 7–33.

F. Ippolito, '(De)Constructing Children's Vulnerability under European Law', in: F. Ippolito & S. Iglesias Sanchez (eds.), *Protecting Vulnerable Groups: The European Human Rights Framework*, Oxford: Hart Publishing 2015.

A.L. James et al., 'The Voice of the Child in Family Mediation: Norway and England', *International Journal of Children's Rights*, Vol. 18, 2010, pp. 313–333.

I. Jansen, 'Europees Verdrag inzake de uitoefening van rechten van kinderen', *Tijdschrift voor Familie- en Jeugdrecht*, No. 6, 1996, pp. 132–138.

R. Jensdottir, 'The Council of Europe Action in Favour of Children's Rights: Helping Professionals Working with Children Make the Best Use of the Available Standards', *Irish Journal of Applied Social Sciences*, Vol. 15, No. 2, 2015, pp. 12–24.

H. Keller & L. Grover, 'General Comments of the Human Rights Committee and Their Legitimacy', in: H. Keller & G. Ulfstein (eds.), *UN Human Rights Treaty Bodies: Law and Legitimacy*, Cambridge: Cambridge University Press 2012, pp. 116–198.

J.B. Kelly & J.R. Johnston, 'The Alienated Child: A Reformulation of Parental Alienation Syndrome', *Family and Conciliation Courts Review*, Vol. 39, No. 3, 2001, pp. 249–266.

T. Kerikmäe, 'EU Charter: Its Nature, Innovative Character, and Horizontal Effect', in: T. Kerikmäe (ed.), *Protecting Human Rights in the EU*, Berlin: Springer-Verlag 2014, pp. 5–19.

U. Kilkelly, *The Child and the European Convention on Human Rights*, Aldershot: Ashgate 1999.

——, 'The Best of Both Worlds for Children's Rights? Interpreting the European Convention on Human Rights in the Light of the UN Convention on the Rights of the Child', *Human Rights Quarterly*, Vol. 23, No. 2, 2001, pp. 308–326.

——, *Listening to Children about Justice: Report of the Council of Europe Consultation with Children on Child-Friendly Justice*, CJ-S-CH (2010) 14 rev., Strasbourg, 5 October 2010.

——, 'The CRC in Litigation under the ECHR', in: T. Liefaard & J.E. Doek (eds.), *Litigating the Rights of the Child: The UN Convention on the Rights of the Child in Domestic and International Jurisprudence*, Dordrecht: Springer 2015, pp. 193–209.

L. Krappmann, 'The Weight of the Child's View (Article 12 of the Convention on the Rights of the Child)', *International Journal of Children's Rights*, Vol. 18, No. 4, 2010, pp. 501–513.

K. Krippendorff, *Content Analysis: An Introduction to its Methodology*, London: SAGE 2004.

T. Kruger & F. Maoli, 'Child Participation in Private International Law: The Hague Conventions and EU Instruments', in: W.M. Schrama et al. (eds.), *International Handbook on Child Participation in Family Law*, Cambridge: Intersentia 2021, pp. 69–86.

T. Kruger & L. Samyn, 'Brussels II *bis*: Successes and Suggested Improvements', *Journal of Private International Law*, Vol. 12, No. 1, 2016, pp. 132–168.

U. Kuckartz, *Qualitative Text Analysis: A Guide to Methods, Practice & Using Software*, London: SAGE 2014.

R. Lamont, 'Article 24', in: S. Peers et al. (eds.), *The EU Charter of Fundamental Rights: A Commentary*, Oxford: Hart Publishing 2014, pp. 661–691.

G. Lansdown, *The Evolving Capacities of the Child*, Florence: United Nations Children's Fund 2005.

——, *Every Child's Right to Be Heard: A Resource Guide on the UN Committee on the Rights of the Child General Comment No. 12*, London: Save the Children Fund 2011.

G. Letsas, 'The Truth in Autonomous Concepts: How to Interpret the ECHR', *European Journal of International Law*, Vol. 15, No. 2, 2004, pp. 279–305.

——, *A Theory of Interpretation of the European Convention on Human Rights*, Oxford: Oxford University Press 2007.

Z. Levite & O. Cohen, 'The Tango of Loving Hate: Couple Dynamics in High-Conflict Divorce', *Clinical Social Work Journal*, Vol. 40, No. 1, 2012, pp. 46–55.

M. Liebel, 'From Evolving Capacities to Evolving Capabilities: Contextualizing Children's Rights', in: D. Stoecklin and J.-M. Bonvin (eds.), *Children's Rights and the Capability Approach*, Dordrecht: Springer Science+Business Media 2014, pp. 67–84.

J.H. Lieber, 'De rechter en de taal van het kind', *Tijdschrift voor Familie- en Jeugdrecht*, No. 6, 2018, pp. 172–179.

T. Liefaard, 'Child-Friendly Justice: Protection and Participation of Children in the Justice System', *Temple Law Review*, Vol. 88, No. 4, 2016, pp. 906–927.

——, 'Access to Justice for Children', in: *Preadviezen KNVIR: Protecting the Rights of Families and Children in a Changing World*, Asser Press: Den Haag 2017, pp. 35–88.

T. Liefaard & J.E. Doek, 'Litigating the Rights of the Child: Taking Stock after 25 Years of the CRC', in: T. Liefaard & J.E. Doek (eds.), *Litigating the Rights of the Child*, Dordrecht: Springer 2015, pp. 1–10.

L. Lixinski, 'Comparative International Human Rights Law: An Analysis of the Right to Private and Family Life across Human Rights "Jurisdictions"', *Nordic Journal of Human Rights*, Vol. 32, No. 2, 2014, pp. 99–117.

N. Lowe, 'The Impact of the Council of Europe on European Family Law', in: J.M. Scherpe (ed.), *European Family Law Volume I: The Impact of Institutions and Organisations on European Family Law*, Cheltenham: Edward Elgar 2016, pp. 95–123.

M-F. Lücker-Babel, 'The Right of the Child to Express Views and to Be Heard: An Attempt to Interpret Article 12 of the UN Convention on the Rights of the Child', *International Journal of Children's Rights*, Vol. 3, Nos. 3/4, 1995, pp. 391–404.

L. Lundy, '"Voice" is Not Enough: Conceptualizing Article 12 of the United Nations Convention on the Rights of the Child', *British Educational Research Journal*, Vol. 33, No. 6, 2007, pp. 927–942.

L. Lundy, J. Tobin & A. Parkes, 'Art. 12: The Right to Respect for the Views of the Child', in: J. Tobin (ed.), *The UN Convention on the Rights of the Child: A Commentary*, Oxford: Oxford University Press 2019, pp. 397–434.

G. Mantle et al., 'Whose Wishes and Feelings? Children's Autonomy and Parental Influence in Family Court Enquiries', *British Journal of Social Work*, Vol. 37, No. 5, 2007, pp. 785–805.

P. Mayring, 'Qualitative Content Analysis', *Forum: Qualitative Social Research Sozialforschung*, Vol. 1, No. 2, 2000.

C. McGlynn, 'Rights for Children?: The Potential Impact of the European Union Charter of Fundamental Rights', *European Public Law*, Vol. 8, No. 3, 2002, pp. 387–400.

J.E. McIntosh, 'Four Young People Speak about Children's Involvement in Family Court Matters', *Journal of Family Studies*, Vol. 15, No. 1, 2009, pp. 98–103.

E. Merckx, 'Het EHRM over ouderlijk gezag en verblijf in het belang van het kind na relatiebreuk', *Tijdschrift voor Familierecht*, No. 9, 2017, pp. 241–264.

——, 'The ECtHR on Parental Authority and Contact after Separation: Towards a More Child-Centered Perspective', in: P. Czech et al. (eds.), *European Yearbook on Human Rights 2020*, Cambridge: Intersentia 2020, pp. 97–133.

B. Milne, *Rights of the Child: 25 Years after the Adoption of the UN Convention*, Cham: Springer 2015.

C.R. Mol, 'Maturity and the Child's Right to Be Heard in Family Law Proceedings: Article 12 UNCRC and Case Law of the ECtHR Compared', in: K. Boele-Woelki & D. Martiny (eds.), *Plurality and Diversity of Family Relations in Europe*, Cambridge: Intersentia 2019a, pp. 237–254.

——, 'Children's Representation in Family Law Proceedings: A Comparative Evaluation in Light of Article 12 of the United Nations Convention on the Rights of the Child', *International Journal of Children's Rights*, Vol. 27, No. 1, 2019b, pp. 66–98.

——, 'Child Participation in Family Law Proceedings Compared', in: W.M. Schrama et al. (eds.), *International Handbook on Child Participation in Family Law*, Cambridge: Intersentia 2021a, pp. 335–358.

——, 'Kinderparticipatie in Nederland: Wat kunnen we leren van het IVRK en het EVRM?', in: J. Tigchelaar (ed.), *Actuele ontwikkelingen in het familierecht: Vijftiende UCERF symposium*, Nijmegen: Ars Aequi 2021b, pp. 59–76.

C.R. Mol, S. Bou-Sfia & J. Huijer, 'Mijn wil is wet! De autonomie van minderjarigen in het Nederlandse personen- en familierecht', in: W.M. Schrama & S. Burri (eds.), *De rol van de staat in het personen- en familierecht*, The Hague: Boom juridisch 2020, pp. 91–147.

T. Morag & Y. Sorek, 'Children's Participation in Israeli Family Courts: An Account of an Ongoing Learning Process', in: T. Gal & B. Duramy (eds.), *International Perspectives and Empirical Findings on Child Participation: From Social Exclusion to Child-Inclusive Policies*, Oxford: Oxford University Press 2015, pp. 157–179.

F. Morrison, E.K.M. Tisdall & J.E.M. Callaghan, 'Manipulation and Domestic Abuse in Contested Contact: Threats to Children's Participation Rights', *Family Court Review*, Vol. 58, No. 2, 2020, pp. 403–416.

A. Mowbray, 'The Creativity of the European Court of Human Rights', *Human Rights Law Review*, Vol. 5, No. 1, 2005, pp. 57–79.

R. Nordeide, 'The ECHR and its Normative Environment: Difficulties Arising from a Regional Human Rights Court's Approach to Systematic Integration', in: O.K. Fauchald & A. Nollkaemper (eds.), *The Practice of International and National Courts and the (De-)Fragmentation of International Law*, Oxford: Hart Publishing 2012, pp. 117–138.

A. Nussberger, *The European Court of Human Rights*, Oxford: Oxford University Press 2020.

D. O'Donnell, *The Right of Children to Be Heard: Children's Right to Have Their Views Taken into Account and to Participate in Legal and Administrative Proceedings*, London: UNICEF 2009.

A. Parkes, *Children and International Human Rights Law: The Right of the Child to Be Heard*, Abingdon: Routledge 2013.

P. Parkinson & J. Cashmore, *The Voice of a Child in Family Law Disputes*, Oxford: Oxford University Press 2008.

P. Parkinson, J. Cashmore & J. Single, 'Parents' and Children's Views on Talking to Judges in Parenting Disputes in Australia', *International Journal of Law, Policy and the Family*, Vol. 21, No. 1, 2007, pp. 84–107.

C. Piper, 'Assumptions about Children's Best Interests', *Journal of Social Welfare and Family Law*, Vol. 22, No. 3, 2000, pp. 261–276.

R.A. Posner, 'In Memoriam: Bernard D. Meltzer (1914–2007)', *University of Chicago Law Review*, Vol. 72, No. 2, 2007, pp. 435–438.

M.K. Pruett & R. Barker, 'Children of Divorce: New Trends and Ongoing Dilemmas', in: J.H. Bray & M. Stanton (eds.), *The Wiley-Blackwell Handbook of Family Psychology*, Malden, MA: Blackwell 2009, pp. 463–474.

A. Quennerstedt, 'Children, But Not Really Humans? Critical Reflections on the Hampering Effect of the "3 P's"', *International Journal of Children's Rights*, Vol. 18, No. 4, 2010, pp. 619–635.

B. Rainey, E. Wicks & C. Ovey, *The European Convention on Human Rights*, Oxford: Oxford University Press 2014.

F.E. Raitt, 'Judicial Discretion and Methods of Ascertaining the Views of a Child', *Child & Family Law Quarterly*, Vol. 16, No. 2, 2004, pp. 151–164.

S. Rap, 'The participation of juvenile defendants in the youth court: A comparative study of juvenile justice procedures in Europe', Ph.D. diss., Utrecht University, 2013.

S. Rap, E. Schmidt & T. Liefaard, 'Safeguarding the Dynamic Legal Position of Children: A Matter of Age Limits', *Erasmus Law Review*, No. 1, 2020, pp. 4–12.

S.W. Sacino, 'Article 17: Access to a Diversity of Mass Media Sources', in: A. Alen et al. (eds.), *A Commentary on the United Nations Convention on the Rights of the Child*, Leiden: Martinus Nijhoff 2012.

M. Saini et al., 'Empirical Studies of Alienation', in: L. Drozd, M. Saini & N. Olsesen (eds.), *Parenting Plan Evaluations: Applied Research for the Family Court*, Oxford: Oxford University Press 2016, pp. 374–430.

C. Sawyer, 'One Step Forward, Two Steps Back: The European Convention on the Exercise of Children's Rights', *Child and Family Law Quarterly*, Vol. 11, No. 2, 1999, pp. 151–166.

M. Schreier, *Qualitative Content Analysis in Practice*, London: SAGE 2012.

——, 'Qualitative Content Analysis', in: U. Flick (ed.), *The SAGE Handbook of Qualitative Data Analysis*, Los Angeles: SAGE 2014, pp. 170–183.

O.J. Settem, *Applications of the 'Fair Hearing' Norm in ECHR Article 6(1) to Civil Proceedings*, Cham: Springer International 2016.

H. Shier, 'Pathways to Participation: Openings, Opportunities and Obligations: A New Model for Enhancing Children's Participation in Decision-Making, in Line with Article 12.1 of the United Nations Convention on the Rights of the Child', *Children & Society*, Vol. 15, No. 2, 2001, pp. 107–117.

D.J.H. Smeets & S. Rap, 'Child Participation in Family Law Proceedings: Pedagogical Insights on Why and How to Involve Children', in: W.M. Schrama et al. (eds.), *International Handbook on Child Participation in Family Law*, Cambridge: Intersentia 2021, pp. 41–66.

R. Smith, 'The Third Optional Protocol to the UN Convention on the Rights of the Child? – Challenges Arising Transforming the Rhetoric into Reality', in: M. Freeman (ed.), *The Future of Children's Rights*, Leiden: Koninklijke Brill NV 2014, pp. 178–195.

J.M. Smits, *The Mind and Method of the Legal Academic*, Cheltenham: Edward Elgar 2012.

——, 'What is Legal Doctrine? On the Aims and Methods of Legal-Dogmatic Research', in: R. van Gestel, H-W. Micklitz & E.L. Rubin (eds.), *Rethinking Legal Scholarship*, Cambridge: Cambridge University Press 2017, pp. 207–228.

M.V.R. Snel, 'Source-Usage within Doctrinal Legal Inquiry: Choices, Problems and Challenges', *Law and Method*, 2014, pp. 1–22.

R.M. Stahl, '"Don't Forget about Me": Implementing Article 12 of the United Nations Convention on the Rights of the Child', *Arizona Journal of International & Comparative Law*, Vol. 24, No. 3, 2007, pp. 803–842.

H. Stalford & M. Schuurman, 'Are We There Yet?: the Impact of the Lisbon Treaty on the EU Children's Rights Agenda', *International Journal of Children's Rights*, Vol. 19, No. 3, 2011, pp. 381–403.

H. Stalford & K. Hollingworth, '"This Case is about You and Your Future": Towards Judgments for Children', *Modern Law Review*, Vol. 83, No. 5, 2020, pp. 1030–1058.

C.J.J.M. Stolker, '"Ja, geléérd zijn jullie wel!" Over de status van de rechtswetenschap', *Nederlands Juristenblad*, No. 15, 2003, pp. 766–778.

E.E. Sutherland, 'Listening to the Voice of the Child: The Evolution of Participation Rights', *New Zealand Law Review*, Vol. 26, No. 3, 2013, pp. 335–355.

——, 'The Enigma of Article 5 of the United Nations Convention on the Rights of the Child: Central or Peripheral?', *International Journal of Children's Rights*, Vol. 28, No. 3, 2020, pp. 447–470.

N. Thomas, 'Towards a Theory of Children's Participation', *International Journal of Children's Rights*, Vol. 15, No. 2, 2007, pp. 199–218.

N. Thomas & C. O'Kane, 'When Children's Wishes and Feelings Clash with Their "Best Interests"', *International Journal of Children's Rights*, Vol. 6, No. 2, 1998, pp. 137–154.

R. Thorburn Stern, *Implementing Article 12 of the UN Convention on the Rights of the Child: Participation, Power and Attitudes*, Leiden: Brill Nijhoff 2017.

E.K.M. Tisdall, 'Children and Young People's Participation: A Critical Consideration of Article 12', in: W. Vandenhole et al. (eds.), *Routledge International Handbook of Children's Rights Studies*, London: Routledge 2015, pp. 185–200.

——, 'Challenging Competency and Capacity? Due Weight to Children's Views in Family Law Proceedings', *International Journal of Children's Rights*, Vol. 26, No. 1, 2018, pp. 159–182.

——, 'Scotland', in: W.M. Schrama et al. (eds.), *International Handbook on Child Participation in Family Law*, Cambridge: Intersentia 2021, pp. 287–301.

E.K.M. Tisdall, F. Morrison & J. Warburton, 'Challenging Undue Influence? Rethinking Children's Participation in Contested Child Contact', *Journal of Social Welfare and Family Law*, Vol. 43, No. 1, 2021, pp. 8–22.

J. Tobin, 'Justifying Children's Rights', *International Journal of Children's Rights*, Vol. 21, No. 3, 2013, pp. 395–441.

——, 'Introduction: The Foundation for Children's Rights', in: J. Tobin (ed.), *The UN Convention on the Rights of the Child: A Commentary*, Oxford: Oxford University Press 2019, pp. 1–20.

J. Tobin & J. Cashmore, 'Art. 9 The Right Not to Be Separated from Parents', in: J. Tobin (ed.), *The UN Convention on the Rights of the Child: A Commentary*, Oxford: Oxford University Press 2019, pp. 307–341.

J. Tobin & E. Handsley, 'Art. 17 The Mass Media and Children: Diversity of Sources, Quality of Content, and Protection against Harm', in: J. Tobin (ed.), *The UN Convention on the Rights of the Child: A Commentary*, Oxford: Oxford University Press 2019, pp. 600–644.

J. Tobin & S. Varadan, 'Art. 5 The Right to Parental Direction and Guidance Consistent with a Child's Evolving Capacities', in: J. Tobin (ed.), *The UN Convention on the Rights of the Child: A Commentary*, Oxford: Oxford University Press 2019, pp. 159–185.

P. Treseder, *Empowering Children and Young People: Training Manual; Promoting Involvement in Decision-Making*, London: Save the Children 1997.

F. Tulkens, 'The European Convention on Human Rights and Children's Rights', in: Council of Europe, *International Justice for Children*, Strasbourg: Council of Europe Publishing 2008, pp. 17–33.

G. Ulfstein, 'Evolutive Interpretation in the Light of Other International Instruments: Law and Legitimacy', in: A. van Aaken & I. Motoc (eds.), *The European Convention on Human Rights and General International Law*, Oxford: Oxford University Press 2018, pp. 83–94.

G.G. van Bijleveld, C.W.M. Dedding & J.F.G. Bunders-Aelen, 'Children's and Young People's Participation within Child Welfare and Child Protection Services: A State-of-the-Art Review', *Child & Family Social Work*, Vol. 20, No. 2, 2015, pp. 129–138.

M. van Hoecke (ed.), *Methodologies of Legal Research: Which Kind of Method for What Kind of Discipline?* Oxford: Hart Publishing 2011.

C.M.M. van Leeuwen, 'Het hoorrecht in het civiele jeugdrecht gaat over grenzen: Over de functie en de waarde van de leeftijdsgrens in het hoorrecht in het civiele jeugdrecht', *Tijdschrift voor Familie- en Jeugdrecht*, No. 10, 2017, pp. 260–265.

E.M.J.M.C. van Wijk-Verhagen, *Redelijkheid en billijkheid in het personen- en familierecht, meer in het bijzonder in het huwelijks- en echtscheidingsvermogensrecht*, The Hague: Boom juridisch 2018.

W. Vandenhole, 'Belgium: The Convention on the Rights of the Child in Belgian Case Law', in: T. Liefaard & J.E. Doek (eds.), *Litigating the Rights of the Child*, Dordrecht: Springer 2015, pp. 105–122.

W. Vandenhole, G.E. Türkelli & S. Lambrechts, *Children's Rights: A Commentary on the Convention on the Rights of the Child and its Protocols*, Cheltenham: Edward Elgar 2019.

S. Varadan, 'The Principle of Evolving Capacities under the UN Convention on the Rights of the Child', *International Journal of Children's Rights*, Vol. 27, No. 2, 2019, pp. 306–338.

E. Verhellen, 'Children's Rights in Europe', *International Journal of Children's Rights*, Vol. 1, No. 3–4, 1993, pp. 357–376.

M. Verheyde & G. Goedertier, 'Articles 43–45: The UN Committee on the Rights of the Child', in: A. Alen et al. (eds.), *A Commentary on the United Nations Convention on the Rights of the Child*, Leiden: Martinus Nijhoff 2006.

E. Vertommen, 'Balancing the Rights of Parent and Child in Case of Non-compliance with Contact Arrangements: A Case Law Analysis', in: K. Boele-Woelki & D. Martiny (eds.), *Plurality and Diversity of Family Relations in Europe*, Cambridge: Intersentia 2019, pp. 175–201.

S. Vité & H. Boéchat, 'Article 21: Adoption', in: A. Alen et al. (eds.), *A Commentary on the United Nations Convention on the Rights of the Child*, Leiden: Martinus Nijhoff 2008.

M. Vonk, 'Het Kind als (Vol)waardige Partij bij Mediation', in: J.H. de Graaf et al. (eds.), *Rechten van het Kind en Waardigheid*, Nijmegen: Ars Aequi Libri 2013, pp. 219–228.

J.B.M. Vranken, *Mr. C. Asser's Handleiding tot de beoefening van het Nederlands Burgerlijk Recht: Algemeen deel****. Een synthese*, Deventer: Kluwer 2014.

N. Vučković Šahović & I. Savić, 'Serbia: Strategic Litigation on the Rights of the Child in Serbia', in: T. Liefaard & J.E. Doek (eds.), *Litigating the Rights of the Child*, Dordrecht: Springer 2015, pp. 139–156.

R.A. Warshak, 'Payoffs and Pitfalls of Listening to Children', *Family Relations*, Vol. 52, No. 4, 2003, pp. 373–384.

L. Wijntjens, *Als ik nu sorry zeg, beken ik dan schuld? Over het aanbieden van excuses in de civiele procedure en de medische tuchtprocedure*, The Hague: Boom juridisch 2020.

C. Willow, *Children's Right to Be Heard and Effective Child Protection: A Guide for Governments and Children's Rights Advocates on Involving Children and Young People in Ending All Forms of Violence*, Bangkok: Save the Children Sweden 2010.

M. Woolf, 'Coming of Age? The Principle of "the Best Interests of the Child"', *European Human Rights Law Review*, 2003, pp. 205–221.

J. Zermatten, 'Foreword', in: T. Liefaard & J.E. Doek (eds.), *Litigating the Rights of the Child*, Dordrecht: Springer 2015, pp. v–vii.

INDEX

ABOUT THE AUTHOR

Dr. Charlotte Mol obtained her doctorate *cum laude* from Utrecht University in January 2022, where she is currently Assistant Professor and member of the Utrecht Centre for European Research into Family Law (UCERF) and the Molengraaff Institute for Private Law. She obtained her bachelor's degree in law at Maastricht University and her master's degree in legal research at Utrecht University. Charlotte received the Jaap Doek Children's rights master thesis award 2017 and the FJR Prijs 2019 for her contribution to *Plurality and Diversity of Family Relations in Europe* (Boele-Woelki & Martiny eds., Intersentia 2019).

European Family Law Series

1. *Legal Recognition of Same-Sex Couples in Europe*, K. Boele-Woelki and A. Fuchs (eds.)
2. *European Family Law in Action Volume I: Grounds for Divorce*, K. Boele-Woelki, B. Braat and I. Sumner (eds.)
3. *European Family Law in Action Volume II: Maintenance Between Former Spouses*, K. Boele-Woelki, B. Braat and I. Sumner (eds.)
4. *Perspectives for the Unification and Harmonisation of Family Law in Europe*, K. Boele-Woelki (ed.)
5. *Family Law Legislation of the Netherlands*, I. Sumner and H. Warendorf
6. *Indépendance et interdépendance patrimoniales des époux dans le régime matrimonial légal des droits néerlandais, français et suisse*, B. Braat
7. *Principles of European Family Law Regarding Divorce and Maintenance Between Former Spouses*, K. Boele-Woelki, F. Ferrand, C. González Beilfuss, M. Jänterä-Jareborg, N. Lowe, D. Martiny and W. Pintens
8. *Inheritance Law Legislation of the Netherlands*, I. Sumner and H. Warendorf
9. *European Family Law in Action Volume III: Parental Responsibilities*, K. Boele-Woelki, B. Braat and I. Curry-Sumner (eds.)
10. *Common Core and Better Law in European Family Law*, K. Boele-Woelki (ed.)
11. *All's well that ends registered?*, I. Curry-Sumner
12. *Model Family Code – From a global perspective*, I. Schwenzer and M. Dimsey
13. *Harmonisation of Family Law in Europe. A Historical Perspective*, M. Antokolskaia
14. *Brussels II bis: Its Impact and Application in the Member States*, K. Boele-Woelki and C. González Beilfuss (eds.)
15. *Tensions between Legal, Biological and Social Conceptions of Parentage*, I. Schwenzer (ed.)
16. *Principles of European Family Law Regarding Parental Responsibilities*, K. Boele-Woelki, F. Ferrand, C. González Beilfuss, M. Jänterä-Jareborg, N. Lowe, D. Martiny and W. Pintens
17. *Juxtaposing Legal Systems and the Principles of European Family Law on Divorce and Maintenance*, E. Örücü and J. Mair (eds.)
18. *Convergence and Divergence of Family Law in Europe*, M. Antokolskaia (ed.)
19. *European Challenges in Contemporary Family Law*, K. Boele-Woelki and T. Sverdrup (eds.)
20. *Children and their parents*, M. Vonk
21. *La capacité de l'enfant dans les droits français, anglais et écossais*, L. Francoz Terminal
22. *Joint Parental Authority*, C.G. Jeppesen de Boer
23. *Debates in Family Law around the Globe at the Dawn of the 21st Century*, K. Boele-Woelki (ed.)
24. *European Family Law in Action Volume IV: Property Relations between Spouses*, K. Boele-Woelki, B. Braat and I. Curry-Sumner (eds.)

25. *Foundational Facts, Relative Truths. A Comparative Law Study on Children's Right to Know Their Genetic Origins*, R. Blauwhoff
26. *Imperative Inheritance Law in a Late-Modern Society. Five Perspectives*, C. Castelein, R. Foqué and A. Verbeke (eds.)
27. *Juxtaposing Legal Systems and the Principles of European Family Law on Parental Responsibilities*, E. Örücü and J. Mair (eds.)
28. *La justice des mineurs en Europe*, Y. Favier and F. Ferrand (eds.)
29. *The Future of Family Property in Europe*, K. Boele-Woelki, J. Miles and J. M. Scherpe (eds.)
30. *The Place of Religion in Family Law: A Comparative Search*, J. Mair and E. Örücü (eds.)
31. *Reconstructing Marriage. The Legal Status of Relationships in a Changing Society*, C. Sörgjerd
32. *Legal Recognition of Same-Sex Relationships in Europe*, K. Boele-Woelki and A. Fuchs (eds.)
33. *Principles of European Family Law Regarding Property Relations Between Spouses*, K. Boele-Woelki, F. Ferrand, C. González Beilfuss, M. Jänterä-Jareborg, N. Lowe, D. Martiny and W. Pintens
34. *Der nacheheliche Unterhalt: Grundlagen und Ausgestaltung im deutschen Unterhaltsrecht und in den Prinzipien der Commission on European Family Law*, P. Beuermann
35. *Family Law and Culture in Europe: Developments, Challenges and Opportunities*, K. Boele-Woelki, N. Dethloff and W. Gephart
36. *Children's Rights in Intercountry Adoption. A European Perspective*, C. Fenton-Glynn
37. *Nordic Cohabitation Law*, J. Asland, M. Brattström, G. Lind, I. Lund-Andersen, A. Singer and T. Sverdrup
38. *European Family Law in Action Volume V: Informal Relationships*, K. Boele-Woelki, C. Mol and E. van Gelder (eds.)
39. *Divided Parents, Shared Children. Legal Aspects of Residential Co-Parenting in England, the Netherlands and Belgium*, N. Nikolina
40. *Family Forms and Parenthood. Theory and Practice of Article 8 ECHR in Europe*, A. Büchler and H. Keller (eds.)
41. *The Child's Interests in Conflict. The Intersections between Society, Family, Faith and Culture*, M. Jänterä-Jareborg (ed.)
42. *Same-Sex Relationships and Beyond. Gender Matters in the EU*, K. Boele-Woelki and A. Fuchs (eds.)
43. *Nacheheliche Verantwortung in Frankreich und Deutschland*, K. Kaesling
44. *The Future of Registered Partnerships: Family Recognition Beyond Marriage?*, J.M. Scherpe and A. Hayward
45. *Plurality and Diversity of Family Relations in Europe*, K. Boele-Woelki and D. Martiny (eds.)
46. *Principles of European Family Law Regarding Property, Maintenance and Succession Rights of Couples in* de facto *Unions*, K. Boele-Woelki, F. Ferrand, C. González Beilfuss, M. Jänterä-Jareborg, N. Lowe, D. Martiny and V. Todorova
47. *Die Familienschiedsgerichtsbarkeit in Recht und Praxis: Eine Rechtsvergleichende Untersuchung des Deutschen und Englischen Rechts*, S.C. Zellerhoff
48. *Elderly Care and Upwards Solidarity: Historical, Sociological and Legal Perspectives*, E. Alofs and W. Schrama (eds.)

49. *Party Autonomy in EU Private International Law: Choice of Court and Choice of Law in Family Matters and Succession*, J. Gray
50. *The Interaction between Family Law, Succession Law and Private International Law: Adapting to Change*, J.M. Scherpe and E. Bargelli (eds.)
51. *International Handbook on Child Participation in Family Law*, W. Schrama, M. Freeman, N. Taylor and M. Bruning (eds.)